World Economic and Financial Surveys

WORLD ECONOMIC OUTLOOK
September 2004

The Global Demographic Transition

International Monetary Fund

Production: IMF Graphics Section
Cover and Design: Luisa Menjivar-Macdonald
Figures: Theodore F. Peters, Jr.
Typesetting: Choon Lee

World economic outlook (International Monetary Fund)
World economic outlook: a survey by the staff of the International Monetary Fund.—1980– —Washington, D.C.: The Fund, 1980–

v.; 28 cm.—(1981–84: Occasional paper/International Monetary Fund ISSN 0251-6365)
Annual.
Has occasional updates, 1984–
ISSN 0258-7440 = World economic and financial surveys
ISSN 0256-6877 = World economic outlook (Washington)
1. Economic history—1971– —Periodicals. I. International Monetary Fund. II. Series: Occasional paper (International Monetary Fund)

HC10.W7979 84-640155
338.5'443'09048—dc19
AACR 2 MARC-S

Library of Congress 8507

Published biannually.
ISBN 1-58906-406-2

Price: US$49.00
(US$46.00 to full-time faculty members and students at universities and colleges)

Please send orders to:
International Monetary Fund, Publication Services
700 19th Street, N.W., Washington, D.C. 20431, U.S.A.
Tel.: (202) 623-7430 Telefax: (202) 623-7201
E-mail: publications@imf.org
Internet: http://www.imf.org

recycled paper

CONTENTS

Boxes

Tables

Figures

ASSUMPTIONS AND CONVENTIONS

A number of assumptions have been adopted for the projections presented in the *World Economic Outlook*. It has been assumed that real effective exchange rates will remain constant at their average levels during July 7–August 4, 2004, except for the currencies participating in the European exchange rate mechanism II (ERM II), which are assumed to remain constant in nominal terms relative to the euro; that established policies of national authorities will be maintained (for specific assumptions about fiscal and monetary policies in industrial countries, see Box A1); that the average price of oil will be $37.25 a barrel in 2004 and 2005, and remain unchanged in real terms over the medium term; that the six-month London interbank offered rate (LIBOR) on U.S. dollar deposits will average 1.6 percent in 2004 and 3.4 percent in 2005; that the six-month euro deposits rate will average 2.2 percent in 2004 and 2.8 percent in 2005; and that the six-month Japanese yen deposit rate will yield an average of 0.1 percent in 2004 and of 0.3 percent in 2005. These are, of course, working hypotheses rather than forecasts, and the uncertainties surrounding them add to the margin of error that would in any event be involved in the projections. The estimates and projections are based on statistical information available through mid-September 2004.

The following conventions have been used throughout the *World Economic Outlook:*

. . . to indicate that data are not available or not applicable;

— to indicate that the figure is zero or negligible;

– between years or months (for example, 2002–03 or January–June) to indicate the years or months covered, including the beginning and ending years or months;

/ between years or months (for example, 2002/03) to indicate a fiscal or financial year.

"Billion" means a thousand million; "trillion" means a thousand billion.

"Basis points" refer to hundredths of 1 percentage point (for example, 25 basis points are equivalent to ¼ of 1 percentage point).

In figures and tables, shaded areas indicate IMF staff projections.

Minor discrepancies between sums of constituent figures and totals shown are due to rounding.

As used in this report, the term "country" does not in all cases refer to a territorial entity that is a state as understood by international law and practice. As used here, the term also covers some territorial entities that are not states but for which statistical data are maintained on a separate and independent basis.

FURTHER INFORMATION AND DATA

This report on the *World Economic Outlook* is available in full on the IMF's Internet site, www.imf.org. Accompanying it on the website is a larger compilation of data from the WEO database than in the report itself, consisting of files containing the series most frequently requested by readers. These files may be downloaded for use in a variety of software packages.

Inquiries about the content of the *World Economic Outlook* and the WEO database should be sent by mail, electronic mail, or telefax (telephone inquiries cannot be accepted) to:

World Economic Studies Division
Research Department
International Monetary Fund
700 19th Street, N.W.
Washington, D.C. 20431, U.S.A.
E-mail: weo@imf.org Telefax: (202) 623-6343

PREFACE

The analysis and projections contained in the *World Economic Outlook* are integral elements of the IMF's surveillance of economic developments and policies in its member countries, of developments in international financial markets, and of the global economic system. The survey of prospects and policies is the product of a comprehensive interdepartmental review of world economic developments, which draws primarily on information the IMF staff gathers through its consultations with member countries. These consultations are carried out in particular by the IMF's area departments together with the Policy Development and Review Department, the International Capital Markets Department, the Monetary and Financial Systems Department, and the Fiscal Affairs Department.

The analysis in this report has been coordinated in the Research Department under the general direction of Raghuram Rajan, Economic Counsellor and Director of Research. The project has been directed by David Robinson, Deputy Director of the Research Department, together with James Morsink, Division Chief, Research Department.

Primary contributors to this report also include Nicoletta Batini, Tim Callen, Xavier Debrun, Hamid Faruqee, Dalia Hakura, Thomas Helbling, Toh Kuan, Nikola Spatafora, and Marco Terrones. Hussein Allidina, Harald Anderson, Paul Atang, Angela Cabugao, Nathalie Carcenac, Yutong Li, Paul Nicholson, and Bennett Sutton provided research assistance. Nicholas Dopuch, Mahnaz Hemmati, Casper Meyer, and Ercument Tulun managed the database and the computer systems. Sylvia Brescia, Celia Burns, and Seetha Milton were responsible for word processing. Other contributors include Anders Åslund, Roel Beetsma, Robin Brooks, Jean Chateau, Milan Cuc, Markus Haacker, Peter Heller, Simon Johnson, Cem Karacadag, Kalpana Kochhar, Laura Kodres, M. Ayhan Kose, Thomas Krueger, Warwick McKibbin, G.A. Mackenzie, Gian Maria Milesi-Ferretti, Christopher Otrok, Sam Ouliaris, Thomas Rumbaugh, Martin Sommer, and Mehmet Tosun. Marina Primorac of the External Relations Department edited the manuscript and coordinated the production of the publication.

The analysis has benefited from comments and suggestions by staff from other IMF departments, as well as by Executive Directors following their discussion of the report on September 1 and 3, 2004. However, both projections and policy considerations are those of the IMF staff and should not be attributed to Executive Directors or to their national authorities.

FOREWORD

Let me start by thanking David Robinson, James Morsink, members of the World Economic Studies Division, and all the other IMF staff who have worked many long hours to bring this to you.

Unless events take an awful turn, the world economy will enjoy one of its strongest years of growth this year. It is but natural then that the equilibrating forces bringing growth back to trend will come into play. Commodity prices are increasing, while central banks are slowly withdrawing the accommodative conditions that were put in place to deal with the recession. This is as it should be.

The key development in the past few months has been that oil prices, which had been quiescent for many years except for short spikes in times of heightened geopolitical risk, shot up once again. This time it has been a volatile combination of heightened demand, very limited spare capacity, and geopolitical threats to existing capacity. While as of this writing oil prices had fallen back somewhat, there is no guarantee that volatility will abate. It would be myopic not to draw lessons from this experience.

The first lesson, as I emphasized in the last *World Economic Outlook*, is that policymakers need to take every opportunity to recover the policy options that have been expended in ensuring the recovery. Without these options, we have little with which to manage the unknown risks that surely are out there.

The second lesson is that long-term trends will eventually, and most unexpectedly, become short-term policy concerns. For instance, we always knew that the phenomenal growth of China and, to a lesser extent, India, would eventually weigh on global energy resources. But that future is now upon us. There are some obvious steps countries can take to ensure that growth is sustainable, such as greater efforts at conservation and efficiency and a reduction of unnecessary impediments to exploration and production. There may also be a need to explore new ways of reducing energy-related risk in the world economy.

More generally, almost any economic issue seems to have international spillovers nowadays. The analytical section in this *World Economic Outlook* highlights four such issues.

The first essay in Chapter II focuses on the current house price boom in industrial countries. House prices across countries are surprisingly highly synchronized, with about 40 percent of the movement in house prices explained by global factors, which in turn reflect key variables such as changes in world interest rates. Since what goes up excessively must come down, policymakers should be aware that they will likely be dealing with the consequences of depressed house prices at a time when house prices elsewhere, and thus external demand, are also likely to be low.

The IMF was set up, in part, because of the recognition that exchange arrangements have spillover effects. In the past few years, the IMF has been advocating more exchange rate flexibility for some countries in emerging Asia, not only because it believes more flexibility will be in the best interest of the countries themselves but also because increased flexibility will contribute to reducing global imbalances. The second essay examines the shift from fixed exchange rates to floating exchange rates in emerging market countries in the 1990s. Countries typically moved in steps from fixed to floating, and those who did it voluntarily spent time strengthening monetary and financial policy frameworks. However, countries did not typically have all frameworks in place before making the change. For example, many who decided to float introduced an inflation targeting regime only after the transition. This suggests that while countries need to prepare for floating, some key institutions can be put in place after the float.

Common currency arrangements again have obvious cross-border effects. Five years after the adoption of the euro, the third essay in Chapter II finds that there is still considerable divergence in member countries' cyclical positions. As a result, the common monetary policy in the euro area has differed from what country-specific conventional policy rules suggest would be appropriate. This means fiscal policy still has a role to play in stabilizing growth outcomes. Unfortunately, the essay finds that while governments have tended to spend more in bad times after the adoption of the euro, they have also tended to spend more in good times. The latter is not only destabilizing; it also creates an unsustainable deficit bias in government policies. The essay reinforces the point that the euro area needs a better mechanism to ensure government spending is disciplined in good times.

This loss of discipline is especially worrying given the looming fiscal costs of aging. Let me highlight some results from Chapter III, which is on demographic change.

Given the magnitude of the demographic changes facing us, there will be no single magic bullet. For instance, if we intended to stabilize the ratio of labor force to population at current levels by 2050 in a group of advanced economies, using only an increase in labor force participation, we would require an average increase of 11 percent. Using only immigration, immigrants would make up on average more than 30 percent of advanced economies' populations by 2050. Relying only on an increase in retirement age, we would require an average extension of our working lives by more than 7 years. These not only exceed the limits of what is politically feasible, but in some countries they also exceed what is physically possible: in Japan, participation rates would have to be above 100 percent.

But if a multipronged approach is adopted, a solution seems well within political reach. One would only require an increase in participation of 3¾ percent, an increase in immigration to 10 percent of population and an increase in retirement age of 2.3 years to stabilize the ratio of labor force to population.

Also, even if solutions achieve similar ends—such as ensuring solvency of pensions—they may have very different implications for economic growth during the transition. For instance, raising the retirement age appears to be more friendly to consumption growth than a decrease in retirement benefits. The latter induces workers to save more for retirement, thus inhibiting consumption, while the former may induce additional consumption as workers know they have a longer period in which to save.

Chapter III emphasizes the role that international movement in goods, people, and capital will play in reducing the costs of aging and exploiting its benefits. We need better international rules of the game to govern such movement, to ensure that trade is free, to ensure that investor rights are protected, and to ensure that the universal human rights of immigrants are respected. International organizations like ours will have an increasingly important role.

In sum then, if there is one message in this *World Economic Outlook*, it is that no country is an island. Policies in one country spill over to the rest of the world through many channels—prices, interest rates, trade, capital flows, people, ideas, conflict, and even through example. This is why it is increasingly important for the outside world that countries that need to reform do not succumb to reform fatigue.

And that fatigue is spreading. Politicians seem to be giving up on reform because people seem to reject it. But, if people are merely rational and self-interested rather than myopic or deaf, there may be ways to bring them around to accept reforms. In fact, there may be no better time to reform than the present: a time of recovery when recent adversity reminds citizens of the cost of standing still, while growing surpluses help ease the pain of reform. Sensible design can help. A reform that increases retirement age should be accompanied by measures to increase labor market flexibility and adult education so that the older workers have more opportunities. Even with good timing and clever design, people will need to be spoken to plainly and convinced to come along. But that is where leadership needs to take over from mere politics as usual. I am hopeful we will see such leadership in the years to come.

Raghuram Rajan
Economic Counsellor and Director, Research Department

CHAPTER I ECONOMIC PROSPECTS AND POLICY ISSUES

Over the past year, the global recovery has become increasingly well established, with global GDP growth now projected to average 5 percent in 2004, the highest for nearly three decades (Figure 1.1 and Table 1.1). That said, growth momentum has slowed from the second quarter of 2004, notably in the United States, Japan, and China, while oil prices have risen sharply. Looking forward, the global expansion—while still solid—will therefore likely be somewhat weaker than earlier expected; the balance of risks has shifted to the downside with further oil price volatility a particular concern. On the policy side, interest rates will need to rise further as the recovery proceeds, although the pace and timing vary considerably across countries, depending on their relative cyclical positions. However, the key challenge—perhaps even more important in light of the somewhat less favorable short-term situation—is to take advantage of the upturn to make progress in addressing fundamental medium-term problems, including difficult fiscal positions, growth-restraining structural weaknesses, financial and corporate vulnerabilities, and—last but not least—continuing global current account imbalances. While progress is being made, it is generally limited; without further action there is a serious risk of shortfalls in many regions, leaving the world significantly more vulnerable to the shocks it will inevitably face in the future.

Over the past year, the global recovery has become increasingly well established. Between mid-2003 and mid-2004, global growth has averaged 5 percent—well in excess of the 4 percent historical trend—with strong growth in industrial countries and exceptionally rapid expansion in emerging markets, notably China. This has been accompanied by a strong upturn in industrial production and global trade flows; a pickup in private consumption growth, underpinned by generally improving labor market conditions; and continued strength in investment, as post-bubble corporate balance sheet restructuring has proceeded (Figure 1.2). While global growth in the first quarter was much stronger than earlier expected, the momentum of the recovery slowed thereafter. While some slowdown was both inevitable and desirable following three quarters of exceptionally rapid expansion, GDP growth in several major countries—including the United States and Japan—fell below expectations, raising concerns of an emerging "soft patch." GDP growth in China also eased—a welcome development, given concerns about incipient overheating—although recent data suggest a soft landing is not yet assured.

From a regional perspective, the recovery has become increasingly broad based, but some regions continue to grow more vigorously than others. Despite the weakness in the second quarter, global growth continues to be driven by the United States, with strong support from Asia; activity in Latin America and some other emerging markets has also picked up strongly. The recovery in the euro area is becoming more established, but remains relatively weak and is heavily dependent on external demand (particularly in Germany, which comprises one-third of the euro area). Despite stronger growth outside the United States, the U.S. current account deficit has continued to deteriorate over the past year, offset by higher surpluses in Japan and the euro area. Current account surpluses in emerging Asia have remained very high—notwithstanding generally strengthening domestic demand—aided by buoyant electronics exports but also by the competitiveness of exchange rates in that region.

Buoyant global demand, accompanied increasingly by a variety of supply-side factors, has led to a strong pickup in commodity prices, which have risen by 27 percent in SDR terms since December 2003 (Appendix 1.1). In the oil market, prices have risen sharply, underpinned by a combination of surging demand and—particularly from the second quarter—supply-side concerns in several major oil-exporting countries, including Iraq, Russia, and Venezuela (see Appendix 1.1 for a detailed discussion). This has been exacerbated by low excess capacity and speculative activity. Amidst considerable volatility, oil prices peaked at $44.71 a barrel on August 19 (a record high in U.S. dollar terms, although well below past peaks in real terms—see Figure 1.1). Thereafter, oil prices initially fell back, partly reflecting easing geopolitical concerns, but since mid-September have turned up once more. In contrast, nonfuel commodity prices, which rose substantially through early 2004, have since shown signs of easing, partly owing to slowing growth in China (which accounts for a substantial proportion of global consumption of some key commodities).

The sharp rise in oil prices has contributed to the weakening of the expansion in recent months, and will likely continue to do so for several quarters. To date, however, the overall impact appears moderate. As of early September, futures markets suggest that average oil prices in 2005 will be about $8 a barrel higher than in 2003; standard economic models suggest that such an increase would reduce global GDP by about ½ percentage point.[1] In contrast to previous episodes, the rise in oil prices has owed much to stronger global demand rather than supply concerns (although this has been less the case since the first quarter); and consumer confidence, which fell significantly in earlier episodes, has so far held up reasonably well.

Figure 1.1. Global Indicators[1]

(Annual percent change unless otherwise noted)

Global growth in 2004 will be the most rapid in nearly three decades, with a slower, but still solid, expansion projected for 2005.

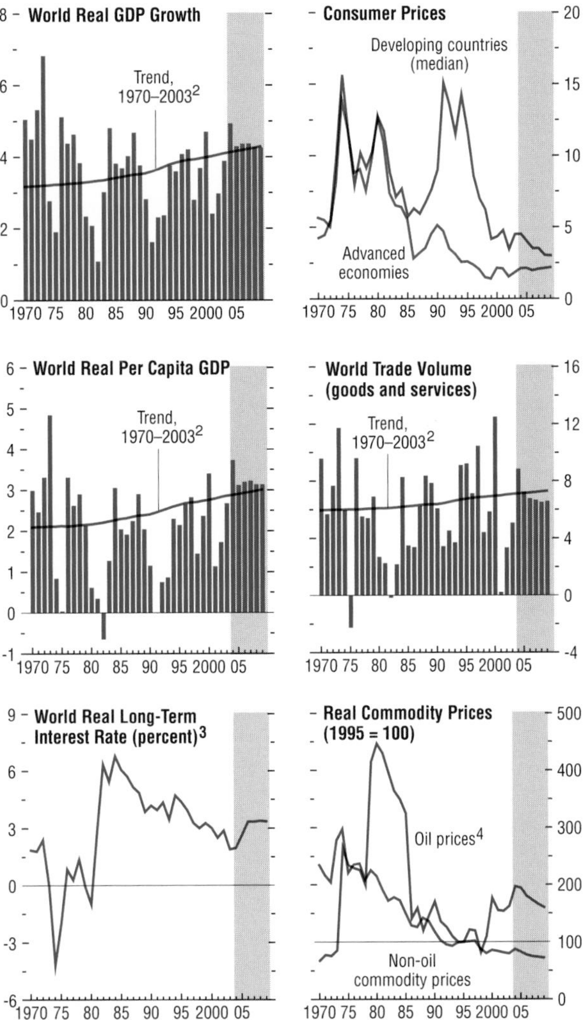

[1]Shaded areas indicate IMF staff projections. Aggregates are computed on the basis of purchasing-power-parity weights unless otherwise noted.

[2]Average growth rates for individual countries, aggregated using purchasing-power-parity weights; the aggregates shift over time in favor of faster growing countries, giving the line an upward trend.

[3]GDP-weighted average of the 10-year (or nearest maturity) government bond yields less inflation rates for the United States, Japan, Germany, France, Italy, the United Kingdom, and Canada. Excluding Italy prior to 1972.

[4]Simple average of spot prices of U.K. Brent, Dubai, and West Texas Intermediate crude oil.

[1]As discussed in Appendix 1.1, the size of this shock is less than one-tenth of the shocks experienced in the 1970s.

Table 1.1. Overview of the *World Economic Outlook* Projections
(Annual percent change unless otherwise noted)

			Current Projections		Difference from April 2004 Projections[1]	
	2002	2003	2004	2005	2004	2005
World output	**3.0**	**3.9**	**5.0**	**4.3**	**0.3**	**–0.1**
Advanced economies	1.6	2.1	3.6	2.9	0.2	–0.2
United States	1.9	3.0	4.3	3.5	–0.3	–0.3
Euro area	0.8	0.5	2.2	2.2	0.4	–0.1
Germany	0.1	–0.1	2.0	1.8	0.5	–0.1
France	1.1	0.5	2.6	2.3	0.9	–0.1
Italy	0.4	0.3	1.4	1.9	0.2	–0.1
Spain	2.2	2.5	2.6	2.9	–0.1	–0.4
Japan	–0.3	2.5	4.4	2.3	1.1	0.5
United Kingdom	1.8	2.2	3.4	2.5	–0.1	–0.1
Canada	3.4	2.0	2.9	3.1	0.3	—
Other advanced economies	3.6	2.4	4.3	3.5	0.3	–0.5
Newly industrialized Asian economies	5.0	3.0	5.5	4.0	0.2	–1.0
Other emerging market and developing countries	4.8	6.1	6.6	5.9	0.5	—
Africa	3.5	4.3	4.5	5.4	0.3	—
Sub-Sahara	3.6	3.7	4.6	5.8	0.4	0.1
Central and eastern Europe	4.4	4.5	5.5	4.8	1.0	0.3
Commonwealth of Independent States[2]	5.4	7.8	8.0	6.6	2.0	1.4
Russia	4.7	7.3	7.3	6.6	1.3	1.4
Excluding Russia	7.0	9.0	9.6	6.5	3.7	1.5
Developing Asia	6.6	7.7	7.6	6.9	0.2	–0.1
China	8.3	9.1	9.0	7.5	0.5	–0.5
India	5.0	7.2	6.4	6.7	–0.4	0.6
ASEAN-4[3]	4.3	5.1	5.5	5.4	—	–0.1
Middle East	4.3	6.0	5.1	4.8	1.0	–0.1
Western Hemisphere	–0.1	1.8	4.6	3.6	0.7	—
Brazil	1.9	–0.2	4.0	3.5	0.5	—
Mexico	0.8	1.3	4.0	3.2	0.8	–0.1
Memorandum						
European Union	1.2	1.1	2.6	2.5	0.4	–0.1
World growth based on market exchange rates	1.7	2.7	4.1	3.4	0.3	–0.1
World trade volume (goods and services)	**3.3**	**5.1**	**8.8**	**7.2**	**2.0**	**0.7**
Imports						
Advanced economies	2.6	3.7	7.6	5.6	1.9	0.2
Other emerging market and developing countries	6.0	11.1	12.8	11.9	2.6	2.4
Exports						
Advanced economies	2.2	2.6	8.1	6.3	1.8	0.2
Other emerging market and developing countries	6.6	10.9	10.8	10.6	2.7	1.9
Commodity prices (U.S. dollars)						
Oil[4]	2.5	15.8	28.9	—	25.1	10.0
Nonfuel (average based on world commodity export weights)	0.6	7.1	16.8	–3.9	9.2	–3.1
Consumer prices						
Advanced economies	1.5	1.8	2.1	2.1	0.4	0.4
Other emerging market and developing countries	6.0	6.1	6.0	5.5	0.3	0.5
Six-month London interbank offered rate (LIBOR, percent)						
On U.S. dollar deposits	1.9	1.2	1.6	3.4	0.3	–0.1
On euro deposits	3.3	2.3	2.2	2.8	0.1	0.2
On Japanese yen deposits	0.1	0.1	0.1	0.3	—	–0.1

Note: Real effective exchange rates are assumed to remain constant at the levels prevailing during July 7–August 4, 2004.

[1]Using updated purchasing-power-parity (PPP) weights, summarized in the Statistical Appendix, Table A.

[2]Mongolia, which is not a member of the Commonwealth of Independent States, is included in this group for reasons of geography and similarities in economic structure.

[3]Includes Indonesia, Malaysia, the Philippines, and Thailand.

[4]Simple average of spot prices of U.K. Brent, Dubai, and West Texas Intermediate crude oil. The average price of oil in U.S. dollars a barrel was $28.89 in 2003; the assumed price is $37.25 in 2004 and $37.25 in 2005.

Figure 1.2. Current and Forward-Looking Indicators
(Percent change from previous quarter at annual rates unless otherwise noted)

Industrial production and global trade growth have slowed somewhat recently, but remain strong; forward-looking indicators in particular suggest a continued solid recovery.

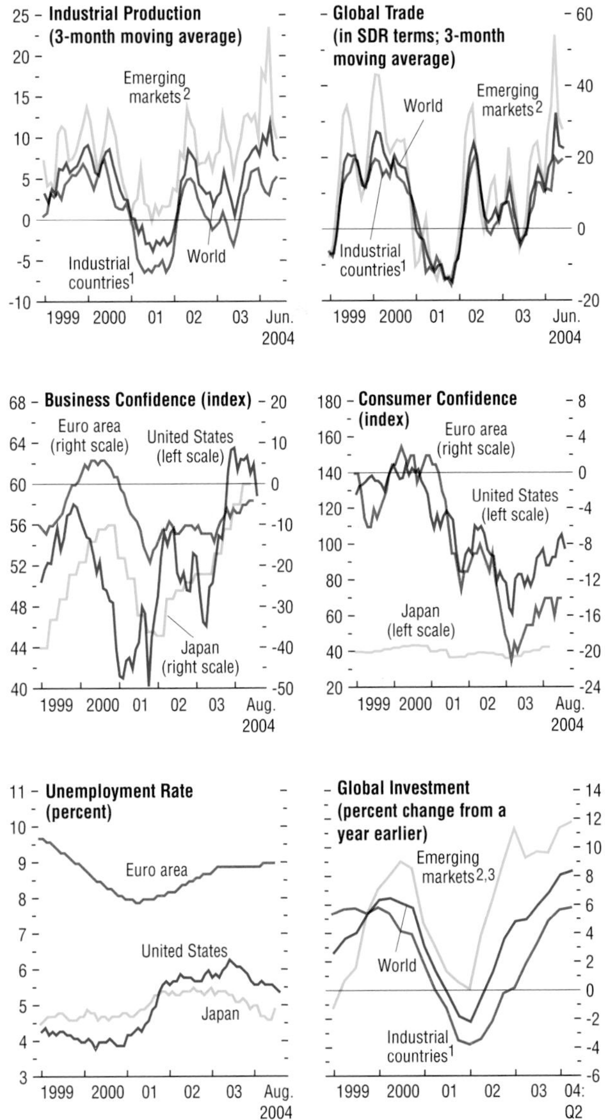

Sources: Business confidence for the United States, the Institute for Supply Management; for the euro area, the European Commission; and for Japan, Bank of Japan. Consumer confidence for the United States, the Conference Board; for the euro area, the European Commission; and for Japan, Cabinet Office. All others, Haver Analytics.

[1] Australia, Canada, Denmark, euro area, Japan, New Zealand, Norway, Sweden, Switzerland, the United Kingdom, and the United States.

[2] Argentina, Brazil, Bulgaria, Chile, China, Colombia, Czech Republic, Estonia, Hong Kong SAR, Hungary, India, Indonesia, Israel, Korea, Latvia, Lithuania, Malaysia, Mexico, Pakistan, Peru, the Philippines, Poland, Romania, Russia, Singapore, Slovak Republic, Slovenia, South Africa, Taiwan Province of China, Thailand, Turkey, Ukraine, and Venezuela.

[3] Data for China, India, Pakistan, and Russia are interpolated.

From a regional perspective, as discussed in more detail in Appendix 1.1, the impact of higher oil prices varies significantly, depending on—among other things—the energy intensity of production and consumption; the impact on the terms of trade; and the flexibility with which the economy adapts to shocks. Among industrial countries, the impact is somewhat larger in the United States and the euro area than in Japan and the United Kingdom. Among developing countries, oil producers clearly benefit; in aggregate, the adverse impact is largest in emerging Asia and Europe, and relatively small in Latin America. The impact on the poorest oil-importing countries—particularly in Africa and the Commonwealth of Independent States—is of particular concern, although in a number of cases it has been partly or fully offset by higher nonfuel prices (Figure 1.3).

After falling to unusually low levels in mid-2003, inflation across the world has turned up, with earlier concerns about deflation replaced by fears that inflation is making a comeback. Headline inflation has inevitably increased with higher oil prices, but in a number of countries—including the United States—core inflation has also picked up, in part reflecting temporary or one-off factors, as well as higher prices of crude and intermediate materials (Box 1.1, pp. 16–18). Inflationary risks vary across countries and regions, but in most appear moderate, given substantial excess capacity in many countries; generally moderate wage settlements relative to productivity growth; strong corporate profitability, particularly in the United States, providing scope for firms to absorb price pressures; and reasonably well-anchored inflationary expectations (Table 1.2). Even so, central banks will need to be vigilant to ensure that the second-round effects of higher headline inflation are well contained, a task that will be easier in those countries where central bank credibility is well established.

Financial market developments have been dominated by changing expectations about the pace and timing of monetary tightening in the United States. The growing strength of the recovery, combined with the changing language in Federal Open Market Committee statements, triggered a significant rise in long-run interest rates through mid-June (Figure 1.4), accompanied by widespread deleveraging. To date—as described in the September 2004 *Global Financial Stability Report*—the market adjustment to these developments has been orderly, and has not posed a threat to financial stability or the health of financial institutions. Mature market equity valuations and corporate bond spreads generally held up relatively well, aided by rising corporate profitability and continued progress in balance sheet restructuring. The biggest impact was in emerging markets, where bond spreads—which had been close to historical lows—widened significantly, and new issuance slowed (Figure 1.5; Table 1.3). Since June, these trends have partially reversed, as weaker U.S. data have prompted a downward revision in the expected pace of U.S. monetary tightening. Long-run interest rates have fallen back, equity markets have weakened, and risk appetite has strengthened, accompanied by a corresponding improvement in emerging market financing conditions. Despite the apparent uncertainty as to future U.S. monetary developments—and other factors, notably oil prices and geopolitical risks—expected volatility in major stock and bond markets is at historically low levels, raising concerns that markets may be becoming unduly complacent.

In foreign exchange markets, rising expectations of higher U.S. interest rates and buoyant growth contributed to a moderate appreciation in the U.S. dollar through the International Monetary and Financial Committee (IMFC) meetings in April. Since then, despite some volatility, the major currencies have moved rather little in trade-weighted terms, with a moderate depreciation of the U.S. dollar and yen accompanied by small appreciations of the euro and the pound (Figure 1.6). Outside central Europe, most emerging market currencies have depreciated, notably in Asia and in Latin America, partly reflecting the deterioration in external financing conditions. Aided by rising

Figure 1.3. Trade Gains and Losses from Commodity Price Movements Between 2003 and 2004[1]
(Percent of GDP)

The impact of higher oil prices on many developing countries has been broadly offset by rising nonfuel commodities prices, although some countries—particularly in Africa and the CIS—have been harder hit.

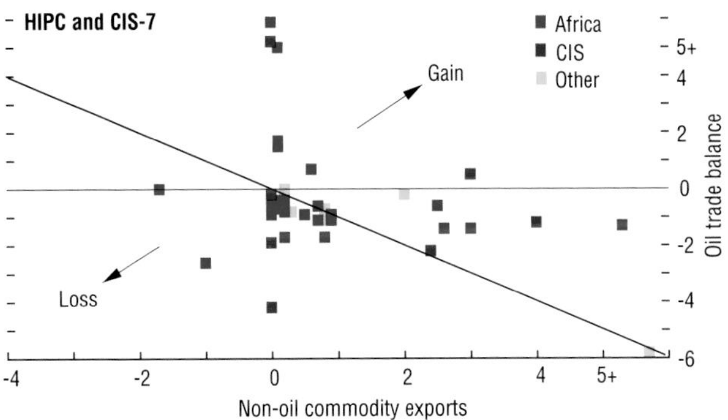

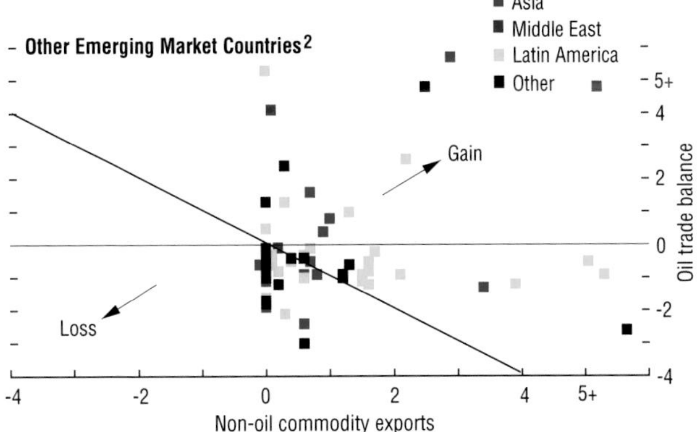

Source: IMF staff estimates.
[1]The figure shows the impact of the projected rise in commodity prices between 2003 and 2004 on nonfuel exports (horizontal axis) and the oil trade balance (vertical axis).
[2]Excluding oil exporters.

Table 1.2. Advanced Economies: Real GDP, Consumer Prices, and Unemployment
(Annual percent change and percent of labor force)

	Real GDP				Consumer Prices				Unemployment			
	2002	2003	2004	2005	2002	2003	2004	2005	2002	2003	2004	2005
Advanced economies	**1.6**	**2.1**	**3.6**	**2.9**	**1.5**	**1.8**	**2.1**	**2.1**	**6.4**	**6.6**	**6.3**	**6.1**
United States	1.9	3.0	4.3	3.5	1.6	2.3	3.0	3.0	5.8	6.0	5.5	5.4
Euro area[1]	0.8	0.5	2.2	2.2	2.3	2.1	2.1	1.9	8.5	8.9	9.0	8.7
Germany	0.1	−0.1	2.0	1.8	1.3	1.0	1.8	1.3	8.7	9.6	9.7	9.5
France	1.1	0.5	2.6	2.3	1.9	2.2	2.4	2.1	8.9	9.4	9.4	9.0
Italy	0.4	0.3	1.4	1.9	2.6	2.8	2.1	2.0	9.0	8.7	8.3	8.2
Spain	2.2	2.5	2.6	2.9	3.9	3.0	2.8	2.7	11.4	11.3	11.1	10.3
Netherlands	0.6	−0.9	1.1	1.8	3.9	2.2	1.4	1.1	2.5	4.3	5.3	5.8
Belgium	0.7	1.1	2.5	2.3	1.6	1.5	1.8	1.6	7.3	8.1	8.3	8.3
Austria	1.4	0.7	1.6	2.4	1.7	1.3	1.7	1.6	4.3	4.4	4.4	4.2
Finland	2.3	2.0	2.8	2.6	2.0	1.3	0.1	1.3	9.1	9.0	8.8	8.5
Greece	3.9	4.3	3.9	3.0	3.9	3.4	3.3	3.4	10.0	9.0	8.9	8.8
Portugal	0.4	−1.2	1.4	2.2	3.7	3.3	2.5	2.2	5.1	6.4	7.1	6.8
Ireland	6.1	3.7	4.7	5.0	4.7	4.0	2.3	2.1	4.4	4.7	4.4	4.1
Luxembourg	1.7	2.1	2.8	3.4	2.1	2.6	2.1	2.0	2.9	3.8	4.5	4.8
Japan	−0.3	2.5	4.4	2.3	−0.9	−0.2	−0.2	−0.1	5.4	5.3	4.7	4.5
United Kingdom[1]	1.8	2.2	3.4	2.5	1.3	1.4	1.6	1.9	5.2	5.0	4.8	4.8
Canada	3.4	2.0	2.9	3.1	2.3	2.7	1.9	2.2	7.7	7.6	7.2	6.8
Korea	7.0	3.1	4.6	4.0	2.8	3.5	3.8	3.8	3.1	3.4	3.5	3.6
Australia	3.8	3.0	3.6	3.4	3.0	2.8	2.8	2.5	6.4	6.1	5.7	5.7
Taiwan Province of China	3.6	3.3	5.6	4.1	−0.2	−0.3	1.1	1.5	5.2	5.0	4.7	4.5
Sweden	2.1	1.6	3.0	2.5	2.0	2.3	0.9	1.4	4.0	4.9	5.6	5.0
Switzerland	0.2	−0.5	1.8	2.2	0.6	0.6	0.7	0.8	2.5	3.5	3.4	3.0
Hong Kong SAR	1.9	3.2	7.5	4.0	−3.0	−2.6	—	1.0	7.3	7.9	6.7	5.8
Denmark	1.0	0.5	2.1	2.5	2.3	2.1	1.7	1.8	4.9	5.8	5.9	5.6
Norway	1.4	0.4	2.7	2.7	1.3	2.5	0.5	1.8	3.9	4.5	4.3	4.0
Israel	−0.7	1.3	3.6	3.5	5.7	0.7	−0.3	1.4	10.3	10.8	10.7	10.1
Singapore	2.2	1.1	8.8	4.4	−0.4	0.5	1.8	1.6	4.4	4.7	4.3	3.9
New Zealand[2]	4.3	3.4	4.2	2.0	2.7	1.8	2.4	2.8	5.2	4.7	4.6	5.0
Cyprus	2.0	2.0	3.0	3.5	2.8	4.1	2.2	2.6	3.2	3.5	3.4	3.2
Iceland	−0.5	4.0	4.4	5.3	4.8	2.1	3.3	3.2	2.5	3.3	3.0	2.3
Memorandum												
Major advanced economies	1.2	2.2	3.7	2.9	1.3	1.7	2.1	2.1	6.5	6.7	6.4	6.2
Newly industrialized Asian economies	5.0	3.0	5.5	4.0	0.9	1.4	2.4	2.6	4.1	4.3	4.1	4.1

[1]Based on Eurostat's harmonized index of consumer prices.
[2]Consumer prices excluding interest rate components.

real yields, the U.S. current account deficit has continued to be financed without major difficulty, with over half of net portfolio inflows continuing to come from Asia.

Against this background, and given the stronger-than-expected economic momentum in the first quarter of the year—consistent with the upside risks identified in the last *World Economic Outlook*—global GDP growth has been revised up to 5 percent in 2004. This has been underpinned by continued accommodative macroeconomic policies, rising corporate profitability, wealth effects from rising equity markets and house prices, rising employment, and—particularly relevant for Asian countries—the very strong growth in China. Looking forward, however, global growth is expected to moderate from the second quarter of 2004 (Figure 1.7) as these positive factors are offset by the steady decline in output gaps across the world; the ongoing withdrawal of fiscal and monetary stimulus (Figure 1.8); and the impact of higher oil prices. Correspondingly, global growth is projected to fall to 4.3 percent in 2005, slightly lower than expected last April, but still significantly above the historical trend.

Looking across individual countries and regions, we find the following.

- In *industrial countries*, the expansion continues to be led by the United States, with ebbing fiscal and monetary stimulus balanced by strong labor productivity growth. However, second-quarter GDP growth—especially private consumption—was weaker than expected, and employment growth has slowed. While this emergent "soft patch"—as discussed below—is most likely to be temporary, growth forecasts have been marked downward in both 2004 and 2005, and much continues to depend on a solid rebound in employment. In Japan, the upturn has also been strong, amid increasing signs that its long-standing problems—deflation and financial and corporate sector weaknesses—are easing. While growth slowed sharply in the second quarter, recent data suggest the near-term outlook remains solid. However, there are some downside risks to the staff forecast, with the key concerns including a further increase in oil prices and an eventual hard landing in China. The recovery is also taking root in the euro area with the 2004 forecast marked up significantly, but it remains heavily dependent on external demand. Final domestic demand—especially in Germany—has remained relatively weak. Looking forward, given the euro area's past history of slow adjustment to shocks, and with employment likely to strengthen only gradually, the pace of the expansion is expected to remain moderate.
- *Emerging market and developing countries* continue to experience a generally strong recovery, with GDP growth forecasts for 2004 revised upward markedly in all major regions. In *emerging Asia*, GDP growth is projected to remain at 7¼ percent in 2004, led by booming activity in China—fueled by very rapid investment and credit growth—and in India, where—despite recent adverse weather conditions—growth is being underpinned by the global expansion and supportive monetary conditions. For the region as a whole, domestic demand growth is generally strong, and current account surpluses—and in some cases capital inflows—remain very high. With output gaps declining

Figure 1.4. Developments in Mature Financial Markets

Long-term interest rates have risen significantly since the first quarter of 2004, but have since fallen back, accompanied by some weakening of equity markets.

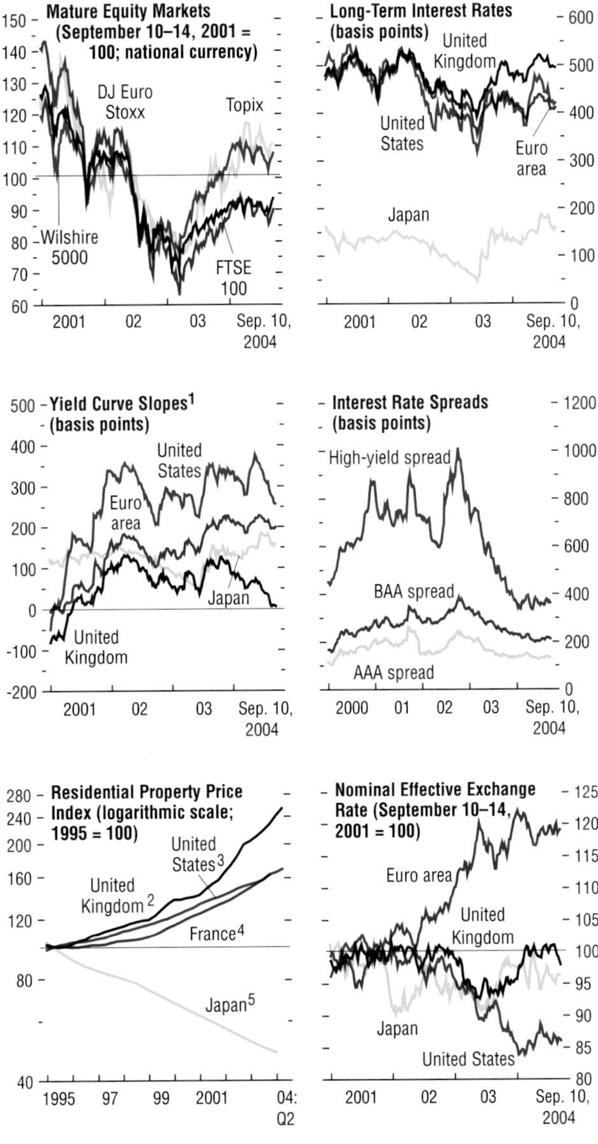

Sources: Bloomberg Financial Markets, LP; State Street Bank; HBOS Plc.; Office of Federal Housing Enterprise Oversight; National Sources; Japan Real Estate Institute; and IMF staff calculations.

[1]10-year government bond minus 3-month treasury bill rate.

[2]Halifax housing index as measured by the value of all houses.

[3]House price index as measured by the value of single-family homes in the United States as a whole, in various regions of the country, and in the individual states and the District of Columbia.

[4]Residential property prices: existing dwellings.

[5]Urban land price index: average of all categories in six large city areas.

Figure 1.5. Emerging Market Financial Conditions

After deteriorating in April and May 2004, emerging market financing conditions have improved, partly reflecting the decline in global long-term interest rates.

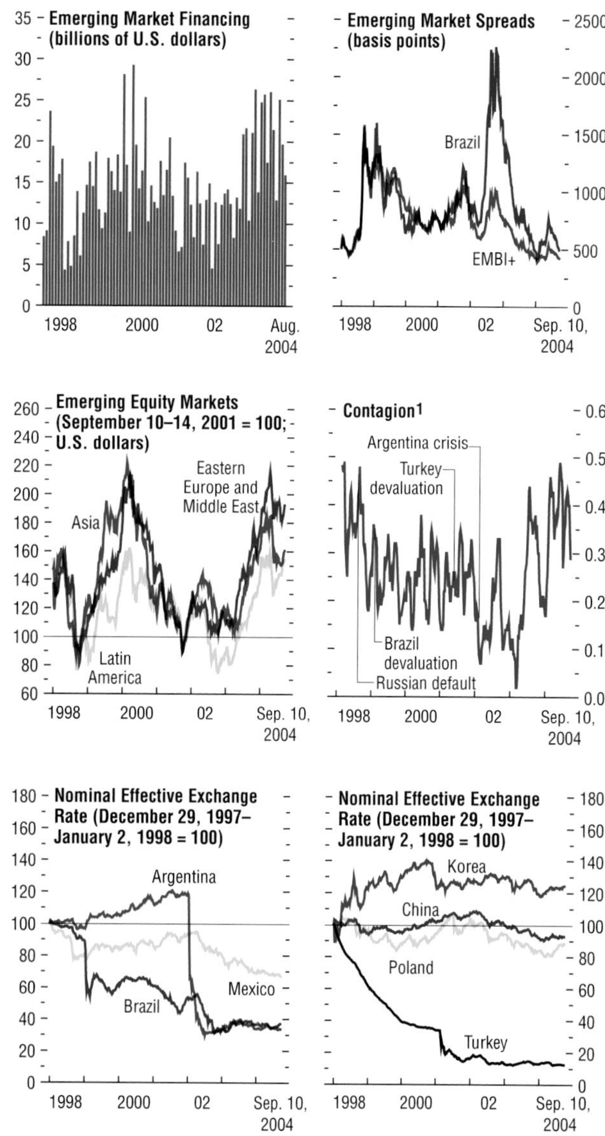

Sources: Bloomberg Financial Markets, LP; Capital Data; and IMF staff calculations.
[1]Average of 30-day rolling cross-correlation of emerging debt market spreads.

and exchange rates competitive, continuing very large reserve increases will increasingly complicate the conduct of monetary policy. The region remains relatively vulnerable to external developments, notably oil prices and a downturn in the information technology sector. A hard landing in China would also adversely affect a number of countries, particularly the newly industrialized and ASEAN economies, although the global consequences would likely be moderate (see Box 1.2, pp. 19–21). In *Latin America*, the recovery appears increasingly well established, with regional GDP growth projected to jump to 4.6 percent in 2004, supported by the global recovery, rising commodity prices, and, increasingly, domestic demand. With most countries taking advantage of earlier benign financing conditions to prefinance sovereign debt repayments for 2004, the deterioration in external financing conditions has so far proved manageable; however, with underlying regional vulnerabilities remaining large, adverse external shocks remain a key source of risk. In the *Middle East*, notwithstanding the still-fragile security situation, GDP forecasts have been revised upward in response to higher oil production and prices. GDP growth in *Turkey* is also exceeding expectations, although the widening current account deficit—exacerbated by higher oil prices—is a source of concern. Turning to the *Commonwealth of Independent States (CIS) countries*, rising global demand for oil and metals has boosted the already strong growth momentum in the region, with growth forecasts for Russia and Ukraine revised upward sharply, although some CIS-7 oil importers have been adversely affected. The expansion in *central and eastern Europe* also continues, with large fiscal and current account deficits remaining the central vulnerability.

- In the *poorest countries*, projected GDP growth in sub-Saharan Africa has been revised upward to 4.6 percent in 2004, mainly owing to higher-than-expected growth in Nigeria, and to 5.8 percent in 2005 (which, if achieved, would be the highest in three decades). This is being

Table 1.3. Emerging Market and Developing Countries: Net Capital Flows[1]

(Billions of U.S. dollars)

	1996	1997	1998	1999	2000	2001	2002	2003	2004	2005
Total										
Private capital flows, net[2]	196.7	195.0	70.5	88.1	46.6	47.8	61.2	120.4	81.6	47.5
Private direct investment, net	116.0	144.9	155.0	173.4	177.1	191.2	143.5	147.6	166.9	175.2
Private portfolio flows, net	86.3	63.3	41.9	66.6	16.1	−91.3	−99.6	−11.0	−21.3	−23.4
Other private capital flows, net	−5.6	−13.2	−126.4	−151.8	−146.6	−52.0	17.3	−16.2	−64.0	−104.4
Official flows, net	−6.8	34.6	49.7	6.5	−27.7	15.7	1.7	−24.8	−31.0	−42.1
Change in reserves[3]	−90.3	−103.8	−33.9	−92.5	−115.6	−113.2	−197.1	−367.0	−350.1	−291.2
Memorandum										
Current account[4]	−93.8	−83.3	−52.7	38.0	126.3	89.7	145.0	235.3	285.7	269.2
Africa										
Private capital flows, net[2]	4.5	12.3	8.3	12.2	5.6	13.5	11.9	14.8	16.6	13.7
Private direct investment, net	3.1	7.9	6.6	9.0	8.0	23.8	13.1	13.6	14.4	15.5
Private portfolio flows, net	2.9	7.0	3.7	8.7	−1.7	−8.4	−0.5	−0.1	1.4	1.1
Other private capital flows, net	−1.5	−2.6	−2.0	−5.5	−0.7	−2.0	−0.7	1.3	0.8	−2.9
Official flows, net	−2.6	−6.4	1.8	1.5	0.9	0.5	3.7	5.2	2.3	2.6
Change in reserves[3]	−5.9	−10.5	3.3	−2.9	−12.8	−12.3	−7.6	−20.0	−22.9	−23.4
Central and eastern Europe										
Private capital flows, net[2]	23.0	20.2	27.2	36.7	39.1	12.1	55.3	51.5	53.2	49.3
Private direct investment, net	10.4	11.6	19.2	22.6	23.9	24.2	25.1	14.9	22.7	24.7
Private portfolio flows, net	1.9	5.4	−1.4	5.7	3.1	0.5	1.5	7.0	9.2	10.0
Other private capital flows, net	10.7	3.2	9.4	8.4	12.1	−12.6	28.7	29.6	21.2	14.6
Official flows, net	0.1	−3.3	0.3	−2.6	1.6	5.5	−7.6	−5.5	−6.6	−5.5
Change in reserves[3]	−7.4	−10.6	−9.5	−11.3	−3.3	5.8	−14.4	−13.6	−9.4	−5.7
Commonwealth of Independent States[5]										
Private capital flows, net[2]	−3.8	19.6	7.2	−6.1	−12.6	−1.7	−9.2	15.2	−19.2	−5.8
Private direct investment, net	4.9	5.9	5.3	4.3	2.4	4.6	3.9	3.8	5.7	6.0
Private portfolio flows, net	−0.1	17.6	7.7	−3.0	−6.0	−9.2	−8.2	−5.0	−7.9	−8.2
Other private capital flows, net	−8.6	−3.9	−5.8	−7.4	−9.0	2.9	−4.8	16.4	−17.1	−3.5
Official flows, net	10.6	8.4	9.9	−0.1	−4.0	−4.2	−1.5	−4.7	−2.6	−2.5
Change in reserves[3]	2.2	−3.8	7.5	−2.2	−17.1	−11.2	−11.8	−33.6	−27.8	−34.7
Emerging Asia[6]										
Private capital flows, net[2,7]	119.4	37.6	−52.2	8.6	−4.5	9.6	25.4	52.8	79.8	8.6
Private direct investment, net	53.4	56.5	56.1	66.4	67.4	60.5	53.8	70.0	77.2	77.5
Private portfolio flows, net	32.5	6.7	8.1	56.1	19.8	−56.9	−59.6	5.5	12.0	−1.8
Other private capital flows, net[7]	33.5	−25.5	−116.4	−113.9	−91.7	6.0	31.2	−22.8	−9.4	−67.1
Official flows, net	−14.5	22.6	17.9	2.2	4.5	−1.8	−1.8	−16.3	−6.9	−8.8
Change in reserves[3]	−46.3	−36.4	−52.7	−87.2	−60.9	−90.9	−158.4	−234.2	−232.6	−158.0
Middle East[8]										
Private capital flows, net[2]	−1.0	7.8	13.3	−0.6	−20.6	−7.9	−23.6	−14.0	−45.5	−32.5
Private direct investment, net	4.6	5.3	5.8	5.3	6.4	7.8	5.8	13.4	8.8	12.2
Private portfolio flows, net	1.0	−2.7	−2.1	−2.3	−0.3	−7.9	−15.6	−16.7	−33.3	−27.5
Other private capital flows, net	−6.6	5.2	9.6	−3.5	−26.7	−7.8	−13.8	−10.7	−21.0	−17.2
Official flows, net	7.1	6.2	1.0	−1.0	−24.4	−10.7	−13.0	−26.3	−25.0	−28.1
Change in reserves[3]	−18.0	−16.1	10.2	−0.2	−26.1	−9.6	−3.3	−29.9	−44.8	−56.3
Western Hemisphere										
Private capital flows, net[2]	54.8	97.4	66.6	37.3	39.6	22.2	1.4	—	−3.3	14.2
Private direct investment, net	39.6	57.7	61.9	65.8	69.0	70.2	41.7	31.8	38.0	39.3
Private portfolio flows, net	48.2	29.4	25.8	1.5	1.3	−9.4	−17.1	−1.7	−2.8	3.0
Other private capital flows, net	−33.0	10.4	−21.1	−30.0	−30.6	−38.6	−23.2	−30.1	−38.5	−28.2
Official flows, net	−7.4	7.1	18.8	6.5	−6.1	26.5	22.0	22.7	7.8	0.2
Change in reserves[3]	−15.0	−26.3	7.3	11.3	4.7	4.9	−1.6	−35.7	−12.7	−13.2
Memorandum										
Fuel exporters										
Private capital flows, net[2]	−24.4	30.2	15.6	−17.7	−52.4	−11.8	−33.3	1.8	−66.7	−46.9
Nonfuel exporters										
Private capital flows, net[2]	221.1	164.8	54.9	105.8	99.0	59.6	94.5	118.6	148.3	94.4

[1]Net capital flows comprise net direct investment, net portfolio investment, and other long- and short-term net investment flows, including official and private borrowing. In this table, Hong Kong SAR, Israel, Korea, Singapore, and Taiwan Province of China are included.
[2]Because of data limitations, "other private capital flows, net" may include some official flows.
[3]A minus sign indicates an increase.
[4]The sum of the current account balance, net private capital flows, net official flows, and the change in reserves equals, with the opposite sign, the sum of the capital and financial account and errors and omissions. For regional current account balances, see Table 25 of the Statistical Appendix.
[5]Historical data have been revised, reflecting cumulative data revisions for Russia and the resolution of a number of data interpretation issues.
[6]Consists of developing Asia and the newly industrialized Asian economies.
[7]Excluding the effects of the recapitalization of two large commercial banks in China with foreign reserves of the Bank of China (US$45 billion), net private capital flows to emerging Asia in 2003 were US$97.8 billion while other private capital flows net to the region amounted to US$22.2 billion.
[8]Includes Israel.

underpinned by improved macroeconomic stability; sharply increasing oil production, as new facilities come on stream in several countries; improved political stability; and a recovery in agricultural production following severe droughts in 2003. It should be noted that IMF forecasts have consistently overestimated African GDP growth in the past, in part owing to unanticipated political instability and natural disasters.[2] Moreover, developments in some specific countries—notably, the humanitarian catastrophe unfolding in western Sudan and the economic collapse in Zimbabwe—are of deep concern. Nonetheless, prospects for much of Africa appear more favorable than they have been for many years, a particularly welcome aspect of the current outlook.

Given the continued uncertainties in the oil market, as well as the softer-than-expected incoming data in the United States and some other countries, the risks to the outlook have shifted to the downside. In the short run, geopolitical risks, while hard to quantify, remain very much present and, in contrast to the past, the room for policy easing in response to geopolitical disturbances is relatively limited. Beyond that, the two following risks appear most immediate.

- *With spare capacity at historical lows, and concentrated in one country, the oil market remains highly vulnerable to shocks.* As the *World Economic Outlook* went to press, oil prices had risen somewhat above the World Economic Outlook baseline, and supply-side risks are substantial, with a sustained $5 a barrel increase in oil prices tending to reduce global growth by about 0.3 percent (Appendix 1.1). This would be of particular concern in countries where domestic demand remains weak; for highly indebted oil importers (including the Philippines and Turkey); and for many poor countries. Looking forward, spare capacity in the oil market is expected to remain low

Figure 1.6. Global Exchange Rate Developments

Trade-weighted exchange rates in most industrial countries are broadly unchanged since the last IMFC meeting in April; outside central Europe, exchange rates in emerging markets have remained stable or depreciated.

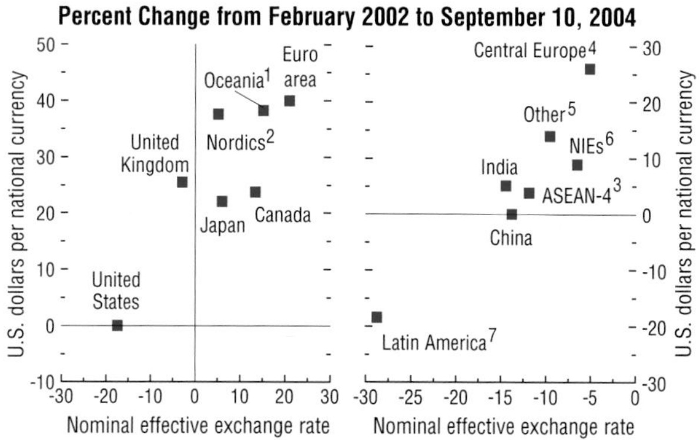

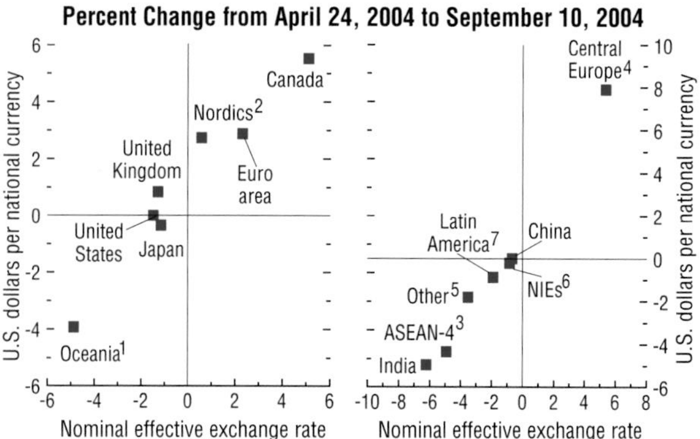

Sources: Bloomberg Financial, LP; and IMF staff calculations.
[1]Australia and New Zealand.
[2]Denmark, Norway, and Sweden.
[3]Indonesia, Malaysia, the Philippines, and Thailand.
[4]Czech Republic, Hungary, and Poland.
[5]Russia, Turkey, and South Africa.
[6]Hong Kong SAR, Korea, Singapore, and Taiwan Province of China.
[7]Argentina, Brazil, Chile, Colombia, Mexico, Peru, and Venezuela.

[2]See "The Accuracy of World Economic Outlook Growth Forecasts: 1991–2000," Box 3.1, *World Economic Outlook*, December 2001.

through the remainder of the decade. Consequently, with terrorist attacks on oil supply a continuing risk, higher and more volatile oil prices may persist. This underscores the need to reduce vulnerability to such conditions, both through concerted measures to restrain the growth of oil demand and through investment in capacity expansion in oil-producing countries.

- *Inflationary pressures could prove stronger than expected—although this concern is tempered by downside risks to global growth—necessitating a sharper rise in interest rates than markets presently price in.* This seems unlikely to give rise to major problems in mature financial markets,[3] but there could be a significant impact on housing markets, which are surprisingly synchronized across countries (see the first essay in Chapter II). This would be of particular concern in countries where housing prices appear richly valued—notably, the United Kingdom, Australia, Ireland, and Spain—and where a large share of mortgage debt is at adjustable rates. Nonetheless, slower house price growth could also adversely affect domestic demand in other countries. Higher interest rates would also result in a further deterioration in emerging market financing conditions. While this by itself would in most cases be manageable, the risks would be significantly greater if it were accompanied by other adverse shocks.

Looking beyond the short term, there are both opportunities and significant risks.

- *The information technology (IT) revolution, along with China's emergence, presents an opportunity for sustained higher global productivity growth.*[4] To date, the benefits of the IT revolution have come primarily from higher productivity in the IT sector itself and from higher investment. However, history suggests that the

[3]See the September 2004 *Global Financial Stability Report* for a detailed discussion.

[4]See Martin Wolf, "Three Reasons To Be Cheerful About The World Economy," *Financial Times*, Wednesday, June 30, 2004, for an eloquent statement of this view.

Figure 1.7. Global Outlook

(Real GDP; percent change from four quarters earlier)

Following the very rapid expansion since mid-2003, global growth has slowed since the first quarter of 2004, but is expected to remain relatively strong.

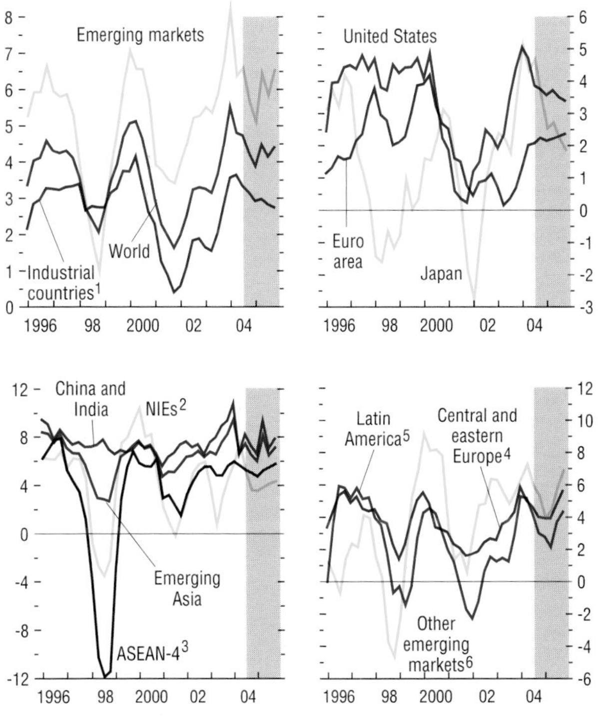

Sources: Haver Analytics; and IMF staff estimates.

[1]Australia, Canada, Denmark, euro area, Japan, New Zealand, Norway, Sweden, Switzerland, the United Kingdom, and the United States.

[2]Hong Kong SAR, Korea, Singapore, and Taiwan Province of China.

[3]Indonesia, Malaysia, the Philippines, and Thailand.

[4]Czech Republic, Estonia, Hungary, Latvia, and Poland.

[5]Argentina, Brazil, Chile, Colombia, Mexico, Peru, and Venezuela.

[6]Israel, Russia, South Africa, and Turkey.

Figure 1.8. Fiscal and Monetary Easing in the Major Advanced Countries

Monetary and fiscal policies in most industrial countries are projected to tighten in 2005, most rapidly in the United States.

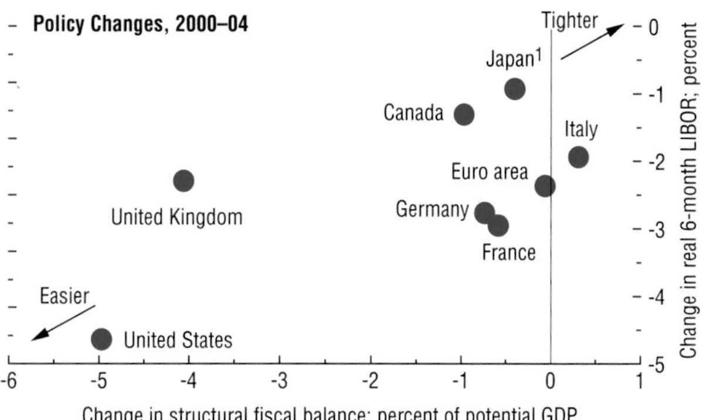

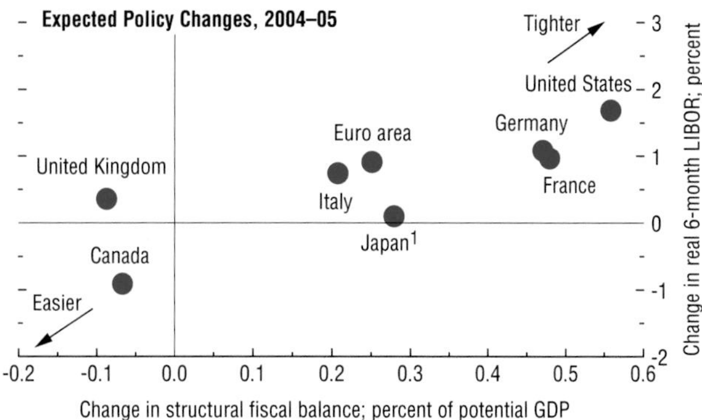

Source: IMF staff estimates.
[1]For Japan, excludes bank support.

largest gains will come from the reorganization of production processes to take advantage of the new technology,[5] a process that has only just begun—outsourcing being one example—and is likely to continue for a considerable period. China's rapid growth, which may well be sustained for two decades or more, will also result in a substantial—although smaller-scale—reorganization of global production, the more so if it is joined by India.[6] Both these developments suggest the scope for substantial productivity gains in coming years, coming most rapidly in those countries that are sufficiently adaptable to take advantage of them.

- However, *significant economic vulnerabilities remain in both industrial and emerging market countries,* particularly on the fiscal side (Figure 1.9 and Table 1.4). With much still to do on pension and health reform (see Chapter III), many industrial countries are still far from prepared for the impact of aging populations. In emerging markets, external vulnerabilities have generally been reduced. However, high and poorly structured public debt is for many an Achilles' heel, which if not addressed is very likely to lead to further financial crises in the future. Corporate and financial sector vulnerabilities—in both industrial and emerging markets—also remain significant, particularly in countries where nonperforming loans remain large or private credit growth is rapid.
- *The global imbalances, notably the large U.S. current account deficit and surpluses elsewhere, remain a key risk.* The U.S. current account deficit has continued to increase through the first half of 2004 and, despite the past depreciation of the U.S. dollar, is projected to remain above 4 percent of GDP over the medium term (Table 1.5). The question is not whether the U.S. deficit will adjust—it will—but when and how

[5]One such example is the invention of electricity, which allowed the introduction of the production line. For a detailed discussion, see "The Information Technology Revolution," Chapter III, *World Economic Outlook,* September 2001.

[6]See "China's Emergence and Its Impact on the Global Economy," *World Economic Outlook,* April 2004.

that adjustment will take place, and in particular whether it will be associated with an abrupt exchange rate adjustment. Some factors—notably strong U.S. productivity growth and deepening global capital markets—are supportive of an orderly adjustment; however, others—including the high level of the U.S. deficit in relation to exports—are less so. And since current account corrections have historically tended to be associated with a slowdown in growth in the deficit country, even an orderly adjustment carries risks, given the central role that the United States has played in supporting global growth in recent years.

With the global expansion expected to remain solid, the key short-term policy challenge is still to manage the transition toward higher interest rates, ensuring that nascent inflationary pressures are contained while facilitating—through effective communication—a continued orderly adjustment in financial markets. Within that, the desirable pace and timing vary significantly, ranging from China—where monetary conditions have already been tightened and more may be needed to prevent incipient overheating—to Japan, where despite stronger growth and easing deflationary pressures, monetary policy should remain accommodative until deflation and deflationary expectations turn around decisively. In the United States, the long-awaited tightening cycle began in June; with considerable economic slack persisting, the Federal Reserve has appropriately indicated that future interest rate increases are likely to be measured, although with uncertainties about both the pace of recovery and the strength of inflationary pressures, much will depend on the nature of incoming data. In the euro area, headline inflation has again risen above 2 percent, in part reflecting higher oil prices and one-off factors. But with underlying inflationary pressures—including wage increases—still moderate, the European Central Bank (ECB) has appropriately remained on hold, and monetary policies should remain accommodative until a self-sustaining pickup in domestic demand is clearly under way.

Figure 1.9. Fiscal Vulnerability Indicators
(Percent of GDP unless otherwise indicated)

Fiscal deficits in many countries have increased since 2000, accompanied by rising public debt.

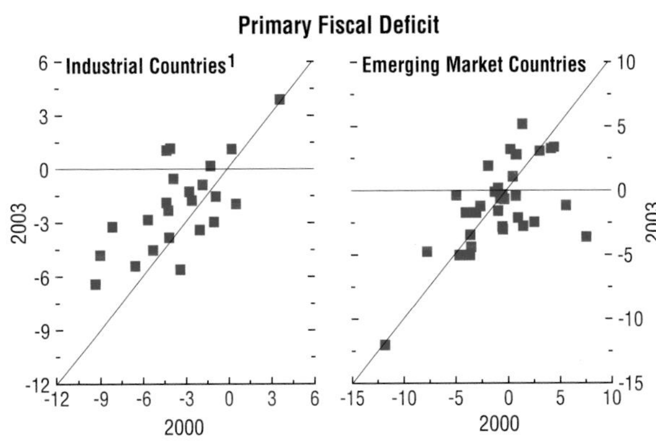

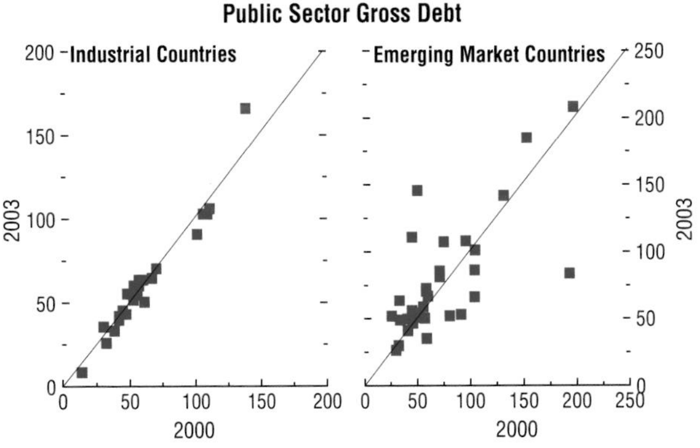

Source: IMF staff calculations.
[1]Structural primary deficit in percent of potential GDP.

Table 1.4. Major Advanced Economies: General Government Fiscal Balances and Debt[1]
(Percent of GDP)

	1988–97	1998	1999	2000	2001	2002	2003	2004	2005	2009
Major advanced economies										
Actual balance	–3.7	–1.5	–1.2	–0.2	–1.8	–4.0	–4.6	–4.5	–4.0	–2.8
Output gap[2]	–0.2	0.1	0.5	1.2	–0.4	–1.8	–2.3	–1.3	–1.0	—
Structural balance	–3.6	–1.5	–1.3	–1.2	–1.7	–3.4	–3.6	–3.9	–3.5	–2.8
United States										
Actual balance	–3.8	0.1	0.6	1.3	–0.7	–4.0	–4.6	–4.9	–4.3	–2.9
Output gap[2]	–0.9	0.9	1.9	2.2	–0.4	–2.0	–2.3	–1.3	–1.0	—
Structural balance	–3.5	–0.3	–0.1	0.5	–0.6	–3.3	–3.8	–4.4	–3.9	–2.9
Net debt	55.3	52.8	48.2	43.3	41.9	44.5	47.0	48.9	50.3	52.3
Gross debt	69.1	66.2	62.8	57.1	56.6	58.6	60.5	61.5	62.2	61.9
Euro area										
Actual balance	. . .	–2.3	–1.3	–0.9	–1.7	–2.3	–2.8	–2.9	–2.5	–1.1
Output gap[2]	. . .	–0.4	0.2	1.3	0.7	–0.5	–1.9	–1.8	–1.7	—
Structural balance	. . .	–1.9	–1.3	–1.6	–2.1	–2.2	–1.7	–1.7	–1.4	–1.0
Net debt	. . .	62.0	61.6	59.1	58.9	58.8	60.2	60.6	60.5	57.1
Gross debt	. . .	73.8	72.7	70.4	69.4	69.2	70.6	70.9	70.6	66.3
Germany[3]										
Actual balance	–2.4	–2.2	–1.5	1.3	–2.8	–3.7	–3.8	–3.9	–3.3	–1.6
Output gap[2]	0.6	–0.4	–0.1	0.9	0.3	–1.1	–2.6	–2.2	–2.0	—
Structural balance[4]	–2.7	–1.7	–1.2	–1.6	–2.9	–2.9	–2.2	–2.4	–1.9	–1.7
Net debt	35.3	53.3	54.9	52.8	53.5	55.5	58.7	60.8	62.3	62.8
Gross debt	48.4	60.9	61.2	60.2	59.4	60.9	63.8	65.7	67.1	67.0
France										
Actual balance	–3.7	–2.7	–1.8	–1.4	–1.4	–3.2	–4.1	–3.4	–2.8	–1.0
Output gap[2]	–0.9	–1.5	–0.6	1.2	1.0	—	–1.4	–1.1	–1.0	—
Structural balance[4]	–3.0	–1.8	–1.4	–2.0	–2.1	–3.2	–3.2	–2.6	–2.1	–1.0
Net debt	35.2	49.8	48.8	47.5	48.2	49.1	54.0	54.6	54.7	52.5
Gross debt	44.2	59.5	58.5	57.1	56.8	58.7	63.7	64.3	64.4	62.2
Italy										
Actual balance	–9.2	–2.8	–1.7	–0.6	–2.6	–2.3	–2.4	–2.9	–2.8	–1.6
Output gap[2]	0.1	–0.1	—	1.0	0.6	–1.0	–2.5	–2.8	–2.7	—
Structural balance[4]	–9.0	–2.8	–1.8	–2.4	–3.1	–2.6	–1.4	–2.1	–1.9	–1.6
Net debt	104.4	110.1	108.4	104.5	103.9	101.4	99.8	99.4	97.9	91.4
Gross debt	110.3	116.4	114.6	111.2	110.6	108.0	106.2	105.8	104.2	97.3
Japan										
Actual balance	–1.3	–5.5	–7.2	–7.5	–6.1	–7.9	–8.2	–6.9	–6.5	–6.1
Excluding social security	–3.7	–6.9	–8.2	–8.0	–6.2	–7.7	–7.7	–6.4	–5.9	–5.2
Output gap[2]	1.2	–1.2	–2.4	–1.4	–2.6	–4.3	–3.4	–0.8	–0.2	0.1
Structural balance	–1.7	–5.1	–6.3	–6.9	–5.1	–6.2	–6.9	–6.6	–6.4	–6.2
Excluding social security	–3.9	–6.6	–7.7	–7.7	–5.6	–6.8	–7.0	–6.2	–5.9	–5.3
Net debt	20.2	45.8	53.5	59.1	65.1	71.4	79.7	85.2	90.8	107.2
Gross debt	81.0	117.9	131.0	139.3	148.8	158.4	166.2	169.6	173.8	180.7
United Kingdom										
Actual balance	–3.7	0.1	1.0	3.9	0.8	–1.7	–3.4	–3.0	–2.9	–2.6
Output gap[2]	—	0.6	—	1.1	0.9	–0.1	–0.6	—	—	—
Structural balance[4]	–3.7	–0.2	0.9	1.3	0.2	–1.9	–3.2	–2.8	–2.9	–2.6
Net debt	31.4	42.4	40.2	34.4	33.0	33.0	34.8	34.8	35.9	39.4
Gross debt	43.3	47.3	44.8	41.9	38.6	38.2	39.6	39.9	40.9	44.5
Canada										
Actual balance	–5.6	0.1	1.6	2.9	1.1	0.3	0.6	0.7	0.9	1.2
Output gap[2]	—	–0.8	0.6	2.0	0.3	0.4	–0.8	–0.7	–0.3	—
Structural balance	–5.4	0.5	1.4	2.1	1.0	0.3	1.1	1.1	1.0	1.2
Net debt	76.1	83.8	75.4	65.3	59.5	56.5	51.9	48.3	45.0	33.2
Gross debt	108.0	114.8	111.6	101.5	99.1	95.4	90.9	85.0	79.8	62.0

Note: The methodology and specific assumptions for each country are discussed in Box A1 in the Statistical Appendix.

[1]Debt data refer to end of year. Debt data are not always comparable across countries. For example, the Canadian data include the unfunded component of government employee pension liabilities, which amounted to nearly 18 percent of GDP in 2001.

[2]Percent of potential GDP.

[3]Data before 1990 refer to west Germany. Beginning in 1995, the debt and debt-service obligations of the Treuhandanstalt (and of various other agencies) were taken over by general government. This debt is equivalent to 8 percent of GDP, and the associated debt service, to ½ to 1 percent of GDP.

[4]Excludes one-off receipts from the sale of mobile telephone licenses (the equivalent of 2.5 percent of GDP in 2000 for Germany, 0.1 percent of GDP in 2001 and 2002 for France, 1.2 percent of GDP in 2000 for Italy, and 2.4 percent of GDP in 2000 for the United Kingdom). Also excludes one-off receipts from sizable asset transactions.

The central issue, however, must be to address the medium-term vulnerabilities and concerns discussed above. The key issues include the following.

- *Strengthening medium-term fiscal positions, through both consolidation and reforms of pension and health systems.* While most industrial countries target a gradual fiscal consolidation, in many cases this depends on relatively optimistic fiscal assumptions (the United States), and the policies to achieve it are not well defined (the euro area and Japan). Despite some progress on pension reform, notably in the euro area and Japan, much remains to be done to address the pressures from aging, the more so since past population projections have systematically underestimated the size of the problem (see Chapter III). In emerging markets, fiscal consolidation is under way in much of Latin America and beginning in some countries in Asia, but is lagging in much of emerging Europe. For many countries, large primary surpluses will need to be sustained for a considerable period to bring public debt down to manageable levels, in the face of substantial—and understandable—pressures for additional social and infrastructure spending. This underscores the importance of other measures to improve public debt sustainability, especially broadening tax bases, strengthening frameworks for public expenditure management, and last, but not least, structural measures to boost growth (historically the key to most successful debt reduction efforts).
- *Strengthening the foundations for sustained and sustainable growth.* In industrial countries, the price of economic inflexibility has risen with increasingly rapid technological change and globalization, and in a number of countries past tradeoffs between social and economic goals may need to be reevaluated. There has been progress in the euro area (notably, labor market reforms under Agenda 2010 in Germany) and in Japan (where banking and corporate sectors have been strengthened), but a substantial agenda remains. In emerging markets, priorities include completing financial and corporate sector reform in Asia; improving the investment climate—including through tax reform—in Latin America; strengthening banking supervision in eastern Europe; and, in the Middle East, putting in place the institutional infrastructure to underpin non-oil private sector development. From a multilateral perspective, the central objective is to achieve substantive trade liberalization under the Doha Round. The end-July package of agreements reached in Geneva is therefore a welcome step forward, putting the

Table 1.5. Selected Economies: Current Account Positions
(Percent of GDP)

	2002	2003	2004	2005
Advanced economies	**–0.8**	**–0.8**	**–0.8**	**–0.8**
United States	–4.5	–4.8	–5.4	–5.1
Euro area[1]	0.8	0.3	0.8	0.9
Germany	2.2	2.2	4.4	4.8
France	1.0	0.3	–0.6	–0.6
Italy	–0.6	–1.5	–1.1	–0.8
Spain	–2.4	–2.8	–3.4	–3.6
Netherlands	2.5	2.2	2.9	3.1
Belgium	5.3	3.8	4.5	4.6
Austria	0.3	–0.9	–1.0	–1.1
Finland	6.8	5.7	5.8	6.2
Greece	–6.0	–5.7	–6.0	–5.7
Portugal	–6.8	–5.1	–6.1	–6.3
Ireland	–1.3	–1.4	–1.6	–1.3
Luxembourg	11.5	9.3	10.1	11.4
Japan	2.8	3.2	3.4	3.2
United Kingdom	–1.7	–1.9	–2.0	–1.9
Canada	2.0	2.0	2.9	2.4
Korea	1.0	2.0	3.1	3.3
Australia	–4.4	–5.9	–5.3	–4.9
Taiwan Province of China	9.1	10.2	6.9	6.0
Sweden	5.4	6.4	6.7	5.7
Switzerland	8.5	10.2	10.3	10.6
Hong Kong SAR	7.9	10.7	10.0	9.6
Denmark	2.0	3.0	1.8	1.9
Norway	12.9	13.0	15.9	16.0
Israel	–1.6	0.1	–0.5	–0.1
Singapore	21.4	30.9	25.7	23.9
New Zealand	–3.1	–4.2	–4.4	–4.4
Cyprus	–5.4	–4.4	–4.3	–4.2
Iceland	–0.3	–5.4	–5.9	–9.7
Memorandum				
Major advanced economies	–1.5	–1.6	–1.5	–1.5
Euro area[2]	0.8	0.4	0.3	0.5
Newly industrialized Asian economies	5.8	7.6	6.8	6.5

[1]Calculated as the sum of the balances of individual euro area countries.
[2]Corrected for reporting discrepancies in intra-area transactions.

Box 1.1. Is Global Inflation Coming Back?

Over the past 15 years, global consumer price inflation has been reduced dramatically, in advanced and developing countries alike, underpinned by a combination of more effective and independent central banking institutions and, just as important, the pressures from globalization (Appendix 2.1 of the April 2002 *World Economic Outlook;* and Rogoff, 2003). As of 2003, only three countries had annual inflation rates in excess of 40 percent, the level above which it is generally considered to be acutely damaging. In none of the G-7 countries did inflation exceed 3 percent (and in Japan, of course, deflation persisted). Moreover, in many middle-income countries where high inflation had once been almost a permanent feature of the economic landscape, inflation has been brought well into single digits.

Since 2000, annual global headline and core inflation (based on the CPI excluding energy products) has averaged about 3 percent (see the figure), although this historically low figure has masked some volatility.[1] In particular, in the middle of 2003, headline inflation fell to unusually low levels, in industrial and emerging countries alike, which—with the recovery still weak—raised fears of global deflationary pressures. From end-2003, with global output growing rapidly and commodity prices rising sharply, headline inflation turned up significantly, although it still remains moderate. Correspondingly, deflationary fears dissipated, and—with monetary policies across the globe still quite accommodative—there have been concerns that inflation could make a comeback.

A significant proportion of the recent rise in headline inflation appears to have been due to higher commodity prices (as of July 2004, oil

Global Inflation

(Annualized percent change of three-month moving average over previous three-month average)

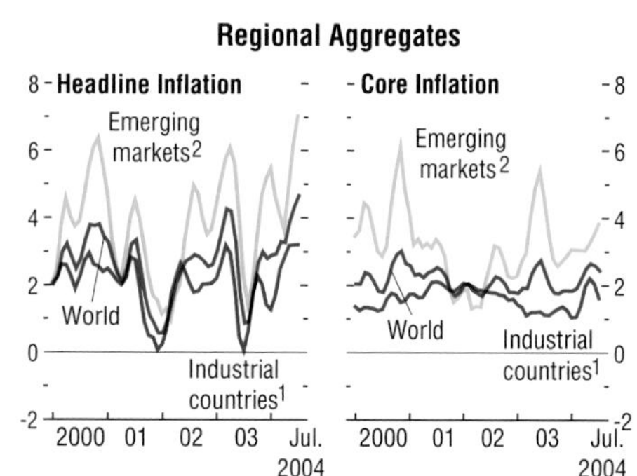

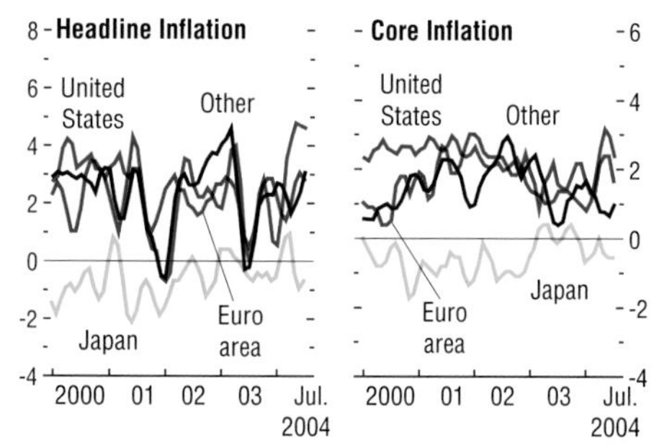

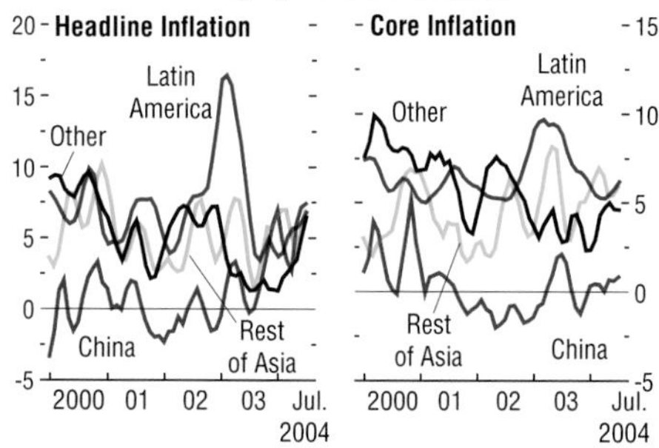

Sources: Haver Analytics; and IMF staff calculations.
[1]Canada, Denmark, euro area, Japan, Norway, Sweden, United Kingdom, and United States.
[2]Brazil, Chile, China, India, Indonesia, Hungary, Korea, Mexico, Poland, and South Africa.

prices were 27 percent and non-oil commodity prices were 9 percent above their end-December,

Note: The main authors of this box are David J. Robinson and Sandy Mackenzie.

[1]The remainder of this box focuses on inflation in a group of 29 industrial and emerging market countries, covering about 80 percent of global output, for which monthly data on both headline and core CPI inflation are available.

2003 level). Core inflation has risen by considerably less than headline inflation (see the figure), and remains at relatively moderate levels.[2] From a regional perspective, headline inflation has increased almost everywhere, but developments in core inflation have varied considerably. The rise in core inflation in the United States has been surprisingly steep,[3] possibly partly reflecting a rebound from the abnormally low levels experienced in 2003, although it has eased in recent months. In contrast, the increase in the euro area is not pronounced. Despite substantial monthly fluctuations, some upward trend in core inflation is also discernable in China, other emerging Asian countries, and emerging Europe and Latin America.

A key question for monetary policymakers is whether the recent rise in both headline and core inflation will be one-off in nature, or whether it could feed through to wages, and thereby become more entrenched. Such risks would be greater if excess capacity in the economy is small (since labor markets are then correspondingly tight and putting pressure on profit margins) or if inflationary expectations are rising (making it more likely that higher inflation will be built into future wage awards). Looking at the evidence across the globe, we find the following.

- *Margins of spare capacity are declining, but in most countries are still significant.* Given the robust growth of the global economy—projected to reach 4.9 percent in 2004, almost 1 percentage point above its trend—capacity utilization rates must be on the rise. Even so, spare capacity in most industrial countries, except the United Kingdom, Australia, and Norway, appears significant, with estimated output gaps still sizable. This is particularly so in the euro area, where output gaps of close to 2 percent of GDP are expected to persist over the next several years. In the United States, the output gap is smaller, but not expected to close until 2007. That said, it should be recognized that such estimates are subject to both large margins of error and substantial revisions (one key uncertainty—particularly relevant in the United States—being the pace of labor productivity growth in the future). In emerging market and developing countries, output gaps are even more difficult to measure, but—as discussed in the main text—overheating pressures are becoming a concern in some countries in Asia and in the CIS.
- *Inflationary expectations have risen moderately, but still appear relatively well grounded.* Since December, the consensus forecast for global inflation in 2005 has been revised upward by 0.3 percent to 2.6 percent. The largest upward revisions have been for emerging markets—notably China, Poland, and Brazil (where domestic measures of inflationary expectations have also picked up)—with smaller increases in industrial countries (see the table). Looking over the longer term, professional forecasts—where available—have remained relatively well grounded. Financial market expectations for long-run U.S. inflation—proxied by the spread between the rates of nominal and indexed 10-year treasury bills[4]—rose by 0.25 percent between December and June—with similar increases observed for the United Kingdom, France, and Canada—but have since fallen back, perhaps because the latest monthly statistics implied some abatement of inflation.

Overall, the combination of higher global growth and rising commodity prices will mean that monetary policies will generally need to be tightened somewhat faster than earlier

[2]For most countries, core inflation is defined as the CPI excluding food and energy. For countries where these data are not readily available, another relatively stable price index is used.

[3]Federal Reserve economists estimate that only one-fourth to one-half of the increase in core inflation in 2004 over 2003 reflects higher commodity prices (Federal Reserve Board, 2004).

[4]The spread between nominal and index-linked bonds is only an imperfect measure of inflationary expectations, since it can also increase when investors are more uncertain about their forecasts and willing to pay a premium for a hedge.

Box 1.1 *(concluded)*

Consensus Forecasts: Projected Inflation in 2005[1]
(Percent)

	January	March	August
World	2.3	2.3	2.6
United States	2.1	1.9	2.4
Euro area	1.7	1.6	1.8
Japan	–0.2	–0.2	0.0
China	2.4	2.8	3.2
Brazil	5.4	5.2	6.0
Poland	2.7	2.8	3.2[2]

Source: Consensus Forecasts.
[1]World projection based on 18-country sample, including the euro area.
[2]July.

expected, depending—as discussed in the main text—on the cyclical positions in individual countries and regions. In most cases the risks of a marked pickup in inflation appear moderate, given still-significant margins of excess capacity; well-grounded inflationary expectations; and—outside the most cyclically advanced countries—relatively moderate labor market pressures and rising profit margins. That said, policymakers will need to respond promptly if inflationary pressures intensify or capacity utilization tightens more rapidly than expected, not least since waiting too long to respond to signs of incipient inflation could be costly to reverse, and would lose central banks some of the credibility that took so long to build up in the 1980s and 1990s.

Looking beyond the short term, however, is there a risk that the long-term factors that supported the recent global disinflation could go into reverse? At the present juncture, the fundamental forces underlying disinflation—more effective and independent central banks, and globalization—remain broadly in place. While this appears most likely to continue, as Rogoff (2003) notes, "one must acknowledge that any pronounced or widespread relapses in the relatively favorable backdrop of globalization, deregulation, productivity increase, and relatively benign fiscal policies could begin to roll back the extraordinary achievements of recent years." Two particular concerns—relevant to the current policy challenges discussed in the main text—include the possibility of reversals in globalization through rising terrorist risks or renewed protectionist pressures, and a failure to address medium-term fiscal problems, increasing the incentives to inflate debt away at some time in the future.

Round formally back on track (Box 1.3, pp. 22–23). That said, the agreements provide the minimum necessary in terms of ambition and specificity for continuing the next phase of negotiations—particularly in the key areas of agriculture, industrial products, trade facilitation, and development issues—and much work remains to be done before the December 2005 Ministerial Meeting in Hong Kong SAR.

- *All countries and regions need to play their part in addressing the global imbalances.* The key policy requirements include medium-term fiscal consolidation in the United States to boost savings; structural reforms to boost growth prospects outside the United States; and greater exchange rate flexibility in Asia, consistent with an orderly reduction in current account surpluses. The first two are to varying degrees moving forward, although much remains to be done, but little progress has been made on the third. The continued rapid buildup in reserves in Asia, the dependence of the United States on financial inflows from that region, and the uncertainty about how the situation will be resolved remain important sources of potential instability, and the longer this is expected to persist, the more likely the situation is to be resolved in a disorderly fashion.
- *Poverty reduction must remain at the top of the international agenda.* The recent strength of growth in the regions where poverty is most concentrated—China, India, and sub-Saharan Africa—is welcome; nevertheless, Africa is still likely to fall well short of the Millennium

Box 1.2. What Are the Risks of Slower Growth in China?

China's economic growth has been marked by periods of cyclical surges in economic activity and inflation, followed by periods of retrenchment. In the 1980s, two cycles ended with hard landings characterized by sharp slowdowns in growth. These periods were often influenced by political changes and typically began with an early relaxation of monetary and fiscal policies to support state-owned enterprises, leading to a significant increase in inflation. The authorities eventually responded with a heavy reliance on direct controls and other administrative measures. Inflation was quickly brought under control, but growth slowed sharply, and the administrative measures adopted were not based on market criteria, with adverse implications for the efficiency of resource allocation.

This general pattern was repeated during the 1991–97 cycle. By 1992, an easing in monetary and fiscal policies led to an investment boom with real GDP growth exceeding 14 percent and an acceleration in inflation. Early attempts at tightening policies hit state-owned enterprises hard, prompting a relaxation of policies. This easing, and a devaluation of the official exchange rate when it was unified with the swap rate, resulted in inflation rising to a peak of over 24 percent in 1994 (see the figure). The authorities eventually achieved a "soft landing" of the economy, with inflation in single digits by 1996 and only a modest slowdown in growth. Factors contributing to this included structural reforms to increase the market orientation of the economy, a record grain harvest in 1996 that reduced food prices, the buildup of excess capacity that put downward pressure on prices, and a tightening of monetary policy. However, this episode is directly linked to the key current problems in the financial sector as the rapid pace of credit growth in 1992–96 contributed to the weakness of the financial sector today. It is thought that many of the nonperforming loans in the banking system date from this period, reflecting bank funding of state-owned enterprises with little regard for credit risk.

China: Another Soft Landing?

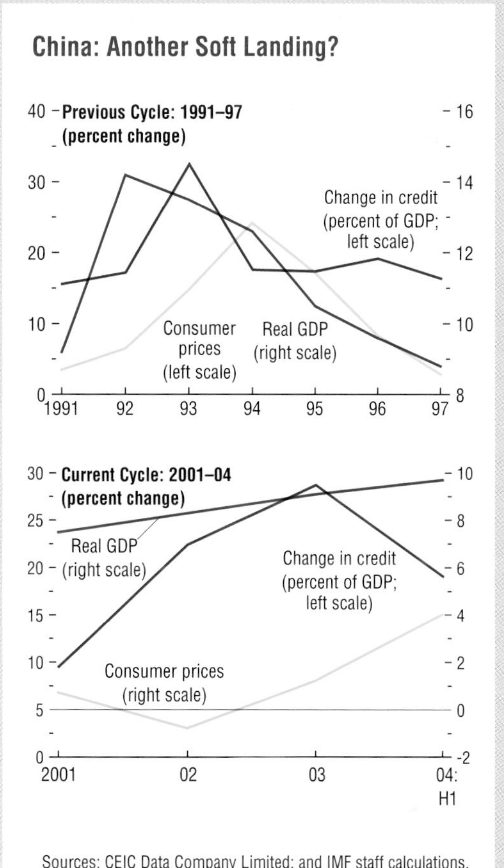

Sources: CEIC Data Company Limited; and IMF staff calculations.

The current cycle (2002–04) bears some of the characteristics of previous overheating cycles, such as high GDP growth, rapid credit growth, and high investment rates (see the figure). Actions to address these pressures were delayed during the Severe Acute Respiratory Syndrome (SARS) outbreak in the second quarter of 2003, but the authorities moved to tighten monetary policies beginning in mid-2003. As a result, credit growth has slowed. However, investment has remained high, and inflation has increased. In current circumstances, a soft landing, which would maintain underlying growth momentum, appears achievable. However, this will require taking into account the lessons

Note: The main author of this box is Thomas Rumbaugh.

Box 1.2 *(concluded)*

learned from earlier cycles. In addition to the early action to rein in credit and investment growth already initiated by the authorities, these include the consistent implementation of monetary tightening actions to restrain the upswings, contain inflation, and mitigate eventual nonperforming loans problems; introducing greater interest rate liberalization and hard budget constraints for state-owned enterprises to support the effectiveness of monetary policy; and increasing the use of indirect monetary policy instruments rather than administrative measures to improve resource allocation and reduce the severity of the cycles. In the near term, it will be important to avoid the tendency seen in earlier cycles to loosen policies prematurely. Moreover, there is scope for fiscal policy to play a more supportive role by using strong growth in revenue to reduce the overall fiscal deficit.

Given China's rapid integration with the global economy, the prospect of a slowing in growth and imports has raised concerns about the impact this would have on other countries. For example, China's share of global trade (6 percent) has tripled since the early 1990s, revealing much stronger trade linkages and the prospect that changes in China's growth could have significant repercussions. The current World Economic Outlook baseline envisages that China's real growth momentum would slow to about 7½ percent by the end of 2004 and remain at that level in 2005. Import growth would also slow from 40 percent in 2003 to a projected 30 percent in 2004 and 24 percent in 2005. Despite the slowdown in Chinese import growth, the growth of global imports is projected to remain strong, given the generally positive prospects in industrial countries and other emerging markets.

But what if there is a sharper slowdown in China? Simulations were conducted to assess the impact on other countries in the region (relative to the World Economic Outlook baseline) of an additional one-time 10-percentage-point decline in the growth of China's imports for domestic use arising from a further slowdown in domestic investment (i.e., the export processing trade was assumed not to be affected).[1] Such a decline would roughly correspond to a 7 percent decline in China's overall imports and is estimated to be consistent with an initial drop of 5½ percentage points in real investment growth. This would correspond to an initial drop of 2½ percentage points in GDP and eventually a 4 percentage point decline if multiplier effects are taken into account, assuming no offsetting policy adjustments.

The impact on the rest of Asia, after allowing for multiplier effects, is estimated to be a 0.4 percentage point drop in GDP growth. The impact varies considerably across the economies of the region, with declines in growth rates ranging from near zero to as high as 0.6 percentage point, depending on the importance of China as an export destination. Asian newly industrialized economies are most affected, with their GDP growth slowing by 0.6 percentage point (see the table). These estimates are subject to a number of caveats: (1) offsetting policy adjustments by affected economies are not considered; (2) the secondary impact of slower growth in each economy on the other economies in the region also is not taken into account; and (3) import and export prices are assumed to remain unchanged, thus excluding possible terms of trade effects.

The IMF's new Global Economy Model (GEM) provides additional insights regarding the impact on the rest of the world within a general equilibrium framework. While the GEM model does not yet allow for the more detailed investigations into the different impacts within Asia excluding Japan, a four-region model was developed consisting of the United States, Japan, Asia excluding Japan, and the rest of the world. The model was used to simulate the

[1]The estimates derived are based on a framework that captures the main trade flows within Asia. Because economic relationships in the framework are assumed to be linear, the results can be adjusted for impacts of different magnitude. The estimated impacts derived from this exercise are expressed relative to the World Economic Outlook baseline forecasts.

Estimated Impact of a 10-Percentage-Point Decline in China's Nonprocessing Import Growth

	Real GDP Growth (percentage points reduction)	Current Account Balance (reduction in billions of US$)
Asia excluding China	−0.4	−6.5
Japan	−0.5	−3.5
Asian newly industrialized economies	−0.6	−2.0
Other Asia	−0.3	−0.7
ASEAN-4	−0.3	−0.5

Source: IMF staff calculations.

impact of a slowdown in China of the same order of magnitude as in the above experiment. Results suggest that such a slowdown could reduce world GDP growth by about ⅓ of a percentage point (at world market prices). In line with the above results, Japan would be affected more than the other areas, because of its stronger trade linkages with China, while the United States and the rest of the world would only be marginally affected. However, the effects on Japan would be more muted relative to the partial equilibrium analysis because of offsetting real exchange-rate changes. It is also important to note that China has played an important role in the increase in global commodity prices over the past two years, and a slowing in China's growth could help reverse some of these increases. The effect could be particularly strong for nonfuel commodities, of which China is a large importer. This would produce positive terms of trade effects for many consuming countries, but raises the prospect of some adverse effects for commodity producers.[2]

While both the partial and general equilibrium results show a significant impact for several Asian economies, such a shock would still be manageable given the fairly robust outlook for Asia and the global economy. Despite China's increasingly important role in the region, other Asian economies are still largely dependent on the U.S. and EU markets for their exports, and the share of the region's exports to China is still only about 15 percent (*including* exports for processing). As a result, a substantial drop in the growth of exports to China would still leave countries in the region with relatively robust export growth rates provided that growth momentum in industrial markets is sustained.

[2]See Appendix 1.1 for a discussion of the effects of commodity prices on economic activity in both producer and consumer countries.

Development Goal target.[7] With macroeconomic stability generally achieved, the key challenge—as recognized in the New Partnership for Africa's Development—is to strengthen institutions and governance. The global community, in turn, needs to support strengthened reform efforts with substantially increased and better coordinated financial and technical assistance and, perhaps even more important, by eliminating barriers to exports, particularly of agricultural goods.

Against this background, a central question now is whether countries will take full advantage of the recovery to address these medium-term problems. To date, progress is at best mixed, and in some countries signs of reform fatigue have already emerged. There is a clear need for politicians—in industrial and developing countries alike—to be more forthright about the costs of doing too little. At the same time, politicians are often responding to genuine popular fears, given that the benefits of reform are usually

[7]See the September 2004 *Global Monitoring Report*.

Box 1.3. Is the Doha Round Back on Track?

On July 31, the General Council of the World Trade Organization (WTO) reached consensus on a set of framework agreements for pursuing negotiations under the Doha Round of multilateral trade talks—thus finishing the task left undone when discussions collapsed during the September 2003 WTO Ministerial Meeting in Cancún, Mexico. The framework agreements lay out the modalities for how trade liberalization is to occur, leaving the details of how much and how fast for later discussion. The decision to adopt the package of agreements puts the Round "back on track" in that formal negotiations can resume on the specific commitments that would lead to a successful conclusion. As noted by WTO Director-General Supachai Panitchpakdi, the July package is "a minor victory for multilateralism"—recognizing that negotiators still face a long and difficult road ahead.

Some significant compromises were made on the original Doha Development Agenda to facilitate agreement before the end-July deadline. A number of thorny issues, for example, were either dropped from the agenda or folded into a larger framework. The WTO General Council also agreed to postpone the original January 2005 target for completing the Round to a yet-unspecified date, at least until the sixth WTO Ministerial Meeting to be held in Hong Kong SAR in December 2005. The result is a "slimmer" formal agenda, with a longer and more realistic timeline for completion. Key points of the July package include the following.

- The agreement on agriculture calls for the elimination of export subsidies, the reduction of trade-distorting domestic support by 20 percent in the first year, and substantial tariff reductions. Developing countries will continue to benefit from special and differential treatment, including the possibility of maintaining state trading monopolies.
- The sectoral initiative on cotton advanced by several African countries during the Cancún Ministerial will be handled within the agriculture framework, rather than as a stand-alone issue. A committee will be established to address the trade-related aspects affecting cotton. The WTO Director-General is also to work with international organizations, including the Bretton Woods institutions, on the economic development of countries where cotton is an important export.
- The agreement is less ambitious and specific on industrial products (non–agricultural market access—NAMA), as members could not bridge all their differences. The text is largely identical to the last version produced in Cancún and is viewed as little more than a platform for discussion rather than an agreed framework.
- The agreement launches negotiations on trade facilitation, the least controversial of the so-called Singapore issues, which were supported by the European Union, Japan, and others. The remaining three Singapore issues (investment, competition, and transparency in government procurement) have been removed from the formal agenda.
- The agreement recommits members to fulfilling the development dimension of the Doha Round through enhanced market access, a balanced approach to trade rules, and well-targeted technical assistance and capacity-building programs. The WTO General Council reiterated the Doha Declaration's call for the provisions for special and differential treatment in all WTO agreements to be made more precise, effective and operational, with clear recommendations for a decision no later than July 2005.

The July package of agreements opens the way for more detailed negotiations to start in September, but it is generally expected that a cooling-off period in the negotiations will last until after the forthcoming U.S. presidential elections and the installation of the new European Commission. It is hoped that significant progress can be made before the December 2005 WTO Ministerial Meeting in Hong Kong SAR. Another key deadline, how-

Note: The main authors of this box are Todd Schneider and Jean-Pierre Chauffour.

ever, is June 2007, when legislation granting trade promotion authority (also known as "fast-track") to the U.S. president expires. Trade promotion authority enables the administration to submit trade agreements to the U.S. Congress for a yes/no vote, without amendment.

Filling out the framework agreements for agriculture, industrial products, trade facilitation, and special and differential treatment with detailed commitments—the nuts and bolts of how far and how fast to eliminate subsidies, reduce tariffs, and allow other forms of market access—is expected to be difficult. Further, some of the agreements are less developed than others. Discussions on NAMA have thus far fallen in the shadow of the discussions on agriculture. Limited progress has been made in other key areas, such as services, where only a small number of countries have tabled offers. It thus remains to be seen whether the July package represents a solid platform for negotiation or a hastily concluded set of agreements that may reveal significant fault lines in the coming months.

longer-term, there are substantial and unpredictable effects on income distribution within and across generations, and also concern that the fruits of reform will not be spread widely. Moreover, with limited political capital, simultaneous structural reform and fiscal consolidation—as are required now—are particularly difficult, even in a recovery.

How can progress be accelerated? While there is probably no single or simple answer to this question, greater efforts to build national consensus are clearly required, with—for example—reductions in barriers to competition accompanied by measures to equip people to compete by improving education, health care, access to finance, and safety nets. Policymakers should also take advantage of trade-offs. For example, a temporary deterioration in fiscal positions could be an acceptable price to pay to facilitate structural reform (especially when, as with pension and health reform, this improves medium-term fiscal sustainability). However, international leadership and cooperation could also play a supporting role, particularly since the global implications of every aspect of the current reform agenda are significant. For example, strong reform efforts by a small group of large countries could increase pressures on others to adjust, and multilateral trade liberalization could also play a central role. Looking further into the future, one key issue will be how best to strengthen the international economic infrastructure in the face of the coming demographic transition; as discussed in Chapter III, greater mobility of goods, capital, and labor will all have important roles to play. The benefits of multilateral cooperation in trade are already evident, and will need to continue. To supplement this, greater multilateral cooperation on capital and labor mobility may also be required.

United States and Canada: How Long Will the U.S. Soft Patch Persist?

In the United States, the economic expansion remained generally strong early this year, but hit a soft patch in the second quarter, with real GDP growth slowing to 2¾ percent from an above-potential 4½ percent in the first quarter. Personal consumption growth fell back markedly, apparently reflecting a combination of higher oil prices, weaker-than-expected employment growth, and a sharp fall in spending on durable goods, due in part to temporarily lower incentives for purchases of motor vehicles. Net exports made a large negative contribution to growth, mainly the result of a sharp increase in imports, and the current account deficit widened to 5¾ percent of GDP. By contrast, business fixed investment accelerated, underpinned by the continued healthy growth of profits and temporary accelerated depreciation allowances.

Economic slack remained, with manufacturing capacity utilization below its long-term average and the unemployment rate higher than most estimates of the natural rate, reflecting continued rapid labor productivity growth. The rise in core CPI inflation from 1.1 percent in December to 1.7 percent in August was due in part to increases in the prices of crude and intermediate materials, reflecting the strength of the global expansion, and the elimination of one-off factors that lowered inflation in 2003.

Looking forward, output growth is projected to pick up in the second half of 2004, supported by continuing strength in profits and household labor income, as well as the restoration of incentives for automobile purchases, and stay above potential through 2005–06, though growth this year and next has been revised down since the April 2004 *World Economic Outlook*. Slowdowns in household demand—responding to higher energy prices, the waning effects of mortgage refinancing and tax cuts, and a gradual rebound in the saving rate—and government spending, as the fiscal position improves, are balanced by continued strength in business fixed investment, reflecting firms' healthy balance sheets and strong profitability, and a modest improvement in external demand, as trade volumes respond to the depreciation of the dollar since 2002. The current account deficit is projected to narrow to 5 percent of GDP in 2005 but—assuming no further real depreciation of the U.S. dollar and a moderate fiscal consolidation (Table 1.4)—is expected to remain above 4 percent of GDP through the rest of the decade.

Given the recent rise in oil prices and declines in some forward-looking indicators, downside risks and uncertainties have increased in recent months. On the positive side, business confidence and indicators of investment spending remain healthy, and labor productivity, which has consistently exceeded expectations, could continue to grow faster than projected. The annual growth rate of output an hour in the nonfarm business sector increased to about 2½ percent in the late 1990s, reflecting capital deepening, gains in total factor productivity in the information technology sector, and—more recently—an acceleration in total factor productivity in industries using information technology. During 2001–03, labor productivity growth increased further to about 3¾ percent, reflecting in part the typical rise during the early phase of economic recovery. The baseline forecast treats the recent acceleration conservatively, assuming that labor productivity growth will slow over the medium term to slightly below the average in the late 1990s, but still well above the average for 1975–95. Faster growth would boost domestic incomes, ease policy challenges by moderating pressures on prices and raising government revenues, and encourage capital inflows needed to fund the current account deficit.

On the downside, however, there is increasing concern that the soft patch in consumption—the reasons for which are not fully understood—could persist for longer than assumed in the IMF staff's baseline projection. While most forward-looking indicators signal continued expansion, weaker labor market conditions and higher oil prices will reduce consumption growth (and to a lesser extent investment growth) in the third quarter and beyond. More generally, risks to household spending include the possibility of an increase in the household saving ratio (which recent revisions to the national accounts suggest is lower than originally thought) or a moderation of house price appreciation. Both the ratio of house prices to disposable income per worker and the ratio of house prices to rent (equivalent to a price-earnings ratio for housing) have risen rapidly (Figure 1.10), though—as discussed in Chapter II—the unexplained portion of the increase in house prices is smaller than in some other countries. Unusually, the pace of house price appreciation in recent years (about 7–8 percent) has been greater than fixed mortgage rates (about 5–6 percent), raising the possibility that some housing purchases may have been motivated in part by the expectation of capital gains. Assuming house prices rise less rapidly as interest rates increase, this will weaken the support for household spending from capital gains on housing, though this effect may take some time to materialize, given the usual transmission lags. The adverse impact on household spending could be exacerbated by the high levels of household debt and debt service as shares of disposable income, though much of this debt is at fixed interest rates.

Given impending demographic pressures and the need to establish a sustainable fiscal position, fiscal policy should aim to bring the federal government budget back to balance, excluding Social Security, by the end of the decade. This is also important for the orderly resolution of global current account imbalances. Although the pace of deficit reduction targeted for FY2005 and FY2006 in the budget is appropriate, the size of the fiscal imbalance suggests that the better-than-projected outcome for FY2004 (as revenues have exceeded projections) should be used to strengthen the targeted outcomes in the coming two years. Beyond that, the fiscal objective that has been set for the medium term—of halving the budget deficit over five years—does not appear sufficiently ambitious. In addition, the government's revenue projections are predicated on a significant increase in the number of tax filers falling under the Alternative Minimum Tax, which will likely trigger legislative action at potentially significant fiscal cost. Finally, the government's targets depend largely on expenditure restraint, which by FY2009 would take nondefense discretionary spending as a share of GDP to its lowest level since the early 1960s. In light of the magnitude of the required fiscal adjustment, tax revenues may also need to rise. To avoid unwinding the supply-side benefits of recent cuts in marginal tax rates, consideration could be given to broadening the tax base, for example by cutting tax exemptions, and introducing a national indirect tax. Early steps to reform Social Security and, more important, Medicare are essential to ensure their long-term sustainability.

The challenge for monetary policy is to return interest rates to neutral, in the face of uncertainties about the inflationary effects of oil prices and moderating growth. Starting early this year, the Federal Reserve prepared financial markets for

Figure 1.10. United States: House Prices

The ratio of house prices to rent and the ratio of house prices to disposable income per worker have both increased sharply. House prices have risen more rapidly since late 2000 than the cost of mortgage finance. Household debt and debt service relative to disposable income have surged to record levels.

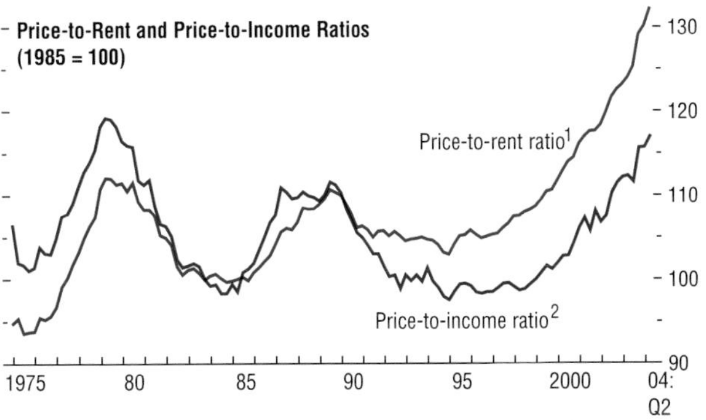

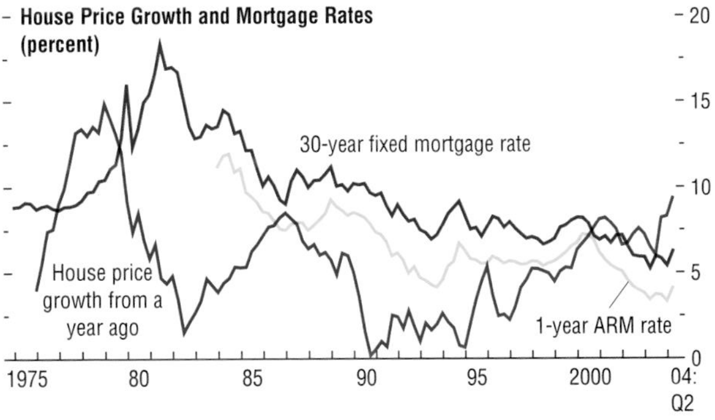

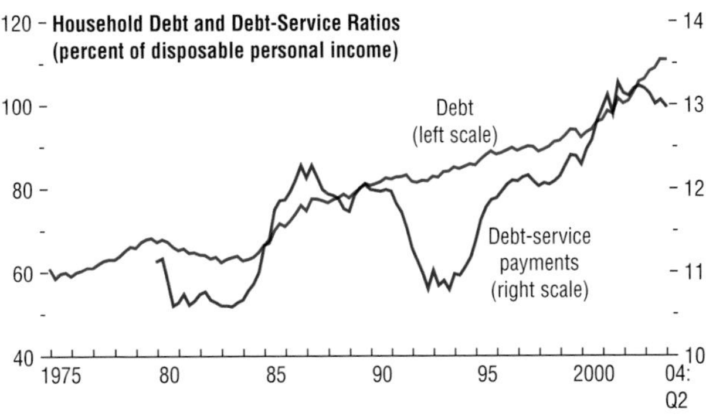

Sources: Office of Federal Housing Enterprise Oversight (OFHEO); Global Insight; and IMF staff calculations.

[1]OFHEO house price index divided by CPI rent of primary residence.

[2]OFHEO house price index divided by disposable personal income per worker.

Figure 1.11. United States: Interest Rates
(Percent)

The Federal Reserve raised interest rates in June from their 40-year low. Financial markets are anticipating a steady rise in interest rates over the coming year at a pace broadly in line with the average post-1985 tightening, though somewhat slower than that implied by a Taylor rule estimated over the past 20 years.

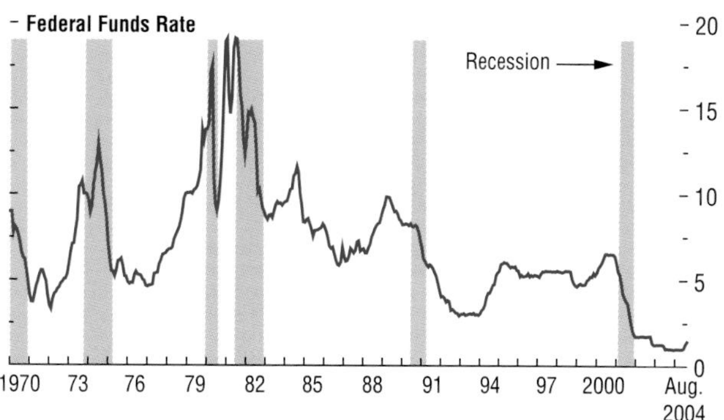

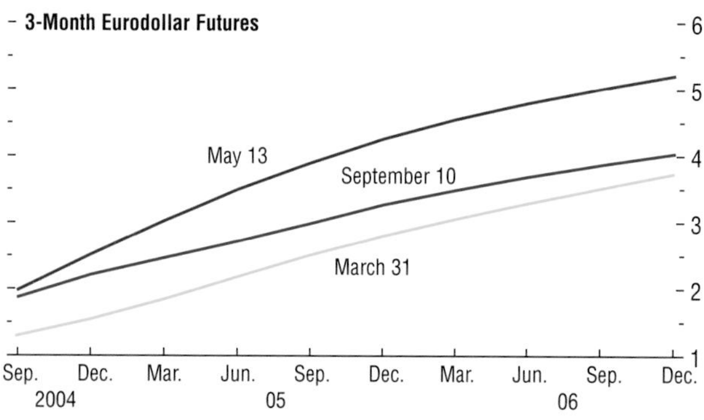

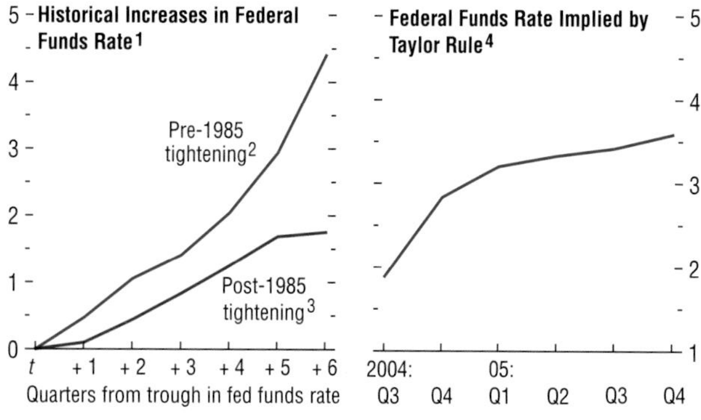

Sources: Haver Analytics; Bloomberg Financial, LP; and IMF staff estimates.
[1]For turning point methodology, see Chapter III of the April 2002 *World Economic Outlook*.
[2]Average increases in 1972–74, 1977–81, and 1983–84.
[3]Average increases in 1986–89, 1993–95, and 1999–2000.
[4]Estimated over 1982–2003. See Rabanal (2004).

the gradual withdrawal of monetary stimulus and—since late June—has raised the key federal funds rate by ¾ percentage point (Figure 1.11). As of early September, financial markets were expecting a steady rise in interest rates over the coming year at a pace broadly in line with the average post-1985 tightening, though somewhat slower than that implied by a Taylor rule estimated over the past 20 years. While the spread between nominal and inflation-indexed bonds rose sharply through May, it has subsequently fallen, and surveys indicate that inflationary expectations remain well anchored. Looking forward, the Federal Reserve's approach of "measured tightening" appears generally appropriate, but, with considerable uncertainties about both the short-term strength of the expansion and the extent of underlying inflationary pressures, much will depend on the nature of the incoming data.

Strong fundamentals have left the financial system well prepared for the expected rise in interest rates, and ongoing reforms of corporate governance have helped increase investor confidence in market integrity. However, the large and increasing share of mortgage-backed securities held by Fannie Mae and Freddie Mac (the government-sponsored housing enterprises) has concentrated interest rate risk, the hedging of which could amplify interest rate movements, underlining the importance of improving supervisory oversight and establishing an independent regulator.

In Canada, the economic expansion has gained momentum, reflecting both the global expansion and low domestic interest rates, and the forecast for growth in 2004 has been revised up. Real GDP growth accelerated from 3 percent in the first quarter to 4¼ percent in the second quarter. Personal consumption is being driven by surging employment, rising disposable income, and a buoyant housing market; business investment, by robust profitability; and exports, by global demand, especially from the United States, despite the appreciation of the Canadian dollar. Strong export volumes and higher world commodity prices are projected to boost the current account surplus to about 3 percent of GDP this year. With the acceleration in growth helping to close the output gap and gradually push core inflation nearer to the midpoint of the Bank of Canada's 1–3 percent target range, the increase in interest rates in September was appropriate. Given the generally robust economic outlook, monetary policy will likely need to continue removing stimulus gradually over the coming months. While Canada's fiscal position is the most favorable among G-7 countries, the government's efforts to sustain surpluses and maintain the federal debt to GDP ratio on a downward track remain appropriate, given impending fiscal pressures from population aging.

Western Europe: A Solidifying, but Uneven, Recovery

The recovery in the euro area has finally gained some momentum, with GDP growth projected to rise to 2.2 percent in 2004, 0.4 percentage point higher than expected in April. However, the upturn remains moderate and has so far been heavily dependent on external demand; and while industrial production and business confidence are gradually improving, consumer confidence and retail sales continue to lag. That said, aggregate figures disguise substantial differences within the region. In particular, the composition of growth varies markedly, with final domestic demand growing strongly in France and Spain, but weaker in Italy and dormant in Germany. Developments in Germany partly reflect slow household income growth in the context of ongoing labor market adjustments, and some increased savings by households in response to cuts in future benefits under recent pension reforms (see Chapter III).

Looking forward, the recovery is projected to be increasingly supported by domestic demand, as private consumption is boosted by rising disposable incomes, and investment picks up as corporate balance sheet restructuring—which has proceeded relatively more slowly than elsewhere—continues. Nonetheless, with GDP growth in the remainder of 2004 and 2005 expected to exceed potential only modestly, the output gap will remain substantial, and area-wide unemployment will decline only marginally. Overall, the risks appear tilted to the downside, and include a further rise in oil prices, especially in those countries where domestic demand is still weak; a slower-than-anticipated pickup in employment—which was unusually resilient during the recession; and a renewed appreciation of the euro. Elevated housing prices in some countries, notably Ireland and Spain (see the second essay in Chapter II), are also a concern.

After slowing in early 2004, headline inflation has again risen above 2 percent, driven by higher energy prices and hikes in indirect taxes and administrative prices; core inflation[8] has remained stable at 1¾ percent. Given substantial excess capacity, the lagged effect of the past appreciation of the euro, and continued wage moderation, inflation is projected to fall back below 2 percent in 2005. While the ECB will need to watch carefully for second-round effects from recent shocks, short- and long-term inflationary expectations still appear well-grounded and monetary policy should therefore remain accommodative until a self-sustaining upturn in domestic demand is in place.

Since 2000, fiscal policies for the euro area as a whole have been broadly neutral, with automatic stabilizers allowed to operate fully (Table 1.4). This has clearly been appropriate in the cyclical circumstances, despite the resulting serial breaches of the Stability and Growth Pact (SGP) deficit limit in some countries; however, the longer-term fiscal situation in many countries remains difficult (Figure 1.12) and the onset of population aging is now only 5 to 10 years away. While fiscal positions and risks vary widely, those countries with the weakest underlying positions should seek to reduce underlying deficits by at least ½ percent a year (more if the upswing were to prove more rapid than

[8]Defined to exclude energy, food, alcohol, and tobacco.

Figure 1.12. European Union: Fiscal Challenges

(Percent of GDP unless otherwise noted)

Fiscal positions vary widely across the European Union, with the four largest countries, Portugal, Greece, and the Netherlands having the largest deficits, but France, Italy, and the United Kingdom face more moderate pressure from aging. Tax rates outside Ireland, Spain, and the United Kingdom are high, and public debt is a serious problem in Belgium, Greece, and Italy.

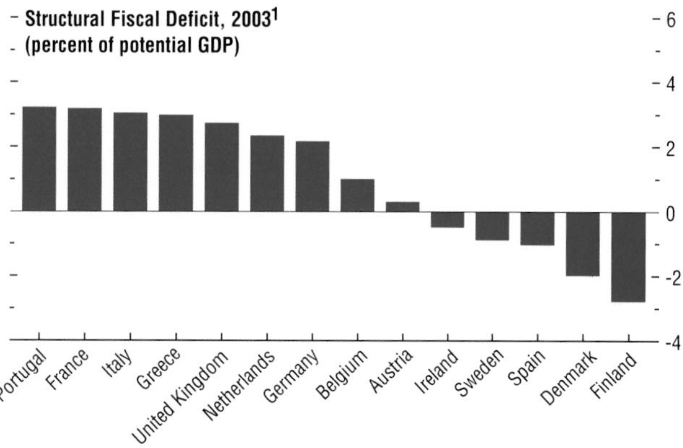

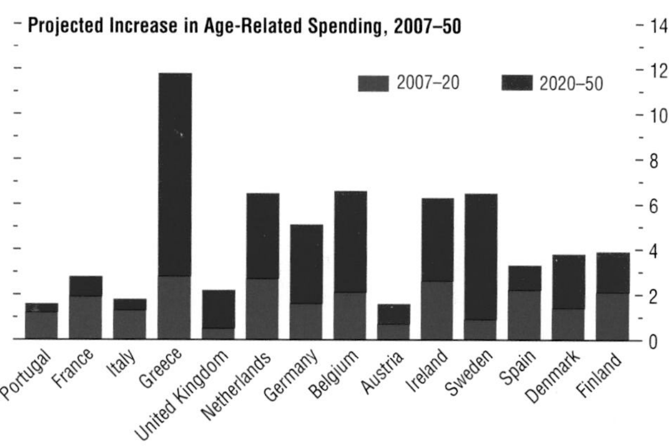

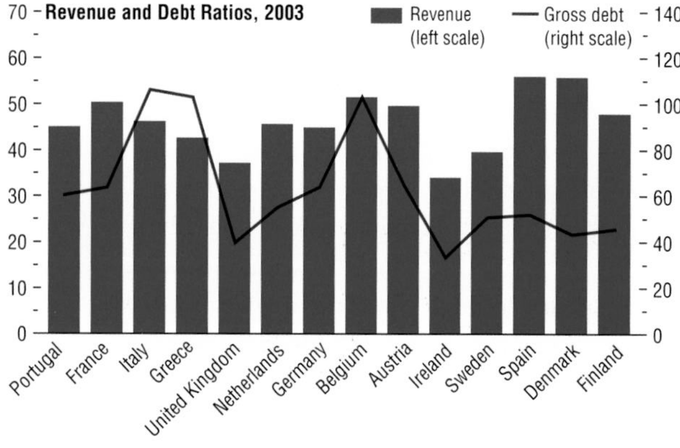

Sources: European Commission; and IMF staff calculations.

[1]For Italy, excluding 1.7 percent of GDP of one-off measures. For Portugal, excluding 2.5 percent of GDP of one-off measures.

expected) while allowing the automatic stabilizers to operate. Reductions in tax burdens in many countries are also highly desirable, but—unless financed through offsetting measures—are a lower priority until a significant downpayment on fiscal adjustment is in place.

While most countries have broadly committed to adjustment along these lines in their Stability Programs, in a number of countries the underlying adjustment required is substantial, and the measures to achieve it have not yet been identified. Among the three largest countries, the near-term budgetary objectives are most likely to be achieved in France, aided by higher-than-expected growth; given the relatively strong expansion, the targets for 2005 and beyond should be made more ambitious. In Germany, little progress is expected in 2004, and further measures will be required to achieve the targeted reduction in 2005. In Italy, significant one-off measures have been required to keep the deficit within the 3 percent of GDP limit in 2004; the government's recent annual update of its medium-term economic plan targets a small decline in the deficit in 2005, followed by a steady ½ percent annual deficit reduction thereafter. Substantial measures will be required to achieve the 2005 target, especially given the intention to implement tax cuts. On the positive side, the recent further pension reform will moderate spending trends over the medium term. Overall, as emphasized in the third essay of Chapter II, a repeat of the experience of 1999–2000—when many euro area countries failed to take advantage of strong growth to accelerate fiscal consolidation—remains a serious danger.

While the recent judgment by the European Court of Justice has clarified a number of issues relating to the implementation of the SGP, there is a growing consensus on the need for reform. A strong fiscal framework remains an essential element of the monetary union, especially given Europe's history of procyclical fiscal policies, the accession of new members with significant deficits, and the likelihood that market discipline would be too little, too late. In many respects, current problems can be traced to the failure to adjust in 1999–2000, and much of the basic design of the SGP remains appropriate. However, recent experience and the reform proposals put forward by the European Commission underscore the desirability of strengthening the incentives for adjustment in good times; of greater focus on medium-term sustainability issues; and for SGP procedures—including the pace and timing of required adjustments—to be conditioned more closely on the proximate reasons for any breach. Greater flexibility should be accompanied by efforts to improve political incentives to comply with the Pact. In this connection, published assessments of fiscal sustainability by independent national institutions could be helpful, including through stimulating public discussion and awareness.

The widespread endorsement of the Lisbon reform agenda has not been matched by equally widespread implementation, and the goal of transforming the European Union into the world's most dynamic and competitive economy remains far off. Progress has been greatest in centrally led reform, notably the Financial Services Action Plan and the Single Market; nationally sponsored reforms have lagged, particularly in labor markets (although recent developments in Germany are encouraging), but also in product markets, where some countries' new focus on creating "national champions" is a retrograde step. The recovery provides a renewed opportunity for progress, but increasing signs of reform fatigue and the political economy difficulties of simultaneously undertaking structural reform and fiscal consolidation[9] are complicating factors. While political leadership—especially in major countries—remains key, greater prioritization of the Lisbon Agenda, focused on the key issue of raising labor utilization, could be helpful. Renewed central initiatives for product market deregulation—by putting competitive pressure on profit margins—might also add to incentives for national labor market reforms.

In the United Kingdom, activity remains robust. Despite higher oil prices, private consumption remains strong, underpinned by sustained income growth and rising housing wealth; private investment has turned up; and government expenditures have continued to support domestic demand. The central risk remains an abrupt adjustment in the housing market, where—despite signs of cooling in recent months—prices still appear higher than can be explained by developments in fundamentals (see the first essay of Chapter II). With interest rates on a rising trend, and most house purchases financed with adjustable rate mortgages, house buyers should exercise particular caution at the present juncture.[10] While inflation remains low, the economy is now running at close to capacity and cost pressures are increasing; the Bank of England has appropriately raised interest rates five times since November 2003, and a continued "early but gradual" approach appears desirable. Following the large increase in the fiscal deficit in recent years, some consolidation is expected in 2004, mainly reflecting higher revenues. In 2005 and beyond, stronger fiscal consolidation than presently seems in prospect would be desirable, both from a cyclical perspective and to reduce the risk of a breach in the golden rule in the future.

Elsewhere in Europe, GDP growth in the Nordic countries is also accelerating, aided by the global recovery and generally accommodative fiscal and monetary policies. Despite higher oil prices, inflation is still moderate, owing to continued excess capacity and past currency appreciation. As the recovery proceeds, monetary policies will need to tighten (in Denmark, with the krone linked to the euro, in line with the ECB); in Norway and to a lesser extent Sweden, the impact of higher interest rates on highly indebted households will need to be carefully

[9]See "Fostering Structural Reforms in Industrial Countries," *World Economic Outlook*, April 2004.

[10]See Bank of England Governor King's speech to the CBI Scotland Dinner, Glasgow, June 14, 2004 (http://www.bankofengland.co.uk/speeches/speech221.pdf).

monitored. Fiscal positions are generally solid, although in Sweden and Norway tight expenditure control will be needed in coming years to ensure that medium-term fiscal targets are met; pension reform (Norway) and further structural measures to boost labor supply (Sweden and Denmark) are also priorities. In Switzerland, which was particularly hard hit by the global slowdown, activity is also starting to pick up and deflationary risks have eased, prompting an increase in benchmark interest rates to ½ percent in mid-June. Fiscal balance will need to be restored gradually, in line with the authorities' medium-term fiscal framework, accompanied by reform of sheltered domestic markets, notably agriculture and network industries, which continue to weigh on productivity growth.

Japan: Is Deflation Finally Coming to an End?

In Japan, real GDP grew very strongly in the first quarter of 2004, with exports, especially to Asia, and business fixed investment remaining key driving forces, although a pickup in private consumption growth also contributed, as consumer confidence improved with the increasingly sustained recovery and firming labor market conditions. In contrast, second-quarter growth turned out to be weaker than expected, primarily on account of a sharp drop in inventory accumulation and a larger-than-expected decline in public investment. The expansion in private fixed investment was also more tepid than expected on the basis of other indicators and private consumption growth moderated by more than was anticipated after the spurt during the previous two quarters. That said, recent forward-looking indicators generally suggest that underlying private domestic demand and external demand remain robust, with profits continuing to grow strongly and household surveys indicating steady consumer demand growth. Against this background, the outlook remains for a sustained, broad-based expansion, and GDP growth is now projected to accelerate to 4.4 percent in 2004, more than 1 percentage point higher than projected in the April 2004 *World Economic Outlook*, and to fall back to 2.3 percent—still higher than potential—during 2005. Nevertheless, the slowdown has highlighted short-term downside risks—notably those arising from higher oil prices, a slowdown in export growth due, for example, to a hard landing in China, higher long-term U.S. rates, or a renewed yen appreciation.

Looking beyond 2005, prospects are underpinned by continued progress in reducing financial vulnerabilities in the corporate and banking sectors (Figure 1.13). Specifically, improved profitability—due to rising sales proceeds, cost restructuring, including by reducing employment costs, and low interest rates—has allowed corporations to increase capital spending and at the same time reduce their balance sheet leverage—the average debt-equity ratio of nonfinancial corporations (measured at book value) has reached levels last observed in the early 1960s—and income gearing (debt service as percent of profits and depreciation). Moreover, as reflected in improved ratings for some banks, banking sector health has improved in this recovery—new loan-loss provisions have been reduced and the share of nonperforming loans has declined further. Nevertheless, the adjustment process still has some way to go, and vulnerabilities remain.

- Corporate debt levels in terms of sales remain high and overall return-on-assets is still low by historical standards. Manufacturing firms have reduced their debt-to-sales ratios close to the levels that prevailed in the first half of the 1980s, but nonmanufacturing firms' debt ratios remain higher. The return-on-assets ratio has recovered slowly in part because of unproductive assets that do not generate sales and thus profits. Corporate restructuring, including closures of firms with little prospect for return to profitability, would be facilitated by a strengthened banking system, by allowing banks to more easily shoulder the losses involved in dealing with weak borrowers.
- Progress in restoring the financial soundness of the banking system has been uneven—with larger banks having progressed faster than

regional banks, which still grapple with substantial nonperforming loans. Bank profitability is still generally low and the quality of bank capital needs to be improved, which could restrain a turnaround in bank lending at precisely the time that the external funding needs of nonfinancial corporations are increasing because of the sustained expansion.

With the gradual reduction in economic slack over the past year, deflationary pressures have eased. The 12-month fall in the core CPI (which excludes fresh food) narrowed to 0.2 percent in July, reflecting the declining output gap and temporary influences such as oil prices; net of transitory factors, the core CPI is falling by about 0.3 percent. The GDP deflator has continued to fall more rapidly than the CPI, reflecting the interaction between differences in the composition of the two indices (with the GDP deflator putting higher weight on electrical goods, the prices of which have generally been falling faster than for other categories while their share in real demand has increased) and in the methodology (with the changes in the CPI—a Laspeyres index—biased upward and in the GDP deflator—a Paasche index—biased downward in this particular constellation of price and demand behavior). Looking forward, deflationary pressures are likely to ease further as economic slack diminishes, and 12-month CPI deflation is projected to ebb to about zero during 2005.

As the prospects for an end to deflation have improved significantly but such an outcome is far from guaranteed, the current monetary stance is appropriate and should be maintained until inflation is firmly positive. If financial markets became concerned that the policy of quantitative easing might end too early, the Bank of Japan could increase the current account target to signal its resolve to maintain the framework until deflation is decisively subdued. Looking forward, as the onset of inflation draws nearer, enhancements to the Bank of Japan's communication strategy could help to focus inflation expectations, including by setting a suitably positive medium-term inflation objective and by pub-

Figure 1.13. Japan: The End of Deflation?
(Percent change from a year ago)

Deflationary pressures have eased, partly reflecting the reduction in economic slack. With a sustained expansion increasingly likely, underpinned by continued progress in reducing financial vulnerabilities, prospects for ebbing deflationary expectations appear better than during other recent post-bubble recoveries.

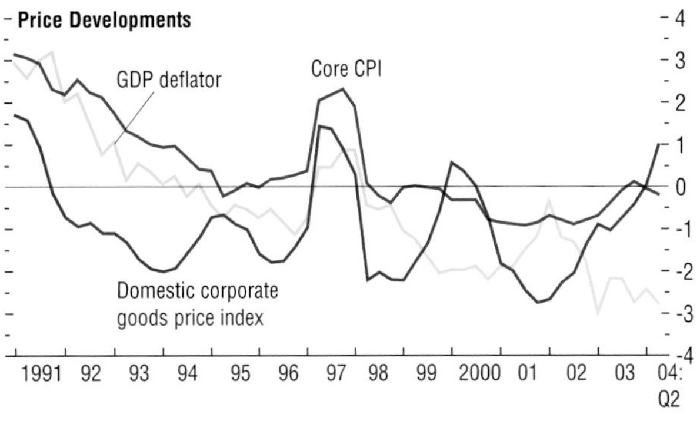

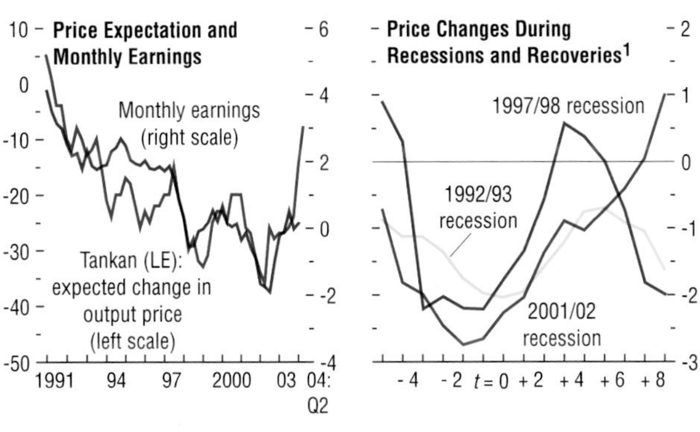

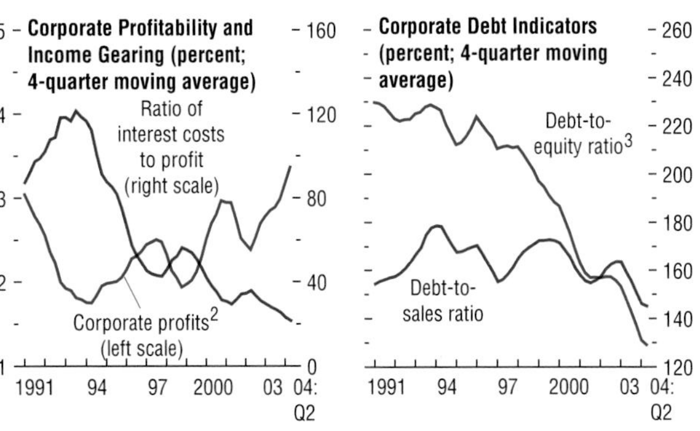

Sources: Haver Analytics; Bank of Japan; and Ministry of Finance.
[1]Based on domestic corporate goods price index. Quarters before and after output trough.
[2]Corporate profit to sales ratio.
[3]Equity valued at book value.

lishing more of the Bank's views on monetary policy and the inflation outlook.

With improved economic prospects, policymakers now face the daunting task of addressing Japan's difficult fiscal position. Gross public debt stood at 166 percent of GDP at end-2003—the highest among advanced economies by a substantial margin, although net debt, while rising, is considerably lower at 80 percent of GDP at end-2003—and the structural deficit (including social security but excluding bank support) was 6½ percent of GDP in FY2003. Against that background, the government aims for a primary surplus (excluding social security) by the early 2010s, which is in part to be achieved through expenditure restraint in FY2004 and FY2005, but further measures to achieve this target are yet to be defined. In light of the favorable economic environment, achieving savings in FY2004 relative to the budget would be desirable. Looking ahead, options for consolidation include further cuts in capital spending, broadening the personal income tax base, and—in the medium term—raising the consumption tax.

With population aging posing further challenges in the medium term, as discussed in Chapter III, the recent reform of the public pension system was a step in the right direction. However, the reform relies heavily on increases in contribution rates, which are likely to hurt economic growth, and it deepens intergenerational inequality as the younger generations will bear most of the burden of the reform. Looking ahead, a further increase in the retirement age is likely to be needed for financial viability of the public pension system—which would most likely increase growth—as are reforms of the medical and long-term care systems to contain rapidly growing costs. Besides fiscal adjustment, stepped-up structural reforms could also improve Japan's fiscal position by increasing potential output growth. The priorities are public enterprise reforms, strengthened competition policy, and enhanced labor market flexibility, including an increase in pension portability.

Emerging Asia: Prospects Are Bright but Can Macroeconomic Policies Rise to the Challenges?

Growth in emerging Asia has continued to exceed expectations, despite the adverse impact of higher oil prices on many countries, underpinned by the global recovery; very strong growth in China; the recovery in the global information technology sector; generally supportive macroeconomic policies, including highly competitive exchange rates; and, increasingly, solid domestic demand growth, including in fixed investment. From mid-2003 to the first quarter in 2004, the regional growth rate averaged over 10 percent, with particularly rapid growth in China and the Asian newly industrialized economies. This has raised fears that China, despite some slowing in the second quarter, is at risk of overheating; some other economies, including Singapore, also appear to be increasingly close to capacity.

Looking forward, on the assumption of a soft landing in China, the regional outlook is for continued solid but slowing growth. Given the strong first half, regional GDP growth is projected to average 7.3 percent in 2004, 0.1 percentage point higher than expected in April, moderating to 6.5 percent in 2005, 0.3 percentage point lower than projected earlier—with the revisions largely reflecting a more delayed slowdown in China and a growth surge in most newly industrialized economies in early 2004 compared with the last *World Economic Outlook* (Table 1.6). The outlook for China plays a particularly important role in the risks to the regional outlook. If China's growth were to slow less than expected, both external and domestic demand—particularly in the newly industrialized economies and the ASEAN-4—would be stronger, although this would clearly come at the risk of a harder landing later on, with significant but manageable regional repercussions (Box 1.2). The region is also relatively more vulnerable to higher oil prices—with the impact on growth and inflation being greater than elsewhere (see Appendix 1.1)—and to the outlook for the information technology sector, where there is some concern

Table 1.6. Selected Asian Economies: Real GDP, Consumer Prices, and Current Account Balance
(Annual percent change unless otherwise noted)

	Real GDP				Consumer Prices[1]				Current Account Balance[2]			
	2002	2003	2004	2005	2002	2003	2004	2005	2002	2003	2004	2005
Emerging Asia[3]	**6.4**	**7.2**	**7.3**	**6.5**	**1.9**	**2.5**	**4.3**	**3.9**	**3.8**	**4.4**	**3.6**	**3.3**
China	8.3	9.1	9.0	7.5	–0.8	1.2	4.0	3.0	2.8	3.2	2.4	2.8
South Asia[4]	**4.9**	**6.9**	**6.2**	**6.5**	**4.2**	**3.9**	**4.9**	**5.1**	**1.3**	**1.3**	**0.3**	**–0.2**
India	5.0	7.2	6.4	6.7	4.3	3.8	4.7	5.0	1.0	1.1	0.5	—
Pakistan	4.4	6.2	6.3	6.0	3.2	2.9	4.6	4.5	4.5	3.5	0.3	–0.3
Bangladesh	4.9	5.4	5.5	5.7	3.8	5.4	6.4	6.1	0.6	0.4	–0.5	–1.3
ASEAN-4	**4.3**	**5.1**	**5.5**	**5.4**	**5.8**	**4.0**	**4.7**	**4.8**	**5.8**	**6.1**	**5.0**	**3.5**
Indonesia	3.7	4.1	4.8	5.0	11.8	6.8	6.5	6.5	4.5	3.5	2.9	1.9
Thailand	5.4	6.8	6.2	6.4	0.6	1.8	2.7	1.8	5.5	5.6	3.8	2.0
Philippines	4.3	4.7	5.2	4.2	3.1	3.0	5.4	6.8	5.8	4.9	2.8	1.8
Malaysia	4.1	5.3	6.5	6.3	1.8	1.1	2.2	2.5	8.4	12.9	12.4	10.1
Newly industrialized Asian economies	**5.0**	**3.0**	**5.5**	**4.0**	**0.9**	**1.4**	**2.4**	**2.6**	**5.8**	**7.6**	**6.8**	**6.5**
Korea	7.0	3.1	4.6	4.0	2.8	3.5	3.8	3.8	1.0	2.0	3.1	3.3
Taiwan Province of China	3.6	3.3	5.6	4.1	–0.2	–0.3	1.1	1.5	9.1	10.2	6.9	6.0
Hong Kong SAR	1.9	3.2	7.5	4.0	–3.0	–2.6	—	1.0	7.9	10.7	10.0	9.6
Singapore	2.2	1.1	8.8	4.4	–0.4	0.5	1.8	1.6	21.4	30.9	25.7	23.9

[1]In accordance with standard practice in the *World Economic Outlook*, movements in consumer prices are indicated as annual averages rather than as December/December changes during the year, as is the practice in some countries.
[2]Percent of GDP.
[3]Consists of developing Asia, the newly industrialized Asian economies, and Mongolia.
[4]Includes Bangladesh, India, Maldives, Nepal, Pakistan, and Sri Lanka.

that recent high rates of investment could lead to the emergence of excess capacity in 2005 (Appendix 1.1). Higher real interest rates in the United States could adversely affect countries relying on external budget financing (Indonesia and the Philippines), but in countries experiencing large capital inflows, this could facilitate monetary policy management.

External current account surpluses have generally remained strong across the region, reflecting in part a relatively faster acceleration in external demand growth compared with domestic demand growth; stable or depreciating real exchange rates; gains in market shares in services, especially in South Asia; and, in the case of South Asia and China, increased remittances (Figure 1.14). While current account surpluses are expected to narrow in 2004 and thereafter as domestic demand strengthens further, the decreases as a percent of GDP are small considering that higher-than-expected oil prices alone contribute some 0.3–0.4 percentage point on average in net oil importers. Net private capital flows to the region—with China and India being the largest recipients—while slowing, have remained large. Allowing for the effects of the recapitalization of two large commercial banks in China with official foreign exchange reserves at end-2003, net private capital flows to emerging Asia are expected to fall by about $18 billion to $80 billion this year. Correspondingly, gross external reserves are projected to increase by some further $230 billion to nearly $1.5 trillion by end-2004, equivalent to nine months of imports, and about eight times larger than short-term debt.

While buoyant activity and rising commodity prices have led to some pickup in inflationary pressures—most obviously in China—headline and core inflation have remained moderate. Looking forward, with growth expected to remain strong and policies generally still highly accommodative, monetary policies will need to be tightened—at varying paces—across the region, a process that has already begun in China and, more recently, in Thailand. Given the continued strength of external positions—and the increasing difficulty and cost of steriliz-

Figure 1.14. Emerging Asia: Current Account Surpluses Remain Strong

External current account surpluses have remained strong, partly reflecting relatively faster acceleration in external demand growth compared with domestic demand growth but also stable or depreciating real exchange rates. Together with substantial capital inflows, this has led to the rapid accumulation of gross external reserves.

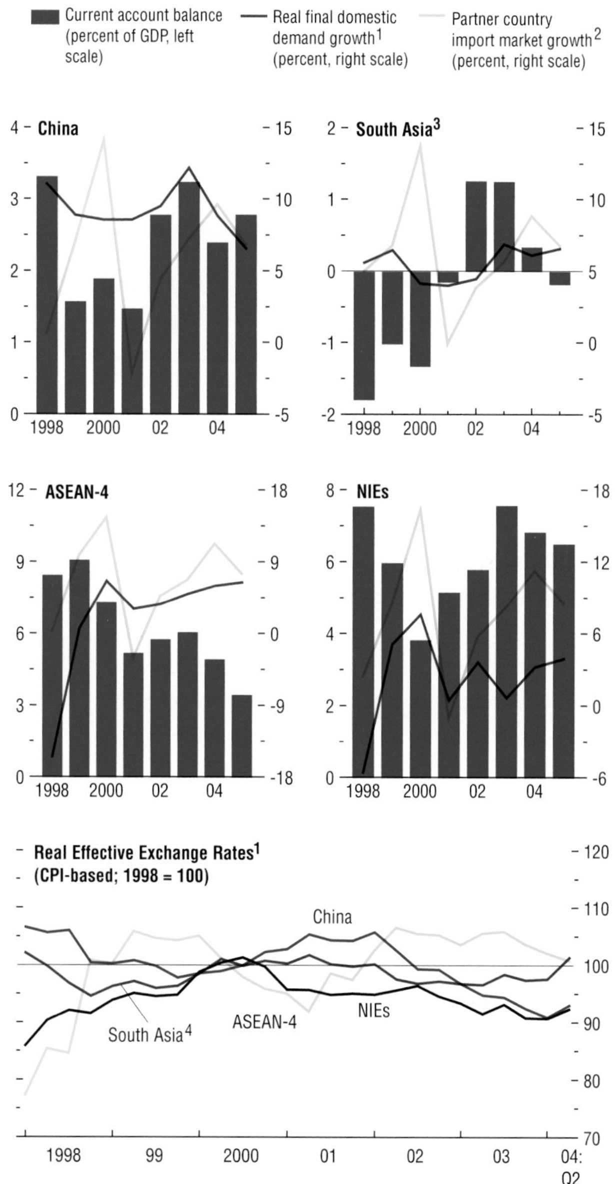

Sources: Haver Analytics; Global Insight; and IMF staff calculations.
[1]Regional aggregates are purchasing-power-parity-weighted averages.
[2]Export-weighted import demand for individual countries; regional aggregated are PPP-weighted averages.
[3]Includes Bangladesh, India, Maldives, Pakistan, and Sri Lanka.
[4]Includes India, Nepal, Pakistan, and Sri Lanka.

ing their impact on domestic liquidity—this would in many countries be facilitated by greater exchange rate flexibility. As discussed above, this would also play an important role in helping resolve global imbalances in an orderly fashion. From both an external and a domestic perspective, the strong regional and global recovery, combined with buoyant export growth, would seem to provide near-ideal conditions for such a move. Moreover, as discussed in Chapter II, voluntary transitions to more exchange rate flexibility do not seem to have been associated with disruptions to macroeconomic stability, or to have led to sustained exchange rate volatility.

Turning to individual countries, growth in China—particularly fixed investment—moderated in the second quarter in response to tightening measures. However, activity remains very strong and growth in fixed investment accelerated again in June and July. This suggests that risks of overheating have not yet abated. Against this background and considering that short-term real interest rates have remained negative, further monetary tightening is likely to be needed, which would be aided, as discussed above, by greater exchange rate flexibility. Fiscal policy also has a key role to play in cooling down the economy, including through saving revenue overperformance and reducing public investment at both central and local government levels. This would also contribute to the needed fiscal consolidation over the medium term, given still sizable contingent liabilities associated with banking sector weaknesses, pension obligations, and pressures to increase social safety net, health care, and environmental expenditures. On the structural side, banking reform remains crucial, especially since buoyant credit growth may well lead to an increase in nonperforming loans, as was the case during the boom in the early 1990s (Box 1.2). The recent recapitalization of two major banks was an important step forward, and needs to be accompanied by recapitalization of other banks and enforcement of capital requirements and adequate loan-loss provisioning throughout the banking system. Linked to that, imposition of hard budget constraints on public enterprises, labor market reform to help absorb the rapidly growing labor force, and trade liberalization in line with World Trade Organization (WTO) commitments are also key priorities.

The boost from strong growth in China has fed through to the rest of east Asia, although GDP growth rates vary significantly across countries depending on the strength of domestic demand. In the ASEAN-4, economic activity has continued to expand at a solid pace in Malaysia. In Thailand, growth slowed in the first half of 2004, owing to the avian flu, a drought, and higher oil prices. Among the newly industrialized economies, export-based growth has recently been bolstered by a pickup in domestic demand in Hong Kong SAR (where deflation appears to have ended and asset prices have begun to recover), Singapore, and Taiwan Province of China. In contrast, domestic demand in Korea remains relatively weak, weighed down by the legacy of debt problems of households and domestically oriented enterprises. Correspondingly, monetary and fiscal policies should remain supportive for relatively longer than elsewhere in the region until the recovery is firmly established.

Both Asian newly industrialized economies and the ASEAN-4 have made significant progress in reducing external and domestic vulnerabilities since the 1997–98 crisis, and the strong global environment provides an opportunity to advance further. In particular, banking sector weaknesses, including still-substantial unresolved nonperforming assets, remain a key vulnerability in most countries, underscoring the need for stepped-up banking supervision and strengthened incentives to resolve nonperforming assets, including through the enforcement of adequate loan-loss recognition and provisioning. With many countries facing difficult medium-term fiscal problems, and public debt having risen sharply since the crisis, fiscal consolidation is also a priority. This is particularly the case in the Philippines, where long-standing vulnerabilities related to fiscal and financial imbalances underscore the need for the new administration to press ahead with measures to secure the increases in the tax revenue required to reduce the budget deficit, restructure the power sector and restore its financial viability, and increase banking system capitalization. In Indonesia, where public debt—while decreasing—remains high and market confidence eroded during the prolonged election period, early implementation of the fiscal adjustment for 2004–05 envisaged by the outgoing administration is key, including, if needed, through additional measures.

In India, GDP growth is projected at 6.4 percent in 2004, underpinned by the global expansion and supportive monetary conditions, although unfavorable patterns in this year's monsoon are raising concerns about agricultural growth. Large budget deficits and high and rising levels of public debt remain the Achilles' heel of the economy. Beyond long-run sustainability concerns, high public borrowing may choke off the nascent recovery in private investment needed to sustain the expansion. The newly elected ruling coalition intends to effect ambitious fiscal adjustment to balance the current budget by 2009 (targeting annual adjustment of at least ⅓ percent of GDP in the overall central government balance) while increasing expenditure in priority areas—including health and education, and infrastructure investment. While this target path appears broadly appropriate, the supporting measures that were recently proposed will take time to be implemented and yield results. In view of this uncertainty, expenditure increases should be contingent on progress on the revenue front. Accelerating structural reforms—including agricultural and trade liberalization—remains key to step up potential growth and reduce poverty.

Elsewhere in south Asia, the improved macroeconomic performance in Pakistan has reduced external vulnerabilities and provided some room to address long-standing fiscal adjustment and development issues, including the need for increased development and social spending. In view of the large outstanding public debt, it will, however, be critical that the increased development expenditure planned for the current fiscal

Figure 1.15. Latin America: Trade Share Rising, But Scope for Further Reduction in Restrictiveness

The ratio of merchandise exports to GDP rose by 10 percentage points between 1998–2003, reflecting in particular growing exports to the United States and emerging Asia and increasing exports of manufactured goods. However, Latin America's trade share is still substantially lower than in other developing country regions and there remains considerable scope to reduce trade restrictions.

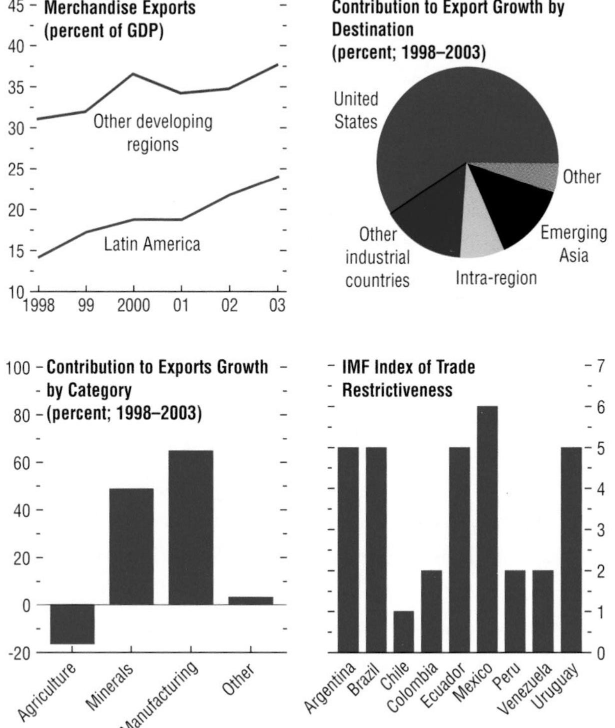

Sources: IMF, *Direction of Trade Statistics*; United Nations Commodity Trade database; and IMF staff calculations.

year be offset by other measures. In Bangladesh, growth has remained solid, aided by a strong recovery in exports, particularly ready-made garments, but recent floods may adversely affect economic activity for the remainder of 2004. Looking forward, the removal of quotas in textile trade under the Multifiber Arrangement at the end of 2004 poses a key risk, as the country is expected to experience a sharp reduction in export market shares without a timely policy response. The latter could include an exchange rate adjustment, reductions in trade taxes to enhance competitiveness, and infrastructure reforms.

In both Australia and New Zealand, GDP growth is expected to remain robust in 2004, underpinned by strong exports and commodity prices and buoyant domestic demand. Monetary policy has been tightened in both countries over the past year, most recently in New Zealand in early September. While core inflation appears subdued, aided by past real exchange rate appreciation, further interest rate increases are likely to be necessary, particularly in New Zealand, given favorable near-term growth prospects, low unemployment rates, and high rates of capacity utilization. Fiscal positions in both countries are very strong, although further actions will be needed to sustain this over the medium term in the face of pressures from rising populations, including reforms to the pension and health systems and measures to increase labor participation and promote high productivity growth.

Latin America: Will the Economic Rebound Be Used To Build Resilience?

In Latin America, economic activity is rebounding strongly this year, supported by a pickup in domestic demand—underpinned by easier monetary conditions in most countries and improved confidence—and the robust global expansion, reinforced by the rising share of trade in GDP (Figure 1.15 and Table 1.7). Higher oil prices are benefiting major oil exporters, such as Colombia, Ecuador, Mexico, and Venezuela, but hurting oil importers, espe-

Table 1.7. Selected Western Hemisphere Countries: Real GDP, Consumer Prices, and Current Account Balance
(Annual percent change unless otherwise noted)

	Real GDP				Consumer Prices[1]				Current Account Balance[2]			
	2002	2003	2004	2005	2002	2003	2004	2005	2002	2003	2004	2005
Western Hemisphere	**–0.1**	**1.8**	**4.6**	**3.6**	**9.0**	**10.6**	**6.5**	**6.1**	**–1.0**	**0.3**	**0.5**	**–0.3**
Mercosur[3]	**–0.9**	**2.0**	**4.8**	**3.7**	**11.3**	**13.5**	**5.8**	**6.0**	**0.1**	**1.6**	**1.1**	**–0.2**
Argentina	–10.9	8.8	7.0	4.0	25.9	13.4	4.8	7.1	9.0	6.2	1.1	–1.4
Brazil	1.9	–0.2	4.0	3.5	8.4	14.8	6.6	5.9	–1.7	0.8	1.2	0.4
Chile	2.2	3.3	4.9	4.7	2.5	2.8	1.1	2.9	–1.3	–0.8	0.5	–1.9
Uruguay	–11.0	2.5	10.0	3.5	14.0	19.4	9.8	9.3	1.6	0.7	0.1	0.2
Andean region	**0.1**	**1.6**	**5.8**	**4.0**	**9.1**	**10.2**	**8.4**	**8.8**	**1.4**	**2.7**	**4.7**	**3.6**
Colombia	1.6	3.7	4.0	4.0	6.3	7.1	6.0	5.0	–1.8	–1.9	–1.1	–2.2
Ecuador	3.3	2.6	5.4	4.0	12.6	7.9	3.2	2.7	–5.0	–1.7	2.8	3.0
Peru	4.9	4.1	4.5	4.5	1.5	2.5	3.5	2.5	–2.0	–1.7	–0.4	–0.7
Venezuela	–8.9	–7.6	12.1	3.5	22.4	31.1	23.7	31.3	7.9	11.3	13.5	12.1
Mexico, Central America, and Caribbean	**1.2**	**1.6**	**3.6**	**3.3**	**5.2**	**5.9**	**6.7**	**5.0**	**–2.7**	**–1.8**	**–1.6**	**–1.9**
Mexico	0.8	1.3	4.0	3.2	5.0	4.5	4.4	4.0	–2.2	–1.5	–1.2	–1.5
Central America[4]	2.3	3.2	3.3	3.3	6.3	5.9	6.5	5.5	–4.9	–5.2	–5.2	–4.6
The Caribbean[5]	3.1	1.9	0.3	3.3	5.2	18.6	30.3	12.5	–5.5	–0.2	–1.2	–2.0

[1]In accordance with standard practice in the *World Economic Outlook*, movements in consumer prices are indicated as annual averages rather than as December/December changes during the year, as is the practice in some countries.
[2]Percent of GDP.
[3]Includes Argentina, Brazil, Paraguay, and Uruguay, together with Bolivia and Chile (associate members of Mercosur).
[4]Includes Costa Rica, El Salvador, Guatemala, Honduras, Nicaragua, and Panama.
[5]Includes Antigua and Barbuda, The Bahamas, Barbados, Dominica, Dominican Republic, Grenada, Guyana, Haiti, Jamaica, St. Kitts and Nevis, St. Lucia, St. Vincent and the Grenadines, and Trinidad and Tobago.

cially countries in Central America, the Dominican Republic, and Uruguay. The rise in nonfuel commodity prices is leading to trade gains in exporters of metals (Chile, Jamaica, and Peru) and agricultural products (Argentina, Bolivia, Brazil, Ecuador, and Paraguay). Inflationary pressures are increasing in some countries, reflecting higher oil prices and exchange rate depreciations.

External financing conditions became less buoyant in late spring, as the rise in U.S. interest rates prompted investors to reduce their demand for Latin American securities. However, sovereign borrowers had already fulfilled most of their funding requirements for 2004 and spreads have since returned to near their historical lows. Gross debt issuance remained heavy in the first half of the year, as borrowers locked in low interest rates and extended maturities. Looking beyond 2004, many countries have large external financing requirements and remain vulnerable to external shocks (such as an abrupt rise in global interest rates, commodity price volatility, or a weakening of global growth) and adverse domestic developments (such as political uncertainties, policy slippages, or social upheaval).

The economic rebound and still relatively favorable external financing conditions provide a window of opportunity for governments to build resilience and set the stage for sustained growth. Given that stable inflation expectations may be less well entrenched in some countries, central banks may need to be relatively more proactive about stemming any second-round effects of higher oil prices. The key to reducing vulnerability is to cut public debt ratios, which remain high (well over 100 percent in some countries), by pressing ahead with fiscal reforms needed to improve debt sustainability. To lay the foundation for stronger and more durable growth—which would also improve debt sustainability—and lower unemployment, it is crucial not only to entrench macroeconomic stability but also to strengthen the rule of law and investor rights, foster financial sector development, further liberalize trade, and promote labor market flexibility. Actions to address poverty and income inequality are crucial to ensure the sustainability of policies, including broader access to education and health care.

Turning to individual countries, the economic recovery in Argentina is continuing, but structural reforms have been delayed. Low interest rates and high commodity prices have helped maintain the recovery, but recent data suggest that the economic expansion is gradually moderating, with growth projected to slow further in 2005. Tax revenues have been buoyant and, on current trends, the consolidated public sector primary surplus in 2004 could end well above the authorities' target of 3 percent of GDP. Inflation has picked up recently, to 5.3 percent year-on-year in August, but remains consistent with the low end of the central bank's end-2004 target band of 7–11 percent. To sustain growth in the medium term, the key priorities are reaching a comprehensive agreement with creditors on the restructuring of defaulted sovereign debt, fiscal reforms, finalizing compensation to banks for losses from asymmetric pesoization and reforming state-owned banks, and establishing an appropriate legal framework for public services. In Uruguay, the economy is also recovering strongly, supported by robust consumption, and the primary surplus target of 3.2 percent of GDP in 2004 is likely to be surpassed. However, the October presidential election is heightening uncertainty, so it is important to push ahead with the reform of tax administration, improve the oversight of asset disposals, and restructure the state-owned banks. In Bolivia, economic activity is recovering gradually, following the political upheavals in late 2003. The policy priorities are to contain the fiscal deficit while increasing propoor spending, strengthen the financial and corporate sectors, and develop an appropriate legal framework for the hydrocarbons sector aimed at fostering investment.

In Brazil, the economic recovery is gathering strength, boosted by robust export growth and increasing domestic demand, and the forecast for real GDP growth in 2004 has been revised up. While Brazil has taken important steps to boost resilience, including increasing international reserves, reducing the share of foreign-exchange-linked public debt, and improving banks' net foreign exchange position, the rise in sovereign spreads in April and May was nevertheless a reminder that vulnerabilities remain. Reflecting the favorable impact of the recovery on tax revenues, as well as expenditure restraint by the federal government, the consolidated public sector primary surplus in 2004 is projected to be about 4¼ percent of GDP. The government has set a primary surplus target for the nonfinancial public sector of 4¼ percent of GDP for 2005–07 and limited the increase in the minimum wage. On monetary policy, the announcement of an inflation target of 4½ percent and the narrowing of the band for 2006 was welcome. With higher oil prices slowing the deceleration in core inflation, the recent increase in the policy interest rate to 16¼ percent was appropriate. To ensure that the current rebound in growth is sustained, structural reforms need to be extended and deepened, including by increasing labor market flexibility, implementing judicial and regulatory reform, improving the business environment, reforming state-level taxes, and de-earmarking federal taxes.

In Chile, real GDP growth is projected to accelerate to about 5 percent in 2004–05, underpinned by a pickup in investment. Risks from the disruption in the supply of natural gas from Argentina appear manageable. Notwithstanding the increase in oil prices, inflation remains below the 2–4 percent target band. In September, the central bank raised the policy interest rate by ¼ percent to 2 percent. Fiscal policy remains anchored by the structural balance rule (a central government surplus of 1 percent of GDP) and the government has successfully resisted pressures to increase spending in the context of high copper prices. To sustain high growth, the priorities are to encourage greater competition in the financial sector and lower rigidities in the labor market, including by promoting part-time work, increasing the flexibility of working hours, and reducing severance payments. The recent implementation of a well-targeted social program for the poor (*Chile Solidario*) is welcome.

In the Andean region, higher oil production and prices are providing a large boost to economic activity in Ecuador and Venezuela, but difficult political situations remain important risks. In Ecuador, inflation is declining, confidence in the financial sector is broadening, and fiscal performance remains broadly positive, but further fiscal consolidation is needed to reduce financing needs and public debt. In Venezuela, the recent improvement in economic conditions is not sustainable without major changes in policies, including a reduction in the non-oil fiscal deficit, the phasing out over time of foreign exchange controls, and an improvement in the business environment.

The favorable external environment has also helped to support growth in Colombia and Peru. In Colombia, private investment has been especially strong, reflecting improved confidence and low interest rates. However, public debt—though declining—is still high and the security situation—while improving—remains fragile. In Peru, growth continues to be solid and inflation moderately low. However, given high public debt, further gradual fiscal consolidation is important.

In Mexico, economic growth is projected to accelerate to 4 percent this year, reflecting both still relatively easy monetary conditions and strong demand from the United States, reinforced by rising trade and financial integration due to the North American Free Trade Agreement (Box 1.4). However, prospects for 2005 and beyond are clouded by the stalling of structural reforms. With headline inflation projected to remain above the Bank of Mexico's target range of 2–4 percent, the recent tightening of monetary policy was appropriate, and further tightening may be necessary to bring inflation expectations back within the target range. Given the desirability of bringing down the level of public debt from about 50 percent of GDP, fiscal priorities are to resist pressures for spending increases in the absence of new revenue measures, establish a fiscal rule that will ensure that future windfall oil revenues are saved, undertake comprehensive tax and pension reforms, and continue to strengthen the structure of public debt. While the banking system appears healthy, lending by nonbanks—especially mortgage lending—is rising rapidly, underlining the importance of improving oversight of such institutions. To raise potential growth and maintain competitiveness, it is essential to reform the energy and telecommunications sectors and the labor market, including reducing impediments to hiring and firing workers, and lowering nonwage costs. In Central America and the Caribbean, it is important to strengthen the institutional basis for macroeconomic stability, private sector development, and effective social policies, so as to boost growth, increase resilience to shocks, and reduce poverty in a lasting way.

Emerging Europe: Will the Recovery Be Used to Address Fiscal Vulnerabilities?

In emerging Europe, GDP growth is projected to rise to 5.5 percent in 2004, with a stronger-than-expected upturn in much of central and southern Europe, led by Poland and Turkey, more than offsetting moderating—but still very strong—growth in the Baltics (Table 1.8). Looking forward, GDP growth is expected to remain well-sustained in the remainder of 2004 and in 2005, underpinned by rising domestic demand and strong export growth. Stronger activity, combined with higher oil prices, has led to a pickup in inflation—except in Turkey and Romania—and in some new European Union (EU) members is significantly above the Maastricht target. For similar reasons, regional current account deficits remain very high, and outside Turkey little improvement is expected in 2005.

In the immediate future, the risks to the outlook appear broadly balanced. With recent data generally surprising on the upside, the underlying momentum of the recovery could be stronger than projected. However, most countries are vul-

Table 1.8. Emerging Europe: Real GDP, Consumer Prices, and Current Account Balance
(Annual percent change unless otherwise noted)

	Real GDP				Consumer Prices[1]				Current Account Balance[2]			
	2002	2003	2004	2005	2002	2003	2004	2005	2002	2003	2004	2005
Emerging Europe	**4.3**	**4.5**	**5.5**	**4.8**	**15.3**	**9.5**	**7.1**	**5.9**	**–3.3**	**–4.1**	**–4.3**	**–4.1**
Turkey	7.9	5.8	7.0	5.0	45.0	25.3	11.4	10.8	–0.8	–2.9	–4.0	–3.5
Excluding Turkey	3.0	3.9	4.9	4.7	5.3	3.8	5.3	4.0	–4.3	–4.6	–4.5	–4.5
Baltics	**6.8**	**7.7**	**6.6**	**6.3**	**1.5**	**0.6**	**2.6**	**2.8**	**–6.7**	**–8.8**	**–8.7**	**–7.9**
Estonia	7.2	5.1	5.8	5.4	3.6	1.3	3.0	2.5	–10.2	–13.2	–11.2	–9.5
Latvia	6.4	7.5	6.5	6.0	1.9	2.9	5.8	3.5	–6.5	–8.6	–9.3	–8.2
Lithuania	6.8	9.0	7.0	7.0	0.3	–1.2	0.6	2.5	–5.2	–6.7	–7.1	–6.9
Central Europe	**2.1**	**3.5**	**4.8**	**4.4**	**2.8**	**2.2**	**4.5**	**3.7**	**–4.1**	**–3.9**	**–3.8**	**–3.9**
Czech Republic	1.5	3.1	3.3	3.4	1.8	0.1	3.2	3.0	–5.6	–6.2	–5.5	–4.9
Hungary	3.5	2.9	3.5	3.7	5.3	4.7	6.9	4.4	–7.2	–8.9	–8.8	–8.2
Poland	1.4	3.8	5.8	5.1	1.9	0.8	3.7	3.8	–2.6	–1.9	–1.7	–2.1
Slovak Republic	4.4	4.2	4.8	4.3	3.3	8.5	7.7	3.0	–8.0	–0.9	–2.3	–2.6
Slovenia	3.4	2.3	3.9	4.1	7.5	5.6	3.7	3.2	1.4	0.1	–0.6	–1.4
Southern and south-eastern Europe	**4.6**	**4.3**	**4.8**	**4.9**	**16.1**	**10.7**	**9.3**	**5.8**	**–4.0**	**–6.2**	**–5.8**	**–5.7**
Bulgaria	4.9	4.3	5.2	5.2	5.8	2.3	6.3	3.6	–5.3	–8.4	–8.7	–8.3
Cyprus	2.0	2.0	3.0	3.5	2.8	4.1	2.2	2.6	–5.4	–4.4	–4.3	–4.2
Malta	1.2	–1.7	1.3	1.7	2.2	1.3	3.0	2.0	–1.1	–6.0	–4.0	–2.6
Romania	5.0	4.9	5.0	5.0	22.5	15.3	11.5	7.2	–3.4	–5.9	–5.2	–5.3

[1]In accordance with standard practice in the *World Economic Outlook*, movements in consumer prices are indicated as annual averages rather than as December/December changes during the year, as is the practice in some countries.
[2]Percent of GDP.

nerable to higher oil prices, which, apart from adversely affecting growth, could also add to pressures on inflation and current accounts. The weakness in euro area domestic demand—especially in Germany, a key regional trading partner—remains sluggish. Looking forward, high external deficits—and linked to that, the high fiscal deficits—in a number of countries remain a key concern, especially given that they are increasingly debt financed. With most countries facing substantial future expenditure pressures—notably from rapidly aging populations (see Chapter III), the need to upgrade infrastructure, and contributions to the EU budget—it is now critical to take advantage of the upturn to make progress with fiscal consolidation (Figure 1.16). Prudential risks from rapid private credit growth as financial deepening proceeds also bear close monitoring—especially when financing consumption rather than investment—underscoring the need to make additional progress in strengthening bank supervision.

On May 1, 2004, 10 countries in the region joined the European Union, with Bulgaria and Romania—and possibly Croatia, which will begin accession negotiations in early 2005—expected to follow later this decade. Following this historic enlargement, Estonia, Lithuania, and Slovenia have moved quickly to join the Exchange Rate Mechanism (ERM2), the precursor to Economic and Monetary Union (EMU), with Latvia expected to follow shortly. Most other countries aim to join toward the end of the decade, although much remains to be done—especially on the fiscal side—if this timetable is to be met. More generally, as the experience of previous entrants—notably Greece through the mid-1990s—has shown, EU accession facilitates, but does not guarantee, rapid growth. With the spur of qualification for EU entry no longer present, it will be important to avoid any slowdown in implementing key structural reforms, particularly in those countries—notably Poland—where growth has disappointed in past years.

Turning to individual countries, Poland has continued to experience a strong recovery, underpinned by the substantial easing of monetary policy over the past two years. Since early 2004, inflation and inflation expectations have picked up sharply, prompting a 125-basis-point increase in interest rates since late June. The external current account deficit is moderate, with export growth boosted by the depreciation of the zloty. Despite the favorable short-run outlook, investment and employment growth have remained moderate, and financial markets are still concerned about fundamental impediments to growth. Notably, since 1999 four successive finance ministers have failed to rein in the rising fiscal deficit, and a further substantial increase is projected in 2004. While recent parliamentary approval of the modification of indexation of pension benefits—an important part of the Hausner medium-term fiscal consolidation plan—is a step forward, without substantial further measures fiscal deficits will remain very high for the remainder of the decade. With unemployment still close to 20 percent, labor market reform—focused on improving employability of low-skilled workers—is a central priority.

In Hungary, GDP growth is also picking up after last year's slowdown, underpinned by strong growth of exports and investment, accompanied by a significant upturn in inflation (now among the highest in central Europe). Foreign exchange markets have stabilized following the turbulence at end-2003, but interest rates are still high and the twin fiscal and current account deficits remain significant vulnerabilities. Looking forward, decisive and credible fiscal adjustment will be a key challenge for the new government, both to reduce external vulnerabilities and to stay on course for euro adoption.

Turning to the Czech Republic, activity is picking up more slowly than in the rest of central Europe, underpinned by exports and export-related investment. With rising inflation and increasing signs of cost push pressures, the Czech National Bank has appropriately raised interest rates by 50 basis points since June; looking forward, monetary policy will likely need to be tightened further, with the pace and timing depending on the strength of the recovery as well as on exchange rate developments. On the fiscal side, the cash general government deficit is expected to increase to about 6 percent of GDP,

Figure 1.16. How Close Are the New EU Members to the Convergence Criteria for EMU Membership?

The Baltic countries and Slovenia meet—or are very close to—Maastrich fiscal and inflation targets; most central European countries have considerably further to go.

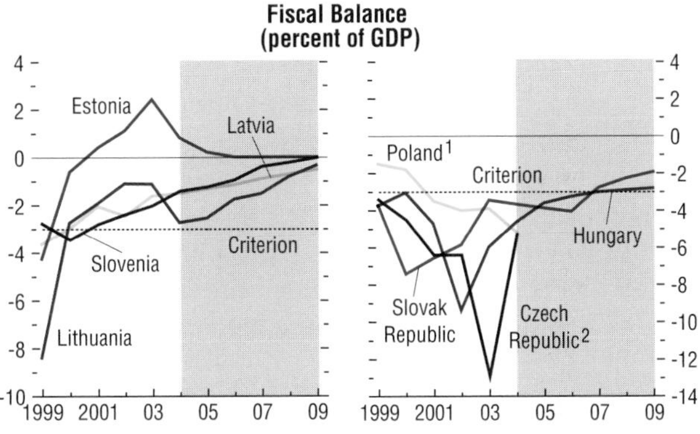

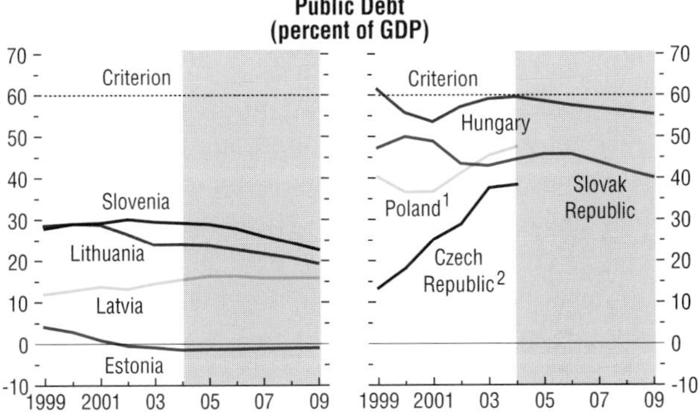

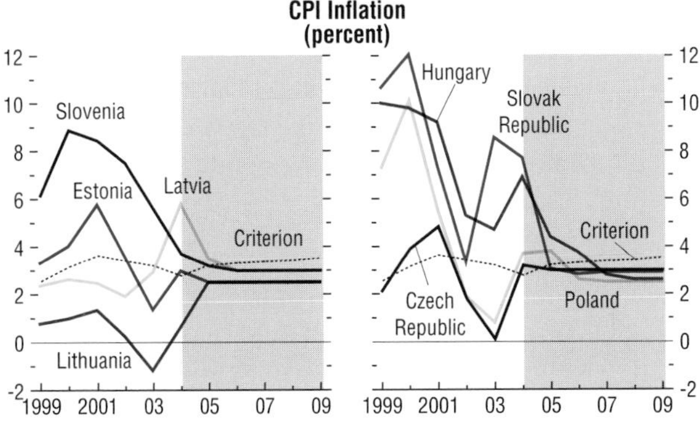

Sources: National authorities; and IMF staff estimates.

[1]European System of Accounts (ESA95) definition with pension funds inside general government. If pension funds are excluded from general government, an issue that is presently under discussion with EUROSTAT, the deficit in 2004 would be 1.5 percent of GDP higher, and debt 4.1 percent of GDP higher.

[2]For 2003, 5.9 percentage points of the deficit were due to the inclusion of a guarantee that was partially called. The 2004 deficit and debt reflect the authorities' projections.

Box 1.4. Regional Trade Agreements and Integration: The Experience with NAFTA

Ten years ago, Canada, Mexico, and the United States launched the North American Free Trade Agreement (NAFTA). This agreement was a milestone in several respects. It created the world's largest free trade area. Its coverage was more comprehensive than in most other regional trade agreements, ranging from merchandise trade to issues related to investment, services, labor markets, environment, and settlement of trade disputes. Finally, it was the first comprehensive free trade agreement between advanced and developing economies. This box briefly reviews the effects of the agreement on trade and financial flows; on business cycle linkages; and on the productivity dynamics in Canada and Mexico, drawing on recent research.[1]

The creation of NAFTA was followed by a sharp acceleration in trade flows among member countries, especially to and from Mexico, leading to an increase in intra-NAFTA relative to extra-NAFTA trade (see the figure).[2] During the recent downturn, however, some of these increases were partially reversed. Perhaps more significantly, the composition of trade flows also changed, as vertical specialization (the amount of imported goods embodied in exports), intra-industry, and intrafirm trade among the NAFTA partners increased substantially. Factors other than NAFTA also contributed to the increased trade integration among member countries, including Mexico's unilateral reduction of tariffs following its entry into GATT in 1986 and the sharp depreciation of the Mexican peso in 1994 (Krueger, 1999). While it is difficult to isolate empirically the effects of NAFTA on member countries' trade patterns, given other shocks during this period that may have affected trade flows, most studies conclude that the agreement played a major role in the growth of trade in the region. For Mexico, it has been estimated that between one-fourth and one-half of the increase in exports to the United States can be attributed to the country's preferential access under NAFTA (Romalis, 2002; Agama and McDaniel, 2002; and Wall, 2003).

NAFTA and Trade Integration in North America

(Trade with NAFTA partners as a percent of total trade)[1]

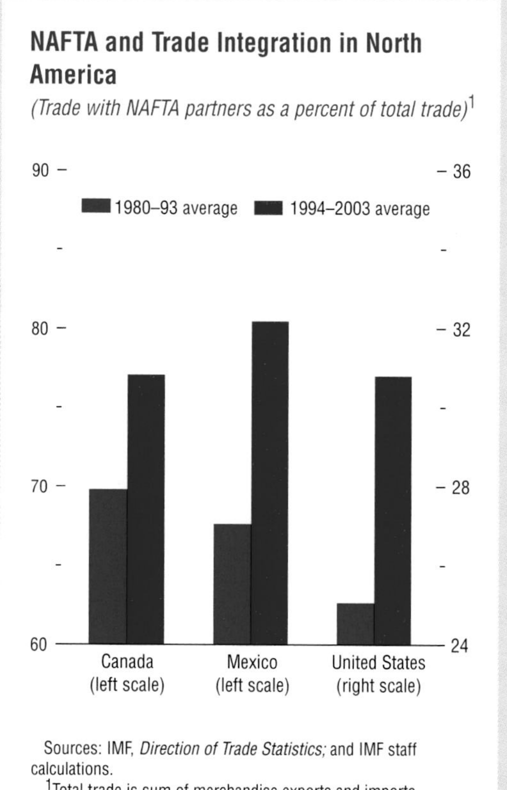

Sources: IMF, *Direction of Trade Statistics;* and IMF staff calculations.

[1]Total trade is sum of merchandise exports and imports.

Intraregional foreign direct investment flows to Mexico rose substantially after the inception of NAFTA. Cuevas, Messmacher, and Werner (2002) and Waldkirch (2003) estimate that NAFTA induced a 40–70 percent increase in the volume of foreign direct investment flows into Mexico, which was partly related to the increase in vertical trade and partly to the signaling

Note: The main author of this box is M. Ayhan Kose.

[1]For detailed reviews of the impact of the agreement on Mexico and Canada, see Kose, Meredith, and Towe (2004) and Cardarelli and Kose (2004), and the references therein.

[2]To date, most studies, including Krueger (1999, 2000), and Lederman, Maloney, and Serven (2003), concluded that NAFTA was not a trade-diverting agreement—that is, the expansion of trade was not at the expense of other countries. However, Romalis (2002) found some evidence of substantial trade diversion.

effects associated with the agreement—signaling Mexico's commitment to liberalization and reform programs. However, NAFTA had no discernible impact on foreign direct investment flows between Canada and the United States (Globerman and Shapiro, 2003).

Increased trade and financial linkages led to an increase in the synchronicity of business cycles among member countries. Cross-country correlations of major macroeconomic aggregates rose, although in some cases, especially for correlations between the United States and Canada, the statistical significance of the increases remains subject to debate (e.g., Doyle and Faust, 2003). The increased synchronicity could reflect the greater role of regional shocks compared with country-specific idiosyncratic shocks since the inception of NAFTA. This, in turn, likely reflects the increase in vertical specialization and intra-industry trade among the member countries, which leads to the transmission of shocks along the production chain. Indeed, some recent studies have found that the share of output fluctuations explained by regional shocks increased while the role of country-specific, idiosyncratic shocks decreased (e.g., Kose, Otrok, and Whiteman, 2003; Bordo and Helbling, 2003; and Helbling and Bayoumi, 2003). Moreover, since regional shocks were less volatile than idiosyncratic shocks in Mexico, cyclical fluctuations in the country became more moderate in size.

Despite the increased importance of regional shocks in business cycle linkages among NAFTA members, country-specific shocks continue to play an important role, given that interindustry trade and differences in industrial structure remain considerable. As a result, cycles can diverge, as happened, for example, during the most recent downturn, when Canada experienced a shallower slowdown and a relatively stronger recovery than the United States. This has been partly ascribed to Canada's smaller information, communication, and technology sector.

NAFTA also appears to have boosted member countries' productivity growth over the past decade. The speed of convergence of total factor productivity among NAFTA partners accelerated after the inception of NAFTA (Easterly, Fiess, and Lederman, 2003). In addition, Lopez-Cordova (2002) and Schiff and Wang (2003) estimate that NAFTA increased the level of total factor productivity in Mexico by 5½–10 percent.

In sum, NAFTA led to significant increases in trade and financial integration in North America, with, so far, little evidence of trade diversion. Moreover, the agreement helped to boost welfare in member countries by accelerating productivity growth and reducing output volatility. Looking forward, additional gains could be derived from further deepening economic linkages. Currently, trade and investment flows are restricted by differences in regulatory frameworks, security procedures, and rules-of-origin requirements. As an illustration of the potential efficiency gains from deeper economic integration, Ghosh and Rao (2004) find that the removal of rules-of-origin requirements and the harmonization of external tariffs—which has been under discussion among NAFTA member countries—could raise Mexico's GDP by more than 5 percent and Canada's GDP by as much as 1¼ percent.

in excess of the government's target. To restore the credibility of the 2004–06 deficit reduction plan, it is essential for the new government to bring forward the adjustment now planned for 2006, and strengthen the fiscal framework for future years. In the Slovak Republic, GDP growth remains solid with buoyant exports supported increasingly by a revival in domestic demand. Fiscal consolidation appears on track and core inflation is low, although headline inflation will remain high through end-2004. Monetary policy has been steadily eased in response to the strength of the koruna.

In the Baltic countries, output growth remains very strong, supported by robust export performance and increased domestic demand—

underpinned inter alia by transfers from the European Union. Macroeconomic policies are well aligned with the euro area, with all three countries expected to meet the Maastricht fiscal criteria in 2004 (although inflation in Latvia is relatively high, partly due to one-off factors, including oil). Relatively flexible economies and the previous history of fixed exchange rates should facilitate a smooth transition to EMU. However, with current account deficits very high and potential risks of increased capital inflows and overheating in the run-up to EMU, further efforts to raise public savings along with continued strengthening of bank supervision would be prudent. Slovenia was also well placed to join ERM2, despite inflation significantly above the EU average.

In both Bulgaria and Romania, growth of output and domestic demand has remained robust, underpinned by rapid credit growth and accompanied by continued high external current account deficits. To restrain external vulnerabilities, both countries need to press ahead with fiscal consolidation; wage restraint in the state-owned sector; measures to moderate private credit growth and strengthen banking supervision; and, in Romania, energy price adjustments. There is also substantial room to improve the business environment, including through accelerated privatization, labor market reform, and strengthening governance. Growth in the Balkans has been solid, aided by buoyant exports, but external vulnerabilities remain a serious concern (especially in Bosnia and Herzegovina, Croatia, and Serbia and Montenegro), underscoring the need for further fiscal consolidation. With poverty widespread, most countries—especially the post-conflict states—face enormous challenges in establishing a political, macroeconomic, and institutional environment conducive to private sector–led growth.

In Turkey, GDP growth is projected to exceed the authorities' 5 percent target in 2004, underpinned by buoyant domestic demand; along with higher oil prices, this has contributed to a further widening in the external current account deficit. To date, the deficit has been relatively comfortably financed, but mainly with short-term flows; looking forward, the recent depreciation of the lira, together with buoyant tourism receipts, should lead to a significant current account improvement in 2005. Nonetheless, the widening deficit—as well as the financial turbulence in April/May—serves as a reminder of Turkey's continued economic vulnerabilities, especially in a period of rising global interest rates and oil price instability, underscoring the need for policy discipline. On the monetary side, performance has been strong, with inflation now reduced to single digits—the lowest in more than 30 years; however, the lagged impact of higher oil prices and lira depreciation will need to be closely monitored. Higher-than-expected growth is leading to an overperformance of budget revenues and a better fiscal performance than targeted in 2004. Given the widening of the current account, it will be critical to hold the line on expenditures, and—given Turkey's high domestic debt—maintain a 6½ percent primary surplus in 2005 and beyond. On the structural side, the key issues remain to implement the newly designed strategy to restructure and privatize state banks; adopt comprehensive new banking legislation; assure a smooth transition to limited deposit insurance; and regain momentum in privatization following recent setbacks.

Commonwealth of Independent States: Maintaining Stability During a Commodity Boom

Sharply higher than expected world prices and demand for crude oil and metals have added to the already strong growth momentum in the CIS region, with economic activity expanding rapidly in the first half of 2004 (Figure 1.17). Buoyant export growth has increasingly been supported by strong domestic demand, with production in most manufacturing sectors and construction rising strongly. The latter reflects in part the spillover from the external stimulus, including the massive oil and gas sector expansion (which has boosted investment in related sectors such as transportation and infrastructure), but also strong wage growth and favorable liquidity conditions.

Given the stronger-than-expected current growth momentum, and with oil and metals prices projected to remain high for longer, short-term prospects are considerably more favorable than anticipated in the April 2004 *World Economic Outlook.* Regional GDP growth is now projected to remain at 8 percent in 2004 and to moderate to 6.6 percent in 2005, as consumption and investment growth slows to more sustainable levels (Table 1.9). Near-term risks appear broadly balanced, with movements in oil prices—in either direction—having a critical impact on the outlook. While domestic demand could continue to surprise on the upside, a slowdown in commodity demand in China could adversely affect a number of countries, especially metals producers. Prudential risks associated with continued rapid credit growth are also a serious concern. Continued discretionary government interference contributes to uncertainty regarding governance and property rights and, as the example of the Yukos affair illustrates, remains a deterrent to investor confidence in the region.

Despite continued rapid money and credit growth—and rising producer prices for intermediate goods and raw materials since late 2003—inflationary pressures have not so far intensified. In part, this reflects the fact that liquidity increases have been absorbed by rising money demand, reflecting rapid remonetization, strong income growth, and improved confidence. Nonetheless, the combination of very rapid growth and booming commodity prices will increasingly lead to overheating and inflationary pressures, most immediately in Russia, where some sectors are already close to capacity limits. To avoid exacerbating such pressures, it will be important to resist pressures to relax fiscal policies—including to spend all or a portion of the windfall gains from commodity prices—even when fiscal positions are in surplus. Monetary policy will also need to tighten, particularly

Figure 1.17. CIS: Riding on the Crest of a Global Commodity Boom

Rising world prices and demand for crude oil and metals have strongly boosted growth while the massive oil and gas sector expansion has added to the momentum. As a result, growth has become dependent on commodity market developments.

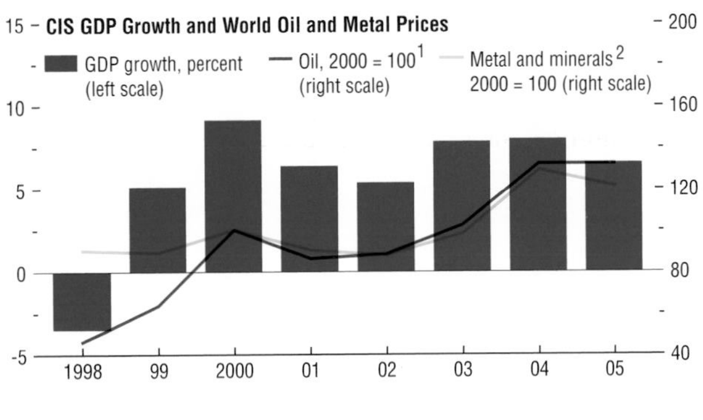

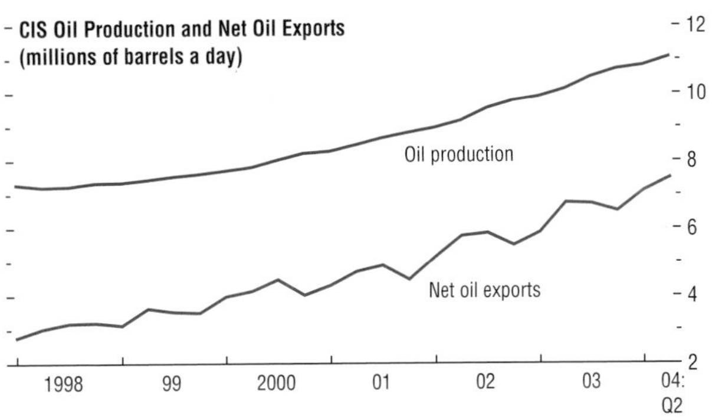

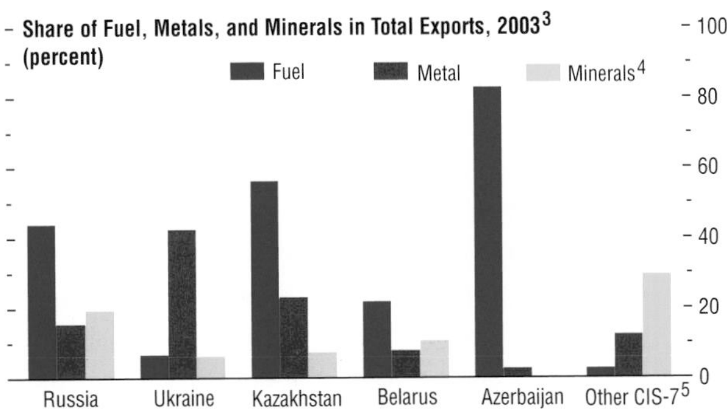

Sources: International Energy Agency, *Monthly Oil Market Report;* OPEC, *Monthly Oil Market Report;* United Nations Commodity Trade database; and IMF staff calculations.

[1]Simple average of U.K. Brent, Dubai, and West Texas Intermediate spot prices.

[2]Simple average of copper, aluminum, iron ore, tin, nickel, zinc, lead, and uranium prices.

[3]Data for Ukraine are as of 2002.

[4]Includes mineral products, precious stones, and precious metals.

[5]Export-weighted average of Armenia, Georgia, Kyrgyz Republic, and Moldova.

Table 1.9. Commonwealth of Independent States: Real GDP, Consumer Prices, and Current Account Balance
(Annual percent change unless otherwise noted)

	Real GDP				Consumer Prices[1]				Current Account Balance[2]			
	2002	2003	2004	2005	2002	2003	2004	2005	2002	2003	2004	2005
Commonwealth of Independent States	**5.4**	**7.9**	**8.0**	**6.6**	**13.8**	**12.0**	**9.9**	**8.7**	**7.0**	**6.4**	**8.3**	**6.2**
Russia	4.7	7.3	7.3	6.6	15.8	13.7	10.3	8.9	8.9	8.3	9.9	7.8
Ukraine	5.3	9.4	12.5	6.0	0.8	5.2	8.3	8.1	7.5	5.8	10.2	4.1
Kazakhstan	9.8	9.2	9.0	8.5	5.9	6.4	6.8	6.7	−3.5	−0.2	2.1	−0.7
Belarus	5.0	6.8	6.4	5.5	42.6	28.4	19.5	17.4	−2.6	−2.9	−3.6	−3.5
CIS-7	**6.4**	**7.2**	**6.0**	**6.2**	**17.7**	**8.6**	**7.8**	**6.7**	**−4.5**	**−7.2**	**−6.8**	**−3.4**
Armenia	12.9	13.9	7.0	6.0	1.1	4.8	3.0	3.0	−6.6	−7.1	−5.9	−5.2
Azerbaijan	10.6	11.2	9.1	11.4	2.8	2.2	5.3	5.0	−12.3	−28.3	−24.2	−8.1
Georgia	5.5	11.1	8.5	6.0	5.6	4.8	5.8	4.8	−6.0	−7.5	−8.1	−8.4
Kyrgyz Republic	—	6.7	5.5	4.9	2.1	3.1	4.5	4.6	−2.2	−2.3	−3.7	−5.7
Moldova	7.8	6.3	5.0	4.0	5.3	11.7	10.7	5.8	−6.0	−9.3	−6.6	−6.3
Tajikistan	9.1	10.2	10.0	8.0	12.2	16.4	7.2	5.7	−2.7	−1.3	−2.2	−2.5
Uzbekistan	3.1	1.5	2.5	2.5	44.3	14.8	11.8	10.5	1.2	8.9	8.2	5.5
Memorandum												
Net energy exporters[3]	5.4	7.6	7.3	6.7	15.5	12.8	9.9	8.6	7.6	7.1	8.8	6.9
Net energy importers[4]	5.5	9.1	10.9	5.9	7.1	8.9	9.7	9.0	3.4	2.1	4.9	1.1

[1]In accordance with standard practice in the *World Economic Outlook*, movements in consumer prices are indicated as annual averages rather than as December/December changes during the year, as is the practice in some countries.
[2]Percent of GDP.
[3]Includes Azerbaijan, Kazakhstan, Russia, Turkmenistan, and Uzbekistan.
[4]Includes Armenia, Belarus, Georgia, Kyrgyz Republic, Moldova, Tajikistan, and Ukraine.

where inflation remains relatively high, accompanied in those countries that continue to experience large external surpluses by greater upward exchange rate flexibility.

Over the medium term, the dependence of many countries on commodity market developments remains a key vulnerability. A good part of the recent boost to growth has reflected temporary factors, including oil and other commodity prices above their long-term averages, and while more persistent than expected earlier, they are nevertheless unlikely to sustain growth at recent high rates. Thus, increased sectoral diversification is needed and, despite encouraging signs that investment outside the energy sector is picking up in Russia and Ukraine, much remains to be done to improve the investment climate and fully develop the institutions and structures for market-based economies, including regulatory frameworks for natural monopolies and competition and effective and transparent public institutions. Progress in this domain has been limited in recent years; a notable exception is the improvement in governance and transparency in Armenia. It will therefore be essential for countries in the region to take advantage of the expansion and press ahead with the reforms needed to improve medium-term prospects.

Turning to individual countries, economic activity in Russia has remained buoyant, while the external position has continued to strengthen with soaring oil exports. With labor markets tightening and growing indications that some sectors are approaching capacity limits, there is a danger that macroeconomic policies could become procyclical. With core inflation entrenched at 10–11 percent, monetary policy needs to focus on decisive disinflation, supported by more exchange rate flexibility. Fiscal policy, in turn, should avoid adding further stimulus, implying additional measures beyond those set out in the 2005 draft budget; pressures to spend a proportion of oil revenues once the cap on accumulation in the oil stabilization fund is reached should also be resisted. The central bank's prompt intervention to restore depositor confidence after some runs on private banks was welcome, but the incident underscores the need for the more determined enforcement of prudential regulations and for sharpening the instruments available to address banking sector problems—including to limit moral hazard related to the extension of interim deposit insurance to all banks after the runs. Regrettably, many structural reforms that would foster economic diversification by improving investment climate and governance have stalled, including reform of natural monopolies and public sector reforms addressing the still-excessive government influence in the economy.

In Ukraine, GDP growth has increased further after accelerating sharply in 2003 despite a poor grain harvest, owing to strong domestic demand and booming exports—particularly of metals and related manufacturing products. Fiscal policy remained appropriately prudent through the first half of 2004, while monetary policy has recently been tightened to contain inflation and credit risks, although this needs to be supported by greater exchange rate flexibility. Progress has been made in reforming the tax system (Box 1.5) and in addressing banking sector risks and vulnerabilities after several years of high credit growth, including through increased capital requirements, but further measures are needed, including restrictions on connected lending and strengthened supervision. In Kazakhstan, economic activity has been booming with the expansion of the oil and gas sector, and medium-term prospects remain favorable, with continued large-scale investment in that sector and enhanced regional market access. With fiscal policy turning more expansionary in 2004 because of welcome increases in social spending, a tightening of monetary policy accompanied by some greater exchange rate flexibility is needed.

On the back of the strong regional growth momentum, economic activity in the low-income CIS-7 countries has generally expanded rapidly, although lagging reformers, including Uzbekistan, have gained considerably less. Higher oil and gas prices benefit Azerbaijan and Uzbekistan, which are net energy exporters. As in other regions, the adverse effect on net energy importers has been partly offset by increases in other commodity prices—including cotton (Tajikistan), aluminum (Tajikistan), and gold (Armenia and the Kyrgyz Republic). Nevertheless, external current account deficits have begun to widen in net energy importers in 2003, a concern given very high external debt—except for Armenia—and vulnerability to external shocks. This underscores the need to sustain fiscal discipline and raise the effectiveness of public institutions—including through better revenue mobilization and expenditure rationalization to improve the delivery of high-priority public services and investment—accompanied by additional assistance from the international community.

Africa: Can Improved Economic Performance Be Sustained?

Real GDP growth in sub-Saharan Africa is projected to rise to 4¾ percent in 2004 and 5¾ percent in 2005, and—while some individual countries continue to face serious problems, with the humanitarian catastrophe in western Sudan of particular concern—the outlook is better than it has been for some time (Table 1.10). Underlying the pickup in growth are improving macroeconomic stability; the global expansion, notably through higher demand for commodities at higher prices; easing external debt burdens through the Heavily Indebted Poor Country (HIPC) Initiative; and somewhat better access to industrial country markets. In addition, growth this year has been boosted by a variety of country-specific developments, including large increases in oil production (in Angola, Chad, and Equatorial Guinea), recoveries of agricultural output from the drought-affected depressed levels of 2003 (in Ethiopia, Malawi, and Rwanda), and improved security situations (Burundi and Central African Republic).

Although higher oil prices are hurting oil importers, the general rise in global commodity prices is projected to have a positive net impact on the trade balances of many countries this

Box 1.5. Bringing Small Entrepreneurs into the Formal Economy

In almost all cases of successful economic development, small-scale entrepreneurs have played a prominent role. In parts of east Asia over the past 40 years, for example, investments by entrepreneurs have resulted in a dynamic small-scale business sector that not only provides suppliers and subcontractors for larger firms but also exports, contests markets, and in a few important cases produces the next generation of large firms. In contrast, in many developing countries, entrepreneurs stay small and "underground" to avoid the costs associated with operating officially. For these countries, sustained economic development requires that the small-scale private sector be brought into the formal economy—that is, that entrepreneurs register their businesses and pay taxes.

In transition economies there has been a divergence with regard to small business. One group of countries, especially in central and eastern Europe and the Baltics, initially gave firms complete freedom and secure property rights. As a result, after 1989, legal small enterprises in these countries swiftly accounted for 50–60 percent of GDP, which is similar to the average for advanced economies. In complete contrast, other postcommunist countries quickly found themselves with numerous entrepreneurs who stayed in the shadow economy to avoid onerous regulation, prohibitive taxation, and the associated corruption. Because these firms operated largely underground, they lacked a political voice. The interests of large firms predominated in the form of tax breaks, special credits, and one-off deals in the judicial system. No one spoke up for lower barriers to entry, for transparency in the fiscal system, or for the fair adjudication of contract disputes. The politics of this situation were largely self-perpetuating because no one with political representation or power wanted change.

In the past decade, two mainstream approaches emerged to entice entrepreneurs out from underground: regulatory reform and improved access to credit. Following the first approach, the World Bank now has an extensive set of recommendations intended to lower the regulatory cost of entry into the formal sector. In particular, countries are encouraged to reduce the time needed to obtain business permits. A second approach follows the work of Hernando de Soto in Peru. It focuses on improving access to credit for small entrepreneurs by making sure they have legal title over their real estate. Both approaches are sensible, and have helped change attitudes toward small-scale entrepreneurs, but the measurable effects so far around the world have been limited.

A third approach is presumptive taxation, meaning simplified taxes for small firms that are designed to reduce the administrative burden and the scope for discretion (and therefore corruption) on the part of tax inspectors. This system has been tried in various parts of the world, and—if properly implemented—is a way to improve tax compliance. Some countries in the Commonwealth of Independent States (CIS) have recently introduced presumptive taxation for small business.[1] For example, this has been the approach in Ukraine since 1998 (Barbone and Sanchez, 2003). After multiple failures to simplify regulations and reduce taxes during the mid-1990s, a presidential decree simply changed the basis of taxation for small firms. Specifically, it offered small firms the choice of paying a single low flat tax that replaced many, but not all, taxes. The rules changed slightly over time, but in 2003 small incorporated businesses could choose between a 5 percent turnover tax with an obligation to pay value-added tax (VAT), and a 10 percent tax with a VAT exemption. This reduced effective tax rates and greatly simplified tax administration for legally registered small

Note: The main authors of this box are Anders Åslund and Simon Johnson.

[1]Strictly speaking, this was a reintroduction. Ironically, given that the overall economic system was not at all favorable to entrepreneurs, a low fixed tax or "patent" fee for small entrepreneurs was present in some parts of the Soviet Union and eastern Europe under communism.

firms. The main significance of the presumptive taxation in this case, however, was that it relieved entrepreneurs from costly visits by tax inspectors.

In terms of direct economic impact, the quantifiable effects of the Ukrainian presumptive tax are significant. The number of registered small and medium-sized enterprises rose by 10 percent in 2000 alone, and the presumptive tax helped reduce the size of the shadow economy by perhaps 11–14 percentage points of GDP during 1999 and 2000 (Thiessen, 2001, 2003). Along with subsequent modest reductions in business licensing requirements and improved access to credit, these tax changes helped launch Ukraine into a period of strong economic growth. Despite the increased business registrations, there was some small loss of revenue associated with the switch to presumptive taxation—that is, there is no sign of favorable supply-side revenue effects being greater than the direct revenue loss. However, the switch to presumptive taxation and other (more costly in terms of revenue) tax cuts did not compromise macroeconomic stabilization because government spending declined by 8 percent of GDP from 1997 to 1999.

Further effects of presumptive taxation and the concomitant growth of the official small business sector are evident at the level of national economic policymaking. In particular, both the executive and the legislature now pay closer attention to the interests of the small-scale private sector. The causality is hard to establish, but this is a complete change in attitude from the situation of the mid-1990s. As entrepreneurs increased their investments in the formal sector, they definitely obtained more political voice, legitimacy, and power collectively. It also became harder to expropriate any of them individually.

There are definite disadvantages to a presumptive tax of any kind. Numerous categories—by separate types of business—introduce room for bureaucratic discretion and haggling. If the simplified tax is very low, as in some parts of the CIS, it operates as a pure tax concession or loophole, which is neither fair nor a good way to build the tax base. Even in the best case, there is obvious scope for rearranging the assets of larger firms so that they appear to be those of smaller firms; this is particularly a problem with high eligibility thresholds, as in Ukraine. It is also not a good idea to permanently create an advantage to being small—firms should want to grow if possible. So ideally a presumptive system should be temporary, until entrepreneurs feel the full advantages of operating in the formal sector, but experience around the world indicates there is a tendency toward permanence in any advantages granted to small business.

Economic development requires improvement in institutions, that is, in the laws, rules, and practices that govern property rights for a broad cross-section of society. When a firm operates unofficially, the entrepreneur does not have secure property rights. Effectively, a government needs to offer property rights in return for tax payments and compliance with regulations. But if taxes are high and regulations too costly—or if registered businesses are much more vulnerable to corruption—operating in the official sector is not attractive. Entrepreneurs can still do business but they invest less and stay small. The political representation of these firms is weak because they are not legal. This difficult economic and political situation exists in many poor countries.

Presumptive taxation can help break an economic and political logjam, as it did in Ukraine. Tax reform of this kind is not a panacea, but under some circumstances it is consistent with broader economic reforms that build a large legal tax-paying entrepreneurial class with legitimate political interests. Reducing regulations and improving access to credit are also helpful. The message from Ukraine confirms what we have learned from other parts of the world in the past 20 years. Macroeconomic stabilization is necessary but not generally sufficient for economic growth. Sustaining growth requires finding ways to offer more secure property rights to a large number of entrepreneurs.

Table 1.10. Selected African Countries: Real GDP, Consumer Prices, and Current Account Balance
(Annual percent change unless otherwise noted)

	Real GDP				Consumer Prices[1]				Current Account Balance[2]			
	2002	2003	2004	2005	2002	2003	2004	2005	2002	2003	2004	2005
Africa	**3.5**	**4.3**	**4.5**	**5.4**	**9.7**	**10.3**	**8.4**	**8.1**	**–1.5**	**–0.1**	**0.4**	**0.7**
Maghreb	**3.3**	**6.2**	**4.2**	**4.4**	**2.1**	**2.2**	**4.0**	**3.4**	**4.5**	**7.0**	**6.1**	**6.8**
Algeria	4.0	6.8	4.5	4.4	1.4	2.6	5.4	4.5	7.8	13.4	13.1	15.2
Morocco	3.2	5.5	3.0	4.0	2.8	1.2	2.0	2.0	4.1	3.1	0.2	–1.3
Tunisia	1.7	5.6	5.6	5.0	2.8	2.8	3.4	2.7	–3.5	–2.9	–2.8	–3.0
Sub-Sahara	**3.6**	**3.7**	**4.6**	**5.8**	**12.1**	**12.9**	**9.9**	**9.6**	**–3.5**	**–2.4**	**–1.4**	**–1.2**
Horn of Africa[3]	**4.1**	**2.0**	**8.6**	**6.8**	**1.3**	**10.5**	**7.7**	**5.7**	**–8.4**	**–7.2**	**–6.0**	**–6.1**
Ethiopia	1.6	–3.9	11.6	5.7	–7.2	15.1	9.6	5.4	–5.7	–4.7	–3.8	–8.5
Sudan	6.0	6.0	6.6	7.6	8.3	7.7	6.5	6.0	–9.6	–8.2	–6.8	–4.8
Great Lakes[4]	**4.8**	**4.1**	**5.2**	**5.8**	**8.3**	**8.3**	**5.5**	**4.2**	**–3.0**	**–2.9**	**–5.3**	**–7.0**
Congo, Dem. Rep. of	3.5	5.6	6.3	7.0	25.3	12.8	5.0	5.0	–2.8	0.6	–3.0	–5.9
Kenya	1.0	1.6	2.3	3.6	2.0	9.8	8.1	4.0	—	–2.5	–7.7	–8.3
Tanzania	7.2	7.1	6.3	6.5	4.6	4.5	4.3	4.0	–3.8	–2.4	–5.2	–6.2
Uganda	6.8	4.7	5.7	6.0	5.7	5.1	3.5	3.5	–6.0	–5.9	–1.2	–5.3
Southern Africa[5]	**2.3**	**2.8**	**4.8**	**6.7**	**44.2**	**54.3**	**44.6**	**38.4**	**–2.9**	**–3.1**	**1.0**	**2.6**
Angola	14.4	3.4	11.2	15.5	108.9	98.3	56.1	16.5	–1.4	–4.9	9.2	14.5
Zimbabwe	–11.1	–9.3	–5.2	1.8	140.0	431.7	350.0	450.0	–2.6	–4.4	–7.1	–10.9
West and Central Africa[6]	**3.6**	**6.7**	**5.4**	**7.9**	**8.4**	**9.5**	**8.3**	**6.5**	**–6.9**	**–2.8**	**—**	**0.5**
Ghana	4.5	5.2	5.2	5.0	14.8	26.7	10.8	6.0	0.5	1.7	0.3	–1.0
Nigeria	1.5	10.7	4.0	5.9	13.7	14.4	15.8	11.4	–11.1	–2.8	2.9	1.7
CFA franc zone[7]	**4.4**	**4.6**	**6.8**	**10.7**	**4.0**	**1.5**	**1.5**	**2.7**	**–4.3**	**–2.9**	**–1.9**	**0.5**
Cameroon[8]	6.5	4.5	4.8	5.1	6.3	0.6	0.8	1.9	–7.0	–2.5	–2.1	–2.3
Côte d'Ivoire	–1.6	–2.8	1.7	4.3	3.1	3.3	1.5	2.0	6.1	3.6	–0.2	1.4
South Africa	**3.6**	**1.9**	**2.6**	**3.3**	**9.2**	**5.8**	**2.6**	**5.7**	**0.6**	**–0.8**	**–2.0**	**–2.1**
Memorandum												
Oil importers	3.2	3.1	4.3	4.5	8.9	9.6	7.2	8.2	–1.8	–1.9	–2.9	–3.3
Oil exporters	4.5	8.0	5.2	8.3	12.3	12.6	12.6	7.8	–0.7	4.8	8.6	10.2

[1]In accordance with standard practice in the *World Economic Outlook*, movements in consumer prices are indicated as annual averages rather than as December/December changes during the year, as is the practice in some countries.
[2]Percent of GDP.
[3]Includes Djibouti.
[4]Includes Burundi and Rwanda.
[5]Includes Botswana, Comoros, Lesotho, Madagascar, Malawi, Mauritius, Mozambique, Rep. of, Namibia, Seychelles, Swaziland, and Zambia.
[6]Includes Cape Verde, The Gambia, Guinea, Mauritania, São Tomé and Príncipe, Sierra Leone, and CFA franc zone.
[7]Includes Benin, Burkina Faso, Central African Republic, Chad, Congo, Rep. of, Equatorial Guinea, Gabon, Guinea-Bissau, Mali, Niger, Senegal, and Togo.
[8]The percent changes in 2002 are calculated over a period of 18 months, reflecting a change in the fiscal year cycle (from July–June to January–December).

year (Figure 1.18). The countries with the largest net gains are mostly oil exporters, followed by countries with substantial gains from higher prices of metal ores. For the majority of countries, gains from higher-priced nonfuel commodity exports are roughly equivalent to losses from higher-priced oil imports, though a few countries face substantial net losses, reflecting mainly higher oil import bills and—for Côte d'Ivoire—lower cocoa prices. A hard landing in China would pose a risk to many countries, as the general increase in nonfuel commodity prices has owed much to the surge in growth there.

While the increases in commodity prices are welcome, the windfall gains will need to be managed carefully to avoid boom-bust cycles that can result from price volatility. Africa's own experience shows that when prices are high, fiscal revenues tend to increase, often leading to an increase in government expenditures, which boosts aggregate demand. When prices subse-

Figure 1.18. Sub-Saharan Africa: Net Impact of Commodity Price Changes on Trade Balances[1]
(Percent of GDP)

Higher commodity prices are projected to have a positive net impact on the trade balances of many countries this year. The countries with the largest net gains are mostly oil exporters, followed by exporters of metals. For the majority of countries, gains from higher-priced nonfuel commodity exports are roughly equivalent to losses from higher-priced oil imports, though a few—mainly small—countries face substantial net losses.

Source: IMF staff estimates.
[1]Change in prices between 2003 and 2004. Assumes unchanged trade volumes.

quently fall, fiscal revenues decline, resulting in a decrease in government spending or an unsustainable increase in government debt, both of which tend to undermine macroeconomic stability and discourage private sector activity. Given the volatility of commodity prices, fiscal policy should aim to accumulate precautionary savings when prices and thus fiscal revenues are high. To ensure that the benefits of higher commodity prices are well used, fiscal institutions need to be strengthened.

Looking ahead, it is crucial to build on the achievements that have been made and lay the foundation for sustained strong growth. On present policies, per capita growth is projected to fall back to about 2 percent in the medium term, far short of what is needed to meet the Millennium Development Goals. Thus, it is essential not only to entrench macroeconomic stability but also to further reduce government involvement in the economy, promote private investment, develop infrastructure, and deepen institutional reforms. As discussed in Box 1.6, several countries in Africa have achieved governance levels that compare favorably with countries outside of Africa, and these could serve as examples for other countries in the region. In this regard, it is encouraging that 23 countries have already joined the African Peer Review Mechanism, which was launched through the New Partnership for Africa's Development and will peer-review economic and political governance. To mitigate the impact of the HIV/AIDS pandemic, an effective strategy will be critical, including strengthening health care systems, expanding prevention programs, and increasing the provision of life-prolonging antiretroviral therapy. The international community has a key role to play in Africa's development, including through lower restrictions on developing country exports, lower subsidies for agricultural products, higher aid flows, and continued debt relief.

Turning to individual countries, growth in South Africa is projected to rise to 2½ percent in 2004 and 3¼ percent in 2005, underpinned by low interest rates and a mildly expansionary fiscal stance. The appreciation of the rand since the end of 2001 has helped to reduce inflation to about the middle of the target band of 3–6 percent, allowing a significant reduction in short-term interest rates. However, the strength of domestic demand, the recent pickup in money supply growth, and wage settlements that have exceeded productivity gains are giving rise to inflationary pressures, which will likely require an increase in policy interest rates over the coming year. While fiscal policy has generally been prudent over the past few years, resulting in a decline in public sector debt, the projected increase in the government deficit to 3.1 percent of GDP in 2004/05 is now at the upper limit of what is desirable to avoid placing undue pressure on long-term interest rates. Any further rise in social spending will need to be funded through increased tax revenue or cuts in lower priority expenditures. With the unemployment rate at 28 percent, it is imperative to remove rigidities in the labor market and provide skills training for unemployed workers.

In Nigeria, real GDP growth is projected to slow to 4–6 percent in 2004–05, as the boom in oil production in 2003 wanes. While the overall fiscal balance is being boosted by windfall oil revenues, the non-oil deficit is large and rising. The government's new economic team has already made some progress in strengthening the federal budget position by cutting non-priority outlays, while increasing spending on education, health, and infrastructure. To increase savings from the oil windfall, the federal and state governments need to agree on a prudent fiscal rule, and the Fiscal Responsibility Bill needs to be enacted. To support disinflation, the central bank should allow interest rates to rise, absorb excess liquidity, and allow greater exchange rate flexibility. Looking further ahead, the central bank's independence needs to be strengthened and the soundness of the banking system needs to be improved. Other structural reform priorities include privatization, trade liberalization, unification of the foreign exchange market, and civil service reform. Nigeria is participating in the Extractive Industry Transparency

Initiative—an international initiative to improve the transparency of payments by companies to governments and of the use of these revenues by governments—and has established an Economic and Financial Crimes Commission.

Elsewhere in sub-Saharan Africa, the economic outlook has generally improved, but further efforts are needed to ensure sustainable growth. In the Horn of Africa, the rebound in economic activity in Ethiopia is largely due to the return of normal weather conditions, and structural reforms need to be accelerated to enhance the investment climate, while in Sudan oil production is rising and a peace agreement has ended the rebellion in the south, but the armed conflict in the west has led to a humanitarian crisis. In the Great Lakes region, the projected increase in real GDP growth in the Democratic Republic of Congo partly reflects progress toward effective reunification, but the security situation in the eastern part of the country remains fragile. In southern Africa, real GDP growth in Angola is projected to accelerate to 11 percent, mainly reflecting increasing oil output, but urgent action is needed to establish sustainable fiscal and external positions, while in Zimbabwe the economy is in sharp decline, with the disorderly land reform reducing agricultural production and concerns about governance discouraging investment and promoting capital flight and emigration. In the CFA franc zone, it is key to restore political stability in Côte d'Ivoire to improve economic prospects.

In north Africa, real GDP growth in Algeria is projected to remain relatively strong in 2004–05, but expansionary fiscal and monetary policies are fueling inflationary pressures. To preserve macroeconomic stability, government spending needs to be de-linked from oil revenues to put fiscal policy firmly on a sustainable path. With unemployment of about 23 percent, it is also essential to initiate the privatization of state-owned banks and further modernize financial intermediation, decrease the role of government in the economy, and reduce labor taxes and the bureaucratic burden on private sector activity. Similarly, the short-term outlooks in Morocco and Tunisia are relatively favorable, but early and vigorous policy action is needed to accelerate underlying growth, reduce high unemployment rates, and cut public debt. The priorities are fiscal consolidation and structural reforms, including trade liberalization, improvements in the business environment, and financial sector reform.

Middle East: Fiscal Consolidation Challenges Ahead

In the Middle East, higher oil production and prices boosted growth in 2003 but, with oil production now close to capacity, the pace of economic expansion has begun to taper off (Figure 1.19). GDP growth in the region is now projected to decline by 1 percentage point to about 5 percent in 2004–05, reflecting a combination of lower growth in the oil sector and, in both oil exporters and the Mashreq, a substantial pickup in non-oil growth (Table 1.11). The latter is predicated on the global upturn, including in Europe, and reform prospects, especially renewed efforts at trade liberalization (including free trade agreements with the European Union and preparations for WTO membership). While most countries in the region have benefited from higher oil prices, they remain exposed to medium-term oil price volatility, especially if windfall gains from above-average oil revenues are not used to accumulate adequate buffer stock savings. Another key concern is the still-fragile security situation.

Looking forward, fiscal consolidation remains a priority in most countries, although the urgency and extent of problems differ. In some non-oil-exporting countries—most seriously Lebanon but also other parts of the Mashreq—public debt burdens are high, and need to be reduced for medium-term sustainability (see the September 2003 *World Economic Outlook*). In contrast, most oil-exporting countries have generally low public debt burdens and are currently running budget surpluses, as substantial shares of the large, oil-related revenue windfalls have been

Box 1.6. Governance Challenges and Progress in Sub-Saharan Africa

A record of poor governance in sub-Saharan Africa has hindered stronger economic growth and poverty reduction, but there are also important exceptions and related challenges being addressed more forcefully across the continent. The focus on good governance—quality of public institutions, transparency, accountability, and control of corruption—has intensified in Africa in recent years with the growing recognition of its critical role for progress toward the Millennium Development Goals (see Mauro, 1997; Kaufmann, Kraay, and Zoido-Lobatón, 1999; Acemoglu, Johnson, and Robinson, 2001; Subramanian and Roy, 2001; and the April 2003 *World Economic Outlook*). Available evidence, even if subject to statistical weaknesses, consistently points to a weak starting point for the region as a whole. For example, the World Bank's governance index places only five countries in the region above the world average.

At the same time, important differences in the quality of governance exist between countries in sub-Saharan Africa (see figure, top panel). Governance in oil-producing countries has been noticeably weaker—probably attributable to relatively large rents, which often are conducive to corruption and an institutional emphasis on preserving the powers of a small elite (see Katz and others, 2004; and Sala-i-Martin and Subramanian, 2003). Conflict is typically associated with a widespread breakdown of governance, and no other region in the world has been more affected by armed conflicts than sub-Saharan Africa.

Sub-Saharan Africa: Selected Governance Indicators

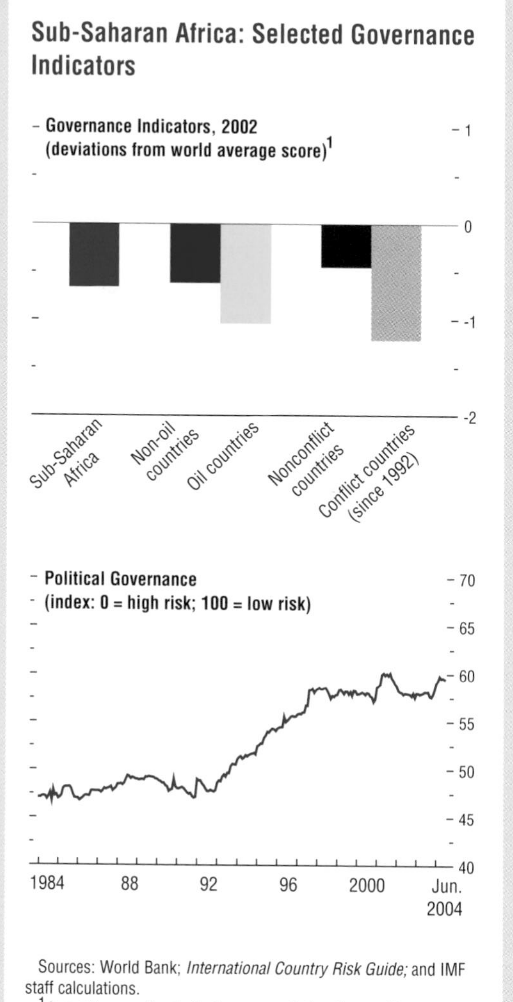

Sources: World Bank; *International Country Risk Guide;* and IMF staff calculations.

[1]A negative number indicates a score below the world average. The scores are normalized with a standard deviation of 1.

Several countries in Africa have achieved governance levels that compare, at least in some areas, quite favorably with other countries, and these could serve as important examples for the region (see also Box 1.5 in the April 2004 *World Economic Outlook*). For example, in South Africa, the institutional framework for macroeconomic policies emphasizes transparency and accountability, the financial sector is well regulated and supervised, and well-defined standards for corporate governance are generally in line with international best practice. Superior economic performance and financial stability in Mauritius have been underpinned by a tradition of good governance, including respect for the law and property rights, a culture of transparency and participatory politics, and an implicit social contract among government, firms, and labor. Comparatively strong legal rights have also fostered development in Namibia in the past, while Botswana's public finance management has been characterized by transparent institutional

Note: The main authors of this box are Milan Cuc and Thomas Krueger.

arrangements for budget formulation and implementation (including for key aspects related to its extractive industry), and by a rule-based approach to fiscal policy.

The challenge is to ensure that these successes spread more broadly across countries in sub-Saharan Africa—with important progress, especially on the political front, already secured over the past two decades (see figure, lower panel). Even so, progress has been uneven, and in many cases formalistic—focusing on legal arrangements without providing adequate resources and lacking frequently political support to actually implement the necessary steps. Moreover, armed conflicts quickly reversed earlier gains and led to a general deterioration in the rule of law in some countries (for example, in Côte d'Ivoire and Liberia).

Several important initiatives—both at national and international levels—are under way to secure improvements in governance. With some elements of governance clearly costly, such as increasing transparency or expanding the judiciary, resource limitations and capacity constraints point to an important role for international support in improving governance in sub-Saharan Africa. Indeed, fundamental progress will require concerted efforts at three levels.

- *Homegrown domestic efforts.* The key task here is to set up the institutional underpinnings for good governance, as well as to move more decisively beyond formalistic applications to actual implementation. Within the public sector, there remains room in many countries to limit official discretion, improve accountability, and strengthen monitoring and oversight—with the regional success stories noted above offering valuable lessons. Property rights and the rule of law will also be indispensable if the hoped-for dynamism in private sector activity is to be achieved. Steps taken within a broad-based participatory process, as is increasingly the case across the continent in the context of a broader poverty reduction strategy, can be particularly effective.
- *Multilateral African initiatives.* The New Partnership for Africa's Development (NEPAD) is a clear expression of Africa's determination to tackle governance problems. One of its central pillars is the African Peer Review Mechanism (APRM), covering several key governance areas. A more determined approach is now needed to turn this vision into reality: while 23 countries had joined the APRM by early July, only three (Ghana, Mauritius, and Rwanda) had entered the preliminary stage of the reviews. With conflict countries presenting particular governance challenges, African peacekeeping initiatives are also noteworthy.
- *Other international efforts.* The international financial institutions have taken a number of initiatives to promote greater transparency and accountability in member countries. The IMF has taken the lead in work on standards and codes in the fiscal and statistical areas and, jointly with the World Bank and the Bank for International Settlements, in the promotion of standards and codes in the monetary and banking areas. The IMF–World Bank Financial Sector Assessment Programs also aim to strengthen transparency and governance in the financial sector. Future steps could target specific revenue transparency issues facing oil-producing countries (or countries with other extractive industries), where governance problems are particularly severe (see above). This is also envisaged by the Extractive Industries Transparency Initiative (EITI), launched by the United Kingdom in 2003. Several African countries, including Equatorial Guinea, Ghana, São Tomé and Príncipe, Gabon, and Republic of Congo, are participating or have announced their intention to participate in the EITI. More efforts are also needed in developed countries that are often party to governance problems in the developing world, including in Africa. The OECD's Convention on Combating Bribery, for example, is an expression of the desire of developed countries to play their part in tackling international business corruption. Effectiveness of this initiative will now depend on how it is enforced under the signatories' national legal frameworks.

Figure 1.19. Middle East: Resisting Pressure to Spend Higher Oil Revenue

Most oil exporters are currently running budget surpluses, as substantial shares of the large, oil-related revenue windfalls have been saved. In contrast, budget deficits have widened in some countries in the Mashreq.

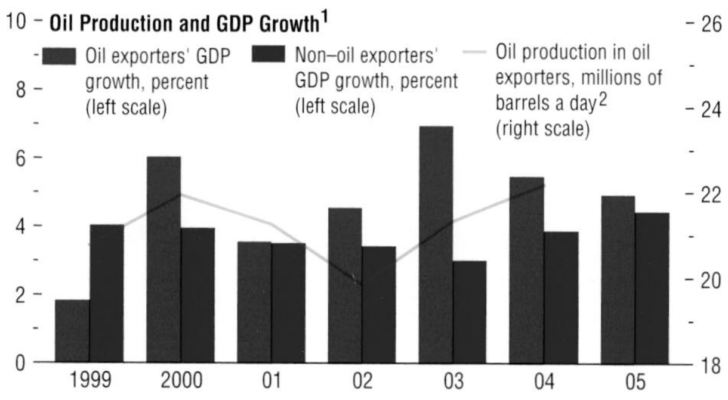

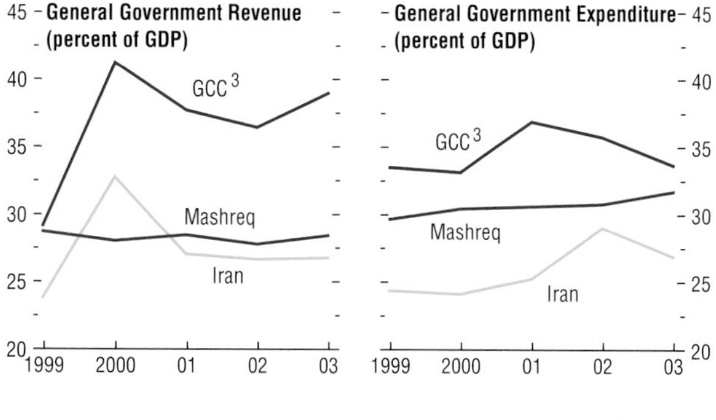

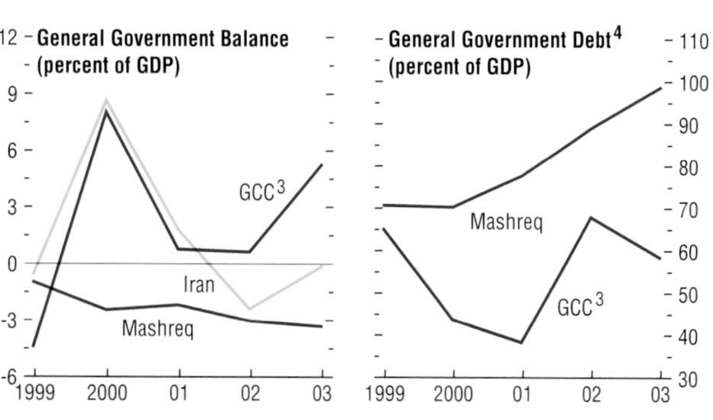

Sources: International Energy Agency, *Monthly Oil Market Report;* and IMF staff calculations.

[1]See Table 1.10 for country compositions of oil exporters and non–oil exporters.

[2]Average of January–June 2004.

[3]The Cooperation Council of the Arab States of the Gulf (GCC) includes Bahrain, Kuwait, Oman, Qatar, Saudi Arabia, and United Arab Emirates.

[4]Data for Bahrain, Iran, Jordan, and Kuwait are not available.

saved. However, budget deficits could reemerge, as oil prices are expected to decline, highlighting the vulnerability of fiscal positions to oil market developments. Accordingly, expenditure ratios need to be aligned with oil revenue based on average prices while at the same time saving some oil wealth for future generations. In addition, in Bahrain, Oman, and Yemen, other revenue sources need to be developed, as oil production will be declining.

Creating the environment for a sustained increase in medium-term growth is the second policy priority, given generally high unemployment rates and a rapidly growing labor force. Specific priorities vary, depending on differences in the origins of low per capita growth, as discussed in Chapter II of the September 2003 *World Economic Outlook.* In the countries of the Cooperation Council of the Arab States of the Gulf (GCC)—Bahrain, Kuwait, Oman, Qatar, Saudi Arabia, and the United Arab Emirates—the priority is to reduce the role of government in the economy, including the large share of public sector employment and associated high wages and benefits, which distort incentives against private sector employment. (The related expenditure reductions would also help in medium-term fiscal consolidation.) In the other countries of the region, oil exporters and non-oil countries alike, priorities are the strengthening of institutions, including the rule of law and the capacity of public institutions, and further trade liberalization.

Turning to individual countries, growth in Iran has remained stronger than in other major oil-exporting countries in the region, owing to a larger and buoyant non-oil sector. This has partly reflected expansionary macroeconomic policies—including procyclical spending of oil revenue—but also recent reforms, including trade liberalization and exchange rate reform, though efforts to support private sector development and to strengthen the banking sector need to be intensified. Inflation has been in the range of 15–16 percent, well above the average in the region, and the external current account has weakened despite higher oil prices due to strong

Table 1.11. Selected Middle Eastern Countries: Real GDP, Consumer Prices, and Current Account Balance
(Annual percent change unless otherwise noted)

	Real GDP				Consumer Prices[1]				Current Account Balance[2]			
	2002	2003	2004	2005	2002	2003	2004	2005	2002	2003	2004	2005
Middle East	**4.3**	**6.0**	**5.1**	**4.8**	**7.5**	**8.0**	**9.2**	**8.7**	**4.5**	**8.1**	**12.7**	**12.5**
Oil exporters[3]	**4.6**	**7.0**	**5.5**	**5.0**	**9.5**	**9.6**	**10.7**	**9.9**	**5.7**	**9.6**	**14.9**	**14.8**
Iran, I.R. of	7.5	6.6	6.6	5.2	15.8	15.6	15.6	15.0	3.1	1.5	3.4	1.6
Saudi Arabia	0.1	7.2	3.6	3.9	–0.6	0.5	2.5	0.8	6.2	13.5	19.5	20.1
United Arab Emirates	1.9	7.0	3.6	4.5	3.1	2.8	3.4	2.1	4.9	8.5	14.2	16.9
Kuwait	–0.4	10.1	2.8	2.3	1.4	1.2	1.7	1.6	12.1	18.1	28.8	29.6
Mashreq	**3.4**	**3.0**	**3.9**	**4.5**	**2.0**	**3.4**	**4.9**	**5.0**	**—**	**1.1**	**1.1**	**0.3**
Egypt	3.2	3.1	3.7	4.5	2.4	3.2	5.2	5.7	0.7	2.4	3.2	1.8
Syrian Arab Republic	4.2	2.6	3.6	4.0	0.6	5.0	5.0	4.5	6.7	3.5	3.3	3.3
Jordan	5.0	3.2	5.5	5.5	1.8	2.3	3.5	1.8	4.5	11.2	5.6	1.8
Lebanon	2.0	3.0	5.0	4.0	1.8	1.3	3.0	2.0	–13.8	–13.1	–12.2	–10.0
Memorandum												
Israel	–0.7	1.3	3.6	3.5	5.7	0.7	–0.3	1.4	–1.6	0.1	–0.5	–0.1

[1]In accordance with standard practice in the *World Economic Outlook*, movements in consumer prices are indicated as annual averages rather than as December/December changes during the year, as is the practice in some countries.

[2]Percent of GDP.

[3]Includes Bahrain, Iran, I.R. of, Iraq, Kuwait, Libya, Oman, Qatar, Saudi Arabia, United Arab Emirates, and Yemen.

import growth. To lower the vulnerability to oil price reversals and reduce inflation to single digit levels, monetary and fiscal policies need to be tightened.

In Iraq, oil production and exports have generally stayed close to prewar levels, with some temporary disruptions owing to continued difficult security conditions. A number of indicators suggest that economic activity has begun to recover—at a slower than initially expected pace—but unemployment and underemployment remain pervasive. Broad consumer prices appear to have stabilized and the nominal exchange rate of the dinar against the U.S. dollar has remained steady since early 2004. Looking forward, policy priorities for the new interim government must be the reconstruction of the country's infrastructure, the maintenance of macroeconomic stability, and, most important, capacity building to develop institutions that can support a market-based economy.

In Egypt, a moderate, export-driven recovery has begun to take hold, reflecting the global upturn and the earlier depreciation of the pound. The latter, in conjunction with higher commodity prices and monetary policy easing, has led to some pickup in inflation, especially at the wholesale price level, where administered prices play less of a role. With steadily increasing net public debt, on course to rise above 70 percent of GDP by end-2005, fiscal consolidation efforts need to be stepped up. Renewed efforts at exchange rate unification and greater rate flexibility remain a priority, given that the dual exchange rate regime—with a de facto inflexible exchange rate—is an impediment to private sector development.

Elsewhere in the Mashreq, economic activity has picked up in Jordan, owing to surging exports and a rebound in domestic demand. Strengthened revenue administration has helped to improve budget balances, although further measures are needed for sustained debt reduction. In Lebanon, growth has similarly picked up, led by strong export, tourism, and construction activities. However, financial vulnerabilities associated with the very high level of public debt, the banking system's exposure to rollover risks in the deposit base, and large capital inflows remain high and, along with correspondingly high real interest rates, weigh on domestic demand. A favorable external environment and a high level of international reserves help to cushion the vulnerabilities in

Figure 1.20. Oil Prices, Futures, and Production

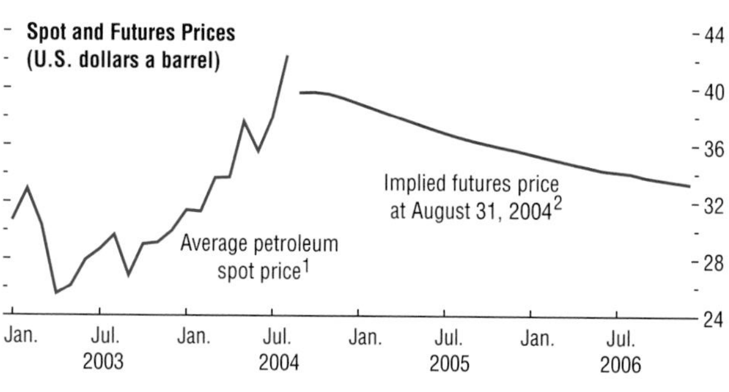

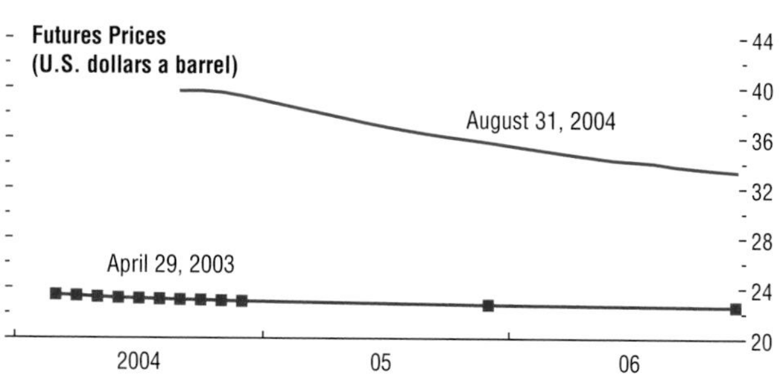

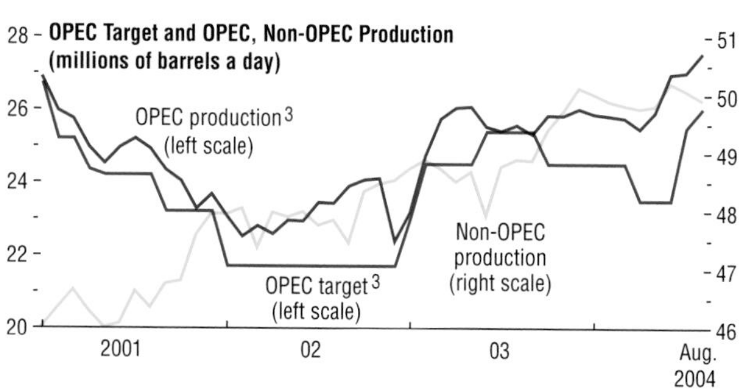

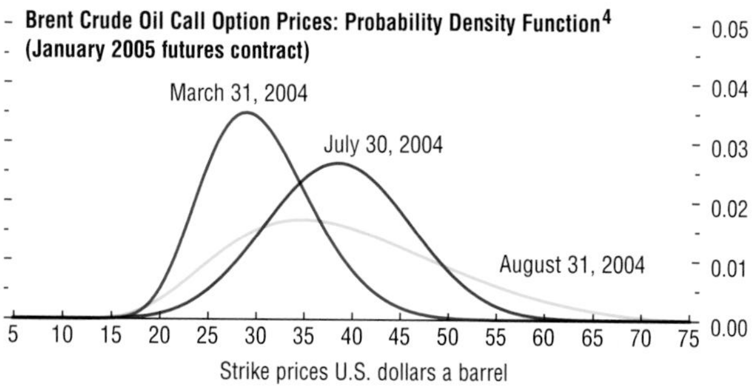

Sources: International Energy Agency; Bloomberg Financial, LP; and IMF staff calculations.

[1]Average petroleum spot price of West Texas Intermediate, U.K. Brent, and Dubai Fateh crude.

[2]Five-day weighted average of NYMEX Light Sweet Crude, IPE Dated Brent, and implied Dubai Fateh.

[3]Excluding Iraq.

[4]Call options are European style options for an option to buy (call) International Petroleum Exchange Brent Contract for January 2005 delivery.

the near term but lasting improvement requires continued fiscal consolidation and structural reforms.

In Israel, the recovery in economic activity has gathered pace, driven by the global upturn, especially in information technology spending, and private consumption. Despite some recent upward creep, core inflation and inflation expectations have remained in the Bank of Israel's target range of 1–3 percent. With a still-substantial output gap and a welcome renewed emphasis on fiscal consolidation, monetary policy has appropriately been relaxed to support recovery. In the West Bank and Gaza, the modest recovery that began in 2003 has continued but output remains some 30 percent below the level reached in 1999, the year before renewed conflict began. Without a lasting improvement in the security situation, general economic conditions will remain depressed.

Appendix 1.1. Commodity Markets

The main authors of this appendix are Kalpana Kochhar and Sam Ouliaris, with support from Hussein Allidina and Paul Nicholson.

Building on the robust increase in commodity prices during the last quarter of 2003, the index of overall primary commodity prices increased by about 27 percent in both U.S. dollar and SDR terms during the first eight months of 2004. The increase can be attributed to sizable movements in energy, raw materials, and metals prices, reflecting a surge in global demand—particularly in Asia. In energy markets, a series of geopolitical events raised concerns about the adequacy and stability of the supply of crude oil, especially with the seasonal pickup in demand approaching. Semiconductor markets consolidated their gains of late 2003 and early 2004.

Crude Oil

The main developments in oil markets during 2004 have been the rise in crude oil prices to record nominal highs, and higher price volatility.

Average[11] oil prices rose substantially during the first eight months of 2004, surpassing the record nominal highs set during the Iraqi invasion of Kuwait in 1990 (Figure 1.20). While OPEC's decision to increase official quotas by 2 million barrels a day (mbd) in July and a further 0.5 mbd in August helped to lower average prices markedly to about US$33 by mid-June, subsequent tensions in oil-exporting nations—particularly Iraq, Nigeria, Russia, and Venezuela—pushed average prices to a new record high of US$44.71 on August 19. Average prices fell to US$38.13 by early September as these tensions eased, but have since turned up once more, reflecting renewed supply concerns in Russia and an unexpected decline in U.S. inventories.

Looking ahead, futures markets suggest that oil prices will remain high for the remainder of 2004 and 2005. Higher prices are corroborated by options data on futures contracts, which reveal a steady rise—since March 2004—in the median strike price for the January 2005 Brent contract. Moreover, the range of strike prices has recently widened, especially at the upper end, suggesting greater uncertainty about the strike price and higher odds of a large price hike relative to existing levels (Figure 1.20). Finally, as of mid-September, future oil prices as far forward as 2010 were uniformly above US$30.

The surge in spot prices has been largely unanticipated—futures markets at the end of September 2003 indicated a spot price of about US$24.90 for September 2004 delivery—and appears to have reflected a number of factors.

- *Perhaps most important, as the global economic recovery has taken hold over the past year, the fact that both the level and growth in the global demand for oil have consistently outpaced expectations.* Despite significantly higher oil prices, the International Energy Agency's (IEA) latest projections envisage oil demand to increase by 3.2 percent in 2004, compared with a July 2003 forecast of only 1.3 percent. This projected increase represents the fastest annual increase in oil demand since 1980, reflecting sizable increases in demand from China, North America, and other non-OECD countries (Brazil and India in particular). The IEA expects Asia to be the principal region of growth, predicting that Chinese oil demand in particular will expand by about 15 percent in 2004—accounting for one-third of total growth in global demand in 2004. This compares with a previously projected increase for China—released in July 2003—of about 5 percent.
- *On the supply side, OPEC's February announcement of lower output targets together with disappointing growth in non-OPEC production.* While OPEC-10 members (OPEC excluding Iraq) actually kept production well above official quotas, the announcement of quota reductions from April 1 surprised the market—raising fears of actual production cuts—and was followed by large increases in oil prices. Moreover, oil production in Venezuela remains below prestrike levels, while production in Iraq—where ongoing security issues as well as aging infrastructure are complicating the task of maintaining production—has been slow to recover to prewar levels. Recent declines in U.S. and U.K. production have also limited the growth in global supply. The net result has been a sizable and somewhat unanticipated increase in the call on OPEC at a time when oil demand is rising rapidly.
- *Very low levels of spare global oil production capacity, raising concerns that the global production system will not be able to cope with an unanticipated, short-term supply shock.* The unexpected surge in oil prices prompted OPEC-10 to announce on June 10 an immediate increase in actual production by 0.8 mbd and a gradual increase in

[11]Unless noted otherwise, all subsequent references to the oil price, which is meant to reflect the global price of oil, are to the equally weighted average petroleum spot price (APSP) of three different grades of oil, namely, West Texas, Brent, and Dubai crude. The APSP is necessarily different from the price of any of these individual crudes, usually falling between the West Texas and Dubai crude prices. While the three crude oil prices move together over time, the APSP is likely to be a better estimate of global cost of oil since the world depends on a variety of crude oils for its energy.

Figure 1.21. OPEC Spare Capacity, Commercial Oil Inventories, and Speculative Activity

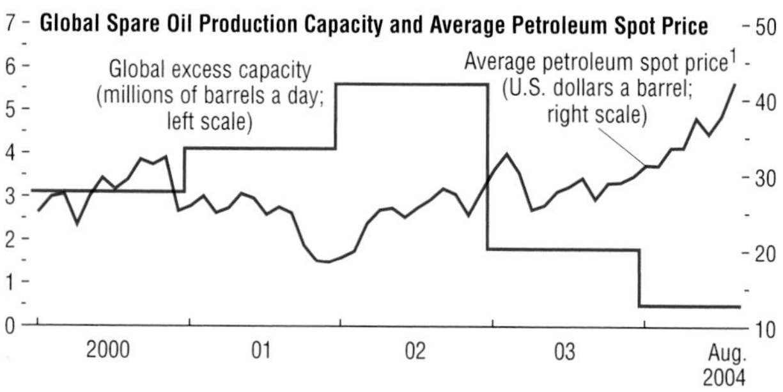

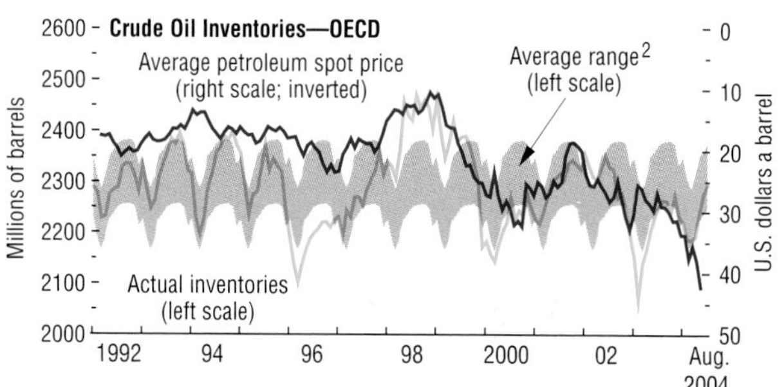

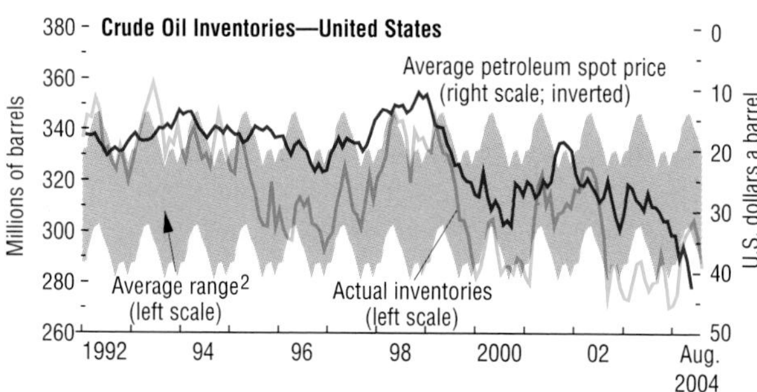

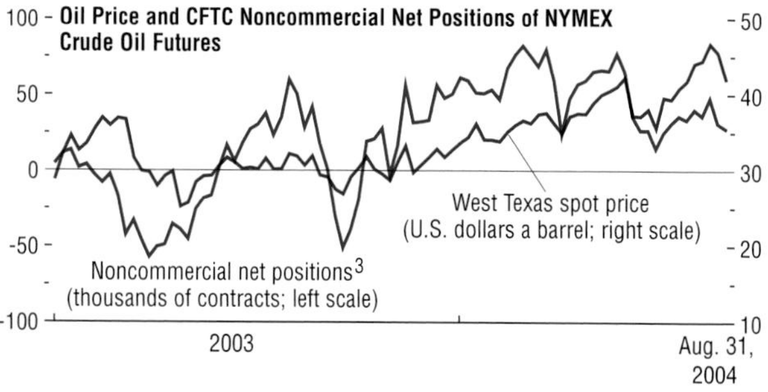

Sources: Commodity Futures Trading Commission (CFTC); Bloomberg Financial, LP; U.S. Department of Energy; International Energy Agency; and IMF staff calculations.

[1]Average petroleum spot price of West Texas Intermediate, U.K. Brent, and Dubai Fateh crude.

[2]Average of each calendar month during 1992–2002, plus a 60 percent confidence interval based on past deviations.

[3]Noncommercial net position is calculated by subtracting the short position from long positions.

official quotas to 26 mbd (effective August 1)—thereby legitimizing OPEC-10's actual end-May production levels. While this decision helped to reduce prices from the record highs recorded in early June, spare global oil production capacity is now extremely low compared with the projected growth in overall demand for 2004 and 2005. According to the IEA, OPEC-10's actual production averaged around 27.5 mbd in August 2004 and its excess capacity fell to about 0.3 mbd—less than 1 percent of global demand—compared with 5.5 mbd in July 2002 (prior to supply disruptions in Venezuela) (Figure 1.21). On September 15, OPEC decided to increase official quotas by a further 1 mbd to 27 mbd effective November 1, thereby raising quotas nearer to actual (and capacity) production levels.

A number of additional factors have also put upward pressure on oil futures prices in recent months.

- *Commercial inventories of crude oil in the OECD, though rising in recent months, remain low by historical standards—especially in the United States.* While low inventories reflect the underlying strength of global demand, and persistent backwardation in the futures market discourages inventory rebuilding, existing inventories may be too low for the normal draw that occurs in the final quarter of 2004, when the northern hemisphere enters the heating season.
- *Product markets are tighter.* Though the level of gasoline inventories measured in terms of the number of days of consumption is close to its long-run trend, strong demand for gasoline and a lack of refinery flexibility in the United States led to higher gasoline prices and gasoline crack spreads from May to July. Gasoline futures peaked at US$61.74 a barrel (US$1.47 a gallon) in May, more than US$12 a barrel above the previous peak set in 2003. More generally, though the efficiency of existing refineries has improved, global refining capacity has not kept pace with crude oil output in recent years, limiting the ability of producers to satisfy surging demand (including inventory needs). These pressures are likely to become especially

acute toward the end of 2004, as the northern hemisphere approaches its winter season.

- *Tight inventories in the context of greater geopolitical uncertainty have encouraged speculative activity in futures markets.* Speculators built a large net long position during the first half of 2004, placing further upward pressure on futures prices and increasing the sensitivity of the market to a sudden reversal in expectations. While causality is difficult to assess, net noncommercial long positions unwound as crude oil prices eased from then record highs in the first half of June.[12] Using first differences, the correlation between the net noncommercial long positions and average crude oil prices since the beginning of 2003 is about 0.6.
- *Geopolitical concerns in the Middle East have raised questions about the stability of supply, both in the short and long term.* Recent terrorist attacks in Iraq and Saudi Arabia in particular have heightened such concerns, although similar attacks in the past have not always been associated with oil price increases.
- *There is continued uncertainty regarding the status of the Russian oil firm OAS Yukos and its ability to continue to produce and sell crude oil.* The Yukos affair began last October when the Russian government made a claim for key production facilities and cash accounts of OAS Yukos as payment for US$3.4 billion in back taxes from 2000. The affair has raised concerns about the reliability of oil supplies from Russia, which recently surpassed Saudi Arabia as the world's largest producer of oil. Yukos currently produces about 2 percent of daily world oil supplies, and exports about 10 percent of its output to China.

As the *World Economic Outlook* went to press, futures markets implied an average crude oil price of US$37.66 in 2004, and $39.17 in 2005 (somewhat above the World Economic Outlook baseline). In addition, longer-term futures remain significantly higher than summer 2003 levels, reflecting expectations of a structural increase in global demand relative to supply, ongoing concerns about potential long-term disruptions to crude oil supply from the Middle East, and the likelihood of slower growth in oil production from non-OPEC countries.

While proven reserves remain plentiful, the key issue in the global oil market appears to be low excess capacity and the adequacy of existing capacity expansion projects relative to the potential increase in global demand. Today's limited spare capacity reflects in part stalled investment in capacity expansion projects by OPEC-11 members during the 1990s owing to persistently low real oil average oil prices during 1985–2000 (Figure 1.22). Existing capacity expansion projects appear limited even though futures markets suggest that crude oil prices will remain above the minimum levels needed to justify additional investment. Though productive capacity is expected to increase by approximately 1 mbd before the end of 2004 owing to expansion projects in Saudi Arabia, Kuwait, and United Arab Emirates, spare capacity is likely to remain tight because of a seasonal surge in demand during the second half of 2004. Moreover, trend growth in demand is expected to consume any additional capacity coming on stream in 2005, while growth in non-OPEC oil production may slow from its present highs. As such, the oil market is likely to remain dependent on all oil-exporting nations producing at close to maximum capacity, raising the likelihood of price spikes if productive capacity is compromised.

Nonenergy Commodity Prices

Following a marked increase in nonenergy commodity prices during the second half of 2003, nonenergy commodity prices experienced further but relatively modest gains during the first eight months of 2004. The slower increases coincided with attempts by China—a large consumer of nonenergy commodities—to cool the pace of its economic expansion, and moves by

[12]The September 2004 *Global Financial Stability Report* reviews hedge fund activity in oil markets in greater detail.

Table 1.12. Commodity Consumption in Selected Countries[1]
(Percent of world consumption)

	China	United States	Japan	India
Wheat	17.2	5.5	1.0	11.8
Soybeans	16.0	24.7	2.1	2.7
Cotton	34.1	5.8	0.7	13.6
Copper	19.8	14.9	7.8	2.0
Aluminum	19.0	20.3	7.4	2.8
Steel	26.5	11.9	8.0	. . .
Petroleum	7.7	25.2	6.6	2.8

Sources: Commodity Research Bureau, U.S. Geological Survey, U.S. Department of Agriculture, International Cotton Advisory Committee, CRU International, International Energy Agency, U.N. Commodity Trade Statistics Database, World Bureau of Metal Statistics, and IMF staff estimates.
[1]Most recent estimates of consumption.

Figure 1.22. Global Production Capacity and Real Average Petroleum Spot Price
(Millions of barrels a day)

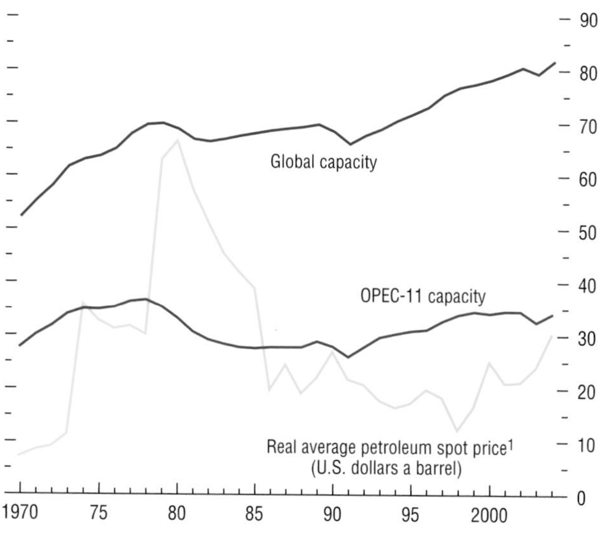

Sources: U.S. Department of Energy (Energy Information Agency); British Petroleum Review; and IMF staff calculations.
[1]Average petroleum spot price of West Texas Intermediate, U.K. Brent, and Dubai Fateh crude. Adjusted by the U.S. CPI with 1994 = 100.

the Federal Reserve to raise U.S. interest rates (Table 1.12). The IMF index of nonenergy commodity prices increased by 8 percent in both U.S. dollar and SDR terms since the start of 2004 (Table 1.13). Growth in the index has recently paused, owing to weakness in food prices in particular, reflecting the impact of favorable harvests. Additional downward pressure on prices has resulted from liquidation in speculative long positions as a number of commodities peaked at multiyear highs (Figure 1.23). Looking forward, nonenergy commodity prices are expected to remain flat or decline marginally in the coming months, but with upside potential toward the end of 2004 owing to depleted inventories (especially of metals) and a robust global economy.

Turning to specific components of the index, by the end of August the overall index of food prices had increased by 3 percent since the beginning of 2004. Rice prices, after a lackluster performance in 2003, increased by 28 percent as a disappointing harvest in China resulted in above-average imports. Relatively low global rice stocks have also supported prices. Maize prices continued their ascent from 2003, recording an increase of 10 percent during the first half of 2004. However, favorable harvests in the United States eventually caused prices to dip by 7 percent by end-August. After increasing to their highest level in over a decade, soybean prices have fallen by 21 percent as Chinese imports declined significantly and farmers in Brazil and

Table 1.13. Nonenergy Commodity Prices
(Percent change from December 2003 to August 2004)

	U.S. Dollar Terms	Contribution[1]	SDR Terms
Food	2.7	43.1	1.9
Beverages	5.2	3.0	5.4
Agricultural raw materials	9.0	21.4	9.2
Metals	15.3	32.5	15.5
Overall nonenergy	8.2	100.0	8.0

Sources: IMF, Primary Commodity Price Database; and IMF staff estimates.
[1]Contributions to change in overall nonenergy price index in U.S. dollar terms, in percent. Contributions to change in SDR terms are similar.

Argentina delivered a newly harvested crop. Favorable harvests in the United States also contributed to the recent move toward lower prices. Meat prices increased by a sizable 24 percent on strong demand reflecting the shift toward low-carbohydrate diets.

Beverage prices increased by 5 percent by end-August. Coffee prices increased by 8 percent, reaching a three-year high on speculation concerning adverse Brazilian weather conditions. However, coffee prices have since eased as the Brazilian concern proved unfounded. Fundamentals for coffee remain weak, as consumption remains static and global stockpiles are abundant. Cocoa prices, which fell sharply during 2003, increased by 5 percent on strong demand and reduced harvests in Côte d'Ivoire.

Agricultural raw materials prices increased by 9 percent, buoyed by growth in softwood lumber prices. As the trade dispute between Canada and the United States continues, softwood lumber prices have increased by over 40 percent on robust demand deriving from the U.S. housing market. Cotton prices declined considerably, falling by 27 percent on expectations of record harvests in the United States and China.

After surging to multiyear highs and recording growth of nearly 20 percent in the second half of 2003, metals prices increased by 15 percent through the end of August and their volatility remained high. Liquidation of speculative long positions resulted in prices easing markedly during the second quarter of 2004. Nickel prices led the decline, plunging by 21 percent through

Figure 1.23. Nonenergy Commodities

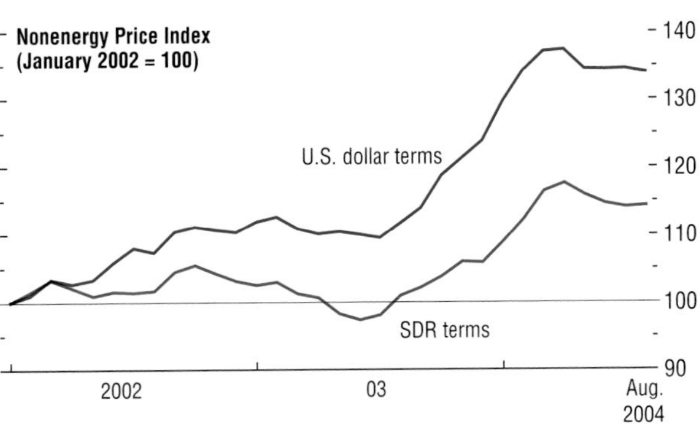

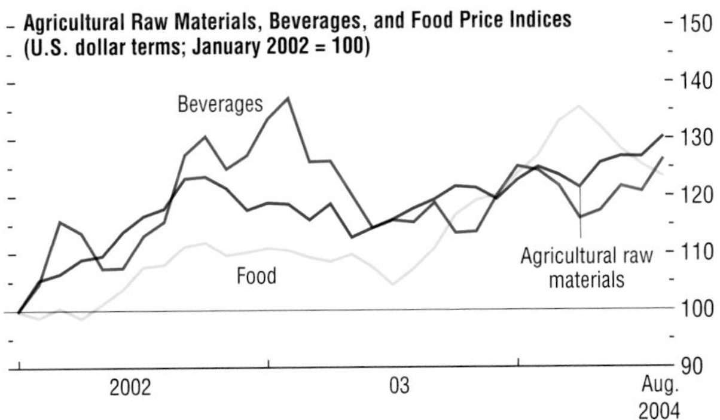

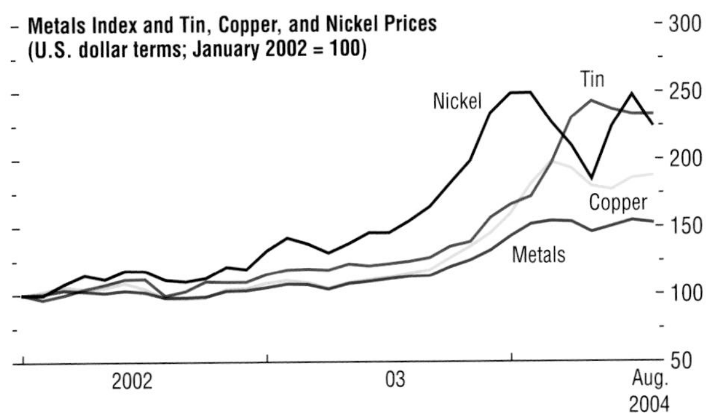

Sources: IMF, *International Financial Statistics;* and IMF staff calculations.

May, owing to substitution, de-stocking, and higher production. In spite of this, nickel prices have recently rebounded and are now down from 2003 levels by only 4 percent. Nickel prices are expected to firm as inventories have fallen significantly, prompting renewed speculative interest. Copper prices increased by 29 percent on robust global demand and falling stocks. Tin prices have appreciated by 49 percent as supply tightness and strong demand have buoyed prices. Citing low metals inventories and the strong pace of growth in the global economy, market analysts are suggesting a second price peak in metals will occur later this year and into the beginning of next year.

Figure 1.24. Semiconductor Market

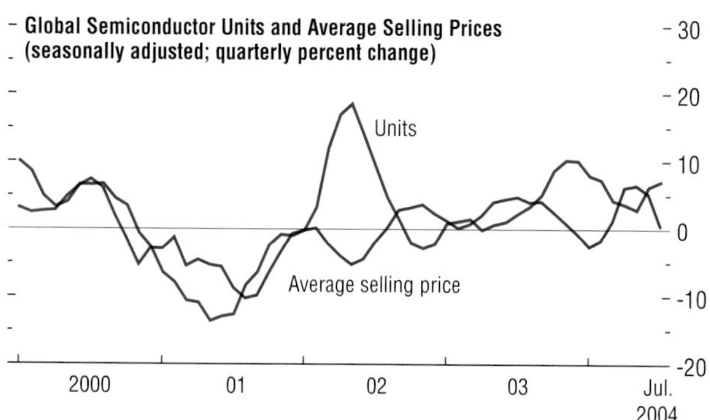

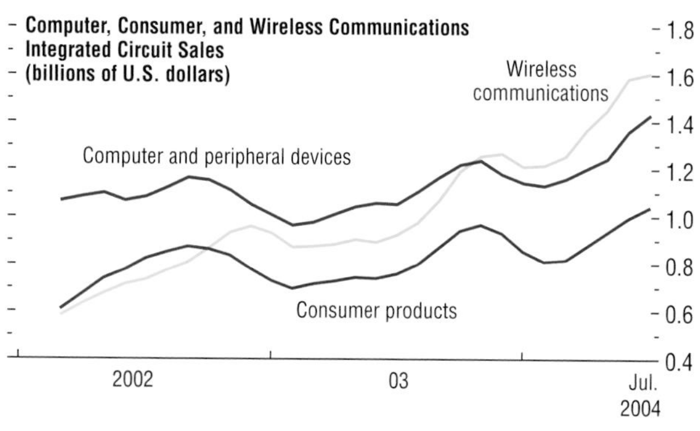

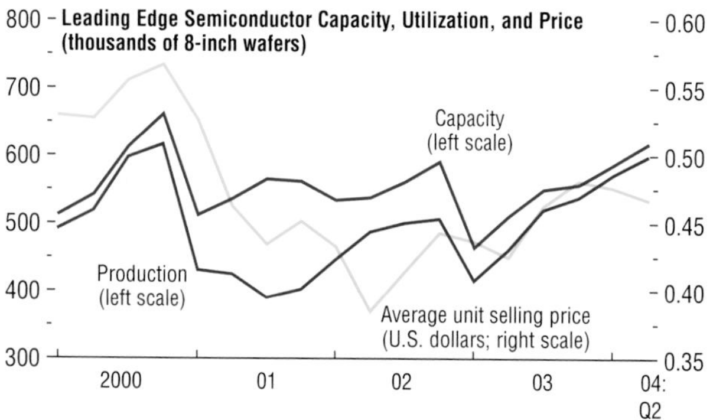

Sources: World Semiconductor Trade Statistics; Semiconductor International Capacity Statistics; and IMF staff calculations.

Semiconductor Markets

Sales in semiconductor markets strengthened further during the first half of 2004, building on the strong recovery in 2003. Seasonally adjusted figures show 15 consecutive months of substantial growth in receipts—especially in the Asia-Pacific region excluding Japan. Moreover, sales for July are 15 percent higher than December 2003 levels, while unadjusted semiconductor receipts are 4 percent higher than corresponding sales in the boom year of 2000—confirming that the recovery has indeed taken hold. Analysts expect 2004 to be a very strong year for semiconductor sales. Much of the strength in receipts comes from unit sales rather than higher prices, while most of the volume can be attributed to surging demand for wireless goods in particular (Figure 1.24).

Capacity utilization in the leading-edge facilities is extremely tight—running at over 97 percent—owing to the surge in demand for wireless goods. While tight capacity had raised concerns that the market would not be able to cope with surging demand this year, average prices for the industry remain well below 2000 levels, and price rallies on spot markets caused by shortages for key integrated circuits have stalled or even reversed. However, given that some business and consumer technology purchasing indicators remain strong, prices are expected to increase in the third and fourth quarters—traditionally the strongest quarters for sales. Though 2004 is likely to be a good year for the semiconductor market, some analysts are expressing reservations about the market's prospects in 2005. Compared with the broader stock market, more companies in the technology sector are reporting earnings below expectations. Investment in capacity expansion is at a record high. In particular, global semiconductor equipment sales remain strong (the ratio of future orders to current shipments is 1.05, implying further increases in productive capacity). High levels of actual production are now outpacing demand, leading to an increase in inventory levels in key segments of the industry and forcing average selling prices down. Some market observers fear that the extra investment and the higher production that will result will lead to a large increase in inventories, placing further downward pressure on prices in the first quarter of 2005, when demand is at its seasonal low. Any inventory overhang and/or excess capacity could depress prices for the remainder of 2005.

Macroeconomic Impact of Higher Crude Oil Prices

Crude oil prices remain a key determinant of global economic prospects. Higher prices affect the global economy through a variety of channels.

- There is a transfer of income from oil consumers to oil producers. As oil producers have a lower propensity to consume than oil consumers on average, global demand falls.
- The cost of production of goods and services rises, possibly reducing profit margins. In the case of advanced countries, this supply-side effect, which was sizable during the 1970s, has fallen in the past three decades in line with their reduced dependency on oil. In contrast, for developing countries, which have not reduced their dependency on oil as much as industrial nations, the supply-side impact is likely to be relatively higher.
- Inflation rises by an amount that depends on the degree of monetary tightening associated with the oil price rise and the extent to which consumers and producers can offset the declines in incomes and profits, respectively.
- Associated movements in actual and anticipated economic activity, corporate earnings, inflation, and monetary policy affect equity and bond valuations, causing financial markets to react adversely to higher oil prices. The follow-on effects in terms of investor confidence and willingness to commit to longer-term capital projects may lower growth prospects further.
- Depending on the duration and extent of the price increases, the change in relative prices creates incentives for suppliers of energy to increase production and investment, and for oil consumers to move toward other sources of energy.

Table 1.14. Impact of a Permanent US$5 a Barrel Increase in Crude Oil Prices After One Year
(Percent of GDP)

	Real GDP	Inflation	Trade Balance
World GDP	–0.3	. . .	
Industrial Countries	–0.3	0.2	–0.1
United States	–0.4	0.3	–0.1
Euro area	–0.4	0.3	–0.1
Japan	–0.2	0.1	–0.2
Other	–0.2	0.1	0.1
Developing Countries			
Latin America	–0.1	0.6	0.0
Argentina	–0.2	0.1	0.1
Brazil	–0.2	1.0	–0.2
Chile	–0.2	1.0	–0.7
Mexico	—	0.1	0.2
Asia	–0.4	0.7	–0.5
China	–0.4	0.4	–0.3
India	–0.5	1.3	–0.6
Emerging Europe and Africa	0.1	0.3	0.2
Poland	–0.3	—	–0.4
Russia	0.7	—	1.8
South Africa	–0.4	1.2	–0.9
Turkey	–0.2	. . .	–0.3

Sources: IMF (2000), and IMF staff estimates.

Estimates of the impact of oil price shocks on the global economy, as reported in IMF (2000), suggest that a US$5 increase in oil prices would reduce global growth by about 0.3 percentage point after one year (Table 1.14). The overall response of a specific region or country differs

Table 1.15. Impact of Nominal Oil Price Hikes
(US$ unless otherwise stated)

	Oil Prices				Direct Impact on Net Trade Balance of Advanced Countries	
	Pre-hike[1]	Post-hike[2]	Change	Percent change	US$ billions	Percent of GDP
1973–74	3.3	11.6	8.3	252	−88	−2.6
1978–80	12.9	35.9	23.1	179	−232	−3.7
1989–90	17.9	28.3	10.4	58	−38	−0.2
1999–2000	18.0	28.2	10.3	57	−96	−0.4
2003–04	28.9	37.3	8.4	29	−107	−0.3

Source: IMF staff estimates.
[1]The average price in the first year of each episode.
[2]The average price in the last episode, except for 1990 and 2004. For 1990 it is the average price for the second half of the year. For 2004, the price is projected using futures market data.

depending on the relative importance of the (first four) short-run links between activity and oil prices indicated above, as well as the underlying flexibility of individual economies to absorb shocks (especially real wage rigidity). The estimated impact is higher in the United States and euro area—about 0.4 percentage point—largely because of their higher dependence on oil and, in the case of the euro area, rigidities in labor markets that limit the pace and extent of real wage adjustments. The impact on the group "other industrial countries" is smaller because the largest two members of this group—the United Kingdom and Canada—are net oil exporters. The negative impact on Japan at 0.2 percentage point is smaller than other industrial countries because of high efficiency in energy consumption and heavy reliance on nuclear power. For emerging market economies, the negative impact on Asia is the largest at 0.4 percentage point because of a larger presence of net-oil-importing nations in its aggregate economic activity. Africa and emerging Europe are less affected by the shock owing to the larger influence of net oil exporters. While oil exporters clearly stand to benefit from the direct impact of higher oil prices, lower domestic demand and substantial second-round effects cause overall activity to decline for some oil-exporting countries (e.g., Argentina)—see IMF (2000) for a detailed analysis.

Turning to the price level effects of higher oil prices, core inflation rises in all countries, with the magnitude depending in part on the extent of labor market rigidities. Inflation is higher by 0.3 percentage point in the United States and euro area, 0.6 percentage point in Latin America, and 0.7 percentage point in Asia. Asia tends to experience the largest increase in inflation because a rapid pass-through of oil price rises to domestic prices.[13]

As of mid-September 2004, futures prices implied an average 2004 oil price of around US$37 a barrel, or about US$8 (or 30 percent) a barrel higher than average 2003 levels. According to IMF (2000), this increase, if permanent, would be likely to reduce world output by approximately ½ percentage point after one year—a relatively small amount compared with the 4.3 percent World Economic Outlook global growth projection for 2005.[14] Moreover, the negative impact of the increase appears moderate when compared with the impact of four previous oil price spikes that have occurred since 1973 (Table 1.15). The estimated impact of the US$8 increase on the net trade balance for advanced

[13]While these price level and activity effects are calibrated for only a single year, it should be noted that the higher oil prices will also affect activity and inflation—both core and headline—in subsequent years.

[14]The World Economic Outlook global growth projection would likely be revised by less than 0.3 percentage point to the extent that higher oil prices reflect stronger activity than envisaged in the last set of projections.

Table 1.16. Movements in the IMF Commodity Price Index
(U.S. dollar terms, 1995 = 100)

	2003	2004[1]	Percent Change
All commodities and energy	119.7	148.8	24.3
Nonfuel commodities	82.1	95.9	16.8
Food	86.1	98.9	14.9
Beverages	66.5	65.0	–2.2
Agricultural	81.1	84.6	4.3
Raw materials			
Metals	80.4	105.6	31.3
Energy	160.6	206.4	28.5
Petroleum crude spot	167.9	216.5	29.0

Source: IMF staff estimates.
[1]Projected value for 2004.

countries in 2004 is at about –0.3 percent of GDP, which is less than one-tenth of the average effect attributable to the two oil price shocks in the 1970s. The smaller impact reflects both the reduced dependency of industrial countries on crude oil compared with the 1970s and the significantly smaller percentage increase in nominal (and hence real) crude oil prices relative to the oil price shocks of the 1970s.

How Will Recent Commodity Price Changes Affect Emerging Markets and Developing Countries?

Though the share of primary commodities in global output has declined in recent decades, movements in commodity prices can still have a substantial impact on the global economy and individual countries. The impact of the recent broad-based run-up in commodity prices is therefore of interest, given that it was largely driven by strong global demand (Table 1.16). In particular, it would be useful to gauge the extent to which the impact of significantly higher oil prices on net oil-importing commodity producers is offset by the higher nonenergy commodity prices.

Movements in specific nonenergy prices can affect activity by raising the costs of production, though typically by a much smaller amount than oil prices because of their smaller share in global output. Even if the ultimate impact on global activity is relatively minor, a rise in nonenergy commodity prices will obviously cause a redistribution of income from net-importing to net-exporting nations. Given that many developing countries rely on only a few nonenergy commodities for the bulk of their export earnings and often have limited access to capital markets, a rise in nonenergy commodity prices may have a significant impact on their gross domestic product—one that could be transmitted to other developing countries via the normal channels of international trade.

Table 1.17. Trade Gains and Losses from Commodity Price Movements: Emerging Market and Developing Countries
(Percent of nominal GDP for 2003)

	Nonenergy[1]	Oil	Total
HIPC			
Oil exporters	0.35	6.14	6.48
Oil importers	0.80	–1.02	–0.22
CIS and Mongolia			
Oil exporters	0.79	3.35	4.14
Oil importers	0.19	–1.28	–1.09
Other emerging market countries			
Oil exporters	0.34	3.22	3.56
Oil importers	0.38	–0.53	–0.15
Overall impact	0.40	0.95	1.35
Oil exporters	0.40	3.32	3.72
Oil importers	0.40	–0.56	–0.16

Source: IMF staff estimates.
[1]Excludes impact of increases in non-oil commodity imports.

The first-round effect of commodity price movements on individual countries can be approximated by the initial change in net export earnings without accounting for second-round effects (Table 1.17). This approach suggests that the projected increase in the average crude oil price in 2004 since 2003—namely, US$8 or 30 percent—will increase the import bill of emerging market and developing countries by approximately 0.6 percent (measured relative to nominal GDP for 2003). This negative impact, however, will be more than offset by the increase in oil revenue accruing to its oil-exporting members—about 3.3 percent of GDP. The overall oil-related net trade balance effect is estimated to be around 1 percent.

The negative impact of the oil price increase for net oil importers is of course tempered by the rise in nonenergy commodity prices. Indeed, for some oil-importing nations, the gains from movements in nonenergy commodity prices exceed the losses from higher crude oil prices. Emerging market economies and developing countries typically benefit from the increase in nonenergy commodity prices, reflecting in part their dependence on such commodities for export revenue. The overall gain in the net trade balance owing to nonenergy price movements, expressed as a percentage of nominal GDP for 2003, is estimated at 0.4 percent, leaving only a moderate net impact on emerging market economies and developing countries. While there are in fact overall losers—mainly some CIS and sub-Saharan African nations—their losses typically amount to less than 1 percent of nominal GDP.

A similar outcome arises for the "other emerging market" grouping of countries, which for the most part consists of exporters of nonenergy commodities. Relative to the HIPC and CIS-7 grouping, however, there will be a greater number of net losers, reflecting the dominance of the negative oil price impact on the trade balance. The list of countries with an overall loss of nominal GDP exceeding 1 percent is led by Cape Verde, which is a net importer of oil that derives little, if any, gains from the increase in nonenergy commodity prices.

References

Acemoglu, Daron, Simon Johnson, and James A. Robinson, 2001, "The Colonial Origins of Comparative Development: An Empirical Investigation," *American Economic Review*, Vol. 91 (December), pp. 1369–401.

Agama, Laurie-Ann, and Christine A. McDaniel, 2002, "The NAFTA Preference and U.S.-Mexico Trade," Office of Economics Working Paper No. 2002–10-A (Washington: U.S. International Trade Commission).

Arora, Vivek B., and Athanasios Vamvakidis, 2004, "How Much Do Trading Partners Matter for Economic Growth?" IMF Working Paper 04/26 (Washington: International Monetary Fund).

Barbone, Luca, and Luis-Alvaro Sanchez, 2003, "The Political Economy of Taxation in CIS Countries," Bank of Italy workshop, Perugia, April 3–5. Available via the Internet at www.bancaditalia.it/ricerca/statist/conv_svo/tax_policy/session_4.pdf.

Bordo, Michael D., and Thomas Helbling, 2003, "Have National Business Cycles Become More Synchronized?" NBER Working Paper No. 10130 (Cambridge, Massachusetts: National Bureau of Economic Research).

Cardarelli, Roberto, and M. Ayhan Kose, 2004, "Economic Integration, Business Cycle, and Productivity in North America," IMF Working Paper 04/138 (Washington: International Monetary Fund).

Cuevas, Alfred, Miguel Messmacher, and Alejandro Werner, 2002, "Changes in the Patterns of External Financing in Mexico Since the Approval of NAFTA," Working Paper (Mexico City: Central Bank of Mexico).

Doyle, Brian, and Jon Faust, 2003, "Breaks in the Variability and Comovement of G-7 Economic Growth," International Finance Discussion Paper No. 786 (Washington: Board of Governors of the Federal Reserve System).

Easterly, William, Norbert Fiess, and Daniel Lederman, 2003, "NAFTA and Convergence in North America: High Expectations, Big Events, Little Time," *Economia*, Vol. 4, No. 1, pp. 1–40.

Federal Reserve Board, 2004, "Outlook for Inflation," remarks by Governor Donald L. Kohn, National Economists Club luncheon meeting, Washington, June 4, 2004, published on June 17, 2004. Available via the Internet: www.federalreserve.gov/boarddocs/speeches/2004/20040604/default.htm.

Ghosh, Madanmohan, and Someshwar Rao, 2004, "Possible Economic Impacts in Canada of a Canada-U.S. Customs Union: Simulation Results from a Dynamic CGE Model," *Policy Research Initiative*, Vol. 7 (June).

Globerman, Steven, and Daniel Shapiro, 2003, "Assessing Recent Patterns of Foreign Direct Investment in Canada and the United States," in *North American Linkages: Opportunities and Challenges*, ed. by Richard G. Harris (Calgary: University of Calgary Press), pp. 279–308.

Helbling, Thomas F., and Tamim A. Bayoumi, 2003, "Are They All in the Same Boat? The 2000–01

Growth Slowdown and the G-7 Business Cycle Linkages," IMF Working Paper 03/46 (Washington: International Monetary Fund).

International Monetary Fund, 2000, *The Impact of Higher Oil Prices on the Global Economy* (Washington). Available via the Internet: http://www.imf.org/external/pubs/ft/oil/2000/oilrep.pdf.

Katz, Menachem, Ulrich Bartsch, Harinder Malothra, and Milan Cuc, 2004, *Lifting the Oil Curse: Improving Petroleum Revenue Management in Sub-Saharan Africa* (Washington: International Monetary Fund).

Kaufmann, Daniel, Aart Kraay, and Pablo Zoido-Lobatón, 1999, "Governance Matters," Policy Research Working Paper No. 2196 (Washington: World Bank).

Kose, M. Ayhan, C. Otrok, and C. H. Whiteman, 2003, "International Business Cycles: World, Region, and Country-Specific Factors," *American Economic Review*, Vol. 93 (September), pp. 1216–39.

Kose, M. Ayhan, Guy M. Meredith, and Christopher M. Towe, 2004, "How Has NAFTA Affected the Mexican Economy? Review and Evidence," IMF Working Paper 04/59 (Washington: International Monetary Fund).

Krueger, Anne O., 1999, "Trade Creation and Trade Diversion under NAFTA," NBER Working Paper No. 7429 (Cambridge, Massachusetts: National Bureau of Economic Research).

———, 2000, "NAFTA's Effects: A Preliminary Assessment," *World Economy*, Vol. 23 (June), pp. 761–75.

Lederman, Daniel, William F. Maloney, and Luis Serven, 2003, *Lessons from NAFTA for Latin America and the Caribbean Countries: A Summary of Research Findings* (Washington: World Bank).

Lopez-Cordova, Jóse E., 2002, "NAFTA and Mexico's Manufacturing Productivity: An Empirical Investigation Using Micro-Level Data" (unpublished; Washington: Inter-American Development Bank).

Mauro, Paolo, 1997, *Why Worry About Corruption?* IMF Economic Issues No. 6 (Washington: International Monetary Fund).

Rabanal, Pau, 2004, "Monetary Policy and the U.S. Business Cycle: Evidence and Implications," IMF Working Paper No. 04/164 (Washington: International Monetary Fund).

Rogoff, Kenneth, 2003, "Globalization and Global Disinflation," in *Economic Review*, Fourth Quarter (Kansas City, Missouri: Federal Reserve Bank of Kansas City), pp. 45–78.

Romalis, John, 2002, "NAFTA's and CUSFTA's Impact on North American Trade" (unpublished; Chicago: University of Chicago).

Sala-i-Martin, Xavier, and Arvind Subramanian, 2003, "Addressing the Natural Resource Curse: An Illustration from Nigeria," IMF Working Paper 03/139 (Washington: International Monetary Fund).

Schiff, Maurice, and Yanling Wang, 2003, "Regional Integration and Technology Diffusion: The Case of NAFTA," Policy Research Working Paper No. 3132 (Washington: World Bank).

Subramanian, Arvind, and Devesh Roy, 2001, "Who Can Explain the Mauritian Miracle: Meade, Romer, Sachs, or Rodrik?" IMF Working Paper 01/116 (Washington: International Monetary Fund).

Thiessen, Ulrich, 2001, "Presumptive Taxation for Small Enterprises in Ukraine," Working Paper No. 6 (Kiev: Institute for Economic Research and Policy Consulting).

———, 2003, "The Impact of Fiscal Policy and Deregulation on Shadow Economies in Transition Countries: The Case of Ukraine," *Public Choice*, Vol. 114 (March), pp. 295–318.

Waldkirch, A., 2003, "The New Regionalism and Foreign Direct Investment: The Case of Mexico," *Journal of International Trade and Economic Development*, Vol. 12 (June), pp. 151–84.

Wall, Howard J., 2003, "NAFTA and the Geography of North American Trade," *Federal Reserve Bank of St. Louis Review* (March–April), pp. 13–26.

CHAPTER II THREE CURRENT POLICY ISSUES

This chapter consists of three essays on current policy issues: the global house price boom, the experience with greater exchange rate flexibility in emerging market countries, and fiscal policy in euro area countries.

House prices in many industrial countries have increased unusually rapidly in recent years and in some cases these increases do not seem to be fully explained by economic fundamentals. More importantly, the analysis in the first essay shows that, even though housing is not traded, house prices are highly synchronized across industrial countries. Specifically, a large share (about 40 percent on average) of house price movements is due to global factors, which reflect global co-movements in interest rates, economic activity, and other macroeconomic variables, which in turn result from common underlying shocks. A key implication of this finding is that, just as the upswing in house prices has been a global phenomenon, it is likely that any downturn would also be highly synchronized, with corresponding implications for global economic activity.

Several emerging market countries have moved to more flexible exchange rate regimes over the past decade, but others remain concerned about potential costs of exchange rate volatility, including inflationary and balance sheet effects ("fear of floating"). The second essay finds that voluntary transitions to greater exchange rate flexibility were generally *not* associated with greater macroeconomic instability, though the results are based on a small sample and could reflect selection bias. An important reason for these results could be that transitions to greater exchange rate flexibility were on the whole associated with a strengthening of monetary and financial policy frameworks ("learning to float"), which directly address the key vulnerabilities that give rise to the fear of floating. Many countries adopted more flexible regimes while still in the process of improving policy frameworks.

Five years after the adoption of a single currency in the euro area, is there still a need for country-specific stabilization policies? The third essay finds that, despite progress toward greater trade and financial integration in the euro area, cross-country cyclical disparities remain important and adjustment mechanisms are still relatively weak, so there is a need for national fiscal policies to dampen output fluctuations—that is, to be countercyclical. However, over the past few decades the countercyclicality of fiscal policies in the euro area, which operates mainly through automatic stabilizers, has often been undermined by procyclical discretionary fiscal measures. While there has been some reduction in the procyclicality of discretionary fiscal policies under the monetary union's fiscal framework, owing mainly to fiscal expansions in bad times, many euro area member states, especially large countries, have continued to adopt expansionary measures in good times. This causes a deterioration in underlying fiscal balances in bad times without a corresponding improvement in good times. The key policy implications are that euro area countries should strive to improve structural fiscal balances during the current expansion and that the Stability and Growth Pact (SGP) should be strengthened to ensure discipline in good times.

The Global House Price Boom

The main author of this essay is Marco Terrones, with support from Christopher Otrok. Nathalie Carcenac provided research assistance.

House prices in industrial countries have increased unusually rapidly in recent years, with their momentum seemingly little affected by the bursting of the stock market bubble or the subsequent global economic downturn. In some cases, notably Australia, Ireland, Spain, and the United Kingdom, prices have risen by 50 percent or more since 1997—increases that are difficult to explain in terms of economic fundamentals alone, including record-low interest rates (Box 2.1). In addition, some housing indicators—including the housing affordability ratio, the ratio of house prices to rent, and mortgage debt—have reached record-high levels in several industrial countries (Table 2.1). This has led some observers to suggest that a house price correction is imminent, possibly triggered by the tightening of monetary policy as economic recovery takes hold. Even an orderly correction would clearly weaken growth in the countries in which it occurred; as discussed in Chapter II of the April 2003 *World Economic Outlook*, an abrupt price correction could have significantly more serious adverse effects.

The profound economic implications of changes in house prices reflect the key role housing plays in societies. Housing satisfies people's basic need for shelter and for a place to carry on family activities, including childrearing. Moreover, housing conditions are often considered a yardstick of economic development and prosperity. Because of this, there is a long tradition of government involvement in the housing markets aimed at improving housing quality and fostering homeownership, for example through subsidized financing and special tax treatment.[1] Yet the bulk of housing activities is carried out by the private sector. Housing activities account for a large fraction of GDP and households' expenditures in industrial countries. Housing is the main asset and mortgage debt, the main liability held by households in these countries, and therefore large house price movements, by affecting households' net wealth and their capacity to borrow[2] and spend, have important economic implications.

This essay studies house price fluctuations in industrial countries, paying particular attention to the current house price boom. In particular, the essay addresses the following questions.

- What are the main features of house price fluctuations in industrial countries? Is the current boom in house prices "atypical"?
- Is there a global house price cycle? Are the fluctuations in house prices mainly related to global factors or to country-specific factors?
- What are the implications of global house price cycles for the future? What are the risks associated with an increase in world interest rates?

An important theme running through the essay is that house prices are highly procyclical, volatile, and synchronized across industrial countries, and that these features have evolved over time. In addition, the essay reports evidence suggesting that the current house price boom in many industrial countries is unusual in both its strength and duration. Innovative aspects of the analysis are the use of dynamic factor models to determine the extent to which house price comovements are explained by global or country-specific factors and of simple forecasting models that combine country-specific variables with world factors, obtained from the dynamic factor models.

The analysis of this essay uses data taken from diverse sources, including the European Mortgage Federation, Eurostat, Haver Analytics, and national authorities. The first section and boxes of the essay use annual data for 18 industrial countries during 1970–2003, while the second section uses quarterly data for 13 industrial countries during 1980:QI–2004:Q2 (see

[1]In many countries mortgage debt risks are carried by public institutions.

[2]Houses are typically used as collateral of mortgage loans. Changes in house prices, by affecting the value of collateral, can lead to significant credit expansions/contractions (see, for instance, Chapter IV of the April 2004 *World Economic Outlook*). Debelle (2004) finds that the current high levels of debt in industrial countries might have left households more sensitive to changes in interest rates, income, house prices, and stock prices, particularly if they are unexpected.

Table 2.1. Housing Indicators in Some Industrial Countries

Country	Year[1]	Mortgage Loans (percent of GDP)	Ownership Ratio (percent)	Affordability Ratio (1985 = 100)[2]	Price-Rent Ratio (1985 = 100)[3]	Population Density (people per square km.)
United States	1970	28.82	64.18	100.34	96.51	22.39
	1980	33.87	65.58	113.36	106.32	24.81
	1990	44.59	63.95	107.14	112.68	27.23
	2003	63.73	68.25	113.66	136.48	31.80
Germany	1970	. . .	. . .	129.41	96.97	217.90
	1980	41.88	41.00	114.45	115.73	219.53
	1990	42.52	39.00	94.81	99.32	222.70
	2003	54.31	43.60	79.71	73.07	231.19
France	1970	. . .	. . .	122.75	90.97	92.30
	1980	16.94	47.00	124.70	119.74	97.95
	1990	19.73	55.02	118.64	115.96	103.14
	2003	24.75	56.22	124.56	129.70	108.65
Italy	1970	. . .	. . .	. . .	. . .	183.00
	1980	3.06	59.00	134.72	. . .	191.88
	1990	3.62	68.00	129.89	100.00	192.85
	2003	13.33	80.00	130.66	91.43	196.69
Spain	1970	. . .	. . .	146.83	62.03	67.59
	1980	8.61	73.00	127.32	102.81	74.85
	1990	10.59	78.00	198.92	207.05	77.76
	2003	42.11	82.90	288.78	249.92	82.70
Netherlands	1970	. . .	. . .	136.69	120.20	384.86
	1980	33.62	42.00	151.42	161.13	417.65
	1990	40.18	45.00	111.43	109.94	441.32
	2003	99.88	53.00	243.14	203.58	478.34
Ireland	1970	. . .	. . .	. . .	57.07	42.82
	1980	. . .	74.00	135.63	126.82	49.37
	1990	18.45	79.30	110.47	100.79	50.89
	2003	45.00	76.92	200.81	272.45	57.03
Japan	1970	5.59	. . .	107.96	76.44	284.55
	1980	21.29	60.00	91.21	87.34	318.82
	1990	30.26	61.00	121.72	123.32	338.83
	2003	36.40	62.00	79.26	75.23	349.57
United Kingdom	1970	. . .	50.00	97.21	89.61	230.95
	1980	22.80	55.00	108.58	116.69	233.85
	1990	52.65	66.00	137.00	117.20	238.96
	2003	63.83	70.00	155.83	194.28	245.64
Canada	1970	27.57	60.00	112.51	79.17	2.31
	1980	33.73	62.00	124.23	122.25	2.67
	1990	39.81	63.00	138.47	140.73	3.01
	2003	42.79	65.20	155.54	182.59	3.42
Australia	1970	. . .	. . .	107.31	96.67	1.63
	1980	15.66	71.00	101.00	96.57	1.91
	1990	19.90	72.00	122.90	101.61	2.22
	2003	57.30	70.00	183.12	212.93	2.57

Sources: European Central Bank; European Mortgage Federation; Eurostat; OECD; national sources; RICS, *European Housing Review;* World Bank, *World Development Indicators;* and IMF staff calculations.

[1]If an observation is not available for the indicated year, data from the nearest year are used.

[2]Ratio of house prices to disposable income per worker.

[3]Ratio of house prices to rents (from CPI).

Appendix 2.1 for details). Differences in the sample coverage primarily reflect the availability of reliable quarterly data on house prices. The quality of the data is in many cases weak and nonstandardized; notably, countries use different coverage and methodologies to calculate house

Box 2.1. What Explains the Recent Run-Up in House Prices?

Over the past eight years, house prices have risen very rapidly in many industrial countries. While some observers argue that the run-up in house prices reflects strong fundamentals—such as income growth and low interest rates—others argue that house prices have been exuberant and divorced from market fundamentals. This box seeks to assess the extent to which fundamentals explain the recent run-up in house prices, building on and extending a dynamic panel model developed by Lamont and Stein (1999). This model is estimated for a sample of 18 countries during 1971–2003.

The model postulates that the growth rate of real house prices, in any given country and period, is explained by the following factors.

- *Past growth rates of real house prices.* If the growth rate of house prices is persistent, then the current growth rate must be serially correlated with the past growth rate. Higher values of this correlation coefficient imply higher persistence.[1]
- *Past housing affordability ratio.* If the growth rate of house prices shows long-run reversion to fundamentals, this implies that prices would tend to fall when they are out of line relative to income levels. Hence, the coefficient of the housing affordability ratio—the ratio of real house prices to (per capita) real income—must be negative.
- *Economic fundamentals.* The growth rate of house prices is positively affected by (per capita) real income growth—as this increases households' purchasing power and borrowing capacity—and negatively affected by interest rates (lower rates increase households' capacity to borrow). Other fundamentals influencing house prices include the growth rate of real credit, a proxy for mortgage debt, as this indicates that households are less credit rationed; the past growth rate of real stock prices—which captures households' efforts to rotate their portfolio in favor of housing; population growth, as this proxies for the growth rate of households; and a bank crisis dummy (a bank crisis is typically associated with a drop in house prices).

The econometric results confirm that real house prices in industrial countries show high persistence, long-run reversion to fundamentals, and dependence on economic fundamentals (see the table). The growth rate of real house prices in industrial countries is very persistent—with a serial correlation coefficient of 0.5—

Note: The main author of this box is Marco Terrones.

[1]If the absolute value of this coefficient exceeds one, the growth rate of real house prices would be explosive.

Table B2.1. What Determines House Prices in Industrial Countries?

(Summary of empirical results, 1971–2003)

Explanatory Variables	Dependent Variable: Real house price (growth)
Lagged dependent variable	
Lagged real house price (growth)	0.521
	[0.030]*
Reversion	
Lagged housing affordability ratio	–0.144
	[0.021]*
Fundamentals	
Real disposable income (per capita, growth)	0.530
	[0.119]*
Short-term interest rate (percent)	–0.507
	[0.109]*
Real credit (growth)	0.109
	[0.036]*
Lagged real stock price (growth)	0.033
	[0.009]*
Population growth	1.754
	[0.623]*
Bank crisis	–2.426
	[0.952]*
Memorandum	
Number of observations	524
Sargan test[1]	
p-value	0.211
Arellano-Bond test[2]	
p-value	0.200

Sources: IMF, *International Financial Statistics*; Haver Analytics; OECD; national sources; World Bank, *World Development Indicators;* and IMF staff calculations.

Note: Country dummies are included in the regression but not reported here. The symbol * denotes significance at the 1 percent level. Significance is based on robust standard errors. Estimated using the Generalized Method of Moments estimator as suggested by Arellano and Bond (1991).

[1]Test of the validity of overidentifying restrictions.

[2]Test of no second-order autocorrelation.

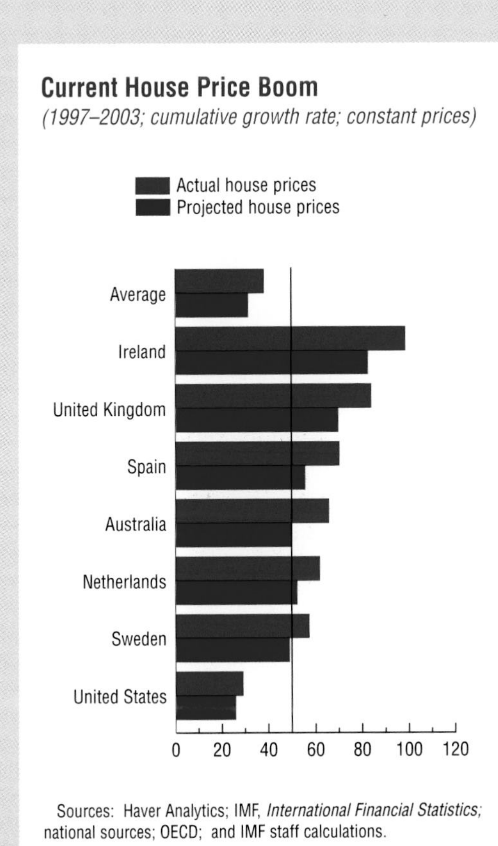

meaning that there is a strong tendency for real house prices to rise tomorrow if they rise today.[2] In addition, the growth rates of real house prices show fundamental reversion: if house prices are out of line with income, there is a gradual tendency for this misalignment to be corrected (about 15 percent every year). All of the economic fundamentals have the expected sign and are highly significant. Improvements in these fundamentals—such as higher income growth and lower interest rates[3]—lead to increases in the growth rate of real house prices over time. For instance, an increase in income growth by 1 percent would over time imply an increase of 1⅒ percentage points in the growth rate of real house prices. Likewise, a reduction in interest rates by 1 percent would over time imply an increase of 1 percent in real house

[2]Lamont and Stein (1999) find a similar result for house prices at the city level in the United States.

[3]Some have argued that the relevant interest rate affecting house prices is the real after-tax rate. This rate, however, is not readily available. When this variable was proxied by real ex post interest rates, the coefficient had the wrong sign and was statistically insignificant.

Box 2.1 *(concluded)*

price inflation.[4] Demographic factors do also have an effect on house prices; for example, an increase in the population growth rate by ¼ percent would over time lead to an increase of about 1 percent in real house price inflation.

How does the increase in house prices during 1997–2003 compare with the model's prediction? The first figure shows that, on average, the model is able to explain most of the increase in house prices during this period. There are, however, important differences across countries. For instance, house prices in Australia, Ireland, Spain, and the United Kingdom exceed their predicted values by 10 to 20 percent—thus suggesting that the sharp increase in prices observed in these countries over the past seven years can not be explained by movements in fundamentals alone.[5] In the case of other countries, including the United States, the differences between observed and predicted values are below 10 percent.

To understand the extent to which market fundamentals explain the run-up in house prices in the past seven years, compared, say, with the previous seven years, the IMF staff has made use of the above-described model. The second figure shows the rate of growth of real house prices and the contributions of the main fundamentals to this growth—between 1997–2003 and 1990–96 across countries. In particular, the following results stand out.

- The fall in average short-term interest rates explains the bulk of the house price increases across industrial countries. This is particularly true in Ireland and Spain, where real interest rates fell since the launch of European Monetary Union, reflecting nominal interest rate convergence and the relatively high inflation rates in these countries. Conversely, this suggests that real house price growth will slow down as interest rates rise.
- The increases in the average growth rate of disposable income and credit have also contributed to the current buoyancy in houses prices relative to the early to mid-1990s.
- In contrast, the rapid increase in the affordability ratio (house prices relative to income per capita) in Ireland and the Netherlands may have contained the pace of increase in real house prices in these countries.

All in all, the model explains most of the increase in real house prices in industrial countries; however, an important portion of the increase in some countries (Australia, Ireland, Spain, and the United Kingdom) remains unexplained.

[4]Short-term interest rates fell by 320 basis points in the United Kingdom and by 450 basis points in the United States during 1997–2003.

[5]The house price increases in France and Italy also appear out of line with fundamentals.

price indexes and mortgage debt. In addition, in most countries the house price indexes do not correct for changes in housing quality over time. Given the importance of the housing sector in modern industrial economies, improvements in the statistics in this area should be a priority for statistical agencies.

House Prices: The Stylized Facts[3]

Over the past three decades, real house prices in industrial countries have grown at an average rate of 1¾ percent a year, broadly similar to the growth of both per capita output and consumption.[4] Real house prices, however, have fluctuated over time—with the current boom standing

[3]Although there is an extensive literature in real estate cycles (surveyed by Pyhrr, Roulac, and Born, 1999), the cyclical behavior of real house prices in industrial countries has not been, to our knowledge, systematically examined. Henley and Morley (2001) and European Central Bank (2003) examine the volatility and co-movement of house prices in countries of the European Union.

[4]Davis and Heathcote (2004) develop a growth model with housing and find that, because land enters in the production of new housing, the relative price of houses will trend upward.

out because of its duration and strength (Figure 2.1).[5] Real house prices in industrial countries are very volatile, with an average standard deviation of the growth rate of real house prices of almost 7 percent a year, although volatility has declined substantially recently, partly reflecting the widespread reduction in macroeconomic volatility and a stable low-inflation environment across industrial countries.[6]

Turning to individual countries, the average growth of real house prices differs significantly—ranging from less than ½ percent a year in Germany, New Zealand, and Switzerland to over 3 percent a year in Ireland, Spain, and the United Kingdom (Figure 2.2). Interestingly, most of the countries that exhibited rapid growth of real house prices in 1986–2003 were laggards in 1971–85. House price volatility also varies significantly across countries, and—consistent with the well-known principle in finance that return and risk of an asset go hand-in-hand—is generally higher the more rapid the rate of underlying house price growth,[7] although this relationship has weakened over the past decade. It is perhaps more interesting that there is no evidence that house price volatility is directly related to the volatility of the economy, although it does appear to be related to the institutional structure of financial markets (see Box 2.2 for a more detailed discussion).

House prices and economic activity are tightly linked. Changes in house prices influence

[5]House prices are not buoyant in all industrial countries. House prices in Germany and Japan have fallen in real terms over the past years, reflecting country-specific developments associated with the excessive supply of houses following the construction boom after the German unification and the bursting of house bubble in Japan in the early 1990s.

[6]See, for instance, Stock and Watson (2003) and Kose, Prasad, and Terrones (2004). Girouard and Blondal (2001) also report that house price volatility has declined in several OECD countries during the 1990s (relative to 1970–99). Low and more stable inflation has also created the conditions for financial deepening in industrial countries, which in turn has resulted in deeper mortgage markets.

[7]A similar result holds for real stock prices. However, the growth and volatility observed in house prices are much smaller than those observed for stock prices.

Figure 2.1. Average Growth and Volatility of House Prices in Industrial Countries

(Percent; constant prices; 10-year rolling window)

Real house prices fluctuate over time, but the recent boom is exceptional; while house prices have been buoyant, their volatility has declined markedly.

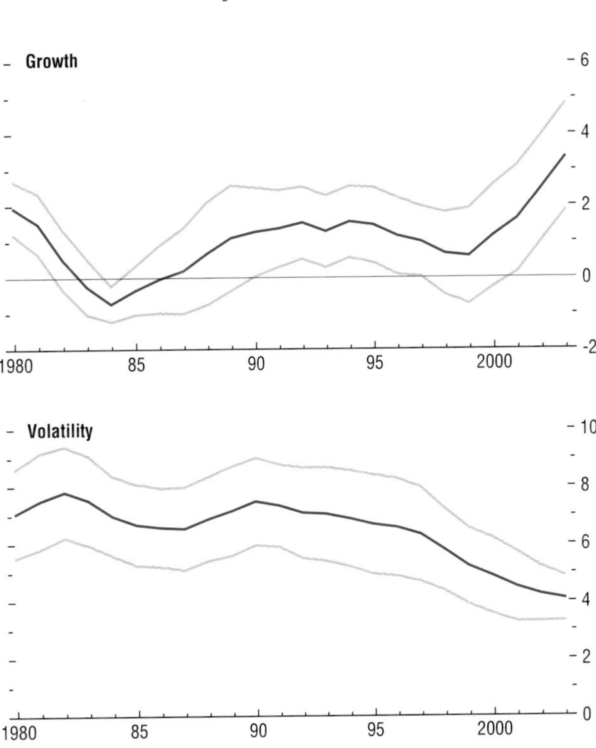

Sources: IMF, *International Financial Statistics;* national sources; and IMF staff calculations.

Figure 2.2. Growth and Volatility of House Prices in Industrial Countries
(Percent; constant prices)

The average growth rates of real house prices and their volatility differ significantly across countries and over time.

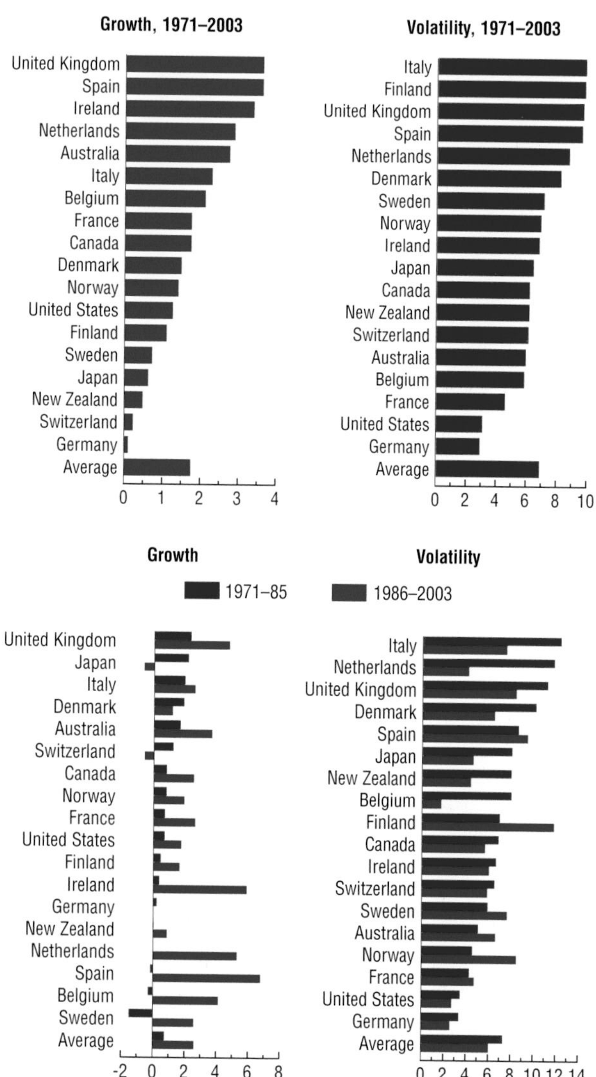

Sources: IMF, *International Financial Statistics;* national sources; and IMF staff calculations.

demand and output by affecting households' wealth and capacity to borrow.[8] Likewise, changes in economic activity, reflected in households' disposable income and employment prospects, can move house prices. Simple correlations between house prices and some key macroeconomic aggregates suggest the following (Figure 2.3).[9]

- *Real house prices in industrial countries are procyclical,* rising in a boom and falling in a recession.[10] The strength of the co-movement between real house prices and output, however, varies across countries, being weakest in Belgium, France, Italy, and Norway and strongest in Finland, Ireland, Switzerland, and the United Kingdom. The procyclicality of real house prices reflects the strong co-movement between these prices and private sector absorption.
- *The average correlation between house prices and long- and short-term interest rates is negative,* and particularly strong in Ireland, the Netherlands, and the United States.
- *The average correlation between real house prices and output (and consumption) has declined since the mid-1990s, reaching unprecedented low levels by 2003.* This tends to strengthen the notion that the current house price boom in industrial countries is atypical: prices have continued to rise while economic activity has weakened. Owing in part to record-low interest rates, the negative correlation between real house prices and interest rates has strengthened since the mid-1990s (Figure 2.3).
- *There is no contemporaneous correlation between housing and stock prices.* However, real stock

[8]Indeed, there is evidence suggesting that the strength of these effects varies across countries, reflecting differences in households' wealth composition and in the structure of the financial sector (see, for instance, Chapter II of the May 2002 *World Economic Outlook*).

[9]Co-movement is measured as the contemporaneous correlation between the growth rates of real house prices and the corresponding aggregate of interest (for instance, consumption).

[10]The average correlation between real house price growth and output growth is about 0.5 during 1971–2003. A related finding is reported by the OECD (2004).

prices often lead movements in house prices, particularly in Finland, Japan, and Norway.[11]

As is well known, industrial countries have become more integrated over the past two decades, reflecting rising trade and financial linkages. Some researchers have argued that increased international linkages led to more synchronized business cycles, whereby macroeconomic fluctuations spill over across countries (Figure 2.4).[12] Indeed, the co-movement of output/consumption across industrial countries increased during most of the 1990s, although it has reversed the past four years, reflecting in part the different intensities of the recent recession and the correction in stock prices following the burst of the stock market bubble.[13] With increasingly integrated financial markets, the synchronization of stock prices and long-term interest rates across industrial countries is high and increasing.

What are the implications of increased international linkages for the dynamics of house prices? While housing is the quintessential nontradable asset, house price cycles across countries may be synchronized if the forces driving house prices (such as output and interest rates) tend to move together across countries. There is growing evidence that

Figure 2.3. Co-movement Between Macroeconomic Aggregates and House Prices

(Rolling 10-year correlation coefficients of growth rates; constant prices unless otherwise noted)

Real house prices are procyclical. The average correlation between house prices and output (consumption) has declined sharply since the late 1990s.

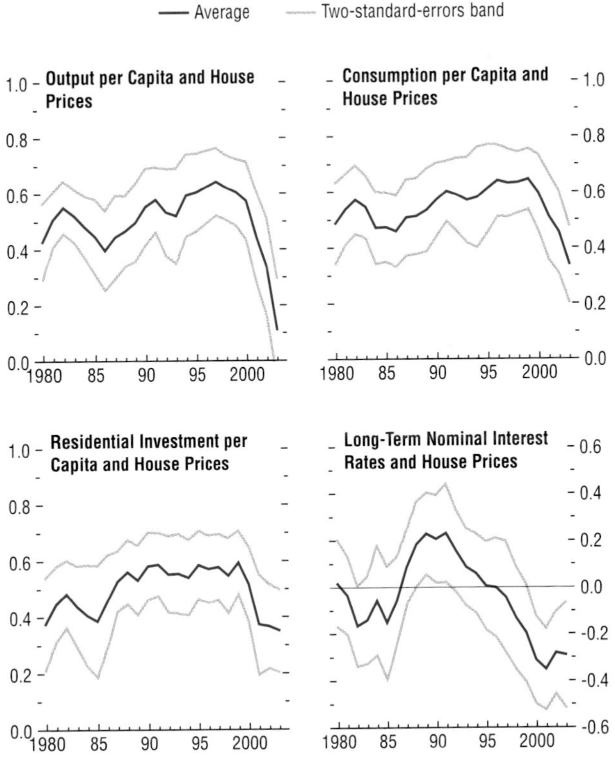

Sources: Haver Analytics; IMF, *International Financial Statistics;* national sources; OECD; and IMF staff calculations.

[11]Quan and Titma (1998) find no significant contemporaneous correlation between the growth of real estate prices and stock prices for a sample of 17 industrial countries. However, they find a positive correlation between these rates of growth in the longer term.

[12]The evidence on this issue is, however, ambiguous. Some have found that the synchronization of business cycles across industrial countries has increased (Kose, Prasad, and Terrones, 2003; and Otto, Voss, and Willard, 2003) while others have found evidence that the synchronization among some industrial countries has either remained unchanged or declined in the globalization period (Helbling and Bayoumi, 2003; Stock and Watson, 2003; and Doyle and Faust, 2003). Differences stem from different sample composition, time coverage, and construction of the "world" aggregates.

[13]The rates of growth of country *i*'s rest-of-the-world aggregate, say output, is calculated as the simple average of the output growth rates of all the industrial countries excluding *i*. (The results do not change much when the world aggregate is calculated instead using a PPP-weighted average of the output growth rates.)

Figure 2.4. Is There International Synchronization?
(Rolling 10-year correlation coefficients of growth rates; constant prices unless otherwise noted)

Industrial countries have become more synchronized over the past two decades. Although housing is the quintessential nontradable asset, house prices have also become more synchronized.

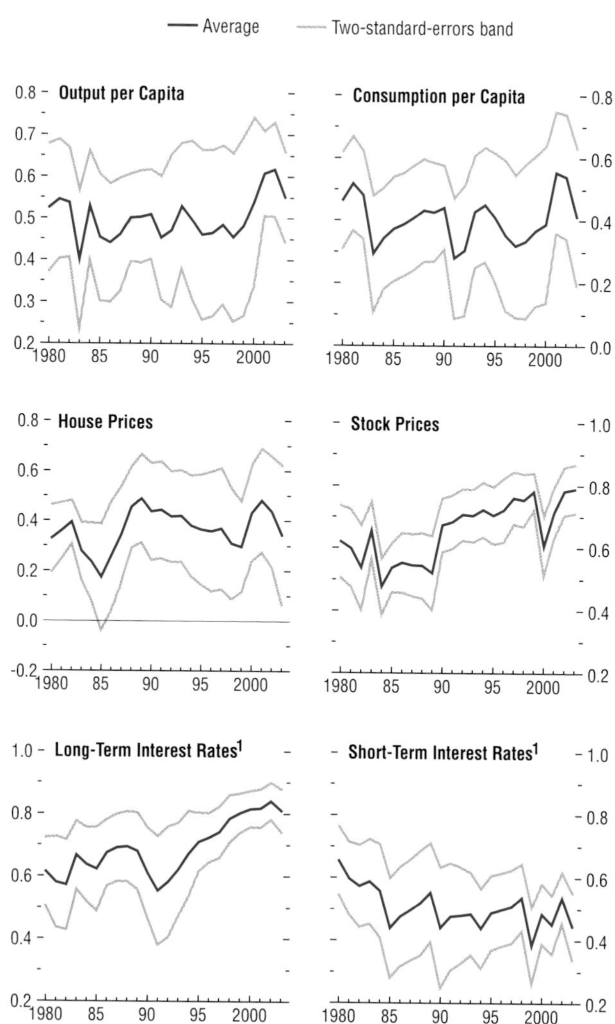

Sources: Haver Analytics; IMF, *International Financial Statistics;* national sources; OECD; and IMF staff calculations.
[1]Annual differences, in nominal terms.

house prices in some industrial countries have moved in tandem, at least during certain periods. For instance, Helbling and Terrones (2003) find evidence of synchronization of house price booms/busts across countries, which, they argue, is a reflection of the synchronization of monetary policy and financial liberalization—in addition to general business cycle linkages.[14]

The following stylized facts stand out from the analysis of the international co-movement of house prices across industrial countries (Figure 2.4):

- *House prices in industrial countries tend to move together*—the average cross-country correlation of house prices is 0.4. France, Sweden, the United Kingdom, and the United States show the strongest correlations with the rest of the industrial countries and Denmark, Germany, and Italy the weakest correlations.
- *House prices have become relatively more synchronized in the 1990s,* although this relationship has weakened somewhat over the past three years, as house prices in some industrial countries have continued to grow at a rapid clip while in others prices have moderated.

What Explains House Price Fluctuations and Co-movement?

To examine the nature of house price movements in industrial countries, and particularly the linkages between them, the IMF staff constructed a "dynamic factor" model for house price growth—and for six other key variables, including real stock prices, per capita output, per capita consumption, per capita residential investment, and changes in the short- and long-term interest rates—for 13 industrial

[14]The European Central Bank (2003) reports evidence that house price cycles were synchronized among some European Union (EU) countries. In contrast, PricewaterhouseCoopers (2002) finds little evidence of house price synchronization among the EU economies over the past 30 years.

Box 2.2. Adjustable- or Fixed-Rate Mortgages: What Influences a Country's Choices?

With interest rates on the rise in many industrial countries, concerns about the effect of higher rates on housing markets have moved to the fore. Although there are several channels through which higher interest rates can affect housing, the household sector is likely to play a key role in countries with predominantly adjustable-rate mortgage (ARM) contracts since households bear the risk of higher rates directly through their higher mortgage payments and smaller remaining income. In fact, analysis suggests that countries with ARMs have typically displayed higher house price growth and volatility than countries with fixed-rate mortgages (FRMs) (see the figure).[1]

But a deeper question remains: what factors influence the types of mortgage contracts that are prevalent in a country? In short, why do ARMs predominate in some and fixed-rate mortgages in others? To answer these questions it is useful to look at how consumers make their mortgage decisions and the reasons lenders offer the specific types of contracts they do.

As regards consumers, one might start by asking whether there are national reasons why consumers might prefer certain types of mortgages over others. There are few cross-country studies that examine mortgage choices by consumers and, in general, their predictions do not match the evidence very well. Campbell and Cocco (2003) conduct a normative analysis, attempting to discover characteristics of a household that should lead it to prefer one form of mortgage over another. In a calibration of their theoretical model to the U.S. economic environment and household

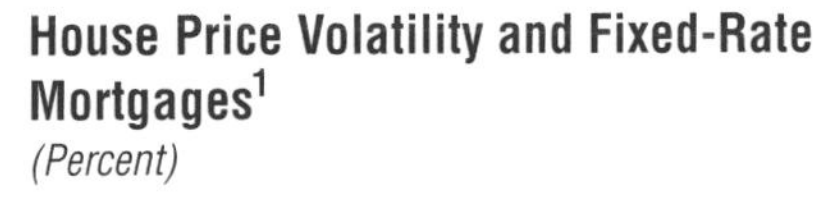

House Price Volatility and Fixed-Rate Mortgages[1]
(Percent)

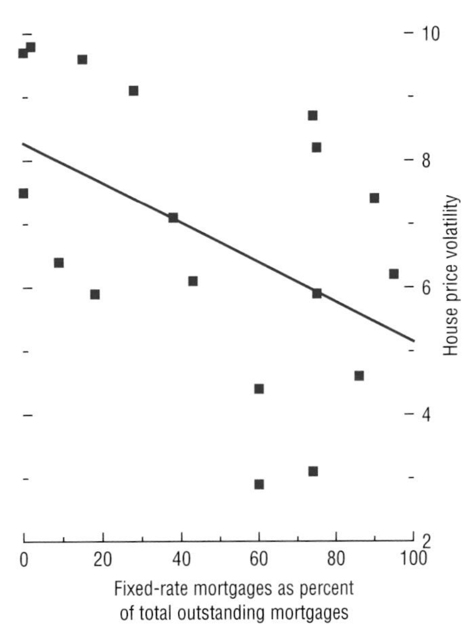

Sources: European Central Bank; European Mortgage Federation; national sources; OECD; and IMF staff calculations.

[1]Volatility calculated as standard deviation of annual growth rates over 1971–2003.

circumstances (with parameters reflecting inflation and its variability, interest rates, differential mortgage costs, and measures of income dependability), they find that ARMs have substantial advantages for most households, in contrast to the tendency for U.S. consumers to choose fixed-rate mortgages. The advantages stem from the typically short period many homeowners stay in a given house, allowing them to benefit from the low initial rates in an ARM, and the relatively stable income of homeowners. Interestingly, an application of the model to U.K. data suggests that a substantial proportion of households in the United Kingdom should find mortgages with longer-term fixed rates attractive, despite the very low take-up (about 2 percent of total

Note: The main author of this box is Laura Kodres.

[1]Using a different grouping—bank-based and market-based financial systems—it is found that market-based economies have typically higher house price growth and lower volatility than bank-based economies. Appendix 2.1 provides a definition of bank- and market-based economies, the corresponding country grouping, and the criteria used to classify a country as having a predominance of fixed- or adjustable-rate mortgages.

Box 2.2 *(concluded)*

mortgages).[2] It appears, therefore, that either the models leave out relevant decision-making variables or make inaccurate assumptions—or many consumers fail to take up mortgage contracts that would best suit their needs. One assumption that bears further examination is whether consumers can accurately gauge their own future circumstances and, even if so, can freely choose either an ARM or a fixed-rate mortgage as appropriate.

There is evidence that consumers tend to prefer mortgage contracts that they consider to have the "most competitive rate" (that is, the ones with the lowest initial cost) and that they can understand. For most households a mortgage loan is large, long, and complex—and households are often not well-informed about the options available to them. Survey data from the United Kingdom suggest that, given the complexity and high degree of long-term uncertainty, U.K. households tend to focus on the immediate monthly mortgage costs, perhaps ignoring longer-term income or wealth risks.[3] The survey also found that the advice households receive about various mortgage products greatly influences their decisions. Much of this advice is, however, provided by lenders, whose interests may not be aligned with borrowers. Even with mandatory disclosure forms and other consumer protection mechanisms, research shows that professional advice was often taken at face value as consumers apparently feel that they have to meet the lenders' criteria and not vice versa.[4]

What then determines the type of mortgage contracts that lenders prefer to offer? The underlying structure of a country's financial markets greatly influences the various funding possibilities, and thus the risk-adjusted profits from mortgage contracts and their offerings. For instance, where covered bond markets or mortgage-backed securities markets are small and illiquid, mortgages tend to be funded through the use of short-term deposits. In order to reduce potential interest rate risks produced by different repricing terms (even when deposits are a stable form of funding), short-term interest rates are used to reprice mortgages at intervals close to that of deposits. Thus, in countries where funding for mortgages is based on short-term deposits (e.g., Australia, Spain, and United Kingdom), ARMs are prevalent. Though lenders tend to choose funding methods based on lowest cost, passing some of it onto their customers, in a few cases there are legal impediments to the use of longer-dated funds. In the United Kingdom, for instance, by law at least 50 percent of funds raised by building societies must be in the form of members' funds (e.g., short-term deposits), limiting building societies' use of longer-term funding sources.

Alternatively, countries with well-developed covered bond markets or deep and liquid mortgage-backed securities markets tend to have a higher proportion of fixed-rate mortgages.[5] The most obvious case is the United States, where the mortgage-backed securities market is aided by the perception of implicit government-backed guarantees of the dominant Freddie Mac and Fannie Mae mortgage institutions. This permits lower funding costs and thus cheaper long-term

[2]Miles (2004). A descriptive examination of housing leverage in Australia, although not explicitly modeling the type of mortgage contract chosen, shows that typical variables such as age, life-cycle stage, and time at a particular address explain much of the variation in Australian households' leverage. At the same time, the study finds a minority of households have higher leverage than similar households because they are involved in leveraged investment in both owner-occupied and rental housing. Overall, the study concludes that households' use of leverage in the Australian housing stock remains fairly moderate (see Ellis, Lawson, and Roberts-Thomson, 2003).

[3]Miles (2004) provides evidence of such myopic behavior among U.K. consumers.

[4]Research commissioned by the U.K. Financial Services Consumer Panel, 1999.

[5]A covered bond market refers to securities issued based on collateral (e.g., mortgage loans) that remain on the balance sheet of the issuer of such bonds, whereas mortgage-backed securities are typically held off balance sheet, often in a legally separate special purpose vehicle.

mortgage pricing (as some of the lower costs are passed onto consumers), spurring the popularity of long-term mortgages. Similarly, long-term fixed-rate mortgages are more prevalent in Denmark and Germany, where specialized private mortgage banks are granted licenses to issue long-term debt against mortgages. In fact, in Denmark, the size of the mortgage-backed securities market exceeds that of government debt.

While a long-term covered bond or mortgage-backed securities market can sometimes develop de novo (or with helpful government legislation), the close association between the liquidity of long-term government securities' markets and these markets is striking for some countries, such as the United States, Germany, and Denmark, since these markets are frequently used as benchmarks for pricing and for hedging activities. Liquid swap markets can also be used by lenders to transfer the receipt of long-term fixed mortgage payments into the payment of short-term variable deposit interest. There are some notable exceptions, however. Australia and the United Kingdom have fairly liquid long-term government bond markets, but few fixed-rate mortgages are offered there. And the Netherlands has mostly fixed-rate mortgages but its banks mostly fund themselves with deposits.

Moreover, the existence of other financial markets to hedge prepayment risks—the risk that a borrower may decide to prepay the mortgage before the term of the loan ends (allowable in some countries)—is also important to lower the costs of fixed-rate mortgages since the longer the loan maturity, the more difficult it is for the lender to replace it with one earning the same rate. Thus, markets where such contract provisions can be hedged through callable debt, swaptions (an option on a swap), options on government debt, and other derivative contracts tend to lower costs to lenders and permit contracts that make prepayment easier, thereby contributing to the increased use of longer-term fixed-rate mortgages.

Aside from funding sources for lenders, other country-specific institutional features may encourage or discourage certain types of mortgage contracts. For instance, bankruptcy laws and the ability to seize property influence the type of mortgage contracts. In Italy, for instance, lengthy and expensive procedures for repossession have meant higher operating costs and the desire to limit the length of contracts to lower the probability of default. Accounting standards also influence mortgage contract availability. For example, some countries permit the matching of an underlying portfolio of mortgages with the derivatives used to hedge the portfolio's maturity and prepayment risks while others do not. The ability to use matching techniques would make hedging longer-term fixed-rate mortgages more cost-effective. Limitations on the information about mortgage contracts to lenders can also influence the types of contracts. Countries in which there are readily available data on prepayment patterns allow these risks to be priced more efficiently and thus permit longer-term fixed-rate mortgages to be offered at lower costs.

In sum, it appears the supply side of mortgage markets—characterized by the types of contracts lenders are willing and able to offer—plays a large role in the preponderance of adjustable-rate- or fixed-rate-type mortgages in a country. Without complete information, consumers gravitate to the incentives provided by lenders, who are able to offer relatively cheaper mortgage contracts based on the funding sources readily available to them. Since it appears that countries with predominantly fixed-rate mortgages have better behaved housing prices and fewer negative spillover effects on their economies, countries where fixed-rate mortgages are inhibited by structural impediments, such as restrictions on financial institutions or accounting regulations, could usefully remove them. Other measures to strengthen long-term markets and the ability of institutions to use derivatives to hedge could also ultimately lower economic risks, strengthen financial stability, and enhance consumer welfare through better risk-sharing. As well, consumer education and information about the various types of mortgages available with their suitability for different types of borrowers should be encouraged.

countries, using quarterly data for the period 1980:QI to 2004:QI.[15] Dynamic factor models, which are gaining increasing popularity among economists, differ from standard econometric models in that, instead of seeking to estimate the relationship between two observable series—such as house prices and interest rates—they are used to identify the underlying (unobservable) forces, known as factors, which may be driving both.[16] For example, the dynamic factor model used in this essay assumes that house prices—and the other six variables mentioned above—can be explained by the following four types of factors:[17]

- an overall *global factor*, which affects all variables in all countries, capturing the common shocks affecting these variables;
- a *global housing factor*, which captures common shocks affecting house prices in all countries, but not other variables. Similarly, there is a *global interest rate factor* that captures common shocks to global interest rates, and so on.
- a *country-specific* factor, which captures common shocks to variables in a country; and
- an *idiosyncratic* factor that captures the effect of country-specific shocks for each individual variable in each country.[18]

These factors capture movements in the underlying forces driving these economies (i.e., monetary and fiscal policy shocks, productivity shocks, oil price shocks, etc.), the relative importance of which changes over time. For example, the co-movement across countries of variables affecting house prices, such as interest rates and disposable income, would be captured by the two global factors, while regulatory, policy, and structural changes affecting the housing market of a particular country would be captured by the idiosyncratic factor.

Consequently, a dynamic factor model is well suited to investigating movements in house prices across different countries, and assessing whether they primarily reflect underlying global forces affecting all variables (the global component), factors specific to global housing markets, or country-specific developments. While the detailed results are set out in Appendix 2.1, the main results are the following.

- Global developments—the combination of the aggregate global factor and the global variable-specific factors—explain 40 percent of house price movements, underscoring the importance of international linkages in the forces driving housing market developments. (Figure 2.5).[19] Unsurprisingly, global developments also play a substantial role in explaining movements in the six other variables.
- Within this, the overall global component—the global factor affecting all variables—explains about 15 percent of movements in house prices. The global housing factor—capturing global shocks to housing markets alone—explains 25 percent of house price movements.[20]
- The impact of global factors on house prices varies significantly across individual countries. For example, global factors appear to explain about 70 percent of house price movements in

[15]Case, Goetzmann, and Rouwenhorst (1999) were, to our knowledge, the first to apply a related approach to study the international returns on office and retail properties. They find that the surprisingly high international correlation among these returns may reflect changes in world economic activity.

[16]These models were originally introduced by Spearman, a century ago, to study the relationship between a set of (observable) test scores and underlying (unobservable) mental ability.

[17]These components are generally not correlated with each other. However, each component could follow an autoregressive process (that is, each component could be correlated with its own past). See, for instance, Kose, Otrok, and Whiteman (2003).

[18]More precisely, the model encompasses 1 global factor, 7 aggregate factors (one for each variable; i.e., house prices, stock prices, etc.), 13 country-specific factors (1 for each country), and 13 idiosyncratic terms. See Appendix 2.1 for more details.

[19]This result is consistent with the findings of the existing literature focusing on the role of global factors in explaining fluctuations in the main macroeconomic variables (see, for instance, Kose, Otrok and Whiteman, 2003).

[20]The fraction of variance and co-movement of a given time series explained by the world components are typically the same because the global component and the aggregate-specific component are not correlated with each other.

the United Kingdom and the United States, but only about 3 percent of house price movements in New Zealand.

- Country-specific factors play a surprisingly small role in most countries, with the exception of Ireland[21] and to a lesser extent New Zealand. Idiosyncratic factors—capturing country-specific forces affecting housing market developments—account for 50 percent of movements in house prices, and are especially important in Australia, Italy, New Zealand, Norway, and Switzerland.

As can be seen from Figure 2.6, both the global and the country-specific factors fluctuate over time, reflecting the major shocks affecting them. However, it is striking that the overall global component moves quite closely with global GDP, including the recession of the early 1980s, the boom of the mid-1980s, the recession of the early 1990s, the long boom of the 1990s, and the mild recession of 2001. Moreover, the global housing component tracks the main developments in global housing markets over the past 25 years remarkably well, including the housing price bust of the early 1980s, the house price boom of the late 1980s, the bust of the early 1990s, and the current house price boom—which shows, as noted before, an unprecedented strength and duration. The global and house components have typically moved in the same direction, with the exception of the most recent years, during which they have diverged, possibly reflecting the recent "disconnect" between house prices and economic activity documented earlier.

It is reasonable to ask why it might be that global factors have such a significant impact on the price of a nontradable asset. While the dynamic factor model does provide only limited information on this issue; the fact that housing is part of households' wealth alongside interna-

[21]In this period, Ireland's economy was experiencing a strong boom and a strong flow of repatriates. To contain the rapid increase in house prices, in 1999–2000 the government introduced temporary measures to discourage "speculation" in the housing market.

Figure 2.5. Variance Decomposition of House Prices
(Percent change; constant prices)

Global developments explain 40 percent of real house price movements, reflecting the importance of international linkages in the housing markets.

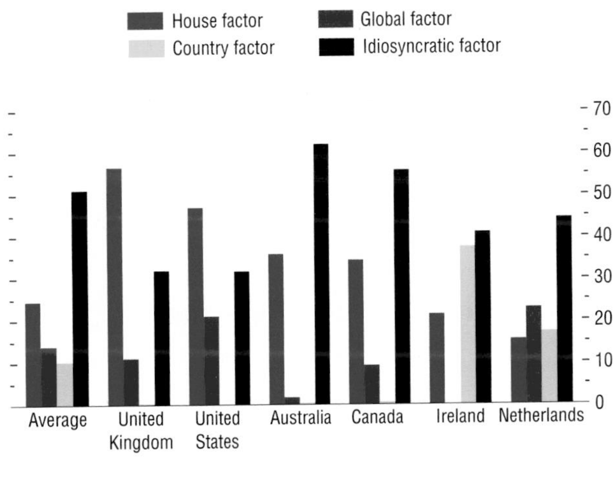

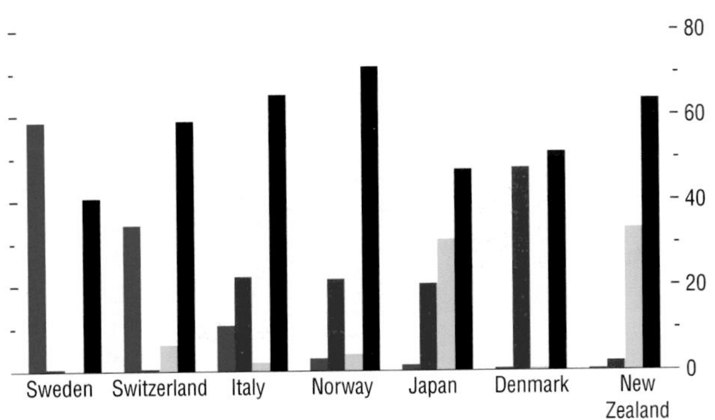

Sources: Haver Analytics; IMF, *International Financial Statistics;* national sources; OECD; and IMF staff calculations.

Figure 2.6. What Explains House Price Fluctuations?
(Percent change; constant prices; demeaned)

The global and country-specific factors fluctuate over time. The global and house factors have typically moved in the same direction, until recently.

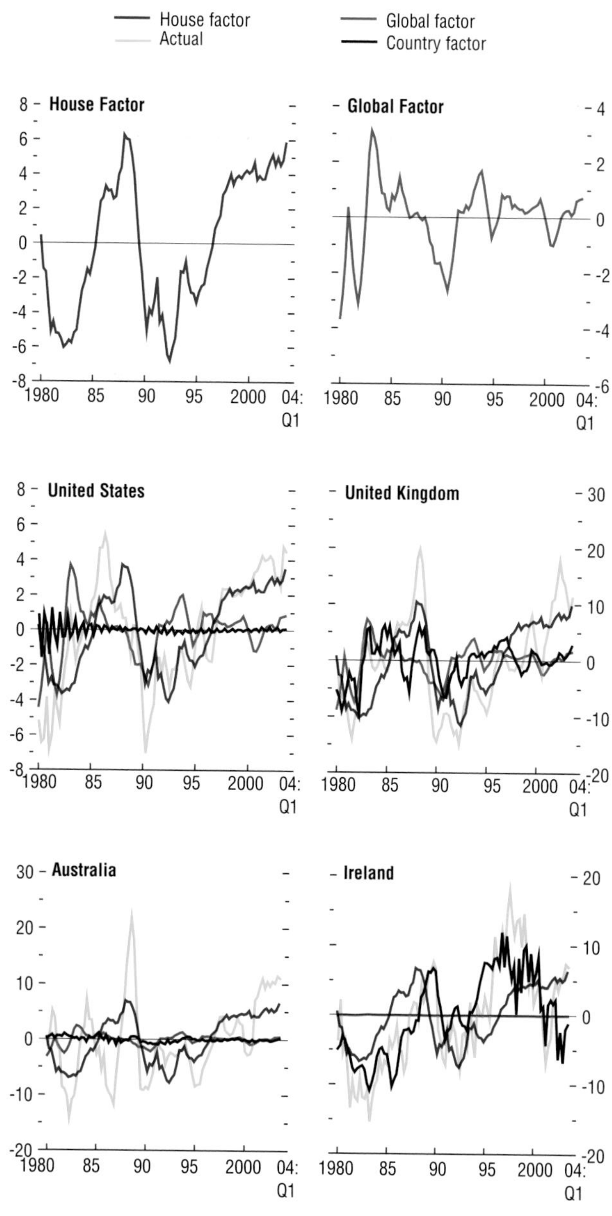

Sources: Haver Analytics; IMF, *International Financial Statistics;* national sources; OECD; and IMF staff calculations.

tionally traded assets suggests that (risk-adjusted) rates of return are likely to move in a coordinated fashion across countries. In addition, recent years have witnessed a process of deepening of financial markets in general, and mortgage markets in particular, across all industrial countries. By easing borrowing constraints, this may also have contributed to a synchronized pickup in housing demand. To further investigate the potential sources of this relationship, the IMF staff regressed the aggregate global factor and the global housing factor against a number of explanatory variables. The main results were as follows.

- The aggregate global factor is positively correlated with output growth in the United States, possibly reflecting the fact that U.S. cycles are exported to the rest of the world.[22] Similarly, the aggregate global factor is negatively correlated with real oil and non-oil commodity prices, in line with the findings in the literature that these prices have a negative effect on global economic activity.
- The global housing factor is negatively correlated with interest rates in the United States—a reflection of the key role played by interest rates in real estate markets. In addition, the global housing factor is positively correlated with the mortgage-to-GDP ratio (perhaps reflecting the fact that the deepening of mortgage markets across industrial countries has been associated with higher global house prices) and the home ownership ratio (the movements of which often reflect cross-country structural and policy changes, including tax/subsidies, aimed at fostering home ownership).

How Could Higher Global Interest Rates Affect House Prices?

Given the importance of global factors in determining house prices, the question arises as to how future global developments—notably, the

[22]Note that the United States has the same weight as all other countries in the calculation of the global factor.

expected rise in interest rates—might affect housing markets in the coming year. To address this, the staff constructed a factor-augmented multivariate vector autoregression model (FAVAR) of housing prices for the United Kingdom and the United States.[23] To formulate the FAVAR, it is necessary first to establish which factors (e.g., world factor, house-price factor) and variables (e.g., interest rates, stock prices) best predict movements in house prices.[24] These tests—along with the analysis of the drivers of the global factors described above—suggested the following.

- Domestic interest rates play a key role in explaining house price movements. Not surprisingly, they are important drivers of house prices in nearly every country in the sample.
- The global interest rate factor is also important in explaining future movements in house prices, both directly and through the global house price component as described above. The former result suggests that global interest rates will affect domestic house prices. The latter result suggests that the co-movement observed in house prices across countries may be in large part due to the interest rate channel.
- At the country level, real sector variables, in addition to interest rates, have an impact on house prices as well.
- There is evidence that U.S. house prices lead the global house factor. This finding, together with the fact that global interest rates—which are also affected by changes in U.S. interest rates—drive world house prices, suggests that movements in both U.S. house prices and interest rates are key sources of global house price fluctuations.

Based on these results, FAVAR models were constructed for two countries—the United States and the United Kingdom—and used to simulate the impact of a rise in interest rates through mid-2005 consistent with current expectations in futures markets. The forecasting analysis suggests the following.

- The growth rate in the U.S. house prices is projected to slow down over the coming year and a half (see Figure 2.7). This slowdown is primarily due to the rise in long-term interest rates expected by the futures markets (i.e., a cumulative 100 basis points during March 2004–June 2005).[25] The analysis, however, does not find compelling evidence suggesting that a real house price drop is in the offing.[26]
- In contrast, the growth rate of real house prices in the United Kingdom is forecast to slow down significantly, and a fall in real house prices cannot be ruled out.[27] This forecast is predicated on the basis of an increase

[23]These models are becoming increasingly popular because they often yield better forecasts than simple VAR models of pure observable variables (see, for instance, Stock and Watson, 2002, and Bernanke, Boivin, and Eliasz, 2004). The use of estimated factors allows the model to capture large amounts of information of the world economy with only a few variables.

[24]This is accomplished through causality tests at the global and country level, with the emphasis on predictive causality. To assess predictive causality among factors and variables a battery of bivariate Granger causality tests are performed (see, for instance, Hamilton, 1994).

[25]The FAVAR used to forecast the growth rate of real house prices in the U.S. comprises, in addition to this variable, the house factor, the country factor, the consumption factor, and yearly changes in the long-term interest rate. Long-term interest rates are thus expected to rise to 5 percent in June 2005 (from 4.02 percent in March 2004). Interestingly, the increase in short-term interest rates expected by the futures markets over the same period is 210 basis points.

[26]This finding, however, does not rule out the possibility of house price drop at a regional level. McCarthy and Peach (2004) also find it unlikely that house prices in the United States would drop in response to deteriorating fundamentals. HSBC (2004) in contrast, argues that because house prices in the United States are 10 to 20 percent overvalued, an increase in short-term interest rates could bring house prices down by mid-2005.

[27]The FAVAR model used to forecast the growth rate of real house prices in the United Kingdom comprises, in addition to this variable, the house price factor, the stock price factor, the consumption factor, and changes in the United Kingdom's short-term interest rates. Interestingly, the consumption factor (and not the output factor) helps predict house prices. This could reflect the fact that, in consumption-based asset pricing models, consumption may be useful in forecasting house prices (Piazzesi, Schneider, and Tuzel, 2004, find that in an asset pricing model with housing, consumption growth helps predict stock returns). Short-term interest rates are expected to rise to 5½ percent in June 2005 (from 4.10 percent in March 2004).

Figure 2.7. How Would House Prices React to an Increase in Interest Rates?
(Percent change; constant prices)

An increase in interest rates as expected by futures markets would slow down house price growth in the United States and the United Kingdom; in the United Kingdom, a drop in prices cannot be ruled out.

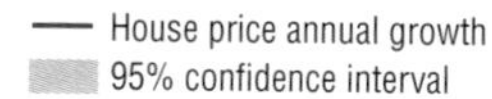

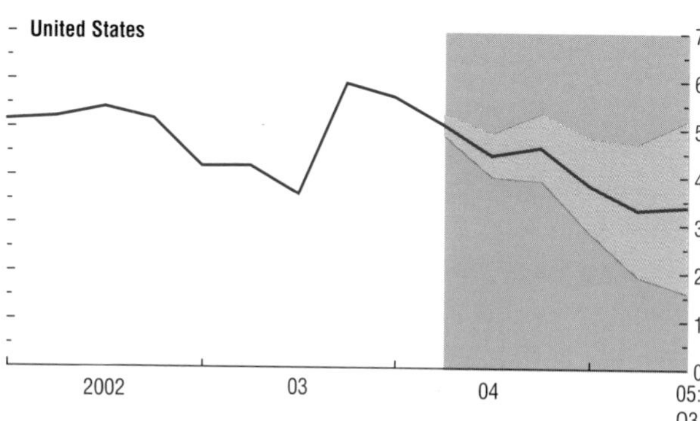

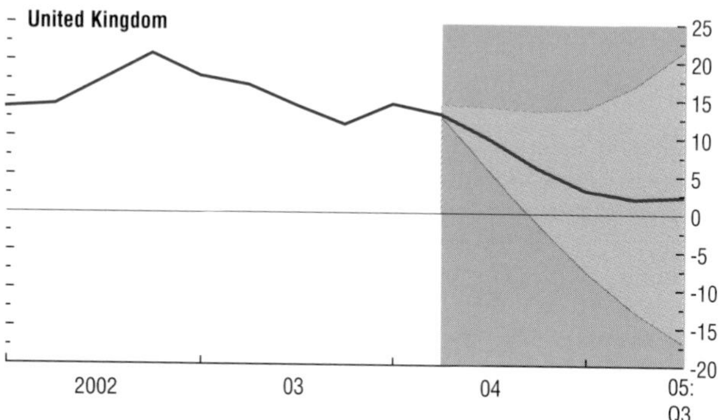

Sources: Bloomberg Financial, LP; Haver Analytics; IMF, *International Financial Statistics;* national sources; OECD; and IMF staff estimates.

in short-term interest rates in line with futures markets (i.e., a cumulative 140 basis points during March 2004–June 2005). There is, however, a substantial degree of uncertainty in the forecast, which indicates that a drop in real house prices is an event with nonzero probability.

Overall, these results tend to suggest that the impact of rising interest rates would be significant—especially in the United Kingdom—but manageable. However, there is one very important caveat. The dynamic factor model/FAVAR analysis assumes that house prices are driven by fundamentals and is not designed to test for the existence of potential bubbles. In cases where house prices may have exceeded fundamentals—which may include Australia, Ireland, Spain, and the United Kingdom, as discussed in Box 2.1—there is a danger that higher interest rates could trigger a much larger downward adjustment in house prices, with considerably more severe consequences for real activity.

Conclusions

Since the mid-1990s, many industrial countries have been experiencing a boom in housing prices, unusual in both its strength and duration; moreover, despite the bursting of the information technology bubble and subsequent global downturn, the momentum of the housing boom has continued almost unabated. This boom has been associated with a very dynamic housing market and record-high levels of mortgage debt. The strength of the housing market has played an important role in supporting activity during and after the downturn. By the same token, the outlook for the housing market will play a key role in shaping the extent and nature of the recovery going forward.

While housing is generally thought to be the quintessential nontradable asset, the analysis in this essay suggests that house prices across countries are surprisingly highly synchronized, reflecting the key role played by global factors, primarily through global interest rates and economic activity. A key implication of this finding is that, just as the upswing in house prices has been mostly a global phenomenon, it is likely that any downturn would also be highly synchronized, with corresponding implications for global economic activity. In particular, higher global interest rates will result in a slowdown in house prices, the extent of which will differ across countries, reflecting in part differences in their sensitivities to global developments. Simulations presented in the paper suggest that an increase of over 100 basis points in interest rates during March 2004–June 2005 would slow down the growth rate of house prices in the United Kingdom and the United States. For the United Kingdom, a drop in house prices cannot be ruled out, reflecting the higher forecasting uncertainty in that country. The evidence provided in Box 2.1 suggests that current house prices appear out of line with fundamentals in some countries, including the United Kingdom, highlighting the risk of a more pronounced drop in prices. Clearly, other factors, such as the size of households' debt and financial structure, could also play an important role, thus exacerbating the risks for an economy.

In those countries where house prices are elevated, central banks face the challenge of containing inflationary pressures while simultaneously seeking to minimize the risks of a house price bust. On the whole, the best compromise would appear to be an "early but gradual" tightening in monetary policy, as appears to be under way in the United Kingdom, maximizing the opportunity for households to adjust to higher interest rates. Indeed, there is evidence that most house prices busts of the past were triggered by a rapid tightening in monetary policy, as reducing inflation became an important policy objective (see, for instance, the April 2003 *World Economic Outlook*). Policymakers should also consider tightening lending requirements and strengthening surveillance of financial entities as household debt may be reaching (or may have reached already) unhealthy levels in some countries. More generally, policymakers should give increasing attention to developing mortgage market infrastructure; in particular, countries should aim at creating the conditions for the introduction of a richer set of mortgage contracts while strengthening their financial sector regulation. This could include reforming their bankruptcy laws and accounting standards, as well as improving the information and disclosure on mortgage contracts (as discussed in Box 2.2). In addition, countries should assess the extent and desirability of their implicit/explicit guarantees to mortgage debt.

Learning To Float: The Experience of Emerging Market Countries Since the Early 1990s

The main author of this essay is Dalia Hakura. Angela Cabugao and Ercument Tulun provided research assistance.

The benefits of more flexible exchange rate regimes increase as economies develop and become more integrated in global financial markets, a process that has been underscored in recent work by Rogoff and others (2003, 2004), and Husain, Mody, and Rogoff (2004). For emerging market economies, moving toward more flexible regimes can help to mitigate the risk from currency crises that have characterized pegged exchange rate regimes. Moreover, in industrial countries, flexible exchange rate regimes have conferred macroeconomic benefits in terms of better growth and inflation performance.

Although several emerging market countries have moved to more flexible exchange rate regimes, others have exhibited a "fear of floating" (Calvo and Reinhart, 2002; and Hausmann, Panizza, and Stein, 2001). The fear of floating derives from the actual or perceived costs of exchange rate volatility. For instance, currency fluctuations may cause a ratcheting up of inflation (exchange rate pass-through) and adversely affect balance sheets and debt-servicing burdens by raising the domestic-currency value of foreign-currency-denominated debt. Because of these costs, some policymakers in emerging market countries feel that the room to pursue an independent monetary policy and increase exchange rate flexibility is, in practice, limited at best.

Against this background, stronger monetary and financial policy frameworks facilitate the introduction of greater exchange rate flexibility by directly addressing the key vulnerabilities that give rise to the fear of floating (Calvo and Mishkin, 2003). For instance, an independent central bank that has price stability as its main objective can help to reduce exchange rate pass-through (Campa and Goldberg, 2001; Choudhri and Hakura, 2001; and Gagnon and Ihrig, 2001). Similarly, strong financial sector supervision helps to reduce currency mismatches on banks' balance sheets (Goldstein and Turner, 2004).

This essay examines empirically the association between transitions to greater exchange rate flexibility, macroeconomic outcomes, and monetary and financial policy frameworks, both systematically across a group of emerging market countries and in three case studies (Box 2.3). Specifically, it addresses the following questions about the experience with exchange rate regimes since the early 1990s.[28]

- Have exchange rate regime transitions in emerging market economies since the early 1990s generally been toward greater flexibility or greater fixity? To what extent have the transitions been driven by crises?
- How have macroeconomic outcomes been associated with changes in exchange rate regimes? Have voluntary transitions been associated with an increase in macroeconomic instability?
- How have countries "learned to float"? Specifically, how have changes in policy frameworks been associated with changes in exchange rate regimes? Have changes in policy frameworks tended to precede or follow moves to more flexible exchange rates? Is the association different for crisis-driven transitions?

How Have Exchange Rate Regimes Changed?

This section investigates how exchange rate regimes in emerging market economies have changed over the past decade using the IMF's de facto classification system.[29] To keep the analysis manageable, the essay distinguishes three categories of exchange rate regimes: pegs, intermediate regimes, and free floats. The data suggest that there has been a trend toward greater flexibility in emerging market countries since the early 1990s (Figure 2.8). Specifically, the share of countries with free floats rose from virtually zero in the early 1990s to more than one-third in recent years.

Overall, there have been 28 transitions over the past decade, of which 20 have been to more flexible regimes. A transition is defined as a change from one exchange rate category, in which a country has been for at least two years, to another, in which a country remains for at least one year or which is followed by another shift in the same direction. The transitions to more flexible exchange rates are from pegs to intermediate regimes and from intermediate regimes to free floats; no emerging market country moved directly from a peg to a free float during the sample period. The transitions to more flexible rates are broadly evenly distributed across all regions—Asia and Latin America, among others—and across the sample period.

Transitions to greater flexibility can be characterized as voluntary or crisis-driven. Following Milesi-Ferretti and Razin (2000), a crisis-driven transition is defined as one that is associated with a depreciation vis-à-vis the U.S. dollar of more than 20 percent, at least a doubling in the

[28]Emerging market economies are defined in the essay as countries in the Morgan Stanley Capital International index (MSCI), which includes Argentina, Brazil, Chile, China, Colombia, the Czech Republic, Egypt, Hungary, India, Indonesia, Israel, Jordan, Korea, Malaysia, Mexico, Morocco, Pakistan, Peru, the Philippines, Poland, Russia, South Africa, Thailand, Turkey, and Venezuela.

[29]The results are robust to using the "Natural Classification" system developed by Reinhart and Rogoff (2004, Appendix 2.2).

Table 2.2. Emerging Market Countries' Transitions to More Flexible Regimes, 1992–2002
(IMF de facto classification)

Transition Type	Voluntary	Crisis-Driven
Peg to intermediate	Czech Republic, 1996 Egypt, 1999 Hungary, 1994 India, 1995 Pakistan, 2000	Argentina, 2001 Philippines, 1997 Thailand, 1997 Venezuela, 1996
Intermediate to free float	Chile, 1999 Peru, 1999 Philippines, 2000 Poland, 2000 South Africa, 1997 Turkey, 2001	Brazil, 1999 Colombia, 1999 Indonesia, 1997 Korea, 1997 Mexico, 1994

Source: IMF staff calculations.

depreciation rate compared with the previous year, and a depreciation in the previous year of less than 40 percent. The transitions that are not crisis-driven are defined as voluntary, though clearly there are different degrees of volition involved, with some occurring under threat of a crisis (such as in Hungary and Turkey).[30] Crisis-driven and voluntary transitions are both nearly evenly split between transitions from pegs to intermediate regimes and transitions from intermediate regimes to free floats (Table 2.2).

How Have Macroeconomic Outcomes Changed?

This section examines the association between transitions to more flexible regimes and macroeconomic outcomes. In contrast to earlier work that has analyzed voluntary and crisis-driven transitions together (Eichengreen and others, 1998 and 1999), the focus here is on voluntary transitions. The key questions are under what macroeconomic conditions have countries made voluntary transitions and whether voluntary transitions have been associated with an increase in macroeconomic instability.

Figure 2.8. Increasing Exchange Rate Flexibility in Emerging Markets
(Percent of annual observations)

The share of countries with freely floating exchange rate regimes has increased from virtually zero in the early 1990s to 40 percent in recent years.

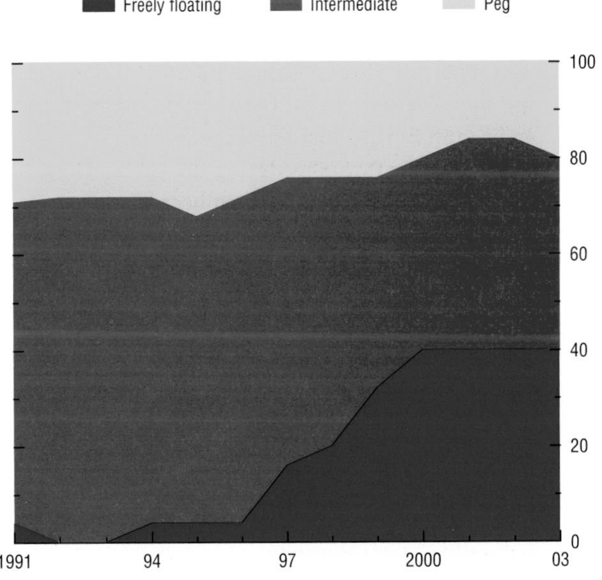

Sources: Bubula and Ötker-Robe (2002); and IMF staff calculations.

[30]Turkey's adoption of a free float in 2001 does not qualify as crisis-driven, because the rate of exchange rate depreciation in that year was not at least double that in the previous year. The results reported in the essay are not sensitive to how this transition is classified.

Box 2.3. How Did Chile, India, and Brazil Learn to Float?

Several emerging market countries moved to greater exchange rate flexibility over the past decade, despite the potential costs of exchange rate fluctuations in terms of output and inflation volatility, and unfavorable balance-sheet and debt-service effects (see, for example, Calvo and Reinhart, 2002; and Hausmann, Panizza, and Stein, 2001). Recent work has emphasized that countries can "learn to float" by improving monetary and financial policy frameworks, which directly addresses the key vulnerabilities (Rogoff and others, 2004). For example, an independent central bank committed to price stability may be able to stabilize inflation expectations and thus reduce the pass-through of exchange rate changes to prices. Similarly, strong prudential regulations can moderate the balance-sheet mismatches in the financial and corporate sectors. This box illustrates these points by examining the experiences of three countries—Chile, India, and Brazil—that moved to greater exchange rate flexibility during the 1990s. These three case studies were selected because they offer a range of experiences across regions, types of transitions, and evolution of policy frameworks.

Chile

Chile made a transition from a crawling band to a free float in September 1999, having significantly enhanced its monetary and financial policy frameworks over the previous decade (see Kalter and others, 2004; Duttagupta, Fernández, and Karacadag, 2004; Morandé, 2001; and Ariyoshi and others, 2000). After gaining full independence in 1989, the central bank started anchoring inflation expectations by publishing short-term inflation targets and over time built a reputation for an anti-inflationary bias. In 1998, the central bank further shifted its policy framework toward influencing expectations by setting the rate of crawl for the peso at expected inflation. When the crawling band was abolished in 1999, the central bank adopted a full-fledged inflation targeting framework, making price stability its only monetary policy objective.

During the 1990s, the crawling band for the peso was widened several times and the central parity adjusted in response to strong capital inflows. To dampen pressures for exchange rate appreciation, Chile maintained restrictions on the capital account, mainly in the form of unremunerated reserve requirements on certain financial inflows (1991–98). Fluctuations of the exchange rate within the crawling band increased incentives for the deepening of forward and futures markets in foreign exchange, which helped to limit the impact of currency fluctuations on the real sector.

Chile had substantially strengthened its banking supervision before the transition to free floating. The banking law of 1986 and the subsequent amendments in 1989 and 1997 gave the regulators the essential tools to control risk taking by banks. The measures strengthened balance sheets by tightening capital requirements, imposing strong liquidity management rules, limiting bank's exposure to foreign exchange risk, and increasing banks' capital requirements in line with the recommendations of the Basel Committee.

India

India announced the transition from the peg of the rupee to the U.S. dollar to a managed float in March 1993, though the IMF de facto classification system dates the transition to August 1995. While India shifted to greater exchange rate flexibility when reforms to policy frameworks were still in progress, the managed float has been maintained without major distress, even during times of international market turbulence.

In 1991, India embarked on a wide-ranging liberalization program. Financial sector reforms were an important component of this reform program and were implemented gradually, beginning with interest rate liberalization, the introduction of greater competition in the banking system, measures to develop domestic securities markets, and steps to strengthen financial sector supervision (see Acharya, 2002; Ariyoshi and others,

Note: The main author of this box is Martin Sommer.

2000; and Chopra and others, 1995). Liquidity in financial markets benefited from fiscal reforms: the government shifted to borrowing at market interest rates (1992/93) and the automatic monetization of fiscal deficits by the central bank was phased out (1994–97). In the period after the floating of the rupee, many of the reforms launched in the early 1990s continued to be implemented and enhanced. Moreover, foreign exchange dealers were allowed to use derivatives to hedge their positions (1996–97) and the prudential requirements regarding the risks of foreign exchange exposures were tightened.

External financial liberalization was also gradual, and focused on long-term foreign direct investment and equity portfolio inflows. Extensive controls on short-term borrowing were retained throughout the 1990s, which together with the existing prudential norms limited foreign exchange vulnerabilities in the banking and corporate sectors and increased India's resilience during international financial crises. The policy of maintaining limited external public debt (and on concessional terms) also diminished the exposure of the economy to exchange rate volatility.

Monetary policy in India has traditionally focused on the twin objectives of maintaining price stability and supporting growth. In the first half of the 1990s, a surge in capital inflows pushed inflation higher but in the second half of the decade, the Reserve Bank of India succeeded in keeping inflation low. After abolishing the peg of the rupee, the central bank actively intervened in the foreign exchange market to reduce volatility. The exchange rate against the U.S. dollar remained quite stable until the end of the 1990s with occasional shifts at the times of large unfavorable shocks. In the past several years, the Reserve Bank of India has allowed even greater exchange rate flexibility but still maintains many controls on residents' capital account transactions.

Brazil

Brazil abandoned the crawling peg of the real to the U.S. dollar in January 1999. However, the rapid adoption of inflation targeting has helped to contain inflation expectations after the initial depreciation and moderate the adverse impact of a more volatile currency (see IMF, 2003; and Bogdanski, Tombini, and Werlang, 2000). To influence expectations, the bank increased the transparency of its decision making, communicated extensively with the public, and explained its performance relative to the inflation targets.

The financial sector weathered the sharp depreciation of the Brazilian real as a result of wide-ranging structural reforms launched in 1994 that reduced systemic foreign exchange and credit risks. In addition, both financial and corporate sectors had little exposure to foreign exchange risk because of extensive hedging through dollar-indexed government securities, derivatives, or foreign receivables. The prudential measures against the foreign exchange risk were further tightened after the crisis.

Restrictions aimed at discouraging short-term capital inflows (1993–97) were ineffective given the sophistication of the Brazilian financial market. This stands in contrast with India, where capital controls were more effective, reflecting in part the relatively less developed financial market.

Concluding Remarks

The three case studies provide us with some interesting insights. First, all three transitions were associated with an improvement in the monetary and financial policy frameworks, which helped to diminish the potential costs of exchange rate flexibility in terms of inflationary and balance-sheet effects. Second, the timing of improvement in policy frameworks varied across the three cases. Chile made significant enhancements to its policy framework before the transition; India started off with partial reforms that continued after the transition; and Brazil quickly adopted a new nominal anchor following a crisis. Finally, the experience of India suggests that even with an imperfect policy framework, the potential costs of exchange rate volatility can be kept in check by capital controls, though—looking forward—gradual liberalization supported by strengthened policy frameworks would likely help to boost growth (see Chapter IV of the October 2001 *World Economic Outlook*).

Figure 2.9. Macroeconomic Indicators[1]
(Percent unless otherwise noted; t = 0 is year of transition)

Voluntary transitions were generally not associated with an increase in macroeconomic instability, unlike crisis-driven transitions.

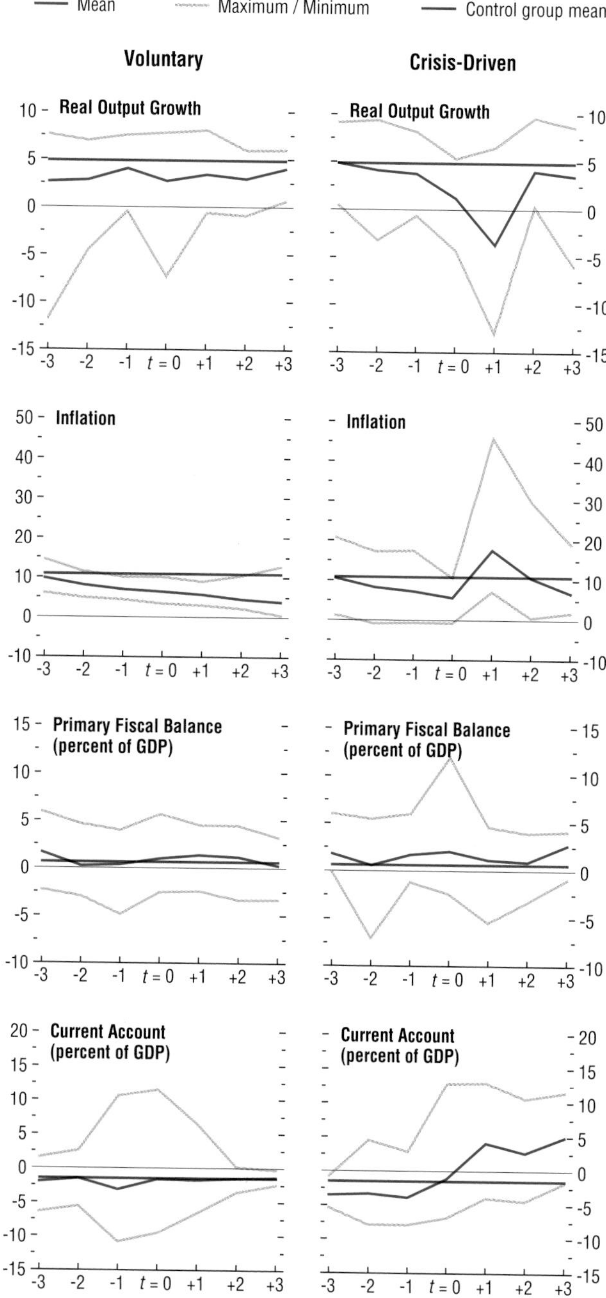

Sources: World Bank, *World Development Indicators;* IMF, *International Financial Statistics;* and IMF staff calculations.
[1]The control group represents countries whose exchange rate regimes are the same as the starting regimes of transitioning countries in periods that are not within three years of a transition. Outliers are excluded from the panel for inflation.

In view of the limited number of transitions identified in the previous section, the analysis is mainly descriptive. Following standard event-study methodology, the paths of key macroeconomic variables in countries making transitions are compared with average values in countries not making transitions (the control group).[31] The analysis yields four key results regarding voluntary transitions.

- Voluntary transitions have been made in a macroeconomic environment not significantly different from that in the control group (Figure 2.9). Pretransition levels of indicators such as growth, the primary fiscal balance, and the current account balance, were, on average, broadly similar.[32]
- Voluntary transitions were mostly orderly in the sense that growth, inflation, and the primary fiscal balance, among other variables, were on average little affected by the transition. Indeed, voluntary transitions appear to have been associated on average with a sustained decline in inflation, which begins in the years preceding the transition and continues after the transition.[33] This finding may partly reflect sample selection bias: the countries that decided to transition may have done so with the expectation that the move would not be disruptive.
- Voluntary transitions were not associated on average with previously over- or undervalued exchange rates, unlike crisis-driven transitions that in most cases occurred against the backdrop of an overvalued exchange rate (Figure 2.10). Correspondingly, the levels of the nominal and real effective exchange rates did not on average change much immediately after the transition, though this reflects some cases

[31]See Appendix 2.2 for data definitions and sources.
[32]In addition, the ratio of reserves to imports in countries making voluntary transitions was, on average, similar to that for the control group.
[33]Forecasts of year-ahead inflation from surveys by *Consensus Forecasts* also suggest that voluntary transitions have on average been associated with a fall in inflation expectations.

where the rate appreciated and others where it depreciated.

- The volatility of real and nominal effective exchange rates increased somewhat in the period immediately after a voluntary transition and returned to pretransition levels soon thereafter (Figure 2.11).[34]

Not surprisingly, voluntary transitions were associated with lower vulnerabilities and far less macroeconomic disruption than crisis-driven transactions, consistent with the findings of earlier work. In the years immediately preceding transitions, the private sector external debt to exports ratio was higher, on average, by 100 percentage points in countries which experienced a crisis-driven transition (Figure 2.12). This is consistent with the hypothesis that, other things equal, extensive liability dollarization is associated with a greater reluctance on the part of the monetary authorities to float the exchange rate, inducing more liability dollarization and creating a situation from which it is hard to exit in an orderly manner (Eichengreen and others, 1998, 1999).[35] In addition, compared with crisis-driven transitions, voluntary transitions have been associated with higher growth, and lower inflation and exchange rate volatility in the years immediately after the transition.

From Fixed To Floating: How Do Policy Frameworks Change?

This section investigates the association between transitions to more flexible exchange rate regimes and changes in monetary and financial policy frameworks. The association with fiscal policy frameworks are not examined because time-series data on fiscal institutions are not available for a large sample of emerging market countries. The main idea is that strong

Figure 2.10. Real Effective Exchange Rate Overvaluation[1]

(Percent deviation from trend; t = 0 is month of transition)

By contrast with crisis-driven transitions, voluntary transitions were generally not associated with previously over- or undervalued exchange rates.

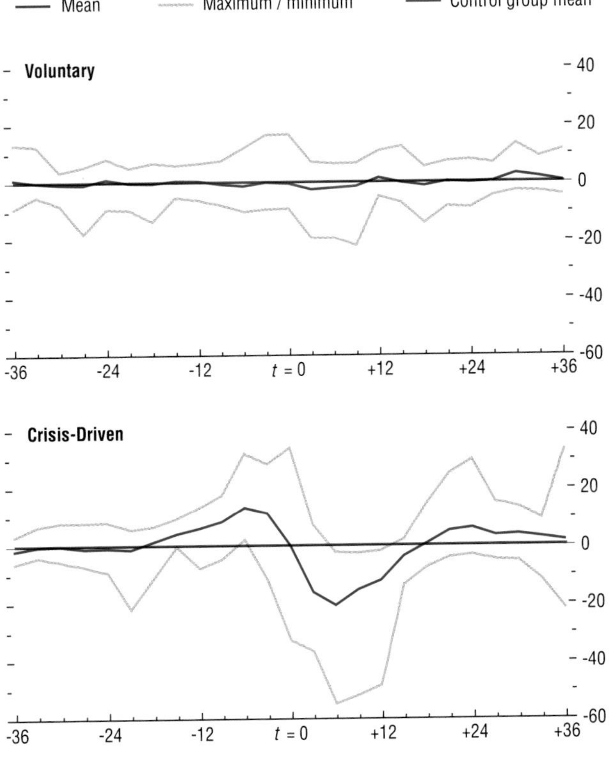

Source: IMF staff calculations.

[1]Real exchange rate overvaluation is calculated using the percentage difference between the actual real effective exchange rate (REER) and the Hodrick-Prescott filter of the REER. The control group represents countries whose exchange rate regimes are the same as the starting regimes of transitioning countries in periods that are not within three years of a transition.

[34]This finding does not imply a problem with the post-transition exchange rate regime classification, because the classification is based on the volatility of a bilateral exchange rate as well as other factors.

[35]Data on total foreign-currency-denominated debt is not available for most countries.

Figure 2.11. Volatility of Exchange Rate[1]

(t = 0 is month of transition)

The volatility of real and nominal exchange rates increased in the period immediately after a voluntary transition but returned to pretransition levels soon thereafter.

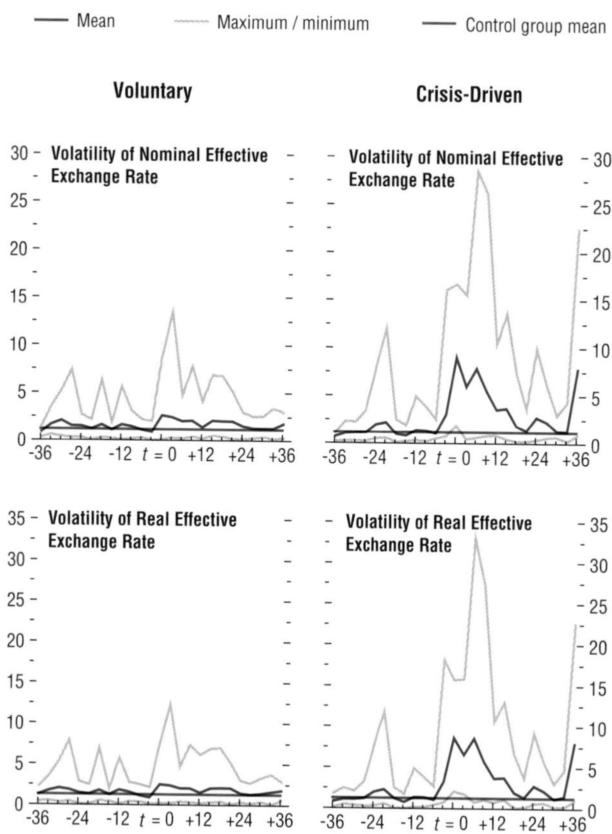

Source: IMF staff calculations.

[1]Volatility is measured as the standard deviation of the monthly growth rate of the exchange rate over the last three months, averaged across transition cases. The control group represents countries whose exchange rate regimes are the same as the starting regimes of transitioning countries in periods that are not within three years of a transition.

policy frameworks address the key vulnerabilities that underlie the "fear of floating." The section first explains how the strength of the policy framework supports greater exchange rate flexibility, and then examines how the framework evolved in the years before and after the transitions to more flexible regimes. As in the previous section, the analysis is based on a limited number of transitions and is thus mainly descriptive. Complementing this analysis, Box 2.4 discusses the development of foreign exchange markets and intervention policies in countries that have moved to more flexible regimes.

Monetary Policy Framework

An independent central bank that has price stability as its main objective is more likely to gain the public's confidence that it can and will control inflation. These attributes help stabilize inflation expectations and lower the pass-through of exchange rate fluctuations to higher prices, directly addressing one of the concerns underlying the "fear of floating." This essay examines two measures of monetary policy frameworks.

- *Central bank independence.* This is measured using an indicator of political and economic independence, where political independence depends inversely on the extent to which the government is involved in the operations of the central bank and economic independence depends inversely on the involvement of the central bank in financing the fiscal deficit and in banking supervision (Grilli, Masciandaro, and Tabellini, 1991; and Arnone and Laurens, 2004). In the early 1990s, emerging market countries had similar levels of central bank independence, but by 2003 countries with free floats had on average more independent central banks than countries with pegs or intermediate regimes (Figure 2.13). However, even among countries with free floats, there is considerable variation in the degree of central bank independence.
- *Inflation targeting.* The explicit announcement of an inflation target and the creation of a

monetary policy framework geared toward achieving the inflation target also help to stabilize inflation expectations. In practice, inflation targeting was not a prerequisite for the move to a more flexible exchange rate regime: only one country (Poland) adopted full-fledged inflation targeting before it transited to a free float. Countries that moved to more flexible regimes introduced inflation targeting on average two years after they made the transition.[36] By 2003, about 90 percent of free floats were associated with inflation targeting, compared with just 40 percent of intermediate regimes (Figure 2.14).

Financial Sector Supervision and Development

Strong financial sector supervision helps banks and other financial market participants to better recognize and price risks, thereby reducing currency and maturity mismatches that can give rise to the fear of floating. Similarly, securities market development helps to improve long-term funding and thus reduces maturity mismatches. Both the quality of bank supervision and the degree of securities market development are measured using indicators put together by Abiad and Mody (2003). The indicators take values from 0 to 3, with increasing values indicating stronger bank supervision and greater securities market development. Figure 2.15 shows the evolution of these indicators in countries making peg-to-intermediate and intermediate-to-free-float transitions, distinguished by voluntary and crisis-driven transitions, compared to the relevant control groups.

- *Quality of bank supervision.*[37] Weak balance sheets, especially currency mismatches, amplify the cost of exchange rate volatility and thus tend to constrain the choice of exchange

[36]Carare and others (2002) provides a review of the initial conditions that can support an inflation-targeting monetary framework.

[37]The indicator for the quality of bank supervision reflects adoption of a capital adequacy regulation, the power and independence of the supervisory agency, and the extent and effectiveness of supervision.

Figure 2.12. Indicators of External Debt[1]
(Percent of exports of goods and services; t = 0 is year of transition)

Voluntary transitions were associated with much lower external debt ratios than crisis-driven transitions.

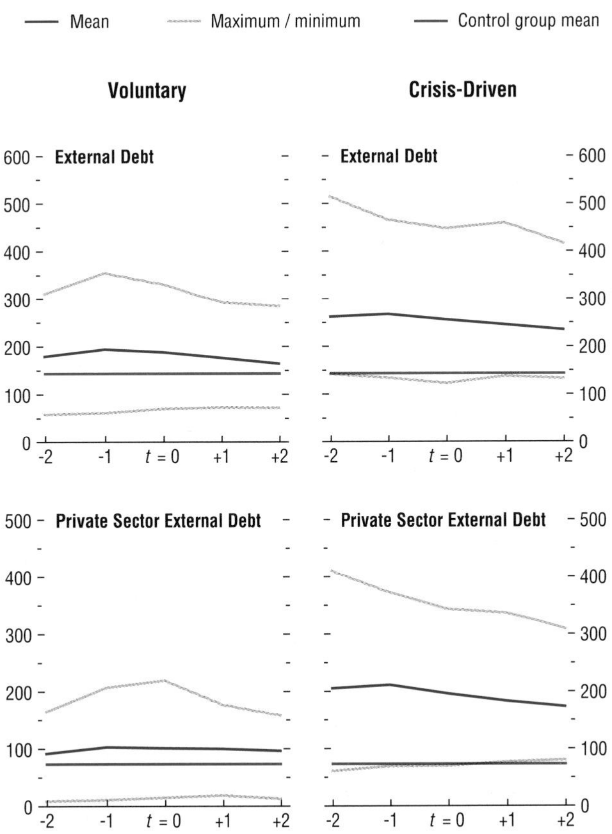

Source: IMF staff calculations.
[1]The control group represents countries whose exchange rate regimes are the same as the starting regimes of transitioning countries in periods that are not within three years of a transition. Only countries with observations for all periods shown around the time of transition are included.

Box 2.4. Foreign Exchange Market Development and Intervention

For the growing number of emerging market countries that have adopted or are considering adopting more flexible exchange rate regimes, the development of the foreign exchange market and official intervention policies is crucial.[1] A sufficiently liquid and efficient foreign exchange market allows the exchange rate to respond to market forces and minimizes instances and durations of excessive volatility and deviations from equilibrium. In addition, whereas the timing and amount of foreign exchange intervention are largely determined by factors out of the control of the central bank under fixed regimes, intervention becomes discretionary under a flexible regime, creating the need to develop policies on the objectives, timing, and amounts of intervention.

Exchange rate rigidity itself hinders the development of the foreign exchange market. In a fixed exchange rate environment, market participants have less incentive to form views on exchange rate trends, take positions, or trade foreign exchange, which keeps them from gaining experience in price formation and exchange rate risk management and constrains interbank activity. A sense of two-way risk created by exchange rate variability encourages market participants to take short and long positions. Thus, an important step to develop the foreign exchange market is to gradually increase exchange rate flexibility, possibly within a band around a peg. For instance, in Israel, the exchange rate was initially allowed to vary within a band introduced in 1989; then, in 1990, the central bank organized daily market clearings on a multilateral basis until the system was replaced by an interbank market in 1994 through which market participants traded among themselves bilaterally and the central bank entered the market only at its own initiative. In fact, foreign exchange market turnover grew between 1998 and 2001 in emerging market countries that adopted more flexible exchange rate regimes, but declined from an already lower base in countries that adopted less flexible regimes or where regimes were unchanged (see the figure).

Foreign Exchange Market Turnover in Emerging Market Countries

(Percent of current and capital account flows)

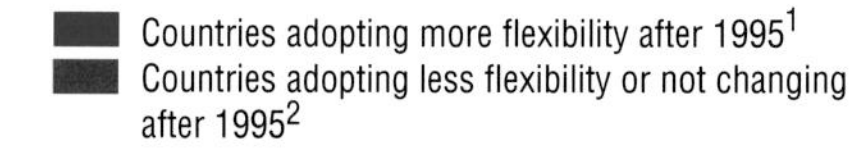

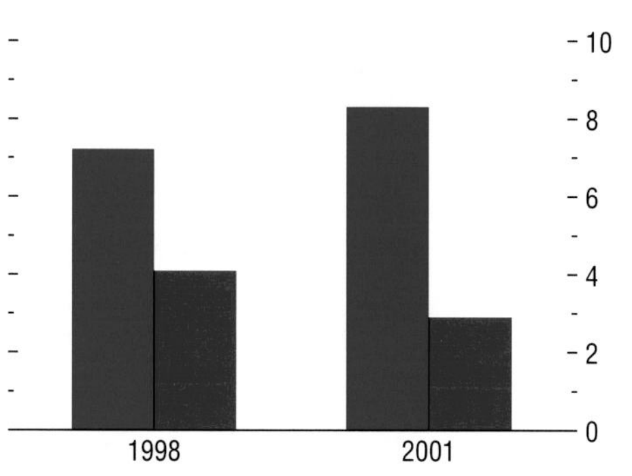

Sources: Bank for International Settlements, *Triennial Central Bank Survey of Foreign Exchange and Derivatives Market Activity,* various issues; and IMF, *International Financial Statistics.*

[1]Brazil, Chile, the Czech Republic, the Philippines, Poland, Russia, South Africa, and Thailand.

[2]Hungary, India, Malaysia, and Mexico.

Emerging market countries have taken other measures to improve the depth and efficiency of their foreign exchange markets.

- *Reducing the central bank's market-making role,* which undercuts other market makers. For example, in Turkey, the central bank gradually withdrew from the market after the lira's flotation in early 2001, forcing market participants to trade among themselves.
- *Increasing market information* on foreign exchange flows and the balance of payments,

Note: The main author of this box is Cem Karacadag. Harald Anderson provided research assistance.

[1]See Duttagupta, Fernández, and Karacadag (2004) for an overview of the operational issues associated with the transition to greater exchange rate flexibility.

as a basis for market participants to develop well-founded views on the exchange rate.

- *Eliminating (or phasing out) regulations that stifle market activity,* among them requirements to surrender foreign exchange receipts to the central bank, taxes and surcharges on foreign exchange transactions, and restrictions on interbank trading.
- *Unifying and simplifying foreign exchange legislation* and avoiding ad hoc and frequent changes to the law to improve market transparency and reduce transaction costs. For example, India (in 1997) and Russia (in 2004) have revised their foreign exchange laws.
- *Facilitating the development of risk-hedging instruments* by lifting controls on forward market activity, once financial institutions achieve a certain level of sophistication in risk management.

Although emerging market countries sometimes announce greater exchange rate flexibility, many are reluctant to actually allow the exchange rate to fluctuate (Calvo and Reinhart, 2002). Central banks frequently intervene to—in their view—correct exchange rate misalignments, contain volatility, and calm disorderly markets. However, the experience of emerging market countries suggests several reasons why interventions should be selective and parsimonious.

- Exchange rate misalignments are difficult to detect, given the variety of methodologies to estimate the equilibrium exchange rate.
- Disorderly markets—defined as a collapse of liquidity—can be hard to distinguish from normal market dynamics. Although signs of market illiquidity include an acceleration in exchange rate changes, a widening of bid-offer spreads, and a sharp increase in interbank trades relative to customer-bank turnover, these can also result from changes in economic fundamentals or the arrival of new information, and may not always warrant intervention by the central bank.
- Official intervention may not always be effective in influencing the exchange rate level or reducing exchange rate volatility. Empirical studies find mixed evidence on the effectiveness of intervention in influencing the exchange rate level and that intervention tends to increase, rather than decrease, exchange rate volatility (Guimarães and Karacadag, 2004; and Tapia and Tokman, 2004).
- Finally, intervention is more effective when it is relatively infrequent, which maximizes the element of surprise and builds market confidence in the official commitment to exchange rate flexibility. Where a band is introduced as part of a gradual transition, intervention episodes may be more frequent, but the central bank should allow full use of the exchange rate flexibility provided by the width of the band.

Transparency in intervention policies also helps to build confidence in the new exchange rate regime, especially in the aftermath of crisis-driven transitions. Many countries, among them the Philippines and Turkey, issued statements and published policy reports affirming their commitment to a market-determined exchange rate and confirming that intervention would not be conducted to target a certain exchange rate level. Moreover, a public commitment to the objectives of intervention enables market scrutiny of and accountability for the central bank's foreign exchange operations. For example, the published intervention policies of Australia and Sweden are clear on the reasons for and the objectives of intervention -(Rankin, 2001; and Sveriges Riksbank, 2002).

In sum, the development of the foreign exchange market and official intervention policies are important to support a more flexible exchange rate regime. Foreign exchange market development and exchange rate flexibility are mutually reinforcing: there is no better way to prepare for operating a flexible exchange rate regime than to introduce some flexibility in the first place. In the same vein, monetary authorities can facilitate market development by reducing their presence in the market, formulating clear and transparent intervention objectives, and intervening selectively and parsimoniously.

Figure 2.13. Central Bank Independence in Emerging Markets[1]

(Countries classified according to exchange rate regime in 2003)

The central banks of emerging market countries that have free floats in 2003 appear to be, on average, more independent than the central banks of emerging market countries classified with peg/intermediate regimes.

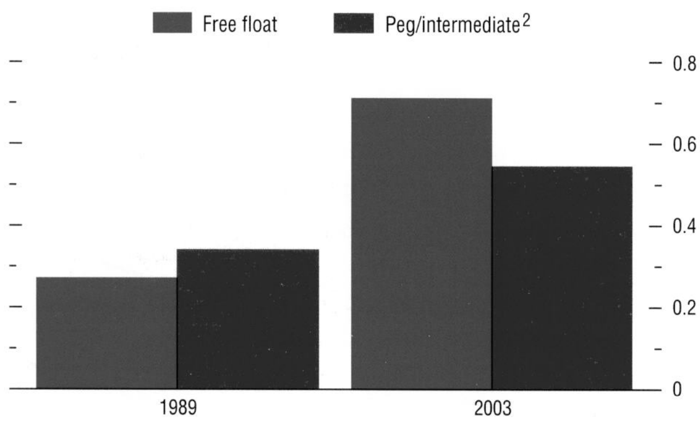

Sources: Arnone and Laurens (2004); and IMF staff calculations.
[1]This measures central bank political and economic independence following the definition by Grilli, Masciandaro, and Tabellini (1991). The indicator ranges from 0 to 1, where a higher score indicates a higher level of central bank independence.
[2]This includes only one country with a peg in 2003.

Figure 2.14. Exchange Rate Regimes of Emerging Markets and Inflation Targeting, 2003

Ninety percent of emerging market countries classified as free floating are inflation targeters, compared with 40 percent of emerging market countries with intermediate floats.

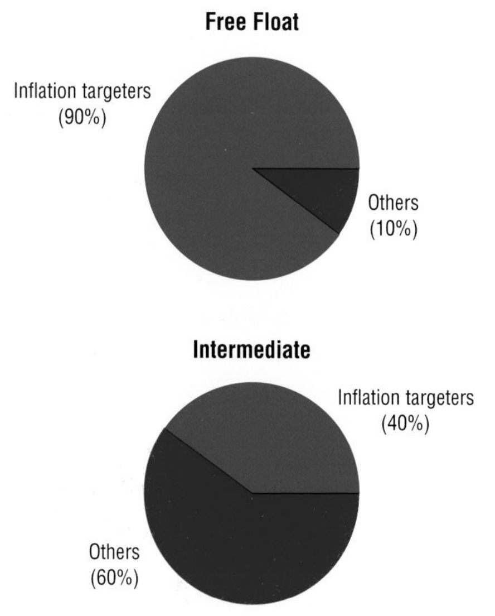

Sources: Stone and Roger (2004); and IMF staff calculations.

rate regime. Therefore, by strengthening balance sheets, bank supervision can support greater exchange rate flexibility. The countries that made transitions to more flexible regimes on average had, before the transition, better bank supervision than their respective control groups. Also, crisis-driven transitions were associated with improvements in bank supervision around the time of transition though the latest available data (for 2002) suggest that countries that effected voluntary transitions on average have better-quality bank supervision than countries that experienced crisis-driven transitions.[38]

- *Securities market development.* In many emerging market countries, banks and nonfinancial firms usually face a shortage of long-term funding. This exposes them to cash flow and liquidity problems, which may constrain the conduct of monetary policy (Mishkin, 1996). The development of longer-term securities markets eases these constraints by lengthening the average maturity of financial instruments in the economy. In fact, countries that moved from intermediate regimes to free floats had above-average securities market development compared with the relevant control group. Again, crisis-driven transitions were associated with further securities market development.

The latest available data (for 2002) suggest that financial sector supervision and development in countries with free floats are on average stronger than those of countries with pegs or intermediate regimes (Figure 2.16). However, even among free floats there is substantial variation in the quality of bank supervision. Moreover, financial sector supervision and development in countries with intermediate regimes are not significantly stronger than those in countries with pegs.

[38]It is possible that the improvements in the quality of banking supervision in the countries that had crisis-driven transitions were a reaction to large costs of cleaning up the banking sector following the crisis, and not a reaction to the adoption of a floating rate per se.

Financial Sector Liberalization

When financial sector supervision is strong and financial institutions are healthy, gradual liberalization generally supports growth.[39] However, if financial sector supervision is weak, then it may be desirable to maintain financial controls, even while moving ahead with exchange rate flexibility. The extent of liberalization is measured using indicators from Abiad and Mody (2003), with increasing values showing greater liberalization.

- *Domestic financial liberalization* that is not supported by good bank supervision can allow risky behavior that weakens balance sheets and thus curtails the central bank's ability to stabilize inflation (Eichengreen and others, 1998). Liberalization may allow insolvent financial institutions to engage in potentially lucrative but risky projects, using expensive funding to "gamble for redemption." Also, by granting banks access to more complex financial instruments, evaluating bank balance sheets may become more difficult. It appears that countries that experienced crisis-driven transitions from pegs to intermediate regimes had, at the time of the transition, on average more liberalized domestic financial systems than countries that made voluntary transitions and countries in the control group (Figure 2.17).[40]
- *External financial liberalization.* As with domestic financial liberalization, if external financial liberalization is not supported by strong financial sector supervision, it can increase risks, such as the potential for sudden reversals of capital inflows. Indeed, countries that made voluntary transitions from pegs to intermediate regimes had, prior to the transition, on average less external financial liberalization

Figure 2.15. Indicators of Financial Sector Supervision and Development[1]

(t = 0 is year of transition; scale 0 to 3 with 3 representing strongest supervision and development)

Voluntary transitions on average had better quality bank supervision than their respective control groups in the period before the transition.

Quality of Bank Supervision

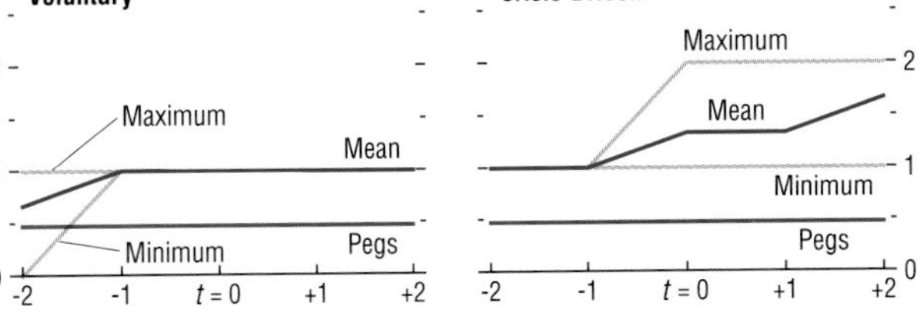

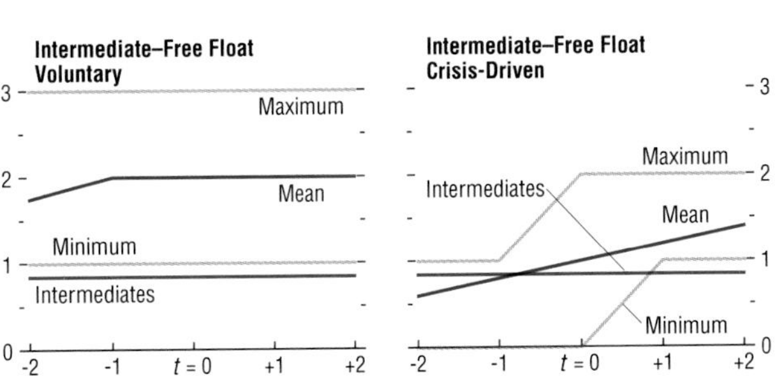

Securities Market Development

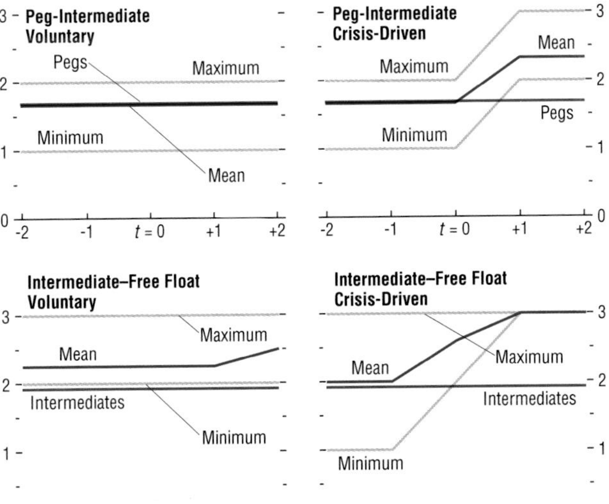

Sources: Abiad and Mody (2003); and IMF staff calculations; see Appendix 2.2 for variable definitions.

[1]The pegs/intermediates control groups are averages for the countries whose exchange rate regime is the same as the starting regime of transitioning countries in periods that are not within three years of a transition. Only countries with observations for all periods shown around the time of transition are included.

[39]Chapter IV of the October 2001 *World Economic Outlook.*

[40]The degree of domestic financial liberalization is measured by a composite index that assesses the extent to which direct credit controls, reserve requirements, and interest rate controls have been abolished, entry barriers against foreign banks eliminated, and the banking system privatized.

Figure 2.16. Financial Policy Frameworks, 2002[1]

(Averages across countries by type of exchange rate regime; scale 0 to 3 with 3 representing strongest policy frameworks)

Although emerging market countries classified as free floats on average have stronger financial policy frameworks than emerging market countries classified as having pegs or intermediate regimes, there is substantial variation in the quality of bank supervision even among the free floaters.

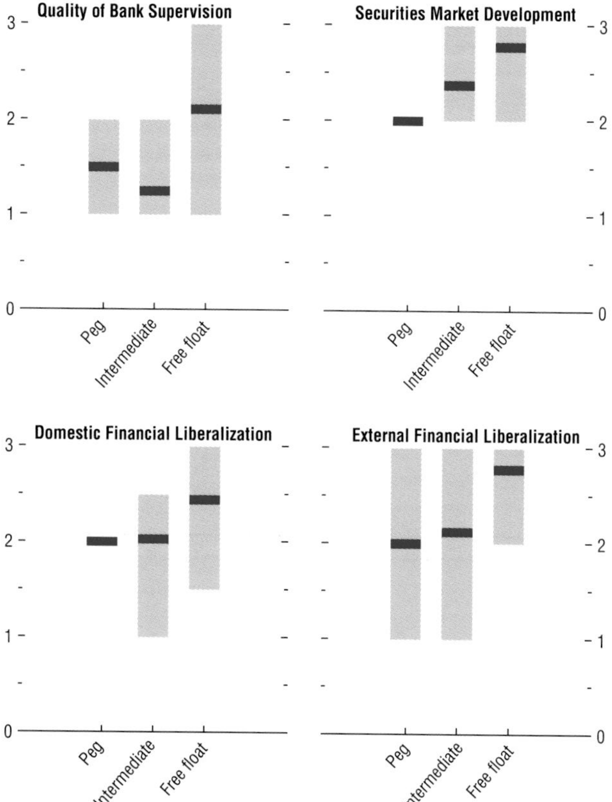

Sources: Abiad and Mody (2003); and IMF staff calculations; see Appendix 2.2 for variable definitions.

[1]The top of the bar represents the maximum; the dark blue line represents the mean; and the bottom of the bar represents the minimum value. Peg includes Morocco and Malaysia; intermediate includes Argentina, Egypt, Israel, Thailand, India, Indonesia, Pakistan, and Venezuela; free float includes Brazil, Chile, Colombia, Korea, Mexico, Peru, the Philippines, South Africa, and Turkey.

than countries that experienced crisis-driven transitions and countries in the control group.[41] By contrast, voluntary transitions from intermediate regimes to free floats were associated with a higher degree of external financial liberalization than in the control group, reflecting in part the higher levels of bank supervision and securities market development than in the control group.

The latest available data (for 2002) suggest that countries with free floats have more liberalized financial systems than countries with pegs or intermediate regimes, consistent with the fact that—in countries with less flexible exchange rates—external financial liberalization reduces the room to pursue independent monetary policy.

Concluding Remarks

Exchange rate flexibility in emerging market countries has increased substantially over the past decade. The share of emerging market countries with free floats rose from virtually zero in the early 1990s to more than one-third in recent years. While there have been some transitions toward less flexible regimes, most have been toward greater flexibility. The numbers of peg-to-intermediate and intermediate-to-free-float transitions were broadly similar, and both were nearly evenly split between voluntary and crisis-driven transitions. There were no transitions from pegs to free floats in the sample. Moreover, the transitions were broadly evenly distributed across regions.

Voluntary transitions were generally not associated with an increase in macroeconomic instability. Although the results are based on a small

[41]External financial liberalization is measured by a composite rules-based index that captures whether there are restrictions on capital inflows and outflows and whether the exchange rate system is unified. The main drawback of rules-based measures of capital controls is that they aim to capture restrictions irrespective of their effectiveness. However, using the outcome-based measure of capital controls constructed by Edison and Warnock (2003) yields similar results.

sample and could reflect sample selection bias, key indicators such as growth and real exchange rate overvaluation, among others, were on average little affected by the transition. Indeed, inflation performance continued to improve after the transitions, and, while exchange rate volatility increased a little immediately after the transitions, it soon returned to a level similar to that in the pretransition period.

Transitions to greater exchange rate flexibility were generally associated with a strengthening of monetary and financial policy frameworks, consistent with the idea that such moves can be facilitated by investing in "learning to float." Compared with the average behavior in the relevant control group, transitions to greater exchange rate flexibility over the past 10 years have been associated with increased central bank independence, the adoption of inflation targeting, and—for crisis-driven transitions—improved bank supervision and further securities markets development (in the case of intermediate to free float transitions). However, there clearly remains scope to further strengthen policy frameworks even in countries that already have free floats.

Many countries moved to more flexible exchange rate regimes while still in the process of strengthening their policy frameworks. It is true that, prior to the transition, bank supervision was generally stronger in countries making voluntary transitions than in the control groups, and that securities markets were more developed in countries that made voluntary transitions from intermediate to free floats. By contrast, only one country had introduced full-fledged inflation targeting before moving to a free float. Also, countries making a voluntary first step toward exchange rate flexibility had on average less financial liberalization than the control group.

Has Fiscal Behavior Changed Under the European Economic and Monetary Union?

The main authors of this essay are Xavier Debrun and Hamid Faruqee, with support from Roel Beetsma. Paul Atang provided research assistance.

Figure 2.17. Indicators of Financial Sector Liberalization[1]

(t = 0 is year of transition; scale 0 to 3 with 3 representing most liberalized)

Voluntary transitions from pegs to intermediate floats on average had less liberalized domestic and external financial systems than the control group.

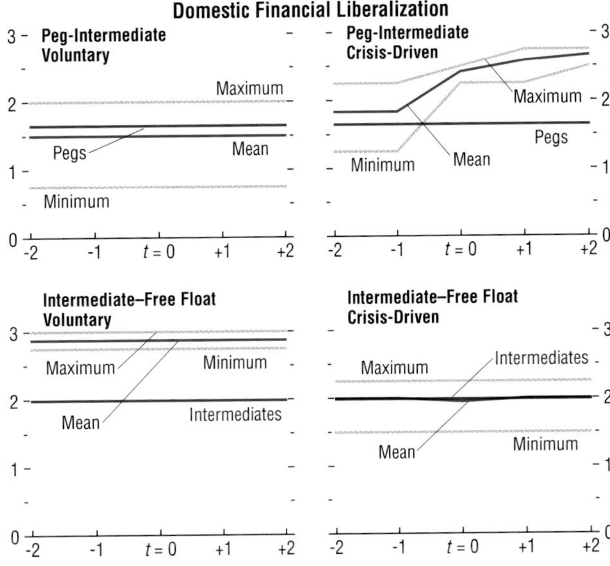

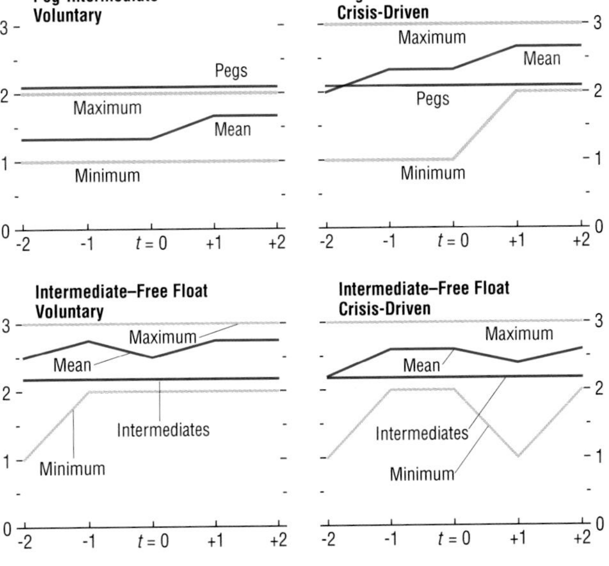

Sources: Abiad and Mody (2003); and IMF staff calculations; see Appendix 2.2 for variable definitions.

[1]The pegs/intermediates control groups are averages for the countries whose exchange rate regime is the same as the starting regime of transitioning countries in periods that are not within three years of a transition. Only countries with observations for all periods shown around the time of transition are included.

The adoption of the euro by 11 member states of the European Union on January 1, 1999 marked the birth of a currency conceived 30 years earlier, when the Heads of States and Governments of the then European Community declared "*. . . that the process of integration should end in a Community of stability and growth . . . with a view to the creation of an economic and monetary union.*" After five years, there is now sufficient experience to make a preliminary assessment of how the European Economic and Monetary Union (EMU) may have affected policymakers' behavior. Of course, any conclusion in that respect inevitably remains tentative as such a profound regime change may take quite some time to impinge on average behaviors. Within this, the impact on fiscal policy—the only macroeconomic instrument available to national policymakers in a currency union—appears particularly important.

Of course, the effects of monetary unification go well beyond the macroeconomic policy sphere. The efficiency gains expected from the symbiosis between a single market and a single currency (Emerson and others, 1990), and the expanding role of the euro as an international currency are clearly critical; indeed, reduced transaction costs, greater price transparency, and lower uncertainty have already contributed to deeper trade and financial integration, aided by progress in regulatory reform (see Box 2.5). These developments are contributing to move EMU[42] closer to an "optimum currency area" (Mundell, 1961), where greater flexibility in product and labor markets lessens the need for country-specific fiscal stabilization policies. Although advancing structural reforms will accelerate this trend, there is still a long way to go, and country-specific macroeconomic stabilization will remain a central issue in the policy debate for the foreseeable future.

The role that national governments can play in providing such stabilization raises the issue of how fiscal policies can best serve that objective. There is a broad consensus that the *automatic stabilizers*—that is, the automatic variations in revenues and expenditures in response to changes in output and employment—should be allowed to operate fully over the business cycle, but the question whether governments should deliberately attempt to further stabilize the economy with *discretionary* budgetary actions is more contentious, particularly in countries where the tax system and social transfers imply large automatic stabilizers. Support for "active" fiscal stabilization policies under EMU is nonetheless growing (Calmfors, 2003; or Taylor, 2000) and, as documented below, appears to have emerged as a key feature of the recent protracted downturn. The potential conflict between active fiscal policies and a rules-based macroeconomic framework[43] (see Buti, In't Veld, and Roeger, 2001) has also been a factor in the increasingly active debate of the reform of the SGP itself, spurred by the fact that half the current members of the euro area are to various degrees at odds with the agreed standards of fiscal discipline.

Against this background, this essay seeks to answer the following three questions.

- To what extent do individual member states still need country-specific macroeconomic stabilization? And does this imply a strong case for deliberate fiscal policy actions to supplement automatic stabilizers?
- How have the fiscal authorities of countries now in the euro area behaved over the past three decades? To what extent were those behaviors consistent with the euro area's rules-based fiscal framework, which pre-supposes efficient stabilization policies and adherence to clear discipline standards?
- How has the SGP affected fiscal behaviors? In particular, has it fundamentally changed the

[42]Although the "first phase" of EMU officially started in March 1990, with the complete liberalization of capital movements, this essay will restrict the use of EMU to the "third phase" of monetary unification—that is, the introduction of the euro in 1999.

[43]Various sources give a detailed description of EMU's macroeconomic framework, including Chapter III of the October 1997 *World Economic Outlook.*

way governments conceive discretionary fiscal actions, for instance by enhancing their macroeconomic stabilization role?[44]

To assess the need for country-specific macroeconomic stabilization, the essay first describes real and nominal disparities within EMU, paying particular attention to the stabilizing response of relative prices (competitiveness) to real divergences. As governments may also try to coordinate the monetary-fiscal *policy mix* at the national level, the analysis looks at the gap between the common monetary policy and a hypothetical monetary stance commensurate to each country. The essay then analyzes fiscal policy behavior in individual euro area member states over the past three decades and examines their potential determinants, emphasizing the effect of EMU's fiscal framework. It concludes with some short-term and medium-term policy implications.

Does EMU Increase the Need for Stabilizing Fiscal Policies?

When economically diverse regions or countries share the same monetary policy, the costs of country-specific disturbances are potentially large. Early analyses of EMU generally concluded that these costs would be greater than in comparable federal currency unions such as Canada or the United States[45] because product and labor markets remained more segmented and price adjustment more sluggish; factors of production, and especially labor, did not move as swiftly from regions in recession to regions in expansion; and no significant centralized transfer system in favor of regions faced with a downturn existed or was likely to be created.

Looking at the magnitude of cross-country disparities (Figure 2.18), the 15 years preceding the

[44]It should be kept in mind that macroeconomic stabilization is only one among three key functions of fiscal policy, which also include redistribution and allocative efficiency.

[45]See Bayoumi and Eichengreen (1997) and Bayoumi and Masson (1998) on the operation of those adjustment mechanisms in the Canadian and U.S. currency unions. For a first assessment of adjustment mechanisms in EMU, see Deroose, Langelijk, and Roeger (2004).

Figure 2.18. Cross-Country Dispersion of Selected Economic Indicators
(Standard deviations)

Although a great deal of convergence has been achieved in financial variables and inflation rates, real divergences remain significant in the euro area.

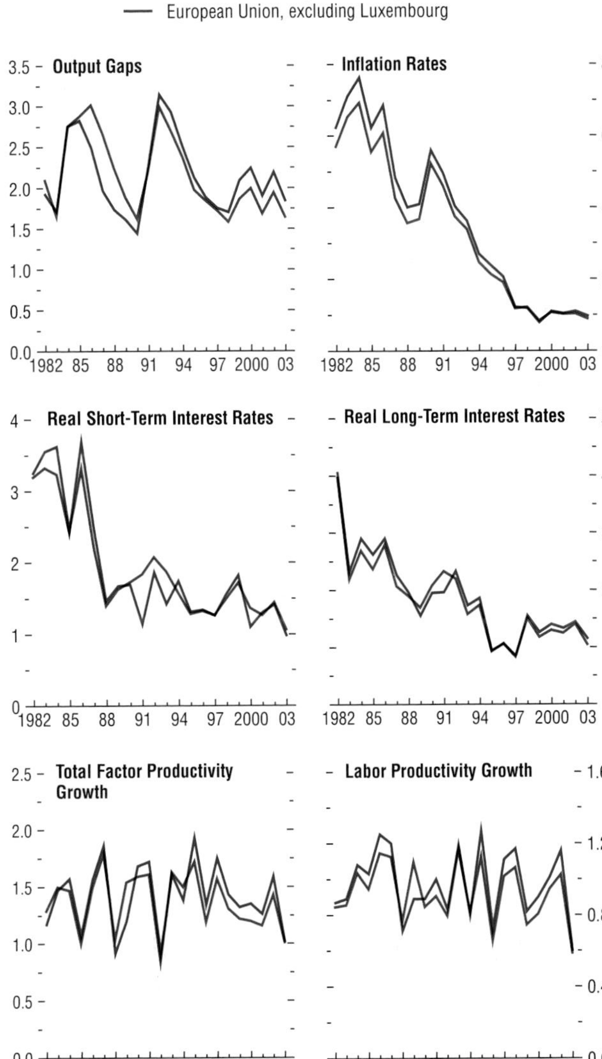

Sources: OECD analytical database; European Commission, Annual Macroeconomic Database; and IMF staff calculations.

Box 2.5. Trade and Financial Integration in Europe: Five Years After the Euro's Introduction

Five years ago, the advent of the euro marked a historic milestone on the path to European integration. Though the nature of this young currency union continues to evolve, the euro's impact on the economic landscape—at both the macroeconomic and microeconomic level—is already quite visible. The most salient change, of course, has been the replacement of member states' national currencies with the euro—the symbol of Economic and Monetary Union (EMU). In conjunction with the new currency, EMU also established new institutions underlying the conduct of area-wide monetary and fiscal policies, most notably the European Central Bank (ECB) and the fiscal framework known as the Stability and Growth Pact (SGP). But in addition to these up-front "macroeconomic" transformations—discussed more in detail in the main text—the euro's existence over the past five years has also had a catalytic role for the functioning of specific markets. Specifically, in the realms of trade and finance, the single currency has impelled changes that have fostered greater market integration—a process that is ongoing.

Trade within the euro area has benefited from lower costs of foreign exchange transactions, the elimination of exchange rate uncertainty, and greater price transparency. Whether trade has appreciably increased since the euro's arrival, however, ultimately remains an empirical question. Estimating the precise trade effects of EMU has been the subject of renewed interest since the work of Rose (2000) and Glick and Rose (2002), who found that trade flows among partner countries belonging to the same currency union were strikingly larger (on the order of 100 to 200 percent) than if these countries had currencies of their own. While much subsequent work has suggested that the trade gains are not that large, the basic finding—that currency unions have significant trade-creating effects—has held up reasonably well (see Rose, 2004, for a survey). Nevertheless, most of these studies did *not* include the euro area in the sample for lack of observations. More recently, Micco, Stein, and Ordoñez (2003) have focused on the trade effects of EMU in the context of the so-called "gravity model" of trade, which essentially assumes that trade flows between countries decrease with the distance between them but increase with their respective economic mass. The study examines whether EMU membership figured as an additional and independent determinant of goods trade. It finds that—when compared with trade among other industrial countries—intra-area trade flows have received a significant boost from monetary union with no harm to extra-area trade flows. Hence, the euro seems to have *created* trade, not *diverted* it.

The figure shows the estimated impact of EMU on goods trade within the euro area, based on the results in Faruqee (2004), which employs a methodology similar to Micco, Stein, and Ordoñez (2003). The trade effects (on average) are significant in a statistical sense and indeed quite sizable considering that the currency union is still quite young. In that sense, these findings should be interpreted as a "progress report" of the effects to date. The figure also shows, however, that the trade benefits of the euro have not been evenly distributed. Some countries have benefited to a greater extent and continue to do so as dispersion measures of trade effects at the country level have not narrowed over time. This may naturally reflect differences in the structure of trade, but also different capacities to reap the benefits that may accrue from joining a currency area. It is thus important not to take these trade gains for granted, but focus instead on structural measures needed to increase them.

Financial integration has taken an even more visible leap forward since the introduction of the euro. Enhanced market competition has been the main driver behind financial integration in Europe, complemented by regulatory harmonization efforts at the EU level—in the form of the Financial Services Action Plan. While overall progress has been considerable, the pace of integration across various euro area financial markets has been uneven. (See

Note: The main author of this box is Hamid Faruqee.

Measuring Trade and Financial Integration in Europe
(Percent)

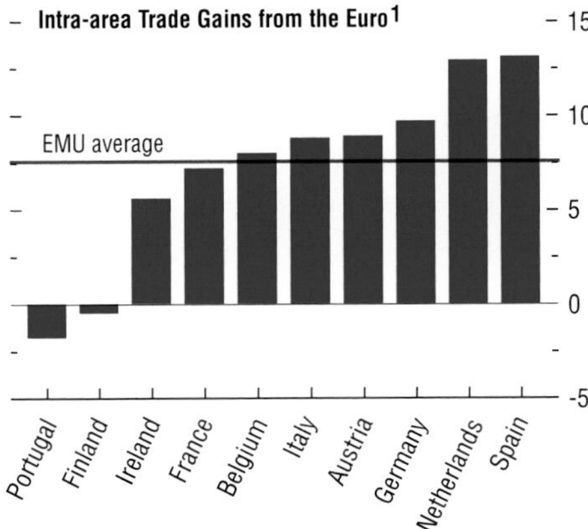

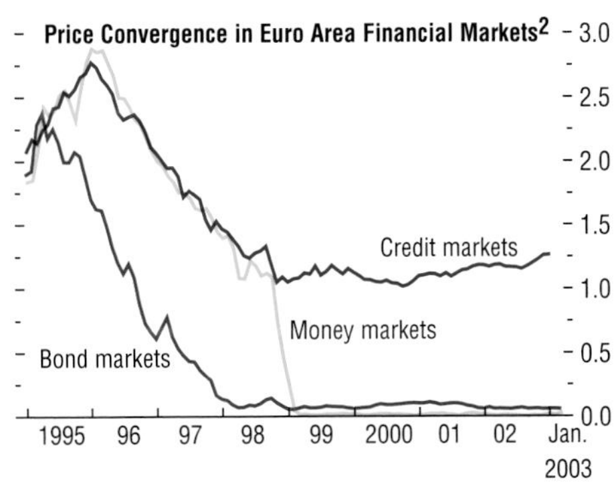

Sources: European Central Bank; and IMF staff calculations.
[1]See Faruqee (2004). Greece joined the euro area in 2001 and is therefore not comparable with the other countries.
[2]Cross-sectional standard deviation in overnight lending rates, 10-year government bond yields, and bank lending and deposit rates.

Commission of the European Communities, 2004; and Baele and others, 2004.) At present, money markets have shown the most integration, essentially forming a single market, particularly for (unsecured) money market (e.g., EONIA and EURIBOR) instruments. Bond markets, particularly for short-term government securities, have also become much more closely integrated. Equity and credit markets—particularly on the retail side—however, remain more fragmented. Major hurdles to further integration include national differences in legal frameworks—e.g., bankruptcy and consumer protection laws—and taxation.

The figure shows the degree of financial integration—as measured by price convergence—across euro area money, bond, and credit markets. In principle, deeper, more integrated financial markets should eliminate price differentials for financial assets with the same risk-return characteristics. Return differentials in money markets have indeed vanished after 1999. Similarly, the dispersion of bond yields has narrowed considerably. Credit markets—represented by various bank lending and deposit rates, however, have shown limited convergence, reflecting barriers such as the importance of geographical proximity. Other measures—for example, based on quantities rather than prices—generally exhibit signs of increasing integration. For example, the "home bias" in portfolios—that is, the tendency to hold a disproportionately large share of assets from one's own country—is on the decline as cross-border diversification across area-wide markets rises, particularly among institutional investors. Cross-border mergers and acquisitions activity, however, has been subdued, particularly in banking where consolidation has predominantly occurred along national boundaries.

Overall, substantial progress has been made in further integrating the euro area's product and financial markets since the birth of the euro. With the five-year-old currency serving as the catalyst, market forces, supported by regulatory harmonization efforts at the EU level, have been the primary driver in that process. Further economic integration holds the promise of substantial gains as the euro area's real and financial resources are allocated more efficiently, but securing additional gains will require addressing national barriers and enhancing market flexibility. In particular, effective national implementation of existing policy initiatives (e.g., the Financial Services Action Plan) and the design of new policy measures (e.g., competition and labor market policies) will be increasingly important.

Figure 2.19. Real Interest Rates and Competitiveness

In sharp contrast with the pre-1999 period, movements in real interest rates were significantly smaller after 1999, hardly contributing to stabilize national economies. In some cases, changes in real interest rates were even destabilizing.

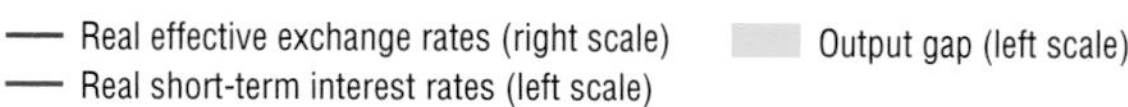

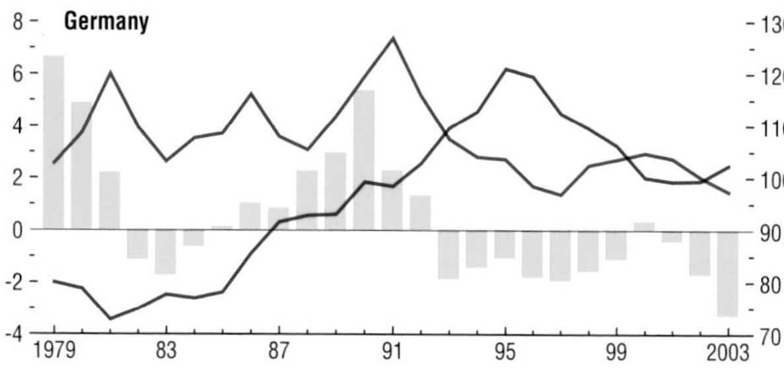

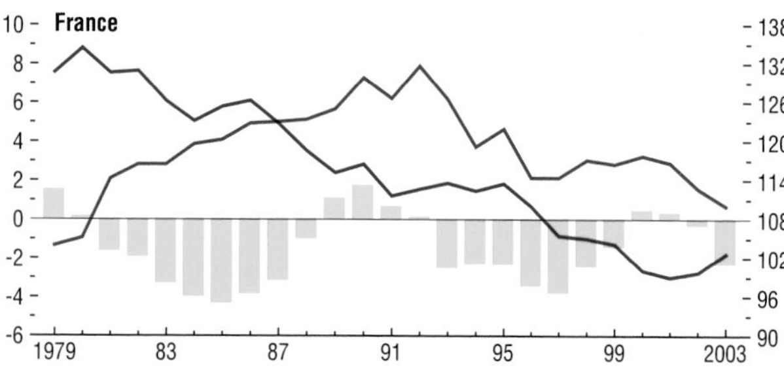

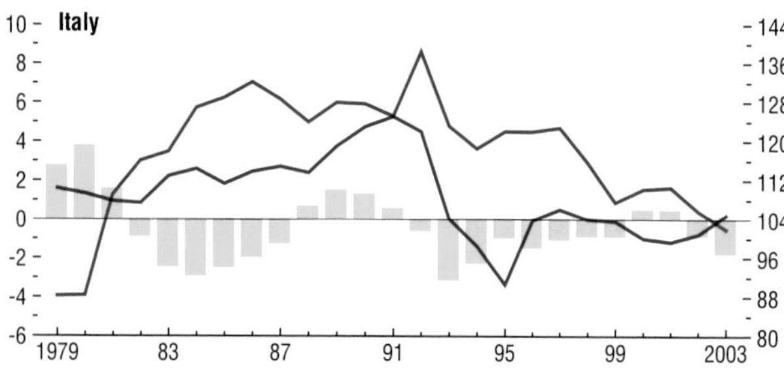

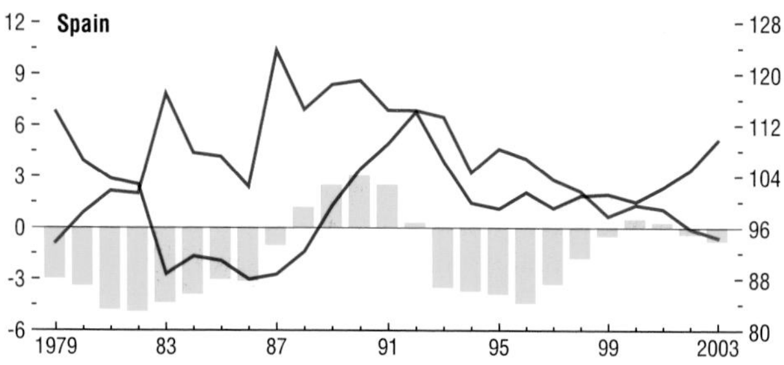

introduction of the euro witnessed a remarkable convergence of inflation and interest rates. The convergence process, driven by increasingly similar policies, received a further impetus from the nominal convergence criteria laid out in the Maastricht Treaty (1992). By contrast, real disparities, in terms of productivity differentials as well as relative business cycle positions,[46] did not exhibit any clear trend. Since 1999, real disparities have persisted—despite the recent synchronized downturn—whereas inflation and real interest rate differentials have increased somewhat. Under EMU, rising inflation differentials partly reflect market-driven price adjustments to dissimilar cyclical patterns, as goods produced in booming economies become more expensive relative to those produced in sluggish regions. Other important factors include the volatility of the euro vis-à-vis other currencies, given different degrees of openness to non-EMU trade (Honohan and Lane, 2003), and productivity growth differentials (productivity gains are often located in sectors exposed to external competition while the corresponding wage pressures are more widespread, forcing other sectors to raise prices to keep up with higher labor costs).

Did inflation differentials ultimately contribute to stabilize output? That is an open question and the answer depends on the country. The effect on real interest rates has tended to be procyclical (Box 2.5 and Figure 2.18) with rising inflation in booming economies, especially Ireland, the Netherlands, and Portugal, leading to lower real interest rates, stimulating domestic demand even further (Figure 2.19). Similarly, in countries experiencing protracted downturns, such as Germany, falling inflation tended to result in relatively high real rates. In fact, the estimated average stabilizing response of the real short-term interest rate to the output gap disap-

[46]Cross-country standard deviations do not account for the relative economic size of member states, and may exaggerate the challenge posed by those disparities to monetary authorities. Given the essay's concern for national fiscal policies, it appears appropriate to consider each individual country on an equal footing throughout the essay.

Table 2.3. Euro Area: Real Short-Term Interest Rates and Competitiveness

	Estimated Average Response of the Real Short-Term Interest Rate to the Output Gap	
	Before EMU[1]	0.18***
	After EMU[1]	−0.01
	Estimated Average Response of the Real Effective Exchange Rate to:	
Output gap	Before EMU[1]	0.44***
	After EMU[1]	−0.20
Real interest rate	Before EMU	−0.26***
	After EMU[2]	−0.64***

Source: IMF staff estimates.

Note: Panel estimates for euro area member states (excluding Luxembourg) over the period 1982–2003. Equations estimated by three-stage least-squares to account for correlation between residuals and dependent variables. *** indicates that the estimated response is significantly different from zero at the 1 percent level.

[1]A positive sign indicates a stabilizing response.

[2]After EMU, a negative sign indicates a stabilizing response.

peared after EMU (Table 2.3). On the other hand, the effect on external competitiveness should be stabilizing, since higher inflation leads to real appreciation (and vice versa). In practice, however, the stabilizing effect of inflation differentials through this channel does not seem to have been particularly strong (Figure 2.19 and Table 2.3), although in the specific case of booming countries confronted with declining real interest rates, the real exchange response appears to have increased since EMU was adopted (bottom panel of Table 2.3).

But to what extent do such disparities make the common monetary policy at odds with each country's needs? One crude but simple way to look into that issue is to compare actual short-term interest rates with country-specific benchmarks generated by a monetary policy "rule" (Taylor, 1993). Despite obvious shortcomings,[47] these rules yield a useful first-order approximation of an "appropriate" monetary policy, assum-

[47]Taylor (1999) shows that these rules perform quite well for the (large and relatively closed) U.S. economy over the 1980s and the 1990s. Significant deviations from the rules are nevertheless inevitable in particular instances (for instance, during asset price bubbles and their aftermath), and when external competitiveness is critical (as in small open economies).

Figure 2.19 ***(concluded)***

Destabilizing moves in the real interest rates were particularly pronounced in Ireland and to a lesser extent in the Netherlands.

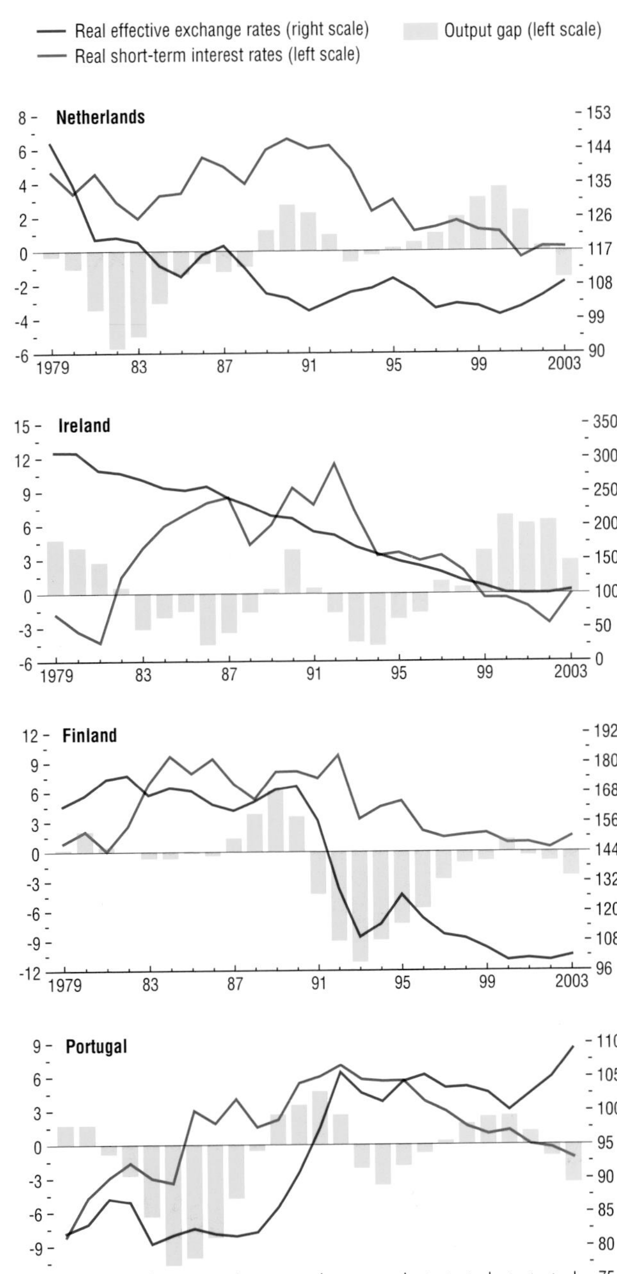

Sources: OECD analytical database; and IMF staff calculations.

Figure 2.20. Monetary Policy Rules for Selected Euro Area Economies
(Percent)

Prior to 1999, short-term interest rates were broadly in line with the benchmarks in Germany only, signaling the leadership position held by the Bundesbank within the European exchange rate mechanism. After the euro, deviations from the benchmarks were smaller in the other two large economies but increased in Germany toward the end of the period. Elsewhere, substantial deviations continued.

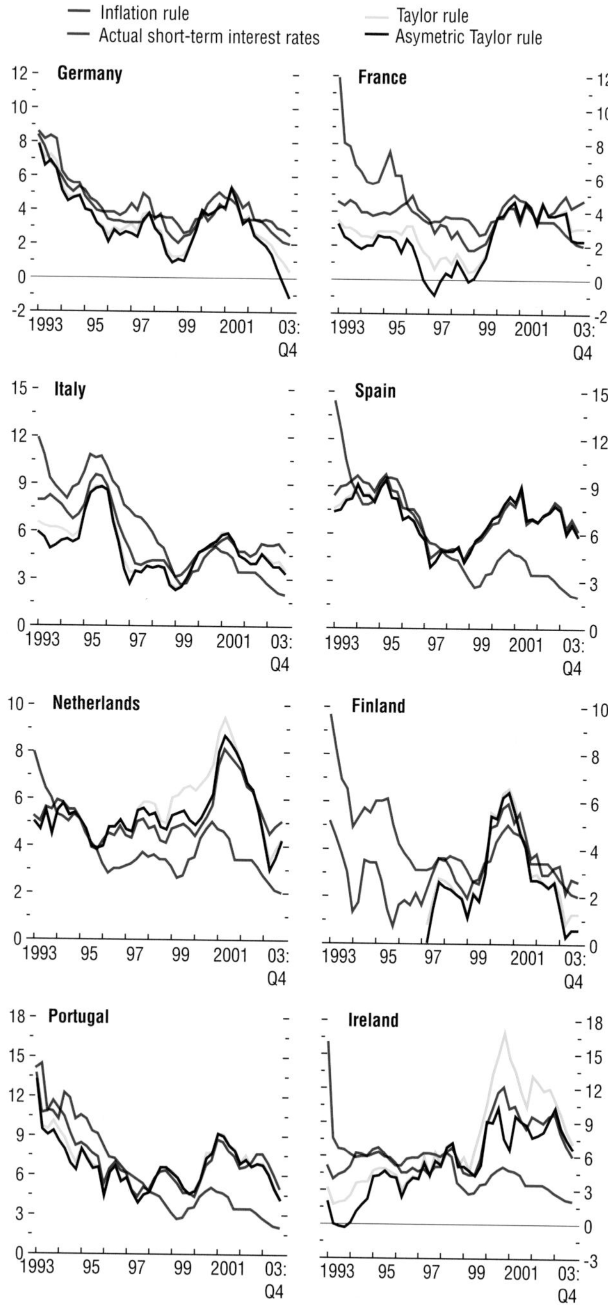

Sources: OECD analytical database; and IMF staff calculations.

ing that short-term interest rates should move to close the output gap and bring inflation in line with a pre-set target. Different policy rules were considered (see Appendix 2.3), each allowing for two country-specific elements—namely, "neutral" policy rates above potential GDP growth[48] and inflation targets in line with cross-country differences in productivity growth (see above) but consistent with the ECB' s objective of keeping area-wide inflation "below but close to 2 percent."

Prior to 1999, monetary gaps (defined here as the difference between actual rates and the relevant benchmarks) were significant and generally positive for all countries except Germany (Figure 2.20)—a clear indication of the Bundesbank's dominant position in the Exchange Rate Mechanism. After the inception of EMU, monetary gaps became more typical of a monetary policy calibrated for the euro area as whole. In Germany, they became larger—especially at the end of the period—reflecting the particularly protracted slowdown in that country; in France and Italy, in contrast, they tended to decline. The smaller economies experiencing different cyclical patterns from the rest of the area—meaning in general above-average growth—continued to face large, and mostly negative, gaps.

Given the persistent cyclical disparities and relatively weak adjustment mechanisms, there would—as noted above—appear to be a prima facie case for active fiscal policies to counteract local disturbances, an argument that seems even more persuasive given the potentially greater effectiveness of fiscal policy in a currency area. Indeed, the typical offsetting effects of a fiscal stimulus through higher interest rates and exchange rate appreciation are much weaker because both variables are determined by area-wide developments.[49] Has greater activism

[48]If that is not the case, no well-defined limit to debt accumulation by economic agents exists, as income growth can always make up for higher interest payments.

[49]This is especially the case if the economy is small (little effect on union-wide interest rates) and if it trades a

indeed been observed? Or has the SGP hampered stabilizing fiscal impulses? To answer these questions, the remainder of this essay is devoted to a more detailed look at the factors explaining fiscal policy behavior in the euro area.

What Drives Fiscal Policies in the Euro Area?

To understand the forces shaping fiscal policymaking in the euro area, the IMF staff began by calculating fiscal "reaction functions" for each euro area country over the past 30 years, building on—and extending—substantial existing work in this area.[50] A fiscal reaction function relates fiscal policy decisions—here proxied by the *cyclically adjusted* primary balance of the general government (Galí and Perotti, 2003)—to the various objectives and constraints that governments face, including the gap between actual and potential GDP, the level of the public debt, and the monetary gap (as above, defined as the differences between actual short-term interest rates and the benchmark interest rate, and capturing the extent to which area-wide monetary policy is inconsistent with local conditions).

The key results—supported by the econometric evidence in Appendix 2.4—are the following (see Figure 2.21):

- *Discretionary fiscal policies in euro area countries over the past three decades have generally been procyclical—that is, expansionary in good times, contractionary in bad times— thereby undermining the role of automatic stabilizers.* Fiscal policy was countercyclical only in Austria (where the effect was statistically insignificant) and Finland.

Figure 2.21. Fiscal Behavior in the Euro Area
(Estimates over 1971–2003)

Country-specific reaction functions reveal a tendency toward policies that destabilize output instead of stabilizing it. Most countries also actively seek to stabilize their debt ratios. Some member states systematically respond to deviations in short-term interest rates from their benchmarks.

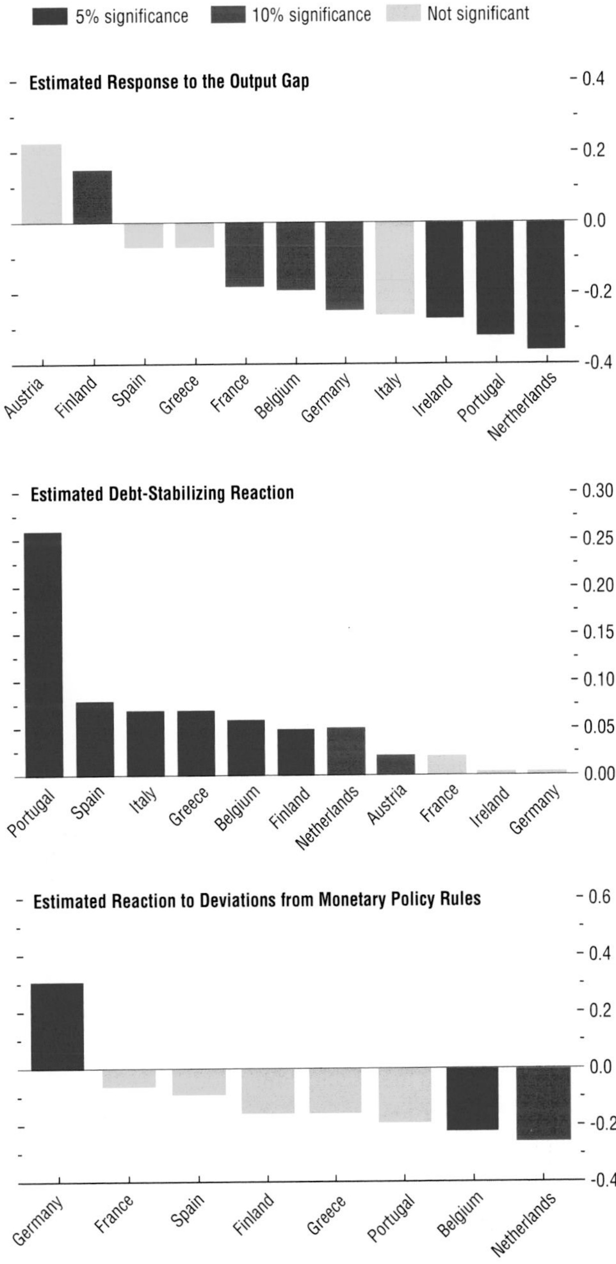

Source: IMF staff calculations.

lot more with other member states than with extra-union partners (the exchange rate of the common currency matters little for competitiveness). Of course, this does not change the fact that fiscal policy effectiveness in small economies is inevitably limited by greater leakages to trading partners.

[50]These studies include, among others, Mélitz (1997), Bohn (1998), Debrun and Wyplosz (1999), von Hagen, Hughes Hallett, and Strauch (2001), Jaeger (2001), Ballabriga and Martinez-Mongay (2002), Favero (2002), Fatás and Mihov (2003), Galí and Perotti (2003), and Muscatelli, Tirelli, and Trecroci (2004).

- *Most countries have tightened fiscal policy in response to high public debt ratios, in line with long-term sustainability requirements.* Only France, Germany, and Ireland exhibit a weaker sensitivity, pointing to large swings in debt ratios over the sample period. Steep upward trends in public debt ratios were indeed observed in the first two countries, whereas in Ireland the prominent role of growth (as opposed to policy) in driving the debt-to-GDP ratio presumably explains the result.
- *Some countries have systematically reacted to monetary policy.* In line with Mélitz (1997) and subsequent studies, it appears that some governments have sought to offset monetary policy gaps, signaling conflicts between monetary and fiscal authorities over the policy mix. Even though the evidence to date is generally weak in a statistical sense, such a pattern may well continue or even amplify under EMU, considering the potential for large monetary gaps illustrated above. In Germany, however, fiscal and monetary policies have been found to generally go hand in hand, pointing to an apparent consensus on the orientation of the policy mix.[51]
- *Only three member states (France, Greece, and the Netherlands) appear to have experienced substantial and lasting changes in fiscal behavior following the Maastricht Treaty.* This suggests either that there was only a limited effect (in scope or time) on government incentives elsewhere or—at least in some cases—that national fiscal setups were already broadly consistent with Maastricht's rules-based approach. Of course, that assessment concerns fiscal policy parameters taken as a whole and, as the remainder of the analysis shows, does not preclude significant changes in specific dimensions of policymaking, nor temporary shifts in overall behavior such as during major adjustment episodes.

These results—broadly in line with those in the existing literature—tend to confirm that country-specific factors have played a substantial role in shaping policymakers' incentives. Among those, fiscal institutions (e.g., von Hagen, Hallerberg, and Strauch, 2004), various features of the political system (e.g., Tornell and Lane, 1999; Lane, 2003; Hallerberg and Strauch, 2002), and structural characteristics of the economy (e.g., Lane, 2003) have been shown to play an important role. Given that EMU's fiscal framework could be expected to operate precisely through such channels, a deeper understanding of the role of these factors is critical to assess its potential impact on national policymaking.

Has EMU Changed Fiscal Policies?

To look into this issue more deeply, the IMF staff undertook a panel analysis of fiscal reaction functions. Besides offering insights on the causes of *cross-country differences* in the estimated reactions, and thereby on the ultimate determinants of fiscal behaviors, panel estimates also allow an assessment of whether *area-wide* changes have occurred in relation to the implementation of the new fiscal framework. In practice, the analysis focuses on *interactions* between the characteristics of fiscal policy and a number of institutional, political, and economic variables likely to influence fiscal behaviors, including the inception of the Maastricht Treaty, the discretion left to the finance ministry in budget preparation (Hallerberg, 2004), the economic situation (good times or bad; asset price boom or bust), the initial fiscal position, and the openness to trade (see Appendix 2.4).

The analysis finds that these factors have a significant effect in determining the response of fiscal policy to cyclical conditions, but have no systematic impact on the response either to public debt or to monetary gaps. The broad conclusion supported by these results is that factors that favor greater discretion also tend to be associated with greater procyclicality, reflecting the difficulty of resisting political pressures to

[51]Of course, the "consensus" may sometimes be "forced." For instance, Berger and Schneider (2000) report various cases of successful political pressures on the Bundesbank.

increase spending (Tornell and Lane, 1999; Talvi and Vegh, 2000).

- *Procyclical behavior is particularly evident in good times,* as incentives to restrain expenditures are generally weak in such circumstances. For the same reason, *strong initial budget positions also lead to more procyclical behaviors* as expansions in good times are likely to be larger if long-term sustainability is not perceived as a pressing issue.
- *Procyclicality is greater in countries where fiscal institutions leave significant discretion* to the finance ministry in the preparation of the budget rather than relying on rules and pre-set targets. That interpretation relies on the distinction between two institutional arrangements designed to ensure that requests from spending ministries remain consistent with fiscal discipline—namely, the "commitment" approach, based on rules and pre-set targets—and the "delegation" approach where the finance ministry is entrusted with the coordination of the budgetary process.[52] Although both approaches have generally proven effective in curbing expenditure requests (Annett, 2004), discretion may weaken the enforcement of spending restraint in good times and strengthen it in bad times—a pattern conducive to more procyclicality. The choice between the two approaches depends on the nature of the political system, with single-party governments often preferring delegation and coalition governments preferring commitment (Hallerberg, 2004). In the euro area, the three *largest economies* have opted for delegation. Large countries may also be particularly encouraged to take advantage of discretion because of the greater effectiveness of fiscal impulses when the domestic market is large.
- *The perceived need for more activist fiscal policies may lead to more procyclical policies.* The larger external disturbances affecting more open economies as well as their revealed preference for fixed exchange rates—especially in the European Union—may have contributed to

[52]See Annett (2004), Hallerberg (2004), and Appendix 2.4.

Figure 2.22. Procyclicality and Output Volatility[1]
(Correlation coefficient = 0.29; 1975–2003)

Greater output volatility is conducive to procyclicality.

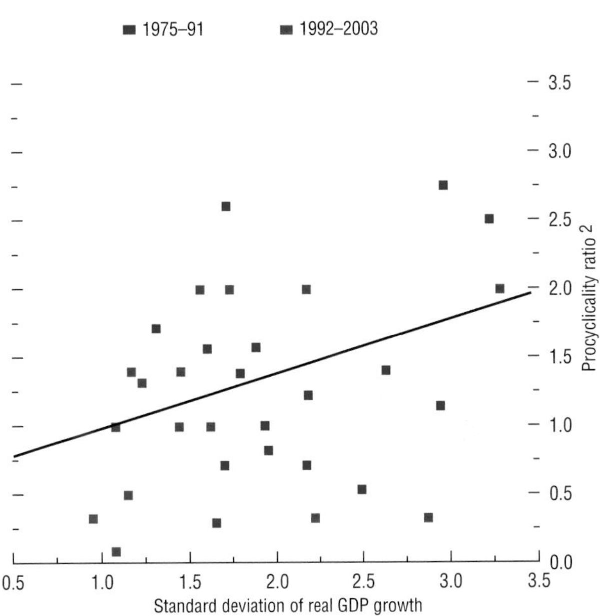

Sources: OECD analytical database; and IMF staff calculations.
[1]Evidence is based on euro area countries (excluding Luxembourg) and Australia, Denmark, Sweden, the United Kingdom, and the United States.
[2]The procyclicality ratio is the frequency of procyclical impulses relative to countercyclical impulses.

Figure 2.23. Fiscal Stance in the Euro Area,1982–2003

While procyclicality remained a prominent feature of fiscal policy in the euro area, it has become tilted toward loosening under EMU. The same is true for countercyclical impulses.

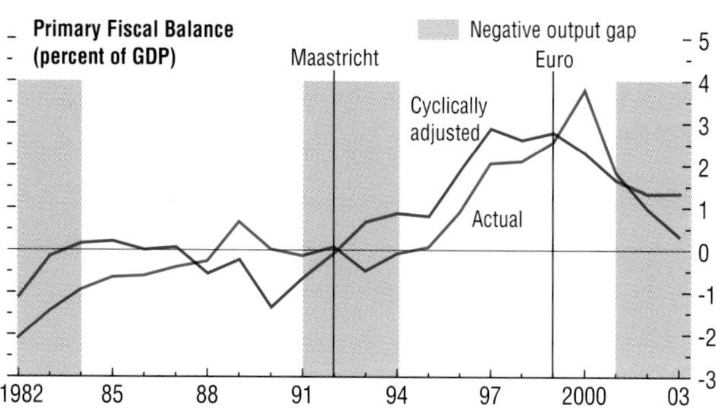

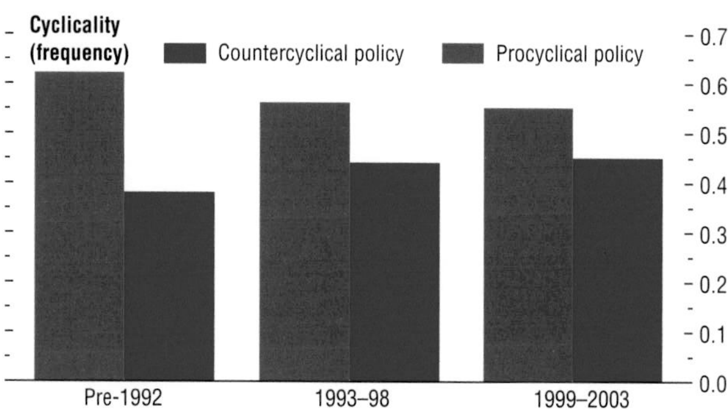

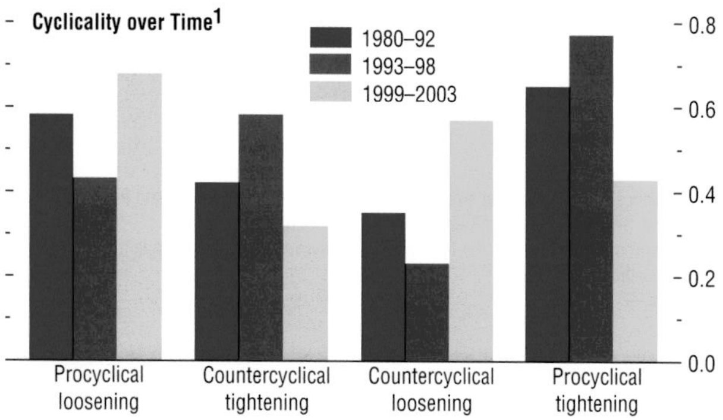

Sources: OECD analytical database; and IMF staff calculations.
[1]Frequency adjusted for the occurence of good versus bad times (defined as growth above or below potential, respectively).

procyclicality in the euro area. In fact, a positive correlation between output volatility and procyclicality seems to exist for industrial countries (Figure 2.22, p. 43).[53]

The apparent link between fiscal discretion and procyclicality tends to suggest that EMU's rules-based, discipline-oriented fiscal framework could be expected to improve fiscal behaviors. Indeed, earlier work by Galí and Perotti (2003) suggests that the average fiscal response to the cycle changed after the Maastricht treaty came into force in 1992, with procyclicality virtually disappearing. This general result is confirmed by the panel analysis above (see Appendix 2.4, including Table 2.8), which also suggests that the other features of fiscal policy, including the concern for debt sustainability, have not been affected. At first sight therefore, automatic stabilizers have indeed been allowed to play more fully than in the past, an undoubtedly welcome development.

However, a more detailed assessment of fiscal behavior since 1992 suggests that this improvement could be more apparent than real, possibly disguising some disturbing post-EMU trends. As illustrated by Figure 2.23, while fiscal policy has in general become less procyclical, it appears that this has come about entirely because there has been more tightening in good times between 1992 and 1997—reflecting adjustments spurred by the desire to secure EMU membership—and less tightening in bad times after 1999. However, fiscal policies have actually become more procyclical in good times under EMU. This assessment is confirmed by Table 2.4, which provides two sets of estimated cyclical responses: before and after Maastricht, and before and after EMU.[54] Although these tests—unlike Figure 2.23—cannot capture the specifics of the 1992–97 period, they confirm the persistent tendency to loosen fiscal policy in

[53]Of course, that positive correlation also partly reflects the lesser stabilizing effect of fiscal policy when discretionary impulses tend to be procyclical.

[54]The other parameters of reaction functions were kept constant over time.

good times—a bent that may have worsened under EMU—whereas the fiscal tightening in bad times has disappeared.[55] Obviously, such a trend cannot be sustained as it would lead to a bias toward increasing deficits in bad and good times alike.

Looking back, procyclical policies have in fact been associated with higher average deficits (Figure 2.24), confirming that a deficit bias inevitably emerges when procyclical impulses occur mainly in good times. In fact, the discretionary fiscal retrenchments observed in bad times may result from unsustainable loosening in good times, an argument supported by the positive association between the frequency of procyclical loosening and procyclical tightening episodes (Figure 2.25). Particularly striking is the fact that, according to the econometric analysis, countries in breach of or close to SGP's deficit limits have on average opted for more procyclical policies than the other member states (see Appendix 2.4).

It could of course be argued that the observed increase in procyclical behavior in good times—in practice mainly in the late 1990s—may have been due to temporary or unexpected factors, rather than deliberate policy actions, and therefore will not persist. For example, overly optimistic growth forecasts in the context of asset price booms and corresponding revenue windfalls may have distorted policymakers' real-time assessment of present and future structural fiscal positions (Jaeger and Schuknecht, 2004).[56] This, along with a temporary adjustment fatigue following long years of pre-EMU austerity, could have made it difficult to resist structural expansionary measures such as tax cuts—indeed much needed in many countries. That said, it should also be noted that pre-EMU adjustments greatly

[55]The power of those tests is inevitably weak, given the relatively small number of observations on which they are based.

[56]The significant downward revision of potential output growth in a number of euro area countries indeed had direct repercussions on estimated output gaps and cyclically adjusted fiscal balances.

Figure 2.24. Procyclicality and Deficit Bias, 1975–2003[1]
(Percent of GDP)

Procyclical fiscal policies ultimately lead to greater average deficits, suggesting a deficit bias.

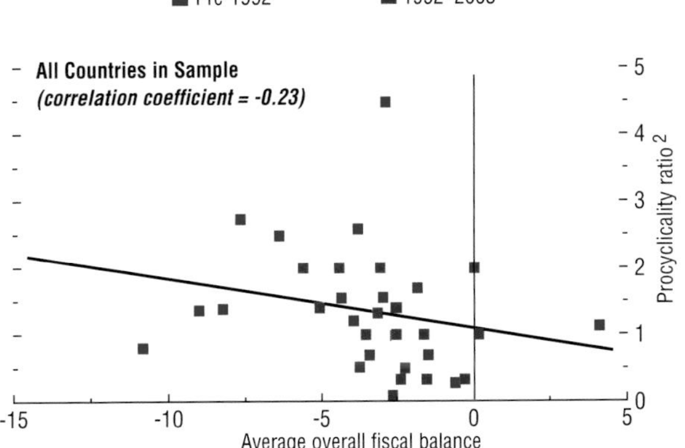

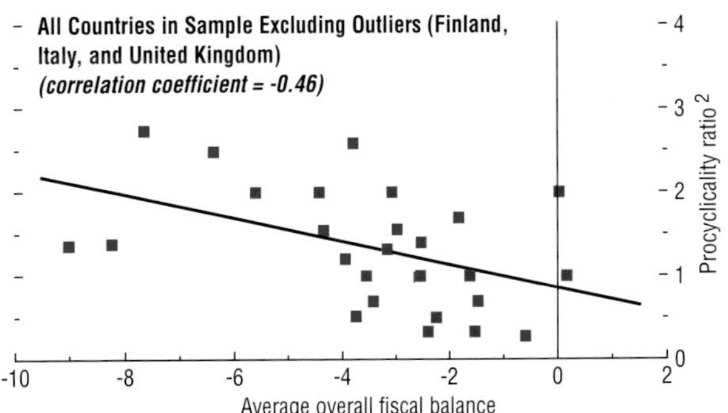

Sources: OECD analytical database; and IMF staff calculations.
[1]Evidence based on the euro area countries (excluding Luxembourg), Australia, Denmark, Sweden, the United Kingdom, and the United States.
[2]Ratio between the frequency of procyclical episodes and the frequency of countercyclical episodes.

Table 2.4. Discretionary Fiscal Policies: Stabilizing or Destabilizing?
(Response of cyclically adjusted primary balance to the output gap; a negative coefficient implies a destabilizing response)

	Before or After Maastrich?			Before or After EMU?		
	Before	After	Different before/after?[1]	Before	After	Different before/after?[1]
Response in good times[2]	−0.173	−0.169	0.001	−0.071	−0.412	3.233
Standard error	0.083	0.087	—	0.080	0.181	—
Significance threshold (*P*-value)	0.037	0.053	0.973	0.373	0.024	0.072
Response in bad times[3]	−0.115	0.013	3.038	−0.175	0.044	1.932
Standard error	0.047	0.051	—	0.037	0.151	—
Significance threshold (*P*-value)	0.014	0.796	0.081	0.000	0.772	0.165
Different in good or bad times?[4]	0.245	3.518		0.954	2.718	
Significance threshold (*P*-value)	0.621	0.061		0.329	0.099	
Number of observations		242			242	

Note: Details about specification and estimation of the underlying model are in Appendix 2.2.
[1]This column reports the Wald test statistic as well as its statistical significance threshold.
[2]Good times correspond to years with positive output gaps.
[3]Bad times correspond to years with negative output gaps.
[4]This line reports the Wald test statistic.

benefited from lower interest rates (Figure 2.26) and one-off measures,[57] and therefore may not have been exceptionally painful nor deeply structural in nature.[58] Also, the advisability of spending uncertain revenue windfalls in the face of certain long-term challenges, such as population aging, is arguably questionable. Overall, while it is admittedly difficult to make a definitive judgment over a relatively short period, the empirical analysis suggests that fiscal behavior under EMU has not improved as much as might have been hoped for, and in some respects—notably, the increase in procyclical fiscal policy in good times—may have slipped, resulting in an increasing bias toward deficits. At the present conjuncture, this underscores the danger that—without a significant change in fiscal behavior relative to the past—euro area countries could once again fail to take advantage of an upturn to make progress in dealing with their substantial medium term fiscal problems (see Beetsma, 2004).

Conclusion

The analysis in this essay builds on and extends a rapidly growing body of research investigating fiscal authorities' behavior along three dimensions potentially affected by EMU—namely, the reaction of discretionary fiscal policy to the business cycle, its sensitivity to long-term debt sustainability, and its reaction to the monetary policy stance. The essay illustrates that the cyclicality of fiscal policy is the central feature of fiscal behavior, affecting both macroeconomic stabilization and long-term sustainability. Fiscal behavior in euro area countries has generally been procyclical, with the degree of procyclicality reflecting, inter alia, country-specific budgetary institutions, structural characteristics—such as the sensitivity to real disturbances—and inher-

[57]Panel estimates of the fiscal reaction function indicate that the year 1997 alone saw an exceptional improvement in cyclically adjusted primary balances, on the order of 0.6 percent of GDP on average across member states, suggesting that some governments indeed took advantage of the margins for "creative accounting" allowed by the Treaty's definition of the fiscal balance. Using government balance sheet data, Milesi-Ferretti and Moriyama (2004) confirm that fiscal adjustments over the period 1992–97 were to a significant extent achieved by measures that had no durable impact on public finances as they left government net worth largely unaffected.

[58]Netting out the cumulative changes in overall balances from those savings, fiscal adjustment does not look particularly ambitious and may explain why most countries failed to meet the SGP's underlying requirement to enter EMU with an overall structural position close to balance or in surplus. Had this been the case, and barring any serious measurement error of structural balances in 1999, none of the countries currently at odds with the SGP would be in that situation today (Figure 2.27).

ited fiscal positions. Procyclical fiscal impulses turn out to be more pronounced in good times (loosening) than in bad (tightening), pointing to the difficulty of resisting pressures to increase spending or cut taxes in the face of revenue windfalls (Tornell and Lane, 1999; Talvi and Vegh, 2000).

Maastricht's fiscal framework appears to have led to some reduction in procyclical fiscal behavior under EMU, owing to a more countercyclical policy stance in bad times. However, this was in general not balanced by sufficient deficit reduction in good times. The continuation of such behavior would result in an underlying—and unsustainable—deficit bias. The ongoing recovery will be a decisive test of whether history will again repeat itself, or whether governments will be able to resist past tendencies to take advantage of the upturn to address underlying fiscal problems before the pressures from aging populations are felt with full force.

In terms of the current debate on the SGP, the essay reinforces the need—as often pointed out by both the IMF staff and the European Commission—to ensure greater adjustment in good times. This could be done by putting a greater emphasis on structural balances in fiscal surveillance. More emphasis on debt reduction (already desirable for sustainability reasons) may also have welcome repercussions by putting a premium on increasing structural surpluses in good times. The country-specific incentives for adjustment could be reinforced by the creation of national bodies that would make and publish independent assessments of fiscal sustainability, raising public awareness of the issues, and strengthening the national debate. Finally, incentives for adjustment would also be strengthened by a more credible enforcement mechanism of the SGP, reserving swift sanctions to flagrant breaches and showing flexibility in the face of *temporary* violations that reflect policies with positive long-term effects on growth (including the possible costs of fiscal measures related to labor and product market reforms) and fiscal sustainability (including tax and pension reforms).

Figure 2.25. Procyclicality in Good and Bad Times[1]

Procyclical loosening (in good times) appears to lead to procyclical tightening (in bad times).

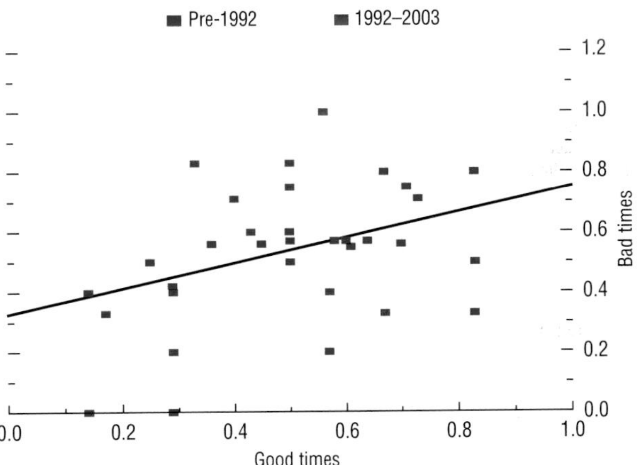

Source: IMF staff calculations.

[1]Evidence based on the euro area countries (excluding Luxembourg), Australia, Denmark, Sweden, the United Kingdom, and the United States. Good and bad times are defined as growth above or below potential, respectively.

Figure 2.26. Interest Payments: Where Did the Savings Go?

EMU member states benefited from significantly lower interest rates on public debt (top panel). Taking that into account, pre-EMU fiscal performance is less impressive (bottom panel).

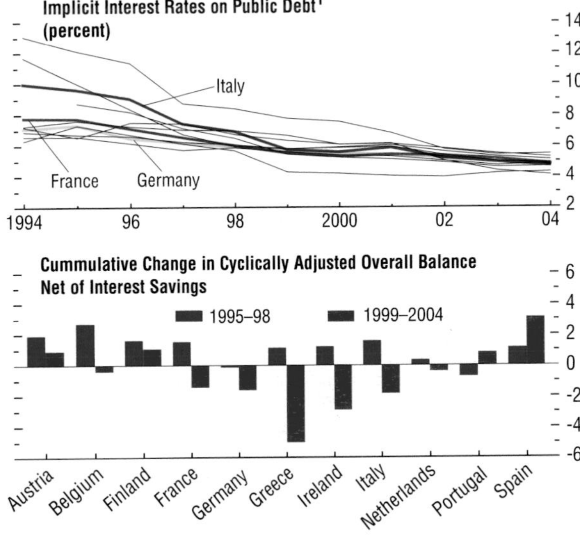

Sources: European Commission, Annual Macroeconomic Database; and IMF staff calculations.

[1]Interest payments divided by the stock of public debt at the end of the previous year.

Figure 2.27. Countries at Odds with the Stability and Growth Pact
(Percent of GDP)

Assuming identical policies, countries currently in breach or close to stability and growth pact deficit caps would have remained within the limits had they entered the EMU with a structural balance.

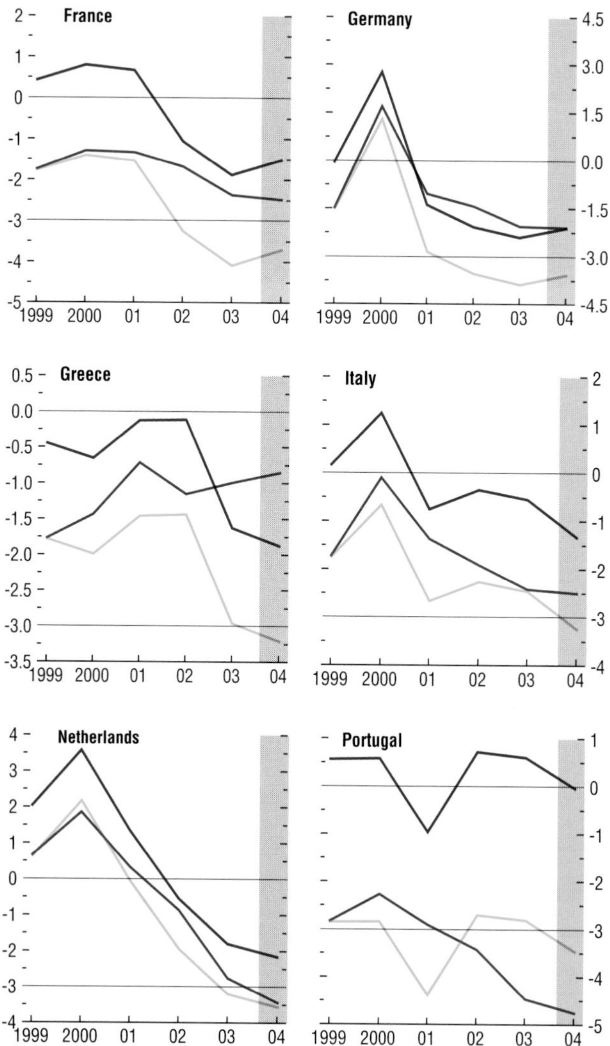

Sources: European Commission, Annual Macroeconomic Database; and IMF staff calculations.

Appendix 2.1. The Global House Boom: Sample Composition, Data Sources, Methods, and Results

The main authors of this appendix are Marco Terrones and Christopher Otrok. Nathalie Carcenac provided research assistance.

This appendix provides details on the data sources, samples, and econometric method and results of the first essay, on the global house boom.

Sample and Data Sources

The sample used in the first two sections of the essay and in Box 2.1 comprises the following 18 countries: Australia, Belgium, Canada, Denmark, Finland, France, Germany, Ireland, Italy, Japan, the Netherlands, New Zealand, Norway, Spain, Sweden, Switzerland, the United States, and the United Kingdom. The data are yearly and cover 1970–2003.

The sample used in the last two sections of the essay includes the following 13 countries: Australia, Canada, Denmark, Ireland, Italy, Japan, the Netherlands, New Zealand, Norway, Sweden, Switzerland, the United States, and the United Kingdom. The data are quarterly and covers 1980:QI–2004:QI.

For purposes of Box 2.2, countries are classified as bank- or market-based depending on the ratio of the value of domestic equities traded on the domestic stock markets to the claims on the private sector by commercial banks (see Beck, Demirgüç-Kunt, and Levine, 1999; and Chapter II of the April 2003 *World Economic Outlook*). The group of bank-based financial system countries comprises Austria, Belgium, Denmark, Finland, France, Germany, Italy, Japan, Norway, New Zealand, and Spain, while the group of market-based financial system countries includes Australia, Canada, Ireland, the Netherlands, Sweden, Switzerland, the United Kingdom, and the United States. Likewise, countries are classified as having a fixed- (variable) rate mortgage system if the fraction of mortgage loans with this characteristic exceeds 74 (72) percent, respectively.[59] Thus, the following countries are characterized as having a fixed-rate mortgage system: Belgium, Canada, Denmark, France, and the United States. Similarly, the following countries are characterized as having a variable-rate mortgage system: Australia, Finland, Ireland, Norway, Spain, and the United Kingdom. The remaining countries are characterized as having a mixed-rate mortgage system.

Data were taken from a variety of sources, including the European Central Bank (ECB), European Mortgage Federation (EMF), Eurostat, Haver Analytics, the IMF's *International Financial Statistics*, national authorities, the OECD Analytical Database, and the World Bank's World Development Indicators.

Main financial and housing series used in the essay are as follows.

- Real asset prices. These are calculated as the ratio of the nominal house price (stock price) index to the consumer price index. The house price index is obtained from national sources, while the stock price index and consumer price indexes are obtained from the IMF *International Financial Statistics.*
- Interest rates. The short- and long-term interest rate series were obtained from the OECD's analytical database and Haver Analytics. Short-term interest rates are the three-month inter-bank rates while long-term rates are government bonds rates (typically 10-year bonds).
- Mortgage loans typically refers to outstanding residential mortgage loans and these data were obtained from a variety of sources including the ECB, the EMF, the OECD, and national sources.
- Data on consumer price index for rents were obtained from the OECD's main economic indicators, national sources, and the ECB.
- The home ownership rates series were obtained from Eurostat, the EMF, the ECB, the Royal Institution of Chartered Surveyors, European Housing Review, and national sources.

Dynamic Factor Model

Dynamic factor models are a generalization of the static factor models that are commonly used in psychology. The motivation underlying these models, which are gaining increasing popularity among economists, is that the covariance or comovement between a group of (observable) time series is the result of the relationship between these variables and a small number of unobservable variables, known as factors, which are thought of as the underlying forces of the economy.[60] The unobserved factors are then indexes of common activity—across the entire data set (e.g., global activity) or across subsets of the data (e.g., a particular country).

One important objective of this literature is to obtain estimates of these unobserved factors to quantify both the extent and nature of comovement in a set of time-series data.[61] Toward this objective, the dynamic factor model decomposes each observable variable—e.g., the house price index for the United Kingdom, output in Japan—into components that are common across all observable variables or common across a subset of variables.

The model used in this essay comprises 13 blocks, 1 for each country; each block comprises 7 equations, 1 for each variable (real house prices, per capita real GDP, per capita consumption, per capita residential investment, short- and long-term interest rates, and real stock prices). These equations relate each variable in the model to a global factor, a country factor—1 for each of the 13 countries, and global factors

[59]These thresholds correspond to the top 33 percent in each case. Data refer to the latest available observation.

[60]The popularity of these models has risen as methods have been developed to perform factor analysis on the large datasets that these models naturally apply to (e.g., Stock and Watson, 2003; Forni and others, 2000; Otrok and Whiteman, 1998).

[61]The second major objective of this literature is using the information in the cross section of time series to forecast one time series.

that are common to each aggregate variable across the data set—1 for each of the 7 observable variables. For example, the block of equations for the first country (the United States) is

$$House_{US,t} = a_{House,US} + b^{Global}_{House,USi} f^{Global}_t + b^{Country}_{House} f^{US}_t + b^{Global}_{House,US} f^{Global\ House}_t + \varepsilon_{House\ US,t}$$

$$GDP_{US,t} = a^{GDP}_{GDP,US} + b^{Global}_{House,US} f^{Global}_t + b^{Country}_{GDP} f^{US}_t + b^{Global\ GDP}_{GDP,US} f^{Global\ GDP}_t + \varepsilon_{GDP\ US,t}$$

$$\vdots$$

$$Stock_{US,t} = a_{Stock,US} + b^{Global}_{Stock,USi} f^{Global}_t + b^{Country}_{Stock} f^{US}_t + b^{Global\ Stock}_{Stock,US} f^{Global\ Stock}_t + \varepsilon_{Stock\ US,t},$$

and the block of variables for the second country (the United Kingdom) is

$$House_{UK,t} = a_{House,UK} + b^{Global}_{House,UKi} f^{Global}_t + b^{Country}_{House} f^{UK} + b^{Global\ House}_{House,UK} f^{Global\ House}_t + \varepsilon_{House\ UK,t}$$

$$GDP_{UK,t} = a_{GDP,UK} + b^{World}_{GDP,UKi} f^{World}_t + b^{Country}_{GDP} f^{U.K}_t + b^{GlobalGDP}_{GDP,UK} f^{GlobalGDP}_t + \varepsilon_{GDP\ UK,t}$$

$$\vdots$$

$$Stock_{UK,t} = a_{Stock,UK} + b^{World}_{Stock,UKi} f^{World}_t + b^{Country}_{Stock} f^{UK}_t + b^{Global\ Stock}_{Stock,UK} f^{Global\ Stock}_t + \varepsilon_{Stock\ UK,t}.$$

The same form is repeated for each of the 13 countries in the system.

In this system we see that the world factor is the component common to all variables in all countries. That is, every variable depends on this common factor and that dependence varies across each variable through the parameter b_i^k, which is called the factor loading of variable i on factor k. The factor loading measures the sensitivity of a variable to a factor. There is a second global factor for each type of aggregate variable. This factor captures co-movement across the world in each variable that is not explained by the common world factor. For example, housing prices in each country are influenced by the world house price factor. There is also a factor for each country that captures co-movement across all variables within each country that is not already captured by either type of global factor.

The model captures dynamic co-movement by allowing the factors (*fs*) and idiosyncratic terms (ε) to be (independent) autoregressive processes. That is, each factor depends on lags of itself and an i.i.d. innovation to the variable:

$$f^{Global}_t = \phi(L) f^{Global}_{t-1} + u_t,$$

where $\varphi(L)$ is a lag polynomial and u_t is normally distributed. All the factor loadings (bs), and lag polynomials are independent of each other. The model is estimated using Bayesian techniques as described in Kose, Otrok, and Whiteman (2003) and in Otrok, Silos, and Whiteman (2003).

To measure the importance of each factor for a particular variable, we calculate variance decompositions that decompose the volatility in each aggregate into components due to each factor. The formula for the variance decomposition is derived by applying the variance operator to each equation in the system. For example, for the first equation, we have

$$var(House_{US}) = (b^{Global}_{House,USi})^2 var(f^{Global}_t) + (b^{Country}_{Global\ House})^2 var(f^{US}) + (b^{Global\ House}_{House,U.S})^2 var(f^{Global\ House}_t) + var(\varepsilon_{House\ US}).$$

The variance in housing prices attributable to the global house factor is then

$$\frac{(b^{Global\ House}_{House,US})^2\ var\ (f^{Global\ House})}{var(House_{US})}.$$

A variance-decomposition analysis is performed to assess the contribution of each of these components to the volatility of a given variable. In particular, for each country, the fraction of the variance of a variable explained by each component is computed. The following findings—in addition to those reported in the essay—stand out from the analysis (Table 2.5).

- Global developments—the combination of the global factor and the global-specific variable—explain between 20–40 percent of the variation of output, consumption, and residential investment. The importance of global developments, however, varies across countries. For example, they account for over 75 percent of the variation of these three variables in the United States and for less than 15 percent in New Zealand.

- Global developments also explain over 50 percent of the variation of stock prices and changes in long-term interest rates as well as 30 percent of the variation of the changes in short-term interest rates. Interestingly, most of the common changes in stock prices and interest rates are captured by the corresponding global-specific factors. This suggests that developments in these markets separate from developments in other markets (and to a lesser extent developments in the global real economic activity) are key to explain the volatility of these variables. Moreover, there are important differences across countries in the strength of the co-movement of stock prices (interest rates) with their global counterparts. Global developments account for over 80 percent of the co-movement in stock prices in the Netherlands and 30 percent in New Zealand. Similarly, global developments account for over 70 percent of the co-movement of long-term interest rates in Canada, the Netherlands, the United Kingdom, and the United States.
- Country-specific factors play a smaller role explaining the movements in output, residential investment, stock prices, and long-term interest rates. However, they explain over 25 percent of the variations of short-term interest rates. This is consistent with the low cross-country correlations of short-term interest rates reported in the main text of the essay.
- The idiosyncratic factors seem to be playing an important role in driving the fluctuations of residential investment. These factors explain on average 70 percent of the fluctuations in this variable; this is consistent with the low cross-country investment correlations reported elsewhere (see, for instance, Kose, Otrok, and Whiteman, 2003).

Appendix 2.2. Learning to Float: Methodology and Data

The main author of this appendix is Dalia Hakura.

This appendix provides details on the methodology used in the second essay to characterize emerging market countries' exchange rate regime transitions, and the definition of the variables used in the analysis and their data sources.

Methodology

The essay examines the evolution of exchange rate regimes in emerging market economies over the past decade using the IMF's de facto classification system.[62] Accordingly, exchange rate regimes are classified based on the behavior of nominal bilateral exchange rates and reserves in combination with information on countries' exchange rate and monetary policy frameworks and policy intentions obtained during bilateral discussions between IMF staff and country authorities (see Bubula and Ötker-Robe, 2002). The IMF de facto system classifies countries' exchange rate regimes into eight categories, which—for the analysis in the essay—are aggregated into three broad categories: pegs, intermediates, and free floating. The pegs category includes countries with currency board arrangements and conventional pegs. The intermediates category includes countries with limited flexible regimes—that is, pegs within horizontal bands, crawling pegs, and crawling bands—and the managed floats. The free floats are countries classified as independently floating. To check robustness, a comparison is also made with the "natural classification" system developed by Reinhart and Rogoff (2004).[63]

[62]Alternatively, exchange rate regimes can be classified based on official notifications to the IMF (de jure classification system). Other de facto classification systems include Reinhart and Rogoff (2004), Levy-Yeyati and Sturzenegger (2002, 2003), and Ghosh and others (1997).

[63]The essay extends the Reinhart-Rogoff classification system from 2001 to 2003.

Table 2.5. Variance Decomposition for Selected Countries
(Percent)

Country	Factor	Real House Price	Real Stock Price	Long-Term Interest Rate	Short-Term Interest Rate	Consumption[1]	Output[1]	Residential Investment[1]
United States	Global	21	10	2	1	65	57	78
	Country	0	0	1	7	1	0	1
	Aggregate	47	53	69	69	8	23	0
United Kingdom	Global	11	12	2	2	26	32	23
	Country	0	12	24	56	1	3	0
	Aggregate	57	46	62	16	31	17	1
Italy	Global	22	6	30	29	4	0	1
	Country	2	1	20	56	5	2	12
	Aggregate	11	34	30	9	33	48	1
Netherlands	Global	23	20	9	3	4	7	14
	Country	17	1	15	21	40	46	5
	Aggregate	15	62	65	33	15	32	1
Canada	Global	9	26	7	1	36	41	41
	Country	0	0	0	0	6	0	0
	Aggregate	34	41	76	93	18	37	1
Ireland	Global	0	30	22	9	11	1	14
	Country	37	0	2	0	27	49	16
	Aggregate	21	4	37	3	10	35	5
Australia	Global	2	21	6	3	0	13	5
	Country	0	2	34	39	15	0	0
	Aggregate	36	27	43	23	7	34	3
New Zealand	Global	2	17	0	1	16	12	6
	Country	33	5	0	2	66	34	31
	Aggregate	0	12	2	4	7	2	2
Average	Global	14	16	10	8	15	16	19
	Country	10	5	15	26	19	16	8
	Aggregate	25	37	42	23	19	26	3

Source: IMF staff calculations.
[1]Per capita.

Unlike the IMF's de facto classification system, the Reinhart-Rogoff classification system relies entirely on an examination of the behavior of official or parallel market exchange rates vis-à-vis the currency to which the national currency is permanently or occasionally pegged. There are merits to having a classification system that incorporates a wider set of information, because the behavior of the exchange rate on its own does not always give an accurate picture of exchange rate policy. For example, in an emerging market country with a free float, high exchange rate pass-through, and inflation targeting, exchange rate depreciation (as a leading indicator of inflation) may prompt an increase in interest rates, which in turn will tend to dampen the exchange rate depreciation. Thus, moving to a float does not necessarily mean that key nominal bilateral exchange rates have to fluctuate very much (see also Genberg and Swoboda, 2004).

Exchange rate regimes in emerging market countries are classified in the same way by the IMF de facto and Reinhart-Rogoff systems nearly two-thirds of the time. Also, both classification systems suggest that there has been a trend toward greater exchange rate flexibility in emerging market countries since the early 1990s. According to the IMF de facto classification system, in 1991–92 there were virtually no emerging market countries classified as having free floats, compared with 40 percent in 2003. Although the proportion is slightly different, the Reinhart-Rogoff classification picks up the same trend of a marked increase in the number of countries classified as free floaters.[64]

An exchange rate regime transition is defined as a shift from one exchange rate category, in which a country has been for at least two years, to another, in which a country remains for at least one year or which is followed by another shift in the same direction. A crisis-driven transition is defined as a transition that is associated with an exchange rate depreciation vis-à-vis the U.S. dollar of at least 20 percent, at least a doubling in the rate of depreciation with respect to the previous year, and a rate of depreciation the previous year below 40 percent (following Milesi-Ferretti and Razin, 2000).[65]

The essay compares the countries that move to a more flexible exchange rate category with a control group. The control group consists of the countries whose exchange rate regime is the same as the starting regime of transiting countries in periods that are not within three years of a transition. Depending on the availability of data, the pegs control group includes the following countries in the relevant years: Argentina, China, Colombia, Jordan, Malaysia, Morocco, and Thailand. Similarly, the intermediates control group includes the following countries in the relevant years: Chile, Colombia, Czech Republic, Hungary, India, Indonesia, Israel, Korea, Russia, South Africa, Thailand, and Turkey.

Data Definitions and Sources

Depending on availability of the data, the indicators cover the period 1991–2003 for the 25 countries listed in footnote 28 in the main text of this chapter.

Macroeconomic Indicators

Real output growth is measured using the annual growth rate of real per capita GDP. The source of the data is the World Economic Outlook database.

Inflation is measured using the growth rate of the Consumer Price Index. The source of the data is the IMF's International Financial Statistics (IFS).

Real and nominal effective exchange rates are obtained from the IMF's Information Notice System. An increase in the index denotes an exchange rate appreciation. The data are monthly.

Real exchange rate overvaluation is calculated using the percentage difference between the actual real effective exchange rate (REER, reported in the IMF's Information Notice System) and a Hodrik-Prescott filter of the REER.

The primary fiscal balance as a percent of GDP is obtained from Chapter III of the September 2003 *World Economic Outlook*.

The current account as a percent of GDP is obtained from the IMF's International Financial Statistics.

The ratio of external debt to exports of goods and services is calculated as the ratio of total external debt outstanding at year-end divided by exports of goods and nonfactor services plus net total transfers minus net official transfers. The source of the data is the World Economic Outlook database.

The ratio of private sector external debt to exports of goods and services is constructed as total external debt outstanding at year-end minus the debt outstanding to official debtors divided by exports of goods and nonfactor services plus net total transfers minus net official transfers. The source of the data is the World Economic Outlook database.

International Reserves in months of imports is obtained from the IMF's International Financial Statistics.

Indicators of Monetary Policy Frameworks

Central bank independence. This measures central bank political and economic independence fol-

[64]The updated Reinhart-Rogoff classification identifies 7 free floats in 2003, compared with 10 under the IMF de facto system.

[65]Exchange rate movements that meet these criteria in a three-year window around the exchange regime transition are attributed to the transition.

lowing the definition by Grilli, Masciandaro, and Tabellini (1991). Political independence measures the extent to which the government is involved in the operations of the central bank, where a lower degree of government involvement implies a higher degree of central bank political independence. Economic independence measures the involvement of the central bank in financing the fiscal deficit and in banking supervision. The smaller the involvement the greater the economic independence. The indicator ranges from 0 to 1, where higher values indicate a higher level of independence. The data, which is available for only 10 of the emerging market countries in the sample for 1989 and 2003, is obtained from Arnone and Laurens (2004).

Dummy for whether a country is inflation targeting or not. The date of adoption of inflation targeting is obtained from Stone and Roger (2004).

Indicators of Financial Sector Supervision and Development

The aggregate index of the *quality of banking supervision* includes (1) banks' adoption of a capital adequacy regulation in line with standards developed by the Bank for International Settlements; (2) the independence of the supervisory agency from the executive's influence and whether it has sufficient legal power and (material) supervisory power; (3) the effectiveness of the supervision; and (4) the extent to which supervision covers all financial institutions.

The securities market development index captures whether a country has taken measures to develop a securities or bond market and the openness of its equity market to foreign investors. The measures to develop a securities market include the introduction of auctions for government paper and the establishment of a securities commission, the establishment of equity and bond markets, the opening of these markets to foreign participants, and liberalization of portfolio investments for pension funds and other institutional investors.

The data are obtained from Abiad and Mody (2003). The indicators take values from 0 to 3, with increasing values indicating stronger bank supervision and greater securities market development. Data are missing for some of the emerging market countries in the sample.

Indicators of Financial Sector Liberalization

The index for *domestic financial liberalization* is constructed as the average of four indicators that measure the extent to which (1) direct credit controls and reserve requirements have been abolished; (2) interest rate controls have been removed; (3) entry barriers against foreign banks have been eliminated; and (4) the banking system has been privatized.

External financial liberalization is an aggregate index that captures whether there are restrictions on capital inflows and outflows, and whether the exchange rate system is unified.

The data are obtained from Abiad and Mody (2003). The indicators take values from 0 to 3, with increasing values indicating greater liberalization. Data are missing for some of the emerging market countries in the sample.

Appendix 2.3. Monetary Policy Rules for the Euro Area

The main author of this appendix is Xavier Debrun.

This appendix provides details on the monetary policy rules used to obtain the hypothetical interest rate benchmarks for euro area member states (Figure 2.20). The original specification of simple, mechanical policy rules is due to Taylor (1993), who observed that U.S. monetary policy in the 1980s and 1990s moved surprisingly well in line with an interest rate benchmark i_t^* defined as

$$i_t^* = r^* + \pi_t + h(\pi_t - \pi^*) + gy_t, \qquad (1)$$

where π_t is the inflation rate; π^* is the inflation rate implicitly or explicitly targeted by the monetary authorities; y_t is the output gap (difference between actual GDP and some measure of potential GDP in percent of the latter); r^* denotes an "equilibrium" real interest rate; and h and g are the relative weights assigned to output and inflation stabilization in the monetary policy framework. The interest rate level consistent with a "neutral" monetary policy (that is, when both objectives are met: $y_t = 0$ and $\pi_t = \pi^*$) is given by $r^* + \pi^*$.

Taylor (1999) discusses in detail the rationale underlying Equation (1) and suggests using i_t^* as a normative tool, interpreting large deviations of actual interest rates from i_t^* as "mistakes." IMF staff analysis considers i_t^* only as a first-order approximation of what might have been an "appropriate" policy for individual euro area member states. Indeed, these countries are relatively open economies so that external competitiveness, and specifically the real exchange rate or unit labor costs, may also play an independent role in monetary policy choices. Another reason not to give a normative interpretation to the interest rate benchmark at all times is that the monetary rule does not capture the possible need to manage the risk of deflation.

But does the ECB's behavior appear at least broadly consistent with the prescription of Equation (1)? The vast empirical literature on monetary policy has confirmed that models comparable to Equation (1)—but including well-specified dynamics—fitted actual policy relatively well, both for the Bundesbank (Clarida, Galí and Gertler, 1998) and the ECB (see Gerlach and Schnabel, 2000; Siklos, Werner, and Bohl, 2004; Gerlach-Kristen, 2003; or Castelnuovo, 2003).

Taylor's (1993) original calibration of Equation (1) implies $g = h = 0.5$ and $\pi^* = r^* = 2$, meaning that the central bank pays equal attention to real activity and to inflation. The rule also implies that the interest rate response to a unit change in inflation is $1 + h$ so that the *real* interest rate moves to ensure that inflation reverts to its target (that is, a monetary contraction if $\pi_t > \pi^*$ and an expansion when $\pi_t < \pi^*$).

IMF staff constructed five different benchmarks for each individual member state of the euro area, the United States, and the euro area as a whole. While the relative weights h and g were kept constant across countries, r^* and π^* were allowed to differ as follows.

- $r_j^* = k_j + \hat{y}_j$, where $\hat{y}_j$ denotes the average growth rate of potential GDP over the period 2004–08; k_j, a positive constant equal to 0.75 in euro area countries and 0 in the United States; and j, a country index. As a result, $r_j^* \geq \hat{y}_j$ and the dynamic efficiency condition, which requires all debts to be ultimately repaid (see, for instance, Obstfeld and Rogoff, 1996), is satisfied. Indeed, if $r_j^* < \hat{y}_j$, then economic agents could in principle roll over any given amount of debt forever because it would always decrease as a proportion of income. For the United States, k_j was set to zero to be as close as possible to Taylor's (1993) original calibration for that country.
- $\pi_j^* = c + (2/3)[\theta_j^T - \theta_j^{NT}]$, where θ_j^T and θ_j^{NT} symbolize productivity growth in the "tradable" sector (exposed to external competition) and "nontradable" sector (protected from external competition) respectively. This formula allows for inflation differentials linked to the so-called Balassa-Samuelson effect, which claims that prices in the nontradable sector (which represent roughly two-thirds of the economy) have to make up for the economy-wide wage pressures created by faster productivity growth in the tradable sector. According to Sinn and Reutter (2001), Germany exhibits the lowest productivity growth differential between the tradable and nontradable sectors and should thus be expected to experience the weakest "structural" inflationary pressure in the euro area. Hence, the German inflation target was set to 1 percent. To ensure that the weighted average of individual inflation targets is in line with the ECB's objective for the euro area—that is, keeping inflation below but close to 2 percent—c is set to 0.66, corresponding to an average inflation target of 1.75 percent (Table 2.6).

In addition to the traditional specification of monetary rules (Equation (1)), the following alternatives were also considered.

- *Inflation rule.* As in Alesina and others (2001), it is assumed that $g = 0$; that is, the central bank only reacts to deviations of actual inflation from the target.

- *Asymmetric Taylor rule.* The central bank is assumed to be more concerned by negative output gaps than by positive ones. In practice, the rule is written as $i^*_t = r^* + \pi_t + 0.5(\pi_t - \pi^*) + 0.5y_t - 0.1y^2_t$.
- *Augmented Taylor rules.* In small open economies, the central bank may pay attention to elements other than inflation and the output gap, including unit labor cost growth (that is, the extent to which nominal wage growth exceeds or falls short of productivity growth) and the real effective exchange rate (that is, the economy's competitiveness). The response to rising unit labor costs is assumed to be a monetary tightening (with a coefficient of 0.1), whereas a real appreciation is supposed to be counteracted by a monetary loosening (with a coefficient of 0.05).

Table 2.6 reports for two subperiods (1993–98 and 1999–2003 using quarterly data) simple descriptive statistics assessing the relevance of these rules—namely, the average and root-mean-squared deviations of actual interest rates from benchmarks implied by the rule. Bold numbers identify the rule with the smallest root-mean-squared deviation (that is, the best fit to the data). The good fit of the Taylor rule (and its asymmetric variant) is confirmed for the United States and the euro area as a whole. For a majority of euro area member states, however, actual interest rates have on average been closer to the benchmark rate derived from the inflation rules, which precludes country-specific output stabilization.

Appendix 2.4. Estimating Fiscal Reaction Functions

The main author of this appendix is Xavier Debrun.

This appendix provides technical details on the econometric evidence discussed in the third essay, about fiscal behaviors in the euro area, including the specification of the underlying models, and estimation procedures.

Specification

The specification of the econometric equation is similar to Galí and Perotti (2003) and several related studies,[66] focusing on three critical characteristics of discretionary fiscal policy—namely, the response to cyclical fluctuations, the sensitivity to movements in the public debt, and the reaction to deviations of short-term interest rates from benchmarks implied by monetary policy rules (in short, the "monetary gaps"—see Appendix 2.3). The model also allows for persistence in fiscal policy choices. Hence, the basic equation can be written as

$$S_t = \beta_0 + \beta_1 S_{t-1} + \beta_2 GAP_t + \beta_3 B_{t-1} + \beta_4 M_t + \varepsilon_t, \quad (1)$$

where t is a time index; S_t denotes the primary surplus (cyclically adjusted in percent of potential GDP); GAP_t is the output gap; B_t, the gross public debt in percent of potential GDP; M_t represents the deviations of short-term interest rates from the benchmarks; and ε_t is an error term.

Both for data availability reasons and to ease comparability with other studies (especially Galí and Perotti, 2003), regressions use annual data from the OECD's analytical database. The study focuses on euro area member states, excluding Luxembourg.

Estimation and Results

The empirical investigation proceeds in two steps. First, the fiscal policy equation (1) is estimated separately for each individual country (Table 2.7) with the maximum number of observations available, that is from 1971 (at the earliest) to 2003. The fact that the output gap and monetary policy can be expected to react to current fiscal policy actions implies a likely correlation with the error term so that standard

[66]See also the September 2003 *World Economic Outlook* for a detailed discussion of a similar specification.

Table 2.6. Monetary Gaps: Descriptive Statistics

	Austria	Belgium	Finland	France	Germany	Ireland
Inflation target	2.07	1.54	3.37	2.01	1.00	3.45
Equilibrium interest rate	2.25	2.47	2.52	2.34	2.09	4.00
Taylor rule (TR)						
1993–98 Mean	0.16	0.60	5.34	3.07	0.50	2.06
1993–98 RMSE	0.51	1.58	6.16	3.42	0.81	3.48
1999–2003 Mean	−0.73	−1.22	0.12	0.08	0.60	-7.51
1999–2003 RMSE	1.02	1.43	1.06	1.00	0.87	7.92
Inflation rule						
1993–98 Mean	0.18	**0.31**	**2.22**	1.65	−0.32	**1.10**
1993–98 RMSE	0.67	**1.37**	**2.65**	2.39	0.78	**2.58**
1999–2003 Mean	−0.38	**−1.06**	**−0.27**	−0.26	**−0.02**	−4.92
1999–2003 RMSE	0.81	**1.26**	**0.67**	1.25	**0.66**	5.22
Adding ULC to TR[1]						
1993–98 Mean	**0.03**	0.47	5.36	**2.96**	**0.41**	1.94
1993–98 RMSE	**0.50**	1.42	6.25	**1.05**	**0.74**	3.34
1999–2003 Mean	−0.82	−1.44	−0.11	−0.12	0.45	. . .
1999–2003 RMSE	1.07	1.66	1.08	1.05	0.77	. . .
Adding REER to TR[1]						
1993–98 Mean	0.03	0.56	5.22	3.02	0.56	1.70
1993–98 RMSE	0.51	1.65	6.07	3.41	0.94	3.31
1999–2003 Mean	−0.74	−1.26	0.05	**0.06**	0.54	-7.63
1999–2003 RMSE	1.05	1.47	1.14	**0.95**	0.88	8.04
Asymmetric TR						
1993–98 Mean	0.22	0.70	10.46	3.93	0.78	2.97
1993–98 RMSE	0.54	1.68	12.79	4.15	1.01	4.46
1999–2003 Mean	**−0.48**	−1.10	0.36	0.26	0.94	**−4.34**
1999–2003 RMSE	**0.80**	1.30	1.18	1.04	1.32	**4.66**

	Italy	Netherlands	Portugal	Spain	Euro Area	United States
Inflation target	2.17	2.07	1.66	2.16	1.75	2.50
Equilibrium interest rate	2.13	2.50	2.41	3.13	2.36	2.56
Taylor rule (TR)						
1993–98 Mean	2.61	−0.69	1.35	0.73	. . .	**0.00**
1993–98 RMSE	2.80	1.60	2.26	1.87	. . .	**0.95**
1999–2003 Mean	−0.96	−3.09	−3.29	−3.57	**−0.78**	−1.40
1999–2003 RMSE	1.16	3.26	3.44	3.64	**0.99**	1.68
Inflation rule						
1993–98 Mean	**1.78**	**−0.47**	**0.77**	**0.31**	. . .	−0.03
1993–98 RMSE	**1.99**	**1.20**	**1.70**	**1.60**	. . .	1.44
1999–2003 Mean	−1.22	**−2.31**	**−3.03**	**−3.40**	−1.01	−1.31
1999–2003 RMSE	1.51	**2.54**	**3.25**	**3.51**	1.33	2.11
Adding ULC to TR[1]						
1993–98 Mean	2.45	−0.80	. . .	0.43	. . .	**−0.17**
1993–98 RMSE	2.61	1.65	. . .	1.65	. . .	**0.94**
1999–2003 Mean	−1.12	−3.83	. . .	−3.92	. . .	−1.31
1999–2003 RMSE	1.29	3.95	. . .	3.99	. . .	1.77
Adding REER to TR[1]						
1993–98 Mean	2.51	−0.69	. . .	0.63	. . .	0.06
1993–98 RMSE	2.71	1.69	. . .	1.82	. . .	1.00
1999–2003 Mean	−0.95	−3.04	. . .	−3.49	−0.82	−1.35
1999–2003 RMSE	1.12	3.22	. . .	3.55	1.06	1.78
Asymmetric TR						
1993–98 Mean	2.99	−0.58	1.60	0.83	. . .	0.37
1993–98 RMSE	3.23	1.49	2.53	1.97	. . .	1.00
1999–2003 Mean	**−0.84**	−2.43	−3.12	−3.52	−0.82	−0.53
1999–2003 RMSE	**1.03**	2.70	3.28	3.60	1.03	1.41

Source: IMF staff estimates.
Note: Bold numbers identify the rule with the smallest root-mean-squared deviation (that is, the best fit to the data).
[1]ULC stands for unit labor costs and REER, for real effective exchange rate.

Table 2.7. Country-Specific Estimates of Fiscal Reaction Functions
(Dependent variable: cyclically adjusted primary balance in percent of potential GDP)

	Austria	Belgium[1]	Finland	France	Germany	Greece	Ireland	Italy	Netherlands	Portugal	Spain[1]
Lagged dependent variable											
Coefficient	0.50	0.71	0.45	0.63	0.45	0.69	0.86	0.51	0.43	0.22	0.47
Standard error	0.17	0.10	0.16	0.15	0.15	0.16	0.06	0.13	0.15	0.15	0.17
t-statistic	2.99***	6.90***	2.77***	4.17***	3.13***	4.32***	14.04***	3.88***	2.83***	1.52	2.72***
Output gap											
Coefficient	0.22	–0.19	0.15	–0.18	–0.25	–0.06	–0.27	–0.26	–0.36	–0.32	–0.06
Standard error	0.16	0.11	0.08	0.09	0.14	0.20	0.13	0.18	0.17	0.07	0.06
t-statistic	1.35	–1.73*	1.81*	–1.97*	–1.80*	–0.32	–2.06**	–1.45	–2.14**	–4.37***	–0.97
Lagged debt ratio											
Coefficient	0.02	0.06	0.05	0.02	0.00	0.07	0.00	0.07	0.05	0.26	0.08
Standard error	0.01	0.02	0.02	0.01	0.03	0.03	0.02	0.02	0.03	0.11	0.02
t-statistic	1.91*	2.98***	2.89***	1.31	0.09	2.09**	0.23	3.65***	1.86*	2.49**	3.96***
Monetary "gap"[2]											
Coefficient		–0.22	–0.15	–0.06	0.31	–0.15			–0.25	–0.19	–0.09
Standard error	[3]	0.10	0.09	0.05	0.11	0.16	[3]	[3]	0.12	0.17	0.07
t-statistic		–2.29**	–1.57	–1.21	2.87***	–0.93			–1.99*	–1.10	–1.32
Summary statistics											
R^2	0.34	0.92	0.62	0.55	0.78	0.83	0.91	0.92	0.52	0.82	0.84
Number of observations	30	31	27	26	32	27	24	33	28	26	24
Breaks[4]	No	1982	No	1992	1982	1991	No	No	1991	No	No

Source: IMF staff estimates.
[1]Robust standard errors (Newey-West correction) when evidence of first- and/or second-order autocorrelation is found.
[2]Monetary gaps are measured as the deviation of actual short-term interest rates from either the Taylor rule or the inflation rule described in Appendix 2.3.
[3]Likelihood ratio test identifies the monetary gap as a redundant variable and keeping it in the equation seriously affects other estimated coefficients.
[4]Identified on the basis of Chow tests. "Candidate" break dates are selected from a preliminary screening with Cusum-of-squares tests operated on OLS estimates.

ordinary least squares (OLS) estimates are biased. Individual equations are therefore estimated by two-stage least squares using as instruments all exogenous variables, own lagged output gaps, and lagged output gaps of the United States and Germany for all non-German European countries, and of the United States and France for Germany. In several cases, standard specification tests strongly reject the relevance of monetary gaps as an explanatory variable of fiscal behavior. They are consequently ignored for these countries. Finally, country-specific estimates also allow testing for structural breaks in the relationship, to see whether the *overall* fiscal policy behavior significantly changed over the sample period. The results are reported at the bottom of Table 2.7 and commented on in the main text.

The second step in the analysis takes advantage of the cross-country dimension of the dataset, looking at panel estimates of the monetary policy equations. On the one hand, this can be seen as the appropriate approach to check whether *area-wide* changes have occurred over time, for instance as a result of the new fiscal policy framework set out in the Maastricht Treaty and the Stability and Growth Pact. Country-specific estimates may indeed underplay these effects, in part because of the small number of observations over time and the correspondingly low power of the related tests. On the other hand, the panel approach can also offer useful insights on the causes of *cross-country differences* in the estimated coefficients, and thereby on the ultimate determinants of fiscal behaviors.

In practice, dummy variables can discriminate between different groups of countries or between periods in time. Interaction variables can also be used to look into the effect of time-varying country characteristics, such as openness to trade or the fiscal position of the government. The idea is to differentiate the estimated β coefficients according to time- or country-specific features that may influence behaviors. In the case of dummy variables, statistically significant differences between the two sets of coefficients (e.g., before and after the inception of the Maastricht Treaty) will suggest that the criterion used to construct those two sets of estimates matters for fiscal behaviors. Statistical significance of interaction variables indicates that the β coefficients are linear functions of these variables.

To cope with the likely correlation of the output gap and the monetary gap with the error term, both explanatory variables are instrumented using their own lags and exogenous variables. The analysis also accounts for the possibility of common fiscal shocks (as may occur under coordinated discretionary actions) so that a three-stage least squares estimator is preferred.[67] The estimation also includes country dummies (fixed effects) unless particular dummies (such as the one indicating the start of EMU's fiscal framework) are allowed to have country-specific slopes. To account for the structural breaks identified in 1982 in two countries (see Table 2.7), the sample period is 1982–2003, unless otherwise indicated (the other structural breaks occurred in or close to 1992 and are therefore explicitly investigated). Finally, all equations include a dummy for 1997, the year considered by the European Union to evaluate fiscal positions in the perspective of entering EMU.

Tables 2.8 and 2.9 present a number of regressions allowing for two sets of estimates (first and second column associated with each equation). The Wald tests relating to the null hypothesis of identical coefficients between the two groups are reported in the third column of each equation. In Table 2.8, the Maastricht Treaty dummy takes a value of one after 1992 and zero otherwise. Bad times are defined as years with negative output gaps (that is, output below its potential level), the rest being considered as good times.[68] The dummy variables for "commitment states" and "delegation states" refer to a broad classification of budgetary institutions (as set out in Hallerberg, 2004; and Annett, 2004). Although both systems are intended to promote fiscal discipline by solving the common pool problem inherent to budget preparation,[69] they differ by the *degree of discretion* left in the hands of the finance ministry, with delegation models granting more discretion than commitment models. In practice, delegation models have been adopted by France, Germany, Greece, and Italy, with all other countries except Portugal (unclassified) being considered as having adopted the commitment model.

Table 2.8 also presents the distinction between the group of countries in breach (or having been in breach) of the SGP limits (France, Germany, and Portugal) and the rest. A similar exercise is run separating out the six countries in breach or close to breaching the SGP's limits (adding Italy, Greece, and the Netherlands). These regressions were run on a slightly shorter sample period (1982–2000), to capture behaviors *before* any breach. Table 2.9 confirms a conjecture by Jaeger and Schuknecht (2004) about the apparent lack of countercyclicality during asset price booms and busts. The boom/bust dummy was constructed on the basis of Table 2 in Jaeger and Schuknecht (2004).

Table 2.10 considers the impact of trade openness and the initial fiscal position on cyclicality through interaction variables. The interactions between these and the other explanatory variables of the model were found to be insignificant and to reduce the precision of estimates.

[67]As suggested by Judson and Owen (1999), the relatively long time-series dimension of this panel implies that the bias inherent to dynamic panel estimations should not have serious effects on the results.

[68]Notice that Table 2.4 in the main text combines the Maastricht Treaty dummy with the good-times dummy to refine the analysis of cyclicality. However, for that particular exercise, the other parameters were assumed constant over time.

[69]Von Hagen, Hallerberg, and Strauch (2004) show that both models indeed provide fiscal discipline through different channels. They also show that political institutions and constitutional features of countries determine the choice for one system against the other. The dummies are based on Box 2 in Annett (2004).

Table 2.8. Fiscal Authorities' Behavior in the Euro Area: Panel Analysis, 1982–2003
(Dependent variable: cyclically adjusted primary balance in percent of potential GDP)

		Maastricht Treaty			Behavior in:		
	Benchmark	Before	After	Wald test	Good times	Bad times	Wald test
Persistence	0.685	0.498	0.527	0.158	0.668	0.653	0.075
Standard error	0.027	0.048	0.055	—	0.046	0.032	—
P-value	0.000	0.000	0.000	0.691	0.000	0.000	0.784
Output stabilization	−0.120	−0.175	−0.040	5.811	−0.231	−0.073	2.607
Standard error	0.023	0.032	0.046	—	0.091	0.043	—
P-value	0.000	0.000	0.386	0.016	0.012	0.092	0.106
Debt stabilization	0.029	0.059	0.0422	1.145	0.034	0.034	0.000
Standard error	0.004	0.014	0.008	—	0.009	0.005	—
P-value	0.000	0.000	0.000	0.285	0.000	0.000	0.983
Reaction to monetary gap	−0.063	−0.115	−0.050	2.016	−0.122	0.026	4.931
Standard error	0.018	0.031	0.033	—	0.039	0.021	—
P-value	0.001	0.000	0.130	0.156	0.002	0.232	0.026
Number of observations	242		242			242	

		Commitment State?			Delegation State?		
	Benchmark	Yes	No	Wald test	Yes	No	Wald test
Persistence	0.685	0.621	0.632	0.032	0.594	0.674	0.874
Standard error	0.027	0.057	0.037	—	0.084	0.029	—
P-value	0.000	0.000	0.000	0.857	0.000	0.000	0.350
Output stabilization	−0.120	−0.066	−0.142	1.877	−0.248	−0.095	4.641
Standard error	0.023	0.047	0.030	—	0.062	0.027	—
P-value	0.000	0.158	0.000	0.171	0.000	0.001	0.031
Debt stabilization	0.029	0.040	0.030	11.542	0.034	0.029	1.410
Standard error	0.004	0.005	0.004	—	0.005	0.005	—
P-value	0.000	0.000	0.000	0.001	0.000	0.000	0.235
Reaction to monetary gap	−0.063	−0.084	−0.022	1.531	−0.001	−0.063	1.072
Standard error	0.018	0.043	0.024	—	0.055	0.022	—
P-value	0.001	0.051	0.360	0.216	0.989	0.005	0.301
Number of observations	242		242			242	

		3 In Breach of SGP?[1]			6 at Odds With SGP?[1]		
	Benchmark	Yes	No	Wald test	Yes	No	Wald test
Persistence	0.685	0.349	0.714	30.144	0.556	0.677	4.295
Standard error	0.027	0.061	0.031	—	0.052	0.034	—
P-value	0.000	0.000	0.000	0.000	0.000	0.000	0.038
Output stabilization	−0.120	−0.165	−0.066	5.550	−0.230	−0.017	13.860
Standard error	0.023	0.036	0.031	—	0.038	0.038	—
P-value	0.000	0.000	0.036	0.019	0.000	0.667	0.000
Debt stabilization	0.029	0.023	0.032	0.748	0.053	0.028	5.794
Standard error	0.004	0.010	0.005	—	0.008	0.006	—
P-value	0.000	0.019	0.000	0.387	0.000	0.000	0.016
Reaction to monetary gap	−0.063	−0.057	−0.046	0.072	−0.067	−0.039	0.302
Standard error	0.018	0.030	0.029	—	0.027	0.038	—
P-value	0.001	0.057	0.114	0.789	0.014	0.316	0.583
Number of observations	242		209			209	

Source: IMF staff estimates.
[1]Estimated over the period 1982–2000.

Table 2.9. Fiscal Authorities' Behavior in the Euro Area: Panel Analysis, 1982–2003
(Dependent variable: cyclically adjusted primary balance in percent of potential GDP)

		Asset Price Boom/Bust?		
	Benchmark	Yes	No	Wald test
Persistence	0.685	0.660	0.666	0.014
Standard error	0.027	0.039	0.037	—
P-value	0.000	0.000	0.000	0.907
Output stabilization	−0.120	−0.016	−0.175	11.560
Standard error	0.023	0.038	0.032	—
P-value	0.000	0.666	0.000	0.001
Debt stabilization	0.029	0.038	0.032	5.925
Standard error	0.004	0.005	0.005	—
P-value	0.000	0.000	0.000	0.015
Reaction to monetary gap	−0.063	0.010	−0.084	6.045
Standard error	0.018	0.032	0.023	—
P-value	0.001	0.750	0.000	0.014
Number of observations	242		242	

Source: IMF staff estimates.

ables of the model were found to be insignificant and to reduce the precision of estimates.

Table 2.10. Fiscal Authorities' Behavior in the Euro Area: Panel Analysis, 1982–2003
(Dependent variable: cyclically adjusted primary balance in percent of potential GDP)

	Benchmark	Fiscal Position	Openness
Persistence	0.685	0.670	0.614
Standard error	0.027	0.028	0.032
P-value	0.000	0.000	0.000
Output stabilization	−0.120	−0.117	0.009
Standard error	0.023	0.025	0.053
P-value	0.000	0.000	0.863
Output stabilization and trade openness	—	—	−0.002
Standard error	—	—	0.001
P-value	—	—	0.006
Output stabilization and fiscal position[1]	—	−0.026	—
Standard error	—	0.013	—
P-value	—	0.054	—
Debt stabilization	0.029	0.027	0.033
Standard error	0.004	0.004	0.004
P-value	0.000	0.000	0.000
Reaction to monetary gap	−0.063	−0.077	−0.026
Standard error	0.018	0.019	0.021
P-value	0.001	0.000	0.227
Number of observations	242	242	242

Source: IMF staff estimates.
[1]Fiscal position corresponds to the lagged cyclically adjusted primary surplus.

References

Abiad, Abdul, and Ashoka Mody, 2003, "Financial Reform: What Shakes It? What Shapes It?" IMF Working Paper 03/70 (Washington: International Monetary Fund). Also forthcoming in the *American Economic Review*.

Acharya, Shankar, 2002, "Macroeconomic Management in the Nineties," *Economic and Political Weekly*, Vol. 37 (April), pp. 1515–38.

Alesina, Alberto, Olivier Blanchard, Jordi Galí, Francesco Giavazzi, and Harald Uhlig, 2001, *Defining a Macroeconomic Policy Framework for the Euro Area: Monitoring the European Central Bank 3* (London: Centre for Economic Policy Research).

Annett, Tony, 2004, "Enforcement and the Stability and Growth Pact: Where Do We Go from Here?" (unpublished; Washington: International Monetary Fund).

Arellano, Manuel, and Stephen Bond, 1991, "Some Tests of Specification for Panel Data: Monte Carlo Evidence and an Application to Employment Equations," *Review of Economic Studies*, Vol. 58 (April), pp. 277–97.

Ariyoshi, Akira, Karl Habermeier, Bernard Laurens, Inci Ötker-Robe, Jorge Ivan Canales-Kriljenko, and Andrei Kirilenko, 2000, *Capital Controls: Country Experiences with Their Use and Liberalization*, IMF Occasional Paper No. 190 (Washington: International Monetary Fund).

Arnone, Marco, and Bernard Laurens, 2004, "Measures of Central Bank Autonomy: Empirical Evidence for OECD and Developing Countries, and Emerging Market Economies" (unpublished; Washington: International Monetary Fund).

Baele, Lieven, Annalisa Ferrando, Peter Hördahl, Elizaveta Krylova, and Cyril Monnet, 2004, "Measuring Financial Integration in the Euro Area," ECB Occasional Paper No. 14 (Frankfurt: European Central Bank).

Ballabriga, Fernando, and Carlos Martinez-Mongay, 2002, "Has EMU Shifted Policy?" Economic Paper No. 166 (Brussels: European Commission).

Bayoumi, Tamim, and Barry Eichengreen, 1997, "Shocking Aspects of European Monetary Unification," in *European Monetary Unification: Theory, Practice and Analysis*, ed. by Barry Eichengreen (Cambridge, Massachusetts: MIT Press), pp. 73–109.

Bayoumi, Tamim, and Paul Masson, 1998, "Liability-Creating Versus Non-Liability-Creating Fiscal Stabilization Policies: Ricardian Equivalence, Fiscal

Stabilization, and EMU," *Economic Journal*, Vol. 108 (July), pp. 1026–45.

Beck, Thorsten, Asli Demirgüç-Kunt, and Ross Levine, 1999, "A New Database on Financial Development and Structure," World Bank Working Paper No. 2146 (Washington: World Bank).

Beetsma, Roel, 2004, "Europe's Future Fiscal Challenges" (unpublished; Washington: International Monetary Fund).

Berger, Helge, and Friedrich Schneider, 2000, "The Bundesbank's Reaction to Policy Conflicts," in *The History of the Bundesbank*, ed. by Jakob de Haan (London: Routledge), pp. 43–66.

Bernanke, Ben, Jean Boivin, and Piotr Eliasz, 2004, "Measuring the Effects of Monetary Policy: A Factor-Augmented Vector Autoregressive (FAVAR) Approach," Finance and Economics Discussion Series No. 2004-3 (Washington: Board of Governors of the Federal Reserve System).

Bogdanski, Joel, Alexandre Antonio Tombini, and Sérgio Ribeiro da Costa Werlang, 2000, "Implementing Inflation Targeting in Brazil," presented at the International Monetary Fund seminar "Implementing Inflation Targets," Washington, March 20–21.

Bohn, Henning, 1998, "The Behavior of U.S. Public Debt and Deficits," *Quarterly Journal of Economics*, Vol. 113 (August), pp. 949–63.

Bubula, Andrea, and Inci Ötker-Robe, 2002, "The Evolution of Exchange Rate Regimes Since 1990: Evidence from De Facto Policies," IMF Working Paper 02/155 (Washington: International Monetary Fund).

Buti, Marco, Jan In't Veld, and Werner Roeger, 2001, "Stabilising Output and Inflation in EMU: Policy Conflicts and Co-operation Under a Stability Pact," *Journal of Common Market Studies*, Vol. 39, No. 5, pp. 801–28.

Calmfors, Lars, 2003, "Fiscal Policy to Stabilise the Domestic Economy in the EMU: What Can We Learn from Monetary Policy?" *CESifo Economic Studies*, Vol. 49, No. 3, pp. 319–53.

Calvo, Guillermo, and Carmen Reinhart, 2002, "Fear of Floating," *Quarterly Journal of Economics*, Vol. 117 (May), pp. 379–408.

Calvo, Guillermo, and Frederic Mishkin, 2003, "The Mirage of Exchange Rate Regimes for Emerging Market Countries," NBER Working Paper No. 9808 (Cambridge, Massachusetts: National Bureau of Economic Research).

Campa, Jose, and Linda Goldberg, 2001, "Exchange Rate Pass-Through into Import Prices: A Macro or Micro Phenomenon?" Staff Report No. 149 (New York: Federal Reserve Bank).

Campbell, John, and João Cocco, 2003, "Household Risk Management and Optimal Mortgage Choice," *Quarterly Journal of Economics*," Vol. 118 (November), pp. 1449–94.

Carare, Alina, Andrea Schaechter, Mark Stone, and Mark Zelmer, 2002, "Establishing Initial Conditions in Support of Inflation Targeting," IMF Working Paper 02/102 (Washington: International Monetary Fund).

Case, Bradford, William Goetzmann, and K. Geert Rouwenhorst, 1999, "Global Real Estate Markets: Cycles and Fundamentals," Yale ICY Working Paper No. 99–03 (New Haven, Connecticut: Yale International Center for Finance).

Castelnuovo, Efrem, 2003, "Taylor Rules and Interest Rate Smoothing in the US and EMU" (unpublished; Milan: Bocconi University).

Chopra, Ajai, Charles Collyns, Richard Hemming, and Karen Parker, with Woosik Chu and Oliver Fratzscher, 1995, *India: Economic Reform and Growth*, IMF Occasional Paper No. 134 (Washington: International Monetary Fund).

Choudhri, Ehsan, and Dalia Hakura, 2001, "Exchange Rate Pass-Through to Domestic Prices: Does the Inflationary Environment Matter?" IMF Working Paper 01/194 (Washington: International Monetary Fund). Also forthcoming in the *Journal of International Money and Finance*.

Clarida, Richard, Jordi Galí, and Mark Gertler, 1998, "Monetary Policy Rules in Practice: Some International Evidence," *European Economic Review*, Vol. 42 (June), pp. 1033–67.

Commission of the European Communities, 2004, "Financial Integration Monitor: Commission Staff Working Document," SEC(2004) 559. Available via the Internet: http://europa.eu.int/comm/internal_market/en/finances/cross-sector/fin-integration/sec–2004–559_en.pdf.

Davis, Morris, and Jonathan Heathcote, 2004, "Housing and the Business Cycle," Finance and Economics Discussion Series No. 2004–11 (Washington: Board of Governors of the Federal Reserve System).

Debelle, Guy, 2004, "Macroeconomic Implications of Rising Household Debt," BIS Working Paper No. 153 (Basel: Bank for International Settlements).

Debrun, Xavier, and Charles Wyplosz, 1999, "Onze Gouvernements et Une Banque Centrale," *Revue d'Economie Politique*, Vol. 109 (May–June), pp. 387–424.

Deroose, Servaas, Sven Langedijk, and Werner Roeger, 2004, "Reviewing Adjustment Dynamics in EMU: From Overheating to Overcooling," Economic Paper No. 198 (Brussels: European Commission).

Doyle, Brian, and Jon Faust, 2003, "Breaks in the Variability and Co-Movements of G-7 Economic Growth," International Finance Discussion Paper No. 786 (Washington: Board of Governors of the Federal Reserve System).

Duttagupta, Rupa, Gilda Fernández, and Cem Karacadag, 2004, "From Fixed to Floating: Operational Aspects of Moving Toward Exchange Rate Flexibility," IMF Working Paper 04/126 (Washington: International Monetary Fund).

Edison, Hali, and Francis Warnock, 2003, "A Simple Measure of the Intensity of Capital Controls," *Journal of Empirical Finance*, Vol. 10 (February), pp. 81–103.

Eichengreen, Barry, and Paul Masson, with Hugh Bredenkamp, Barry Johnston, Javier Hamann, Esteban Jadresic, and Inci Ötker, 1998, *Exit Strategies: Policy Options for Countries Seeking Greater Exchange Rate Flexibility*, IMF Occasional Paper No. 168 (Washington: International Monetary Fund).

Eichengreen, Barry, Paul Masson, Miguel Savastano, and Sunil Sharma, 1999, "Transition Strategies and Nominal Anchors on the Road to Greater Exchange-Rate Flexibility," Essays in International Finance No. 213 (Princeton, New Jersey: Princeton University).

Ellis, Luci, Jeremy Lawson, and Laura Roberts-Thomson, 2003, "Housing Leverage in Australia," Research Discussion Paper No. 2003–09 (Sydney: Reserve Bank of Australia).

Emerson, Michael, and others, 1990, "One Market, One Money," European Economy No. 44 (Brussels: Commission of the European Communities).

European Central Bank, 2003, "Structural Factors in the EU Housing Markets" (unpublished; Frankfurt).

Faruqee, Hamid, 2004, "Measuring the Trade Effects of EMU," IMF Working Paper (Washington: International Monetary Fund, forthcoming).

Fatás, Antonio, and Ilian Mihov, 2003, "On Constraining Fiscal Policy Discretion in EMU," *Oxford Review of Economic Policy*, Vol. 19, No. 1, pp. 1–28.

Favero, Carlo, 2002, "How Do European Monetary and Fiscal Authorities Behave?" CEPR Discussion Paper No. 3426 (London: Centre for Economic Policy Research).

Forni, Mario, Marc Hallin, Marco Lippi, and Lucrezia Reichlin, 2000, "The Generalized Dynamic-Factor Model: Identification and Estimation," *Review of Economics and Statistics*, Vol. 82 (November), pp. 540–54.

Gagnon, Joseph, and Jane Ihrig, 2001, "Monetary Policy and Exchange Rate Pass-Through," International Finance Discussion Paper No. 704 (Washington: Board of Governors of the Federal Reserve System).

Galí, Jordi, and Roberto Perotti, 2003, "Fiscal Policy and Monetary Integration in Europe," *Economic Policy*, Vol. 37 (October), pp. 535–72.

Genberg, Hans, and Alexander K. Swoboda, 2004, "Exchange Rate Regimes: Does What Countries Say Matter?" (unpublished; Geneva: Graduate Institute of International Studies).

Gerlach, Stefan, and Gert Schnabel, 2000, "The Taylor Rule and Interest Rates in the EMU Area," *Economics Letters*, Vol. 67 (May), pp. 165–71.

Gerlach-Kristen, Petra, 2003, "Interest Rate Reaction Functions and the Taylor Rule in the Euro Area," ECB Working Paper No. 258 (Frankfurt: European Central Bank).

Ghosh, Atish, Anne-Marie Gulde, Jonathan Ostry, and Holger Wolf, 1997, "Does the Nominal Exchange Rate Regime Matter?" NBER Working Paper No. 5874 (Cambridge, Massachusetts: National Bureau of Economic Research).

Girouard, Nathalie, and Sveinbjorn Blondal, 2001, "House Prices and Economic Activity," OECD Economics Department Working Paper No. 279 (Paris: Organization for Economic Cooperation and Development).

Glick, Reuven, and Andrew K. Rose, 2002, "Does a Currency Union Affect Trade? The Time Series Evidence," *European Economic Review*, Vol. 46, No. 6, pp. 1125–51.

Goldstein, Morris, and Philip Turner, 2004, *Controlling Currency Mismatches in Emerging Markets* (Washington: Institute for International Economics).

Grilli, Vittorio, Donato Masciandaro, and Guido Tabellini, 1991, "Political and Monetary Institutions and Public Financial Policies in the Industrial Countries," *Economic Policy: A European Forum*, Vol. 6 (October), pp. 342–91.

Guimarães, Roberto, and Cem Karacadag, 2004, "The Empirics of Foreign Exchange Rate Intervention in Emerging Markets: The Cases of Mexico and

Turkey," IMF Working Paper 04/123 (Washington: International Monetary Fund).

Hallerberg, Mark, 2004, *Domestic Budgets in a United Europe: Fiscal Governance from the End of Bretton Woods to EMU* (Ithaca, New York: Cornell University Press).

———, and Rolf Strauch, 2002, "On the Cyclicality of Public Finances in Europe," *Empirica*, Vol. 29, No. 3, pp. 183–207.

Hamilton, James, 1994, *Time Series Analysis* (Princeton, New Jersey: Princeton University Press).

Hausmann, Ricardo, Ugo Panizza, and Ernesto Stein, 2001, "Why Do Countries Float the Way They Float?" *Journal of Development Economics*, Vol. 66, pp. 387–414.

Helbling, Thomas, and Tamim Bayoumi, 2003, "Are They All in the Same Boat? The 2000–2001 Growth Slowdown and the G-7 Business Cycle Linkages," IMF Working Paper 03/46 (Washington: International Monetary Fund).

Helbling, Thomas, and Marco Terrones, 2003, "Asset Price Booms and Busts—Stylized Facts from the Last Three Decades of the 20th Century," presented at the European Central Bank workshop "Asset Prices and Monetary Policy," Frankfurt, December 11–12.

Henley, Andrew, and Bruce Morley, 2001, "European House Price Volatility and the Macroeconomy: The Implications for European Monetary Union," Royal Economic Society Conference Paper, University of Wales, Aberystwyth.

Honohan, Patrick, and Philip Lane, 2003, "Divergent Inflation Rates in EMU," *Economic Policy*, Vol. 18, No. 37, pp. 357–94.

HSBC, 2004, "The U.S. Housing Bubble: The Case for a Home-Brewed Hangover." U.S. Economics Special Report (New York: HSBC, June).

Husain, Aasim, Ashoka Mody, and Kenneth Rogoff, 2004, "Exchange Rate Regime Durability and Performance in Developing Versus Advanced Economies" (unpublished; Washington, Cambridge, Massachusetts: IMF and Harvard University).

IMF Independent Evaluation Office, 2003, *The IMF and Recent Capital Account Crises: Indonesia, Korea, Brazil* (Washington: International Monetary Fund).

Jaeger, Albert, 2001, "Cyclical Fiscal Policy Behavior in EU Countries," Selected Issues paper for 2001 Euro Area Article IV Consultation (Washington: International Monetary Fund).

———, and Ludger Schuknecht, 2004, "Boom-Bust Phases in Asset Prices and Fiscal Policy," IMF Working Paper 04/54 (Washington: International Monetary Fund).

Judson, Ruth, and Ann Owen, 1999, "Estimating Dynamic Panel Data Models: A Guide for Macroeconomists," *Economics Letters*, Vol. 65 (October), pp. 9–15.

Kalter, Eliot, Steven Phillips, Marco A. Espinosa-Vega, Rodolfo Luzio, Mauricio Villafuerte, and Manmohan Singh, 2004, *Chile: Institutions and Policies Underpinning Stability and Growth,* IMF Occasional Paper No. 231 (Washington: International Monetary Fund).

Kose, Ayhan, Christopher Otrok, and Charles Whiteman, 2003, "International Business Cycles: World, Region, and Country-Specific Factors," *American Economic Review*, Vol. 93 (September), pp. 1216–39.

Kose, Ayhan, Eswar Prasad, and Marco Terrones, 2003, "How Does Globalization Affect the Synchronization of Business Cycles?" *American Economic Review, Papers and Proceedings*, Vol. 92 (May), pp. 57–62.

———, 2004, "Volatility and Co-movement in a Globalized World Economy: An Empirical Exploration," in *Macroeconomic Policies in the World Economy*, ed. by Horst Siebert (Berlin: Springer-Verlag, forthcoming).

Lamont, Owen, and Jeremy Stein, 1999, "Leverage and House Price Dynamics in U.S. Cities," *Rand Journal of Economics*, Vol. 30 (Autumn), pp. 498–514.

Lane, Philip, 2003, "The Cyclical Behavior of Fiscal Policy: Evidence from the OECD," *Journal of Public Economics*, Vol. 87, No. 12, pp. 2661–75.

Levy-Yeyati, Eduardo, and Federico Sturzenegger, 2002, "Classifying Exchange Rate Regimes: Deeds Versus Words" (Buenos Aires: Universidad Torcuato Di Tella). Available via the Internet: http://www.utdt.edu/~fsturzen.

———, 2003, "To Float or to Fix: Evidence on the Impact of Exchange Rate Regimes on Growth," *American Economic Review*, Vol. 93 (September), pp. 1173–93.

McCarthy, Jonathan, and Richard Peach, 2004, "Are Home Prices the Next 'Bubble'?" FRBNY Economic Policy Review (unpublished; New York: Federal Reserve Bank).

Mélitz, Jacques, 1997, "Some Cross-Country Evidence About Debts, Deficits, and the Behavior of Monetary and Fiscal Authorities," CEPR Discussion Paper No. 1653 (London: Centre for Economic Policy Research).

Micco, Alejandro, Ernesto Stein, and Guillermo Ordoñez, 2003, "The Currency Union Effect on Trade: Early Evidence from EMU," *Economic Policy*, Vol. 18 (April), pp. 315–56.

Miles, David, 2004, "The UK Mortgage Market: Taking a Longer-Term View. Final Report and Recommendations" (London: The Stationery Office).

Milesi-Ferretti, Gian Maria, and Assaf Razin, 2000, "Current Account Reversals and Currency Crises: Empirical Regularities," in *Currency Crises*, ed. by Paul Krugman (Washington: International Monetary Fund).

Milesi-Ferretti, Gian Maria, and Kenji Moriyama, 2004, "Fiscal Adjustment in EU Countries: A Balance Sheet Approach," IMF Working Paper (Washington: International Monetary Fund, forthcoming).

Mishkin, Frederic, 1996, "Understanding Financial Crises: A Developing Country Perspective," NBER Working Paper No. 5600 (Cambridge, Massachusetts: National Bureau of Economic Research).

Morandé, Felipe G., 2001, "Exchange Rate Policy in Chile: Recent Experience," presented at the International Monetary Fund conference "Exchange Rate Regimes: Hard Peg or Free Floating?" Washington, March 19–20.

Mundell, Robert, 1961, "A Theory of Optimum Currency Areas," *American Economic Review*, Vol. 51 (September), pp. 657–65.

Muscatelli, V. Anton, Patrizio Tirelli, and Carmine Trecroci, 2004, "Monetary and Fiscal Policy Interactions Over the Cycle: Some Empirical Evidence," in *Monetary Policy, Fiscal Policies and Labour Markets: Macroeconomic Policymaking in the EMU*, ed. by Roel Beetsma and others (Cambridge, Massachusetts: University Press).

Obstfeld, Maurice, and Kenneth Rogoff, 1996, *Foundations of International Macroeconomics*, (Cambridge, Massachusetts: MIT Press).

Organization for Economic Cooperation and Development (OECD), 2004, *Economic Outlook, May*, Chapter IV (Paris).

Otrok, Christopher, and Charles Whiteman, 1998, "Bayesian Leading Indicators: Measuring and Predicting Economic Conditions in Iowa," *International Economic Review*, Vol. 39, No. 4, pp. 997–1014.

Otrok, Christopher, Pedro Silos, and Charles Whiteman, 2003, "Bayesian Dynamic Factor Models for Large Datasets: Measuring and Forecasting Macroeconomic Data" (unpublished; Charlottesville, Virginia: University of Virginia).

Otto, Glenn, Graham Voss, and Luke Willard, 2003, "A Cross Section Study of the International Transmission of Business Cycles" (unpublished; Victoria, British Columbia: University of Victoria).

Persson, Torsten, 2001, "Currency Unions and Trade: How Large is the Treatment Effect?" *Economic Policy*, Vol. 33 (October), pp. 435–48.

Piazzesi, Monika, Martin Schneider, and Selale Tuzel, 2004, "Housing, Consumption, and Asset Pricing" (unpublished; Chicago: University of Chicago).

PricewaterhouseCoopers, 2002, *European Economic Outlook*, May.

Pyhrr, Stephen, Stephen Roulac, and Waldo Born, 1999, "The Real Estate Cycles and Their Strategic Implications for Investors and Portfolio Managers in the Global Economy," *Journal of Real Estate Research*, Vol. 18, No. 1, pp. 7–68.

Quan, Daniel, and Sheridan Titma, 1998, "Do Real Estate Prices and Stock Prices Move Together? An International Analysis," *Real Estate Economics*, Vol. 27, No. 2, pp. 183–207.

Rankin, Bob, 2001, "The Exchange Rate and the Reserve Bank's Role in the Foreign Exchange Market" (Sydney: Reserve Bank of Australia). Available via the Internet: http://www.rba.gov.au/Education/exchange_rate.html.

Reinhart, Carmen, and Kenneth Rogoff, 2004, "The Modern History of Exchange Rate Arrangements: A Reinterpretation," *Quarterly Journal of Economics*, Vol. 119 (February), pp. 1–48.

Rogoff, Kenneth, Aasim Husain, Ashoka Mody, Robin Brooks, and Nienke Oomes, 2003, "Evolution and Performance of Exchange Rate Regimes," IMF Working Paper 03/243 (Washington: International Monetary Fund).

———, 2004, *Evolution and Performance of Exchange Rate Regimes*, IMF Occasional Paper No. 229 (Washington: International Monetary Fund).

Rose, Andrew K., 2000, "One Money, One Market: Estimating the Effect of Common Currencies on Trade," *Economic Policy*, Vol. 15, No. 30, pp. 7–45.

———, 2004, "A Meta-Analysis of the Effect of Common Currencies on International Trade," NBER Working Paper No. 10373 (Cambridge, Massachusetts: National Bureau of Economic Research).

Siklos, Pierre, Thomas Werner, and Martin Bohl, 2004, "Asset Prices in Taylor Rules: Specification, Estimation and Policy Implications for the ECB"(unpublished). Available via the Internet: http://www.wlu.ca/~wwwsbe/faculty/psiklos/papers/buba_ii_04–2004.pdf.

Sinn, Hans-Werner, and Michael Reutter, 2001, "The Minimum Inflation Rate for Euroland," NBER Working Paper No. 8085 (Cambridge, Massachusetts: National Bureau of Economic Research).

Spearman, Charles, 1904, "'General Intelligence,' Objectively Determined and Measured," *American Journal of Psychology*, Vol. 15, pp. 201–93.

Stock, James, and Mark Watson, 2002, "Macroeconomics Forecasting Using Diffusion Indexed," *Journal of Business and Economic Statistics*, Vol. 20 (April), pp. 147–62.

———, 2003, "Understanding Changes in International Business Cycle Dynamics," NBER Working Paper No. 9859 (Cambridge, Massachusetts: National Bureau of Economic Research).

Stone, Mark, and Scott Roger, 2004, "Home on the Range: Country Experiences with Inflation Targeting" (unpublished; Washington: International Monetary Fund).

Sveriges Riksbank, 2002, "The Riksbank's Interventions in the Foreign Exchange Market—Operations, Decision-Making and Communication" (Stockholm).

Talvi, Ernesto, and Carlos Vegh, 2000, "Tax Base Variability and Procyclical Fiscal Policy," NBER Working Paper No. 7499 (Cambridge, Massachusetts: National Bureau of Economic Research).

Tapia, Matias, and Andrea Tokman, 2004, "Effects of Foreign Exchange Intervention Under Public Information: The Chilean Case," Central Bank of Chile Working Paper No. 255 (Santiago: Central Bank of Chile).

Taylor, John, 1993, "Discretion Versus Policy Rules in Practice," *Carnegie-Rochester Conference Series on Public Policy*, Vol. 39 (December), pp. 195–220.

———, 1999, "A Historical Analysis of Monetary Policy Rules," in *Monetary Policy Rules*, ed. by John Taylor (Chicago: University of Chicago Press).

———, 2000, "Reassessing Discretionary Fiscal Policy" (unpublished; Stanford, California: Stanford University).

Tenreyro, Silvana, 2001, "On the Causes and Consequences of Currency Unions"(unpublished; Cambridge, Massachusetts: Harvard University). Available via the Internet: http://www.faculty.haas.berkeley.edu/arose/tenreyro.pdf.

Tornell, Aaron, and Philip Lane, 1999, "The Voracity Effect," *American Economic Review*, Vol. 89 (March), pp. 22–46.

Von Hagen, Jürgen, Mark Hallerberg, and Rolf Strauch, 2004, "The Design of Fiscal Rules and Forms of Governance in European Union Countries" (unpublished; Bonn: Zentrum für Europäische Integrationsforschung/Center for European Integration Studies, Reinische Friedrich-Wilhelms-Universität).

Von Hagen, Jürgen, Andrew Hughes Hallett, and Rolf Strauch, 2001, "Budgetary Consolidation in EMU," Economic Papers No. 148 (Brussels: European Commission).

CHAPTER III

HOW WILL DEMOGRAPHIC CHANGE AFFECT THE GLOBAL ECONOMY?

It seems possible that a society in which the proportion of young people is diminishing will become dangerously unprogressive, falling behind other communities not only in technical efficiency and economic welfare, but in intellectual and artistic achievement as well.

—Extract from the *Report of the Royal Commission on Population*, United Kingdom, 1949

The world is in the midst of a major demographic transition. Not only is population growth slowing, but the age structure of the population is changing, with the share of the young falling and that of the elderly rising. Different countries and regions, however, are at varying stages of this demographic transition. In most advanced countries, the aging process is already well under way, and a number of developing countries in east and southeast Asia and central and eastern Europe will also experience significant aging from about 2020.[1] In other developing countries, however, the demographic transition is less advanced, and working-age populations will increase in the coming decades.

The relationship between population growth and the economy has long been the subject of debate among scholars and policymakers. Thomas Malthus, in his *Essay on the Principle of Population* published in 1798, argued that the rate of population growth was held in equilibrium by the pace of economic growth. If population growth was too rapid, wages would be depressed, causing famine or disease to raise mortality, and inducing marriage, and therefore childbearing, to be postponed. Faster economic expansion and the associated increase in prosperity on the other hand would increase fertility and the population would then quickly rise to its new equilibrium. Today the theories of Malthus appear to be happening in reverse. As economic prosperity has risen around the world, fertility rates have fallen (and large gains in life expectancy have been made), resulting in slower population growth and aging.

The gains in life expectancy that have been achieved in recent years are clearly very desirable and have improved individual welfare. A key question, however, is how ongoing demographic change will affect economic performance in the years ahead. Some argue that there is little reason to be concerned. Aging in the advanced countries has been under way for a considerable time, and has coincided with a period of strong income gains. Further, older people now lead healthier lives than at any time in the past, which allows them to continue to contribute to society well beyond the official age of retirement. Others see greater risks, including the possibility of slower economic growth, less innovation, financial market instability, and difficulties in funding overly generous public pension systems (see, for example, Peterson, 1999; Jackson, 2002; and Center for Strategic and International Studies (CSIS) and Watson Wyatt, 1999). Indeed, such concerns are not new. Over 50 years ago, the Royal Commission on Population in the United Kingdom worried about the consequences of declining fertility and popula-

Note: The main authors of this chapter are Tim Callen, Nicoletta Batini, and Nicola Spatafora with consultancy support from Jean Chateau, Warwick McKibbin, and Mehmet Tosun. Bennett Sutton provided research assistance.

[1]The term developing countries in this chapter refers to emerging market and other developing countries.

Figure 3.1. Global Demographic Transition, 1700–2050

Current demographic changes are unprecedented. After remaining broadly constant for centuries, the age structure of the world's population is now changing dramatically. Population growth is also slowing, following rapid growth in the second half of the twentieth century.

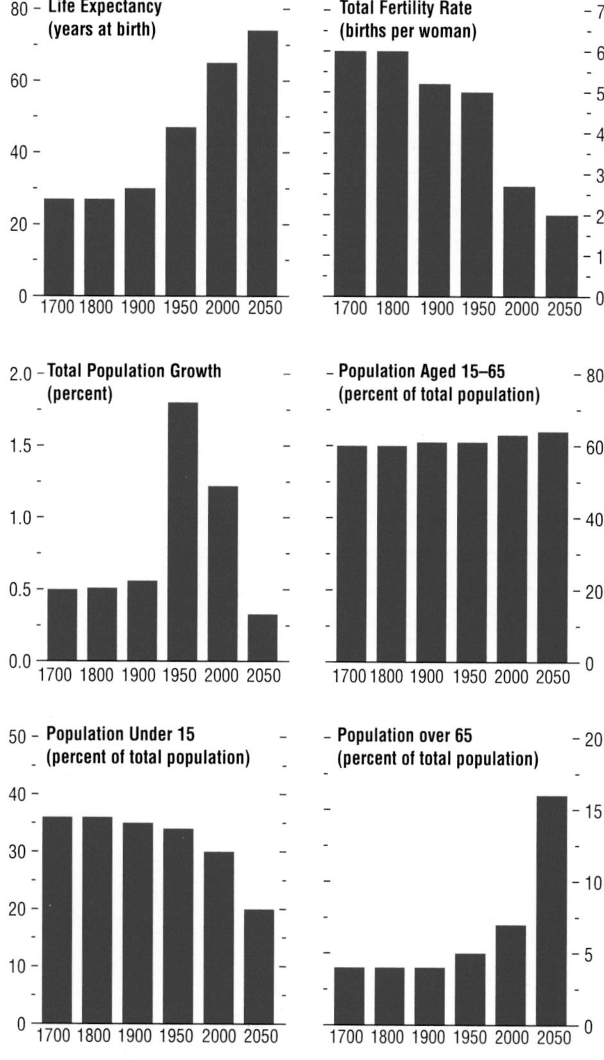

Source: Lee (2003).

tion aging on both the economy and Britain's influence overseas (United Kingdom, 1949). The impact of demographic change on developing countries has received less attention, but is certainly no less important, particularly given that an increasing share of the world's population will reside in these countries in the future.

Despite the uncertainty of demographic projections, the broad trends just described appear to be well established. Nonetheless, some time will elapse before their consequences for macroeconomic behavior are fully manifested. So, if the economic implications of these demographic changes are judged to be significant, policymakers do have the opportunity to respond ahead of time, although this window of opportunity is closing fast, particularly for those countries where the demographic transition is well advanced. The appropriate policy responses, however, are likely to vary between countries, will inevitably involve difficult trade-offs, and will take time to agree and implement.

In light of the changes taking place in the world's demographic structure, this chapter

- identifies more precisely the main demographic trends currently facing the world;
- assesses how these trends may affect the global and regional economies; and
- discusses policy responses to meet the challenges posed by demographic change.

The chapter is organized as follows. The first section discusses current and projected demographic trends, and how these will affect the size and structure of the world's population. The second section presents econometric and model-based evidence on the economic impact of demographic change. The last section explores possible policy options for responding to ongoing demographic developments.

Changing Structure of the World's Population

The world is in the midst of a historically unprecedented demographic transition that is having—and will continue to have—profound effects on the size and age structure of its population (Figure 3.1). Before 1900, world population growth was slow, the age structure of the population was broadly constant, and relatively few people lived beyond age 65. This began to change during the first half of the twentieth century as rising life expectancy boosted population growth, although initially there was little change in the age structure of the population.[2] The second half of the twentieth century saw the start of another phase in this transition. Fertility rates declined dramatically—by almost one-half—causing population growth to slow, the share of the young in the population to decline, and the share of the elderly to increase. The share of the working-age population, however, also rose modestly.

These global developments mask considerable variation between countries and regions that are the result of very different fertility, mortality, and migration trends (Figure 3.2). For example, although fertility rates have fallen almost universally in recent decades, they remain much higher in developing than in advanced countries, where they are generally below the replacement rate.[3] Even among developing countries, considerable differences exist—fertility rates are high in Africa and the Middle East, but are below replacement rates in east Asia and central and eastern Europe. Likewise, while life expectancy has risen across the globe over the past 50 years—and the largest gains have generally been made in developing countries—life expectancy still remains much higher in advanced countries. Exceptions to the generalized increase in life expectancy are Africa—where as a result of the HIV/AIDS

[2]In a number of European countries the demographic transition began much earlier. Lee (2003) dates the beginning of the decline in mortality in northwest Europe to about 1800. Population growth in the United States and Canada also decelerated in the nineteenth century.

[3]Replacement level fertility is estimated to be 2.1 births per woman in advanced countries and 2.4 births per woman in the developing countries. The level exceeds 2 in part because more boys are born than girls and in part because some children do not survive through the reproductive ages.

Figure 3.2. Key Demographic Trends, 1950–2050

Fertility rates are declining, life expectancy is rising, and migration is becoming a more important factor in population growth in the advanced economies.

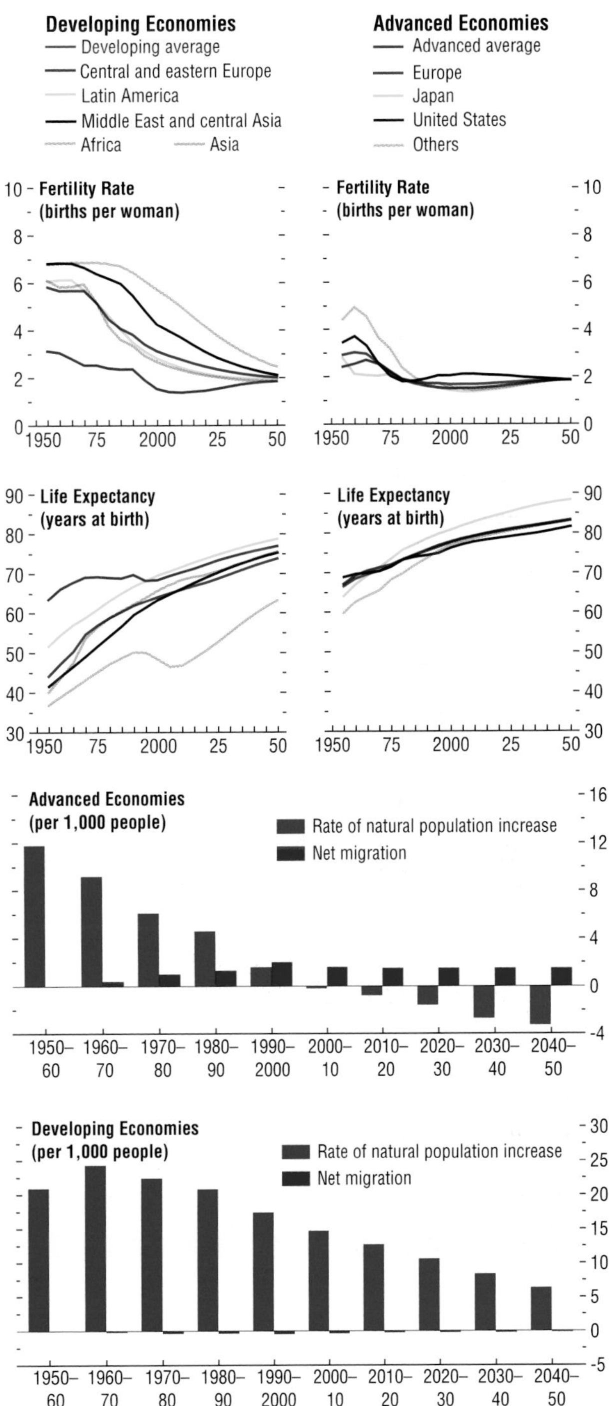

Sources: United Nations, *World Population Prospects: The 2002 Revision* (2003) and *World Population Prospects: The 2000 Revision* (2001).

Figure 3.3. Where the World's Population Lives[1]

The share of the world's population living in developed countries is declining, while that living in the least developed countries is rising.

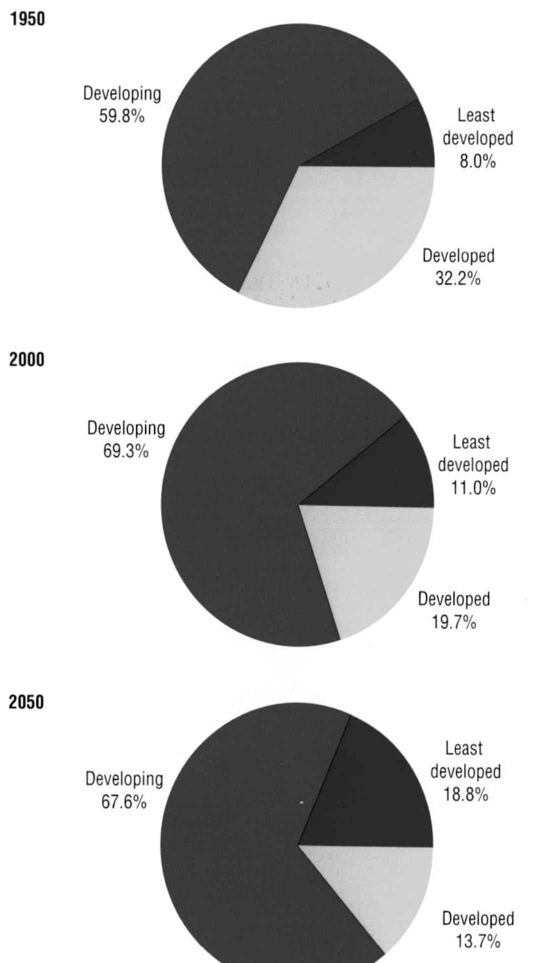

Source: United Nations, *World Population Prospects: The 2002 Revision* (2003).
[1]United Nations definitions of developing, developed, and least developed country groups are used for this figure.

pandemic, life expectancy has declined by more than 25 percent in some countries—and the Commonwealth of Independent States (CIS) countries. Lastly, net immigration has made an important contribution to population growth in recent years in North America, while Europe and Japan have had much lower immigration rates.

As a consequence of all of these trends, population growth is much higher in developing countries—particularly in Africa and the Middle East—than in advanced countries. Indeed, in Japan and Europe, population growth is close to zero. The share of the young in the total population is also higher in developing countries, while the elderly account for a larger share of the population in advanced nations.

Looking ahead, the United Nations' current population projections (which extend to 2050) envisage that fertility rates in low-fertility countries will recover modestly, that fertility in other countries will continue to decline, that further gains in life expectancy will be made in both advanced and developing country regions, and that migration will make an increasingly important contribution to total population growth in advanced countries, but will only modestly reduce population growth in developing countries.[4] This has the following consequences.

- *Global population growth will continue to slow.* By 2050, global population growth is projected to be only ¼ percent a year, compared with 1¼ percent at present. The population in a number of countries is actually expected to decline over the next 50 years, including by over 30 percent in some central and eastern European countries, by 22 percent in Italy, and by 14 percent in Japan. In other countries—particularly in Africa and the Middle East, but also

[4]The projections discussed in this section refer to the "medium variant" of United Nations (2003). The fact that migration will become an increasingly important source of population growth in advanced countries is due to the fact that the rate of natural population increase will slow, or decline. The level of immigration into advanced economies itself is projected to be somewhat lower during 2000–50 than it has been in recent years.

parts of Asia—population growth, although slowing, will remain robust, reflecting their higher fertility rates. These trends will lead to a continuing redistribution of the world's population away from the developed countries (Figure 3.3). Indeed, 19 percent of the world's population will be living in what are now the least developed countries by 2050, compared with 11 percent in 2000.

- *The world's population will continue to age.* The elderly will account for an increasing share of the population—although the pace and timing of aging varies widely between countries and regions—and the median age of the world is expected to increase by over 10 years during 2000–50 to 37 years. The elderly dependency ratio—which shows the population aged 65 and older as a share of the working-age (aged 15–64) population—is projected to rise dramatically in Japan and Europe, with lesser increases anticipated in the United States (Figure 3.4).[5] Further, the elderly themselves are getting older. The number of people aged 80 years and over is increasing at nearly twice the rate of that of those over 65. Among the developing country regions, aging is already under way in central and eastern Europe, a process that is expected to accelerate from about 2015. Aging will also begin to accelerate in Asia and Latin America around this time—with China experiencing particularly rapid aging—but the share of the elderly in Africa and the Middle East, while rising, will remain relatively small.
- *The share of the working-age population will fall in advanced countries, but increase in many developing countries.* In Japan and some European

[5]These elderly dependency ratios are only an approximation of the support needs of an elderly population. Some people continue to work after they have reached 65, while not everyone in the 15–64 age group is in employment—they may be still in school, unemployed, or outside the labor force. Further, in some countries, children younger than 15 are in full-time employment. It is possible to develop a measure of economic dependency that adjusts for these factors, but this alternative measure is difficult to calculate, particularly for developing countries.

Figure 3.4. Population Structure, 1950–2050

In the advanced countries, working-age populations are projected to decline and the share of the elderly to rise. In the developing countries, working-age populations are projected to first rise, before aging sets in.

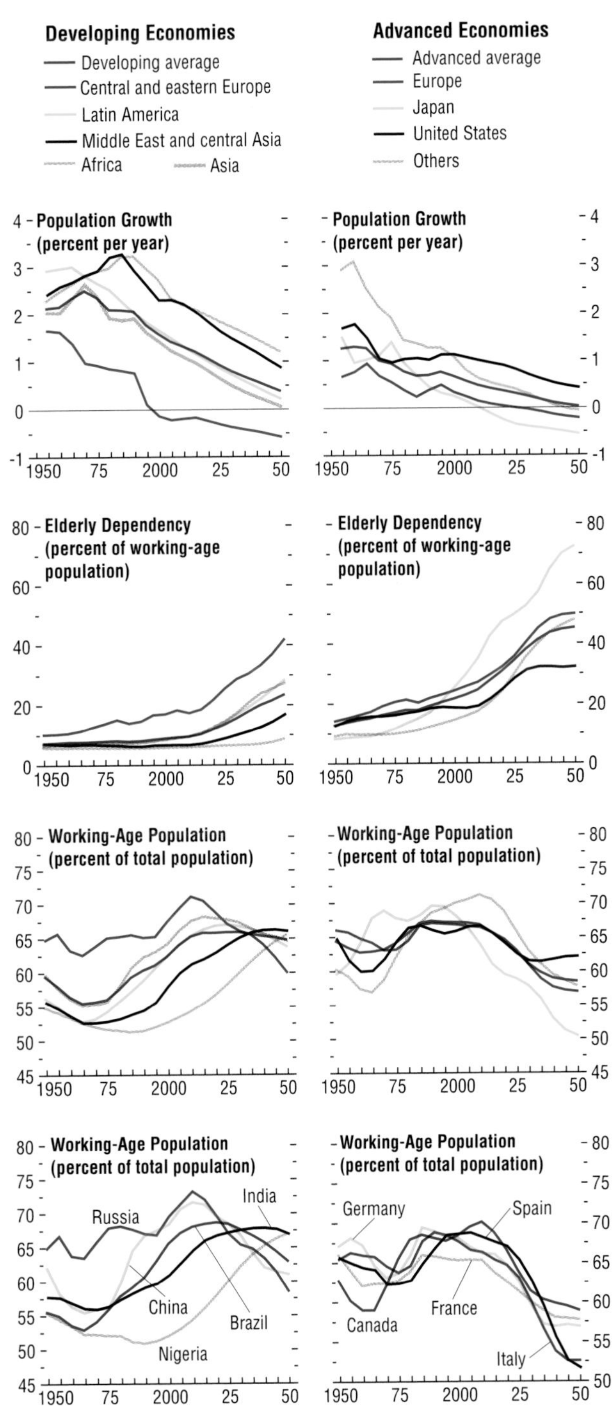

Source: United Nations, *World Population Prospects: The 2002 Revision* (2003).

Figure 3.5. Uncertainty in Population Projections

Demographic projections are uncertain. Past projections have shown a clear tendency to underestimate the share of the elderly in the population.

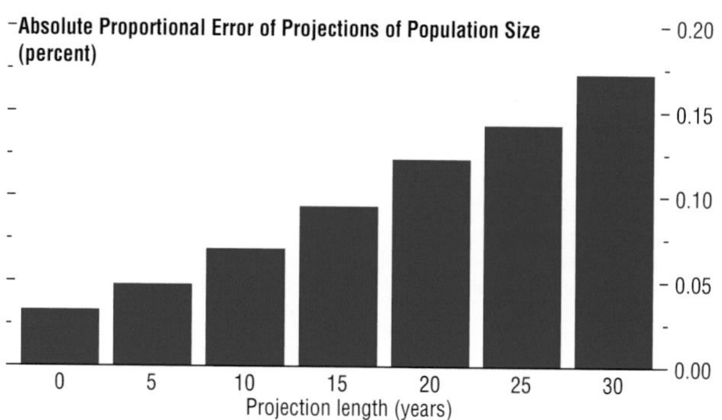

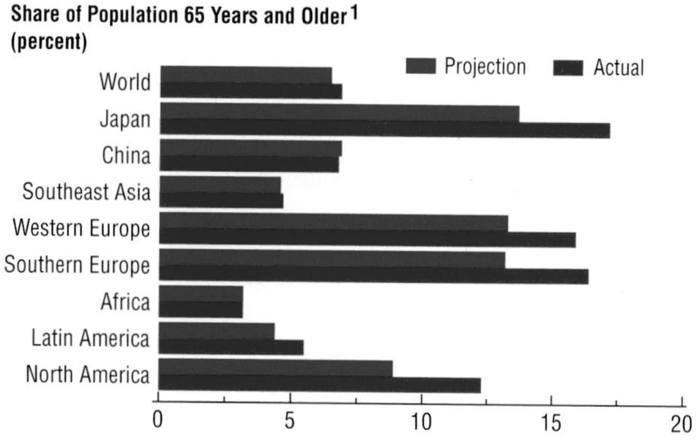

Sources: United Nations; National Research Council; and IMF staff calculations.
[1]Projections made in 1963 of population shares in 2000.

countries, this decline has already started and is projected to accelerate. In the United States, a high rate of immigration and higher fertility rates result in a more modest projected decline until 2025, after which the share of the working-age population stabilizes. In developing countries, the share of the working-age population is projected to increase until 2015, and then remain at this higher level as a declining share of the young offsets a rising share of the elderly. The working-age share will, however, start to decline in some regions before 2050, first in central and eastern Europe, and then in Asia and Latin America. In the Middle East and Africa, increases in the working-age populations are projected out to 2050. Looking at specific countries, large declines in the share of the working-age population are anticipated in Russia and China, while steady increases are expected in India and Nigeria.

The demographic changes that are projected to take place in the coming years are striking, and the important, but difficult, question is whether such projections provide a useful guide to likely future developments. Clearly, caution must be exercised when using long-term projections of any kind, and demographic projections do become much more uncertain the further into the future one goes (Figure 3.5). However, as discussed in Box 3.1, the basic trends outlined in this section—toward an increasing share of the elderly and a declining share of the young in the population—are apparent in most plausible scenarios. The main issue therefore is the extent to which the global population will age over the next 50 years (and beyond). While one cannot say on which side future errors are more likely to fall, a clear feature of past population projections has been the tendency to underestimate the share of the elderly in the total population in advanced countries, by underestimating both the decline in fertility and the increase in life expectancy. If this trend were to continue in the future, it would have important implications, particularly for public pension systems in these countries.

Table 3.1. Macroeconomic Impact of Demographic Changes: Panel Instrumental Variable Regressions[1]

	Growth in Real GDP per Capita	Saving/GDP	Investment/GDP	Current Account/GDP	Budget Balance/GDP
Impact of:					
Share of working-age population[2]	**0.08**	**0.72**	**0.31**	**0.05**	0.06
Share of elderly population[2]	**–0.041**	**–0.35**	–0.14	**–0.25**	**–0.46**

[1]All regressions are panel fixed-effects regressions. The sample includes 115 countries; the data for each country are averaged over each decade. All demographic variables, as well as several other controls, are instrumented using their lagged values. See the appendix for details of the controls and instruments used in each regression. Bold-faced values are statistically significant at the 10 percent level.

[2]The working-age population is defined as the age group 15–64 inclusive. The elderly population is defined as the age group 65 and upward. Increases in the share of either are defined as coming at the expense of the age group 0–14 inclusive. These population shares appear in growth form in the regression for the growth of real GDP per capita, and in level form elsewhere except in the regression for the current account/GDP ratio, where they are expressed as deviations from the world average.

Economic Impact of Demographic Change

The demographic changes projected over the coming years are large, but are they likely to have an important effect on the economies of advanced and developing countries? This section uses two approaches—econometric analysis and simulations from a multicountry macroeconomic model—to investigate this issue.

Econometric Results

A large, 115-country, panel data set covering the period 1960–2000 was used to investigate the relationship between demographic variables and per capita GDP growth, saving, investment, the current account, and fiscal balances. The key results of the analysis—which are shown in Table 3.1 and described in more detail in Appendix 3.1—show the following, after controlling for other explanatory factors.[6]

- *Per capita GDP growth is positively correlated with changes in the relative size of the working-age population, and negatively correlated with changes in the share of the elderly* (Figure 3.6). This result, which is in line with existing studies, partly reflects the direct productive impact of a larger labor force.[7] In addition, as discussed below, lower dependency ratios tend to raise saving, which in turn helps finance more investment and boosts output.[8] Some evidence also suggests that the lower the initial level of per capita income, the larger the net positive impact of a decline in fertility (Bloom, Canning, and Sevilla, 2001). Other studies have suggested that the impact of demography on growth is linked to the strength of the institutional and policy framework in place. For example, relatively open and competitive markets, substantial investments in basic education, fiscal discipline, and a relatively deep financial sector may have helped east Asian countries benefit from the demographic dividend.[9] Per capita growth is also found to be positively associated with life expectancy—which may directly affect labor productivity and the incentives for investment in human and physical capital—although this could partly reflect the difficulty of adequately measuring and controlling for variables such as

[6]The econometric results should be interpreted with some caution as historical correlations may not reflect causality. In particular, econometric analysis of demographic issues is subject to problems of endogeneity and omitted variables. For instance, income itself is an important determinant of fertility, mortality, and hence the age structure of populations (Lee, 2003); this may introduce biases into the estimated coefficients. The analysis does try to minimize such problems through the use of instruments, as described in the appendix.

[7]See Kelley and Schmidt (2001), Bloom, Canning, and Sevilla (2001), and Gomez and Hernandez de Cos (2003). In contrast, increases in the relative size of the young or the elderly are negatively associated with growth.

[8]The association between declining fertility and increased female labor force participation also strengthens the impact of lower youth dependency—the ratio of those aged 0–14 to the working-age population—on per capita growth.

[9]Bloom and Canning (2001), Williamson (2001), and Lee, Mason, and Miller (1997) examine this issue.

Box 3.1. Demographic Projections: Methodologies and Uncertainties

The United Nations (UN) has been the leader in producing global population projections, and the analysis in this chapter is based on the "medium variant" scenario in the UN's "World Population Prospects: The 2002 Revision" (UN, 2003). Global population projections are also published by the World Bank, the United States Census Bureau, and the International Institute for Applied Systems Analysis (IIASA). At present, there is little difference in the projections of the four organizations. World population in 2050 is projected at 8.9 billion by the UN, 9 billion by the U.S. Census Bureau, and 8.8 billion by the IIASA and the World Bank (world population was 6.1 billion in 2000). Projections for individual countries, however, vary more widely. In terms of the age structure of the population, the share of the elderly—here defined as over 60 years of age—in 2050 is projected to be 21.4 percent by the UN, 21.9 percent by IIASA, and 22.2 percent by the U.S. Census Bureau.

A key issue is whether these projections provide a reasonable guide to future demographic developments. While this is clearly a very difficult question to answer because any set of projections can only be judged ex post, an assessment of past projections may provide useful information about the likely accuracy of the current projections. Past projections of world population have generally been quite accurate. The National Research Council (2000) found that while the UN was more likely to overestimate than underestimate future world population, the size of the error was small (an average of less than 3 percent in the projections made between 1957 and 1998). Indeed, the 1957 projection overestimated world population in 2000 by 3½ percent. At the country level, however, projection errors have been larger, particularly over long time horizons; these errors tend to offset when aggregated—hence the greater accuracy of the global projections. In general, population has been overprojected in most regions except the Middle East and North Africa, and projection errors have been smaller for developed than for developing countries, and for large countries compared with small countries. Another feature of past projections—as discussed in the main text—is that there has been a tendency to underestimate the share of the elderly in the total population in developed countries.

Errors in population projections occur for three main reasons. First, the estimate of the population in the base year of the projection may be inaccurate, and may subsequently be revised. Second, the underlying trends in fertility, mortality, and migration may be incorrectly projected. Third, unexpected events may occur that have demographic consequences such as war, famine, or the spread of disease. The HIV/AIDS pandemic, for example, has significantly altered the demographic profile in Africa. The National Research Council found that errors in fertility and migration projections account for most of the projection error in country forecasts over long periods. Looking at past experience, fertility rates have consistently been overestimated for most regions of the world; projections about life expectancy have generally been too pessimistic (Africa and the Commonwealth of Independent States (CIS) countries are exceptions); and net migration has been very difficult to predict.

Looking forward, uncertainties exist about future trends in fertility and life expectancy, and the assumptions made in the projections are crucial; even small projection errors—especially for fertility rates—can lead to very different outcomes in the long run. The UN's latest projections foresee a gradual recovery in fertility rates in developed countries, while fertility rates in developing countries are expected to continue to decline toward replacement levels. Those people expecting fertility to rebound in developed countries point out that the average age of childbearing is rising, leading to fewer births each year during this transition. Once this transition is over, measured fertility rates should rebound. They also note that in a number of countries—Denmark, Finland, Norway, and the United States—fertility has recovered somewhat in recent years, while in surveys conducted in Europe, women consistently say they want two children, which would boost the current fertility

Note: The main author of this box is Tim Callen.

rate if acted upon.[1] Others, however, believe that the decline in fertility will not be reversed because it represents an adjustment to changed social expectations, including the greater career orientation of women and the increased amount of time, attention, and money that are devoted to each child. Life expectancy projections are also the subject of disagreement. Some argue that there is a biological limit to life expectancy—often put at about 85 years of age—while others expect the gains in life expectancy seen in recent decades to continue into the future (see Oeppen and Vaupel, 2002, for example).

The most common way of characterizing the uncertainties with demographic projections is to consider alternate scenarios around the central projection. For example, the UN publishes different scenarios in addition to their "medium" variant projections. In the "low" and "high" variant scenarios, fertility is assumed to level off at half a birth below and half a birth above that in the "medium" variant scenario, respectively (assumptions about mortality and net migration are unchanged). These assumptions lead to very different outcomes, particularly in the long run. In the low-fertility scenario, world population increases only modestly to 7.4 billion by 2050, while in the high variant scenario it increases to 10.6 billion. The proportion of the elderly population in 2050—here defined as over 60 years of age to be consistent with the IIASA projections below—is also very different between scenarios, but in both cases is higher than in 2000 (see the figure).

A criticism of the scenario approach is that it gives no indication of the probability of any particular outcome actually occurring. Probabilistic projections—such as those by the IIASA and Lee, Anderson, and Tuljapurkar (2003)—attempt to address this problem. These projections acknowledge that there is uncertainty about future fertility, mortality, and migration trends, and use a range of possible outcomes to derive a probability distribution for the size and age structure of the future population. The IIASA's projections suggest that at the 95 percent confidence level the world's population in 2050 will be between 6.4 and 11.3 billion, and that the proportion of the population aged over 60 years will be between 15 and 29 percent.

In sum, there are clear uncertainties with projections of future demographic trends, which need to be carefully considered when using the projections for policy purposes. Under almost any scenario, however, the global population will age over the next 50 years (and beyond), and the main question is the extent to which this will happen. Policymakers need to prepare for this aging process, although the magnitude of the policy response will need to be reevaluated on an ongoing basis as more information becomes available about how demographic trends are developing.

Uncertainty in Population Projections

(Population aged 60 years and older in percent of total population)

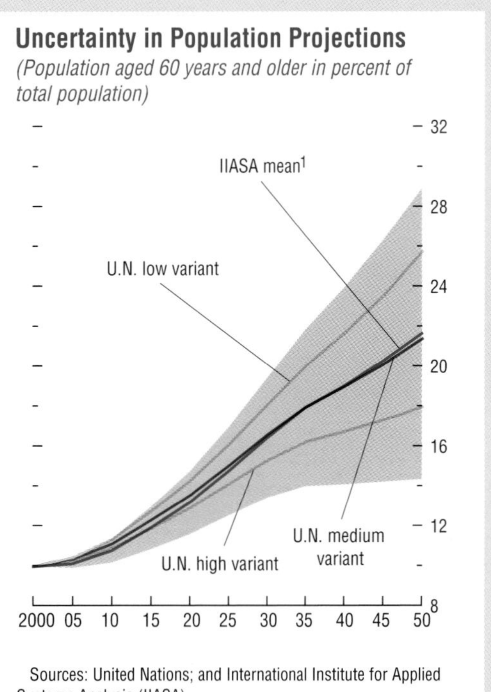

Sources: United Nations; and International Institute for Applied Systems Analysis (IIASA).

[1]Shaded area represents the IIASA mean projection plus and minus two standard deviations.

[1]The reasons for the recovery in fertility in these countries is not clear, although the emphasis in the Scandinavian countries on measures that make motherhood and women's labor force participation more compatible—such as day care services, flexible working hours, and liberal maternity and sick leave allowances—may be important (see Demeny, 2003).

Figure 3.6. Per Capita Growth and Working-Age Population

There is a clear, positive relationship between growth in output per capita and the relative size of the working-age population. This holds for both advanced and developing economies.

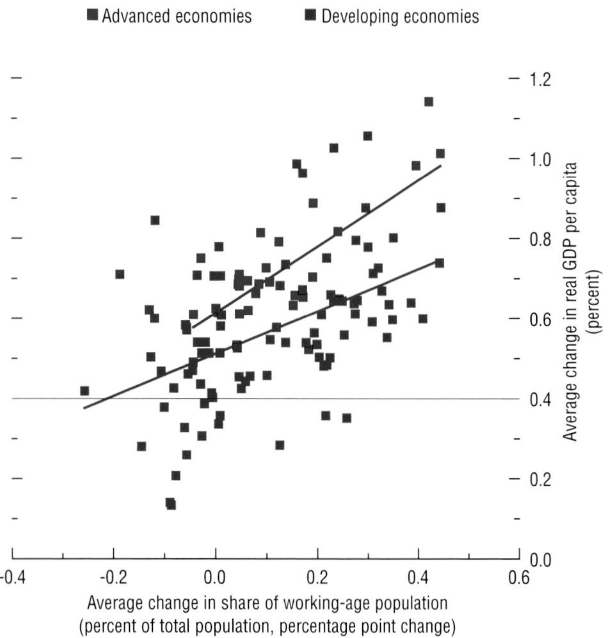

Sources: Penn World Tables; World Bank, *World Development Indicators;* and IMF staff calculations.

institutional quality, which are likely to be correlated with both growth and life expectancy.[10]

- *There is a statistically significant association between demographic variables and saving.* According to the life-cycle hypothesis of saving, people try to maintain a smooth pattern of consumption through their lifetime. This means that when current income is low relative to lifetime average income, saving will also be low, and when current income is high relative to lifetime average income, saving will be high. Younger people tend to be net borrowers; older people at the peak of their earnings potential tend to be high net savers; and the elderly tend to dissave, or at least to save at a lower rate than during their working years. While there is some contention about the validity of the life-cycle hypothesis—particularly whether the elderly actually run down their wealth in retirement—the results in Table 3.1, as well as most other cross-country studies, find that demographic factors (together with income growth, real interest rates, and public saving) play a role in influencing saving behavior.[11] Specifically, saving rises with an increase in the share of the working-age population, and declines with an increase in the elderly share.
- *The share of the working-age population is also correlated with investment.* Demographic change influences investment through its impact on saving, and because changes in the labor supply affect the returns to investment.
- *Current account balances increase with the relative size of the working-age population, and decrease*

[10]Meltzer (1992) started the modern literature on the links between mortality and growth. More recent contributions include Zhang and others (2003), Kalemli-Ozcan and others (2000), and Kalemli-Ozcan (2002, 2003). For a more skeptical viewpoint, see Acemoglu, Johnson, and Robinson (2003).

[11]Recent theoretical and empirical discussions of the link between demographic change and saving include Faruqee (2002), Futagami and Nakajima (2001), Deaton and Paxson (2000), Loayza, Schmidt-Hebbel, and Servén (2000), Disney (1996), Masson, Bayoumi, and Samiei (1995), Malmberg (1994), and Horioka (1991).

when the elderly dependency ratio rises.[12] Although saving and investment are both affected by the age structure of the population, so that it is not immediately obvious what impact demographic change should have on the current account, most empirical studies agree with this result.[13]

- *Demographic factors also affect the fiscal balance.* Specifically, government budgets are adversely affected by population aging due to higher spending on pensions, health care, and long-term residential care (see Heller, 2003, for an analysis of the long term fiscal challenges posed by population aging). Casey and others (2003) estimate that among OECD countries elderly-related spending will rise by an average of nearly 7 percent of GDP between 2000 and 2050 with additional expenditures on health care exceeding those on pensions in a number of countries.[14] A smaller working-age population may also result in lower tax revenues.

Demographic shifts may also have important implications for the performance of financial markets. As discussed in Box 3.2, the aging of populations may put downward pressure on real equity prices in advanced countries in the years ahead if retirees begin to liquidate their assets.[15] Chapter II of this *World Economic Outlook* also finds that demographic changes have been a factor behind the rise in housing prices in a number of countries.

The econometric results suggest that projected demographic changes could have an important impact on future economic performance. Combining the estimated coefficients reported in Table 3.1 with the UN's population projections yields a sense of the potential magnitudes, and how they may vary across regions.

- *In advanced countries, the impact of upcoming demographic changes on growth could be substantial.* The historic association between demographic and macroeconomic variables suggests that the projected increase in elderly dependency ratios and the projected decline in the share of the working-age population could result in slower per capita GDP growth, and lower saving and investment. For example, the estimates suggest that demographic change could reduce annual real GDP per capita growth in advanced countries by an average of ½ percentage point by 2050—i.e., growth would be ½ percentage point lower than if the demographic structure had remained the same as in 2000.[16] Growth would be most severely affected in Japan, while the impact in the United States would be relatively small (Figure 3.7).
- *The impact on growth in developing countries will vary by region.* In Africa and the Middle East, per capita growth could be boosted by the increase in the share of the working-age population.[17] The results suggest that per capita growth in 2050 could be 0.3 and 0.1 percent-

[12]Because separate equations are estimated for saving, investment, and the current account, the effects of the demographic variables on saving and investment do not sum to the aggregate effect on the current account.

[13]Feroli (2003) analyses the experience of the Group of Seven industrial countries (G-7); Chinn and Prasad (2003), Higgins (1998), and Luhrmann (2003) provide a wider cross-country perspective.

[14]Studies of the fiscal impact of population aging have also been carried out by the European Commission (2001), the OECD (2001), the Group of Ten (1998), and many individual countries, including for Australia (Australian Treasury, 2002), New Zealand (Janssen, 2001), and the United States (U.S. CBO, 2001). Other studies include Bohn (1999), Bryant (2004), INGENUE Team (2001), and Heller (1997).

[15]The impact of demographic change on pension funds is discussed in the September 2004 *Global Financial Stability Report.*

[16]This result is not suggesting that real per capita growth *will* be ½ percentage point lower in 2050 than it was in 2000. Many of the other variables that influence growth will also change over the next 50 years, and these changes could offset the impact of demographic factors.

[17]Declining fertility rates in the developing world could also have an important impact on poverty. While causality works in both directions, high fertility increases absolute poverty both by reducing economic growth and by changing the distribution of consumption against the poor—for instance, by increasing the price of food and reducing wages (Eastwood and Lipton, 2001). Consequently, if the UN projections of a sharp decline in fertility in the least developed countries are realized, this could help reduce poverty in these countries.

Figure 3.7. Impact of Demographic Change on Growth and Current Account Balances, 2000–50

Population aging will likely depress growth rates in advanced economies, while relatively more youthful developing countries, in contrast, could enjoy a growth boost as working-age populations increase. Faster-aging countries are also likely to experience a reduction in their current account balances, as the elderly run down their assets during retirement.

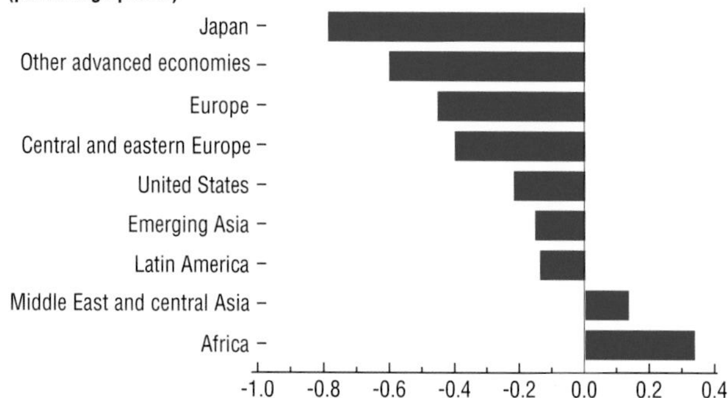

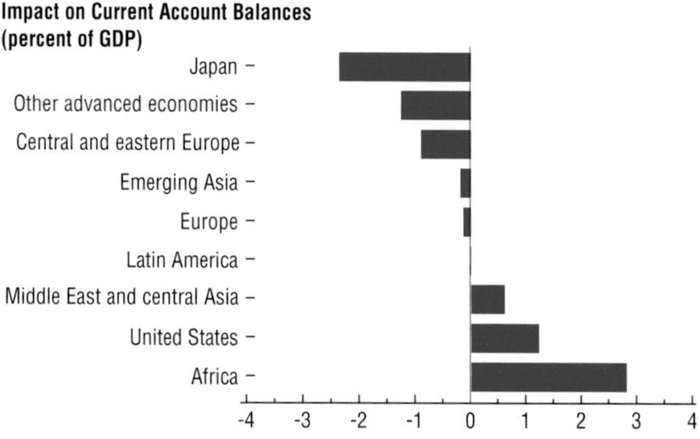

Sources: Penn World Tables; United Nations, *World Population Prospects: The 2002 Revision* (2003); and IMF staff calculations.

age point higher, respectively, in these regions. These results, however, are unlikely to adequately account for the impact of the HIV/AIDS pandemic which will continue to have a significant impact on macroeconomic outcomes in countries with high prevalence rates (see Box 3.3). In contrast, demographic changes are likely to weigh on growth in central and eastern Europe and, to a lesser extent, in Asia and Latin America by 2050 (although in these latter two regions individual country experience will vary).

- *Future demographic changes could lead to large changes in current account balances.* In advanced economies, the negative impact of population aging on saving will in general result in deteriorating current account balances; indeed, for Japan, the results suggest that the deterioration could be on the order of 2½ percentage points of GDP. The major exception is the United States, where demographic developments could lead to an improvement in the current account position of over 1 percentage point of GDP. Among developing countries, demographic change could contribute to an improvement in current account balances in Africa and the Middle East, but result in a deterioration in central and eastern Europe.

Impact of Demographic Change in a Multicountry Model

The econometric analysis provides a useful guide of how demographic change could affect key economic variables, but it suffers from the drawbacks that each variable is considered separately, rather than as part of an integrated economic system, and that the historical correlations that are identified between variables may not reflect causality. To address these issues, the potential impact of demographic change was examined using a multiregion macroeconomic model—the INGENUE model (INGENUE Team, 2001)—that explicitly captures the interactions between variables and across countries within an integrated and consistent framework.

The INGENUE model disaggregates the world economy into six regions: North America and Oceania, Europe, Japan, and three developing country regions that are defined according to their particular demographic characteristics.[18] The model explicitly incorporates the age structure of the population, and adopts the life-cycle hypothesis of saving as one of its cornerstones. The model also accounts for the costs to parents of raising children, and incorporates a pension system in each country/region. Capital is allowed to move freely across regions, but labor is assumed to be immobile (since migration is an important channel through which the global economy could adjust to demographic developments, a model that allows for labor mobility is discussed in the next section).

The results from the model suggest that the demographic changes projected over the next 50 years will lower output growth in all regions although, given slowing population growth, the impact on per capita growth rates will not be as large (Figure 3.8). Per capita growth rates will slow relative to current levels in all the advanced country regions, while they will initially rise in the developing country regions as demographic changes boost the supply of labor.[19]

An important aspect of the results is that saving rates in Europe and Japan—and to a lesser extent the rapidly aging developing region—will decline sharply as the share of the elderly in the population rises and working-age populations fall. Pension systems actually contribute significantly

Figure 3.8. Implications of Projected Demographic Change in the INGENUE Model

(Changes relative to the model predicted outcome in 2000)

Population aging is likely to lower output growth in all regions of the world and could result in large changes in current account balances as staggered aging across the world leads to different saving-investment profiles between regions.

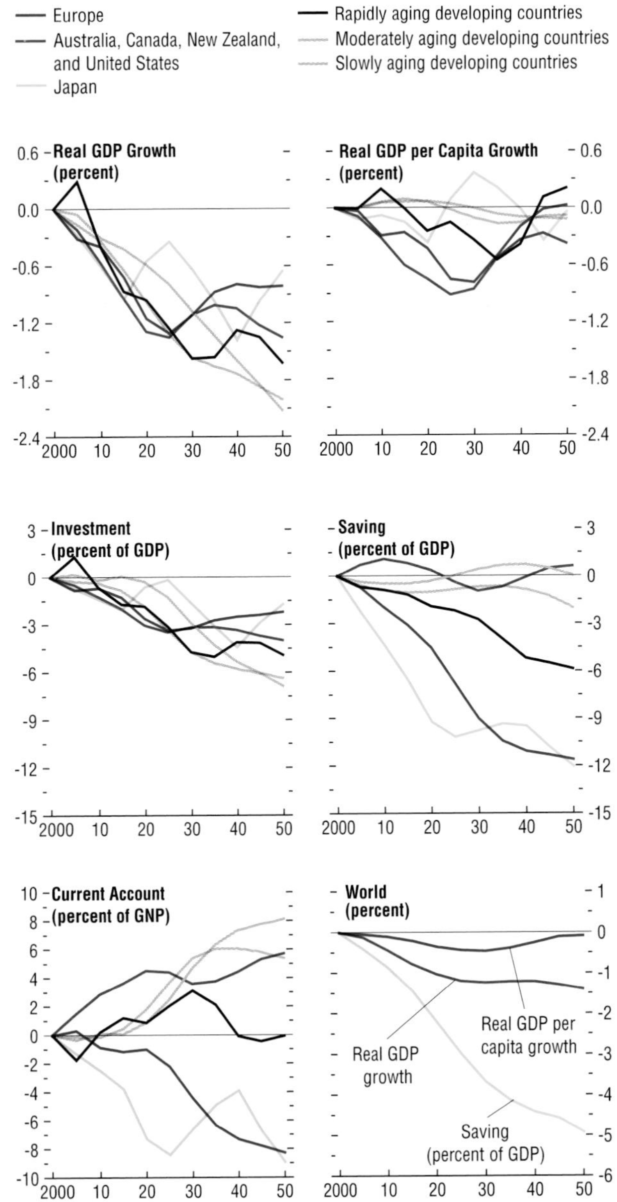

Sources: INGENUE Team; and IMF staff calculations.

[18]The three developing country regions in the INGENUE model are those economies that are well advanced in the demographic transition, such as China, Korea, and Russia (labeled "rapidly aging developing countries"); those economies at an earlier stage of the demographic transition, such as India and many Latin American countries (labeled "moderately aging developing countries"); and, finally, those economies just starting or yet to start the demographic transition, including most African countries and Pakistan (labeled "slowly aging developing countries").

[19]The more modest decline in per capita growth in Europe and Japan relative to North America and Oceania is largely driven by the model's assumption that the former regions close their productivity gap with the United States over the projection period.

Box 3.2. How Will Population Aging Affect Financial Markets?

Even after the bursting of the technology bubble, stock prices in real terms are four times their value at the beginning of 1980. In the United States, this increase has coincided with a dramatic rise in the share of the population aged 40 to 64, as the baby boomers—those born from 1946 to 1964—have moved into their prime saving years. Popular accounts, such as Passell (1996) have linked these two phenomena, arguing that an inflow of private saving from middle-aged baby boomers has been driving up the stock market. These accounts warn that demographic forces will conspire against the stock market after 2010, when the oldest of the baby boomers begin to turn 65. They conjecture that beyond this point, the baby boomers will be selling off their stocks to a much smaller generation of buyers, causing stock prices to decline. During the postwar period, real stock prices in the United States have indeed been positively associated with the relative importance of the population in prime saving years (top panel of the figure). Given the projected path for the population of prime savers, the degree to which real stock prices will fall after 2010 then depends on understanding whether this association is empirically robust and what underlying factors could be driving it.

This box reviews recent advances in the academic literature on the link between demography and the stock market. Broadly speaking, this literature consists of two strands: one empirical and the other theoretical. The former uses a variety of techniques to test the robustness of the link between demographic factors and the stock market, while the latter uses economic models to understand how changes in the age distribution affect the stock market in a controlled environment.[1]

The empirical literature often finds a robust link between the proportion of high net savers in the population and asset prices, suggesting that the aging of the baby boomers could cause real stock prices to fall. Bergantino (1998) uses

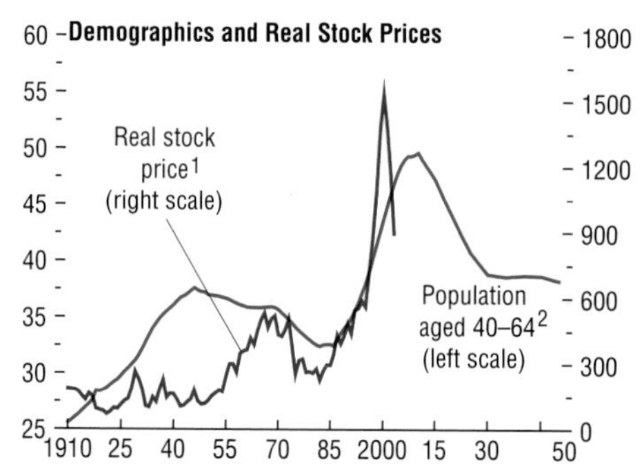

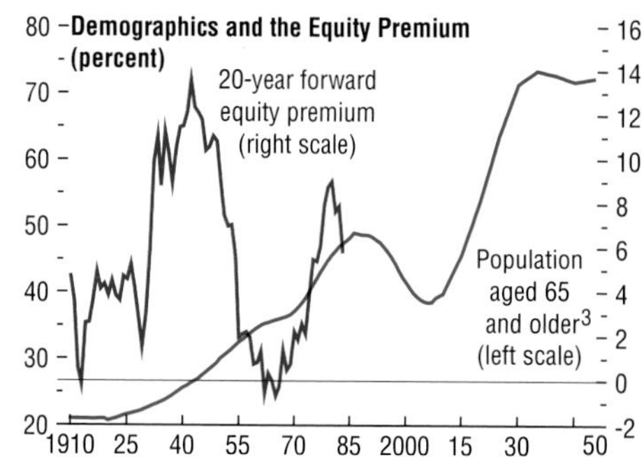

Sources: Shiller (2003); and United States Census Bureau.
[1]Standard and Poors 500 index, deflated by U.S. consumer price index.
[2]As a percent of population aged 0–39 and those aged 65 and older.
[3]As a percent of population aged 40–64.

household surveys from the United States to construct age-specific demand profiles for stocks and other assets and finds that demand for stocks and other financial assets is greatest among households aged 40 to 60. Based on this exercise, he constructs an aggregate demand schedule for financial assets, which explains about three-fourths of the observed annual increase in real stock prices between 1986 and 1997. Brooks (1998) explores the link between real stock and bond prices and demography in an international setting. Using data from 14 advanced economies over the postwar period, he finds that real stock and bond prices are positively associated with the share of the population aged 40 to 64, even after controlling for other fundamentals driving

Note: The main author of this box is Robin Brooks.
[1]More extensive surveys of the empirical and theoretical literature can be found in Young (2002) and Bosworth, Bryant, and Burtless (2004).

financial markets. Davis and Li (2003) report similar results for seven OECD countries—an increase in the fraction of the population aged 40 to 64 tends to boost real asset prices. Most recently, Geanakoplos, Magill, and Quinzii (2004) find that the price-earnings ratio of stock prices in the United States—a normalized measure of the level of equity prices that has the advantage of factoring out growth—is positively associated with the relative importance of middle-aged workers in the population.

This evidence, however, must be interpreted with caution. First, the effective number of observations is small. The relative importance of prime savers rises through the late 1940s, falls through the mid-1980s as the baby boomers enter the young tail of the age distribution, and subsequently rises as they enter their prime saving years. Over the same horizon, the major events in the stock market are the postwar boom in the 1950s and 1960s, the oil-shock induced bust in the 1970s and early 1980s, and the subsequent boom starting in the mid-1980s. The small effective number of observations is exacerbated by the fact that there is little systematic association between real stock prices and demography prior to the postwar period. Second, at long horizons there are common shocks, notably the Great Depression and World War II, which are driving both demography and the stock market. Because these shocks are global, data from other countries do not represent independent observations. In other words, cross-country studies do not add much explanatory power in effective terms. Indeed, Poterba (2001) argues that none of the empirical findings provide a strong and convincing measure of the amount that asset prices will change as a result of population aging.

In part because of the limitations of the empirical analysis, researchers have increasingly turned to economic models as a controlled environment in which to study the effects of demography on the stock market. Abel (2003) and Geanakoplos, Magill, and Quinzii (2004) resolve what is perhaps one of the most puzzling questions in this literature: how can there be a contemporaneous association between changes in the age distribution—a slow-moving, highly predictable process—and stock prices when financial markets are rational and forward looking? Both papers use stylized representations of the age distribution and capital markets to show that real stock prices display a contemporaneous link to the age distribution even when investors are forward looking and rational. This is because only living generations trade in financial markets at a point in time, meaning that differences in the demand and supply of financial assets—a reflection of differences in size across generations—cannot be arbitraged away ahead of time. Moreover, the latter paper shows that demographic fluctuations account for virtually all of the peak-to-trough variation in stock prices over the postwar period once the business cycle is accounted for.

Finally, theoretical approaches are increasingly being used to study the link between demography and the equity premium—the extra return that investors earn for holding equities rather than government bonds. Constantinides, Donaldson, and Mehra (2002) use an economic model to show that retirees are less willing holders of equity than workers because they can no longer count on wage income to offset the consumption effects of adverse stock market movements. Their model suggests that the equity premium should be higher the greater the fraction of old people in the population, consistent with Bakshi and Chen (1994). Indeed, in the United States, as the relative importance of the population over 65 increased after 1970, so did the 20-year forward equity premium (which measures the excess return investors could have earned on stocks under perfect foresight; see the bottom panel of the figure). However, any empirical link between the equity premium and demography is weak (see also Ang and Maddaloni, 2003).

Overall, the empirical and theoretical strands of the literature suggest that stock prices could move against the baby boomers as they retire so that past returns should not be viewed as a benchmark for returns on the retirement savings of this generation. Moreover, there is some evidence that the equity premium could rise as the boomer generation moves into retirement. This has important implications for individual accounts-based reforms to public pension systems, which often assume a constant equity premium over the reform horizon.

Box 3.3. HIV/AIDS: Demographic, Economic, and Fiscal Consequences

The HIV/AIDS epidemic has resulted in a substantial increase in mortality—and a corresponding loss of life expectancy—in many countries, particularly in sub-Saharan Africa. In addition to its devastating human costs, HIV/AIDS disrupts economic activity and erodes a government's ability to deliver public services when the demand for these services—particularly in the health sector—is actually increasing.

Demographic Impact of HIV/AIDS

HIV/AIDS is now the primary cause of death in Africa (the worst-affected region); about 20 percent of all deaths are accounted for by the disease, twice as many as are caused by malaria and 10 times as many as are caused by violence and war combined (WHO, 2004). For sub-Saharan Africa, HIV prevalence rates for the prime-age working population (ages 15–49) were 7.5 percent on average as of end-2003, but they exceeded 20 percent in 6 countries including Botswana and Swaziland where they were above 30 percent. For the worst-affected countries, mortality among the working-age population has increased substantially, and HIV/AIDS now accounts for over 90 percent of deaths in this age range for some countries (see the table). In some countries, life expectancy at birth has decreased by more than 25 percent in recent years, and in Botswana and Zimbabwe it is now lower than it was in 1950. Finally, because of HIV/AIDS, the number of orphans has increased to about 20 percent of the young in the worst-affected countries. In the broader international context, increasing attention is being paid to countries such as China or India—where the largest number of people outside of South Africa live with HIV—and where low aggregate prevalence rates mask more serious epidemics at a regional level.

Economic Impact of HIV/AIDS

The economic impact of HIV/AIDS on households is uneven, depending on whether a household member is infected or not. In households where a member is ill or dies, income falls because of the loss of the person's earnings, and because other household members have to forgo work to devote time to care for the sick. Households also have to reallocate resources to care. A survey from South Africa suggests that health spending accounts for one-third of outlays for households affected by HIV/AIDS, compared with a national average of only 4 percent (Steinberg and others, 2002). In turn, this spending on health care reduces spending on other items—including education—and saving. Orphans of AIDS victims are a particularly vulnerable group as they often live in poorer households and have lower school enrollment rates than non-orphans (which affects human capital formation).

HIV/AIDS has adverse effects on private sector businesses because it disrupts activity, raises the cost of providing benefits, reduces productivity, and increases training costs as workers who retire or die have to be replaced. While disruptions caused by illness and death are the primary cost of HIV/AIDS to small companies and the informal sector, the impact on medical and death-related benefits is more important for larger companies. Faced with rising costs and a deteriorating and uncertain economic outlook, companies may also relocate their production or, in the case of foreign investment, stop investing in countries with severe HIV/AIDS epidemics.

There are a wide range of estimates of the overall impact of HIV/AIDS on growth. For example, some studies for Botswana and Swaziland estimate that HIV/AIDS will lower GDP growth by about 1.5 percent a year. A broader empirical study—using data from 41 countries—suggests a larger decline in GDP growth of up to 4 percent a year (see Dixon, McDonald, and Roberts, 2002). HIV/AIDS in fact not only destroys existing human capital but also severely impairs its formation (see Bell, Devarajan, and Gersbach, 2004).

Income per capita, however, is far from a complete measure of the economic impact of HIV/AIDS. As Crafts and Haacker (2004) show,

Note: The main author of this box is Markus Haacker.

Demographic Impact of HIV/AIDS

	HIV Prevalence Rate Ages 15–49, End-2003 (percent)	Life Expectancy at Birth (years)		Mortality, Ages 15–39, 2003 (percent)		Orphans Ages 0–17 (percent of young population)
		1990–1995	2002	Total	Of which: AIDS	2003
	(1)	(2)	(3)	(4)	(5)	(6)
Botswana	37.3	65.0	40.4	4.3	4.1	20.0
Côte d'Ivoire	7.0	48.3	45.3	1.8	1.3	13.4
South Africa	21.5	61.8	50.7	3.1	2.9	12.9
Zambia	16.5	44.2	39.7	2.7	2.1	18.3
Zimbabwe	24.6	53.3	37.9	2.7	2.5	18.6

Sources: UNAIDS (2004) for column (1); UN (2003), for column (2); WHO (2004), for column (3); estimates provided by the International Programs Center at the U.S. Bureau of the Census, for columns (4) and (5); and UNAIDS/UNICEF/USAID (2004) for column (6).

welfare losses from HIV/AIDS are much larger than losses in per capita income because of the need for higher outlays on health services and increased poverty. More generally, the higher risk of illness and death means that living standards fall (for example, in the UNDP's Human Development Index).

Consequences of HIV/AIDS for the Public Sector

HIV/AIDS has significant implications for government budgets and service delivery. Higher mortality erodes the government's human resource base, undermines domestic revenue collection, raises costs, and causes disruptions to the delivery of public services. Many of these effects are similar to those for the private sector, although the impact on the government's personnel costs is likely to be larger because the government typically offers more comprehensive benefits, including health insurance and pensions to surviving dependants. At the same time as the government's service delivery capacities are eroded, HIV/AIDS increases the demand for a wide array of government services, most notably in the health sector. The HIV epidemic is already having a profound effect on health services in developing countries. Over (2004) estimates that an HIV prevalence rate of 5 percent could result in an increase in the demand for health services of 26 percent for the treatment of opportunistic infections alone. With HIV prevalence rates of 20–30 percent in some countries, this would mean that the demand for health services more than doubles as a result of HIV/AIDS. Available data on the share of hospital beds occupied by HIV positive patients, frequently in a range of 50–70 percent, are broadly consistent with this picture, and indicate that some crowding out of other patients is taking place.

Implementing a broad response to HIV/AIDS remains a major challenge. Substantial declines in the costs of antiretroviral drugs have resulted in a shift in the emphasis of the international response to HIV/AIDS to also include increasing access to these treatments. For example, the WHO's "3 by 5" initiative aims to provide antiretroviral treatment to three million people in developing countries by end–2005, at an estimated cost of $5–6 billion (Gutierrez and others, 2004). This means that many countries can now start to provide treatment to HIV patients. However, in countries where only basic health services are currently provided through the public sector, where the availability of health personnel is limited, or where health expenditures would increase (and sometimes more than double) from a very low base, the delivery of adequate care for patients remains a challenge (Over, 2004). The international community needs to raise the resources available for an adequate response to HIV/AIDS, help countries to mount sustainable and effective AIDS strategies, and assist countries in strengthening their capacities to deliver these strategies (UNAIDS, 2004).

to this decline because social security contribution rates have to be raised to finance the additional pension expenditures that result from the increase in retirees. This effectively transfers resources from the working-age population—which has a higher propensity to save—to older generations who have a lower propensity to save.[20] Changes in saving behavior elsewhere are much smaller. In North America, saving initially rises as the baby boomers move through their high saving years, and then begins to decline modestly after 2010. In the aggregate, world saving declines sharply. As the relative size of the working-age population (and hence the marginal product of capital) declines, investment (relative to GDP) also falls, with the most pronounced changes occurring in the fastest-aging regions.

Demographic change could result in a substantial reallocation of global capital in the long run.[21] The decline in saving causes a large current account deterioration in Japan and Europe in the model (initially, these changes result in a smaller current account surplus, which turns into a deficit around 2020 as capital is repatriated from abroad). Other countries experience offsetting current account increases, although in the moderately and slowly aging developing country regions this change does not occur immediately. An important implication of the results is that developing countries may have access to less external capital in the future, although reforms to improve the investment environment in these countries may help alleviate this problem (see below).

The results from the model and those from the econometric exercise reach broadly similar conclusions about the likely impact of the demographic changes projected over the next 50 years. Specifically, per capita growth rates are likely to decline in advanced economies, but rise in those developing countries where the share of the working-age population is increasing. Saving and investment will be affected in all countries, but the countries that are aging faster—Japan and Europe—will experience a deterioration in their current account positions, which will be offset by improvements elsewhere.

There are, however, substantial uncertainties associated with these results, and different models do project different outcomes. For example, simulations using the MSG3 model—see Batini, Callen, and McKibbin (2004)—suggest a broadly similar impact on per capita GDP to that discussed above, but different future current account paths.[22] Specifically, Europe is projected to experience an improvement in its current account position because investment declines more sharply than saving, while other regions see a corresponding deterioration. The behavior of saving is particularly critical to the results, but it is very difficult to know how households will respond to demographic change. Will the elderly dissave in retirement as expected in the INGENUE model, or will they seek to maintain their wealth in the face of uncertainty about how long they will live? Further, if people expect that incomes in the future will be lower because of demographic change, will they raise saving in the near term by more than the INGENUE model projects to smooth their future consumption? These issues are critical to the macroeconomic outcome, but they very much depend on individuals' understanding of the implications of demographic change and their expectations of the future, both of which are not easily observable.

[20]Even in the absence of a formal pension system, there would be transfers from the young to support the elderly.

[21]As populations in fast-aging regions pass through their high-saving years, they may invest part of their additional saving in regions where labor forces are larger and the rates of return on capital higher. As these populations then move into retirement, this capital should then be repatriated to finance retirement. These capital flows play an important part in the global adjustment process by allowing residents of regions that are aging at different speeds to borrow and lend to each other. These capital flows cushion the impact of demographic change relative to the case of a closed economy. See McKibbin and Nguyen (2004) for an assessment of the relative impact of demographic change in a closed versus an open economy model.

[22]MSG3 is a less regionally disaggregated model than INGENUE and does not incorporate a social security system. It does, however, have more sophisticated financial and production sectors. The model is described in Appendix 3.1.

Policies to Meet the Challenges of Global Demographic Change

What can be done to meet the economic challenges posed by demographic change? Clearly, a wide range of possible policy responses are available—at both the national and international level—and some of these are currently under discussion, particularly in countries facing the most significant and immediate demographic pressures. While the challenges differ between advanced and developing countries, at a broad level, if a policy is to help respond to demographic change, it needs to boost labor supply, saving, or productivity.

Assuming that participation rates do not change, demographic developments will result in a decline in the supply of labor in many advanced countries over the next 50 years. Estimates by Burniaux, Duval, and Jaumotte (2003) suggest that labor supply could drop by as much as 35 percent in Japan, 30 percent in Italy, and 17 percent in Germany. Measures to boost labor force participation rates and labor supply, particularly among the women and the elderly (of both genders)—including through pension system reform and providing other work incentives—have therefore attracted considerable interest (see Casey and others, 2003; Burniaux, Duval, and Jaumotte, 2003; and McMorrow and Roeger, 2004).[23] The increase in the participation rate among the working-age population that would be necessary to keep the workforce-to-population ratio at current levels, however, is large (Figure 3.9). For advanced countries, participation rates would need to increase by an average of 11 percentage points, with the required increase much higher for European countries and Korea than for the United States; for Japan, even raising the participation rate to 100 percent would not by itself be sufficient to offset the pro-

[23]See Chapter IV of the April 2003 *World Economic Outlook* for a discussion of labor market reform in Europe. To increase the participation of the elderly, it is likely that accompanying measures would also be needed to ensure that they have the skills needed for work and that there is no employment discrimination against them.

Figure 3.9. Some Policy Responses to a Declining Labor Force in Advanced Economies

For many advanced economies, maintaining a constant ratio of work force to population over the next 50 years would require large increases in participation rates and retirement ages and/or very substantial amounts of immigration.

Increasing the Labor Participation Rate (percentage point change)

Projected required change in labor participation rate, 2000–50[1]
Historical change in labor participation rate, 1960–2000
Advanced economy average
Japan[2]
Spain
Korea
Italy
Germany
France
United Kingdom
United States
-3 0 3 6 9 12 15 18 21 24

Immigration (percent of end-of-period total population)

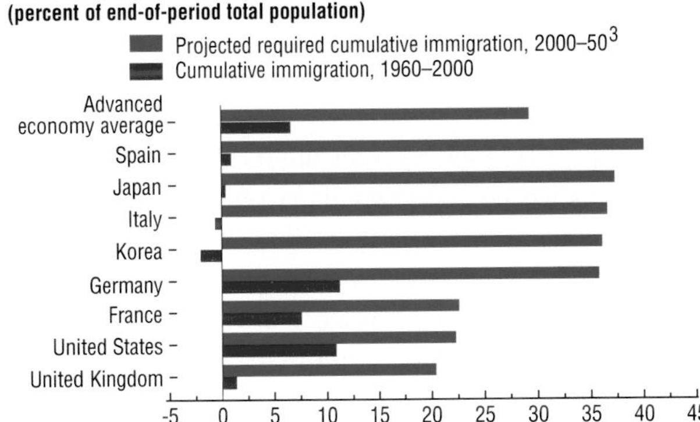

Raising Retirement Age[4] (years)

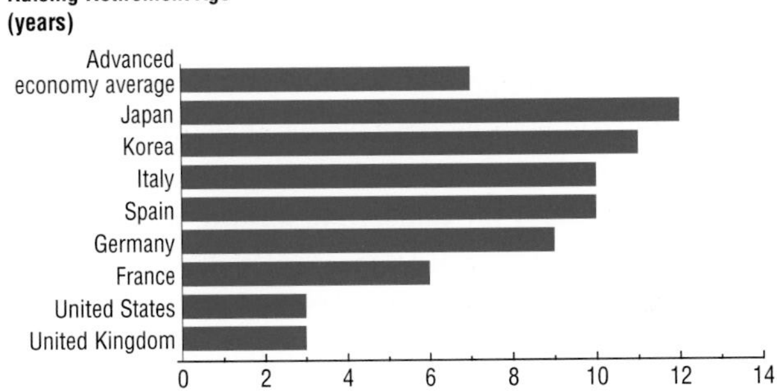

Sources: United Nations, *World Population Prospects: The 2002 Revision* (2003); and IMF staff calculations.

[1]Increase in the labor participation rate necessary to maintain the ratio of labor force to total population in 2050 at its 2000 level.

[2]For Japan, even if the labor participation rate increased from its 2000 value of 78.8 percent to 100 percent, the relative size of the labor force would still decline.

[3]Cumulative immigration over 2000–50 necessary to maintain the ratio of labor force to total population in 2050 at its 2000 level.

[4]Increase in the retirement age necessary to maintain the ratio of labor force to total population in 2050 at its 2000 level.

jected decline in the working-age population. The workforce could also be increased by permitting more immigration. Again, the migration flows that would be required to keep the workforce-to-population ratio constant at current levels are very large, particularly when seen against the background of the generally low levels of migration in recent years.[24] Raising the retirement age could also help offset the impact of population aging on the workforce. An increase of about seven years would be needed, on average, in the advanced countries to keep the share of the working-age population constant at its current level, although individual country requirements again vary widely.

Policies that encourage an increase in fertility rates have also been suggested as a way to counter current demographic changes, although there would be a long lag before these would increase the labor force even if they were effective in raising fertility. While there is considerable evidence that public policy has played an important role in reducing fertility rates in developing countries, there remains much more debate about whether public policies can raise fertility in low fertility countries (see Demeny, 2003). Proponents of an activist public policy to raise fertility often point to the Scandinavian countries, where measures to make motherhood and the participation in the labor force by women more compatible have been implemented, and fertility rates have also increased in recent years (although these policies are aimed at broader social objectives, rather than explicitly at raising fertility). Whether these measures have caused the increase in fertility, of course, is difficult to say, particularly as fertility rates in the United States have also risen in recent years largely in the absence of such policies. In the United States, however, the private sector has responded to the increase in demand for childcare, and this has supported female labor force participation.

In developing countries, in contrast, the key requirement for labor market policies will be to ensure that the larger working-age populations are absorbed into the workforce. This will require reforms to improve the flexibility of labor markets, as well as better education and training to provide the skills necessary for employment (see the April 2003 *World Economic Outlook* and Fasano and Goyal, 2004, for evidence on labor markets in the Middle East).

Equipping the remaining workforce with a larger and more labor-efficient capital stock could help offset the impact of a declining labor supply. To do this, saving would need to increase. One way to achieve higher saving is for the government itself to save more before the onset of its population's aging. The desirability of running primary fiscal surpluses and reducing public debt in advanced countries in this way has been discussed in the May 2001 *World Economic Outlook* and Heller (2003). As discussed in Box 3.4, however, population aging and nondemographic factors—such as the cost of new technologies and drugs—are likely to result in substantial increases in health care expenditures in the years ahead and make this fiscal task more difficult. As well as helping to contain public sector outlays, pension reforms may also contribute to higher private saving, although this will depend on the nature of the reforms themselves and the strength of the signals sent to those in the labor force to bolster their savings for retirement (see Box 3.5). In developing countries, a strong and stable macroeconomic framework—that delivers low inflation and sustainable public debt levels—together with institutional reforms are important elements of an environment conducive to domestic saving, capital inflows, and capital accumulation.[25]

[24]See United Nations (2000) for a detailed analysis of whether migration could help offset declining and aging populations in advanced countries.

[25]The importance of strong institutions for growth is discussed in Chapter III of the April 2003 *World Economic Outlook*. The sustainability of public debt in emerging market economies is considered in Chapter III of the September 2003 *World Economic Outlook*.

More efficient use of existing capital and labor could provide an important offset to the expected decline in labor (and possibly capital) availability in the advanced countries and the more rapidly aging developing countries. Therefore, structural reforms aimed at boosting productivity by reducing the impediments to competition, improving labor market and price flexibility, and spurring innovation will be important (although there is clearly little certainty about the exact impact that such reforms would have).[26] Stronger productivity growth, however, will not help to alleviate financing pressures in pension systems if benefit payments are indexed to wages (which rise with productivity), although by increasing overall income it will provide an environment in which reforms are easier to implement (see Box 3.5). Boosting productivity in other developing countries would also provide an important complement to the positive impact that demographic change may have on per capita growth in the coming years.

A broad mix of measures is likely to be needed to address the consequences of demographic change as the size of the reforms that would be needed in any single area are sufficiently large that they would be politically and economically difficult to achieve. For example, Figure 3.9 shows that for advanced economies as a whole, large increases in participation rates, immigration, or the retirement age would be needed to stabilize the labor force to population ratio at current levels if enacted on their own. These increases are outside the range of historic experience. If reforms were jointly implemented in all three areas, however, the required changes would be much smaller; an increase in the participation rate of 3¾ percentage points, immigration of 10 percent of population, and an increase in the retirement age of 2.3 years would together be sufficient to keep the labor force to population ratio at its current level in 2050. These changes—while not easy—are within the range of what has been seen in some advanced countries during the past 40 years, or, in the case of retirement age, what has been legislated in some countries in recent pension reforms. Further, policy responses are often related and complementary, and this may help maximize the impact of individual reforms—raising the retirement age would not only ease the burden on pension systems, but would also boost the potential supply of labor as the elderly stay longer in the labor force and possibly influence saving behavior.

Policies at the international level will be important for coping with demographic change. Global adjustment to differences in the pace of population aging will take place through the movement of goods, capital, and labor between countries, and these flows could be large. The reallocation of global resources will be achieved most efficiently if all of these channels are allowed to function smoothly, and the more that the adjustment is shared across the channels, the less will be the burden placed on each.[27] Policymakers, however, will need to balance economic, political, and social considerations. For example, if advanced countries allow more immigration, this would help cushion the impact of population aging on their workforces, but social implications also need to be taken into account—including the ability to integrate a large number of migrants into society and the impact that immigration would have on population density (which is already high in Europe and Japan).[28] Capital account liberalization

[26]Population aging itself could affect productivity, although there is no consensus in the economics literature about the direction of this impact. According to one strand of research, population aging is likely to be detrimental to productivity growth if an older labor force turns out to be less dynamic and innovative than a younger one (Jones, 2002; Romer, 1990). Others, however, take the view that technological change may be boosted as a premium is placed on innovation to offset the negative implications of the relative scarcity of labor (Cutler and others, 1990).

[27]In an analysis of Japan, Dekle (2003) finds that capital flows induced by population aging would be substantially reduced if the government were to allow a large increase in immigration.

[28]National security considerations may also play an increasingly important role in determining immigration policy in some countries.

Box 3.4. Implications of Demographic Change for Health Care Systems

Much of the focus of the aging policy debate has centered on the potential for rising pension outlays. Yet population aging will also have important implications for health care systems in both industrial countries and emerging market and middle-income countries. While aging itself will increase health care outlays, the principal challenge for governments in the years ahead will be to address the key nondemographic factors that have continued to increase the cost of medical care. This box discusses some of the key issues with regard to the impact of aging and other factors on health care systems.

Do the Elderly Consume More Medical Care?

In industrial countries, the elderly population—those over 65—spends more on medical care than those under 65. Thus, an increased share of the elderly in the population should imply, all other things equal, an increased average level of medical care spending. But this inference may be misleading; the higher average spending level may be simply due to a significant share of lifetime medical care costs being incurred in the last year(s) of life. If an increased share of the elderly had no effect on the death rate, then the increased share would only affect medical spending if those elderly not in their last years of life spend more, on average, than the working-age population.

Evidence that is just emerging suggests that people are living longer and healthier lives, in part because they are exercising more, smoking less, and watching their weight.[1] Access to high-quality medical care for prevention, diagnosis, and treatment and the availability of new pharmaceuticals is also contributing to additional healthy life years. But the elderly still appear to have a higher average demand for medical care in their later years (excluding the last year of life) in terms of ambulatory, inpatient, and long-term chronic care, than those under age 65. As people become very old, they seem to be subject to more disabling conditions that can require long-term care (which may require the time of those who would otherwise be fully in the labor force). Whether, additionally, the death rate will rise with an increasing elderly share (increasing the weight of those high-cost medical years) will depend on the balance between an increasing elderly population share and increasing life expectancy (which reduces the share of those elderly in their last year of life!).[2]

How Much Will Demographic Factors Contribute to Increased Medical Spending?

Recent studies have sought to estimate how demographic factors will affect medical care spending. OECD and EU studies suggest that demographic factors in isolation will lead to increased medical care spending of 2–3 percentage points of GDP between 2000 and 2050.[3] Inclusion of long-term chronic care would further increase these estimates. Yet these studies still assume that the increasing share of the elderly will spend more on health, independent of whether the elderly are indeed more healthy. More sophisticated analyses under way by the European Commission should more accurately clarify the impact of demographic factors.

Most health economists argue that nondemographic factors are primarily responsible for the surge in medical care costs since the 1960s and that these factors will equally dominate in coming decades. Many point to the United States, where medical care outlays are among the highest in the world, and where national health expenditures have risen faster—by about 2.5 percent annually—than real GDP since 1960. But the pressure for medical costs to rise faster than real GDP per capita is also evident for most other OECD countries, even with their lower medical spending levels (OECD, 2004).

Note: The main author of this box is Peter Heller.

[1]There is much ongoing work on this subject in Europe in the context of a project on Aging, Health, and Retirement sponsored by the European Union (AGIR, 2003a, 2003b). This is providing data on the biodemographic aspects of aging and the use of health care and nursing care by the elderly.

[2]See Wise (2003), Wanless (2002), and AGIR (2003a, 2003b).

[3]OECD (2001) and European Commission (2001).

Interestingly, efforts at improving health behavior by individuals (reduced obesity, curtailed smoking) would not dramatically reduce the pace of spending increases since they would lead to increased life expectancy, more demand for care, and a different composition of care than in a scenario of less behavioral change (Wanless, 2002).

Key factors underlying the strong growth in health care costs are the relatively lower productivity growth in the sector (reflecting the high share of labor costs), the expansion in health insurance coverage, the moral hazard associated with third-party coverage (as households bear only a small share of the costs of increased demand), the development of new but costly pharmaceuticals, technological innovations in diagnosis and treatment, and the increased take-up of these technologies and drugs by households and providers. These innovations have also facilitated an increase in healthy life expectancy and reduced the nonmedical costs associated with treatment and care, even if medical outcomes do not improve (Glied, 2003). Nonetheless, few analysts today expect the pressure for rising medical costs to abate in the near term (U.S. CBO, 2003).

Challenges in Containing Medical Costs in an Aging Society

There are limits as to how much of GDP can be spent on medical care, and concerns about how such spending can be financed and whether there will be equity in access to care. All industrial countries are grappling with how to contain the growth of medical care costs, particularly with the other fiscal burdens borne by governments in aging societies. Two approaches have been adopted.

- The first involves *imposing global budget constraints on health spending*, such as regulation of prices on labor and drugs; budgetary caps in the context of systems where the state is the principal health care provider; and shifting of costs to the private sector by caps on the reimbursement of purchases of goods and services (mostly pharmaceuticals).
- The second seeks to *alter the incentives facing both producers and users of health care*, including through the introduction of cost-sharing arrangements; utilization of "gatekeeper" practitioners to curb excess demand and steer demand to more efficient providers (e.g., ambulatory centers rather than more costly hospitals); an increase in competition among providers (e.g., hospitals, insurance companies); and a strengthening of efficiency through greater use of information technologies.

Emerging market and middle-income countries face similar challenges. But for many, even more complex challenges must be addressed in facilitating the modernization of their health care systems. Middle- and upper-income groups will demand the availability of modern and costly technologies of medical care. Yet for many others in society, there will be an increased prevalence of noncommunicable diseases (as a consequence of tobacco consumption) and exposure to accidents whose treatment will also require the application of modern medical technologies. And yet these countries' medical care systems will also need to treat many still subject to the communicable disease problems common to developing countries. Moreover, as their societies age as well, they will begin to experience similar problems to the industrial countries in financing the medical costs of their elderly populations.

could potentially enable developing countries to attract more external financing—and hence provide them with the opportunity to boost investment and growth—but it may also raise the risk of financial crisis, particularly if economic policies and institutions are not sufficiently robust. Labor mobility may provide an important source of income to developing countries through remittances, but could result in a "brain drain" whereby the country's best educated people leave with a detrimental effect on output. Increased international cooperation will be

Box 3.5. Impact of Aging on Public Pension Plans

Public pension systems play a critical role in supporting the retired and elderly. In the larger countries of Europe, the public pension system provides a large share of retirement income. In the United States, social security provides a lower share of retirement income than the public pension systems of many European countries do, but nonetheless is important for millions of older Americans. In a number of emerging market countries, the public pension system can be an important source—often virtually the only source—of income for many older people. Elsewhere, the coverage of the pension system is typically very narrow.

Most public pension systems are defined-benefit pay-as-you-go plans under which the amount of the pension is determined by the number of years worked and the wage or salary received in the last years of work.[1] In a pay-as-you-go system, current period benefits are financed from current revenues—usually via a payroll tax. No reserve fund is accumulated, as is the case with an employer-provided defined-benefit plan.

Aging has a direct financial impact on a pay-as-you-go system. For pay-as-you-go revenues to equal expenditures, the payroll tax rate should equal the pension bill divided by the wage bill, which is equivalent to the ratio of pensioners to active contributors times the ratio of the average pension to the average wage. Aging increases the ratio of pensioners to employed and, absent changes to the ratio of the pension to the wage, requires an increase in the payroll tax to maintain the balance between revenue and expenditure. In many industrial countries, substantial increases in payroll tax rates have taken place over the past 40 years. In part, these increases were necessary to finance increases in average real pensions, which in turn were due in part to what is known as the maturation effect, whereby the average contributory period of new retirees increases as the plan ages. However, much of the increase is attributable to the increase in the ratio of pensioners to employed—namely, to population aging. The payroll tax increases necessary to keep pay-as-you-go plans financially balanced have contributed to labor market distortions, especially in Europe, and have compounded the aging problem by reducing labor force participation rates.

The aging phenomenon results from both declining birth rates and increasing life expectancies at all ages, but particularly among older people. Life expectancy at retirement in the advanced countries is much greater than it was even 50 years ago. When birth rates began to drop in many countries after World War II, the decline was not recorded by national accounts statisticians as a decline in investment—in human capital formation—but effectively it was. From society's, if not their parents', point of view, children are an economic investment. However, the decline in investment in future workers that declining birth rates entailed was not offset by investment in other areas.

The economic and fiscal problems that aging entails can be viewed as an intergenerational zero-sum game. There are more mouths to feed per economically active person, and the necessary decline in consumption must be shared across generations. However, an increase in saving and investment, which will equip the generation that has to support the baby boomers as they retire with more capital, will increase growth and output per head, and mitigate the generational trade-off. The increase in investment requires an initial decline in the level of consumption, which must be shared in some way across generations, but can lead to higher consumption levels later on. Similarly, any reform that raises productivity can mitigate the problem of financing the pensions of an aging populace.

Some economists have argued that the establishment of a defined contributions plan would have avoided the difficulties that the typical public pension system is now experiencing.[2] Pension pri-

Note: The main author of this box is Sandy Mackenzie.

[1]By way of illustration, a pensioner might receive 1.3 percent of the average of the last three annual salaries for each year worked. Thirty-five years of work would result in a replacement rate (ratio of pension to pensionable salary) of 45.5 percent. Caps and floors may also apply, and the accrual factor (in this example, 1.3 percent) may vary with the number of years worked.

[2]A defined contributions plan determines the contributions the participant makes—usually in terms of a fixed proportion of salary—but does not promise a specific benefit.

vatization, or an individual accounts pension reform, establishes such a scheme. However, this argument overlooks the fact that in an aging society, the working-age population has more people to support regardless of the form the pension system takes. The establishment of a defined contributions plan will not mitigate the effects of aging unless it raises the savings rate. A well-designed reform that establishes an individual accounts system may succeed in doing that, but a saving increase has to be made an explicit objective of the reform.

In considering the options for public pension system reform, it is useful to distinguish between conventional or parametric reform, under which the existing system, remains in place but its parameters are changed, and structural reform, where a new kind of arrangement, like an individual accounts system, is introduced. Conventional reform requires some combination of revenue increases and lower pensions. In many countries the payroll tax is already high, and further increases are likely to have distortive effects on the labor market. This leaves pension reductions, which can be achieved in various ways. One way is postponing the normal retirement age, an option that can be justified on the grounds that people are staying healthy longer. This option, however, requires that people near the normal retirement age be able to continue working or find alternative employment. Achieving this goal may well require both changes in employer attitudes and practices and labor market reform. A second option is to index the starting pension (the pension paid in the first year of retirement) to consumer prices rather than wages, as is done in the United Kingdom, which would require changing the benefit formula. A third is to lower the accrual factor (see footnote 1). Both political considerations and considerations of equity call for these changes to be gradually, not precipitously, introduced.

Parametric reforms reduce the implicit rate of return of the public pension system.[3] Advocates of pension privatization point to declines in the implicit rate of return over time as one of the reasons for privatization. Privatization works by establishing an individual account for each participant in the public system. Part of the participant's current payroll tax is diverted to this account—or an additional contribution may be imposed—and the funds in the account are invested in financial markets, according to the limits that the reform establishes. Upon retirement, these funds and their accumulated earnings can be used to finance the purchase of an annuity or a series of phased withdrawals. Individual accounts can replace the old state pension system in its entirety, or simply complement or supplement it.

Pension reform is not simply about increasing the saving rate to boost investment and growth, but if reform is not simply to redistribute the burden across generations it has to do that at least. This increase in saving can be brought about by changes to the pension system itself, fiscal retrenchment, or both. For example, an add-on individual accounts reform can increase saving if contributors do not respond by a completely offsetting decline in other saving. A conventional reform can increase saving by increases in payroll taxation, which reduce consumption of the current working generation, or a reduction in pension benefits. The impact on saving is not the only test of pension reform: an individual accounts system differs in other important ways from the conventional public system—for example, in the risk borne by contributors. Nonetheless, both conventional and individual accounts reforms must themselves increase saving or be accompanied by measures that increase saving or boost productivity if they are to help mitigate the financial and macroeconomic consequences of aging.[4]

[3]The implicit rate of return is the discount rate that equates what the average member of a given age group can expect to receive in pension benefits with the accumulated value of his payroll tax contributions and the contributions of his employer on his behalf.

[4]For discussions of the merits of individual account systems from various points of view, see Barr (2001), Orszag and Stiglitz (2001), and Samwick (1999).

Figure 3.10. Life Expectancy and Age of Retirement for Males in Selected Advanced Economies

While life expectancy has increased, there has been little change in official retirement ages and the effective age of withdrawal from the labor force has fallen.

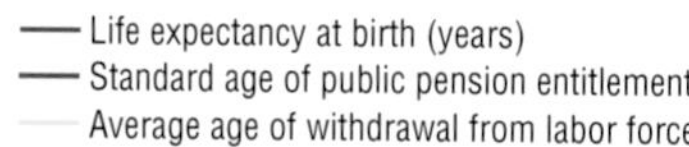

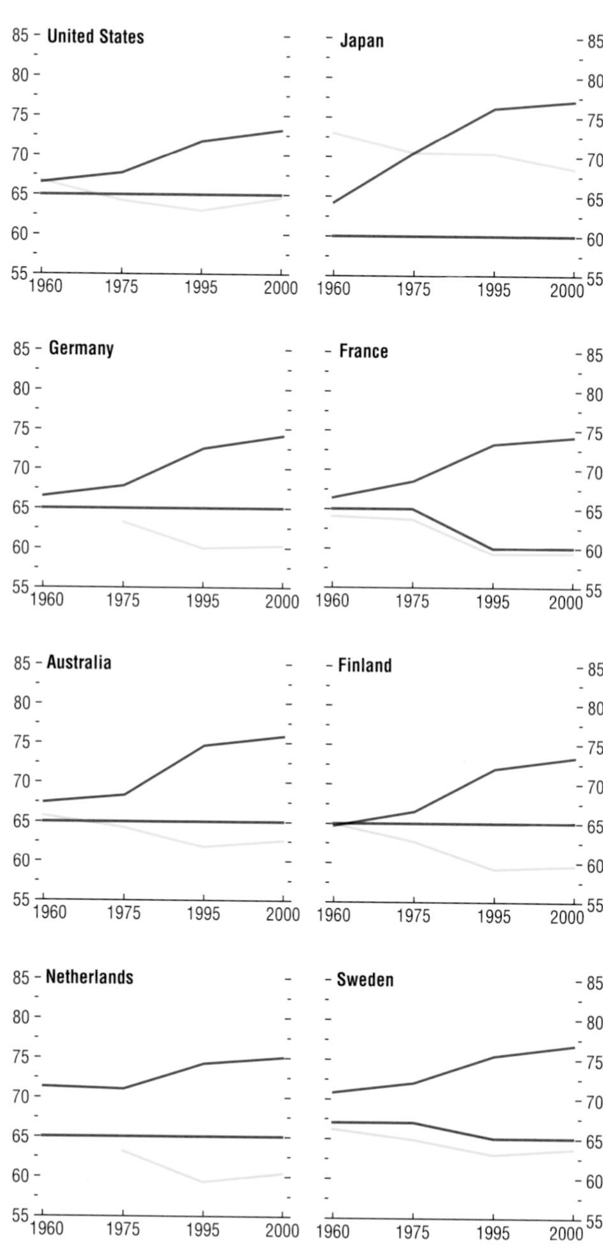

Sources: Scherer (2002); United Nations, *World Population Prospects: The 2002 Revision* (2003); and U.S. Department of Health and Human Services, *Social Security Programs Throughout the World* (various issues).

needed to manage these cross-country flows, and to ensure that the associated risks are minimized to the extent possible.

The remainder of this section takes up three issues related to the policy response to demographic change in greater detail, and assesses both the potential domestic and global implications of the reforms. These issues are (1) pension reforms in advanced countries; (2) the role of labor mobility (migration) in the global adjustment process; and (3) improving access to international capital markets for developing countries to maximize the opportunities presented by the demographic dividend. The choice of these three areas certainly does not suggest that they are more important than others—such as fiscal consolidation and labor market reform—in addressing the challenges of demographic change.

Reforming Pension Systems in Advanced Countries

As discussed previously, the financing of currently promised pension benefits in many advanced countries would require a substantial increase in contribution rates in the future. Given the enormous burden such an increase would place on the working-age population and the adverse effect it would have on the incentive to work, governments are actively considering a range of reforms to improve the sustainability of public pension systems. For example, retirement ages are being raised in France, Italy, and Japan, while in the United States the normal retirement age under social security has been rising gradually from 65 to 67 years of age since the implementation of the recommendations of the 1983 Greenspan Commission. The changes under way, however, are quite modest and come against the background of the substantial gains in life expectancy that have been made over the past 40 years and the general trend toward exit from the workforce before the official retirement age is reached (Figure 3.10). Announced pension reforms in Germany have taken a different approach, whereby future benefits will be reduced but the retirement age left unchanged.

The potential impact of two possible reforms to European public pension systems was assessed using the INGENUE model.[29]

- In the first scenario, the pension replacement rate is reduced to 50 percent by 2050 (from 70 percent in 2000) and the contribution rate held steady at its end-2000 level.
- In the second scenario, the retirement age is gradually raised from 60 to 65 years between 2000 and 2020, but the replacement rate is left unchanged. This requires less of an increase in contribution rates than if reforms were not implemented.

These two reform scenarios are compared with the baseline case—which underlies the results in the previous section—where contribution rates have to be raised substantially, from 22½ percent to 37½ percent, to ensure that pension systems are able to finance their obligations under existing benefit parameters. The reforms in the scenarios are assumed to be fully believed when announced, and hence individuals immediately begin to adjust their behavior.

There are important differences in the macroeconomic impact of these two types of pension reform in the model. In the case where pension benefits are reduced, private saving in Europe increases as households adjust to the realization that they will have to provide more for their own retirement (Figure 3.11).[30] Although this increase in saving lowers real interest rates and

[29]The advantage of studying pension reform within a multicountry macroeconomic model such as INGENUE is that it allows an analysis of both the domestic and international aspects of the reform. A drawback, however, is that the pension systems incorporated in the model are stylized, and thus do not include all the country-specific institutional details. For a more detailed analysis of the impact of pension reforms in Europe, see Rother, Catenaro, and Schwab (2003). Pension reforms in the United States are discussed by Diamond and Orszag (2004) and Samwick (1998), and in Japan by Faruqee and Mülheisen (2001). The September 2004 *Global Financial Stability Report* discusses reforms to private sector pension arrangements in a number of advanced countries.

[30]This model-driven response is not assured. Households may not adjust their saving behavior in reaction to the pension reforms if, for example, they believe the government will ultimately be required to ensure that they attain a reasonable standard of living in retirement.

Figure 3.11. Impact of Pension Reforms in Europe in the INGENUE Model

(Percentage point difference from baseline)

Pension reforms in Europe are key for fiscal sustainability and may help support saving and growth in the face of aging.

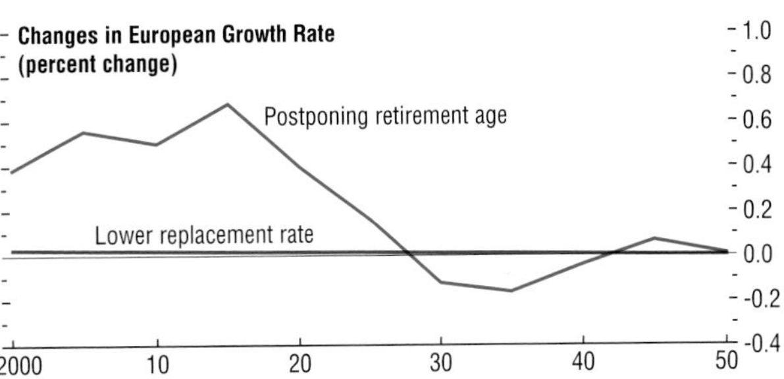

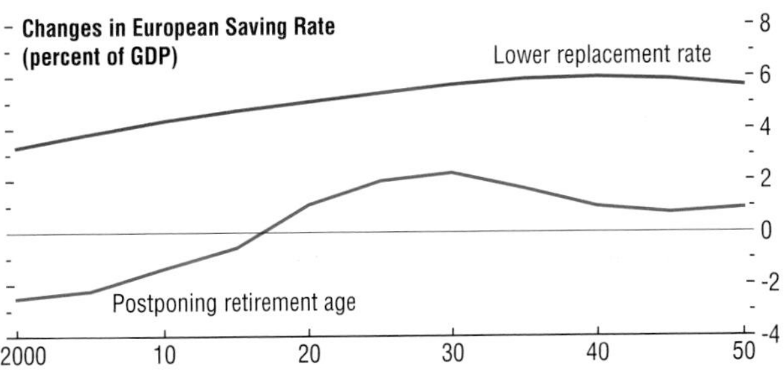

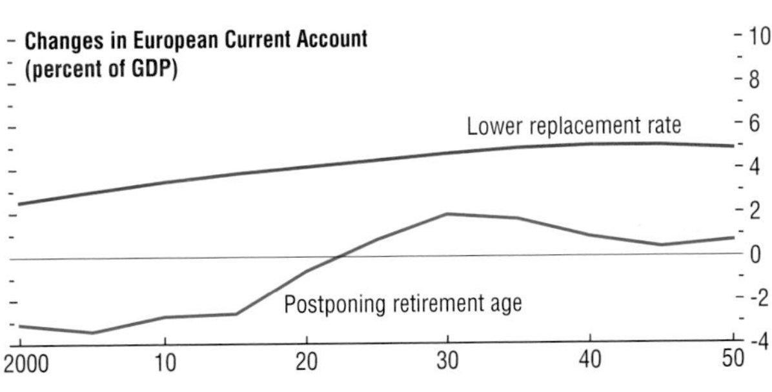

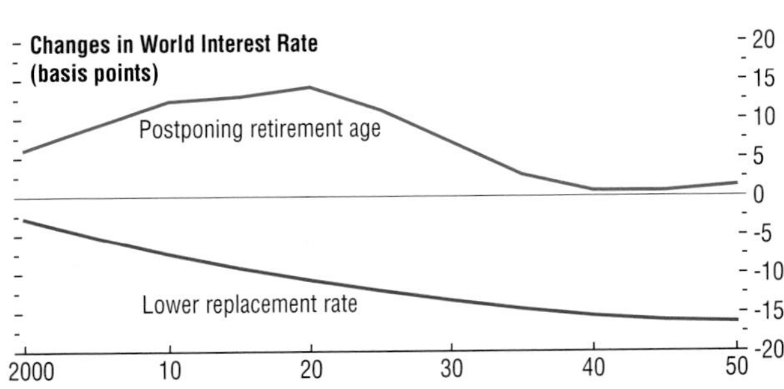

Source: INGENUE Team.

boosts investment, it also reduces consumption, and real GDP growth rates in the model are actually little affected. The effect of raising the retirement age is less straightforward. Private saving initially falls as workers realize that they will need to finance future consumption over a shorter retirement period, and this boosts consumption and growth. In the longer run, however, the increase in real interest rates acts to modestly reduce real growth rates. The changes in saving behavior in Europe that result from the pension reforms have implications for capital flows, the world real interest rate, and external balances. The increase in saving when public pension benefits are reduced pushes down the world real interest rate—which has a small positive impact on global activity—and leads to a substantial improvement in the European current account balance. On the other hand, if the retirement age is raised, the model suggests that the current account balance in Europe would initially deteriorate owing to the decline in saving, and world interest rates would rise modestly. Then, as saving recovers, the current account balance improves, and the world real interest rate declines.

The model's results raise a number of important issues with regard to pension reform. First, alternative approaches to pension reform may affect the macroeconomy in different ways. Reforms that raise the retirement age appear to be more growth friendly than those that reduce pension benefits. Therefore, the design of pension reforms is important. Second, pension reforms in large countries will have implications for the global economy through their impact on interest rates and capital flows. While the impact in the scenarios discussed here is not that large, if advanced countries were all to implement pension reforms at the same time, the impact on the global economy would be much more significant.

An important dynamic for pension reforms is that demographic change—by increasing the political weight of older persons who may have the most to lose—is actually likely to make the implementation of such reforms increasingly difficult in the future. Older people—those over 50 years of age—will soon represent the majority of active voters in many advanced countries once the differing voter turnout between age groups is accounted for (Figure 3.12).[31]

Role of Labor Mobility in the Global Adjustment Process

The INGENUE model—along with most other large multicountry macroeconomic models—does not allow for the possibility of labor mobility between countries. Increased labor mobility, however, is a potentially important mechanism through which the global economy could respond to demographic change, and is an important alternative to the flow of capital. While migration has generally not been an important source of population growth in most advanced countries in recent years—indeed, migration has been tightly constrained by immigration policies—in the past there have been periods when substantial flows of labor have occurred, perhaps most notably during 1820–1913 when large numbers of migrants moved from Europe to the United States and other countries of the new world.

The role that labor mobility could play in helping economies respond to demographic change was investigated in a simple two-country, two-period model that extends the work of Tosun (2003). The model features an advanced and a developing country, each with a population composed of two age groups (workers and the retired). The population characteristics of each country are set to represent actual UN projections for advanced and developing countries, so that the advanced country ages more quickly than the developing country. The model incorporates a pay-as-you-go social security system, public spending on education that enhances the productivity of workers, taxes on both workers

[31]This depends on a number of assumptions, including that the over-50s vote for personal benefit rather than the benefit of society, and that voter turnout patterns remain the same in the future as in the past.

and the retired to finance these expenditures, and a simple voting system in which people vote on their preferred tax rate and in so doing determine the amount of the productivity-enhancing good provided by the government.[32] Migration of workers occurs in response to real-wage differentials between countries (retired people do not move between countries), while capital moves in reaction to real interest rate differentials (see Appendix 3.1 for more details).[33]

The implication of allowing full capital mobility (with no labor mobility) was compared with the situation where there is full labor mobility (with no capital mobility).[34] The results—in terms of per capita consumption, a proxy for household's welfare—of having full capital mobility are broadly similar to those discussed earlier. Specifically, demographic change will reduce per capita consumption growth in advanced countries and will raise it in developing countries over the next half-century (Figure 3.13).

If there is labor mobility but no capital mobility, the results change. Specifically, the advanced country benefits from labor mobility, and its per capita consumption loss is considerably less than when there is no labor mobility. This is because the advanced country already has in place the capital stock, and without inward migration the declining size of the domestic workforce—as its population ages—means this capital stock becomes less productive. Consequently, migration cushions the impact of the declining work-

[32]In the model, workers benefit directly from the impact of education on productivity so they tend to vote for higher taxes and higher spending than the retired, who receive no direct benefit from higher labor productivity and labor income. Consequently, because migration changes the share of working-age people, it also changes voting patterns, and this leads to changes in government spending on the productivity-enhancing public good and may have important growth and welfare effects.

[33]Actual migration flows appear in practice to be driven by a wide range of factors, not only wage differentials; see Greenwood (1985) and Carrington, Detragiache, and Vishwanath (1996), among others.

[34]Of course, capital and labor mobility are likely to move together. Considering these polar opposites, however, not only makes it easier to establish the mechanisms at work but also considerably simplifies the modeling.

Figure 3.12. The Last Train for Pension Reform Departs in . . .[1]

(Year in which voters aged 50 and older comprise at least 50.1 percent of all voters)

In many countries the elderly may soon represent the majority of the voting public, making it harder to implement reforms that adversely affect them.

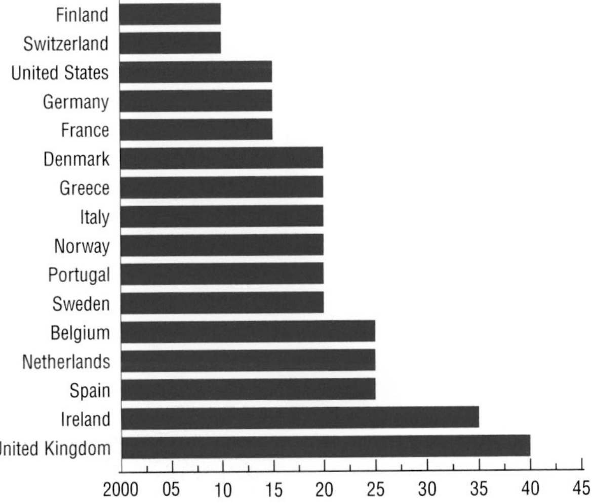

Sources: Institute for Democracy and Electoral Assistance, *Youth Voter Participation* (1999); Statistisches Bundesamt, *Voter Behavior in the Federal Elections 2002 by Gender and Age* (2003); United States Census Bureau (2003); and United Nations, *World Population Prospects: The 2002 Revision* (2003).

[1]Number of voters aged 50 years and older adjusted for voters' turnout by age.

Figure 3.13. Implications of Labor and Capital Mobility for Per Capita Consumption, 2000–60
(Total percent change in per capita consumption over 2000–60)

Capital and labor mobility have different implications for advanced and developing economies. This simple model suggests advanced economies benefit more from labor mobility, and developing economies more from capital mobility.

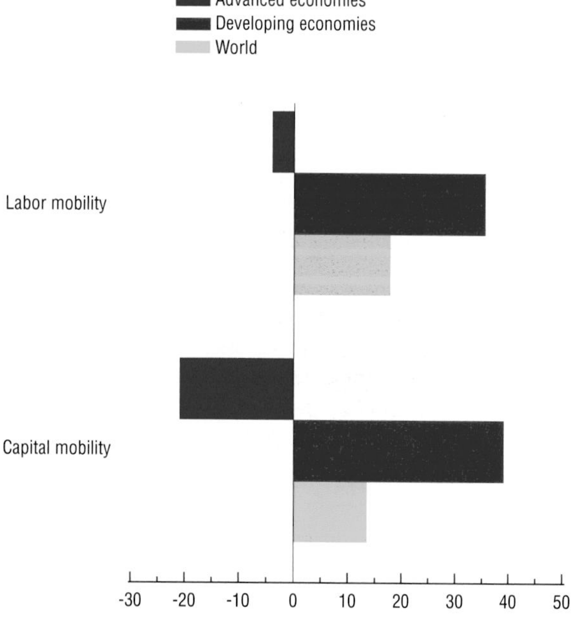

Source: IMF staff calculations.

force, although growth is still slightly negative over the period.

The developing country, however, is slightly better off with capital mobility, although it grows more strongly than the advanced country in both scenarios. It benefits more from capital mobility because it has a large workforce, but labor productivity is low because its capital stock is inadequate. It therefore gains from capital inflows that allow it to invest more and build up its capital stock, thus boosting labor productivity and growth. Of course, this model does not account for some of the other potential channels through which migration benefits the developing country, including increased migrant remittances or reduced domestic unemployment if there is excess labor.[35] At the global level, per capita consumption growth is slightly higher under labor mobility than under capital mobility in the model.

The results in this section suggest that inward migration has the potential to help respond to the effects of population aging in the advanced countries, although—consistent with the evidence discussed earlier—the inflow of migrants to the advanced country is large (immigrants equivalent to 13 percent of the end-period native working-age population move to the advanced country during the 60-year period in the model). While such large-scale immigration may face social and political barriers, some increase in labor flows between countries from existing levels is likely to be an important part of the global adjustment to demographic change.[36]

[35]Cardarelli and Ueda (2004) find that migration to the United States has significantly raised the well-being of a number of developing countries in recent years when account is taken of the income produced by nationals residing at home and in the United States. Further, Ratha (2003) estimates that workers' remittances back to developing countries are very large, generally exceeding official development assistance to low-income countries. Remittances support growth and are a more stable form of financing than private capital flows.

[36]See Borjas (1999, 2001) for a general discussion of the impact of immigration on advanced economies, particularly the United States, including the implications for income distribution.

The results also suggest that labor and capital mobility may benefit developing and advanced countries differently, so ultimately some balance in the adjustment that takes place through these two channels is likely to be needed.

Of course, migration is only a "temporary" remedy to the aging of populations. In the long term, population aging is a global event, and one that migration alone cannot solve, given that immigrants themselves get old and over time also tend to embrace the fertility standards of the host country. The results also emphasize that capital flows will be important for developing countries if they are to maximize the opportunities presented by their rising working-age populations.

Improving Capital Market Access for Developing Countries

An increasing share of the world's working-age population will be located in developing countries in the future. At present, however, international capital flows to these economies are relatively small, and are generally directed at only a few countries, some of which—such as China, which attracted nearly 40 percent of net foreign direct investment to developing countries in 2003—are themselves relatively advanced in the aging process. Indeed, the results of the previous section suggested that the decline in global saving could actually reduce the availability of capital for developing countries in the period ahead. A lack of access to capital would make it more difficult for these countries to maximize the economic benefits from the increase in the relative size of their working-age populations.

What can developing countries do to improve their access to international capital? Steps are certainly needed to strengthen investor confidence in policies and institutions, including through measures to improve the sustainability of public and external debt, strengthen financial sectors, and tackle governance issues. It is very difficult to model the impact that such reforms would have, although the success of Chile in maintaining low spreads on its external debt and uninterrupted access to global capital markets clearly indicates that such reforms are important.

Here, reforms to improve the investment environment are assumed to result in a reduction in the risk premium associated with investing in developing country assets (Figure 3.14 shows the impact in the MSG3 model of a one-off 1 percentage point reduction in this risk premium, which is currently about 5 percentage points as measured by the EMBI spread). The reduction in the risk premium encourages more capital to flow into developing countries, and this reduces real interest rates and has a considerable impact on real GDP. Domestic saving also increases as the rate of return on domestic capital improves as a result of the reforms, further reinforcing the positive effect on growth. The current account position of developing countries deteriorates, while the advanced country regions—the suppliers of the capital to the developing countries—experience improvements in their external balances.

Concluding Remarks

The world is in the midst of a demographic transition that is resulting in an unprecedented aging of its population. Different countries, however, are at different stages of this transition. In most advanced countries, population aging is already well under way, and the share of the working-age population is projected to decline quite significantly over the next 50 years. In contrast, the relative size of the working-age population in many developing countries will rise in the coming years before aging then begins.

The impact of these demographic shifts will be wide ranging. In advanced countries, population aging will strain the finances of governments, especially pension and health care systems, while per capita growth rates are likely to be reduced. In developing countries, however, increases in the relative size of the working-age population could lead to stronger per capita growth provided the additional labor resources

Figure 3.14. Implications of a 1-Percentage-Point Decline in Developing Country Risk Premium in the MSG3 Model
(Deviation from baseline projection)

A reduction in the risk of investing in developing countries would boost their capital inflows, investment, and growth.

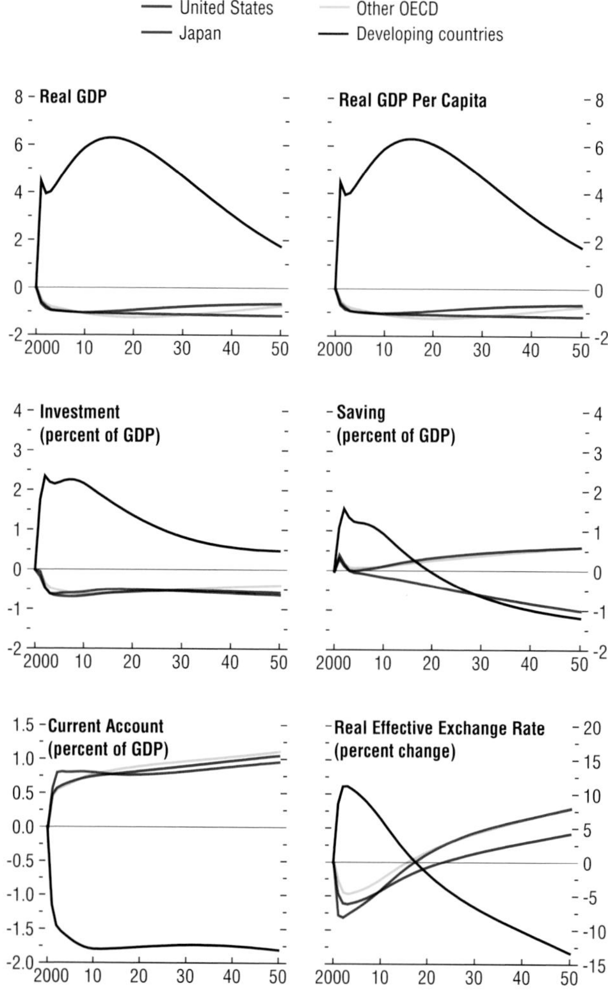

Source: IMF staff estimates.

are effectively utilized. International capital flows could also be substantially affected. The results presented in this chapter have suggested that large changes in saving, investment, and current account balances could take place over the next 50 years.

There are, however, considerable uncertainties, and our understanding of how demographic change will affect economic performance is far from complete. For example, while it is clear that population aging will put strains on pension and health care systems in advanced countries, the magnitudes of the financial impact will depend on demographic outcomes, which are difficult to project. If the pace of aging is more rapid than expected—as has been the case in the advanced countries in the past—the task of reforming pension and health care systems will be even greater than currently envisaged. Even more uncertainty surrounds the impact of demographic change on external balances and capital flows. Here, much will depend on the reaction of private saving, but it remains unclear to what extent households will adjust their behavior as the demographic transition unfolds.

In advanced countries, the key challenge in designing and implementing an effective policy package for responding to demographic change is to identify a broad mix of reforms—politically feasible changes in any single area are likely to prove insufficient—that are as resilient as possible to the uncertainties that exist. The basic aim of these reforms should be to boost labor supply, saving, and productivity. Many countries have already begun to tackle some of the critical issues, including through the modification of pension arrangements and structural reforms to boost productivity, although much more needs to be done, including to improve government budget positions and reduce public debt ahead of the onset of aging. The health care sector—where aging will add to ongoing spending pressures from other sources—is an area where much more attention is necessary.

Given the size of the task, reforms that help tackle multiple aspects of the challenges deserve particular attention; announcing a prospective rise in the retirement age would not only ease pension burdens, but would also increase potential labor supply. Designing reforms that are resilient to uncertainties about the future is clearly a very difficult task. However, one way that uncertainties about life expectancy could be dealt with in pension systems would be to link increases in the retirement age to gains in life expectancy or to link pension benefits to life expectancy (as in Sweden). Lastly, aging may have important implications for financial markets if the elderly run down their assets in retirement, and regulators will need to ensure that financial systems are sufficiently resilient to cope with such possible changes (see the September 2004 *Global Financial Stability Report*).

The policy response to demographic change in developing countries has received less attention, but is very important, particularly as these countries will become an increasingly significant source of global growth in the period ahead. The main priorities for developing countries are to put in place a policy framework that ensures that the potential benefits from the demographic dividend are maximized, while setting the groundwork for eventual population aging. Pension and health care systems will need to be strengthened to ensure that they provide a safety net for the elderly that is both adequate and fiscally sustainable. In doing this, it will be important that governments learn from the current situation in many advanced countries, and do not commit themselves to provide benefits that will be difficult to finance.

The movement of goods, capital, and labor between countries will be an integral part of the global adjustment to the differential rates of population aging. Choices will need to be made about how these channels are allowed to operate, with policymakers having to balance the economic, political, and social implications of each. The more the adjustment is shared between the various channels, however, the less will be the burden on each, and this may help reduce the risks that could accompany large capital flows. At the international level, increased cooperation will be needed to manage these cross-country flows and to ensure that the associated risks are minimized to the extent possible. In this regard, progress toward freer trade—including through the successful completion of the ongoing Doha Round—and the strengthening of the global financial architecture will be important.

Finally, some of the policies to tackle the impact of demographic change will inevitably involve difficult tradeoffs, will take time to agree and implement, and will need to be phased in to allow people sufficient time to adjust their behavior. This is most clearly true of pension reforms—which affect the welfare of the elderly and threaten benefits that people believe they are entitled to—but also of health care. Therefore, while the full impact of demographic change will not be felt in most countries for a number of years, the process of planning a response should not be delayed. This is particularly true for advanced countries, where reforms to pension and health care systems will become increasingly difficult to implement as populations age. Policymakers therefore need to take advantage of the current strong global economic rebound to advance the reform agenda before the window of opportunity begins to close.

Appendix 3.1. Demographic Change and the Global Economy: Data and Modeling Strategy

The main authors of this appendix are Nicoletta Batini, the INGENUE Team, Warwick McKibbin, Nicola Spatafora, and Mehmet Tosun.

This appendix provides further details on the data and the modeling strategy used in the chapter to analyze the global economic impact of demographic change.

Econometric Analysis

The econometric work analyzes a broad panel of 115 advanced and developing countries, representing all major geographic regions, over the

Table 3.2. Selected Summary Statistics, 1960–2000[1]
(Percent unless otherwise noted)

Variable	All Sample Countries
Economic variables	
Output growth per capita	1.7 (6.3)
Saving/GDP	16.9 (15.0)
Investment/GDP	21.8 (8.4)
Current account/GDP	–4.1 (10.4)
Budget balance/GDP	–3.4 (7.0)
Demographic variables	
Working-age population/total population	57.4 (6.3)
Elderly population/total population	5.7 (3.8)
Change in (working-age population/total population)[2]	0.11 (0.32)
Change in (elderly population/total population)[2]	0.05 (0.11)

Sources: World Bank, *World Development Indicators*; United Nations, *World Population Prospects: 2002 Revision*; and IMF staff calculations.
[1]Values are means at an annual frequency, with panel standard deviations provided in parentheses next to each value.
[2]Percentage points.

period 1960–2000.[37] For all variables, and for each country, the data are averaged over each decade. The analysis focuses on the impact of demographic change on each of the following measures of macroeconomic performance: growth of GDP per capita; saving/GDP; investment/GDP; current account balance/GDP; and central government budget balance/GDP.

Demographic change is measured using the following variables:

- ratio of working-age population to total population, and ratio of elderly population to total population, when analyzing any measure of macroeconomic performance except growth of GDP per capita;[38] and
- change in the ratio of working-age population to total population, and change in the ratio of elderly population to total population, when analyzing growth of GDP per capita.

Summary statistics for the key variables used in the analysis are shown in Table 3.2. To examine the importance of demographic change as a determinant of economic performance, the following equation was estimated:

$$Y_{it} = \alpha_i + \beta \cdot Demo_{it} + \gamma \cdot Z_{it} + \varepsilon_{it}, \qquad (1)$$

where Y is the specific macroeconomic variable of interest; *Demo* are the relevant measures of demographic change; Z is a set of control variables; and the subscripts i and t denote the country and the time period, respectively. This equation is estimated using the panel fixed-effects estimator. More specifically:

- in the *growth* regression, the controls include initial income; secondary school enrollment ratios; investment/GDP; budget balance/GDP; inflation rate; external trade/GDP; and country risk (as measured by the ICRG);
- in the regressions for *saving/GDP, investment/GDP*, and *current account/GDP*, the controls include initial income; budget balance/GDP; net foreign assets/GDP; M2/GDP; the standard deviation of a terms of trade index; external trade/GDP; and an oil-producer dummy; and
- in the *budget balance* regression, the controls include initial income; the standard deviation of the terms of trade; and external trade/GDP.

To control for possible endogeneity problems, all demographic variables, as well as several other controls, are instrumented using their lagged values (for all decades except the first, the lagged

[37]These countries are Albania, Algeria, Argentina, Armenia, Australia, Austria, Azerbaijan, Bangladesh, Barbados, Belarus, Belgium, Benin, Bolivia, Botswana, Brazil, Bulgaria, Burkina Faso, Burundi, Cameroon, Canada, Central African Republic, Chad, Chile, China, Colombia, Congo, Dem. Rep. of, Congo, Rep. of, Costa Rica, Côte d'Ivoire, Croatia, Cyprus, Czech Republic, Denmark, Dominican Republic, Ecuador, Egypt, El Salvador, Ethiopia, Finland, France, Gabon, The Gambia, Georgia, Germany, Ghana, Greece, Guatemala, Guinea-Bissau, Guyana, Haiti, Honduras, Hungary, India, Indonesia, Iran, I.R. of, Ireland, Israel, Italy, Jamaica, Japan, Jordan, Kenya, Korea, Kyrgyz Republic, Madagascar, Malawi, Malaysia, Mali, Mauritania, Mauritius, Mexico, Moldova, Morocco, Nepal, Netherlands, New Zealand, Nicaragua, Niger, Nigeria, Norway, Pakistan, Papua New Guinea, Paraguay, Peru, Philippines, Poland, Portugal, Romania, Russia, Rwanda, Senegal, Sierra Leone, Singapore, Slovenia, South Africa, Spain, Sri Lanka, Sweden, Switzerland, Syrian Arab Rep., Thailand, Togo, Trinidad and Tobago, Tunisia, Turkey, Uganda, Ukraine, United Kingdom, United States, Uruguay, Venezuela, Vietnam, Yemen, Zambia, and Zimbabwe.

[38]The working-age population is defined as the age group 15–64 inclusive; the elderly population is defined as the age group 65 years of age and older. When analyzing the determinants of the current account, demographic variables for each country are expressed as deviations from the world average.

Table 3.3. Main Characteristics of the Multiple-Generations Models

Characteristic	INGENUE	Tosun	MSG3
Number of countries/blocks[1]	6	2	4
Intertemporal optimization/ overlapping generations	Yes	Yes	Yes
Expectations	Rational	Rational	Rational and rule of thumb
Sectors	1	1	3
Age cohorts	4 young, 15 adult (including elderly)	0 young, 1 adult, 1 elderly	1 young,1 adult (including elderly)
Period lengths (years)	5	30	1
Life ends at	Fixed at 60–94 years	Fixed at 60 years	Fixed with probability "*p*"
Rigidities	No	No	Yes
Capital mobility	Yes	Yes	Yes
Labor mobility	No	Yes	No
Intergenerational transfers	Adults to young Adults to elderly	Adults to elderly	Adults to young
Public sector	Yes (simple public pension scheme)	Yes (articulated with public pension scheme)	Yes (articulated without public pension scheme)

[1]INGENUE regions include (1) Western Europe; (2) North America: Australia, Canada, New Zealand, and the United States; (3) Japan; (4) developing rapidly aging countries; (5) developing moderately aging countries; and (6) developing slowly aging countries. Tosun's model's regions include an advanced and a developing country bloc. MSG3 regions include (1) the United States; (2) Japan; (3) other OECD economies; and (4) rest of the world.

value is defined as the value in the preceding decade; for the first decade, the lagged value is defined as the value in the first year).[39]

Macroeconomic Models

This section describes in more detail the three multiple generations models (MGM) used in this chapter.[40] Table 3.3 summarizes and contrasts the key features of each model.

The INGENUE Model

The INGENUE model (INGENUE Team, 2001) is a multiregion world model in the spirit of those developed by Obstfeld and Rogoff (1996) in which the structure of each regional economy is similar to that of other applied OLG general equilibrium models such as Auerbach and Kotlikoff (1987) or Cazes and others (1992, 1994), except that labor supply is exogenous.[41]

The world is divided into six regions, including three advanced areas (Europe, North America, and Japan) and three developing country zones ranked according to their stage in the demographic transition (a "rapidly aging," a "moderately aging," and a "slowly aging" zone) (Table 3.4). Each region of the world comprises three categories of economic agents: households, firms, and the public sector. These are described below.

[39]Specifically, secondary school enrollment ratios; investment/GDP; budget balance/GDP; inflation rate; external trade/GDP; and country risk.

[40]Multiple generations models were first proposed by Samuelson (1958) and Diamond (1965). In their purest overlapping-generations (OLG) form, these innovate upon the Ramsey infinitely-lived representative-consumer hypothesis by introducing at each point in time individuals of different generations. Work by Blanchard (1985), Buiter (1988), Weil (1989), and more recently Faruqee (2000a, 2000b, 2003) suggested simplified alternatives to pure OLG models. Multicountry extensions in the OLG tradition include Buiter (1981), Cutler and others (1990), Attanasio and Violante (2000), INGENUE Team (2001), Börsch-Supan, Ludwig, and Winter (2003), and Fehr, Jokisch, and Kotlikoff (2003), among others. Faruqee, Laxton, and Symanski (1997), and Bryant and McKibbin (2004) all proposed multicountry extensions in the Blanchard-Buiter-Weil multiple-generations-model tradition.

[41]A new, more sophisticated version of the INGENUE model with 10 regions, imperfect financial markets, 2 sectors, autonomous population projections based upon UN coefficient methods, stochastic life expectancy, and bequest motives is currently under construction.

Table 3.4. INGENUE Model: Countries Composing Each Demographic Zone

Name of Region	Countries in Region
Western Europe	European Union, Switzerland, Norway, and Iceland
North America and Oceania	United States, Canada, Australia, and New Zealand
Japan	Japan
Developing: rapidly aging	Armenia, Bahrain, Belarus, Bosnia-Herzegovina, Bulgaria, China, Czech Republic, Cyprus, Estonia, Georgia, Hong Kong SAR, Hungary, Korea, Dem. People's Rep., Korea, Rep. of, Latvia, Lithuania, Macao, Moldova, Poland, Qatar, Romania, Russian Federation, Singapore, Slovak Republic, Thailand, Ukraine, United Arab Emirates, and Uruguay.
Developing: moderately aging	Albania, Argentina, Azerbaijan, Bahamas, Brazil, Brunei, Caribbean zone, Chile, Colombia, Dominica, Guyana, India, Indonesia, Israel, Jamaica, Kuwait, Lebanon, Malaysia, Mexico, Panama, Peru, Sri Lanka, Suriname, Trinidad and Tobago, Turkey, and Vietnam.
Developing: slowly aging	Afghanistan, Africa, Bangladesh, Bhutan, Bolivia, Cambodia, Costa Rica, Ecuador, El Salvador, Fiji, Guatemala, Haiti, Honduras, Iran, Islamic Rep. of, Iraq, Jordan, Kazakhstan, Kyrgyz Republic, Lao PDR, Melanesia, Micronesia, Mongolia, Myanmar, Nepal, Nicaragua, Oman, Pakistan, Papua New Guinea, Paraguay, Philippines, Polynesia, Samoa, Saudi Arabia, Syrian Arab Republic, Tajikistan, Turkmenistan, Eastern Timor, Uzbekistan, Vanuatu, Venezuela, West Bank and Gaza, and Yemen, Rep. of.

Households

In each region the household sector consists of 15 overlapping five-year-long cohorts of adults aged 20–94, and four cohorts of "young" who are dependent on their parents: individuals become adults when they turn 20, and remain in the labor force until legal, mandatory retirement age, which differs according to the region. Death occurs with certainty between ages 60 and 94, but is modeled in a way that mimics realistic probabilistic assumptions for the various world regions.

Households are assumed to supply labor, inelastically and locally, during the first periods of their adult life (youth and maturity) and then to retire. In addition, young adults bear the costs of educating children, modeled as a "tax" on the parent's consumption, proportional to the number of births. Households maximize life-cycle utility, with perfect foresight: when working, they save and invest in shares of the capital stock of production firms that are sold on a unified world capital market to finance their consumption during retirement—when they dissave. There is no bequest motive so at the end of each household's life each household's cumulated saving is zero.

Firms

The model assumes that identical firms located in various regions of the world are perfectly competitive, are equipped with a Cobb-Douglas constant-return technology using two factors (capital and labor), and produce a single good that may be used for consumption and investment. In the model this good is used as a numeraire and is freely traded at no cost on a world market. The assumption of a single good traded at no cost in world markets implies that regional real exchange rates are constant and always equal to one. In the model, capital is also perfectly mobile and the world financial market is perfect so that, in the long run, regional interest rates are equalized. Although the production technology is assumed to be identical across regions, the model is simulated assuming a wide initial gap in the level of total factor productivity between regions, which in turn is driven by an exogenous growth and convergence process. A mechanism of exogenous international diffusion of technological progress is specified, whereby the various regions of the world slowly converge to the level of total factor productivity in the North American economy—the world's technological leader—so that in the very long run all regions grow at the same rate.

Public Sector

The public sector is reduced to a pay-as-you-go public pension scheme. It is financed by a payroll tax on all labor incomes and pays pensions to retired households. The replacement rate on the after tax wage is fixed, and the payroll tax is endogenous in order to enforce a balanced-budget rule. The adopted calibration allows the model to reproduce realistic regional intergenerational transfers.

Equilibrium

The general equilibrium of the world economy is solved by equating, in each region, the optimal labor demand emanating from domestic firms to the exogenous local labor supply, and the sum of regional supplies of saving with the sum of regional demand for investment. These equilibrium conditions respectively yield the six regional real wage rates and the world real interest rate, which in turn determine regional GDP, aggregate consumption, and saving, as well as their distribution over living cohorts in the various regions. In any given period, the difference between the flows of domestic saving and domestic investment in any of the six regions gives the inflow or outflow of the capital for the region, while the ratio of the stock of accumulated wealth of resident households to the stock of accumulated productive capital in a particular region, defined as the ownership ratio, measures its net external position—that is, net foreign assets or net external debt.

Calibration

Fertility rates and households' life expectancy in the model are set to mimic demographic projections from the UN's medium-fertility scenario up to 2050. The evolution of regional populations beyond that date is obtained by setting reproduction rates so that populations become stationary after 2100. Parameter values governing households' and firms' behavior together with assumptions on exogenous growth rates, the degree of international technological convergence, and contribution and replacement rates for pension schemes in the various regions of the world are based on historical data in order to match as closely as possible the observed dynamic of key economic variables, notably current account balances and interest rates.

MSG3 Model

The MSG3 model is a three-sector—energy, nonenergy, and capital-producing—version of the G-Cubed model developed by McKibbin and Wilcoxen (1998) building on the earlier MSG2 model developed by McKibbin and Sachs (1989) and the Jorgenson and Wilcoxen (1990) model. The model divides the world into four regions: the United States, Japan, the rest of the OECD, and the rest of the world (in essence, the world's developing bloc). It combines the modern intertemporal optimization approach to modeling economic behavior (as found in Blanchard and Fischer, 1989; and Obstfeld and Rogoff, 1996) with short-run rule-of-thumb behavior. In doing this it brings together features of real business cycle models—with a fully articulated analysis of forward-looking producers and consumers—and modern macroeconometric models—describing the effects of demand downturns in the face of wage (and price) stickiness. The main features of the model are as follows.

- *Demographics.* The model includes demographic considerations, such that economic agents in the model possess finite life spans and their income varies as they age. Specifically, drawing heavily on Faruqee (2000a, 2000b), who extended the Blanchard (1985) model of finitely lived agents to include aging considerations, in the MSG3 economic agents progress from being financially dependent children to being adults who are financially responsible for their own children. Death occurs with a fixed probability.
- *Explicit optimization.* The model is based on explicit intertemporal optimization by agents (consumers and firms) in each economy. Thus, time and dynamics are of fundamental importance in the MSG3 model, making its core theoretical structure like that of real business cycle models.
- *Rule-of-thumb agents.* To track the inertial dynamics of some key macroeconomic vari-

ables, the behavior of agents is modified to allow for short-run deviations from optimal behavior, owing either to myopia or to restrictions on the ability of households and firms to borrow at the risk-free bond rate on government debt.

- *Cash-in-advance constraints.* Holdings of financial assets including money are explicitly modeled. In particular, money is introduced into the model through a restriction that households require money to purchase goods.
- *Nominal rigidities.* The model allows for short-run nominal wage rigidity (by different degrees in different countries) and therefore allows for protracted periods of unemployment depending on the labor market institutions in each country.
- *Two types of capital.* The model distinguishes between the stickiness of physical capital within sectors and within countries and the flexibility of financial capital that can flow immediately where expected returns are highest. This distinction leads to a difference between the quantity of physical capital that is available at any time to produce goods and services and the valuation of that capital as a result of decisions about the geographical allocation of financial capital.
- *Estimation/calibration.* Key parameters in the model—such as the elasticities of substitution in production and consumption decisions—are estimated, enhancing the model's ability to reproduce the dynamics of historical data.

As a result, the model exhibits a rich dynamic behavior, driven on the one hand by asset accumulation and, on the other hand, by wage adjustment to a neoclassical steady state. Details of the model can be found on the Internet at www.gcubed.com.

Tosun's Two-Region OLG Model with International Labor Mobility

This two-period two-country model builds on the standard closed-economy overlapping generations framework developed by Diamond (1965). The model features either capital or labor mobility in line with work by Galor (1986, 1992) and Crettez, Michel, and Vidal (1996, 1998). In the version used here the two countries represent the advanced and developing regions of the world, each with a population that is composed of two age groups (workers and the retired). The population characteristics of each country are calibrated to actual UN projections for advanced and developing blocs of the world so that the advanced countries age more quickly than the developing countries. The model incorporates the interaction of household behavior, firm behavior, political process, and international labor flows. These are described in more detail below.

Households

Individuals live for two (30-year-long) periods and seek to maximize the utility that they derive from consumption over their lifetime. To pay for consumption, households supply labor according to a distribution of abilities that is replicated in each new generation. Effective labor is the product of human capital that is accumulated from the interaction of the ability level of the individual and government spending per young on a productivity-enhancing public good such as education. Both labor and capital income are taxed to finance the provision of public goods.

Firms

Each country produces a single good using a Cobb-Douglas technology. Competitive factor markets require that the real wage and the real interest rate are equalized to the marginal product of labor and capital, respectively.

Political process

The government provides two public goods: a productivity-enhancing good (education) and social security. It is assumed that there is a predetermined "earmarked" level of social security spending. Thus the social security tax is simply determined by the government budget constraint where social security spending per worker is fixed. However, spending on the productivity-enhancing public good is determined through a political process for which a median-voter framework with voter heterogeneity is used. Voter heterogeneity is introduced by assuming a distribution of genetic ability levels for the working generation. The ability level of the individual will, in turn, determine the value that the individual receives from the public good.

The preferred tax rate is increasing with the ability level of the individual and with income per worker and it is decreasing with the social security tax rate. Since retirees do not derive any benefit from this public good, they incur a cost without enjoying any benefits. Therefore, their preferred tax rate will always be zero, regardless of their ability. With an increase in the dependency ratio, retired people will need fewer working voters to form a majority. Since these working voters are at the lower end of the ability distribution, they prefer lower taxes than higher-ability people because their return from the productivity-enhancing public good is lower. Therefore, the median voter becomes a person with lower ability and the preferred tax rate of the median voter falls. The migration of workers increases the number of working voters, the upshot of which is a higher preferred tax rate of the median voter, and thus a larger provision of productivity-enhancing good. In turn, this supports labor income and growth relative to a scenario of aging where no migration takes place.

Equilibrium

In the absence of international capital mobility, capital market equilibrium requires that saving in each period equals accumulated capital in the following period. Two alternatives are also contemplated to close the dynamic model. Either capital is fully mobile internationally (so that rates of return are equalized between the two countries) or labor is perfectly mobile between the two countries (so that net-of-tax real wages are equalized across countries, given that the model uses source-based income taxation for both countries).

In the case of perfect labor mobility, it is assumed that only people of working age move between regions. Additionally, migration is assumed to have no effect on the ability distribution in both regions. This means that migration of labor affects the size rather than the composition of the working-age generation in the two regions.

References

Abel, Andrew, 2003, "The Effects of a Baby Boom on Stock Prices and Capital Accumulation in the Presence of Social Security," *Econometrica*, Vol. 71 (March), pp. 551–78.

Acemoglu, Daron, Simon Johnson, and James Robinson, 2003, "Disease & Development in Historical Perspective," *Journal of the European Economic Association*, Vol. 1 (April), pp. 397–405.

AGIR Project, 2003a, "Bio-Demographic Aspects of Aging, Data for Belgium," Working Paper No. 10–03 (Brussels).

———, 2003b, "Use of Health Care and Nursing Care by the Elderly: Data for Belgium," Working Paper No. 11–03 (Brussels).

Ang, Andrew, and Angela Maddaloni, 2003, "Do Demographic Changes Affect Risk Premiums? Evidence from International Data," NBER Working Paper No. 9677 (Cambridge, Massachusetts: National Bureau of Economic Research); forthcoming in the *Journal of Business*.

Attanasio, Orazio P., and Giovanni L. Violante, 2000, "The Demographic Transition in Closed and Open Economies: A Tale of Two Regions," IADB Working Paper No. 412 (Washington: Inter-American Development Bank).

Auerbach, Alan J., and Laurence J. Kotlikoff, 1987, *Dynamic Fiscal Policy* (Cambridge: Cambridge University Press).

Australia, Commonwealth of, The Treasury, 2002, "Intergenerational Report 2002–2003," 2002–2003 Budget Paper No. 5 (Canberra).

Bakshi, Gurdip, and Zhiwu Chen, 1994, "Baby Boom, Population Aging and Capital Markets," *Journal of Business*, Vol. 67 (April), pp. 165–202.

Barr, Nicholas, 2001, *The Welfare State as Piggy Bank—Information Risk, Uncertainty, and the Role of the State* (Oxford, United Kingdom: Oxford University Press).

Batini, Nicoletta, Timothy Callen, and Warwick McKibbin, 2004, "The Global Impact of Demographic Change," IMF Working Paper (Washington: International Monetary Fund, forthcoming).

Bell, Clive, Shantajanan Devarajan, and Hans Gersbach, 2004, "Thinking About the Long-Run

Consequences of HIV/AIDS," in *The Macroeconomics of HIV/AIDS*, ed. by Markus Haacker (Washington: International Monetary Fund, forthcoming).

Bergantino, Steven, 1998, "Lifecycle Investment Behavior, Demographics, and Asset Prices" (Ph.D. dissertation; Cambridge, Massachusetts: MIT, Department of Economics).

Blanchard, Olivier, 1985, "Debt, Deficits, and Finite Horizons," *Journal of Political Economy*, Vol. 93 (April), pp. 223–47.

———, and Stanley Fischer, 1989, *Lectures on Macroeconomics* (Cambridge, Massachusetts: MIT Press).

Bloom, David, and David Canning, 2001, "Cumulative Causality, Economic Growth, and the Demographic Transition," Chapter 7 in *Population Matters: Demographic Change, Economic Growth, and Poverty in the Developing World*, ed. by Nancy Birdsall, Allen Kelley, and Steven Sinding (New York: Oxford University Press).

———, and Jaypee Sevilla, 2001, "Economic Growth and the Demographic Transition," NBER Working Paper No. 8685 (Cambridge, Massachusetts: National Bureau of Economic Research).

Bohn, Henning, 1999, "Social Security and Demographic Uncertainty: The Risk Sharing Properties of Alternative Policies," NBER Working Paper No. 7030 (Cambridge, Massachusetts: National Bureau of Economic Research).

Borjas, George, 1999, "The Economic Analysis of Immigration," in *Handbook of Labor Economics 3A*, ed. by O. Ashenfelter and D. Card (Amsterdam: North-Holland).

———, 2001, "Does Immigration Grease the Wheels of the Labor Market?" *Brookings Papers on Economic Activity: 1*, Brookings Institution, pp. 69–133.

Börsch-Supan, Axel, Alexander Ludwig, and Joachim Winter, 2003, "Aging, Pension Reform, and Capital Flows: A Multi-Country Simulation Model," MEA Discussion Paper No. 28–30 (Mannheim, Germany: Mannheim Research Institute for the Economics of Aging).

Bosworth, Barry, Ralph Bryant, and Gary Burtless, 2004, "The Impact of Aging on Financial Markets and the Economy: A Survey," Brookings Institution Working Paper (Washington: Brookings Institution).

Brooks, Robin, 1998, "Asset Market and Saving Effects of Demographic Transitions" (Ph.D. dissertation; New Haven, Connecticut: Yale University, Department of Economics).

Bryant, Ralph C., 2004, "Demographic Pressures on Public Pension Systems and Government Budgets in Open Economies," ESRI Discussion Paper No. 109 (Tokyo: Economic and Social Research Institute).

———, and Warwick J. McKibbin, 2004, "Incorporating Demographic Change in Multi-Country Macroeconomic Models: Some Preliminary Results" (unpublished; Brookings Institution and Australian National University).

Buiter, Willem H., 1981, "Time Preference and International Lending and Borrowing in an Overlapping-Generations Model," *Journal of Political Economy*, Vol. 89 (August), pp. 769–97.

———, 1988, "Death, Birth, Productivity Growth and Debt Neutrality," *Economic Journal*, Vol. 98, pp. 279–93.

Burniaux, Jean-Marc, Romian Duval, and Florence Jaumotte, 2003, "Coping with Aging: A Dynamic Approach to Quantify the Impact of Alternative Policy Options on Future Labor Supply in OECD Countries," OECD Economics Department Working Paper No. 371 (Paris: Organization for Economic Cooperation and Development).

Cardarelli, Roberto, and Kenichi Ueda, 2004, "Domestic and Global Perspectives of Migration to the United States," in IMF Country Report No. 04/228 (Washington: International Monetary Fund, July).

Carrington, William J., Enrica Detragiache, and Tara Vishwanath, 1996, "Migration with Endogenous Moving Costs," *American Economic Review*, Vol. 86 (September), pp. 909–30.

Casey, Bernard, Howard Oxley, Edward Whitehouse, Pablo Antolin, Romain Duval, and Willi Leibfritz, 2003, "Policies for an Aging Society: Recent Measures and Areas for Further Reform," OECD Economics Department Working Paper No. 369 (Paris: Organization for Economic Cooperation and Development).

Cazes, Sandrine, Thierry Chauveau, Jacques Le Cacheux, and Rahim Loufir, 1992, "An OG Model of the French Economy: Application to the Long-Run Prospects of the Public Pension Scheme," OFCE Working Paper No. 92–5 (Paris: Observatoire Français des Conjonctures Économiques).

———, 1994, "Public Pensions in an Overlapping-Generations Model of the French Economy," *Keio Economic Studies*, Vol. 31, No. 1, pp. 1–19.

Center for Strategic and International Studies, and Watson Wyatt, 1999, *Global Aging: The Challenge of the New Millennium* (Washington).

Chinn, Menzie D., and Eswar S. Prasad, 2003, "Medium-Term Determinants of Current Accounts in Industrial and Developing Countries: An Empirical Exploration," *Journal of International Economics,* Vol. 59 (January), pp. 47–76.

Constantinides, George, John Donaldson, and Rajnish Mehra, 2002, "Junior Can't Borrow: A New Perspective on the Equity Premium Puzzle," *Quarterly Journal of Economics,* Vol. 117 (February), pp. 269–96.

Crafts, Nicholas, and Markus Haacker, 2004, "Welfare Implications of HIV/AIDS," in *The Macroeconomics of HIV/AIDS,* ed. by Markus Haacker (Washington: International Monetary Fund, forthcoming).

Crettez, Bertrand, Philippe Michel, and Jean-Pierre Vidal, 1996, "Time Preference and Labor Migration in an OLG Model with Land and Capital," *Journal of Population Economics,* Vol. 9, No. 4, pp. 387–403.

———, 1998, "Time Preference and Capital Mobility in an OLG Model with Land," *Journal of Population Economics,* Vol. 11, No. 1, pp. 149–58.

Cutler, David, James M. Poterba, Louise Sheiner, and Laurence Summers, 1990, "An Aging Society: Opportunity or Challenge?" *Brookings Papers on Economic Activity: 1,* Brookings Institution, pp. 1–56.

Davis, E. Philip, and Christine Li, 2003, "Demographics and Financial Asset Prices in the Major Industrial Economies," Department of Economics and Finance Discussion Paper No. 03–07 (Middlesex, England: Brunel University).

Deaton, Angus, and Christina Paxson, 2000, "Growth and Saving Among Individuals and Households," *Review of Economics and Statistics,* Vol. 82 (May), pp. 212–25.

Dekle, Robert, 2003, "Financing Consumption in an Aging Japan: The Role of Foreign Capital Inflows and Immigration" (unpublished; Los Angeles: University of Southern California).

Demeny, Paul, 2003, "Population Policy: A Concise Summary," Policy Research Division Working Paper No. 173 (New York: Population Council).

Diamond, Peter A., 1965, "National Debt in a Neoclassical Growth Model," *American Economic Review,* Vol. 55 (December), pp. 1126–50.

———, and Peter R. Orszag, 2004, *Saving Social Security: A Balanced Approach* (Washington: Brookings Institution Press).

Disney, Richard, 1996, *Can We Afford to Grow Older? A Perspective on the Economics of Aging* (Cambridge, Massachusetts: MIT Press).

Dixon, Simon, Scott McDonald, and Jennifer Roberts, 2002, "The Impact of HIV and AIDS on Africa's Economic Development," *British Medical Journal,* Vol. 324, pp. 232–4.

Eastwood, Robert, and Michael Lipton, 2001, "Demographic Transition and Poverty: Effects via Economic Growth, Distribution, and Conversion," Chapter 9 in *Population Matters: Demographic Change, Economic Growth, and Poverty in the Developing World,* ed. by Nancy Birdsall, Allen Kelley, and Steven Sinding (New York: Oxford University Press).

European Commission, Economic Policy Committee, 2001, *Budgetary Challenges Posed by Ageing Populations: The Impact on Public Spending on Pensions, Health and Long-Term Care for the Elderly and Possible Indicators of the Long-Term Sustainability of Public Finances* (Brussels).

Faruqee, Hamid, 2000a, "Population Aging and Its Macroeconomic Implications," in Japan: Selected Issues, IMF Staff Country Report No. 00/144 (Washington: International Monetary Fund).

———, 2000b, "Population Aging and Its Macroeconomic Implications: A Framework for Analysis" (unpublished; Washington: International Monetary Fund).

———, 2002, "Population Aging and Its Macroeconomic Implication: A Framework for Analysis," IMF Working Paper 02/16 (Washington: International Monetary Fund).

———, 2003, "Debt, Deficits, and Age-Specific Mortality," *Review of Economic Dynamics,* Vol. 6, No. 2, pp. 300–12.

———, Douglas Laxton, and Stephen Symansky, 1997, "Government Debt, Life-Cycle Income and Liquidity Constraints: Beyond Approximate Ricardian Equivalence," *IMF Staff Papers,* Vol. 44, No. 3, pp. 374–82.

Faruqee, Hamid, and Martin Mühleisen, 2001, "Population Aging in Japan: Demographic Shock and Fiscal Sustainability," IMF Working Paper 01/40 (Washington: International Monetary Fund).

Fasano, Ugo, and Rishi Goyal, 2004, "Emerging Strains in GCC Labor Markets," IMF Working Paper 04/71 (Washington: International Monetary Fund).

Fehr, Hans, Sabine Jokisch, and Laurence J. Kotlikoff, 2003,"The Developed World's Demographic Transition—The Roles of Capital Flows, Immigration, and Policy," NBER Working Paper No. 10096 (Cambridge, Massachusetts: National Bureau of Economic Research).

Feroli, Michael, 2003, "Capital Flows Among the G-7 Nations: A Demographic Perspective," Finance and Economics Discussion Series No. 2003–54 (Washington: Federal Reserve Board).

Futagami, Koichi, and Tetsuya Nakajima, 2001, "Population Aging and Economic Growth," *Journal of Macroeconomics,* Vol. 23, No. 1, pp. 31–44.

Galor, Oded, 1986, "Time Preference and International Labor Migration," *Journal of Economic Theory,* Vol. 38 (February), pp. 1–20.

———, 1992, "The Choice of Factor Mobility in a Dynamic World," *Journal of Population Economics,* Vol. 5 (May), pp. 135–44.

Geanakoplos, John, Michael Magill, and Martine Quinzii, 2004, "Demography and the Long-Run Predictability of the Stock Market," *Brookings Papers on Economic Activity: 1,* Brookings Institution, pp. 241–307.

Glied, Sherry, 2003, "Health Care Costs: On the Rise Again," *Journal of Economic Perspectives,* Vol. 17 (Spring), pp. 125–48.

Gómez, Rafael, and Pablo Hernández de Cos, 2003, "Demographic Maturity and Economic Performance: The Effect of Demographic Transitions on per Capita GDP Growth," Bank of Spain Working Paper No. 318 (Madrid: Bank of Spain).

Greenwood, Michael J., 1985, "Human Migration: Theory, Models, Empirical Studies," *Journal of Regional Science,* Vol. 25 (November), pp. 521–44.

Group of Ten, 1998, *The Macroeconomic and Financial Implications of Ageing Populations* (Paris, Washington, Basel: OECD, IMF, and Bank for International Settlements).

Gutierrez, Juan Pablo, and others, 2004, "Achieving the WHO/UNAIDS Antiretroviral Treatment 3 by 5 Goal: What Will It Cost?," *The Lancet,* Vol. 364, pp. 63–4.

Heller, Peter, 1997, "Aging in the Asian 'Tigers': Challenges for Fiscal Policy," IMF Working Paper 97/143 (Washington: International Monetary Fund).

———, 2003, *Who Will Pay? Coping with Aging Societies, Climate Change, and Other Long-Term Fiscal Challenges* (Washington: International Monetary Fund).

Higgins, Matthew, 1998, "Demography, National Savings, and International Capital Flows," *International Economic Review,* Vol. 39, No. 2, pp. 343–69.

Horioka, Charles, 1991, "The Determinants of Japan's Savings Rate," *Economic Studies Quarterly,* Vol. 42, No. 3, pp. 237–53.

INGENUE Team, 2001, "INGENUE: Une Modélisation Intergénérationnelle et Universelle" (Paris: Banque de France).

Jackson, Richard, 2002, *The Global Retirement Crisis: The Threat to World Stability and What to Do About It* (Washington: Center for Strategic and International Studies).

Jannsen, John, 2001, "New Zealand's Fiscal Policy Framework: Evolution and Experience," New Zealand Treasury Working Paper 01/25 (Wellington: The Treasury).

Jones, Charles, 2002, "Sources of U.S. Economic Growth in a World of Ideas," *American Economic Review,* Vol. 92 (March), pp. 220–39.

Jorgenson, Dale W., and Peter J. Wilcoxen, 1990, "Environmental Regulation and U.S. Economic Growth," *RAND Journal of Economics,* Vol. 21, No. 2, pp. 314–40.

Kalemli-Ozcan, Sebnem, 2002, "Does Mortality Decline Promote Economic Growth?" *Journal of Economic Growth,* Vol. 7 (December), pp. 411–39.

———, 2003, "A Stochastic Model of Mortality, Fertility, and Human Capital Investment," *Journal of Development Economics,* Vol. 70, No. 1, pp. 103–18.

———, Harl Ryder, and David Weil, 2000, "Mortality Decline, Human Capital Investment, and Economic Growth," *Journal of Development Economics,* Vol. 62, No. 1, pp. 1–23.

Kelley, Allen, and Robert Schmidt, 2001, "Economic and Demographic Change: A Synthesis of Models, Findings, and Perspectives," Chapter 4 in *Population Matters: Demographic Change, Economic Growth, and Poverty in the Developing World,* ed. by Nancy Birdsall, Allen Kelley, and Steven Sinding (New York: Oxford University Press).

Lee, Ronald, 2003, "The Demographic Transition: Three Centuries of Fundamental Change," *Journal of Economic Perspectives,* Vol. 17, No. 4, pp. 167–90.

———, Andrew Mason, and Timothy Miller, 1997, "Saving, Wealth, and the Demographic Transition in East Asia," East-West Center Working Paper No. 88–24 (Honolulu, Hawaii: East-West Center).

Lee, Ronald, Michael Anderson, and Shripad Tuljapurkar, 2003, "Stochastic Forecasts of the Social Security Trust Fund," CEDA Paper No. 2003-0005CL (Berkeley, California: University of California, Center for the Economics and Demography of Aging).

Loayza, Norman, Klaus Schmidt-Hebbel, and Luis Servén, 2000, "Saving in Developing Countries: An Overview," *World Bank Economic Review,* Vol. 14, No. 3, pp. 393–41.

Luhrmann, Melanie, 2003, "Demographic Change, Foresight, and International Capital Flows" (unpublished; Mannheim, Germany: Mannheim University).

Malmberg, Bo, 1994, "Age Structure Effects on - Economic Growth—Swedish Evidence," *Scandinavian Economic History Reviews,* Vol. 42, No. 3, pp. 279–95.

Malthus, Thomas, 1798, *An Essay on the Principle of Population* (London: Macmillan, 1926).

Masson, Paul, Tamim Bayoumi, and Hossein Samiei, 1995, "International Evidence on the Determinants of Private Saving," IMF Working Paper 95/51 (Washington: International Monetary Fund).

McKibbin, Warwick J., and Jeremy Nguyen, 2004, "Modelling Global Demographic Change: Results for Japan," paper presented at the conference on the International Collaborations Projects for the Economic and Social Research Institute, Cabinet Office, Government of Japan, Tokyo, February 18.

McKibbin, Warwick J., and Jeffrey D. Sachs, 1989, "The McKibbin-Sachs Global Model: Theory and Specifications," NBER Working Paper No. 3100 (Cambridge, Massachusetts: National Bureau of Economic Research).

McKibbin, Warwick J., and Peter J. Wilcoxen, 1998, "The Theoretical and Empirical Structure of the G-Cubed Model," *Economic Modelling,* Vol. 16, No. 1, pp. 123–48.

McMorrow, Kieran, and Werner Roeger, 2004, *The Economic and Financial Market Consequences of Global Ageing* (New York: Springer-Verlag Press).

Meltzer, David, 1992, *Mortality Decline, the Demographic Transition, and Economic Growth* (Ph.D. dissertation; Chicago, Illinois: University of Chicago, Department of Economics).

National Research Council, 2000, *Beyond Six Billion: Forecasting the World's Population* (Washington: National Academy Press).

Obstfeld, Maurice, and Kenneth Rogoff, 1996, *Foundations of International Macroeconomics*" (Cambridge, Massachusetts: MIT Press).

Oeppen, Jim, and James Vaupel, 2002, "Broken Limits to Life Expectancy," *Science Magazine,* Vol. 296 (May), pp. 1029–31.

Organization for Economic Cooperation and Development (OECD), 2001, "Fiscal Implications of Aging: Projections of Age-Related Spending," *Economic Outlook,* Vol. 69 (September), pp. 145–67.

———, 2004, *Ensuring the Financial Sustainability of Health Systems* (Paris).

Orszag, Peter R., and Joseph E. Stiglitz, 2001, "Rethinking Pension Reform: Ten Myths About Social Security Systems," in *New Ideas About Old Age Security: Toward Sustainable Pension Systems in the 21st Century,* ed. by Robert Holzmann and Joseph Stiglitz (Washington: World Bank).

Over, Mead, 2004, "The Impact of the HIV/AIDS Epidemic on the Health Sectors of Developing Countries," in *The Macroeconomics of HIV/AIDS,* ed. by Markus Haacker (Washington: International Monetary Fund, forthcoming).

Passell, Peter, 1996, "The Year Is 2010. Do You Know Where Your Bull Is?" *New York Times,* March 10, Section 3, pp. 1–16.

Peterson, Peter, 1999, "Gray Dawn: How the Coming Age Wave Will Transform America—and the World" (New York: Times Books).

Poterba, James, 2001, "Demographic Structure and Asset Returns," *Review of Economics and Statistics,* Vol. 83, pp. 565–84.

Ratha, Dilip, 2003, "Workers' Remittances: An Important and Stable Source of External Development Finance," Chapter 7 in *Global Development Finance 2003* (Washington: World Bank), pp. 157–75.

Romer, Paul M., 1990, "Endogenous Technological Change," *Journal of Political Economy,* Vol. 98 (October), pp. 71–102.

Rother, P., M. Catenaro, and G. Schwab, 2003, "Ageing and Pensions in the Euro Area: Survey and Projection Results," Social Protection Discussion Paper No. 0307 (Washington: World Bank).

Samuelson, Paul A., 1958, "An Exact Consumption-Loan Model of Interest With or Without the Social Contrivance of Money," *Journal of Political Economy,* Vol. 66 (December), pp. 467–82.

Samwick, Andrew A., 1998, "New Evidence on Pensions, Social Security, and the Timing of Retirement," NBER Working Paper No. W6534 (Cambridge, Massachusetts: National Bureau of Economic Research).

———, 1999, "Social Security Reform in the United States," *National Tax Journal,* Vol. 52 (December), pp. 819–42.

Steinberg, Malcolm, and others, 2002, "Hitting Home: How Households Cope with the Impact of the HIV/AIDS Epidemic" (Washington: Kaiser Family Foundation).

Tosun, Mehmet S., 2003, "Population Aging and Economic Growth: Political Economy and Open Economy Effects," *Economics Letters,* Vol. 81, No. 3, pp. 291–96.

UNAIDS (Joint United Nations Program on HIV/AIDS), 2004, *Report on the Global AIDS Epidemic* (Geneva, Switzerland).

UNAIDS/UNICEF/USAID, 2004, "Children on the Brink 2004: A Joint Report of New Orphan

Estimates and a Framework for Action" (Geneva, New York, Washington).

United Kingdom, Royal Commission on Population, 1949, *Report to Parliament* (June) (London).

United Nations, 2000, "Replacement Migration: Is It a Solution to Declining and Ageing Populations?" Population Division, Department of Economic and Social Affairs, United Nations (New York).

———, 2003, "World Population Prospects: The 2002 Revision," Population Division, Department of Economic and Social Affairs, United Nations (New York).

United States, Congressional Budget Office, 2001, *Uncertainty in Social Security's Long-Term Finances: A Stochastic Analysis* (Washington).

———, 2003, *The Long-Term Budget Outlook* (December) (Washington).

Wanless, Derek, 2002, *Securing Our Future Health: Taking a Long-Term View* (April) (London: Public Enquiry Unit, HM Treasury).

Weil, Philippe, 1989, "Overlapping Families of Infinitely-Lived Agents," *Journal of Public Economics,* Vol. 38 (March), pp. 183–98.

Williamson, Jeffrey, 2001, "Demographic Change, Economic Growth, and Inequality," Chapter 5 in *Population Matters: Demographic Change, Economic Growth, and Poverty in the Developing World,* ed. by Nancy Birdsall, Allen Kelley, and Steven Sinding (New York: Oxford University Press).

Wise, David, 2003, "Program Report on Economics of Aging," *NBER Reporter,* June 22.

World Health Organization, 2004, *World Health Report* (Geneva: WHO).

Young, Gary, 2002, "The Implications of an Aging Population for the UK Economy," Working Paper No. 159 (London: Bank of England).

Zhang, Jie, Junsen Zhang, and Ronald Lee, 2003, "Rising Longevity, Education, Savings, and Growth," *Journal of Development Economics,* Vol. 70, No. 1, pp. 83–101.

ANNEX SUMMING UP BY THE ACTING CHAIR

The following remarks by the Acting Chair were made at the conclusion of the Executive Board's discussion of the World Economic Outlook on September 3, 2004.

Executive Directors noted that the global recovery remains solid, with economic growth in 2004 projected to reach its highest rate in nearly 30 years. The expansion is underpinned by continued accommodative macroeconomic policies, rising corporate profitability, and wealth effects from rising equity and house prices. It has become increasingly broad-based geographically, although some regions continue to grow more vigorously than others. Global growth remains driven by the United States, with strong support from Asia, particularly China and Japan. Activity in Latin America and some other emerging markets has also picked up strongly, while the outlook for Africa has improved. There is growing economic momentum in the euro area, although the strength of the upturn varies across countries and in some cases is heavily dependent on external demand.

While welcoming these developments, Directors noted that risks to the expansion have increased in recent months. First, oil prices rose sharply through mid-August, driven by strong global demand and, increasingly, supply-side concerns. While prices have since fallen back somewhat, they are still significantly higher than in 2003; and with spare capacity near historical lows, the oil market remains highly vulnerable to shocks and speculative pressures. Against this backdrop, Directors urged greater cooperation between consumers and producers toward a more stable global oil market, with some Directors emphasizing the importance of measures to promote more efficient use of oil and other nonrenewable resources. Second, and partly related, second-quarter growth slowed in some major countries—including the United States and Japan. Directors noted the risk that this slowdown could persist, especially if employment growth in the United States remains relatively modest. Overall, while Directors generally expected a continued solid expansion of the world economy, they considered that the balance of risks has shifted to the downside, with further oil price volatility and geopolitical risks becoming the central short-term concerns.

Directors noted that inflationary risks remain generally moderate. Nevertheless, after falling to unusually low levels in mid-2003, inflation has turned up around the world, reflecting a combination of strong growth and higher commodity prices. Directors cautioned that, going forward, inflationary pressures could prove stronger than expected, necessitating a sharper-than-expected rise in interest rates. While acknowledging that monetary policy in many countries remains appropriately accommodative, Directors underscored that the key short-term policy challenge will be to continue to manage the transition toward higher interest rates to ensure that nascent inflationary pressures are contained, while facilitating—through continued good communication of the stance of monetary policy—sustained economic recovery and orderly adjustment in financial markets. In this connection, Directors viewed further sustained increases in oil prices as a complicating factor. While first-round oil price effects should be accommodated, central banks will need to ensure that second-round effects are well contained.

Directors called on policymakers to take advantage of the current cyclical expansion to address three key medium-term vulnerabilities and concerns.

- First, global imbalances—which remain an important medium-term risk to the economic outlook—need to be tackled. Directors reiterated that eliminating these will require medium-term fiscal consolidation in the United States to increase domestic saving, structural reforms to boost growth in Europe, Japan, and elsewhere, and steps toward greater exchange rate flexibility in Asia, as appropriate. In all three areas, much remains to be done; it will be important to make strong progress on each of them.
- Second, the pace of structural reforms needs to be quickened to increase economic flexibility and resilience, so that countries are well positioned to take full advantage of the opportunities from globalization and the information technology revolution, while strengthening their resistance to future shocks. Noting the key role of open markets in promoting competitiveness and efficiency, Directors looked forward to far-reaching trade liberalization under the Doha Round, building on the welcome progress in Geneva in July.
- Third, medium-term fiscal positions need to be strengthened in both industrial and developing countries. This will require a combination of fiscal consolidation, while allowing automatic stabilizers to work; structural measures to improve debt sustainability, including tax reform and stronger public expenditure frameworks; and reforms of pension and health care systems.

Industrial Countries

Directors welcomed the strong expansion in the *United States*, which has provided important support to global growth. Although business investment remains strong, Directors cautioned that the slowdown in consumption in the second quarter may be a source of concern going forward, especially since support from past macroeconomic stimulus and mortgage refinancing will decline in coming quarters. Nevertheless, in the context of the strong expansion expected for 2004, Directors agreed that a measured pace of tightening of monetary policy—calibrated according to the strength of the expansion and the extent of underlying inflationary pressures—is likely to be appropriate. Regarding fiscal policy, most Directors considered the pace of deficit reduction targeted for fiscal years 2005 and 2006 as appropriate, but many encouraged the authorities to capitalize on the better-than-expected budget outcome for fiscal year 2004 by further strengthening the near-term deficit reduction objective. For the medium term, most Directors suggested that the objective of halving the budget deficit over five years is not sufficiently ambitious. Directors generally reiterated the long-standing call for the establishment of a clear long-term fiscal goal embedded within the context of a credible medium-term fiscal framework.

Directors were encouraged that the *euro area* expansion has finally gained momentum, although the upturn remains moderate and heavily dependent on external demand, with substantial differences across countries. Looking forward, rising disposable incomes and progress in corporate balance sheet restructuring should help the euro area boost private consumption and investment, and contribute to a more balanced area-wide recovery. With underlying inflationary pressures still relatively moderate, Directors agreed that monetary policy should remain accommodative until a self-sustaining upturn in domestic demand is in place. Although recently enacted structural reforms have strengthened the prospects for medium-term growth, further reforms will be needed to provide critically needed impetus to employment creation and domestic demand. Directors stressed that the recovery provides a renewed opportunity for progress, focused particularly on the key issue of raising labor utilization. In this connection, some Directors recalled that, based on past experience, renewed initiatives at the European Union level for product market deregulation can also play a useful role, as they strengthen incentives for reforms, especially in labor markets.

Directors were encouraged by the finding of the staff's analysis of fiscal behavior under the EMU that fiscal policies in the euro area have become less procyclical over the past decade. However, they also highlighted the persisting tendency toward fiscal expansion in good times, which they saw as an important reason why some member states are currently breaching the Stability and Growth Pact (SGP) deficit limits. Accordingly, Directors urged euro area governments to take full advantage of the current expansion to strengthen fiscal positions. Many Directors underlined that reducing the procyclical bias of fiscal policy should be an important objective of ongoing reflection on the improvements needed in the design and effectiveness of SGP fiscal rules.

Directors welcomed the strong expansion in *Japan* over the last year. They noted that this was accompanied by a gradual easing of deflationary pressures, and continued progress in addressing corporate and financial sector vulnerabilities—although a substantial reform agenda remains to be completed in both areas. Despite the slowdown in GDP growth in the second quarter, most high-frequency indicators remain supportive of a continued solid expansion, with external sector developments—including with respect to oil prices and the exchange rate, as well as labor market conditions—remaining keys to the outlook. Directors underscored that to ensure an end to deflation, the current highly accommodative monetary stance should be maintained until inflation is firmly positive. Most Directors emphasized that, given Japan's difficult fiscal position and the favorable economic environment, it is now opportune to start the process of fiscal consolidation, including by achieving savings in fiscal year 2004 relative to the budget. Some Directors noted that stepped-up structural reforms should also improve Japan's fiscal position by increasing potential output growth—with the priorities being public enterprise reforms, strengthened competition policy, and enhanced labor market flexibility.

Directors welcomed the staff's analysis of the global house price boom and the impact that rising interest rates in industrial countries might have on housing markets. They noted the staff's analysis, which, reflecting linkages in economic activity and interest rates, shows a remarkable degree of synchronization of house prices across industrial countries—although the data limitations need to be recognized. Given the importance of house prices for private consumption, through wealth and credit channels, many Directors suggested that policymakers should monitor developments in the housing market closely, and they noted that a tightening of monetary policy during the transition to a more neutral policy stance could trigger a slowing or reversal of house price growth. Some Directors also underscored the need to further develop the mortgage market infrastructure and improve housing statistics.

Emerging Markets and Developing Countries

Directors welcomed the continued strength of the expansion in *emerging Asia*, reflecting the combined influence of the global upturn, especially in the electronics sector; the generally supportive macroeconomic policies, including highly competitive exchange rates; and the progressively stronger domestic demand growth. Looking forward, regional growth is expected to slow somewhat, but to remain solid, with much depending on developments in China, where—despite signs of slowing growth—a soft landing is not yet guaranteed. Other potential risks include the region's relatively greater exposure to oil price volatility and to higher global real interest rates, especially on countries reliant on external financing.

Given the prospects for solid growth and the still generally accommodative policies in emerging Asia, Directors agreed that monetary policies may need to be tightened, albeit by varying degrees, in most countries. Most Directors noted that, given continued current account and balance of payments surpluses, monetary tightening would be facilitated by greater exchange rate flexibility. In this connection, a number of Directors called on the authorities to use the current favorable conditions to initiate the transition to more flexible exchange rates. Directors stressed the importance of sound underlying macroeconomic policies and structural reforms in ensuring a smooth transition to more flexible exchange rate regimes. Directors were encouraged by the staff's finding that voluntary transitions to more flexible exchange rate regimes are generally not associated with an increase in macroeconomic instability. This probably reflects the strengthening of monetary and financial policy frameworks through greater central bank independence, the adoption of inflation targeting, the improvements in bank supervision, and the development of securities markets that frequently accompanied the transitions. Directors stressed the importance of proper timing and sequencing of reforms in these areas, tailored to individual country circumstances, in order to prepare the transition. Several Directors also pointed out that sound policies are essential for the success of any exchange rate regime.

Directors were encouraged by the strong rebound in economic activity in *Latin America,* supported by easier monetary conditions in most countries, improved confidence, rising commodity prices, and the global expansion. They noted that while sovereign borrowers have already largely met their funding requirements for 2004, external financing requirements remain high, and constitute an important vulnerability going forward. Directors emphasized that cutting high public debt ratios will be key to reducing vulnerabilities, and urged countries to press ahead with fiscal reforms. To boost medium-term growth, Directors pointed to the importance of strengthening the rule of law and investor rights, fostering financial sector development, further liberalizing trade, and promoting labor market flexibility. They noted that the success of these reforms will also require actions to address income inequality and reduce poverty.

Directors welcomed the continued strong growth momentum in *emerging Europe* and the *Commonwealth of Independent States (CIS),* while cautioning that policymakers in some of these countries need to guard against overheating. They underscored the need for fiscal consolidation, especially in light of substantial expenditure pressures and—in much of emerging Europe and the CIS-7—large external deficits. They also called for tighter monetary policies in the CIS, including through upward exchange rate flexibility in countries with large external surpluses; and for strengthening bank supervision in both regions to curb the prudential risks arising from rapid private sector credit growth. In addition, countries will need to persist with key structural reforms to further improve investment climates and fully develop the institutions and structures for market-based economies. In the *Middle East,* Directors noted the fading impetus to growth from higher oil production and prices as production reaches capacity. At the same time, they noted that the region will benefit from an expected substantial pickup in non-oil growth stemming from the global expansion and progress with reforms, especially trade liberalization. Fiscal consolidation will remain a priority in most countries, as will the need to boost employment by improving the environment for sustained private sector–led growth.

Directors were encouraged by the improved outlook for *Africa.* This has been underpinned by greater macroeconomic stability, higher export commodity prices, lower external debt burdens, somewhat better access to industrial country markets, and a variety of country-specific developments. Nevertheless, with most countries likely to fall significantly short of achieving the Millennium Development Goals, key challenges going forward will be to promote private investment and develop infrastructure, deepen institutional reforms, and reduce government involvement in the economy. Directors were encouraged that several countries have achieved more favorable governance levels. They called on the international community to support the region's strengthened reform efforts—through increased and better-coordinated assistance, continued debt relief, and elimination of barriers to exports, particularly in agriculture.

Demographic Change

Directors welcomed the work undertaken by the staff on demographic change, which is becoming an increasingly urgent concern. To meet the demographic challenges from population aging, industrial countries should boost labor supply, saving, and productivity, which, given the size of prospective demographic changes, will require a combination of reforms to be politically acceptable. Particularly important will be the selection of reforms, especially with respect to pension and health care systems: they will need to be resilient to a wide range of possible future demographic changes. For developing countries, Directors agreed that the key policy priorities will be to increase the flexibility of labor and product markets, and to ensure that labor resources and savings are effectively utilized. It will be important in these countries to move early to lay the groundwork for eventual population aging, including by strengthening pension and health care systems. This will be particularly challenging where medium-term fiscal positions are already under strain. Directors agreed that a broad longer-term implication of the staff's work on demographic change is that the effectiveness of actions to facilitate movements of goods, capital, and labor smoothly and efficiently across countries will significantly influence the pace, and pattern, of global adjustment to different rates of population aging. This promises to be a subject in which the international community—including the Fund—has a shared interest.

STATISTICAL APPENDIX

The statistical appendix presents historical data, as well as projections. It comprises five sections: Assumptions, What's New, Data and Conventions, Classification of Countries, and Statistical Tables.

The assumptions underlying the estimates and projections for 2004–05 and the medium-term scenario for 2006–09 are summarized in the first section. The second section presents a brief description of changes to the database and statistical tables. The third section provides a general description of the data, and of the conventions used for calculating country group composites. The classification of countries in the various groups presented in the *World Economic Outlook* is summarized in the fourth section.

The last, and main, section comprises the statistical tables. Data in these tables have been compiled on the basis of information available through mid-September 2004. The figures for 2004 and beyond are shown with the same degree of precision as the historical figures solely for convenience; since they are projections, the same degree of accuracy is not to be inferred.

Assumptions

Real effective *exchange rates* for the advanced economies are assumed to remain constant at their average levels during the period July 7–August 4, 2004. For 2004 and 2005, these assumptions imply average U.S. dollar/SDR conversion rates of 1.468 for 2004 and 1.461 for 2005, U.S. dollar/euro conversion rate of 1.22 and 1.21, and yen/U.S. dollar conversion rates of 109.7 and 109.8, respectively.

It is assumed that the *price of oil* will average $37.25 a barrel in 2004 and 2005.

Established *policies* of national authorities are assumed to be maintained. The more specific policy assumptions underlying the projections for selected advanced economies are described in Box A1.

With regard to *interest rates*, it is assumed that the London interbank offered rate (LIBOR) on six-month U.S. dollar deposits will average 1.6 percent in 2004 and 3.4 percent in 2005, that six-month euro deposits will average 2.2 percent in 2004 and 2.8 percent in 2005, and that six-month Japanese yen deposits will average 0.1 percent in 2004 and 0.3 percent in 2005.

With respect to *introduction of the euro*, on December 31, 1998, the Council of the European Union decided that, effective January 1, 1999, the irrevocably fixed conversion rates between the euro and currencies of the member states adopting the euro are as follows.

1 euro	=	13.7603	Austrian schillings
	=	40.3399	Belgian francs
	=	1.95583	Deutsche mark
	=	5.94573	Finnish markkaa
	=	6.55957	French francs
	=	340.750	Greek drachma[1]
	=	0.787564	Irish pound
	=	1,936.27	Italian lire
	=	40.3399	Luxembourg francs
	=	2.20371	Netherlands guilders
	=	200.482	Portuguese escudos
	=	166.386	Spanish pesetas

See Box 5.4 in the October 1998 *World Economic Outlook* for details on how the conversion rates were established.

What's New

- The European Union added 10 new member nations on May 1, 2004, enlarging the group

[1]The conversion rate for Greece was established prior to inclusion in the euro area on January 1, 2001.

Box A1. Economic Policy Assumptions Underlying the Projections for Selected Advanced Economies

The short-term ***fiscal policy assumptions*** used in the *World Economic Outlook* are based on officially announced budgets, adjusted for differences between the national authorities and the IMF staff regarding macroeconomic assumptions and projected fiscal outturns. The medium-term fiscal projections incorporate policy measures that are judged likely to be implemented. In cases where the IMF staff has insufficient information to assess the authorities' budget intentions and prospects for policy implementation, an unchanged structural primary balance is assumed, unless otherwise indicated. Specific assumptions used in some of the advanced economies follow (see also Tables 12–14 in the Statistical Appendix for data on fiscal and structural balances).[1]

United States. The fiscal projections are based on the Administration's mid-session review projections (July 30, 2004) adjusted to take into account: (1) differences between macroeconomic assumptions; (2) additional Alternative Minimum Tax (AMT) relief; and (3) higher defense spending in line with Congressional Budget Office projections and IMF staff assumptions. Most provisions of the 2001 and 2003 tax cuts are assumed to be made permanent.

Japan. The medium-term projections for social security revenue and expenditure assume implementation of the pension reform recently passed by the Diet. For the rest of the general government (excluding social security), expenditure and revenue are adjusted in line with the current government target of achieving primary balance by the early 2010s.

[1]The output gap is actual less potential output, as a percent of potential output. Structural balances are expressed as a percent of potential output. The structural budget balance is the budgetary position that would be observed if the level of actual output coincided with potential output. Changes in the structural budget balance consequently include effects of temporary fiscal measures, the impact of fluctuations in interest rates and debt-service costs, and other noncyclical fluctuations in the budget balance. The computations of structural budget balances are based on IMF staff estimates of potential GDP and revenue and expenditure elasticities (see the October 1993 *World Economic Outlook*, Annex I). Net debt is defined as gross debt less financial assets of the general government, which include assets held by the social security insurance system. Estimates of the output gap and of the structural balance are subject to significant margins of uncertainty.

Germany. Fiscal projections for 2004–09 are based on the IMF staff's macroeconomic assumptions and estimates of fiscal adjustment measures and structural reforms.

France. Projections for 2004 are based on the budget adjusted for the IMF staff's growth projections and budget execution to date. For 2005–07, projections are based on the IMF staff's macroeconomic assumptions and the intentions underlying the 2005–07 Stability Program Update, except for a higher growth of health care spending. For 2008–09, the IMF staff assumes unchanged tax policies and real expenditure growth at the average rate of 2005–07.

Italy. Fiscal projections for 2004 assume measures of about ½ percent of GDP committed to by the authorities in July. In 2005, the planned tax cuts are assumed to be fully matched by expenditure cuts. Beyond 2005, projections start with the assumption of a constant structural primary balance, and are then adjusted for the savings from the ongoing pension reform (impact starting from 2008).

United Kingdom. The fiscal projections are based on information provided in the 2004 Budget Report. Additionally, the projections incorporate the most recent statistical releases from the Office for National Statistics, including provisional budgetary outturns throughout 2004:Q1.

Canada. Projections are based on the 2004 budget, released on March 23, 2004. The federal government balance is the IMF staff's estimate of the planning surplus (budgetary balance less contingency and economic reserves).

Australia. Fiscal projections through the fiscal year 2007/08 are based on the 2004 Budget published in May 2004. Subsequently, the IMF staff assumes no change in policies.

Austria. Fiscal projections for 2004 are based on the authorities' most recent projections. Projections for 2005–07 are based on the Stability Program objectives, adjusted for IMF staff projections of yields of spending and tax measures in 2005–06. Projections for 2008 assume further improvements in fiscal balances based on expenditure measures, consistent with the authorities' plan to balance the budget in 2008.

Belgium. Fiscal projections for 2004 are consistent with the budget and developments through midyear. Projections for subsequent years are based on the government's tax reform plans, and historical expenditure trends, adjusted for IMF staff macroeconomic assumptions.

Denmark. Projections for 2004 are aligned with the authorities' latest projections and budget, adjusted for the IMF staff's macroeconomic projections. For 2005–09, projections are in line with the authorities' medium-term framework—adjusted for the IMF staff's macroeconomic projections—targeting an average budget surplus of 1.5–2.5 percent of GDP, supported by a ceiling on real public consumption growth.

Greece. Historical data and projections do not take into account revisions to the fiscal data announced in mid-September, which raised general government deficits and debt substantially. The projections assume (1) constant ratio of revenue to GDP; (2) EU transfers falling in the medium term; (3) continuation of the increase in social contributions until 2007; (4) continuation of recent trends for wage growth, social spending, and operational spending; (5) a gradual decline in investment spending from its peak level in 2003–04 owing to the 2004 Olympic games; and (6) a constant ratio to GDP for other spending.

Korea. For 2004, it is assumed that the fiscal outcome will be in line with the budget. In the medium term, fiscal policy is assumed consistent with achieving a balanced budget excluding social security funds.

Netherlands. Fiscal projections for 2004 and 2005 build on the latest government estimates and include the additional policy measures announced in the spring. Projections for subsequent years are based on the latest Stability Program, adjusted for the IMF staff's macroeconomic assumptions.

Portugal. Fiscal projections for 2004 build on the preliminary figures for the 2003 deficit and the authorities' 2004 targets (including the 2004 budget target for one-off measures), adjusted for the IMF staff's macroeconomic projections for 2004. Projections for 2005 and beyond assume a constant structural primary balance.

Spain. Fiscal projections through 2007 are based on the national authorities' updated stability program of January 2004, adjusted for the IMF staff's macroeconomic projections. Projections also reflect the combined effect of the recently announced decision to pay the historical debt with Andalusia (0.3 percent of GDP) this year and additional spending associated with this transfer; a small deficit is also envisaged for regional governments (0.2 percent of GDP). In subsequent years, the fiscal projections assume no significant changes in policies.

Sweden. The fiscal projections are based on information provided in the 2004 Spring Budget Bill. Additionally, the projections incorporate the most recent statistical releases from Statistics Sweden, including provisional budgetary outturns throughout May 2004.

Switzerland. Projections for 2004 are based on federal budget and IMF staff projections for lower levels of government. Projections for 2005–07 are based on official financial plans (which incorporate measures to restore balance in the federal accounts) adjusted for the effects of recent referenda and for the IMF staff's macroeconomic projections.

Monetary policy assumptions are based on the established policy framework in each country. In most cases, this implies a nonaccommodative stance over the business cycle: official interest rates will therefore increase when economic indicators suggest that prospective inflation will rise above its acceptable rate or range, and they will decrease when indicators suggest that prospective inflation will not exceed the acceptable rate or range, that prospective output growth is below its potential rate, and that the margin of slack in the economy is significant. On this basis, the London interbank offered rate (LIBOR) on six-month U.S. dollar deposits is assumed to average 1.6 percent in 2004 and 3.4 percent in 2005. The projected path for U.S. dollar short-term interest rates reflects the assumption implicit in prevailing forward rates that the U.S. Federal Reserve will continue to raise interest rates in 2004–05. The rate on six-month euro deposits is assumed to average 2.2 percent in 2004 and 2.8 percent in 2005. The interest rate on six-month Japanese yen deposits is assumed to average 0.1 percent in 2004 and 0.3 percent in 2005, with the current monetary policy framework being maintained. Changes in interest rate assumptions compared with the April 2004 *World Economic Outlook* are summarized in Table 1.1.

to a total of 25 countries. The new members are Cyprus, the Czech Republic, Estonia, Hungary, Latvia, Lithuania, Malta, Poland, Slovak Republic, and Slovenia.

Data and Conventions

Data and projections for 175 countries form the statistical basis for the *World Economic Outlook* (the World Economic Outlook database). The data are maintained jointly by the IMF's Research Department and area departments, with the latter regularly updating country projections based on consistent global assumptions.

Although national statistical agencies are the ultimate providers of historical data and definitions, international organizations are also involved in statistical issues, with the objective of harmonizing methodologies for the national compilation of statistics, including the analytical frameworks, concepts, definitions, classifications, and valuation procedures used in the production of economic statistics. The World Economic Outlook database reflects information from both national source agencies and international organizations.

The completion in 1993 of the comprehensive revision of the standardized *System of National Accounts 1993 (SNA)* and the IMF's *Balance of Payments Manual (BPM)* represented important improvements in the standards of economic statistics and analysis.[2] The IMF was actively involved in both projects, particularly the new *Balance of Payments Manual*, which reflects the IMF's special interest in countries' external positions. Key changes introduced with the new *Manual* were summarized in Box 13 of the May 1994 *World Economic Outlook*. The process of adapting country balance of payments data to the definitions of the new *BPM* began with the May 1995 *World Economic Outlook*. However, full concordance with the *BPM* is ultimately dependent on the provision by national statistical compilers of revised country data, and hence the *World Economic Outlook* estimates are still only partially adapted to the *BPM*.

The members of the European Union have adopted a harmonized system for the compilation of the national accounts, referred to as ESA 1995. All national accounts data from 1995 onward are presented on the basis of the new system. Revision by national authorities of data prior to 1995 to conform to the new system has progressed, but has in some cases not been completed. In such cases, historical *World Economic Outlook* data have been carefully adjusted to avoid breaks in the series. Users of EU national accounts data prior to 1995 should nevertheless exercise caution until such time as the revision of historical data by national statistical agencies has been fully completed. See Box 1.2, "Revisions in National Accounts Methodologies," in the May 2000 *World Economic Outlook*.

Composite data for country groups in the *World Economic Outlook* are either sums or weighted averages of data for individual countries. Unless otherwise indicated, multiyear averages of growth rates are expressed as compound annual rates of change. Arithmetically weighted averages are used for all data except inflation and money growth for the other emerging market and developing country group, for which geometric averages are used. The following conventions apply.

- Country group composites for exchange rates, interest rates, and the growth rates of monetary aggregates are weighted by GDP converted to U.S. dollars at market exchange rates (averaged over the preceding three years) as a share of group GDP.
- Composites for other data relating to the domestic economy, whether growth rates or ratios, are weighted by GDP valued at purchas-

[2]Commission of the European Communities, International Monetary Fund, Organization for Economic Cooperation and Development, United Nations, and World Bank, *System of National Accounts 1993* (Brussels/Luxembourg, New York, Paris, and Washington, 1993); and International Monetary Fund, *Balance of Payments Manual, Fifth Edition* (Washington: IMF, 1993).

Table A. Classification by World Economic Outlook Groups and Their Shares in Aggregate GDP, Exports of Goods and Services, and Population, 2003[1]
(Percent of total for group or world)

	Number of Countries	GDP		Exports of Goods and Services		Population	
		Advanced economies	World	Advanced economies	World	Advanced economies	World
Advanced economies	**29**	**100.0**	**55.5**	**100.0**	**73.4**	**100.0**	**15.4**
United States		38.0	21.1	15.1	11.1	30.4	4.7
Euro area	12	28.6	15.9	43.6	32.0	32.2	5.0
Germany		8.1	4.5	12.9	9.5	8.6	1.3
France		5.8	3.2	6.8	5.0	6.4	1.0
Italy		5.5	3.0	5.4	4.0	6.0	0.9
Spain		3.2	1.8	3.5	2.6	4.3	0.7
Japan		12.6	7.0	7.8	5.7	13.3	2.1
United Kingdom		5.7	3.2	6.7	4.9	6.2	1.0
Canada		3.5	1.9	4.9	3.6	3.3	0.5
Other advanced economies	13	11.7	6.5	21.9	16.1	14.6	2.2
Memorandum							
Major advanced economies	7	79.1	43.9	59.7	43.8	74.3	11.4
Newly industrialized Asian economies	4	5.9	3.3	12.7	9.3	8.6	1.3
		Other emerging market and developing countries	World	Other emerging market and developing countries	World	Other emerging market and developing countries	World
Other emerging market and developing countries	**146**	**100.0**	**44.5**	**100.0**	**26.6**	**100.0**	**84.6**
Regional groups							
Africa	48	7.3	3.2	7.9	2.1	14.6	12.4
Sub-Sahara	45	5.5	2.5	5.8	1.5	13.3	11.2
Excluding Nigeria and South Africa	43	2.9	1.3	2.8	0.7	9.7	8.2
Central and eastern Europe	15	7.5	3.3	15.0	4.0	3.5	3.0
Commonwealth of Independent States	13	8.2	3.7	9.1	2.4	5.3	4.5
Russia		5.7	2.6	6.2	1.7	2.7	2.3
Developing Asia	23	53.5	23.8	38.8	10.3	61.9	52.4
China		28.3	12.6	19.8	5.3	24.6	20.9
India		12.9	5.7	3.4	0.9	20.3	17.2
Excluding China and India	21	12.4	5.5	15.6	4.2	17.0	14.3
Middle East	14	6.3	2.8	13.7	3.6	4.7	4.0
Western Hemisphere	33	17.2	7.6	15.6	4.1	9.9	8.4
Brazil		6.2	2.8	3.4	0.9	3.3	2.8
Mexico		4.1	1.8	4.8	1.3	1.9	1.6
Analytical groups							
By source of export earnings							
Fuel	19	7.2	3.2	16.5	4.4	7.3	6.1
Nonfuel	127	92.8	41.3	83.5	22.2	92.7	78.5
of which, primary products	29	2.6	1.2	2.6	0.7	7.1	6.0
By external financing source							
Net debtor countries	129	59.6	26.5	59.5	15.8	69.2	58.5
of which, official financing	54	10.4	4.6	8.5	2.3	23.7	20.0
Net debtor countries by debt-servicing experience							
Countries with arrears and/or rescheduling during 1997-2001	55	18.4	8.2	15.7	4.2	27.1	22.9
Other groups							
Heavily indebted poor countries	36	2.8	1.2	1.9	0.5	9.9	8.4
Middle East and north Africa	20	8.4	3.7	15.9	4.2	6.8	5.7

[1]The GDP shares are based on the purchasing-power-parity (PPP) valuation of country GDPs. The number of countries comprising each group reflects those for which data are included in the group aggregates.

Table B. Advanced Economies by Subgroup

Major Currency Areas	Other Subgroups						
	Euro area		Newly industrialized Asian economies	Major advanced economies	Other advanced economies	
United States Euro area Japan	Austria Belgium Finland France Germany Greece	Ireland Italy Luxembourg Netherlands Portugal Spain	Hong Kong SAR[1] Korea Singapore Taiwan Province of China	Canada France Germany Italy Japan United Kingdom United States	Australia Cyprus Denmark Hong Kong SAR[1] Iceland Israel	Korea New Zealand Norway Singapore Sweden Switzerland Taiwan Province of China

[1]On July 1, 1997, Hong Kong was returned to the People's Republic of China and became a Special Administrative Region of China.

ing power parities (PPPs) as a share of total world or group GDP.[3]

- Composites for data relating to the domestic economy for the euro area (12 member countries throughout the entire period unless otherwise noted) are aggregates of national source data using weights based on 1995 ECU exchange rates.
- Composite unemployment rates and employment growth are weighted by labor force as a share of group labor force.
- Composites relating to the external economy are sums of individual country data after conversion to U.S. dollars at the average market exchange rates in the years indicated for balance of payments data and at end-of-year market exchange rates for debt denominated in currencies other than U.S. dollars. Composites of changes in foreign trade volumes and prices, however, are arithmetic averages of percentage changes for individual countries weighted by the U.S. dollar value of exports or imports as a share of total world or group exports or imports (in the preceding year).

For central and eastern European countries, external transactions in nonconvertible currencies (through 1990) are converted to U.S. dollars at the implicit U.S. dollar/ruble conversion rates obtained from each country's national currency exchange rate for the U.S. dollar and for the ruble.

Classification of Countries

Summary of the Country Classification

The country classification in the *World Economic Outlook* divides the world into two major groups: advanced economies and other emerging market and developing countries.[4] Rather than being based on strict criteria, economic or otherwise, this classification has evolved over time with the objective of facilitating analysis by providing a reasonably meaningful organization of data. A few countries are presently not included in these groups, either because they are not IMF members and their economies are not monitored by the IMF, or because databases have not yet been fully developed. Because of data limitations, group composites do not reflect the following countries: Afghanistan, Bosnia and Herzegovina, Brunei Darussalam, Eritrea, Liberia, Serbia and Montenegro, Somalia, and Timor-Leste. Cuba and the Democratic People's Republic of Korea

[3]See Box A1 of the May 2000 *World Economic Outlook* for a summary of the revised PPP-based weights and Annex IV of the May 1993 *World Economic Outlook.* See also Anne-Marie Gulde and Marianne Schulze-Ghattas, "Purchasing Power Parity Based Weights for the *World Economic Outlook,*" in *Staff Studies for the World Economic Outlook* (International Monetary Fund, December 1993), pp. 106–23.

[4]As used here, the term "country" does not in all cases refer to a territorial entity that is a state as understood by international law and practice. It also covers some territorial entities that are not states, but for which statistical data are maintained on a separate and independent basis.

Table C. European Union

Austria	France	Latvia	Portugal
Belgium	Germany	Lithuania	Slovak Republic
Cyprus	Greece	Luxembourg	Slovenia
Czech Republic	Hungary	Malta	Spain
Denmark	Ireland	Netherlands	Sweden
Estonia	Italy	Poland	United Kingdom
Finland			

are examples of countries that are not IMF members, whereas San Marino, among the advanced economies, is an example of an economy for which a database has not been completed.

Each of the two main country groups is further divided into a number of subgroups. Among the advanced economies, the seven largest in terms of GDP, collectively referred to as the major advanced countries, are distinguished as a subgroup, and so are the 12 members of the euro area, and the four newly industrialized Asian economies. The other emerging market and developing countries are classified by region, as well as into a number of analytical and other groups. Table A provides an overview of these standard groups in the *World Economic Outlook*, showing the number of countries in each group and the average 2003 shares of groups in aggregate PPP-valued GDP, total exports of goods and services, and population.

General Features and Composition of Groups in the *World Economic Outlook* Classification

Advanced Economies

The 29 advanced economies are listed in Table B. The seven largest in terms of GDP—the United States, Japan, Germany, France, Italy, the United Kingdom, and Canada—constitute the subgroup of *major advanced economies,* often referred to as the Group of Seven (G-7) countries. The euro area (12 countries) and the *newly industrialized Asian economies* are also distinguished as subgroups. Composite data shown in the tables for the euro area cover the current members for all years, even though the membership has increased over time.

Table D. Other Emerging Market and Developing Countries by Region and Main Source of Export Earnings

	Fuel	Nonfuel, of Which Primary Products
Africa		
Sub-Sahara	Angola Congo, Rep. of Equatorial Guinea Gabon Nigeria	Botswana Burkina Faso Burundi Chad Congo, Dem. Rep. of Côte d'Ivoire Ethiopia Ghana Guinea Guinea-Bissau Malawi Mali Mauritania Namibia Niger Rwanda Sierra Leone Togo Uganda Zambia Zimbabwe
North Africa	Algeria	
Commonwealth of Independent States	Azerbaijan Turkemenistan	Tajikistan Uzbekistan
Developing Asia		Papua New Guinea Solomon Islands
Middle East	Bahrain Iran, I.R. of Iraq Kuwait Libya Oman Qatar Saudi Arabia United Arab Emirates Yemen	
Western Hemisphere	Venezuela	Bolivia Chile Guyana

In 1991 and subsequent years, data for *Germany* refer to west Germany *and* the eastern Länder (i.e., the former German Democratic Republic). Before 1991, economic data are not available on a unified basis or in a consistent manner. Hence, in tables featuring data expressed as annual percent change, these apply

Table E. Other Emerging Market and Developing Countries by Region and Net External Position

Countries	Net Creditor	Net Debtor[1]
Africa		
Sub-Sahara		
Angola		•
Benin		★
Botswana	•	
Burkina Faso		★
Burundi		★
Cameroon		★
Cape Verde		•
Central African Republic		★
Chad		★
Comoros		★
Congo, Dem. Rep. of		★
Congo, Rep. of		★
Côte d'Ivoire		•
Djibouti		★
Equatorial Guinea		•
Eritrea		★
Ethiopia		★
Gabon		★
Gambia, The		•
Ghana		★
Guinea		★
Guinea-Bissau		★
Kenya		•
Lesotho		•
Madagascar		★
Malawi		★
Mali		★
Mauritania		★
Mauritius		•
Mozambique, Rep. of		★
Namibia	•	
Niger		★
Nigeria		★
Rwanda		★
São Tomé and Príncipe		★
Senegal		•
Seychelles		•
Sierra Leone		•
South Africa		•
Sudan		•
Swaziland		•
Tanzania		•
Togo		★
Uganda		•
Zambia		•
Zimbabwe		★
North Africa		
Algeria	•	
Morocco		•
Tunisia		•
Central and eastern Europe		
Albania		★
Bosnia and Herzegovina		★
Bulgaria		•
Croatia		•
Czech Republic		•
Estonia		•
Hungary		•
Latvia		•
Lithuania		•
Macedonia, FYR	•	
Malta		•
Poland		•
Romania		•
Serbia and Montenegro		★
Slovak Republic		•
Slovenia	•	
Turkey	•	
Commonwealth of Independent States[2]		
Armenia		•
Azerbaijan		•
Belarus		•
Georgia		★
Kazakhstan		•
Kyrgyz Republic		★
Moldova		•
Mongolia		★
Russia	•	
Tajikistan		★
Turkmenistan	•	
Ukraine		•
Uzbekistan		•
Developing Asia		
Bangladesh		★
Bhutan		★
Brunei	•	
Cambodia		★
China		•
Fiji		★
India		★
Indonesia		★
Kiribati	•	
Lao PDR		★
Malaysia		•
Maldives		•
Myanmar		★
Nepal		★
Pakistan		★
Papua New Guinea		★
Philippines		•
Samoa		•
Solomon Islands		★
Sri Lanka		•
Thailand		•
Tonga		★
Vanuatu		★
Vietnam		★

Table E *(concluded)*

Countries	Net Creditor	Net Debtor[1]	Countries	Net Creditor	Net Debtor[1]
Middle East			Costa Rica		•
Bahrain		•	Dominica		•
Egypt		•	Dominican Republic		•
Iran, I.R. of	•		Ecuador		★
Iraq		•	El Salvador		★
Jordan		★	Grenada		★
Kuwait	•		Guatemala		•
Lebanon		•	Guyana		•
Libya	•		Haiti		★
Oman		•	Honduras		★
Qatar	•		Jamaica		•
Saudi Arabia	•		Mexico		•
Syrian Arab Republic		•	Netherlands Antilles		•
United Arab Emirates	•		Nicaragua		•
Yemen		★	Panama		•
Western Hemisphere			Paraguay		•
Antigua and Barbuda		•	Peru		•
Argentina		•	St. Kitts and Nevis		•
Bahamas, The		•	St. Lucia		★
Barbados		•	St. Vincent and the Grenadines		•
Belize		•	Suriname		•
Bolivia		•	Trinidad and Tobago		•
Brazil		•	Uruguay		•
Chile		•	Venezuela		•
Colombia		•			

[1]Star instead of dot indicates that the net debtor's main external finance source is official financing.

[2]Mongolia, which is not a member of the Commonwealth of Independent States, is included in this group for reasons of geography and similatiries in economic structure.

to west Germany in years up to and including 1991, but to unified Germany from 1992 onward. In general, data on national accounts and domestic economic and financial activity through 1990 cover west Germany only, whereas data for the central government and balance of payments apply to west Germany through June 1990 and to unified Germany thereafter.

Other Emerging Market and Developing Countries

The group of other emerging market and developing countries (146 countries) includes all countries that are not classified as advanced economies.

The *regional breakdowns* of other emerging market and developing countries—*Africa, central and eastern Europe, Commonwealth of Independent States, developing Asia, Middle East, and Western Hemisphere*—largely conform to the regional breakdowns in the IMF's *International Financial Statistics.* In both classifications, Egypt and the Libyan Arab Jamahiriya are included in the *Middle East* region rather than in Africa. Three additional regional groupings—two of them constituting part of Africa and one a subgroup of Asia—are included in the *World Economic Outlook* because of their analytical significance. These are *sub-Sahara, sub-Sahara excluding Nigeria and South Africa,* and *Asia excluding China and India.*

Other emerging market and developing countries are also classified according to *analytical criteria* and into *other groups.* The analytical criteria reflect countries' composition of export earnings and other income from abroad, a distinction between net creditor and net debtor countries, and, for the net debtor countries, financial criteria based on external financing source and experience with external debt servicing. Included as "other groups" are the heavily indebted poor countries (HIPCs), and Middle East and north Africa (MENA). The

Table F. Other Developing Country Groups

Countries	Heavily Indebted Poor Countries	Middle East and North Africa
Africa		
Sub-Sahara		
Benin	•	
Burkina Faso	•	
Burundi	•	
Cameroon	•	
Central African Republic	•	
Chad	•	
Comoros		
Congo, Dem. Rep. of	•	
Congo, Rep. of	•	
Côte d'Ivoire	•	
Ethiopia	•	
Gambia, The	•	
Ghana	•	
Guinea	•	
Guinea-Bissau	•	
Madagascar	•	
Malawi	•	
Mali	•	
Mauritania	•	•
Mozambique, Rep. of	•	
Niger	•	
Rwanda	•	
São Tomé and Príncipe	•	
Senegal	•	
Sierra Leone	•	
Sudan	•	•
Tanzania	•	
Togo	•	
Uganda	•	
Zambia	•	
North Africa		
Algeria		•
Morocco		•
Tunisia		•
Developing Asia		
Lao PDR	•	
Myanmar	•	
Middle East		
Bahrain		•
Egypt		•
Iran, I.R. of		•
Iraq		•
Jordan		•
Kuwait		•
Lebanon		•
Libya		•
Oman		•
Qatar		•
Saudi Arabia		•
Syrian Arab Republic		•
United Arab Emirates		•
Yemen		•
Western Hemisphere		
Bolivia	•	
Guyana	•	
Honduras	•	
Nicaragua	•	

detailed composition of other emerging market and developing countries in the regional, analytical, and other groups is shown in Tables D through F.

The first analytical criterion, by *source of export earnings*, distinguishes between categories: *fuel* (Standard International Trade Classification—SITC 3) and nonfuel and then focuses on *nonfuel primary products* (SITC 0, 1, 2, 4, and 68).

The financial criteria focus on *net creditor* and *net debtor countries*. Net debtor countries are further differentiated on the basis of two additional financial criteria: by *official external financing* and by *experience with debt servicing*.[5]

The *other groups* of developing countries constitute the HIPCs and MENA countries. The first group comprises the countries considered by the IMF and the World Bank for their debt initiative, known as the HIPC Initiative.[6] Middle East and north Africa, also referred to as the MENA countries, is a *World Economic Outlook* group, whose composition straddles the Africa and Middle East regions. It is defined as the Arab League countries plus the Islamic Republic of Iran.

[5]During 1997–2001, 54 countries incurred external payments arrears or entered into official or commercial bank debt-rescheduling agreements. This group of countries is referred to as *countries with arrears and/or rescheduling during 1997–2001*.

[6]See David Andrews, Anthony R. Boote, Syed S. Rizavi, and Sukwinder Singh, *Debt Relief for Low-Income Countries: The Enhanced HIPC Initiative*, IMF Pamphlet Series, No. 51 (Washington: International Monetary Fund, November 1999)

List of Tables

Output

Inflation

Financial Policies

Foreign Trade

Current Account Transactions

Balance of Payments and External Financing

External Debt and Debt Service

Flow of Funds

Medium-Term Baseline Scenario

Table 1. Summary of World Output[1]

(Annual percent change)

	Ten-Year Averages											
	1986–95	1996–2005	1996	1997	1998	1999	2000	2001	2002	2003	2004	2005
World	**3.3**	**3.8**	**4.1**	**4.2**	**2.8**	**3.7**	**4.7**	**2.4**	**3.0**	**3.9**	**5.0**	**4.3**
Advanced economies	**3.0**	**2.8**	**3.0**	**3.4**	**2.7**	**3.5**	**3.9**	**1.2**	**1.6**	**2.1**	**3.6**	**2.9**
United States	2.9	3.4	3.7	4.5	4.2	4.4	3.7	0.8	1.9	3.0	4.3	3.5
Euro area	. . .	2.0	1.4	2.3	2.9	2.8	3.5	1.6	0.8	0.5	2.2	2.2
Japan[2]	3.1	1.6	3.5	1.8	–1.2	0.2	2.8	0.4	–0.3	2.5	4.4	2.3
Other advanced economies[3]	3.7	3.4	3.7	4.1	2.0	4.6	5.2	1.7	3.0	2.3	3.8	3.1
Other emerging market and developing countries	**3.7**	**5.1**	**5.6**	**5.3**	**3.0**	**4.0**	**5.9**	**4.0**	**4.8**	**6.1**	**6.6**	**5.9**
Regional groups												
Africa	1.9	3.9	5.7	3.2	3.1	2.7	2.9	4.0	3.5	4.3	4.5	5.4
Central and eastern Europe	0.8	3.6	4.8	4.2	2.8	0.4	4.9	0.2	4.4	4.5	5.5	4.8
Commonwealth of Independent States[4]	. . .	4.1	–3.9	1.1	–3.5	5.1	9.1	6.4	5.4	7.8	8.0	6.6
Developing Asia	7.7	6.6	8.2	6.5	4.1	6.2	6.7	5.5	6.6	7.7	7.6	6.9
Middle East	2.7	4.5	4.6	5.3	3.8	2.4	5.5	3.6	4.3	6.0	5.1	4.8
Western Hemisphere	2.8	2.6	3.7	5.2	2.3	0.4	3.9	0.5	–0.1	1.8	4.6	3.6
Memorandum												
European Union	2.3	2.4	1.9	2.8	3.1	2.9	3.7	1.8	1.2	1.1	2.6	2.5
Analytical groups												
By source of export earnings												
Fuel	2.0	4.5	3.9	4.8	3.4	1.6	5.5	4.0	3.8	6.5	6.0	5.8
Nonfuel	3.8	5.1	5.7	5.3	3.0	4.2	5.9	4.0	4.9	6.1	6.6	5.9
of which, primary products	3.0	3.5	5.9	4.0	2.7	1.7	2.0	3.4	2.6	2.5	5.2	4.8
By external financing source												
Net debtor countries	3.1	4.0	5.3	4.5	1.8	2.9	4.7	2.5	3.4	4.6	5.4	5.2
of which, official financing	4.3	3.8	6.2	4.2	–1.9	2.8	4.4	4.0	3.9	4.7	5.3	5.3
Net debtor countries by debt-servicing experience												
Countries with arrears and/or rescheduling during 1997–2001	2.3	3.5	4.2	3.8	–0.6	1.9	4.5	3.7	3.5	3.3	5.4	5.1
Memorandum												
Median growth rate												
Advanced economies	3.0	3.0	3.3	3.8	3.6	3.8	4.2	1.6	1.8	2.0	3.0	2.7
Other emerging market and developing countries	3.1	4.0	4.4	4.6	3.7	3.4	4.0	3.5	3.5	4.3	4.5	4.5
Output per capita												
Advanced economies	2.3	2.2	2.3	2.8	2.0	2.9	3.3	0.6	1.0	1.6	3.1	2.4
Other emerging market and developing countries	1.9	3.7	4.0	3.8	1.5	2.5	4.4	2.6	3.4	4.8	5.3	4.6
World growth based on market exchange rates	**2.6**	**2.9**	**3.3**	**3.5**	**2.2**	**3.1**	**4.0**	**1.4**	**1.7**	**2.7**	**4.1**	**3.4**
Value of world output in billions of U.S. dollars												
At market exchange rates	22,262	33,325	29,870	29,736	29,508	30,613	31,436	31,175	32,357	36,238	40,108	42,213
At purchasing power parities	26,735	45,292	35,719	37,918	39,404	41,394	44,236	46,292	48,176	50,431	53,070	56,282

[1]Real GDP.
[2]Annual data are calculated from seasonally adjusted quarterly data.
[3]In this table, "other advanced economies" means advanced economies excluding the United States, euro area countries, and Japan.
[4]Mongolia, which is not a member of the Commonwealth of Independent States, is included in this group for reasons of geography and similarities in economic structure.

Table 2. Advanced Economies: Real GDP and Total Domestic Demand
(Annual percent change)

	Ten-Year Averages												Fourth Quarter[1]		
	1986–95	1996–2005	1996	1997	1998	1999	2000	2001	2002	2003	2004	2005	2003	2004	2005
Real GDP															
Advanced economies	**3.0**	**2.8**	**3.0**	**3.4**	**2.7**	**3.5**	**3.9**	**1.2**	**1.6**	**2.1**	**3.6**	**2.9**	. . .	. . .	. . .
United States	2.9	3.4	3.7	4.5	4.2	4.4	3.7	0.8	1.9	3.0	4.3	3.5	4.4	3.7	3.4
Euro area	. . .	2.0	1.4	2.3	2.9	2.8	3.5	1.6	0.8	0.5	2.2	2.2	0.7	2.2	2.4
Germany	2.7	1.4	0.8	1.4	2.0	2.0	2.9	0.8	0.1	–0.1	2.0	1.8	—	1.8	2.3
France	2.1	2.3	1.0	1.9	3.6	3.2	4.2	2.1	1.1	0.5	2.6	2.3	1.0	3.0	2.1
Italy	2.1	1.5	1.1	2.0	1.8	1.7	3.0	1.8	0.4	0.3	1.4	1.9	0.1	1.5	2.5
Spain	3.0	3.2	2.4	4.0	4.3	4.2	4.4	2.8	2.2	2.5	2.6	2.9	2.8	2.6	3.1
Netherlands	2.7	2.3	3.0	3.8	4.3	4.0	3.5	1.4	0.6	–0.9	1.1	1.8	–0.5	1.2	2.2
Belgium	2.3	2.1	0.9	3.7	2.1	3.2	3.7	0.7	0.7	1.1	2.5	2.3	1.3	3.0	1.7
Austria	2.5	2.0	2.0	1.6	3.9	2.7	3.4	0.8	1.4	0.7	1.6	2.4	0.8	2.5	2.2
Finland	1.1	3.4	3.9	6.3	5.0	3.4	5.1	1.1	2.3	2.0	2.8	2.6	1.6	3.6	1.8
Greece	1.2	3.6	2.4	3.6	3.4	3.4	4.4	4.0	3.9	4.3	3.9	3.0	4.3	3.9	2.8
Portugal	4.0	2.4	3.5	4.0	4.6	3.8	3.4	1.6	0.4	–1.2	1.4	2.2	–0.2	1.8	2.9
Ireland[2]	4.4	7.4	8.1	10.8	8.9	11.1	9.9	6.0	6.1	3.7	4.7	5.0	5.1	4.1	4.3
Luxembourg	6.2	4.6	3.3	8.3	6.9	7.8	9.0	1.3	1.7	2.1	2.8	3.4	. . .	. . .	. . .
Japan[3]	3.1	1.6	3.5	1.8	–1.2	0.2	2.8	0.4	–0.3	2.5	4.4	2.3	3.5	3.5	1.9
United Kingdom	2.5	2.8	2.8	3.3	3.1	2.9	3.9	2.3	1.8	2.2	3.4	2.5	2.9	3.1	2.2
Canada	2.3	3.4	1.6	4.2	4.1	5.5	5.2	1.8	3.4	2.0	2.9	3.1	1.7	3.4	3.0
Korea	8.5	4.4	7.0	4.7	–6.9	9.5	8.5	3.8	7.0	3.1	4.6	4.0	3.9	2.9	4.7
Australia	3.1	3.7	4.3	3.9	5.2	4.3	3.2	2.5	3.8	3.0	3.6	3.4	3.9	3.7	2.2
Taiwan Province of China	8.1	4.3	6.1	6.7	4.6	5.4	5.9	–2.2	3.6	3.3	5.6	4.1	5.6	3.9	3.7
Sweden	1.6	2.6	1.3	2.4	3.6	4.6	4.3	0.9	2.1	1.6	3.0	2.5	2.3	2.2	2.8
Switzerland	1.4	1.5	0.5	1.9	2.8	1.3	3.7	1.0	0.2	–0.5	1.8	2.2	–0.1	1.8	2.2
Hong Kong SAR	6.6	3.4	4.3	5.1	–5.0	3.4	10.2	0.5	1.9	3.2	7.5	4.0	4.7	4.8	4.3
Denmark	1.6	2.1	2.5	3.0	2.5	2.6	2.8	1.6	1.0	0.5	2.1	2.5	1.5	2.1	2.7
Norway	2.8	2.8	5.3	5.2	2.6	2.1	2.8	2.7	1.4	0.4	2.7	2.7	0.5	2.2	3.3
Israel	5.4	2.9	4.6	3.5	3.7	2.5	8.0	–0.9	–0.7	1.3	3.6	3.5	1.7	6.7	1.1
Singapore	8.8	4.6	8.1	8.6	–0.9	6.9	9.7	–1.9	2.2	1.1	8.8	4.4	4.9	6.4	5.0
New Zealand	2.5	3.0	4.0	2.0	–0.1	4.0	3.8	2.6	4.3	3.4	4.2	2.0	3.1	3.3	2.5
Cyprus	5.7	3.3	1.9	2.3	4.8	4.7	5.0	4.0	2.0	2.0	3.0	3.5	. . .	. . .	. . .
Iceland	1.7	4.1	5.2	4.7	5.6	4.2	5.6	2.7	–0.5	4.0	4.4	5.3	. . .	. . .	. . .
Memorandum															
Major advanced economies	2.7	2.6	2.8	3.2	2.7	3.1	3.5	1.0	1.2	2.2	3.7	2.9	3.0	3.2	2.8
Newly industrialized Asian economies	8.1	4.3	6.4	5.6	–2.2	7.2	7.9	1.1	5.0	3.0	5.5	4.0	5.1	4.1	4.8
Real total domestic demand															
Advanced economies	**3.0**	**2.8**	**3.0**	**3.3**	**3.1**	**4.0**	**3.8**	**1.1**	**1.6**	**2.3**	**3.5**	**2.7**	. . .	. . .	. . .
United States	2.7	3.8	3.8	4.8	5.3	5.3	4.4	0.9	2.5	3.3	4.6	3.3	4.3	4.0	3.1
Euro area	. . .	1.9	1.0	1.8	3.6	3.5	2.9	1.0	0.4	1.2	1.8	2.1	1.4	1.4	2.4
Germany	2.8	0.7	0.3	0.6	2.4	2.8	1.9	–0.8	–1.9	0.5	0.2	1.4	0.8	–0.3	2.2
France	2.1	2.5	0.7	0.7	4.2	3.7	4.5	2.0	1.5	1.4	3.6	2.6	2.0	3.9	2.2
Italy	1.8	1.9	0.9	2.7	3.1	3.2	2.3	1.4	1.3	1.2	1.4	1.8	0.1	1.4	2.5
Spain	3.7	3.7	1.9	3.5	5.7	5.6	4.6	2.9	2.8	3.2	3.3	3.1	3.5	2.7	3.5
Japan[3]	3.4	1.3	4.0	0.8	–1.5	0.3	2.3	1.2	–1.0	1.8	3.5	2.0	2.6	2.9	1.5
United Kingdom	2.6	3.3	3.1	3.5	4.8	3.9	3.8	2.9	2.9	2.5	3.5	2.5	2.7	2.5	2.6
Canada	2.0	3.3	0.9	5.7	2.4	4.1	4.9	1.3	3.4	4.4	2.7	3.3	3.7	2.7	3.1
Other advanced economies	5.3	3.0	4.8	3.9	–1.1	5.2	5.1	0.4	3.3	1.1	3.8	3.2	. . .	. . .	. . .
Memorandum															
Major advanced economies	2.7	2.8	2.8	3.1	3.4	3.8	3.6	1.1	1.4	2.5	3.5	2.7	3.1	3.1	2.6
Newly industrialized Asian economies	8.8	2.9	6.9	4.6	–7.5	7.3	7.5	–0.3	3.7	–0.3	4.6	3.7	1.8	3.8	4.5

[1]From fourth quarter of preceding year.
[2]Fourth-quarter data are calculated from seasonally adjusted data.
[3]Annual data are calculated from seasonally adjusted quarterly data.

Table 3. Advanced Economies: Components of Real GDP

(Annual percent change)

	Ten-Year Averages											
	1986–95	1996–2005	1996	1997	1998	1999	2000	2001	2002	2003	2004	2005
Private consumer expenditure												
Advanced economies	**3.1**	**2.8**	**2.9**	**2.9**	**3.1**	**4.0**	**3.7**	**2.3**	**2.3**	**2.1**	**2.7**	**2.4**
United States	2.9	3.7	3.4	3.8	5.0	5.1	4.7	2.5	3.1	3.3	3.4	2.7
Euro area	. . .	1.9	1.6	1.6	3.0	3.5	2.7	1.9	0.6	1.0	1.5	2.1
Germany	2.9	1.1	1.0	0.6	1.8	3.7	2.0	1.7	–0.7	—	0.1	1.2
France	1.8	2.3	1.3	0.2	3.6	3.5	2.9	2.8	1.8	1.7	2.5	2.5
Italy	2.2	1.9	1.2	3.2	3.2	2.6	2.8	0.8	0.5	1.3	1.3	2.1
Spain	2.9	3.3	2.2	3.2	4.4	4.7	4.1	2.8	2.9	2.9	3.2	2.9
Japan[1]	3.3	1.3	2.4	1.0	—	0.2	0.8	1.8	0.9	0.8	3.1	1.7
United Kingdom	3.0	3.4	3.6	3.6	3.9	4.4	4.6	2.9	3.3	2.3	2.7	2.3
Canada	2.3	3.3	2.6	4.6	2.8	3.8	4.0	2.7	3.4	3.1	3.2	2.6
Other advanced economies	5.1	3.2	4.7	4.1	–0.6	5.8	5.4	2.5	3.6	1.3	2.9	3.0
Memorandum												
Major advanced economies	2.9	2.8	2.6	2.7	3.4	3.8	3.5	2.3	2.1	2.2	2.8	2.3
Newly industrialized Asian economies	8.3	3.4	6.3	5.1	–5.0	8.0	7.4	3.2	4.6	–0.2	1.9	3.7
Public consumption												
Advanced economies	**2.2**	**2.3**	**1.6**	**1.4**	**1.8**	**2.7**	**2.4**	**2.9**	**3.4**	**2.3**	**2.0**	**2.8**
United States	1.5	2.5	0.4	1.8	1.6	3.1	1.7	3.1	4.0	2.9	2.0	4.2
Euro area	. . .	1.9	1.7	1.3	1.4	1.8	2.1	2.5	3.1	1.7	1.5	1.5
Germany	1.6	1.0	1.8	0.3	1.9	0.8	1.1	1.0	1.9	0.1	0.2	0.7
France	2.3	2.4	2.2	2.1	–0.1	1.5	3.0	2.9	4.6	2.5	3.0	1.9
Italy	1.3	1.6	1.1	0.3	0.3	1.4	1.7	3.8	1.9	2.2	1.2	1.8
Spain	4.7	3.6	1.3	2.9	3.7	4.2	5.6	3.5	4.1	3.9	4.0	3.5
Japan[1]	3.4	2.4	2.9	1.0	2.0	4.6	4.9	3.0	2.4	1.0	1.6	0.9
United Kingdom	1.0	2.4	1.3	–0.4	1.2	3.5	2.3	2.6	3.8	3.5	4.0	2.8
Canada	1.6	2.2	–1.2	–1.0	3.2	2.1	3.1	3.7	2.8	3.8	2.8	2.7
Other advanced economies	3.9	2.7	5.3	2.8	2.9	1.2	2.0	2.8	3.2	2.0	2.1	2.6
Memorandum												
Major advanced economies	1.9	2.2	1.2	1.1	1.5	2.9	2.4	2.9	3.3	2.3	1.9	2.9
Newly industrialized Asian economies	5.6	3.1	7.8	4.0	3.1	–0.1	2.4	3.0	3.4	2.4	2.9	2.0
Gross fixed capital formation												
Advanced economies	**3.3**	**3.5**	**5.6**	**5.4**	**5.2**	**5.5**	**5.3**	**–0.9**	**–2.0**	**2.5**	**5.7**	**3.5**
United States	2.8	5.0	8.1	8.0	9.1	8.2	6.1	–1.7	–3.1	4.5	8.7	3.3
Euro area	. . .	2.1	1.3	2.5	5.2	6.0	4.9	–0.3	–2.7	–0.6	2.1	3.4
Germany	3.3	–0.2	–0.8	0.6	3.0	4.1	2.7	–4.2	–6.4	–2.2	–0.9	2.6
France	2.3	3.3	–0.1	–0.2	7.2	8.3	8.4	2.1	–1.8	0.1	4.4	5.4
Italy	1.5	2.8	3.6	2.1	4.0	5.0	6.9	1.9	1.2	–2.1	3.6	2.4
Spain	5.0	4.6	2.1	5.0	10.0	8.8	5.7	3.0	1.7	3.2	3.2	3.3
Japan[1]	3.7	0.9	7.0	0.6	–4.3	–0.5	2.8	–1.3	–6.1	3.2	4.7	3.7
United Kingdom	2.7	4.7	5.7	6.8	12.7	1.6	3.6	2.6	2.7	2.2	6.3	3.5
Canada	2.0	5.6	4.4	15.2	2.4	7.3	4.7	4.1	2.4	4.9	6.0	4.7
Other advanced economies	6.5	3.0	6.3	5.5	–0.7	2.9	6.9	–3.9	2.9	2.1	4.5	4.1
Memorandum												
Major advanced economies	2.9	3.5	5.7	5.1	5.7	5.6	5.2	–0.8	–2.9	2.7	6.2	3.4
Newly industrialized Asian economies	11.5	2.1	7.5	4.6	–9.1	2.4	10.6	–6.8	1.5	1.1	6.4	4.9

Table 3 *(concluded)*

	Ten-Year Averages											
	1986–95	1996–2005	1996	1997	1998	1999	2000	2001	2002	2003	2004	2005
Final domestic demand												
Advanced economies	**3.0**	**2.9**	**3.2**	**3.1**	**3.1**	**4.0**	**3.9**	**1.7**	**1.5**	**2.2**	**3.2**	**2.7**
United States	2.7	3.8	3.8	4.3	5.3	5.4	4.5	1.8	2.1	3.4	4.1	3.0
Euro area	. . .	2.0	1.6	1.7	3.2	3.7	3.1	1.5	0.4	0.8	1.6	2.2
Germany	2.7	0.8	0.7	0.5	2.1	3.2	2.0	0.2	−1.5	−0.4	−0.1	1.4
France	2.0	2.5	1.3	0.6	3.3	4.0	4.1	2.7	1.7	1.6	3.0	3.0
Italy	1.9	2.0	1.7	2.4	2.8	2.9	3.4	1.5	0.9	0.7	1.7	2.1
Spain	3.6	3.7	2.0	3.5	5.5	5.5	4.7	3.0	2.8	3.1	3.3	3.1
Japan[1]	3.4	1.3	3.8	0.9	−1.0	0.7	2.0	1.1	−0.8	1.5	3.3	2.1
United Kingdom	2.5	3.4	3.4	3.3	4.8	3.8	4.0	2.8	3.3	2.5	3.6	2.6
Canada	2.1	3.5	2.1	5.4	2.8	4.2	4.0	3.2	3.1	3.6	3.7	3.1
Other advanced economies	5.2	3.0	5.2	4.0	−0.5	4.1	5.2	0.9	3.4	1.6	3.1	3.2
Memorandum												
Major advanced economies	2.7	2.8	3.0	2.9	3.4	3.9	3.7	1.7	1.3	2.3	3.3	2.6
Newly industrialized Asian economies	8.7	3.0	7.0	4.6	−5.6	5.1	7.6	0.4	3.6	0.6	3.2	3.9
Stock building[2]												
Advanced economies	**—**	**—**	**−0.2**	**0.2**	**—**	**—**	**—**	**−0.6**	**0.1**	**0.1**	**0.4**	**0.1**
United States	—	0.1	—	0.5	—	—	−0.1	−0.9	0.4	−0.1	0.9	0.3
Euro area	. . .	−0.1	−0.5	0.1	0.4	−0.2	−0.1	−0.6	—	0.3	0.2	−0.2
Germany	—	−0.1	−0.5	—	0.3	−0.4	−0.1	−1.0	−0.4	0.9	0.3	—
France	0.1	—	−0.6	0.1	0.8	−0.2	0.4	−0.6	−0.2	−0.2	0.6	−0.3
Italy	—	−0.1	−0.7	0.3	0.3	0.3	−1.1	−0.1	0.5	0.5	−0.3	−0.3
Spain	—	—	−0.1	—	0.2	0.1	−0.1	−0.1	—	0.1	—	—
Japan[1]	—	—	0.3	−0.1	−0.6	−0.4	0.3	—	−0.2	0.3	0.2	−0.1
United Kingdom	—	—	−0.3	0.3	0.1	0.2	−0.1	0.1	−0.4	—	−0.1	−0.1
Canada	0.1	—	−0.7	0.7	−0.3	0.1	0.8	−1.9	0.6	0.9	−0.6	0.1
Other advanced economies	0.1	−0.1	−0.3	−0.2	−0.5	0.9	−0.1	−0.5	−0.1	−0.4	0.6	—
Memorandum												
Major advanced economies	—	—	−0.1	0.3	—	−0.1	—	−0.6	0.1	0.2	0.5	0.1
Newly industrialized Asian economies	0.1	−0.1	−0.1	−0.1	−1.9	1.9	−0.2	−0.7	0.1	−0.8	1.1	−0.1
Foreign balance[2]												
Advanced economies	**—**	**−0.1**	**—**	**0.2**	**−0.4**	**−0.5**	**—**	**0.1**	**−0.1**	**−0.2**	**0.1**	**0.2**
United States	0.1	−0.5	−0.1	−0.3	−1.2	−1.0	−0.9	−0.2	−0.7	−0.4	−0.5	0.1
Euro area	. . .	0.1	0.4	0.6	−0.6	−0.6	0.6	0.7	0.5	−0.7	0.4	0.2
Germany	−0.1	0.6	0.5	0.8	−0.4	−0.7	1.0	1.6	1.9	−0.6	1.9	0.5
France	—	−0.2	0.4	1.2	−0.5	−0.4	−0.2	0.1	−0.4	−0.8	−1.0	−0.3
Italy	0.2	−0.4	0.2	−0.6	−1.2	−1.4	0.8	0.3	−0.9	−0.9	—	0.1
Spain	−0.6	−0.5	0.5	0.6	−1.3	−1.4	−0.3	−0.2	−0.6	−0.8	−0.8	−0.3
Japan[1]	−0.2	0.3	−0.4	1.0	0.3	−0.1	0.5	−0.7	0.7	0.7	1.1	0.5
United Kingdom	−0.1	−0.6	−0.2	−0.3	−1.6	−1.0	−0.1	−0.7	−1.2	−0.4	−0.2	−0.1
Canada	0.1	0.1	0.3	−1.7	1.7	1.4	0.6	0.7	−0.1	−2.4	0.1	—
Other advanced economies	−0.2	0.8	−0.1	0.7	2.2	0.5	0.8	1.0	0.3	1.2	0.8	0.5
Memorandum												
Major advanced economies	—	−0.2	—	0.1	−0.7	−0.7	−0.2	—	−0.2	−0.4	—	0.1
Newly industrialized Asian economies	−0.6	1.5	−0.5	1.1	5.6	0.6	0.7	1.3	1.3	3.2	1.7	0.5

[1]Annual data are calculated from seasonally adjusted quarterly data.
[2]Changes expressed as percent of GDP in the preceding period.

Table 4. Advanced Economies: Unemployment, Employment, and Real Per Capita GDP

(Percent)

	Ten-Year Averages[1]											
	1986–95	1996–2005	1996	1997	1998	1999	2000	2001	2002	2003	2004	2005
Unemployment rate												
Advanced economies	**6.9**	**6.5**	**7.1**	**6.9**	**6.8**	**6.4**	**5.8**	**5.9**	**6.4**	**6.6**	**6.3**	**6.1**
United States[2]	6.2	5.0	5.4	4.9	4.5	4.2	4.0	4.8	5.8	6.0	5.5	5.4
Euro area	. . .	9.3	10.8	10.8	10.2	9.4	8.5	8.0	8.5	8.9	9.0	8.7
Germany	7.3	8.9	8.7	9.7	9.1	8.4	7.8	7.9	8.7	9.6	9.7	9.5
France	10.3	10.0	11.9	11.8	11.4	10.7	9.3	8.5	8.9	9.4	9.4	9.0
Italy	11.2	10.1	11.6	11.7	11.8	11.4	10.6	9.5	9.0	8.7	8.3	8.2
Spain	19.9	14.6	22.2	20.8	18.7	15.7	13.9	10.5	11.4	11.3	11.1	10.3
Netherlands	6.9	4.2	6.6	5.5	4.2	3.2	2.6	2.0	2.5	4.3	5.3	5.8
Belgium	8.4	8.2	9.5	9.2	9.3	8.6	6.9	6.7	7.3	8.1	8.3	8.3
Austria	3.3	4.2	4.4	4.4	4.5	4.0	3.7	3.6	4.3	4.4	4.4	4.2
Finland	8.8	10.3	14.6	12.6	11.4	10.2	9.8	9.1	9.1	9.0	8.8	8.5
Greece	8.2	10.1	9.8	9.8	11.1	11.9	11.1	10.5	10.0	9.0	8.9	8.8
Portugal	6.0	5.7	7.3	6.7	5.0	4.4	3.9	4.1	5.1	6.4	7.1	6.8
Ireland	15.0	6.1	11.9	10.3	7.6	5.6	4.3	3.9	4.4	4.7	4.4	4.1
Luxembourg	1.8	3.4	3.3	3.3	3.1	2.9	2.6	2.6	2.9	3.8	4.5	4.8
Japan[3]	2.5	4.5	3.4	3.4	4.1	4.7	4.7	5.0	5.4	5.3	4.7	4.5
United Kingdom	8.9	5.8	8.1	7.1	6.3	6.0	5.5	5.1	5.2	5.0	4.8	4.8
Canada	9.5	7.8	9.6	9.1	8.3	7.6	6.8	7.2	7.7	7.6	7.2	6.8
Korea	2.7	4.0	2.1	2.6	7.0	6.4	4.2	3.8	3.1	3.4	3.5	3.6
Australia	8.4	6.8	8.2	8.2	7.7	6.9	6.3	6.8	6.4	6.1	5.7	5.7
Taiwan Province of China	1.7	3.8	2.6	2.7	2.7	2.9	3.0	4.6	5.2	5.0	4.7	4.5
Sweden	4.1	5.6	8.0	8.0	6.5	5.6	4.7	4.0	4.0	4.9	5.6	5.0
Switzerland	1.8	3.0	4.1	4.5	3.5	2.5	1.8	1.7	2.5	3.5	3.4	3.0
Hong Kong SAR	1.9	5.4	2.8	2.2	4.7	6.2	5.0	5.1	7.3	7.9	6.7	5.8
Denmark	9.8	6.1	8.6	7.8	6.4	5.5	5.1	4.9	4.9	5.8	5.9	5.6
Norway	4.6	3.9	4.9	4.1	3.2	3.2	3.4	3.5	3.9	4.5	4.3	4.0
Israel	8.4	9.2	6.6	7.7	8.5	8.9	8.8	9.3	10.3	10.8	10.7	10.1
Singapore	3.1	3.4	2.0	1.8	3.2	3.5	3.1	3.3	4.4	4.7	4.3	3.9
New Zealand	7.3	5.7	6.1	6.6	7.4	6.8	6.0	5.3	5.2	4.7	4.6	5.0
Cyprus	2.7	3.3	3.1	3.4	3.4	3.6	3.4	2.9	3.2	3.5	3.4	3.2
Iceland	2.4	2.7	4.4	3.9	2.8	1.9	1.3	1.4	2.5	3.3	3.0	2.3
Memorandum												
Major advanced economies	6.7	6.3	6.7	6.6	6.3	6.1	5.7	5.9	6.5	6.7	6.4	6.2
Newly industrialized Asian economies	2.4	4.0	2.3	2.6	5.4	5.3	3.9	4.1	4.1	4.3	4.1	4.1
Growth in employment												
Advanced economies	**1.2**	**1.1**	**1.0**	**1.4**	**1.1**	**1.4**	**2.1**	**0.7**	**0.3**	**0.6**	**0.9**	**1.2**
United States	1.5	1.3	1.5	2.3	1.5	1.5	2.5	—	–0.3	0.9	1.2	1.8
Euro area	. . .	1.0	0.5	0.9	1.8	1.8	2.2	1.4	0.5	0.1	0.5	0.9
Germany	0.6	0.2	–0.3	–0.2	1.1	1.2	2.0	0.3	–0.5	–1.1	–0.4	0.3
France	0.4	1.0	0.4	0.4	1.5	2.0	2.7	1.7	0.7	—	0.3	0.9
Italy	–0.3	1.1	0.5	0.4	1.1	1.3	1.9	2.1	1.5	1.0	0.8	0.5
Spain	1.6	3.4	2.6	3.3	4.1	5.5	5.5	3.7	2.0	2.7	2.4	2.7
Japan[3]	1.1	–0.2	0.4	1.1	–0.7	–0.8	–0.2	–0.6	–1.2	–0.2	0.3	0.2
United Kingdom	0.3	1.0	0.9	1.8	1.0	1.3	1.1	0.8	0.7	0.9	0.7	0.5
Canada	1.4	2.0	0.8	2.3	2.7	2.8	2.6	1.1	2.2	2.2	1.8	1.7
Other advanced economies	2.0	1.4	1.6	1.2	–0.5	1.6	2.8	1.1	1.7	1.0	1.6	1.5
Memorandum												
Major advanced economies	1.0	0.9	0.8	1.4	1.0	1.1	1.8	0.3	–0.1	0.5	0.7	1.1
Newly industrialized Asian economies	2.7	1.3	2.1	1.8	–2.9	1.5	3.5	1.0	2.0	0.3	1.7	1.7

Table 4 *(concluded)*

	Ten-Year Averages[1]											
	1986–95	1996–2005	1996	1997	1998	1999	2000	2001	2002	2003	2004	2005
Growth in real per capita GDP												
Advanced economies	**2.3**	**2.2**	**2.3**	**2.8**	**2.0**	**2.9**	**3.3**	**0.6**	**1.0**	**1.6**	**3.1**	**2.4**
United States	1.7	2.3	2.5	3.3	3.0	3.3	2.5	–0.3	0.8	2.0	3.3	2.5
Euro area	. . .	1.8	1.2	2.2	2.6	2.5	3.1	1.1	0.2	–0.2	1.9	1.9
Germany	2.0	1.3	0.5	1.2	2.0	2.0	2.7	0.7	–0.1	–0.1	2.0	1.8
France	1.6	1.8	0.7	1.5	3.2	2.8	3.7	1.6	0.6	—	2.2	1.9
Italy	1.9	1.5	0.9	1.9	1.7	1.6	3.0	1.8	0.4	0.3	1.2	1.7
Spain	2.8	2.7	2.3	3.8	4.1	3.8	3.2	2.2	1.6	1.9	2.0	2.3
Japan[3]	2.8	1.4	3.2	1.6	–1.5	—	2.6	0.2	–0.5	2.3	4.3	2.3
United Kingdom	2.2	2.4	2.6	3.1	2.8	2.5	3.6	1.6	1.3	1.7	2.9	1.9
Canada	1.0	2.4	0.6	3.2	3.2	4.7	4.3	0.7	2.3	1.1	2.0	1.9
Other advanced economies	3.8	2.8	3.7	3.4	–0.1	4.4	5.0	0.6	2.8	1.7	3.6	2.9
Memorandum												
Major advanced economies	2.1	2.1	2.2	2.6	2.1	2.5	2.9	0.5	0.7	1.6	3.1	2.4
Newly industrialized Asian economies	7.0	3.4	5.3	4.5	–3.3	6.2	6.9	0.3	4.2	2.3	4.8	3.5

[1]Compound annual rate of change for employment and per capita GDP; arithmetic average for unemployment rate.
[2]The projections for unemployment have been adjusted to reflect the survey techniques adopted by the U.S. Bureau of Labor Statistics in January 1994.
[3]Annual data are calculated from seasonally adjusted quarterly data.

Table 5. Other Emerging Market and Developing Countries: Real GDP

(Annual percent change)

	Ten-Year Averages											
	1986–95	1996–2005	1996	1997	1998	1999	2000	2001	2002	2003	2004	2005
Other emerging market and developing countries	**3.7**	**5.1**	**5.6**	**5.3**	**3.0**	**4.0**	**5.9**	**4.0**	**4.8**	**6.1**	**6.6**	**5.9**
Regional groups												
Africa	1.9	3.9	5.7	3.2	3.1	2.7	2.9	4.0	3.5	4.3	4.5	5.4
Sub-Sahara	1.9	3.9	5.3	3.9	2.3	2.7	3.1	3.9	3.6	3.7	4.6	5.8
Excluding Nigeria and South Africa	2.2	4.6	5.9	5.1	3.8	3.4	2.4	4.9	4.0	3.6	6.0	7.4
Central and eastern Europe	0.8	3.6	4.8	4.2	2.8	0.4	4.9	0.2	4.4	4.5	5.5	4.8
Commonwealth of Independent States[1]	. . .	4.1	–3.9	1.1	–3.5	5.1	9.1	6.4	5.4	7.8	8.0	6.6
Russia	. . .	3.9	–3.6	1.4	–5.3	6.3	10.0	5.1	4.7	7.3	7.3	6.6
Excluding Russia	. . .	4.7	–4.5	0.5	0.8	2.2	6.9	9.4	7.0	9.0	9.6	6.5
Developing Asia	7.7	6.6	8.2	6.5	4.1	6.2	6.7	5.5	6.6	7.7	7.6	6.9
China	9.9	8.3	9.6	8.8	7.8	7.1	8.0	7.5	8.3	9.1	9.0	7.5
India	5.7	6.0	7.5	5.0	5.8	6.7	5.4	3.9	5.0	7.2	6.4	6.7
Excluding China and India	6.2	3.8	6.6	3.9	–4.7	3.7	5.3	3.0	4.5	5.1	5.6	5.5
Middle East	2.7	4.5	4.6	5.3	3.8	2.4	5.5	3.6	4.3	6.0	5.1	4.8
Western Hemisphere	2.8	2.6	3.7	5.2	2.3	0.4	3.9	0.5	–0.1	1.8	4.6	3.6
Brazil	2.5	2.2	2.7	3.3	0.1	0.8	4.4	1.3	1.9	–0.2	4.0	3.5
Mexico	1.6	3.6	5.2	6.8	5.0	3.6	6.6	–0.2	0.8	1.3	4.0	3.2
Analytical groups												
By source of export earnings												
Fuel	2.0	4.5	3.9	4.8	3.4	1.6	5.5	4.0	3.8	6.5	6.0	5.8
Nonfuel	3.8	5.1	5.7	5.3	3.0	4.2	5.9	4.0	4.9	6.1	6.6	5.9
of which, primary products	3.0	3.5	5.9	4.0	2.7	1.7	2.0	3.4	2.6	2.5	5.2	4.8
By external financing source												
Net debtor countries	3.1	4.0	5.3	4.5	1.8	2.9	4.7	2.5	3.4	4.6	5.4	5.2
of which, official financing	4.3	3.8	6.2	4.2	–1.9	2.8	4.4	4.0	3.9	4.7	5.3	5.3
Net debtor countries by debt-servicing experience												
Countries with arrears and/or rescheduling during 1997–2001	2.3	3.5	4.2	3.8	–0.6	1.9	4.5	3.7	3.5	3.3	5.4	5.1
Other groups												
Heavily indebted poor countries	2.0	4.8	5.4	4.7	4.0	4.4	4.2	5.5	4.6	3.4	5.9	5.5
Middle East and north Africa	2.5	4.5	5.2	4.5	4.3	2.6	4.9	3.8	4.1	6.0	5.0	4.8
Memorandum												
Real per capita GDP												
Other emerging market and developing countries	1.9	3.7	4.0	3.8	1.5	2.5	4.4	2.6	3.4	4.8	5.3	4.6
Africa	–0.9	1.6	3.2	0.8	0.8	0.4	0.6	1.7	1.3	2.1	2.3	3.3
Central and eastern Europe	0.1	3.2	4.4	3.7	2.3	—	4.4	–0.2	3.9	4.1	5.1	4.4
Commonwealth of Independent States[1]	. . .	4.3	–3.8	1.2	–3.3	5.3	9.4	6.6	5.6	8.1	8.2	6.8
Developing Asia	5.9	5.3	6.7	5.0	2.7	4.8	5.3	4.2	5.3	6.5	6.4	5.7
Middle East	–0.1	2.4	2.4	3.1	1.7	0.3	3.4	1.4	2.1	3.8	3.0	2.7
Western Hemisphere	1.0	1.0	2.0	3.6	0.7	–1.2	2.4	–1.1	–1.6	0.4	3.1	2.2

[1]Mongolia, which is not a member of the Commonwealth of Independent States, is included in this group for reasons of geography and similarities in economic structure.

Table 6. Other Emerging and Developing Countries—by Country: Real GDP[1]
(Annual percent change)

	Average 1986–95	1996	1997	1998	1999	2000	2001	2002	2003	2004	2005
Africa	**1.9**	**5.7**	**3.2**	**3.1**	**2.7**	**2.9**	**4.0**	**3.5**	**4.3**	**4.5**	**5.4**
Algeria	0.4	3.8	1.1	5.1	3.2	2.1	2.6	4.0	6.8	4.5	4.4
Angola	–0.9	11.2	7.9	6.8	3.2	3.0	3.1	14.4	3.4	11.2	15.5
Benin	2.5	6.0	5.7	4.6	4.7	5.8	5.0	6.0	4.8	3.0	5.0
Botswana	7.8	5.7	6.7	5.9	5.5	7.5	5.2	3.9	5.4	4.5	3.7
Burkina Faso	4.8	9.9	6.8	8.5	3.7	1.6	6.8	4.6	8.0	4.8	5.3
Burundi	0.6	–8.0	—	4.7	–0.9	–1.1	2.2	4.5	–0.5	5.4	5.7
Cameroon[2]	–2.1	5.0	5.1	5.0	4.4	4.2	5.3	6.5	4.5	4.8	5.1
Cape Verde	4.5	5.5	8.5	8.0	10.9	8.1	4.7	4.9	5.3	5.5	6.0
Central African Republic	0.6	–8.1	7.5	3.9	3.6	1.8	0.3	–0.6	–7.5	2.3	4.4
Chad	3.8	3.1	4.2	7.7	–1.7	1.9	9.1	10.5	9.7	30.8	12.0
Comoros	1.2	–1.3	4.2	1.2	1.9	2.4	2.3	2.3	2.1	1.8	3.5
Congo, Dem. Rep. of	–3.7	–1.1	–5.4	–1.7	–4.3	–6.9	–2.1	3.5	5.6	6.3	7.0
Congo, Rep. of	4.8	4.3	–0.6	3.7	–3.0	8.2	3.6	5.4	0.8	4.0	9.2
Côte d'Ivoire	1.6	7.7	5.7	4.8	1.6	–2.3	0.1	–1.6	–2.8	1.7	4.3
Djibouti	–1.2	–4.1	–0.7	0.1	2.2	0.7	1.9	2.6	3.5	4.1	4.6
Equatorial Guinea	4.1	32.2	82.0	22.6	27.0	18.0	37.5	18.0	14.7	13.6	48.1
Eritrea	. . .	9.3	7.9	1.8	—	–13.1	9.2	0.7	3.0	1.8	0.7
Ethiopia	3.0	10.2	5.1	–1.4	6.0	5.4	7.7	1.6	–3.9	11.6	5.7
Gabon	1.9	3.6	5.7	3.5	–8.9	–1.9	2.0	—	2.8	1.5	0.7
Gambia, The	3.0	6.1	4.9	6.5	6.4	5.5	5.8	–3.2	6.7	7.1	5.0
Ghana	4.8	4.6	4.2	4.7	4.4	3.7	4.2	4.5	5.2	5.2	5.0
Guinea	4.1	5.1	5.0	4.8	4.6	1.9	3.8	4.2	1.2	2.6	3.8
Guinea-Bissau	3.0	4.6	6.5	–27.2	7.6	7.5	0.2	–7.2	0.6	1.0	3.4
Kenya	3.6	4.2	2.1	1.6	1.3	–0.1	1.2	1.0	1.6	2.3	3.6
Lesotho	5.3	9.5	4.8	–3.5	0.5	1.9	3.3	3.7	3.2	3.0	3.4
Madagascar	1.2	2.1	3.7	3.9	4.7	4.8	6.0	–12.7	9.8	5.3	7.0
Malawi	2.6	7.3	3.8	3.3	4.0	1.1	–4.2	1.0	4.4	3.6	4.0
Mali	3.7	7.4	5.3	8.4	3.0	–3.2	12.1	4.3	6.0	4.5	5.6
Mauritania	3.1	5.7	2.8	3.9	5.2	5.2	4.0	3.3	4.9	4.6	5.2
Mauritius	7.1	5.2	6.0	6.0	5.3	2.7	7.6	4.3	2.7	4.4	4.8
Morocco	2.7	12.2	–2.2	7.7	–0.1	1.0	6.3	3.2	5.5	3.0	4.0
Mozambique, Rep. of	4.4	7.1	11.1	12.6	7.5	1.5	13.0	7.4	7.1	8.4	6.8
Namibia	3.5	3.2	4.2	3.3	3.4	3.5	2.4	2.5	3.7	3.5	3.6
Niger	1.6	3.4	2.8	10.4	–0.6	–1.4	7.1	3.0	5.3	4.1	4.1
Nigeria	2.7	6.6	3.2	0.3	1.5	5.4	3.1	1.5	10.7	4.0	5.9
Rwanda	–4.5	12.7	13.8	8.9	7.6	6.0	6.7	9.4	0.9	6.0	6.0
São Tomé and Príncipe	0.1	1.5	1.0	2.5	2.5	3.0	4.0	4.1	4.5	6.5	6.5
Senegal	2.3	5.1	3.3	4.5	6.2	3.0	4.7	1.1	6.5	6.0	5.8
Seychelles	4.3	10.0	12.2	5.7	–1.3	4.8	–2.2	0.3	–5.1	–2.0	1.0
Sierra Leone	–1.4	–24.8	–17.6	–0.8	–8.1	3.8	18.5	26.8	9.4	7.2	7.0
South Africa	1.3	4.3	2.6	0.8	2.0	3.5	2.7	3.6	1.9	2.6	3.3
Sudan	3.7	6.3	9.3	5.7	6.5	6.9	6.1	6.0	6.0	6.6	7.6
Swaziland	6.5	3.9	3.8	3.3	3.6	1.9	1.7	3.6	2.2	1.5	1.3
Tanzania	3.7	4.5	3.5	3.7	3.5	5.1	6.2	7.2	7.1	6.3	6.5
Togo	1.7	7.1	3.5	–2.3	2.4	–0.8	–0.2	4.2	2.7	3.0	2.8
Tunisia	3.4	7.1	5.4	4.8	6.1	4.7	4.9	1.7	5.6	5.6	5.0
Uganda	5.6	9.1	5.5	3.6	8.1	5.6	4.9	6.8	4.7	5.7	6.0
Zambia	–0.8	6.9	3.3	–1.9	2.2	3.6	4.9	3.3	5.1	3.5	4.5
Zimbabwe	2.9	9.7	1.4	0.5	–3.6	–7.9	–2.8	–11.1	–9.3	–5.2	1.8

Table 6 *(continued)*

	Average 1986–95	1996	1997	1998	1999	2000	2001	2002	2003	2004	2005
Central and eastern Europe[3]	**0.8**	**4.8**	**4.2**	**2.8**	**0.4**	**4.9**	**0.2**	**4.4**	**4.5**	**5.5**	**4.8**
Albania	–1.2	9.1	–10.2	12.7	10.1	7.3	7.6	4.7	6.0	6.2	6.0
Bosnia and Herzegovina	. . .	61.9	30.0	15.8	9.6	5.5	4.4	5.5	2.7	5.0	4.0
Bulgaria	–3.5	–8.0	–5.6	4.0	2.3	5.4	4.1	4.9	4.3	5.2	5.2
Croatia	. . .	5.9	6.8	2.5	–0.9	2.9	4.4	5.2	4.3	3.7	4.1
Czech Republic	. . .	4.3	–0.8	–1.0	0.5	3.3	2.6	1.5	3.1	3.3	3.4
Estonia	. . .	4.5	10.5	5.2	–0.1	7.8	6.4	7.2	5.1	5.8	5.4
Hungary	–0.9	1.3	4.6	4.9	4.2	5.2	3.8	3.5	2.9	3.5	3.7
Latvia	. . .	3.8	8.3	4.7	3.3	6.9	8.0	6.4	7.5	6.5	6.0
Lithuania	. . .	4.7	7.0	7.3	–1.7	3.9	6.4	6.8	9.0	7.0	7.0
Macedonia, FYR	. . .	1.2	1.4	3.4	4.4	4.5	–4.5	0.9	3.1	4.0	4.5
Malta	5.9	4.0	4.9	3.4	4.1	6.4	–1.2	1.2	–1.7	1.3	1.7
Serbia and Montenegro	. . .	7.3	—	2.5	–18.0	5.0	5.5	4.0	3.0	4.4	4.5
Poland	1.6	6.0	6.8	4.8	4.1	4.0	1.0	1.4	3.8	5.8	5.1
Romania	–2.0	3.9	–6.1	–4.8	–1.2	2.1	5.7	5.0	4.9	5.0	5.0
Slovak Republic	. . .	6.1	4.6	4.2	1.5	2.0	3.8	4.4	4.2	4.8	4.3
Slovenia	. . .	3.6	4.8	3.6	5.6	3.9	2.7	3.4	2.3	3.9	4.1
Turkey	4.4	6.9	7.6	3.1	–4.7	7.4	–7.5	7.9	5.8	7.0	5.0
Commonwealth of Independent States[3,4]	. . .	**–3.9**	**1.1**	**–3.5**	**5.1**	**9.1**	**6.4**	**5.4**	**7.8**	**8.0**	**6.6**
Russia	. . .	–3.6	1.4	–5.3	6.3	10.0	5.1	4.7	7.3	7.3	6.6
Excluding Russia	. . .	–4.5	0.5	0.8	2.2	6.9	9.4	7.0	9.0	9.6	6.5
Armenia	. . .	5.9	3.3	7.3	3.3	6.0	9.6	12.9	13.9	7.0	6.0
Azerbaijan	. . .	1.3	5.8	10.0	7.4	11.1	9.9	10.6	11.2	9.1	11.4
Belarus	. . .	2.8	11.4	8.4	3.4	5.8	4.7	5.0	6.8	6.4	5.5
Georgia	. . .	10.5	10.6	2.9	3.0	1.9	4.7	5.5	11.1	8.5	6.0
Kazakhstan	. . .	0.5	1.6	–1.9	2.7	9.8	13.5	9.8	9.2	9.0	8.5
Kyrgyz Republic	. . .	7.1	9.9	2.1	3.7	5.4	5.3	—	6.7	5.5	4.9
Moldova	. . .	–5.9	1.6	–6.5	–3.4	2.1	6.1	7.8	6.3	5.0	4.0
Mongolia	0.5	2.4	4.0	3.5	3.2	1.1	1.0	3.9	5.3	6.0	5.5
Tajikistan	. . .	–4.4	1.7	5.3	3.7	8.3	10.2	9.1	10.2	10.0	8.0
Turkmenistan	. . .	–6.7	–11.3	6.7	16.4	18.6	20.4	19.8	16.9	7.5	7.0
Ukraine	. . .	–10.0	–3.0	–1.9	–0.2	5.9	9.2	5.3	9.4	12.5	6.0
Uzbekistan	. . .	1.6	2.5	2.1	3.4	3.2	4.1	3.1	1.5	2.5	2.5

Table 6 *(continued)*

	Average 1986–95	1996	1997	1998	1999	2000	2001	2002	2003	2004	2005
Developing Asia	**7.7**	**8.2**	**6.5**	**4.1**	**6.2**	**6.7**	**5.5**	**6.6**	**7.7**	**7.6**	**6.9**
Afghanistan, I.S. of	. . .	. . .	. . .	. . .	. . .	. . .	. . .	. . .	. . .	. . .	. . .
Bangladesh	4.1	5.0	5.3	5.0	5.4	5.6	4.8	4.9	5.4	5.5	5.7
Bhutan	6.7	5.2	7.2	6.4	7.8	5.5	7.1	6.7	6.5	7.3	7.6
Brunei Darussalam	. . .	2.0	2.6	–4.0	2.6	2.8	3.1	2.8	3.1	1.1	2.2
Cambodia	. . .	5.0	6.8	3.7	10.8	7.0	5.7	5.5	5.2	4.3	1.9
China	9.9	9.6	8.8	7.8	7.1	8.0	7.5	8.3	9.1	9.0	7.5
Fiji	3.3	3.1	–0.9	1.5	9.5	–3.2	4.3	4.4	5.2	3.2	3.0
India	5.7	7.5	5.0	5.8	6.7	5.4	3.9	5.0	7.2	6.4	6.7
Indonesia	6.8	8.0	4.5	–13.1	0.8	4.9	3.5	3.7	4.1	4.8	5.0
Kiribati	1.9	3.8	1.9	12.6	9.5	1.6	1.8	1.0	2.5	1.8	1.5
Lao PDR	5.0	6.9	6.9	4.0	7.3	5.8	5.8	5.8	5.3	5.4	5.8
Malaysia	8.2	10.0	7.3	–7.4	6.1	8.9	0.3	4.1	5.3	6.5	6.3
Maldives	7.5	9.1	10.4	9.8	7.2	4.8	3.5	6.5	8.4	5.0	4.7
Myanmar	1.7	6.4	5.7	5.8	10.9	13.7	11.3	10.0	—	3.6	3.3
Nepal	6.1	5.3	5.3	2.9	4.5	6.1	5.5	–0.6	3.1	3.5	4.6
Pakistan	5.2	2.9	1.8	3.1	4.0	3.4	2.7	4.4	6.2	6.3	6.0
Papua New Guinea	4.9	7.7	–3.9	–3.8	7.6	–1.2	–2.3	–0.8	2.7	2.5	2.9
Philippines	3.4	5.8	5.2	–0.6	3.4	4.4	1.8	4.3	4.7	5.2	4.2
Samoa	2.3	7.3	0.8	2.4	2.6	6.9	6.2	1.8	3.1	3.2	3.2
Solomon Islands	5.5	1.6	–1.4	1.8	–0.5	–14.3	–9.0	–1.6	5.1	4.2	4.4
Sri Lanka	4.4	3.8	6.4	4.7	4.3	6.0	–1.5	3.9	5.9	5.0	5.0
Thailand	9.5	5.9	–1.4	–10.5	4.4	4.8	2.1	5.4	6.8	6.2	6.4
Timor-Leste, Dem. Rep. of	. . .	. . .	. . .	. . .	. . .	15.4	14.6	3.0	–2.7	1.0	1.5
Tonga	2.3	0.3	–3.0	3.6	2.5	5.5	0.9	2.7	1.9	1.0	1.3
Vanuatu	3.1	2.5	8.6	4.3	–3.2	2.7	–2.1	–2.8	1.8	2.5	3.3
Vietnam	6.5	9.3	8.2	3.5	4.2	5.5	5.0	5.8	6.0	7.0	7.0
Middle East	**2.7**	**4.6**	**5.3**	**3.8**	**2.4**	**5.5**	**3.6**	**4.3**	**6.0**	**5.1**	**4.8**
Bahrain	4.1	4.1	3.1	4.8	4.3	5.3	4.5	5.1	5.7	5.5	5.3
Egypt	2.8	4.9	5.9	4.5	6.3	5.1	3.5	3.2	3.1	3.7	4.5
Iran, I.R. of	1.4	7.1	3.4	2.7	1.9	5.1	3.7	7.5	6.6	6.6	5.2
Iraq	. . .	. . .	. . .	. . .	. . .	. . .	. . .	. . .	. . .	. . .	. . .
Jordan	3.5	2.1	3.3	3.0	3.1	4.1	4.2	5.0	3.2	5.5	5.5
Kuwait	2.5	0.6	2.5	3.6	–1.7	1.9	0.6	–0.4	10.1	2.8	2.3
Lebanon	–3.6	4.0	4.0	3.0	1.0	–0.5	2.0	2.0	3.0	5.0	4.0
Libya	–1.0	2.7	4.8	–1.2	–0.4	0.7	1.0	2.7	9.8	5.4	4.8
Oman	4.4	2.9	6.2	2.7	–0.2	5.5	7.5	1.7	1.4	2.5	3.6
Qatar	1.3	4.5	31.1	11.7	4.5	9.1	4.5	7.3	3.3	9.3	5.0
Saudi Arabia	3.4	1.4	2.6	2.8	–0.7	4.9	0.5	0.1	7.2	3.6	3.9
Syrian Arab Republic	4.3	9.8	5.0	6.8	–3.6	0.6	3.8	4.2	2.6	3.6	4.0
United Arab Emirates	3.4	6.1	8.3	1.4	4.4	12.3	3.5	1.9	7.0	3.6	4.5
Yemen	. . .	7.4	6.4	5.3	3.5	4.4	4.6	3.9	3.2	2.7	2.7

Table 6 ***(concluded)***

	Average 1986–95	1996	1997	1998	1999	2000	2001	2002	2003	2004	2005
Western Hemisphere	**2.8**	**3.7**	**5.2**	**2.3**	**0.4**	**3.9**	**0.5**	**–0.1**	**1.8**	**4.6**	**3.6**
Antigua and Barbuda	4.2	6.1	5.6	5.0	4.9	3.3	1.5	2.1	2.5	1.0	0.5
Argentina	2.8	5.5	8.1	3.8	–3.4	–0.8	–4.4	–10.9	8.8	7.0	4.0
Bahamas, The	1.0	4.2	3.3	3.0	5.9	4.9	–3.1	–0.1	1.9	3.0	3.5
Barbados	0.8	3.2	4.6	6.2	0.5	2.4	–3.4	–0.5	2.2	3.0	2.5
Belize	7.8	1.5	3.6	3.7	8.8	12.3	4.9	4.3	9.4	3.0	3.3
Bolivia	3.1	4.4	5.0	5.0	0.4	2.3	1.5	2.8	2.5	3.8	4.5
Brazil	2.5	2.7	3.3	0.1	0.8	4.4	1.3	1.9	–0.2	4.0	3.5
Chile	7.7	7.4	6.6	3.2	–0.8	4.5	3.4	2.2	3.3	4.9	4.7
Colombia	4.6	2.1	3.4	0.6	–4.2	2.9	1.4	1.6	3.7	4.0	4.0
Costa Rica	5.3	0.9	5.6	8.4	8.2	1.8	1.0	2.9	5.6	3.8	3.5
Dominica	3.6	3.1	2.0	2.8	1.6	1.4	–4.2	–4.7	—	1.0	2.0
Dominican Republic	3.5	7.2	8.3	7.3	8.1	7.8	4.0	4.3	–0.4	–1.0	3.2
Ecuador	2.7	2.4	4.1	2.1	–6.3	2.8	5.1	3.3	2.6	5.4	4.0
El Salvador	2.7	1.7	4.2	3.7	3.4	2.2	1.7	2.2	1.8	2.0	2.5
Grenada	3.7	3.1	4.0	7.3	7.5	6.5	–3.3	–0.5	2.5	4.5	4.6
Guatemala	3.6	3.0	4.4	5.0	3.8	3.6	2.3	2.2	2.2	2.6	3.1
Guyana	2.6	7.9	6.2	–1.7	3.0	–1.3	2.3	–0.5	–0.8	2.4	—
Haiti	–1.5	4.1	2.7	2.2	2.7	0.9	–1.0	–0.5	0.4	–5.0	3.0
Honduras	3.3	3.6	5.0	2.9	–1.9	5.7	2.6	2.7	3.2	3.8	4.0
Jamaica	2.6	–1.2	–1.4	–0.4	–0.2	0.9	1.1	1.5	2.2	1.6	1.6
Mexico	1.6	5.2	6.8	5.0	3.6	6.6	–0.2	0.8	1.3	4.0	3.2
Netherlands Antilles	2.1	1.3	–0.5	0.7	–0.7	–2.0	0.6	0.4	1.4	1.0	1.5
Nicaragua	–0.6	6.3	4.0	3.7	7.0	4.2	3.0	1.0	2.3	3.7	3.8
Panama	2.4	7.4	6.4	7.4	4.0	2.7	0.6	2.2	4.1	5.3	3.7
Paraguay	3.6	1.3	2.6	–0.4	0.5	–0.4	2.7	–2.3	2.6	2.1	2.5
Peru	2.0	2.5	6.8	–0.6	0.9	2.8	0.3	4.9	4.1	4.5	4.5
St. Kitts and Nevis	5.2	6.5	6.8	1.1	3.5	4.1	3.3	2.1	2.1	2.4	2.3
St. Lucia	5.9	1.7	0.6	3.4	2.8	0.1	–4.3	—	2.3	2.0	1.5
St. Vincent and the Grenadines	5.0	1.4	3.9	5.2	3.0	1.3	0.9	1.1	2.2	2.8	3.3
Suriname	0.2	1.3	5.7	2.3	–1.4	1.8	4.3	2.8	5.1	5.3	2.2
Trinidad and Tobago	–0.4	3.8	2.8	7.8	4.4	7.3	4.0	7.1	13.1	6.2	6.3
Uruguay	3.9	5.6	5.0	4.5	–2.8	–1.4	–3.4	–11.0	2.5	10.0	3.5
Venezuela	3.0	–0.2	6.4	0.3	–6.0	3.7	3.4	–8.9	–7.6	12.1	3.5

[1]For many countries, figures for recent years are IMF staff estimates. Data for some countries are for fiscal years.

[2]The percent changes in 2002 are calculated over a period of 18 months, reflecting a change in the fiscal year cycle (from July–June to January–December).

[3]Data for some countries refer to real net material product (NMP) or are estimates based on NMP. For many countries, figures for recent years are IMF staff estimates. The figures should be interpreted only as indicative of broad orders of magnitude because reliable, comparable data are not generally available. In particular, the growth of output of new private enterprises of the informal economy is not fully reflected in the recent figures.

[4]Mongolia, which is not a member of the Commonwealth of Independent States, is included in this group for reasons of geography and similarities in economic structure.

Table 7. Summary of Inflation
(Percent)

	Ten-Year Averages											
	1986–95	1996–2005	1996	1997	1998	1999	2000	2001	2002	2003	2004	2005
GDP deflators												
Advanced economies	**3.5**	**1.6**	**1.9**	**1.7**	**1.3**	**0.9**	**1.4**	**1.8**	**1.6**	**1.4**	**1.7**	**1.9**
United States	2.8	1.9	1.9	1.7	1.1	1.4	2.2	2.4	1.7	1.8	2.4	2.6
Euro area	. . .	1.8	2.9	–0.1	1.2	1.7	1.4	2.4	2.5	2.1	2.0	2.0
Japan[1]	1.2	–1.3	–0.8	0.3	–0.1	–1.5	–2.0	–1.5	–1.2	–2.5	–2.5	–1.3
Other advanced economies[2]	4.8	2.1	3.1	2.6	1.9	1.1	2.0	1.9	1.7	1.9	2.4	2.2
Consumer prices												
Advanced economies	**3.6**	**1.9**	**2.4**	**2.0**	**1.5**	**1.4**	**2.1**	**2.1**	**1.5**	**1.8**	**2.1**	**2.1**
United States	3.5	2.5	2.9	2.3	1.5	2.2	3.4	2.8	1.6	2.3	3.0	3.0
Euro area[3]	. . .	1.9	2.2	1.6	1.1	1.1	2.0	2.4	2.3	2.1	2.1	1.9
Japan[1]	1.4	–0.1	—	1.7	0.6	–0.3	–0.9	–0.8	–0.9	–0.2	–0.2	–0.1
Other advanced economies	4.7	2.0	2.9	2.2	2.2	1.2	1.8	2.1	1.7	1.8	1.9	2.1
Other emerging market and developing countries	**58.2**	**8.8**	**18.1**	**11.6**	**11.3**	**10.4**	**7.3**	**6.8**	**6.0**	**6.1**	**6.0**	**5.5**
Regional groups												
Africa	27.4	12.3	28.2	13.5	8.9	11.6	13.1	12.0	9.7	10.3	8.4	8.1
Central and eastern Europe	59.2	21.7	37.3	52.0	33.0	23.3	23.0	19.6	14.8	9.2	6.9	5.9
Commonwealth of Independent States[4]	. . .	24.3	55.5	18.1	23.9	69.6	24.5	20.3	13.8	12.0	9.9	8.7
Developing Asia	11.2	4.1	8.2	4.9	7.8	2.5	1.9	2.7	2.1	2.6	4.5	4.1
Middle East	17.7	9.6	14.4	11.0	10.5	11.0	8.5	7.1	7.5	8.0	9.2	8.7
Western Hemisphere	196.2	9.1	19.5	11.5	8.5	7.3	6.7	6.0	9.0	10.6	6.5	6.1
Memorandum												
European Union	9.7	2.3	3.5	2.6	2.1	1.7	2.4	2.5	2.2	2.0	2.2	2.0
Analytical groups												
By source of export earnings												
Fuel	25.8	15.0	36.7	17.9	15.0	15.0	12.3	10.8	11.0	11.4	11.8	10.6
Nonfuel	61.5	8.4	16.7	11.1	11.0	10.0	6.9	6.5	5.6	5.7	5.6	5.1
of which, primary products	51.7	17.7	33.3	19.8	10.6	19.8	24.4	20.8	11.7	15.3	11.6	12.1
By external financing source												
Net debtor countries	70.1	10.2	18.3	13.5	15.0	10.6	9.2	8.4	8.2	7.5	6.3	6.1
of which, official financing	24.4	11.6	14.9	9.9	23.6	12.8	7.5	11.5	10.0	9.1	8.8	8.4
Net debtor countries by debt-servicing experience												
Countries with arrears and/or rescheduling during 1997–2001	165.4	12.8	23.4	11.8	16.6	14.0	12.1	11.7	10.3	11.9	9.2	8.2
Memorandum												
Median inflation rate												
Advanced economies	3.6	2.0	2.2	1.8	1.6	1.4	2.6	2.5	2.1	2.2	1.8	1.9
Other emerging market and developing countries	10.2	5.1	8.5	7.0	6.2	4.1	4.3	4.8	3.4	4.5	4.5	4.0

[1]Annual data are calculated from seasonally adjusted quarterly data.
[2]In this table, "other advanced economies" means advanced economies excluding the United States, euro area countries, and Japan.
[3]Based on Eurostat's harmonized index of consumer prices.
[4]Mongolia, which is not a member of the Commonwealth of Independent States, is included in this group for reasons of geography and similarities in economic structure.

Table 8. Advanced Economies: GDP Deflators and Consumer Prices

(Annual percent change)

	Ten-Year Averages												Fourth Quarter[1]		
	1986–95	1996–2005	1996	1997	1998	1999	2000	2001	2002	2003	2004	2005	2003	2004	2005
GDP deflators															
Advanced economies	**3.5**	**1.6**	**1.9**	**1.7**	**1.3**	**0.9**	**1.4**	**1.8**	**1.6**	**1.4**	**1.7**	**1.9**	. . .	. . .	. . .
United States	2.8	1.9	1.9	1.7	1.1	1.4	2.2	2.4	1.7	1.8	2.4	2.6	1.7	3.0	2.3
Euro area	. . .	1.8	2.9	–0.1	1.2	1.7	1.4	2.4	2.5	2.1	2.0	2.0	1.9	2.0	1.8
Germany	3.7	0.9	1.0	0.7	1.1	0.5	–0.3	1.3	1.5	1.1	1.1	1.2	1.2	1.2	1.2
France	2.8	1.4	1.4	1.3	0.8	0.4	0.7	1.7	2.4	1.4	2.0	1.9	1.4	2.2	1.8
Italy	6.0	2.8	5.3	2.4	2.7	1.6	2.2	2.6	3.1	2.9	2.7	2.6	2.8	2.4	1.9
Spain	6.4	3.4	3.5	2.3	2.4	2.8	3.4	4.2	4.5	4.0	3.7	3.6	3.8	3.7	3.3
Netherlands	1.5	2.5	1.2	2.0	1.7	1.6	3.9	5.2	3.1	3.0	1.7	1.3	2.3	2.2	0.3
Belgium	2.8	1.6	1.2	1.4	1.7	1.4	1.2	1.8	1.7	1.7	1.7	1.9	2.0	1.6	2.3
Austria	2.9	1.3	1.3	0.9	0.5	0.7	1.4	2.1	1.4	2.0	1.5	1.5	2.1	1.6	1.5
Finland	4.2	1.3	–0.3	2.1	3.5	–0.2	3.2	3.0	0.9	–0.1	0.4	1.1	–0.1	–0.7	3.0
Greece	15.6	4.3	7.4	6.8	5.2	3.0	3.4	3.5	3.9	3.5	3.2	3.1	3.9	2.8	1.9
Portugal	10.0	3.3	3.0	3.8	3.8	3.1	3.5	4.4	4.5	2.3	2.0	2.7	2.0	–0.1	4.6
Ireland	3.1	3.8	2.1	4.1	6.4	3.8	4.8	5.7	4.5	1.6	2.7	2.5	1.1	3.2	1.8
Luxembourg	2.6	2.3	2.0	2.7	2.7	2.2	4.1	1.9	0.7	2.1	2.1	2.1	. . .	. . .	. . .
Japan[2]	1.2	–1.3	–0.8	0.3	–0.1	–1.5	–2.0	–1.5	–1.2	–2.5	–2.5	–1.3	–2.7	–2.0	–1.1
United Kingdom	4.7	2.7	3.2	2.9	2.8	2.3	1.3	2.2	3.2	3.0	2.7	2.9	2.9	3.7	2.1
Canada	2.9	1.9	1.6	1.2	–0.4	1.7	4.1	1.1	1.0	3.2	3.0	2.2	2.2	3.5	2.0
Korea	7.5	3.1	5.1	4.6	5.8	–0.1	0.7	3.5	2.8	2.3	3.5	2.4	2.3	3.9	1.9
Australia	4.2	2.3	2.1	1.4	0.5	0.6	4.4	3.6	2.4	3.0	3.3	1.9	3.5	2.1	1.5
Taiwan Province of China	2.7	0.3	3.1	1.7	2.6	–1.4	–1.7	0.6	–1.0	–2.1	0.1	1.4	–2.5	2.6	1.3
Sweden	5.3	1.5	1.2	1.6	0.8	0.7	1.3	2.3	1.4	2.3	1.1	1.9	1.9	0.8	2.1
Switzerland	2.9	0.6	–0.1	–0.1	–0.3	0.7	0.8	0.6	1.0	1.2	1.0	1.1	2.3	0.9	1.0
Hong Kong SAR	7.8	–1.3	5.9	5.7	0.2	–5.9	–6.2	–1.9	–3.6	–5.2	–2.5	1.3	–4.8	–2.1	4.1
Denmark	3.2	2.0	2.5	2.2	1.0	1.8	3.0	2.1	1.6	2.2	1.6	1.6	2.4	0.8	1.9
Norway	2.7	3.7	4.1	2.9	–0.7	6.6	15.9	1.1	–1.6	2.3	5.2	1.9	2.1	8.0	–2.1
Israel	18.9	4.1	11.7	8.6	6.4	6.6	0.9	2.2	4.4	–0.3	–0.3	1.4	–2.1	1.4	1.7
Singapore	2.7	—	1.1	0.4	–2.3	–4.7	4.3	–1.6	0.4	–0.4	1.8	1.6	–1.1	1.8	1.6
New Zealand	4.7	2.2	1.9	1.4	1.6	1.0	2.5	4.5	0.6	1.8	3.7	2.8	3.7	4.4	2.3
Cyprus	4.6	2.9	1.8	2.7	2.5	2.2	4.5	2.3	2.8	5.3	2.2	2.6	. . .	. . .	. . .
Iceland	12.0	3.7	2.0	3.5	4.9	2.8	2.9	9.4	5.3	–0.4	4.4	2.1	. . .	. . .	. . .
Memorandum															
Major advanced economies	3.0	1.4	1.6	1.4	1.1	0.9	1.2	1.6	1.4	1.3	1.5	1.8	1.1	2.0	1.6
Newly industrialized Asian economies	5.7	1.5	4.3	3.5	3.5	–1.5	–0.7	1.6	0.7	–0.2	1.6	1.9	–0.2	2.8	2.0
Consumer prices															
Advanced economies	**3.6**	**1.9**	**2.4**	**2.0**	**1.5**	**1.4**	**2.1**	**2.1**	**1.5**	**1.8**	**2.1**	**2.1**	. . .	. . .	. . .
United States	3.5	2.5	2.9	2.3	1.5	2.2	3.4	2.8	1.6	2.3	3.0	3.0	1.9	4.1	2.3
Euro area[3]	. . .	1.9	2.2	1.6	1.1	1.1	2.0	2.4	2.3	2.1	2.1	1.9	2.1	2.1	1.8
Germany	2.4	1.3	1.2	1.5	0.6	0.6	1.4	1.9	1.3	1.0	1.8	1.3	1.2	2.2	1.2
France	2.7	1.7	2.1	1.3	0.7	0.6	1.8	1.8	1.9	2.2	2.4	2.1	2.4	2.4	2.1
Italy	5.4	2.4	4.0	1.9	2.0	1.7	2.6	2.3	2.6	2.8	2.1	2.0	2.7	2.0	2.0
Spain	5.9	2.8	3.7	1.9	2.2	2.4	2.5	2.6	3.9	3.0	2.8	2.7	2.7	2.9	2.7
Japan[2]	1.4	–0.1	—	1.7	0.6	–0.3	–0.9	–0.8	–0.9	–0.2	–0.2	–0.1	–0.2	–0.1	0.1
United Kingdom[3]	4.3	1.5	2.5	1.8	1.6	1.4	0.8	1.2	1.3	1.4	1.6	1.9	1.4	2.0	1.8
Canada	3.3	2.0	1.6	1.6	1.0	1.7	2.7	2.5	2.3	2.7	1.9	2.2	1.7	2.4	2.0
Other advanced economies	5.3	2.2	3.4	2.6	2.9	0.9	2.0	2.4	1.7	1.8	2.0	2.3	. . .	. . .	. . .
Memorandum															
Major advanced economies	3.2	1.8	2.2	2.0	1.2	1.4	2.1	1.9	1.3	1.7	2.1	2.1	1.5	2.7	1.8
Newly industrialized Asian economies	5.0	2.2	4.3	3.3	4.4	—	1.1	1.9	0.9	1.4	2.4	2.6	1.5	2.8	2.4

[1]From fourth quarter of preceding year.
[2]Annual data are calculated from seasonally adjusted quarterly data.
[3]Based on Eurostat's harmonized index of consumer prices.

Table 9. Advanced Economies: Hourly Earnings, Productivity, and Unit Labor Costs in Manufacturing
(Annual percent change)

	Ten-Year Averages											
	1986–95	1996–2005	1996	1997	1998	1999	2000	2001	2002	2003	2004	2005
Hourly earnings												
Advanced economies	**5.1**	**3.8**	**3.3**	**2.9**	**3.5**	**3.0**	**5.6**	**3.0**	**3.9**	**4.9**	**3.9**	**3.6**
United States	3.6	5.0	2.2	2.0	6.2	3.9	9.0	2.5	6.7	8.5	5.3	4.0
Euro area	. . .	3.0	4.3	3.1	1.5	2.5	4.0	3.4	3.2	2.8	2.7	2.9
Germany	5.9	2.7	4.9	1.9	1.5	2.3	5.2	3.0	2.0	1.7	2.0	2.5
France	3.9	2.7	2.3	2.1	0.6	1.1	4.3	2.5	3.7	2.5	3.7	4.0
Italy	7.0	2.8	5.8	4.2	–1.4	2.3	3.1	3.3	2.3	3.1	2.8	2.7
Spain	7.0	3.9	5.7	4.5	3.3	2.7	2.8	4.0	5.2	5.1	3.2	3.0
Japan	3.7	0.9	1.8	3.1	0.9	–0.7	—	1.0	–1.1	1.0	1.1	2.5
United Kingdom	7.1	4.1	4.4	4.2	4.6	4.0	4.7	4.3	3.5	3.6	4.0	4.2
Canada	3.9	2.6	1.0	2.2	1.8	3.7	3.3	2.8	1.0	3.2	3.9	3.5
Other advanced economies	9.3	4.8	6.7	4.8	3.2	5.4	5.7	5.5	3.0	3.9	5.1	4.8
Memorandum												
Major advanced economies	4.5	3.6	2.8	2.5	3.6	2.7	5.8	2.5	4.0	5.2	3.8	3.5
Newly industrialized Asian economies	13.5	6.0	9.9	5.6	2.6	7.5	6.6	6.5	2.9	5.7	6.7	6.3
Productivity												
Advanced economies	**3.1**	**3.3**	**2.8**	**3.9**	**2.3**	**3.6**	**5.1**	**0.8**	**4.2**	**3.9**	**3.6**	**2.9**
United States	2.9	4.1	3.6	3.6	4.8	3.6	4.5	2.3	7.0	5.1	3.9	3.0
Euro area	. . .	2.4	1.9	4.4	2.6	1.9	4.5	0.5	1.6	2.2	2.2	2.3
Germany	3.4	2.5	3.0	4.1	1.6	0.2	5.1	–0.3	2.4	2.9	2.8	2.8
France	3.6	3.8	1.0	5.6	5.5	2.9	7.3	2.2	2.3	3.1	3.8	4.1
Italy	3.2	0.5	–0.6	2.7	–0.6	1.5	3.8	–0.8	–2.0	–0.9	0.6	1.4
Spain	3.2	1.3	0.6	2.7	1.4	1.4	0.3	—	2.2	3.6	0.7	0.3
Japan	2.3	3.1	3.8	5.0	–3.6	3.2	6.8	–3.1	3.6	5.5	6.5	4.1
United Kingdom	3.7	3.0	0.2	1.5	1.2	4.4	6.3	3.5	1.4	5.1	4.0	2.2
Canada	2.1	2.3	–2.4	3.4	1.7	5.7	6.3	–1.8	2.8	1.3	2.9	2.9
Other advanced economies	3.9	3.8	4.8	4.5	1.4	8.2	6.2	0.5	3.8	2.5	3.5	2.8
Memorandum												
Major advanced economies	3.0	3.4	2.6	3.8	2.4	3.1	5.3	0.9	4.4	4.2	3.9	3.1
Newly industrialized Asian economies	7.3	5.6	7.8	4.9	0.1	13.7	10.0	0.6	5.6	4.2	5.6	4.3
Unit labor costs												
Advanced economies	**2.0**	**0.5**	**0.6**	**–0.9**	**1.3**	**–0.6**	**0.4**	**2.2**	**–0.2**	**1.0**	**0.2**	**0.7**
United States	0.7	0.8	–1.3	–1.6	1.3	0.3	4.3	0.2	–0.3	3.2	1.4	1.0
Euro area	. . .	0.6	2.4	–1.2	–1.0	0.5	–0.5	2.8	1.5	0.7	0.5	0.6
Germany	2.5	0.2	1.9	–2.1	—	2.1	0.1	3.3	–0.4	–1.2	–0.8	–0.3
France	0.3	–1.0	1.3	–3.3	–4.7	–1.8	–2.8	0.3	1.4	–0.5	–0.1	–0.1
Italy	3.6	2.3	6.4	1.5	–0.8	0.8	–0.7	4.1	4.4	4.0	2.2	1.3
Spain	3.7	2.6	5.1	1.7	1.9	1.2	2.4	4.0	2.9	1.4	2.5	2.7
Japan	1.4	–2.1	–1.9	–1.8	4.6	–3.8	–6.4	4.2	–4.5	–4.3	–5.1	–1.5
United Kingdom	3.3	1.1	4.2	2.6	3.3	–0.4	–1.6	0.8	2.1	–1.5	–0.1	2.0
Canada	1.7	0.4	3.4	–1.2	—	–1.9	–2.8	4.7	–1.7	1.8	1.0	0.5
Other advanced economies	5.2	1.0	2.3	0.6	2.2	–2.5	–0.6	4.8	–0.9	1.0	1.2	1.8
Memorandum												
Major advanced economies	1.5	0.3	0.3	–1.3	1.2	–0.4	0.5	1.7	–0.4	0.9	—	0.5
Newly industrialized Asian economies	5.7	0.3	2.8	1.1	3.2	–5.2	–3.4	5.4	–2.6	0.7	0.4	1.5

Table 10. Other Emerging Market and Developing Countries: Consumer Prices

(Annual percent change)

	Ten-Year Averages											
	1986–95	1996–2005	1996	1997	1998	1999	2000	2001	2002	2003	2004	2005
Other emerging market and developing countries	**58.2**	**8.8**	**18.1**	**11.6**	**11.3**	**10.4**	**7.3**	**6.8**	**6.0**	**6.1**	**6.0**	**5.5**
Regional groups												
Africa	27.4	12.3	28.2	13.5	8.9	11.6	13.1	12.0	9.7	10.3	8.4	8.1
Sub-Sahara	32.4	15.0	33.9	16.5	10.4	14.7	16.9	15.0	12.1	12.9	9.9	9.6
Excluding Nigeria and South Africa	49.2	22.3	60.0	24.7	13.2	23.9	28.4	21.6	13.9	18.0	14.1	12.0
Central and eastern Europe	59.2	21.7	37.3	52.0	33.0	23.3	23.0	19.6	14.8	9.2	6.9	5.9
Commonwealth of Independent States[1]	. . .	24.3	55.5	18.1	23.9	69.6	24.5	20.3	13.8	12.0	9.9	8.7
Russia	. . .	25.0	47.7	14.8	27.7	85.7	20.8	21.5	15.8	13.7	10.3	8.9
Excluding Russia	. . .	22.7	75.8	26.5	15.9	36.9	34.0	17.6	9.3	8.3	8.8	8.2
Developing Asia	11.2	4.1	8.2	4.9	7.8	2.5	1.9	2.7	2.1	2.6	4.5	4.1
China	11.7	1.7	8.3	2.8	–0.8	–1.4	0.4	0.7	–0.8	1.2	4.0	3.0
India	9.4	5.9	9.0	7.2	13.2	4.7	4.0	3.8	4.3	3.8	4.7	5.0
Excluding China and India	11.6	7.4	7.4	6.6	20.9	8.7	2.8	5.9	6.4	4.8	5.5	5.6
Middle East	17.7	9.6	14.4	11.0	10.5	11.0	8.5	7.1	7.5	8.0	9.2	8.7
Western Hemisphere	196.2	9.1	19.5	11.5	8.5	7.3	6.7	6.0	9.0	10.6	6.5	6.1
Brazil	716.1	8.0	16.0	6.9	3.2	4.9	7.1	6.8	8.4	14.8	6.6	5.9
Mexico	41.2	11.8	34.4	20.6	15.9	16.6	9.5	6.4	5.0	4.5	4.4	4.0
Analytical groups												
By source of export earnings												
Fuel	25.8	15.0	36.7	17.9	15.0	15.0	12.3	10.8	11.0	11.4	11.8	10.6
Nonfuel	61.5	8.4	16.7	11.1	11.0	10.0	6.9	6.5	5.6	5.7	5.6	5.1
of which, primary products	51.7	17.7	33.3	19.8	10.6	19.8	24.4	20.8	11.7	15.3	11.6	12.1
By external financing source												
Net debtor countries	70.1	10.2	18.3	13.5	15.0	10.6	9.2	8.4	8.2	7.5	6.3	6.1
of which, official financing	24.4	11.6	14.9	9.9	23.6	12.8	7.5	11.5	10.0	9.1	8.8	8.4
Net debtor countries by debt-servicing experience												
Countries with arrears and/or rescheduling during 1997–2001	165.4	12.8	23.4	11.8	16.6	14.0	12.1	11.7	10.3	11.9	9.2	8.2
Other groups												
Heavily indebted poor countries	56.3	16.8	42.0	22.0	13.6	17.5	18.4	17.9	11.8	11.3	8.5	8.4
Middle East and north Africa	17.8	8.6	16.1	10.5	9.3	9.2	7.0	6.1	6.4	6.7	8.0	7.4
Memorandum												
Median												
Other emerging market and developing countries	10.2	5.1	8.5	7.0	6.2	4.1	4.3	4.8	3.4	4.5	4.5	4.0
Africa	10.8	5.2	7.3	6.1	5.2	4.7	5.3	5.0	4.3	5.3	5.0	4.0
Central and eastern Europe	49.3	6.2	17.6	8.8	8.2	3.3	6.2	5.5	3.3	2.3	3.7	3.2
Commonwealth of Independent States[1]	. . .	15.3	46.8	17.4	10.5	23.5	18.7	11.6	5.9	5.6	6.8	5.7
Developing Asia	8.6	4.7	7.2	6.2	8.3	4.2	2.5	3.8	3.3	3.2	4.6	3.8
Middle East	7.2	2.8	6.8	3.3	3.0	2.1	1.0	1.7	1.6	2.3	3.5	2.5
Western Hemisphere	13.3	4.7	7.1	6.5	4.7	3.5	4.8	3.2	5.0	4.5	4.0	3.5

[1]Mongolia, which is not a member of the Commonwealth of Independent States, is included in this group for reasons of geography and similarities in economic structure.

Table 11. Other Emerging Market and Developing Countries—by Country: Consumer Prices[1]
(Annual percent change)

	Average 1986–95	1996	1997	1998	1999	2000	2001	2002	2003	2004	2005
Africa	**27.4**	**28.2**	**13.5**	**8.9**	**11.6**	**13.1**	**12.0**	**9.7**	**10.3**	**8.4**	**8.1**
Algeria	17.7	18.7	5.7	5.0	2.6	0.3	4.2	1.4	2.6	5.4	4.6
Angola	184.6	4,146.0	221.5	107.4	248.2	325.0	152.6	108.9	98.3	56.1	16.5
Benin	5.9	4.9	3.8	5.8	0.3	4.2	4.0	2.4	1.5	2.6	3.0
Botswana	13.1	10.3	9.4	7.6	6.9	7.9	7.2	5.5	4.7	4.5	4.5
Burkina Faso	2.8	6.1	2.4	5.0	–1.1	–0.3	4.9	2.3	2.0	1.9	2.0
Burundi	8.9	26.4	31.1	12.5	3.4	24.3	9.3	–1.3	10.7	9.1	7.6
Cameroon[2]	4.5	6.6	5.2	—	2.9	0.8	2.8	6.3	0.6	0.8	1.9
Cape Verde	7.2	6.0	8.6	4.4	3.9	–2.4	3.8	1.8	1.2	1.0	2.0
Central African Republic	2.5	3.7	1.6	–1.9	–1.4	3.2	3.8	2.3	4.2	0.8	2.5
Chad	2.1	11.3	5.6	4.3	–8.4	3.8	12.4	5.2	–1.8	–5.0	3.0
Comoros	2.0	2.0	3.0	3.5	6.3	4.5	5.9	3.3	4.5	3.5	3.5
Congo, Dem. Rep. of	648.2	617.0	199.0	29.1	284.9	550.0	357.3	25.3	12.8	5.0	5.0
Congo, Rep. of	2.9	7.4	13.1	1.8	3.1	0.4	0.8	3.1	1.2	2.0	2.0
Côte d'Ivoire	6.7	2.7	4.2	4.5	0.7	2.5	4.4	3.1	3.3	1.5	2.0
Djibouti	6.3	3.5	2.5	2.2	2.0	2.4	1.8	0.6	2.0	2.0	2.0
Equatorial Guinea	2.5	6.0	4.5	3.7	6.0	6.5	6.0	8.8	7.6	8.0	6.0
Eritrea	. . .	10.3	3.7	9.5	8.4	19.9	14.6	16.9	22.7	21.5	20.5
Ethiopia	7.6	0.9	–6.4	3.6	4.8	6.2	–5.2	–7.2	15.1	9.6	5.4
Gabon	4.1	4.5	4.1	2.3	–0.7	0.4	2.1	0.2	2.1	2.0	2.0
Gambia, The	14.3	4.8	3.1	1.1	3.8	0.9	4.5	8.6	17.0	14.5	6.2
Ghana	28.9	46.6	27.9	14.6	12.4	25.2	32.9	14.8	26.7	10.8	6.0
Guinea	21.9	3.0	1.9	5.1	4.6	6.8	5.4	3.0	12.9	16.6	13.8
Guinea-Bissau	53.1	50.7	49.1	8.0	–2.1	8.6	3.3	3.3	3.0	3.0	3.0
Kenya	15.9	8.9	11.9	6.7	5.8	10.0	5.8	2.0	9.8	8.1	4.0
Lesotho	13.3	9.1	8.5	7.8	8.6	6.1	6.9	11.2	7.6	6.0	5.5
Madagascar	19.1	19.8	4.5	6.2	9.9	8.8	6.9	16.2	–1.1	10.5	5.0
Malawi	25.5	37.7	9.1	29.8	44.8	29.6	27.2	14.9	9.6	19.9	20.0
Mali	2.1	6.5	–0.7	4.1	–1.2	–0.7	5.2	5.0	–1.3	2.6	3.0
Mauritania	7.2	4.7	4.5	8.0	4.1	3.3	4.7	3.9	5.5	7.0	3.8
Mauritius	7.2	5.9	7.9	5.4	7.9	5.3	4.4	6.4	5.0	3.9	4.0
Morocco	5.4	3.0	1.0	2.7	0.7	1.9	0.6	2.8	1.2	2.0	2.0
Mozambique, Rep. of	54.6	44.6	6.4	0.6	2.9	12.7	9.0	16.8	13.5	12.9	7.8
Namibia	12.5	8.0	8.8	6.2	8.6	9.3	9.3	11.3	7.2	5.2	6.4
Niger	2.5	5.3	2.9	4.5	–2.3	2.9	4.0	2.7	–1.6	0.4	2.0
Nigeria	33.2	29.3	8.5	10.0	6.6	6.9	18.0	13.7	14.4	15.8	11.4
Rwanda	13.9	13.4	11.7	6.8	–2.4	3.9	3.4	2.0	7.4	6.9	4.0
São Tomé and Príncipe	35.7	42.0	69.0	42.1	12.2	12.2	9.2	10.1	9.8	13.3	14.5
Senegal	3.4	2.8	1.6	1.2	0.8	0.9	3.0	2.3	—	0.8	2.2
Seychelles	1.8	–1.1	0.6	2.7	6.3	6.2	6.0	0.2	7.0	5.0	4.0
Sierra Leone	64.7	23.1	14.6	36.0	34.1	–0.9	2.6	–3.7	8.2	12.4	4.7
South Africa	13.3	7.3	8.6	6.9	5.2	5.4	5.7	9.2	5.8	2.6	5.7
Sudan	78.0	132.8	46.7	17.1	16.0	8.0	4.9	8.3	7.7	6.5	6.0
Swaziland	12.2	6.4	7.9	7.5	5.9	9.9	7.5	11.9	7.3	4.9	7.7
Tanzania	29.1	20.5	15.4	13.2	9.0	6.2	5.2	4.6	4.5	4.3	4.0
Togo	5.2	4.6	5.3	1.0	–0.1	1.9	3.9	3.1	–0.9	2.5	2.5
Tunisia	6.5	3.7	3.7	3.1	2.7	3.0	1.9	2.8	2.8	3.4	2.7
Uganda	62.9	7.7	5.8	0.2	5.8	4.5	–2.0	5.7	5.1	3.5	3.5
Zambia	86.9	43.1	24.4	24.5	26.8	26.1	21.7	22.2	21.5	18.5	17.4
Zimbabwe	19.9	21.4	18.8	31.7	58.5	55.9	76.7	140.0	431.7	350.0	450.0

Table 11 *(continued)*

	Average 1986–95	1996	1997	1998	1999	2000	2001	2002	2003	2004	2005
Central and eastern Europe[3]	**59.2**	**37.3**	**52.0**	**33.0**	**23.3**	**23.0**	**19.6**	**14.8**	**9.2**	**6.9**	**5.9**
Albania	26.9	12.7	32.1	20.9	0.4	—	3.1	5.2	2.4	3.4	3.0
Bosnia and Herzegovina	. . .	–11.5	5.6	–0.4	2.9	5.0	3.2	0.3	0.2	0.9	1.7
Bulgaria	51.0	123.0	1,061.2	18.8	2.6	10.4	7.5	5.8	2.3	6.3	3.6
Croatia	. . .	3.5	3.6	5.7	4.1	6.2	4.9	2.3	1.5	2.5	3.5
Czech Republic	. . .	8.8	8.5	10.6	2.1	3.9	4.8	1.8	0.1	3.2	3.0
Estonia	. . .	23.1	11.2	8.2	3.3	4.0	5.8	3.6	1.3	3.0	2.5
Hungary	19.9	23.5	18.3	14.3	10.0	9.8	9.2	5.3	4.7	6.9	4.4
Latvia	. . .	17.6	8.4	4.6	2.4	2.6	2.5	1.9	2.9	5.8	3.5
Lithuania	. . .	24.7	8.8	5.1	0.8	1.0	1.3	0.3	–1.2	0.6	2.5
Macedonia, FYR	. . .	2.3	2.6	–0.1	–2.0	6.2	5.3	2.4	1.2	2.0	3.0
Malta	2.4	2.0	3.1	2.4	2.1	2.1	3.2	2.2	1.3	3.0	2.0
Poland	77.9	19.9	14.9	11.8	7.3	10.1	5.5	1.9	0.8	3.7	3.8
Romania	71.3	38.8	154.8	59.1	45.8	45.7	34.5	22.5	15.3	11.5	7.2
Serbia and Montenegro	. . .	. . .	. . .	29.5	42.1	69.9	91.1	21.2	11.3	7.9	6.9
Slovak Republic	. . .	5.8	6.1	6.7	10.7	12.0	7.3	3.3	8.5	7.7	3.0
Slovenia	. . .	9.9	8.4	7.9	6.2	8.9	8.4	7.5	5.6	3.7	3.2
Turkey	66.0	82.3	85.7	84.6	64.9	54.9	54.4	45.0	25.3	11.4	10.8
Commonwealth of Independent States[3,4]	**. . .**	**55.5**	**18.1**	**23.9**	**69.6**	**24.5**	**20.3**	**13.8**	**12.0**	**9.9**	**8.7**
Russia	. . .	47.7	14.8	27.7	85.7	20.8	21.5	15.8	13.7	10.3	8.9
Excluding Russia	. . .	75.8	26.5	15.9	36.9	34.0	17.6	9.3	8.3	8.8	8.2
Armenia	. . .	18.7	14.0	8.6	0.6	–0.8	3.1	1.1	4.8	3.0	3.0
Azerbaijan	. . .	19.8	3.7	–0.8	–8.5	1.8	1.5	2.8	2.2	5.3	5.0
Belarus	. . .	52.7	63.8	73.0	293.7	168.6	61.1	42.6	28.4	19.5	17.4
Georgia	. . .	39.3	7.0	3.6	19.1	4.0	4.7	5.6	4.8	5.8	4.8
Kazakhstan	. . .	39.1	17.4	7.3	8.4	13.4	8.3	5.9	6.4	6.8	6.7
Kyrgyz Republic	. . .	32.0	23.4	10.5	35.9	18.7	6.9	2.1	3.1	4.5	4.6
Moldova	. . .	23.5	11.8	7.7	39.3	31.3	9.8	5.3	11.7	10.7	5.8
Mongolia	44.4	46.8	36.6	9.4	7.6	11.6	11.6	6.3	0.9	5.0	5.0
Tajikistan	. . .	418.2	88.0	43.2	27.5	32.9	38.6	12.2	16.4	7.2	5.7
Turkmenistan	. . .	992.4	83.7	16.8	23.5	8.0	11.6	8.8	5.6	5.0	5.1
Ukraine	. . .	80.2	15.9	10.6	22.7	28.2	12.0	0.8	5.2	8.3	8.1
Uzbekistan	. . .	54.0	70.9	16.7	44.6	49.5	47.5	44.3	14.8	11.8	10.5

Table 11 *(continued)*

	Average 1986–95	1996	1997	1998	1999	2000	2001	2002	2003	2004	2005
Developing Asia	**11.2**	**8.2**	**4.9**	**7.8**	**2.5**	**1.9**	**2.7**	**2.1**	**2.6**	**4.5**	**4.1**
Afghanistan, I.S. of	. . .	. . .	. . .	. . .	. . .	. . .	. . .	. . .	. . .	. . .	. . .
Bangladesh	8.1	2.5	5.0	8.6	6.2	2.2	1.5	3.8	5.4	6.4	6.1
Bhutan	10.1	7.4	9.0	9.0	9.2	3.6	3.6	2.7	1.8	3.0	4.0
Brunei Darussalam	. . .	2.0	1.7	–0.4	—	1.2	0.6	–2.3	0.3	1.0	1.3
Cambodia	. . .	7.1	8.0	14.8	4.0	–0.8	0.2	3.3	1.2	2.0	2.9
China	11.7	8.3	2.8	–0.8	–1.4	0.4	0.7	–0.8	1.2	4.0	3.0
Fiji	5.1	4.9	3.4	5.9	2.0	1.1	4.3	1.9	2.0	2.5	2.5
India	9.4	9.0	7.2	13.2	4.7	4.0	3.8	4.3	3.8	4.7	5.0
Indonesia	8.2	7.9	6.2	58.0	20.7	3.8	11.5	11.8	6.8	6.5	6.5
Kiribati	2.7	–1.5	2.2	3.7	1.8	0.4	6.0	3.2	1.4	2.3	2.5
Lao PDR	12.6	19.1	19.5	90.1	128.4	23.2	7.8	10.6	15.5	11.0	5.6
Malaysia	2.7	3.5	2.7	5.3	2.7	1.5	1.4	1.8	1.1	2.2	2.5
Maldives	10.4	6.2	7.6	–1.4	3.0	–1.2	0.7	0.9	–2.8	0.3	2.8
Myanmar	23.7	20.0	33.9	49.1	10.9	–1.7	34.5	58.1	37.0	27.5	37.5
Nepal	11.7	7.2	8.1	8.3	11.4	3.4	2.4	2.9	4.7	3.9	3.8
Pakistan	9.0	10.4	11.4	6.5	4.1	4.4	3.1	3.2	2.9	4.6	4.5
Papua New Guinea	6.1	11.6	3.9	13.6	14.9	15.6	9.3	11.8	14.7	7.4	6.0
Philippines	8.9	9.0	5.9	9.8	6.7	4.3	6.1	3.1	3.0	5.4	6.8
Samoa	5.4	5.4	6.9	2.2	0.3	1.0	3.8	8.1	4.2	2.4	2.3
Solomon Islands	12.3	11.8	8.0	12.3	8.0	6.9	7.6	9.4	10.1	5.6	2.5
Sri Lanka	11.4	15.9	9.6	9.4	4.7	6.2	14.2	9.6	6.3	6.4	9.4
Thailand	4.4	5.9	5.6	8.1	0.3	1.6	1.7	0.6	1.8	2.7	1.8
Timor-Leste, Dem. Rep. of	. . .	. . .	. . .	. . .	. . .	63.6	3.6	4.8	7.1	4.1	3.2
Tonga	8.2	2.7	–31.2	3.0	3.9	5.3	6.9	10.4	11.1	11.0	10.0
Vanuatu	6.0	0.9	2.8	3.3	2.2	2.5	3.7	1.1	2.8	3.2	3.0
Vietnam	101.8	5.7	3.2	7.7	4.2	–1.6	–0.4	4.0	3.2	6.0	3.5
Middle East	**17.7**	**14.4**	**11.0**	**10.5**	**11.0**	**8.5**	**7.1**	**7.5**	**8.0**	**9.2**	**8.7**
Bahrain	0.3	–0.1	4.6	–0.4	–1.3	–3.6	–1.2	–0.5	0.6	1.0	1.2
Egypt	17.0	7.1	6.2	4.7	3.8	2.8	2.4	2.4	3.2	5.2	5.7
Iran, I.R. of	25.5	23.2	17.3	18.1	20.1	12.6	11.4	15.8	15.6	15.6	15.0
Iraq	. . .	. . .	. . .	. . .	. . .	. . .	. . .	. . .	. . .	. . .	. . .
Jordan	4.8	6.5	3.0	3.1	0.6	0.7	1.8	1.8	2.3	3.5	1.8
Kuwait	7.9	3.6	0.7	0.1	3.0	1.8	1.7	1.4	1.2	1.7	1.6
Lebanon	83.2	8.9	7.7	4.5	0.2	–0.4	–0.4	1.8	1.3	3.0	2.0
Libya	7.1	4.0	3.6	3.7	2.6	–2.9	–8.8	–9.9	–2.1	2.1	3.0
Oman	2.8	0.5	–0.5	–0.5	0.5	–1.2	–1.1	–0.6	–0.4	1.0	0.7
Qatar	2.8	8.8	1.1	2.9	2.2	1.7	1.4	1.0	2.3	3.5	3.0
Saudi Arabia	0.7	0.9	–0.4	–0.2	–1.3	–0.6	–0.8	–0.6	0.5	2.5	0.8
Syrian Arab Republic	20.8	8.9	1.9	–1.0	–3.7	–3.9	3.0	0.6	5.0	5.0	4.5
United Arab Emirates	4.4	3.0	2.9	2.0	2.1	1.4	2.8	3.1	2.8	3.4	2.1
Yemen	35.2	40.0	4.6	11.5	8.0	10.9	11.9	12.2	10.8	15.3	15.2

Table 11 ***(concluded)***

	Average 1986–95	1996	1997	1998	1999	2000	2001	2002	2003	2004	2005
Western Hemisphere	**196.2**	**19.5**	**11.5**	**8.5**	**7.3**	**6.7**	**6.0**	**9.0**	**10.6**	**6.5**	**6.1**
Antigua and Barbuda	4.2	3.0	0.2	3.4	1.1	0.7	1.0	2.2	2.5	2.5	2.5
Argentina	212.8	0.2	0.5	0.9	–1.2	–0.9	–1.1	25.9	13.4	4.8	7.1
Bahamas, The	4.4	1.4	0.5	1.3	1.3	1.6	2.0	2.1	2.8	2.5	2.0
Barbados	3.4	2.1	7.7	–1.3	1.6	2.4	2.8	0.2	1.5	1.5	2.0
Belize	2.3	6.4	1.0	–0.9	–1.2	0.6	1.2	2.2	2.5	2.7	2.2
Bolivia	28.0	12.4	4.7	7.7	2.2	4.6	1.6	0.9	3.3	3.9	3.5
Brazil	716.1	16.0	6.9	3.2	4.9	7.1	6.8	8.4	14.8	6.6	5.9
Chile	16.6	7.4	6.1	5.1	3.3	3.8	3.6	2.5	2.8	1.1	2.9
Colombia	24.8	20.8	18.5	18.7	10.9	9.2	8.0	6.3	7.1	6.0	5.0
Costa Rica	18.1	17.5	13.2	11.7	10.0	11.0	11.3	9.2	9.4	10.2	9.5
Dominica	3.4	1.7	2.4	1.0	1.2	–7.3	1.6	0.1	1.6	2.3	1.5
Dominican Republic	22.0	5.4	8.3	4.8	6.5	7.7	8.9	5.2	27.4	55.5	18.6
Ecuador	–0.7	—	4.1	–0.6	–29.2	–7.7	37.7	12.6	7.9	3.2	2.7
El Salvador	18.2	9.8	4.5	2.5	–1.0	4.3	1.4	2.8	2.5	4.5	2.8
Grenada	2.6	2.8	1.3	1.4	0.5	2.2	3.2	3.0	2.5	2.5	2.5
Guatemala	16.1	11.0	9.2	6.6	4.9	5.1	8.9	6.3	5.9	7.0	5.0
Guyana	36.2	7.1	3.6	4.7	8.5	5.9	1.9	5.4	6.0	4.5	3.5
Haiti	15.8	21.9	16.2	12.7	8.1	11.5	16.8	8.7	32.5	28.3	17.5
Honduras	14.6	23.8	20.2	13.7	11.6	11.0	9.7	7.7	7.7	7.7	6.8
Jamaica	27.8	21.5	9.1	8.1	6.3	7.7	8.0	6.5	7.0	7.0	7.0
Mexico	41.2	34.4	20.6	15.9	16.6	9.5	6.4	5.0	4.5	4.4	4.0
Netherlands Antilles	2.6	3.4	3.1	1.2	0.8	5.0	1.8	0.4	1.9	2.5	2.5
Nicaragua	811.9	7.7	11.2	11.6	9.2	13.0	11.2	11.5	7.4	4.0	5.2
Panama	0.8	1.3	1.3	0.6	1.3	1.4	0.3	1.0	1.4	2.1	2.3
Paraguay	23.0	9.8	7.0	11.6	6.8	9.0	7.3	10.5	14.2	5.2	5.3
Peru	288.3	11.8	6.5	6.0	3.7	3.7	–0.1	1.5	2.5	3.5	2.5
St. Kitts and Nevis	2.4	2.0	8.7	3.7	3.4	2.1	2.1	2.1	1.4	1.5	1.6
St. Lucia	3.6	0.9	—	2.8	3.5	3.6	2.1	–0.2	1.0	1.0	1.0
St. Vincent and the Grenadines	3.1	4.4	0.5	2.1	1.0	0.2	0.8	1.0	0.3	2.0	2.0
Suriname	66.7	–0.8	7.3	19.1	98.7	58.6	39.8	15.5	23.1	9.9	10.0
Trinidad and Tobago	8.1	3.3	3.6	–0.5	3.4	5.6	3.2	4.3	3.0	4.0	3.0
Uruguay	69.3	28.3	19.8	10.8	5.7	4.8	4.4	14.0	19.4	9.8	9.3
Venezuela	40.6	99.9	50.0	35.8	23.6	16.2	12.5	22.4	31.1	23.7	31.3

[1]For many countries, figures for recent years are IMF staff estimates. Data for some countries are for fiscal years.

[2]The percent changes in 2002 are calculated over a period of 18 months, reflecting a change in the fiscal year cycle (from July–June to January–December).

[3]For many countries, inflation for the earlier years is measured on the basis of a retail price index. Consumer price indices with a broader and more up-to-date coverage are typically used for more recent years.

[4]Mongolia, which is not a member of the Commonwealth of Independent States, is included in this group for reasons of geography and similarities in economic structure.

Table 12. Summary Financial Indicators

(Percent)

	1996	1997	1998	1999	2000	2001	2002	2003	2004	2005
Advanced economies										
Central government fiscal balance[1]										
Advanced economies	–2.8	–1.6	–1.1	–1.1	0.2	–1.0	–2.5	–2.9	–3.2	–2.8
United States	–1.8	–0.6	0.5	1.2	2.0	0.5	–2.4	–3.3	–4.0	–3.3
Euro area	–3.7	–2.6	–2.5	–1.7	–0.4	–1.6	–2.0	–2.3	–2.2	–2.0
Japan	–4.4	–4.0	–3.8	–8.5	–6.9	–6.3	–7.0	–6.8	–6.5	–6.3
Other advanced economies[2]	–1.6	–0.4	–0.1	0.4	2.3	0.6	–0.3	–0.7	–1.0	–0.8
General government fiscal balance[1]										
Advanced economies	–3.4	–1.9	–1.4	–1.0	—	–1.5	–3.4	–3.9	–3.9	–3.4
United States	–2.5	–1.1	0.1	0.6	1.3	–0.7	–4.0	–4.6	–4.9	–4.3
Euro area	–4.3	–2.7	–2.3	–1.3	–0.9	–1.7	–2.3	–2.8	–2.9	–2.5
Japan	–5.1	–3.8	–5.5	–7.2	–7.5	–6.1	–7.9	–8.2	–6.9	–6.5
Other advanced economies[2]	–2.4	–0.6	–0.1	0.6	2.6	0.4	–0.7	–1.2	–1.3	–0.9
General government structural balance[3]										
Advanced economies	–3.1	–1.8	–1.5	–1.2	–1.0	–1.5	–2.9	–3.1	–3.3	–3.0
Growth of broad money[4]										
Advanced economies	4.9	5.0	6.7	5.9	5.0	8.7	5.7	5.2	. . .	. . .
United States	4.6	5.6	8.4	6.2	6.1	10.2	6.7	5.3	. . .	. . .
Euro area[5]	4.1	4.5	4.8	5.4	4.2	11.2	6.7	6.5	. . .	. . .
Japan	3.0	3.9	4.0	2.7	1.9	3.3	1.8	1.6	. . .	. . .
Other advanced economies[2]	9.6	6.1	9.4	9.0	6.9	7.3	6.2	6.3	. . .	. . .
Short-term interest rates[6]										
United States	5.1	5.2	4.9	4.8	6.0	3.5	1.6	1.0	1.3	2.8
Euro area[5]	5.2	4.4	4.1	3.0	4.4	4.2	3.3	2.4	2.4	3.1
Japan	0.3	0.3	0.2	0.0	0.2	0.0	0.0	0.0	0.0	0.2
LIBOR	5.6	5.9	5.6	5.5	6.6	3.7	1.9	1.2	1.6	3.4
Other emerging market and developing countries										
Central government fiscal balance[1]										
Weighted average	–2.6	–2.9	–3.8	–3.8	–2.9	–3.2	–3.4	–2.8	–2.2	–1.9
Median	–2.5	–2.5	–3.0	–3.2	–2.7	–3.7	–3.7	–2.9	–2.7	–2.3
General government fiscal balance[1]										
Weighted average	–3.5	–3.8	–4.8	–4.8	–3.6	–4.0	–4.4	–3.6	–2.8	–2.5
Median	–2.9	–2.4	–3.3	–3.4	–3.2	–3.6	–4.0	–2.9	–2.7	–2.2
Growth of broad money										
Weighted average	29.9	18.3	17.0	18.2	15.0	14.6	15.8	17.0	14.4	12.5
Median	16.7	17.2	11.1	13.2	13.6	14.0	13.0	12.1	10.7	10.0

[1]Percent of GDP.

[2]In this table, "other advanced economies" means advanced economies excluding the United States, euro area countries, and Japan.

[3]Percent of potential GDP.

[4]M2, defined as M1 plus quasi-money, except for Japan, for which the data are based on M2 plus certificates of deposit (CDs). Quasi-money is essentially private term deposits and other notice deposits. The United States also includes money market mutual fund balances, money market deposit accounts, overnight repurchase agreements, and overnight Eurodollars issued to U.S. residents by foreign branches of U.S. banks. For the euro area, M3 is composed of M2 plus marketable instruments held by euro-area residents, which comprise repurchase agreements, money market fund shares/units, money market paper, and debt securities up to two years.

[5]Excludes Greece prior to 2001.

[6]For the United States, three-month treasury bills; for Japan, three-month certificates of deposit; for the euro area, a weighted average of national three-month money market interest rates through 1998 and three-month EURIBOR thereafter; and for LIBOR, London interbank offered rate on six-month U.S. dollar deposits.

Table 13. Advanced Economies: General and Central Government Fiscal Balances and Balances Excluding Social Security Transactions[1]

(Percent of GDP)

	1996	1997	1998	1999	2000	2001	2002	2003	2004	2005
General government fiscal balance										
Advanced economies	**–3.4**	**–1.9**	**–1.4**	**–1.0**	**—**	**–1.5**	**–3.4**	**–3.9**	**–3.9**	**–3.4**
United States	–2.5	–1.1	0.1	0.6	1.3	–0.7	–4.0	–4.6	–4.9	–4.3
Euro area	–4.3	–2.7	–2.3	–1.3	–0.9	–1.7	–2.3	–2.8	–2.9	–2.5
Germany	–3.4	–2.7	–2.2	–1.5	1.3	–2.8	–3.7	–3.8	–3.9	–3.3
France[2]	–4.1	–3.0	–2.7	–1.8	–1.4	–1.4	–3.2	–4.1	–3.4	–2.8
Italy	–7.1	–2.7	–2.8	–1.7	–0.6	–2.6	–2.3	–2.4	–2.9	–2.8
Spain	–4.9	–3.2	–3.0	–1.2	–0.8	–0.3	0.1	0.3	–0.7	—
Netherlands	–1.8	–1.1	–0.8	0.7	2.2	–0.1	–1.9	–3.2	–3.0	–2.7
Belgium	–3.8	–2.0	–0.8	–0.5	0.1	0.5	—	0.2	–0.2	–0.4
Austria[3]	–3.8	–2.0	–2.5	–2.4	–1.7	0.1	–0.4	–1.4	–1.2	–1.8
Finland	–2.9	–1.3	1.6	2.2	7.1	5.2	4.3	2.1	2.5	2.5
Greece	–7.4	–4.0	–2.5	–1.8	–2.0	–1.4	–1.2	–3.2	–3.4	–3.5
Portugal	–4.0	–3.0	–2.6	–2.8	–2.9	–4.4	–2.7	–2.8	–4.1	–4.0
Ireland[4]	–0.1	1.5	2.3	2.5	4.4	1.1	–0.2	0.2	–0.3	–0.5
Luxembourg	1.9	3.2	3.2	3.7	6.3	6.3	2.7	–0.1	–2.1	–2.7
Japan	–5.1	–3.8	–5.5	–7.2	–7.5	–6.1	–7.9	–8.2	–6.9	–6.5
United Kingdom	–4.2	–2.2	0.1	1.0	3.9	0.8	–1.7	–3.4	–3.0	–2.9
Canada	–2.8	0.2	0.1	1.6	2.9	1.1	0.3	0.6	0.7	0.9
Korea[5]	—	–1.5	–3.9	–3.0	1.1	0.6	2.3	2.8	1.0	0.9
Australia[6]	–1.1	–0.1	0.3	1.4	1.9	0.9	1.0	1.2	0.7	0.5
Taiwan Province of China	–5.1	–3.8	–3.4	–6.0	–4.5	–6.7	–4.3	–4.0	–5.0	–3.4
Sweden	–2.8	–1.0	1.9	2.3	5.1	2.9	–0.3	0.5	0.3	0.6
Switzerland	–2.0	–2.4	–0.4	–0.2	2.2	—	–1.2	–1.9	–2.5	–1.9
Hong Kong SAR	2.1	6.5	–1.8	0.8	–0.6	–5.0	–4.9	–3.3	–4.9	–2.6
Denmark	–1.0	0.4	1.1	3.2	2.5	2.8	1.6	1.2	1.2	1.4
Norway	6.5	7.7	3.6	6.2	15.6	13.6	9.2	8.3	6.6	6.7
Israel	–5.9	–4.5	–3.7	–4.2	–2.1	–4.1	–4.5	–6.4	–4.9	–3.9
Singapore	9.3	9.2	3.6	4.6	8.0	4.8	4.0	5.0	3.7	3.1
New Zealand[7]	2.7	2.2	2.1	1.5	1.3	1.6	1.7	2.9	4.0	3.5
Cyprus	–3.4	–5.3	–4.3	–4.5	–2.4	–2.4	–4.6	–6.3	–5.3	–3.0
Iceland	–1.6	—	0.5	2.4	2.5	0.2	–1.1	–1.4	0.2	1.1
Memorandum										
Major advanced economies	–3.6	–2.0	–1.5	–1.2	–0.2	–1.8	–4.0	–4.6	–4.5	–4.0
Newly industrialized Asian economies	–1.6	0.2	–2.2	–3.2	–2.1	–4.9	–3.4	–2.7	–3.9	–2.4
Fiscal balance excluding social security transactions										
United States	–2.7	–1.5	–0.6	–0.4	0.2	–1.5	–4.4	–5.0	–5.2	–4.7
Japan	–6.8	–5.5	–6.9	–8.2	–8.0	–6.2	–7.7	–7.7	–6.4	–5.9
Germany	–3.1	–2.8	–2.4	–1.8	1.3	–2.6	–3.4	–3.5	–3.5	–3.1
France	–3.6	–2.6	–2.6	–2.1	–1.9	–1.7	–3.0	–3.4	–2.4	–2.1
Italy	–5.3	–0.7	1.3	2.7	3.4	1.3	1.9	1.6	1.2	1.3
Canada	—	3.0	2.7	3.9	4.8	2.8	1.8	2.0	2.1	2.3

Table 13 *(concluded)*

	1996	1997	1998	1999	2000	2001	2002	2003	2004	2005
Central government fiscal balance										
Advanced economies	**–2.8**	**–1.6**	**–1.1**	**–1.1**	**0.2**	**–1.0**	**–2.5**	**–2.9**	**–3.2**	**–2.8**
United States[8]	–1.8	–0.6	0.5	1.2	2.0	0.5	–2.4	–3.3	–4.0	–3.3
Euro area	–3.7	–2.6	–2.5	–1.7	–0.4	–1.6	–2.0	–2.3	–2.2	–2.0
Germany[9]	–1.9	–1.6	–1.8	–1.5	1.4	–1.4	–1.7	–1.9	–1.8	–1.7
France	–3.7	–3.6	–3.9	–2.5	–2.4	–2.2	–3.9	–4.0	–3.1	–2.7
Italy	–7.0	–2.9	–2.7	–1.5	–1.1	–2.8	–2.4	–2.5	–2.7	–2.6
Spain	–3.9	–2.7	–2.4	–1.1	–0.9	–0.5	–0.4	–0.4	–1.5	–0.7
Japan[10]	–4.4	–4.0	–3.8	–8.5	–6.9	–6.3	–7.0	–6.8	–6.5	–6.3
United Kingdom	–4.4	–2.2	0.1	1.0	3.9	0.8	–1.7	–3.4	–3.1	–3.0
Canada	–2.0	0.7	0.8	0.9	1.9	1.3	0.8	0.4	0.6	0.6
Other advanced economies	0.1	0.3	–0.6	–0.2	1.6	0.3	0.1	0.4	–0.5	—
Memorandum										
Major advanced economies	–3.0	–1.7	–1.0	–1.2	0.1	–1.2	–3.0	–3.6	–3.7	–3.3
Newly industrialized Asian economies	1.0	0.8	–1.1	–1.0	0.8	–0.9	–0.5	—	–1.4	–0.7

[1]On a national income accounts basis except as indicated in footnotes. See Box A1 for a summary of the policy assumptions underlying the projections.
[2]Adjusted for valuation changes of the foreign exchange stabilization fund.
[3]Based on ESA95 methodology, according to which swap income is not included.
[4]To maintain comparability, data exclude the impact of discharging future pension liabilities of the formerly state-owned telecommunications company at a cost of 1.8 percent of GDP in 1999.
[5]Data cover the consolidated central government including the social security funds but excluding privatization.
[6]Data exclude net advances (primarily privatization receipts and net policy-related lending).
[7]Government balance is revenue minus expenditure plus balance of state-owned enterprises, excluding privatization receipts.
[8]Data are on a budget basis.
[9]Data are on an administrative basis and exclude social security transactions.
[10]Data are on a national income basis and exclude social security transactions.

Table 14. Advanced Economies: General Government Structural Balances[1]
(Percent of potential GDP)

	1996	1997	1998	1999	2000	2001	2002	2003	2004	2005
Structural balance										
Advanced economies	**–3.1**	**–1.8**	**–1.5**	**–1.2**	**–1.0**	**–1.5**	**–2.9**	**–3.1**	**–3.3**	**–3.0**
United States	–2.1	–1.2	–0.3	–0.1	0.5	–0.6	–3.3	–3.8	–4.4	–3.9
Euro area[2,3]	–3.3	–1.7	–1.9	–1.3	–1.6	–2.1	–2.2	–1.7	–1.7	–1.4
Germany[2,4]	–3.0	–2.0	–1.7	–1.2	–1.6	–2.9	–2.9	–2.2	–2.4	–1.9
France[2]	–2.1	–1.1	–1.8	–1.4	–2.0	–2.1	–3.2	–3.2	–2.6	–2.1
Italy[2]	–6.3	–1.9	–2.8	–1.8	–2.4	–3.1	–2.6	–1.4	–2.1	–1.9
Spain[2]	–3.0	–1.8	–2.3	–1.0	–1.3	–0.8	0.3	0.9	0.8	0.8
Netherlands[2]	–1.4	–1.1	–1.4	–0.7	–0.2	–1.1	–2.5	–2.4	–1.7	–1.3
Belgium[2]	–3.0	–2.0	–0.8	–1.1	–1.7	–0.8	–0.1	–1.0	0.2	–0.1
Austria[2]	–3.7	–1.7	–2.5	–2.7	–2.9	—	0.1	–0.3	–0.1	–1.1
Finland	–1.5	–1.8	—	0.3	6.0	5.2	4.5	2.8	3.0	2.9
Greece	–6.9	–3.9	–2.5	–2.0	–2.5	–2.5	–1.4	–3.0	–3.2	–3.1
Portugal[2]	–3.3	–2.7	–2.8	–3.3	–3.9	–4.6	–2.0	–0.8	–1.8	–1.8
Ireland[2]	0.8	0.7	1.9	0.9	2.2	–0.7	–1.8	0.5	–0.2	–0.5
Japan	–5.5	–4.3	–5.1	–6.3	–6.9	–5.1	–6.2	–6.9	–6.6	–6.4
United Kingdom[2]	–4.2	–2.3	–0.2	0.9	1.3	0.2	–1.9	–3.2	–2.8	–2.9
Canada	–2.0	0.7	0.5	1.4	2.1	1.0	0.3	1.1	1.1	1.0
Other advanced economies	–1.6	–1.0	–0.7	—	0.7	0.3	–0.4	0.4	0.5	0.5
Australia[5]	–2.3	–2.0	–1.8	–0.9	–0.5	–0.8	–0.4	0.7	0.8	0.8
Sweden	–1.1	0.6	2.7	1.7	4.0	2.8	–0.3	1.0	1.0	1.1
Denmark	–1.1	–0.1	0.8	2.2	2.2	2.4	1.6	2.0	1.8	1.6
Norway[6]	–3.1	–2.6	–3.9	–3.1	–1.8	–1.8	–3.0	–3.0	–1.8	–1.8
New Zealand[7]	1.2	1.5	1.7	0.9	1.2	2.0	3.1	3.9	3.7	3.4
Memorandum										
Major advanced economies	–3.2	–1.9	–1.5	–1.3	–1.2	–1.7	–3.4	–3.6	–3.9	–3.5

[1]On a national income accounts basis. The structural budget position is defined as the actual budget deficit (or surplus) less the effects of cyclical deviations of output from potential output. Because of the margin of uncertainty that attaches to estimates of cyclical gaps and to tax and expenditure elasticities with respect to national income, indicators of structural budget positions should be interpreted as broad orders of magnitude. Moreover, it is important to note that changes in structural budget balances are not necessarily attributable to policy changes but may reflect the built-in momentum of existing expenditure programs. In the period beyond that for which specific consolidation programs exist, it is assumed that the structural deficit remains unchanged.

[2]Excludes one-off receipts from the sale of mobile telephone licenses equivalent to 2.5 percent of GDP in 2000 for Germany, 0.1 percent of GDP in 2001 and 2002 for France, 1.2 percent of GDP in 2000 for Italy, 2.4 percent of GDP in 2000 for the United Kingdom, 0.1 percent of GDP in 2000 for Spain, 0.7 percent of GDP in 2000 for the Netherlands, 0.2 percent of GDP in 2001 for Belgium, 0.4 percent of GDP in 2000 for Austria, 0.3 percent of GDP in 2000 for Portugal, and 0.2 percent of GDP in 2002 for Ireland. Also excludes one-off receipts from sizable asset transactions.

[3]Excludes Luxembourg.

[4]The estimate of the fiscal impulse for 1995 is affected by the assumption by the federal government of the debt of the Treuhandanstalt and various other agencies, which were formerly held outside the general government sector. At the public sector level, there would be an estimated withdrawal of fiscal impulse amounting to just over 1 percent of GDP.

[5]Excludes commonwealth government privatization receipts.

[6]Excludes oil.

[7]Government balance is revenue minus expenditure plus balance of state-owned enterprises, excluding privatization receipts.

Table 15. Advanced Economies: Monetary Aggregates[1]

(Annual percent change)

	1996	1997	1998	1999	2000	2001	2002	2003
Narrow money[2]								
Advanced economies	**4.9**	**4.5**	**5.8**	**8.2**	**2.6**	**9.8**	**9.1**	**7.7**
United States	–4.4	–1.2	2.1	1.9	–1.7	7.0	3.3	6.6
Euro area[3]	8.0	7.3	10.6	11.0	5.4	9.7	9.9	9.6
Japan	9.7	8.6	5.0	11.7	3.5	13.7	23.5	4.5
United Kingdom	6.7	6.4	5.3	12.2	4.5	8.0	6.1	7.2
Canada	17.8	10.6	8.7	8.9	14.4	15.3	4.6	10.0
Memorandum								
Newly industrialized Asian economies	5.8	–4.0	0.9	19.8	4.6	11.4	13.4	13.9
Broad money[4]								
Advanced economies	**4.9**	**5.0**	**6.7**	**5.9**	**5.0**	**8.7**	**5.7**	**5.2**
United States	4.6	5.6	8.4	6.2	6.1	10.2	6.7	5.3
Euro area[3]	4.1	4.5	4.8	5.4	4.2	11.2	6.7	6.5
Japan	3.0	3.9	4.0	2.7	1.9	3.3	1.8	1.6
United Kingdom	9.6	5.7	8.3	4.1	8.4	6.6	7.0	6.0
Canada	2.1	–1.3	1.4	4.3	6.9	5.9	5.0	6.0
Memorandum								
Newly industrialized Asian economies	12.7	11.6	20.0	17.3	14.4	7.3	5.7	6.8

[1]Based on end-of-period data.

[2]M1 except for the United Kingdom, where M0 is used here as a measure of narrow money; it comprises notes in circulation plus bankers' operational deposits. M1 is generally currency in circulation plus private demand deposits. In addition, the United States includes traveler's checks of nonbank issues and other checkable deposits and excludes private sector float and demand deposits of banks. Canada excludes private sector float.

[3]Excludes Greece prior to 2001.

[4]M2, defined as M1 plus quasi-money, except for Japan, and the United Kingdom, for which the data are based on M2 plus certificates of deposit (CDs), and M4, respectively. Quasi-money is essentially private term deposits and other notice deposits. The United States also includes money market mutual fund balances, money market deposit accounts, overnight repurchase agreements, and overnight Eurodollars issued to U.S. residents by foreign branches of U.S. banks. For the United Kingdom, M4 is composed of non-interest-bearing M1, private sector interest-bearing sterling sight bank deposits, private sector sterling time bank deposits, private sector holdings of sterling bank CDs, private sector holdings of building society shares and deposits, and sterling CDs less building society of banks deposits and bank CDs and notes and coins. For the euro area, M3 is composed of M2 plus marketable instruments held by euro-area residents, which comprise repurchase agreements, money market fund shares/units, money market paper, and debt securities up to two years.

Table 16. Advanced Economies: Interest Rates

(Percent a year)

	1996	1997	1998	1999	2000	2001	2002	2003	August 2004
Policy-related interest rate[1]									
United States	5.3	5.5	4.7	5.3	6.4	1.8	1.2	1.0	1.4
Euro area[2]	. . .	. . .	. . .	3.0	4.8	3.3	2.8	2.0	2.0
Japan	0.4	0.4	0.3	0.0	0.2	0.0	0.0	0.0	0.0
United Kingdom	5.9	7.3	6.3	5.5	6.0	4.0	4.0	3.8	4.8
Canada	3.0	4.3	5.0	4.8	5.8	2.3	2.8	2.8	2.0
Short-term interest rate[3]									
Advanced economies	**4.3**	**4.1**	**4.1**	**3.4**	**4.4**	**3.2**	**2.0**	**1.6**	**1.9**
United States	5.1	5.2	4.9	4.8	6.0	3.5	1.6	1.0	1.5
Euro area[2]	5.2	4.4	4.1	3.0	4.4	4.2	3.3	2.4	2.1
Japan	0.3	0.3	0.2	0.0	0.2	0.0	0.0	0.0	0.0
United Kingdom	6.1	6.9	7.4	5.5	6.1	5.0	4.0	3.7	4.9
Canada	4.3	3.2	4.7	4.7	5.5	3.9	2.6	2.9	2.1
Memorandum									
Newly industrialized Asian economies	8.7	9.3	10.5	4.6	4.7	3.3	0.6	3.1	3.3
Long-term interest rate[4]									
Advanced economies	**6.1**	**5.5**	**4.5**	**4.7**	**5.1**	**4.4**	**4.2**	**3.7**	**4.0**
United States	6.4	6.4	5.3	5.6	6.0	5.0	4.6	4.0	4.3
Euro area[2]	7.3	6.1	4.8	4.7	5.5	5.0	4.9	4.2	4.2
Japan	3.0	2.1	1.3	1.7	1.7	1.3	1.3	1.0	1.5
United Kingdom	7.8	6.8	5.1	5.2	5.0	5.0	4.8	4.5	4.9
Canada	7.2	6.1	5.3	5.6	5.9	5.5	5.3	4.8	4.7
Memorandum									
Newly industrialized Asian economies	8.2	9.1	9.5	6.8	6.8	5.3	5.3	5.7	4.3

[1]Annual data are end of period. For the United States, federal funds rate; for Japan, overnight call rate; for the euro area, main refinancing rate; for the United Kingdom, base lending rate; and for Canada, overnight money market financing rate.

[2]Excludes Greece prior to 2001.

[3]Annual data are period average. For the United States, three-month treasury bill market bid yield at constant maturity; for Japan, three-month bond yield with repurchase agreement; for the euro area, a weighted average of national three-month money market interest rates through 1998 and three-month EURIBOR thereafter; for the United Kingdom, three-month London interbank offered rate; and for Canada, three-month treasury bill yield.

[4]Annual data are period average. For the United States, 10-year treasury bond yield at constant maturity; for Japan, 10-year government bond yield; for the euro area, a weighted average of national 10-year government bond yields through 1998 and 10-year euro bond yield thereafter; for the United Kingdom, 10-year government bond yield; and for Canada, government bond yield of 10 years and over.

Table 17. Advanced Economies: Exchange Rates

	1996	1997	1998	1999	2000	2001	2002	2003	Exchange Rate Assumption[1] 2004
				U.S. dollars per national currency unit					
U.S. dollar nominal exchange rates									
Euro	. . .	. . .	. . .	1.067	0.924	0.896	0.944	1.131	1.217
Pound sterling	1.562	1.638	1.656	1.618	1.516	1.440	1.501	1.634	1.822
				National currency units per U.S. dollar					
Japanese yen	108.8	121.0	130.9	113.9	107.8	121.5	125.4	115.9	109.7
Canadian dollar	1.363	1.385	1.483	1.486	1.485	1.549	1.569	1.401	1.331
Swedish krona	6.706	7.635	7.950	8.262	9.162	10.329	9.737	8.086	7.543
Danish krone	5.799	6.604	6.701	6.976	8.083	8.323	7.895	6.588	6.124
Swiss franc	1.236	1.451	1.450	1.502	1.689	1.688	1.559	1.347	1.271
Norwegian krone	6.450	7.073	7.545	7.799	8.802	8.992	7.984	7.080	6.953
Israeli new sheqel	3.192	3.449	3.800	4.140	4.077	4.206	4.738	4.554	4.535
Icelandic krona	66.50	70.90	70.96	72.34	78.62	97.42	91.66	76.71	71.59
Cyprus pound	0.466	0.514	0.518	0.543	0.622	0.643	0.611	0.517	0.479
Korean won	804.5	951.3	1,401.4	1,188.8	1,131.0	1,291.0	1,251.1	1,191.6	1,170.0
Australian dollar	1.277	1.344	1.589	1.550	1.717	1.932	1.839	1.534	1.385
New Taiwan dollar	27.458	28.703	33.456	32.270	31.234	33.813	34.579	34.444	33.869
Hong Kong dollar	7.734	7.742	7.745	7.758	7.791	7.799	7.799	7.787	7.793
Singapore dollar	1.410	1.485	1.674	1.695	1.724	1.792	1.791	1.742	1.700
				Index, 1990 = 100					*Percent change from previous assumption*[2]
Real effective exchange rates[3]									
United States	89.5	94.5	100.6	99.1	106.6	116.7	116.1	103.0	–1.8
Japan	125.3	119.7	111.8	127.2	136.6	120.8	110.0	107.4	1.1
Euro[4]	102.1	91.9	88.7	84.3	75.1	74.9	76.7	83.9	0.2
Germany	120.4	113.2	110.3	107.0	100.8	100.0	100.1	103.1	0.1
France	94.5	90.6	90.2	89.4	85.9	85.0	85.6	88.1	0.1
United Kingdom	96.0	114.4	121.7	123.8	130.6	130.3	132.9	127.6	0.5
Italy	84.4	86.3	84.6	84.2	81.4	80.8	82.0	85.3	0.1
Canada	88.7	91.1	85.4	84.4	84.5	81.1	80.8	90.6	3.2
Spain	96.6	94.2	96.0	96.3	95.1	97.2	99.8	104.3	0.1
Netherlands	101.8	97.3	98.5	97.9	95.7	97.6	100.4	103.8	0.1
Belgium	99.4	95.9	95.3	91.7	88.8	89.8	88.9	91.0	0.1
Sweden	90.6	88.3	86.9	84.3	83.8	76.1	77.9	82.4	–0.6
Austria	87.4	83.2	81.9	80.3	78.7	78.5	79.0	80.7	—
Denmark	100.4	97.9	99.6	99.4	96.3	97.7	99.2	103.5	0.3
Finland	68.8	64.8	63.9	61.6	58.7	59.2	58.7	59.9	0.2
Greece	109.3	113.3	109.6	110.4	106.9	107.5	110.8	115.9	—
Portugal	120.4	119.9	121.4	122.1	121.3	124.4	127.6	133.2	0.1
Ireland	66.4	62.3	56.3	52.6	47.6	47.2	47.2	49.4	—
Switzerland	111.6	108.3	114.5	114.1	113.8	119.6	126.2	127.5	–0.1
Norway	105.5	110.2	111.4	116.8	119.0	125.7	140.6	140.4	–2.7
Australia	108.4	112.8	101.0	102.6	96.5	91.2	96.7	107.1	1.1
New Zealand	114.4	118.6	102.7	100.0	88.3	85.8	95.0	110.8	3.3

[1]Average exchange rates for the period July 7–August 4, 2004. See "Assumptions" in the introduction to Statistical Appendix.
[2]In nominal effective terms. Average May 17–June 14, 2004 rates compared with July 7–August 4, 2004 rates.
[3]Defined as the ratio, in common currency, of the normalized unit labor costs in the manufacturing sector to the weighted average of those of its industrial country trading partners, using 1989–91 trade weights.
[4]A synthetic euro for the period prior to January 1, 1999 is used in the calculation of real effective exchange rates for the euro. See Box 5.5 in the *World Economic Outlook*, October 1998.

Table 18. Other Emerging Market and Developing Countries: Central Government Fiscal Balances

(Percent of GDP)

	1996	1997	1998	1999	2000	2001	2002	2003	2004	2005
Other emerging market and developing countries	**–2.6**	**–2.9**	**–3.8**	**–3.8**	**–2.9**	**–3.2**	**–3.4**	**–2.8**	**–2.2**	**–1.9**
Regional groups										
Africa	–2.4	–2.8	–3.7	–3.4	–1.3	–1.9	–2.5	–1.5	–0.8	–0.1
Sub-Sahara	–3.1	–3.5	–3.6	–3.8	–2.5	–2.3	–2.7	–2.0	–1.4	–0.7
Excluding Nigeria and South Africa	–3.1	–3.7	–3.3	–4.8	–4.4	–2.8	–3.3	–2.2	–1.8	–0.7
Central and eastern Europe	–4.1	–3.9	–3.9	–5.0	–4.6	–6.8	–6.5	–4.8	–4.7	–3.6
Commonwealth of Independent States[1]	–6.0	–6.9	–5.3	–4.0	0.3	1.8	1.0	1.2	2.2	2.6
Russia	–6.9	–7.7	–6.0	–4.2	0.8	2.7	1.3	1.5	3.7	3.5
Excluding Russia	–3.3	–4.6	–3.1	–3.2	–1.4	–0.7	0.3	0.2	–2.1	–0.1
Developing Asia	–2.2	–2.7	–3.7	–4.3	–4.4	–4.2	–4.1	–3.6	–3.2	–3.0
China	–1.6	–1.9	–3.0	–4.0	–3.6	–3.1	–3.3	–2.8	–2.2	–2.0
India	–4.2	–4.7	–5.3	–5.5	–5.7	–6.2	–6.1	–5.3	–5.5	–5.4
Excluding China and India	–1.4	–2.2	–3.2	–3.2	–4.6	–4.4	–3.5	–3.3	–3.1	–2.7
Middle East	–1.2	–1.7	–4.8	–1.9	3.6	–0.6	–2.7	–0.6	1.8	1.6
Western Hemisphere	–2.0	–1.9	–3.4	–2.9	–2.4	–2.6	–3.0	–3.1	–2.1	–2.0
Brazil	–2.6	–2.6	–5.4	–2.7	–2.3	–2.1	–0.7	–4.1	–1.9	–1.4
Mexico	–1.0	–1.9	–2.3	–2.2	–1.6	–1.3	–1.5	–1.7	–1.3	–1.8
Analytical groups										
By source of export earnings										
Fuel	0.2	–1.0	–5.6	–2.1	6.0	0.4	–1.9	1.3	4.1	4.6
Nonfuel	–2.8	–3.1	–3.7	–3.9	–3.6	–3.5	–3.6	–3.2	–2.7	–2.4
of which, primary products	–2.6	–2.2	–2.5	–4.2	–4.9	–3.3	–3.3	–2.8	–1.6	–1.9
By external financing source										
Net debtor countries	–2.9	–3.1	–3.8	–3.9	–3.8	–4.2	–4.2	–3.7	–3.4	–3.0
of which, official financing	–2.0	–3.1	–3.8	–3.4	–3.8	–3.8	–3.0	–2.5	–2.0	–1.8
Net debtor countries by debt-servicing experience										
Countries with arrears and/or rescheduling during 1997–2001	–2.1	–3.0	–4.2	–3.0	–3.0	–2.8	–1.9	–2.9	–1.9	–1.2
Other groups										
Heavily indebted poor countries	–3.6	–2.8	–2.9	–3.6	–4.2	–3.4	–3.3	–3.0	–2.4	–2.0
Middle East and north Africa	–1.1	–1.4	–4.5	–1.9	3.2	–0.6	–2.4	–0.4	1.5	1.6
Memorandum										
Median										
Other emerging market and developing countries	–2.5	–2.5	–3.0	–3.2	–2.7	–3.7	–3.7	–2.9	–2.7	–2.3
Africa	–3.4	–2.6	–3.1	–3.3	–2.9	–3.1	–4.0	–3.0	–2.6	–2.5
Central and eastern Europe	–1.7	–2.0	–2.9	–3.2	–2.7	–3.5	–5.0	–3.2	–3.4	–2.9
Commonwealth of Independent States[1]	–4.5	–4.7	–4.4	–3.7	–1.0	–1.7	–0.6	–0.7	–1.9	–1.9
Developing Asia	–3.1	–3.0	–2.4	–3.6	–4.3	–4.4	–3.6	–2.8	–3.4	–3.3
Middle East	–1.4	–2.4	–4.8	–0.9	5.2	0.4	–0.9	–0.3	0.8	0.5
Western Hemisphere	–2.0	–2.5	–2.3	–2.9	–2.5	–3.9	–5.0	–4.0	–3.5	–2.1

[1]Mongolia, which is not a member of the Commonwealth of Independent States, is included in this group for reasons of geography and similarities in economic structure.

Table 19. Other Emerging Market and Developing Countries: Broad Money Aggregates

(Annual percent change)

	1996	1997	1998	1999	2000	2001	2002	2003	2004	2005
Other emerging market and developing countries	**29.9**	**18.3**	**17.0**	**18.2**	**15.0**	**14.6**	**15.8**	**17.0**	**14.4**	**12.5**
Regional groups										
Africa	22.5	19.2	18.8	19.0	19.7	21.5	20.1	20.4	16.7	15.3
Sub-Sahara	26.3	20.8	17.5	21.1	22.3	22.8	23.1	23.4	18.8	17.4
Central and eastern Europe	57.4	51.8	37.1	37.1	24.0	30.6	12.3	11.7	14.7	12.9
Commonwealth of Independent States[1]	35.2	31.8	20.9	60.3	61.2	40.9	32.8	47.3	28.3	19.7
Russia	30.5	30.0	19.8	57.2	62.4	40.1	32.3	51.6	30.9	18.9
Excluding Russia	56.2	39.0	24.8	70.3	58.2	42.8	34.1	35.9	21.0	22.4
Developing Asia	20.8	18.1	18.4	14.4	12.3	13.1	15.5	15.8	13.8	13.2
China	25.3	19.6	14.8	14.7	12.3	14.8	19.7	19.0	14.0	13.0
India	16.9	17.6	20.2	18.6	16.2	13.9	15.1	15.9	17.2	17.3
Excluding China and India	18.4	16.8	21.5	11.5	9.6	9.5	8.4	10.1	10.8	10.7
Middle East	12.9	10.0	8.3	10.7	12.4	13.1	15.7	12.9	16.3	10.8
Western Hemisphere	37.6	8.9	11.1	10.1	7.1	6.5	13.5	15.0	10.3	8.6
Brazil	57.4	–7.3	5.5	7.8	3.3	13.3	23.6	3.7	13.0	10.6
Mexico	31.7	28.3	25.1	19.6	12.9	16.0	10.7	13.3	4.2	3.8
Analytical groups										
By source of export earnings										
Fuel	23.5	18.3	13.5	15.7	18.5	15.5	17.9	20.9	18.9	13.2
Nonfuel	30.6	18.3	17.4	18.4	14.6	14.5	15.6	16.5	13.8	12.4
of which, primary products	33.7	–8.7	16.2	18.3	20.4	19.9	19.3	21.0	19.1	20.2
By external financing source										
Net debtor countries	31.7	16.7	17.8	16.8	12.9	13.3	13.8	13.8	12.6	11.8
of which, official financing	21.4	23.1	30.0	16.3	20.8	18.1	15.4	18.6	13.9	15.1
Net debtor countries by debt-servicing experience										
Countries with arrears and/or rescheduling during 1997–2001	41.9	6.3	16.2	14.7	12.6	17.2	22.1	13.3	15.7	14.4
Other groups										
Heavily indebted poor countries	32.2	22.5	19.1	22.9	28.1	21.4	21.3	15.4	16.1	13.4
Middle East and north Africa	13.0	11.0	10.8	11.2	12.6	14.0	15.3	13.0	15.6	10.6
Memorandum										
Median										
Other emerging market and developing countries	16.7	17.2	11.1	13.2	13.6	14.0	13.0	12.1	10.7	10.0
Africa	15.6	14.2	8.6	12.1	14.1	14.8	16.4	15.4	11.3	10.3
Central and eastern Europe	24.0	34.1	13.0	14.2	16.5	21.4	10.4	10.9	11.8	10.0
Commonwealth of Independent States[1]	35.1	33.9	19.8	32.1	40.1	33.4	32.3	26.8	16.1	13.9
Developing Asia	15.7	17.6	11.7	14.7	12.3	11.7	13.3	13.1	11.1	10.7
Middle East	8.1	9.9	8.3	11.3	10.2	13.4	10.8	8.9	9.7	8.4
Western Hemisphere	17.3	13.5	11.5	10.8	8.4	8.1	8.1	8.3	8.7	7.2

[1]Mongolia, which is not a member of the Commonwealth of Independent States, is included in this group for reasons of geography and similarities in economic structure.

Table 20. Summary of World Trade Volumes and Prices

(Annual percent change)

	Ten-Year Averages											
	1986–95	1996–2005	1996	1997	1998	1999	2000	2001	2002	2003	2004	2005
Trade in goods and services												
World trade[1]												
Volume	6.2	6.5	7.1	10.5	4.4	5.9	12.5	0.2	3.3	5.1	8.8	7.2
Price deflator												
In U.S. dollars	4.2	—	–1.5	–5.9	–5.5	–1.9	–0.6	–3.4	1.1	10.4	7.9	0.8
In SDRs	0.1	0.4	2.9	–0.8	–4.2	–2.7	3.0	0.1	–0.6	2.2	2.8	1.3
Volume of trade												
Exports												
Advanced economies	6.3	5.6	6.2	10.6	4.2	5.6	11.8	–0.7	2.2	2.6	8.1	6.3
Other emerging market and developing countries	6.4	8.9	9.5	12.7	5.3	4.5	14.9	3.5	6.6	10.9	10.8	10.6
Imports												
Advanced economies	6.5	6.0	6.5	9.4	5.9	8.1	11.7	–0.7	2.6	3.7	7.6	5.6
Other emerging market and developing countries	4.7	8.2	10.9	11.6	–0.7	0.6	15.9	3.3	6.0	11.1	12.8	11.9
Terms of trade												
Advanced economies	0.8	–0.1	–0.2	–0.6	1.3	–0.3	–2.4	0.3	0.9	1.0	–0.6	–0.5
Other emerging market and developing countries	–2.4	0.7	3.0	–0.6	–7.2	3.7	7.0	–3.1	0.8	1.2	3.0	–0.2
Trade in goods												
World trade[1]												
Volume	6.4	6.6	7.2	10.9	4.7	5.8	13.3	–0.4	3.5	5.5	9.1	7.4
Price deflator												
In U.S. dollars	4.0	–0.1	–1.8	–6.3	–6.5	–1.6	—	–3.6	0.7	10.4	8.5	0.8
In SDRs	–0.1	0.3	2.6	–1.2	–5.1	–2.4	3.6	–0.2	–1.0	2.3	3.3	1.3
World trade prices in U.S. dollars[2]												
Manufactures	6.0	–0.1	–3.2	–8.1	–1.7	–1.9	–5.6	–2.8	2.4	13.2	7.5	1.5
Oil	–4.5	8.0	18.4	–5.4	–32.1	37.5	57.0	–13.8	2.5	15.8	28.9	—
Nonfuel primary commodities	3.2	–0.8	–1.8	–3.1	–14.3	–6.7	4.4	–4.1	0.6	7.1	16.8	–3.9
World trade prices in SDRs[2]												
Manufactures	1.8	0.3	1.2	–3.1	–0.3	–2.7	–2.1	0.6	0.6	4.9	2.4	2.0
Oil	–8.3	8.4	23.7	–0.2	–31.2	36.4	62.8	–10.7	0.8	7.2	22.8	0.5
Nonfuel primary commodities	–0.9	–0.4	2.6	2.2	–13.0	–7.5	8.3	–0.6	–1.1	–0.8	11.3	–3.4
World trade prices in euros[2]												
Manufactures	0.4	0.8	–0.2	2.8	–0.5	3.0	9.0	0.2	–2.9	–5.5	–0.2	2.4
Oil	–9.6	8.9	22.0	5.8	–31.3	44.4	81.4	–11.1	–2.7	–3.3	19.8	0.8
Nonfuel primary commodities	–2.3	—	1.2	8.4	–13.2	–2.1	20.6	–1.0	–4.6	–10.6	8.5	–3.1

Table 20 *(concluded)*

	Ten-Year Averages											
	1986–95	1996–2005	1996	1997	1998	1999	2000	2001	2002	2003	2004	2005
Trade in goods												
Volume of trade												
Exports												
Advanced economies	6.4	5.5	5.8	11.1	4.4	5.2	12.5	–1.5	1.9	2.6	7.8	6.1
Other emerging market and developing countries	6.7	9.3	10.8	11.5	5.8	4.5	15.9	3.0	7.7	12.3	11.0	10.7
Fuel exporters	7.1	4.3	6.8	7.8	1.3	–3.1	8.2	0.7	1.6	9.8	4.4	6.5
Nonfuel exporters	6.4	10.3	11.6	12.4	6.9	5.7	17.5	3.6	9.1	12.9	12.4	11.5
Imports												
Advanced economies	6.9	6.2	6.1	10.3	6.0	8.5	12.4	–1.6	2.6	4.0	8.2	5.9
Other emerging market and developing countries	4.9	8.8	13.3	11.4	0.4	0.2	16.5	3.4	6.9	11.1	13.8	12.3
Fuel exporters	–1.6	7.9	6.6	17.3	1.1	1.0	12.7	11.4	8.6	3.9	9.0	8.6
Nonfuel exporters	6.2	8.9	14.2	10.6	0.3	0.1	17.0	2.5	6.6	12.1	14.4	12.8
Price deflators in SDRs												
Exports												
Advanced economies	0.6	—	1.8	–2.2	–3.8	–3.4	0.4	—	–0.6	3.5	3.2	1.2
Other emerging market and developing countries	–1.9	1.6	5.9	1.7	–10.9	3.7	13.2	–1.7	–0.4	0.6	5.2	0.7
Fuel exporters	–7.6	6.6	18.7	–1.0	–26.7	35.5	46.5	–9.0	1.2	3.0	16.7	–0.3
Nonfuel exporters	—	0.5	3.2	2.3	–7.4	–1.5	6.4	0.2	–0.8	0.1	2.7	0.9
Imports												
Advanced economies	–0.5	0.1	2.4	–1.7	–5.1	–3.4	3.6	–0.3	–1.7	2.2	3.3	1.8
Other emerging market and developing countries	0.8	0.8	2.8	1.2	–3.7	–1.6	5.3	1.5	–1.0	0.6	1.9	1.0
Fuel exporters	—	0.2	1.9	–1.6	–0.8	–2.0	1.1	2.2	–0.9	1.3	–0.1	0.7
Nonfuel exporters	1.0	0.8	3.0	1.6	–4.1	–1.6	5.8	1.4	–1.0	0.5	2.2	1.0
Terms of trade												
Advanced economies	1.1	–0.1	–0.6	–0.5	1.3	0.1	–3.1	0.3	1.1	1.3	–0.1	–0.6
Other emerging market and developing countries	–2.7	0.9	3.0	0.5	–7.4	5.4	7.6	–3.1	0.6	—	3.2	–0.3
Fuel exporters	–7.7	6.4	16.5	0.6	–26.1	38.3	44.9	–10.9	2.2	1.7	16.8	–0.9
Nonfuel exporters	–1.0	–0.3	0.2	0.7	–3.5	—	0.5	–1.2	0.2	–0.4	0.5	–0.1
Memorandum												
World exports in billions of U.S. dollars												
Goods and services	4,251	8,233	6,630	6,897	6,787	7,027	7,825	7,568	7,936	9,201	10,806	11,659
Goods	3,398	6,581	5,308	5,518	5,386	5,581	6,293	6,030	6,302	7,340	8,680	9,369

[1]Average of annual percent change for world exports and imports.

[2]As represented, respectively, by the export unit value index for the manufactures of the advanced economies; the average of U.K. Brent, Dubai, and West Texas Intermediate crude oil spot prices; and the average of world market prices for nonfuel primary commodities weighted by their 1995–97 shares in world commodity exports.

Table 21. Nonfuel Commodity Prices[1]

(Annual percent change; U.S. dollar terms)

	Ten-Year Averages											
	1986–95	1996–2005	1996	1997	1998	1999	2000	2001	2002	2003	2004	2005
Nonfuel primary commodities	**3.2**	**–0.8**	**–1.8**	**–3.1**	**–14.3**	**–6.7**	**4.4**	**–4.1**	**0.6**	**7.1**	**16.8**	**–3.9**
Food	1.5	–0.5	8.2	–8.9	–11.0	–11.6	1.7	2.3	0.7	5.9	14.9	–4.3
Beverages	–1.2	–4.2	–14.8	31.1	–13.2	–21.3	–15.1	–16.1	16.5	4.9	–2.2	0.3
Agricultural raw materials	7.2	–1.7	–3.7	–4.7	–16.7	1.2	4.4	–4.9	1.8	3.7	4.3	—
Metals	4.5	–0.1	–11.3	1.2	–17.7	–1.1	12.2	–9.8	–2.7	11.9	31.2	–6.1
Advanced economies	**3.6**	**–0.8**	**–2.6**	**–4.3**	**–15.7**	**–5.9**	**5.2**	**–5.1**	**1.8**	**8.2**	**18.6**	**–4.4**
Other emerging market and developing countries	**3.4**	**–1.1**	**–3.6**	**–1.5**	**–16.1**	**–7.8**	**3.9**	**–6.2**	**2.0**	**8.4**	**18.6**	**–4.6**
Regional groups												
Africa	2.9	–1.4	–5.8	–0.5	–14.1	–9.1	1.7	–6.0	5.9	7.9	12.6	–3.4
Sub-Sahara	2.9	–1.4	–6.5	—	–14.1	–9.3	1.6	–6.4	6.4	8.1	12.5	–3.4
Central and eastern Europe	3.9	–0.9	–4.3	–3.2	–16.2	–5.0	6.0	–5.9	0.7	8.1	20.1	–4.8
Commonwealth of Independent States[2]	. . .	–0.6	–9.1	–1.7	–17.9	–2.3	9.7	–8.4	–0.7	10.5	26.0	–5.7
Developing Asia	3.5	–1.3	–1.9	–3.6	–13.6	–7.5	1.8	–5.6	2.5	6.8	14.5	–3.5
Middle East	3.6	–1.1	–4.3	–3.3	–15.2	–7.4	5.4	–6.0	0.5	9.5	18.4	–4.4
Western Hemisphere	2.9	–1.1	–2.5	0.8	–18.3	–10.2	4.1	–6.4	1.8	9.3	21.5	–5.5
Analytical groups												
By source of export earnings												
Fuel	3.8	–0.7	–6.5	–1.7	–16.0	–5.1	7.2	–7.0	—	9.8	21.8	–4.7
Nonfuel	3.4	–1.1	–3.5	–1.5	–16.1	–7.9	3.8	–6.2	2.1	8.3	18.5	–4.6
of which, primary products	3.6	–1.6	–10.4	—	–16.9	–10.7	3.9	–7.0	6.3	9.4	22.2	–7.2
By source of external financing												
Net debtor countries	3.2	–1.2	–3.1	–1.2	–16.1	–8.7	3.2	–6.0	2.5	8.2	17.8	–4.5
of which, official financing	3.1	–1.8	–5.5	–0.6	–13.5	–10.9	–0.3	–6.5	5.1	7.7	13.4	–3.4
Net debtor countries by debt-servicing experience												
Countries with arrears and/or rescheduling during 1997–2001	2.8	–1.3	–3.6	0.9	–15.6	–10.5	1.6	–6.7	4.0	8.8	16.1	–4.0
Other groups												
Heavily indebted poor countries	1.5	–1.9	–7.7	2.9	–13.3	–14.8	–3.3	–6.3	12.9	8.8	9.0	–3.2
Middle East and north Africa	3.3	–1.1	–2.8	–3.6	–14.6	–7.9	4.5	–4.9	0.9	8.6	16.8	–4.1
Memorandum												
Average oil spot price[3]	–4.5	8.0	18.4	–5.4	–32.1	37.5	57.0	–13.8	2.5	15.8	28.9	—
In U.S. dollars a barrel	17.64	25.16	20.37	19.27	13.08	17.98	28.24	24.33	24.95	28.89	37.25	37.25
Export unit value of manufactures[4]	6.0	–0.1	–3.2	–8.1	–1.7	–1.9	–5.6	–2.8	2.4	13.2	7.5	1.5

[1]Averages of world market prices for individual commodities weighted by 1995–97 exports as a share of world commodity exports and total commodity exports for the indicated country group, respectively.
[2]Mongolia, which is not a member of the Commonwealth of Independent States, is included in this group for reasons of geography and similarities in economic structure.
[3]Average of U.K. Brent, Dubai, and West Texas Intermediate crude oil spot prices.
[4]For the manufactures exported by the advanced economies.

Table 22. Advanced Economies: Export Volumes, Import Volumes, and Terms of Trade in Goods and Services

(Annual percent change)

	Ten-Year Averages											
	1986–95	1996–2005	1996	1997	1998	1999	2000	2001	2002	2003	2004	2005
Export volume												
Advanced economies	**6.3**	**5.6**	**6.2**	**10.6**	**4.2**	**5.6**	**11.8**	**–0.7**	**2.2**	**2.6**	**8.1**	**6.3**
United States	9.0	4.6	8.4	11.9	2.4	4.3	8.7	–5.4	–2.3	1.9	9.0	8.1
Euro area	5.1	5.6	4.4	10.6	7.1	5.3	12.2	3.4	1.6	–0.1	6.3	5.8
Germany	3.4	7.0	5.1	11.2	7.0	5.5	13.5	5.7	4.1	1.8	10.7	6.3
France	5.2	5.4	3.2	12.0	8.4	4.2	13.4	1.9	1.7	–2.7	4.8	7.9
Italy	6.2	1.9	0.6	6.4	3.4	0.1	9.7	1.6	–3.4	–3.9	3.3	2.3
Spain	6.9	7.0	10.4	15.3	8.2	7.7	10.1	3.6	1.2	2.6	5.0	6.8
Japan	2.9	6.1	6.4	11.4	–2.4	1.4	12.5	–6.1	7.9	10.1	15.1	6.8
United Kingdom	4.8	4.6	8.6	8.4	2.8	4.3	9.4	2.9	0.1	0.1	4.9	5.3
Canada	6.3	4.7	5.6	8.3	9.1	10.7	8.9	–2.8	1.1	–2.4	6.1	3.5
Other advanced economies	9.0	7.0	7.0	10.4	2.4	8.3	14.7	–2.3	6.1	7.5	10.2	6.6
Memorandum												
Major advanced economies	5.5	5.1	5.9	10.5	3.8	4.2	10.8	–1.1	1.1	1.4	8.4	6.3
Newly industrialized Asian economies	13.4	8.2	7.9	10.9	1.5	9.2	17.0	–4.4	9.3	12.3	13.3	7.0
Import volume												
Advanced economies	**6.5**	**6.0**	**6.5**	**9.4**	**5.9**	**8.1**	**11.7**	**–0.7**	**2.6**	**3.7**	**7.6**	**5.6**
United States	6.1	7.7	8.7	13.6	11.6	11.5	13.1	–2.7	3.4	4.4	9.8	5.0
Euro area	5.5	5.6	3.3	9.1	9.8	7.6	11.2	1.7	0.5	1.9	5.7	5.8
Germany	4.1	5.5	3.1	8.3	9.1	8.4	10.6	1.0	–1.6	4.0	6.5	6.1
France	5.2	6.3	1.7	7.2	11.5	6.1	15.2	1.6	3.3	0.3	8.3	8.8
Italy	5.7	3.5	–0.3	10.1	8.9	5.6	7.1	0.5	–0.2	–0.6	3.3	1.9
Spain	10.5	8.3	8.0	13.3	13.2	12.6	10.5	3.9	3.1	4.8	7.0	6.8
Japan	7.3	3.9	13.2	1.0	–6.6	3.3	9.3	0.2	1.9	5.0	8.8	4.8
United Kingdom	5.2	6.5	9.7	9.8	9.3	7.9	9.1	4.9	4.1	1.3	4.9	5.0
Canada	6.2	5.0	5.1	14.2	5.1	7.8	8.1	–5.0	1.4	3.8	6.5	4.0
Other advanced economies	9.5	5.9	7.0	8.8	–2.2	7.1	13.9	–4.2	5.9	6.7	10.1	6.7
Memorandum												
Major advanced economies	5.6	6.0	6.6	9.5	7.8	8.3	11.2	–0.5	2.0	3.2	7.6	5.3
Newly industrialized Asian economies	15.1	6.2	8.0	8.3	–8.2	8.2	17.3	–6.4	8.0	8.7	13.0	7.4
Terms of trade												
Advanced economies	**0.8**	**–0.1**	**–0.2**	**–0.6**	**1.3**	**–0.3**	**–2.4**	**0.3**	**0.9**	**1.0**	**–0.6**	**–0.5**
United States	–0.3	0.2	0.2	2.0	3.4	–1.2	–2.2	2.4	0.6	–1.3	–1.2	–0.2
Euro area	0.5	—	0.2	–1.0	1.3	0.2	–3.6	0.7	1.5	1.0	–0.2	—
Germany	–0.2	—	–0.7	–1.7	2.1	1.2	–4.3	0.3	1.6	1.7	0.7	–0.4
France	0.6	—	–0.9	–0.5	1.4	0.3	–3.8	1.2	2.2	0.1	–0.8	0.7
Italy	1.4	0.2	4.3	–1.5	2.0	0.3	–7.2	0.6	2.3	1.3	0.1	0.3
Spain	2.5	0.3	1.0	–0.3	0.9	–0.8	–2.2	2.8	2.5	1.0	–1.9	–0.4
Japan	3.3	–2.4	–5.4	–4.0	3.6	–0.4	–4.9	–1.5	0.1	–1.8	–4.9	–4.0
United Kingdom	–0.1	0.8	1.2	3.3	2.1	0.6	–0.9	–0.6	2.7	0.8	–1.5	0.2
Canada	—	0.6	1.8	–0.7	–3.9	1.4	4.0	–1.6	–2.5	6.1	3.0	–1.0
Other advanced economies	0.6	–0.4	0.6	–1.0	–0.3	–1.0	–0.8	–0.4	0.3	0.2	–0.6	–0.4
Memorandum												
Major advanced economies	0.8	—	–0.4	–0.4	2.1	—	–3.2	0.4	1.1	1.3	–0.6	–0.7
Newly industrialized Asian economies	0.6	–1.1	–0.3	–1.3	0.2	–2.4	–3.2	–0.6	0.2	–1.6	–1.7	—
Memorandum												
Trade in goods												
Advanced economies												
Export volume	6.4	5.5	5.8	11.1	4.4	5.2	12.5	–1.5	1.9	2.6	7.8	6.1
Import volume	6.9	6.2	6.1	10.3	6.0	8.5	12.4	–1.6	2.6	4.0	8.2	5.9
Terms of trade	1.1	–0.1	–0.6	–0.5	1.3	0.1	–3.1	0.3	1.1	1.3	–0.1	–0.6

Table 23. Other Emerging Market and Developing Countries—by Region: Total Trade in Goods
(Annual percent change)

	Ten-Year Averages											
	1986–95	1996–2005	1996	1997	1998	1999	2000	2001	2002	2003	2004	2005
Other emerging market and developing countries												
Value in U.S. dollars												
Exports	7.8	10.2	11.1	7.2	–6.9	7.7	25.6	–2.2	8.9	21.9	22.2	10.6
Imports	8.7	8.9	10.5	6.6	–4.6	–1.6	18.1	1.2	7.5	20.6	21.5	12.9
Volume												
Exports	6.7	9.3	10.8	11.5	5.8	4.5	15.9	3.0	7.7	12.3	11.0	10.7
Imports	4.9	8.8	13.3	11.4	0.4	0.2	16.5	3.4	6.9	11.1	13.8	12.3
Unit value in U.S. dollars												
Exports	2.2	1.2	1.4	–3.6	–12.2	4.5	9.2	–5.1	1.3	8.6	10.4	0.2
Imports	5.0	0.4	–1.6	–4.1	–5.1	–0.8	1.5	–2.1	0.7	8.6	7.0	0.5
Terms of trade	–2.7	0.9	3.0	0.5	–7.4	5.4	7.6	–3.1	0.6	—	3.2	–0.3
Memorandum												
Real GDP growth in developing country trading partners	3.5	3.1	3.6	4.0	1.8	3.4	4.7	1.4	2.0	2.8	4.4	3.5
Market prices of nonfuel commodities exported by other emerging market and developing countries	3.4	–1.1	–3.6	–1.5	–16.1	–7.8	3.9	–6.2	2.0	8.4	18.6	–4.6
Regional groups												
Africa												
Value in U.S. dollars												
Exports	3.7	8.0	11.1	3.2	–13.8	7.9	27.9	–6.7	2.6	25.9	20.6	9.1
Imports	5.9	6.1	0.8	4.7	–2.3	1.0	4.2	2.2	7.4	21.6	15.5	7.8
Volume												
Exports	2.8	5.1	8.0	6.2	1.5	3.9	9.0	0.8	0.9	7.1	4.9	9.4
Imports	2.8	5.8	3.4	8.5	4.4	1.7	2.8	6.6	6.8	7.0	7.9	8.9
Unit value in U.S. dollars												
Exports	1.3	2.8	2.9	–2.7	–15.1	4.4	16.9	–7.5	1.8	17.8	14.8	–0.3
Imports	3.9	0.4	–2.1	–3.5	–6.1	–0.8	1.7	–4.3	0.8	13.8	7.1	–0.7
Terms of trade	–2.5	2.3	5.1	0.8	–9.6	5.2	15.0	–3.4	1.0	3.5	7.2	0.5
Sub-Sahara												
Value in U.S. dollars												
Exports	4.0	7.6	10.4	3.3	–14.1	6.7	25.4	–7.0	3.0	26.8	19.4	9.3
Imports	5.9	6.2	3.2	7.6	–4.9	—	4.1	2.3	6.0	24.1	13.6	8.4
Volume												
Exports	3.3	5.2	9.7	6.1	0.5	2.4	9.5	0.8	0.2	7.6	4.8	10.9
Imports	3.2	6.1	7.7	10.0	2.2	0.7	2.0	7.3	5.8	8.2	7.7	9.7
Unit value in U.S. dollars												
Exports	1.2	2.3	0.7	–2.5	–14.6	4.8	13.8	–7.7	2.8	18.3	13.6	–1.4
Imports	3.4	0.2	–4.0	–2.0	–6.6	–0.9	2.4	–5.0	0.4	14.9	5.6	–0.8
Terms of trade	–2.1	2.1	4.9	–0.4	–8.6	5.7	11.1	–2.9	2.4	3.0	7.5	–0.6

Table 23 ***(continued)***

	Ten-Year Averages											
	1986–95	1996–2005	1996	1997	1998	1999	2000	2001	2002	2003	2004	2005
Central and eastern Europe												
Value in U.S. dollars												
Exports	6.7	11.7	9.2	7.9	6.4	–2.5	13.2	10.8	13.8	28.9	23.0	9.5
Imports	8.4	11.4	16.8	9.1	5.9	–4.1	16.0	–0.2	13.5	29.1	23.6	8.7
Volume												
Exports	2.1	10.2	10.4	12.9	9.1	1.3	16.5	10.4	8.3	12.9	12.5	8.8
Imports	4.9	10.2	17.4	16.8	10.8	–2.3	16.7	2.0	8.9	12.9	12.5	8.1
Unit value in U.S. dollars												
Exports	5.5	1.5	–0.7	–4.3	–2.5	–3.5	–3.0	0.8	5.3	14.3	9.4	0.4
Imports	6.1	1.3	—	–6.3	–4.4	–1.7	–0.4	–2.0	4.6	14.8	10.1	0.5
Terms of trade	–0.5	0.1	–0.7	2.1	2.0	–1.8	–2.6	2.8	0.6	–0.4	–0.7	—
Commonwealth of Independent States[1]												
Value in U.S. dollars												
Exports	. . .	9.0	9.1	–1.4	–14.0	—	37.0	–0.9	6.3	26.8	31.5	6.0
Imports	. . .	6.1	13.1	4.0	–15.9	–25.8	14.2	15.0	9.7	25.9	21.8	11.2
Volume												
Exports	. . .	5.4	6.8	1.6	0.2	–1.3	9.2	3.9	6.7	13.4	8.3	6.1
Imports	. . .	6.2	13.3	12.4	–14.4	–22.5	14.3	16.7	8.4	20.6	12.8	9.9
Unit value in U.S. dollars												
Exports	. . .	3.6	2.7	–1.8	–13.5	1.1	24.7	–4.7	–0.4	11.9	21.8	—
Imports	. . .	0.1	0.4	–6.6	–1.9	–4.2	—	–1.4	1.6	4.4	8.2	1.3
Terms of trade	. . .	3.5	2.4	5.1	–11.8	5.5	24.7	–3.3	–2.0	7.2	12.6	–1.3
Developing Asia												
Value in U.S. dollars												
Exports	15.7	12.0	10.1	12.2	–2.4	8.5	22.3	–1.8	14.0	23.0	19.9	17.7
Imports	14.1	10.8	10.3	0.9	–13.6	9.0	28.0	–0.8	13.1	25.5	24.7	18.7
Volume												
Exports	12.5	13.7	16.0	15.5	8.4	8.8	24.0	1.3	14.8	17.5	15.8	16.5
Imports	10.5	11.2	17.1	5.3	–6.9	8.6	24.0	2.0	12.9	16.2	18.2	17.9
Unit value in U.S. dollars												
Exports	3.2	–1.0	–3.4	–2.8	–9.8	1.9	–1.0	–3.0	–0.5	4.8	3.7	0.8
Imports	3.6	0.2	–4.1	–4.0	–7.3	3.7	3.6	–2.5	0.1	7.8	5.6	0.5
Terms of trade	–0.4	–1.3	0.6	1.3	–2.7	–1.7	–4.4	–0.5	–0.7	–2.8	–1.9	0.4
Excluding China and India												
Value in U.S. dollars												
Exports	15.2	6.4	5.8	7.5	–4.2	10.3	18.9	–9.3	6.1	11.7	13.4	6.5
Imports	16.9	4.1	5.4	–1.1	–23.3	6.3	24.2	–6.8	6.2	11.8	16.9	9.2
Volume												
Exports	13.0	5.8	2.5	10.3	9.0	3.3	15.9	–6.4	5.8	6.5	7.1	5.8
Imports	13.6	3.1	4.5	1.6	–15.7	–0.7	20.5	–6.9	7.0	6.7	10.0	8.5
Unit value in U.S. dollars												
Exports	2.2	1.0	3.7	–2.5	–11.8	10.3	2.8	–3.1	0.4	4.9	5.9	0.7
Imports	3.3	1.6	1.5	–2.5	–8.8	12.3	3.2	0.2	–0.7	4.8	6.3	0.6
Terms of trade	–1.0	–0.6	2.2	–0.1	–3.4	–1.8	–0.4	–3.2	1.2	0.1	–0.3	0.1

Table 23 ***(concluded)***

	Ten-Year Averages											
	1986–95	1996–2005	1996	1997	1998	1999	2000	2001	2002	2003	2004	2005
Middle East												
Value in U.S. dollars												
Exports	3.5	9.8	16.4	0.5	–25.2	30.6	45.9	–8.2	5.9	21.0	24.6	3.9
Imports	2.9	6.9	7.8	5.2	–0.9	–1.5	9.3	8.7	8.4	12.6	11.9	8.4
Volume												
Exports	8.4	4.5	5.4	6.8	2.1	–0.1	7.3	3.0	3.4	9.9	3.1	4.4
Imports	–1.4	7.9	11.5	13.2	3.0	2.8	12.3	10.0	9.0	3.5	6.5	7.3
Unit value in U.S. dollars												
Exports	–4.0	5.3	11.4	–6.0	–26.5	31.1	36.6	–10.9	2.9	10.2	21.0	–0.3
Imports	4.9	–0.8	–3.2	–7.2	–3.7	–4.1	–2.5	–1.0	–0.4	9.0	5.4	1.1
Terms of trade	–8.5	6.1	15.1	1.3	–23.6	36.7	40.2	–10.0	3.2	1.1	14.8	–1.4
Western Hemisphere												
Value in U.S. dollars												
Exports	8.4	7.0	11.5	9.8	–3.8	4.0	19.9	–4.3	1.3	10.4	20.8	3.8
Imports	12.2	6.0	10.9	18.7	4.8	–6.9	14.8	–1.7	–8.2	4.3	19.7	8.1
Volume												
Exports	8.1	6.5	8.8	15.1	6.6	3.9	11.3	2.8	–0.3	3.7	8.8	4.8
Imports	10.0	5.4	8.5	18.7	8.7	–3.5	12.4	–0.6	–7.2	0.6	11.3	7.6
Unit value in U.S. dollars												
Exports	2.4	0.7	2.6	–4.4	–9.8	1.6	8.0	–7.0	1.9	6.6	10.7	–0.9
Imports	3.5	0.7	2.4	0.2	–3.5	–3.7	2.1	–1.2	–1.1	3.9	7.6	0.4
Terms of trade	–1.1	0.1	0.2	–4.6	–6.5	5.5	5.8	–5.8	3.0	2.5	2.9	–1.3

[1]Mongolia, which is not a member of the Commonwealth of Independent States, is included in this group for reasons of geography and similarities in economic structure.

Table 24. Other Emerging Market and Developing Countries—by Source of Export Earnings: Total Trade in Goods
(Annual percent change)

	Ten-Year Averages											
	1986–95	1996–2005	1996	1997	1998	1999	2000	2001	2002	2003	2004	2005
Fuel												
Value in U.S. dollars												
Exports	2.5	10.3	20.2	0.5	–27.1	31.2	52.8	–11.4	4.2	22.1	27.5	5.3
Imports	2.2	7.5	3.4	9.5	–0.9	–0.2	10.0	10.2	8.6	13.6	13.9	8.5
Volume												
Exports	7.1	4.3	6.8	7.8	1.3	–3.1	8.2	0.7	1.6	9.8	4.4	6.5
Imports	–1.6	7.9	6.6	17.3	1.1	1.0	12.7	11.4	8.6	3.9	9.0	8.6
Unit value in U.S. dollars												
Exports	–3.9	6.2	13.6	–6.2	–27.7	36.6	41.3	–12.1	2.9	11.2	22.5	–0.8
Imports	4.1	–0.2	–2.4	–6.7	–2.2	–1.2	–2.5	–1.3	0.8	9.4	4.9	0.2
Terms of trade	–7.7	6.4	16.5	0.6	–26.1	38.3	44.9	–10.9	2.2	1.7	16.8	–0.9
Nonfuel												
Value in U.S. dollars												
Exports	9.5	10.1	9.2	8.8	–2.5	3.9	20.0	0.2	9.9	21.9	21.1	11.8
Imports	10.1	9.1	11.4	6.3	–5.1	–1.8	19.2	0.1	7.4	21.6	22.5	13.4
Volume												
Exports	6.4	10.3	11.6	12.4	6.9	5.7	17.5	3.6	9.1	12.9	12.4	11.5
Imports	6.2	8.9	14.2	10.6	0.3	0.1	17.0	2.5	6.6	12.1	14.4	12.8
Unit value in U.S. dollars												
Exports	4.1	0.2	–1.2	–3.0	–8.7	–0.7	2.6	–3.3	0.9	8.1	7.8	0.4
Imports	5.1	0.5	–1.5	–3.7	–5.5	–0.8	2.1	–2.1	0.7	8.5	7.3	0.5
Terms of trade	–1.0	–0.3	0.2	0.7	–3.5	—	0.5	–1.2	0.2	–0.4	0.5	–0.1
Primary products												
Value in U.S. dollars												
Exports	7.7	3.9	2.9	3.5	–9.3	1.5	4.8	–5.3	3.0	17.3	23.3	1.6
Imports	7.2	4.3	14.1	5.4	–5.6	–10.6	5.2	–0.6	0.7	12.6	17.9	7.5
Volume												
Exports	6.0	4.7	8.8	6.4	2.7	5.4	2.4	3.1	0.9	5.1	7.6	5.4
Imports	5.2	4.7	12.9	9.7	3.8	–7.5	2.2	3.7	2.8	4.2	8.4	8.4
Unit value in U.S. dollars												
Exports	3.4	–0.7	–5.2	–2.6	–11.3	–3.5	2.4	–8.1	2.2	11.7	13.5	–3.5
Imports	3.0	–0.2	1.2	–3.7	–9.0	–3.4	3.6	–4.0	–1.9	8.5	8.8	–0.8
Terms of trade	0.4	–0.5	–6.3	1.1	–2.5	–0.1	–1.2	–4.2	4.2	3.0	4.3	–2.8

Table 25. Summary of Payments Balances on Current Account

(Billions of U.S. dollars)

	1996	1997	1998	1999	2000	2001	2002	2003	2004	2005
Advanced economies	**36.3**	**80.7**	**35.0**	**–107.9**	**–250.1**	**–202.9**	**–216.4**	**–246.5**	**–266.1**	**–270.3**
United States	–117.2	–136.0	–209.6	–296.8	–413.5	–385.7	–473.9	–530.7	–631.3	–641.7
Euro area[1]	78.2	98.9	63.1	29.1	–29.7	9.3	52.8	25.5	72.2	87.6
Japan	65.7	96.6	119.1	114.5	119.6	87.8	112.6	136.2	159.4	148.9
Other advanced economies[2]	9.6	21.2	62.4	45.2	73.5	85.7	92.2	122.4	133.6	134.8
Memorandum										
Newly industrialized Asian economies	–2.3	6.0	64.9	58.4	41.4	52.3	62.5	86.4	85.0	86.0
Other emerging market and developing countries	**–86.1**	**–85.3**	**–116.3**	**–18.9**	**86.3**	**39.5**	**84.2**	**148.9**	**201.3**	**183.2**
Excluding Asian countries in surplus[3]	–70.6	–108.9	–173.1	–66.9	41.7	7.3	29.3	77.8	140.3	116.1
Regional groups										
Africa	–4.9	–6.0	–19.3	–15.0	6.3	–1.3	–6.7	–0.4	2.8	5.0
Central and eastern Europe	–17.8	–21.1	–19.3	–26.6	–32.6	–16.3	–24.0	–35.1	–44.2	–45.2
Commonwealth of Independent States[4]	2.5	–8.8	–9.6	20.7	46.3	32.8	32.2	36.6	61.4	53.6
Developing Asia	–37.8	10.3	48.9	48.2	45.6	38.5	70.4	85.9	68.8	68.5
Middle East	11.4	7.8	–25.4	11.6	69.2	38.7	29.1	57.6	103.5	108.2
Western Hemisphere	–39.4	–67.4	–91.6	–57.7	–48.4	–52.9	–16.8	4.4	9.0	–6.8
Memorandum										
European Union	66.5	92.9	47.7	–18.5	–74.4	–24.1	23.7	–3.8	31.7	43.4
Analytical groups										
By source of export earnings										
Fuel	28.0	18.9	–32.2	11.3	100.2	50.2	35.5	71.5	130.6	141.4
Nonfuel	–114.0	–104.2	–84.1	–30.2	–13.9	–10.7	48.7	77.4	70.7	41.9
of which, primary products	–6.6	–8.7	–8.7	–3.9	–4.2	–5.5	–4.2	–2.1	–1.7	–5.4
By external financing source										
Net debtor countries	–129.6	–140.4	–121.7	–72.5	–67.3	–59.0	–22.7	–7.7	–18.6	–50.5
of which, official financing	–18.4	–14.9	–12.9	–3.8	9.9	2.8	–1.4	1.4	2.1	–3.8
Net debtor countries by debt-servicing experience										
Countries with arrears and/or rescheduling during 1997–2001	–46.0	–51.0	–55.8	–34.7	–16.8	–21.6	–8.0	5.6	13.4	3.5
Total[1]	**–49.8**	**–4.6**	**–81.3**	**–126.8**	**–163.8**	**–163.4**	**–132.2**	**–97.7**	**–64.8**	**–87.1**
Memorandum										
In percent of total world current account transactions	–0.4	—	–0.6	–0.9	–1.0	–1.1	–0.8	–0.5	–0.3	–0.4
In percent of world GDP	–0.2	—	–0.3	–0.4	–0.5	–0.5	–0.4	–0.3	–0.2	–0.2

[1]Reflects errors, omissions, and asymmetries in balance of payments statistics on current account, as well as the exclusion of data for international organizations and a limited number of countries. Calculated as the sum of the balance of individual euro area countries. See "Classification of Countries" in the introduction to this Statistical Appendix.

[2]In this table, "other advanced economies" means advanced economies excluding the United States, euro area countries, and Japan.

[3]Excludes China, Malaysia, the Philippines, and Thailand.

[4]Mongolia, which is not a member of the Commonwealth of Independent States, is included in this group for reasons of geography and similarities in economic structure.

Table 26. Advanced Economies: Balance of Payments on Current Account

	1996	1997	1998	1999	2000	2001	2002	2003	2004	2005
					Billions of U.S. dollars					
Advanced economies	**36.3**	**80.7**	**35.0**	**–107.9**	**–250.1**	**–202.9**	**–216.4**	**–246.5**	**–266.1**	**–270.3**
United States	–117.2	–136.0	–209.6	–296.8	–413.5	–385.7	–473.9	–530.7	–631.3	–641.7
Euro area[1]	78.2	98.9	63.1	29.1	–29.7	9.3	52.8	25.5	72.2	87.6
Germany	–13.7	–8.6	–11.8	–24.0	–25.7	1.6	43.1	52.9	118.5	129.7
France	20.5	39.8	38.6	42.0	18.0	21.5	14.5	5.5	–12.8	–13.2
Italy	40.0	32.4	20.0	8.1	–5.8	–0.7	–6.7	–21.9	–18.1	–13.3
Spain	0.4	2.5	–2.9	–14.0	–19.4	–16.4	–15.9	–23.5	–33.1	–36.5
Netherlands	21.4	25.1	13.0	15.6	7.2	7.5	10.6	11.2	16.4	18.3
Belgium	13.8	13.8	13.3	12.9	9.0	8.4	13.0	11.6	15.2	16.1
Austria	–5.4	–6.5	–5.2	–6.8	–4.9	–3.7	0.7	–2.4	–2.9	–3.3
Finland	5.1	6.9	7.3	7.8	9.2	8.6	8.9	9.2	10.4	11.3
Greece	–4.5	–4.8	–3.6	–4.8	–8.4	–8.1	–8.1	–9.8	–11.9	–11.9
Portugal	–4.1	–6.0	–7.8	–9.8	–11.1	–10.4	–8.2	–7.5	–10.0	–10.8
Ireland	2.4	2.5	0.7	0.2	–0.4	–0.7	–1.5	–2.1	–2.7	–2.5
Luxembourg	2.2	1.8	1.7	1.7	2.5	1.7	2.5	2.5	3.0	3.6
Japan	65.7	96.6	119.1	114.5	119.6	87.8	112.6	136.2	159.4	148.9
United Kingdom	–10.9	–1.5	–6.6	–39.5	–36.5	–32.2	–27.4	–33.4	–43.3	–43.1
Canada	3.4	–8.2	–7.7	1.7	19.7	16.1	14.4	17.0	28.2	25.2
Korea	–23.1	–8.3	40.4	24.5	12.2	8.0	5.4	12.3	20.7	23.7
Australia	–15.8	–12.7	–18.0	–22.3	–15.0	–8.6	–17.6	–30.2	–32.0	–30.2
Taiwan Province of China	10.9	7.1	3.4	8.4	8.9	18.2	25.6	29.2	21.3	19.4
Sweden	9.6	10.3	9.7	10.7	9.9	9.7	12.9	19.2	22.6	19.9
Switzerland	22.0	25.5	26.1	30.4	30.9	21.4	23.3	32.7	36.2	39.0
Hong Kong SAR	–4.0	–7.7	2.5	10.3	7.1	9.9	12.6	16.7	16.4	16.6
Denmark	2.7	0.7	–1.5	3.0	2.3	4.9	3.5	6.3	4.3	4.5
Norway	11.0	10.0	0.1	8.5	26.0	26.2	24.6	28.6	38.7	39.6
Israel	–5.4	–4.0	–1.3	–1.5	–1.4	–2.1	–1.7	0.1	–0.5	–0.1
Singapore	13.9	14.9	18.6	15.3	13.2	16.1	18.9	28.2	26.6	26.4
New Zealand	–3.9	–4.3	–2.2	–3.5	–2.5	–1.2	–1.8	–3.3	–4.1	–4.2
Cyprus	–0.5	–0.3	–0.6	–0.2	–0.5	–0.4	–0.5	–0.6	–0.6	–0.7
Iceland	–0.1	–0.1	–0.6	–0.6	–0.9	–0.3	—	–0.6	–0.7	–1.3
Memorandum										
Major advanced economies	–12.2	14.4	–57.9	–193.9	–324.2	–291.6	–323.4	–374.4	–399.3	–407.4
Euro area[2]	. . .	56.8	22.0	–31.0	–71.7	–15.0	51.5	29.3	29.8	43.8
Newly industrialized Asian economies	–2.3	6.0	64.9	58.4	41.4	52.3	62.5	86.4	85.0	86.0

Table 26 *(concluded)*

	1996	1997	1998	1999	2000	2001	2002	2003	2004	2005
					Percent of GDP					
Advanced economies	**0.2**	**0.3**	**0.1**	**–0.4**	**–1.0**	**–0.8**	**–0.8**	**–0.8**	**–0.8**	**–0.8**
United States	–1.5	–1.6	–2.4	–3.2	–4.2	–3.8	–4.5	–4.8	–5.4	–5.1
Euro area[1]	1.1	1.5	0.9	0.4	–0.5	0.2	0.8	0.3	0.8	0.9
Germany	–0.6	–0.4	–0.5	–1.1	–1.4	0.1	2.2	2.2	4.4	4.8
France	1.3	2.8	2.7	2.9	1.4	1.6	1.0	0.3	–0.6	–0.6
Italy	3.2	2.8	1.7	0.7	–0.5	–0.1	–0.6	–1.5	–1.1	–0.8
Spain	0.1	0.5	–0.5	–2.3	–3.4	–2.8	–2.4	–2.8	–3.4	–3.6
Netherlands	5.2	6.6	3.3	3.9	2.0	1.9	2.5	2.2	2.9	3.1
Belgium	5.1	5.6	5.3	5.1	3.9	3.7	5.3	3.8	4.5	4.6
Austria	–2.3	–3.2	–2.5	–3.2	–2.6	–1.9	0.3	–0.9	–1.0	–1.1
Finland	4.0	5.6	5.6	6.1	7.7	7.1	6.8	5.7	5.8	6.2
Greece	–3.6	–4.0	–3.0	–3.8	–7.3	–6.9	–6.0	–5.7	–6.0	–5.7
Portugal	–3.6	–5.7	–6.9	–8.5	–10.4	–9.5	–6.8	–5.1	–6.1	–6.3
Ireland	3.3	3.1	0.8	0.3	–0.4	–0.7	–1.3	–1.4	–1.6	–1.3
Luxembourg	12.2	10.5	8.8	8.3	12.7	8.4	11.5	9.3	10.1	11.4
Japan	1.4	2.2	3.0	2.6	2.5	2.1	2.8	3.2	3.4	3.2
United Kingdom	–0.9	–0.1	–0.5	–2.7	–2.5	–2.3	–1.7	–1.9	–2.0	–1.9
Canada	0.5	–1.3	–1.2	0.3	2.7	2.3	2.0	2.0	2.9	2.4
Korea	–4.1	–1.6	11.7	5.5	2.4	1.7	1.0	2.0	3.1	3.3
Australia	–3.9	–3.1	–5.0	–5.7	–4.0	–2.4	–4.4	–5.9	–5.3	–4.9
Taiwan Province of China	3.9	2.4	1.3	2.9	2.9	6.5	9.1	10.2	6.9	6.0
Sweden	3.6	4.2	3.9	4.3	4.1	4.4	5.4	6.4	6.7	5.7
Switzerland	7.3	9.7	9.7	11.5	12.5	8.5	8.5	10.2	10.3	10.6
Hong Kong SAR	–2.6	–4.4	1.5	6.4	4.3	6.1	7.9	10.7	10.0	9.6
Denmark	1.5	0.4	–0.9	1.8	1.5	3.1	2.0	3.0	1.8	1.9
Norway	6.9	6.3	—	5.4	15.6	15.4	12.9	13.0	15.9	16.0
Israel	–5.5	–3.9	–1.3	–1.5	–1.2	–1.9	–1.6	0.1	–0.5	–0.1
Singapore	15.1	15.6	22.7	18.6	14.3	18.7	21.4	30.9	25.7	23.9
New Zealand	–5.9	–6.5	–4.0	–6.2	–4.8	–2.4	–3.1	–4.2	–4.4	–4.4
Cyprus	–5.2	–4.0	–6.6	–2.3	–5.1	–4.3	–5.4	–4.4	–4.3	–4.2
Iceland	–1.8	–1.8	–6.9	–7.0	–10.1	–4.1	–0.3	–5.4	–5.9	–9.7
Memorandum										
Major advanced economies	–0.1	0.1	–0.3	–0.9	–1.5	–1.4	–1.5	–1.6	–1.5	–1.5
Euro area[2]	. . .	0.9	0.3	–0.5	–1.2	–0.2	0.8	0.4	0.3	0.5
Newly industrialized Asian economies	–0.2	0.6	7.6	6.0	3.8	5.2	5.8	7.6	6.8	6.5

[1]Calculated as the sum of the balances of individual euro area countries.
[2]Corrected for reporting discrepancies in intra-area transactions.

Table 27. Advanced Economies: Current Account Transactions

(Billions of U.S. dollars)

	1996	1997	1998	1999	2000	2001	2002	2003	2004	2005
Exports	4,111.2	4,233.8	4,191.1	4,293.8	4,675.9	4,448.7	4,580.6	5,241.4	6,114.4	6,531.2
Imports	4,044.2	4,152.9	4,129.1	4,362.0	4,897.1	4,634.8	4,750.5	5,442.9	6,377.9	6,844.4
Trade balance	67.0	80.9	62.0	–68.2	–221.2	–186.1	–169.9	–201.5	–263.5	–313.2
Services, credits	1,069.3	1,102.4	1,132.1	1,187.2	1,246.8	1,243.3	1,321.0	1,510.5	1,717.1	1,842.7
Services, debits	999.8	1,018.1	1,054.6	1,117.6	1,173.2	1,180.8	1,244.4	1,424.2	1,596.1	1,675.0
Balance on services	69.5	84.3	77.5	69.7	73.6	62.5	76.5	86.3	121.0	167.7
Balance on goods and services	136.5	165.1	139.6	1.5	–147.6	–123.6	–93.4	–115.2	–142.5	–145.5
Income, net	12.4	29.1	23.5	16.9	32.3	43.0	16.6	43.7	54.2	61.7
Current transfers, net	–112.6	–113.6	–128.1	–126.3	–134.8	–122.3	–139.6	–175.1	–177.7	–186.5
Current account balance	**36.3**	**80.7**	**35.0**	**–107.9**	**–250.1**	**–202.9**	**–216.4**	**–246.5**	**–266.1**	**–270.3**
Balance on goods and services										
Advanced economies	**136.5**	**165.1**	**139.6**	**1.5**	**–147.6**	**–123.6**	**–93.4**	**–115.2**	**–142.5**	**–145.5**
United States	–102.9	–108.2	–164.9	–263.3	–378.3	–362.7	–421.7	–496.5	–596.2	–607.0
Euro area[1]	155.5	163.3	147.1	105.4	49.3	101.5	170.2	179.3	219.7	233.6
Germany	22.5	27.6	29.5	20.4	9.3	40.5	91.0	107.3	165.6	174.2
France	31.2	44.9	42.3	36.3	16.5	21.4	24.7	16.5	–2.8	–3.9
Italy	62.2	47.6	39.8	24.5	10.5	15.5	13.2	8.3	10.0	13.3
Spain	4.2	6.6	1.3	–7.5	–12.5	–8.3	–7.6	–12.0	–24.4	–27.3
Japan	21.2	47.3	73.2	69.2	69.0	26.5	51.7	72.5	87.9	79.9
United Kingdom	–5.4	1.8	–14.1	–25.8	–29.6	–39.5	–46.7	–53.4	–69.6	–70.1
Canada	24.4	12.1	11.8	23.8	41.2	40.5	32.1	33.8	46.9	44.7
Other advanced economies	43.6	48.9	86.5	92.1	100.9	110.1	121.0	149.1	168.7	173.3
Memorandum										
Major advanced economies	53.3	73.2	17.6	–114.8	–261.4	–257.9	–255.7	–311.5	–358.2	–369.0
Newly industrialized Asian economies	–1.8	4.5	63.3	57.5	41.6	47.8	60.1	81.0	85.6	88.5
Income, net										
Advanced economies	**12.4**	**29.1**	**23.5**	**16.9**	**32.3**	**43.0**	**16.6**	**43.7**	**54.2**	**61.7**
United States	24.5	12.6	3.8	13.2	20.6	23.6	7.2	33.3	21.1	24.6
Euro area[1]	–26.4	–16.2	–31.3	–27.6	–31.3	–42.8	–66.8	–84.3	–71.5	–67.9
Germany	–2.3	–5.7	–11.0	–17.7	–8.8	–14.4	–21.5	–21.8	–6.9	–3.5
France	–2.7	7.9	8.7	19.0	15.5	15.0	4.0	7.8	9.9	10.3
Italy	–15.0	–11.2	–12.3	–11.1	–12.0	–10.3	–14.6	–22.1	–18.5	–16.5
Spain	–6.1	–6.8	–7.5	–9.5	–8.3	–9.7	–10.6	–12.0	–13.5	–14.3
Japan	53.5	58.1	54.7	57.4	60.4	69.2	65.8	71.2	80.0	79.6
United Kingdom	1.9	6.4	21.4	–1.8	7.9	16.8	32.2	36.1	45.6	47.1
Canada	–21.6	–20.9	–20.0	–22.6	–22.3	–25.4	–18.3	–16.9	–19.1	–19.9
Other advanced economies	–19.5	–10.9	–5.0	–1.7	–2.9	1.6	–3.5	4.4	–1.8	–1.7
Memorandum										
Major advanced economies	38.4	47.2	45.3	36.4	61.2	74.4	54.8	87.6	112.0	121.7
Newly industrialized Asian economies	3.1	5.9	2.5	3.9	4.5	10.5	9.4	14.0	8.2	6.8

[1]Calculated as the sum of the individual euro area countries.

Table 28. Other Emerging Market and Developing Countries: Payments Balances on Current Account

	1996	1997	1998	1999	2000	2001	2002	2003	2004	2005
					Billions of U.S. dollars					
Other emerging market and developing countries	**–86.1**	**–85.3**	**–116.3**	**–18.9**	**86.3**	**39.5**	**84.2**	**148.9**	**201.3**	**183.2**
Regional groups										
Africa	–4.9	–6.0	–19.3	–15.0	6.3	–1.3	–6.7	–0.4	2.8	5.0
Sub-Sahara	–5.7	–8.8	–17.6	–14.4	–1.6	–9.1	–11.7	–10.0	–6.8	–6.4
Excluding Nigeria and South Africa	–6.3	–8.4	–12.4	–10.8	–6.0	–10.4	–7.3	–7.0	–5.4	–3.8
Central and eastern Europe	–17.8	–21.1	–19.3	–26.6	–32.6	–16.3	–24.0	–35.1	–44.2	–45.2
Commonwealth of Independent States[1]	2.5	–8.8	–9.6	20.7	46.3	32.8	32.2	36.6	61.4	53.6
Russia	8.3	–2.6	–2.1	22.2	44.6	33.4	30.9	35.8	56.6	52.3
Excluding Russia	–5.8	–6.3	–7.5	–1.5	1.6	–0.7	1.2	0.7	4.8	1.3
Developing Asia	–37.8	10.3	48.9	48.2	45.6	38.5	70.4	85.9	68.8	68.5
China	7.2	37.0	31.5	15.7	20.5	17.4	35.4	45.9	38.5	49.5
India	–6.0	–3.0	–6.9	–3.2	–5.1	–0.8	4.8	6.5	3.4	0.2
Excluding China and India	–38.9	–23.7	24.3	35.8	30.2	21.9	30.1	33.6	27.0	18.8
Middle East	11.4	7.8	–25.4	11.6	69.2	38.7	29.1	57.6	103.5	108.2
Western Hemisphere	–39.4	–67.4	–91.6	–57.7	–48.4	–52.9	–16.8	4.4	9.0	–6.8
Brazil	–23.0	–30.3	–33.3	–25.4	–24.2	–23.2	–7.6	4.0	6.5	2.1
Mexico	–2.5	–7.7	–16.1	–14.0	–18.2	–18.2	–14.1	–9.3	–8.0	–10.5
Analytical groups										
By source of export earnings										
Fuel	28.0	18.9	–32.2	11.3	100.2	50.2	35.5	71.5	130.6	141.4
Nonfuel	–114.0	–104.2	–84.1	–30.2	–13.9	–10.7	48.7	77.4	70.7	41.9
of which, primary products	–6.6	–8.7	–8.7	–3.9	–4.2	–5.5	–4.2	–2.1	–1.7	–5.4
By external financing source										
Net debtor countries	–129.6	–140.4	–121.7	–72.5	–67.3	–59.0	–22.7	–7.7	–18.6	–50.5
of which, official financing	–18.4	–14.9	–12.9	–3.8	9.9	2.8	–1.4	1.4	2.1	–3.8
Net debtor countries by debt-servicing experience										
Countries with arrears and/or rescheduling during 1997–2001	–46.0	–51.0	–55.8	–34.7	–16.8	–21.6	–8.0	5.6	13.4	3.5
Other groups										
Heavily indebted poor countries	–9.0	–9.9	–11.7	–12.5	–9.8	–8.6	–8.5	–8.1	–9.3	–10.5
Middle East and north Africa	10.8	9.1	–28.8	9.3	75.1	44.3	32.7	65.5	111.4	117.9

Table 28 *(concluded)*

	Ten-Year Averages											
	1986–95	1996–2005	1996	1997	1998	1999	2000	2001	2002	2003	2004	2005
	Percent of exports of goods and services											
Other emerging market and developing countries	**–8.0**	**5.6**	**–5.9**	**–5.5**	**–7.9**	**–1.2**	**4.5**	**2.1**	**4.1**	**6.1**	**6.8**	**5.6**
Regional groups												
Africa	–13.3	2.0	–3.8	–4.5	–16.1	–11.7	4.0	–0.9	–4.3	–0.2	1.2	2.0
Sub-Sahara	–12.8	–3.5	–5.8	–8.6	–19.5	–15.1	–1.4	–8.4	–10.5	–7.0	–4.1	–3.5
Excluding Nigeria and South Africa	–17.4	–4.1	–12.9	–17.0	–27.5	–22.4	–11.1	–19.8	–12.7	–10.4	–6.6	–4.1
Central and eastern Europe	–4.2	–9.2	–9.2	–10.0	–8.5	–12.5	–13.5	–6.3	–8.3	–9.6	–9.9	–9.2
Commonwealth of Independent States[1]	. . .	17.5	1.7	–6.0	–7.6	16.7	28.1	19.8	18.1	16.3	21.2	17.5
Russia	. . .	25.0	8.0	–2.5	–2.4	26.2	38.9	29.7	25.7	23.6	28.5	25.0
Excluding Russia	. . .	1.3	–13.1	–13.6	–18.6	–4.0	3.3	–1.3	2.2	1.0	5.3	1.3
Developing Asia	–9.3	5.1	–7.5	1.8	9.1	8.4	6.5	5.6	8.9	9.0	6.0	5.1
China	1.1	6.5	4.2	17.8	15.2	7.2	7.3	5.8	9.7	9.5	6.4	6.5
India	–14.6	0.2	–14.7	–6.7	–15.1	–6.3	–8.3	–1.2	6.5	7.9	3.2	0.2
Excluding China and India	–14.2	4.1	–13.4	–7.6	8.5	11.7	8.4	6.7	8.6	8.8	6.2	4.1
Middle East	–0.2	25.1	5.7	3.8	–15.9	5.7	24.5	14.7	10.4	17.2	25.0	25.1
Western Hemisphere	–15.5	–1.4	–14.4	–22.5	–31.4	–19.1	–13.5	–15.4	–4.8	1.1	2.0	–1.4
Brazil	–36.3	2.0	–43.5	–50.6	–56.4	–46.0	–37.5	–34.4	–10.9	4.8	6.4	2.0
Mexico	–2.5	–7.1	–3.3	–9.0	–18.6	–14.3	–15.4	–16.0	–12.3	–7.8	–5.7	–7.1
Analytical groups												
By source of export earnings												
Fuel	0.4	26.2	11.6	7.7	–17.5	4.8	28.3	15.8	10.7	17.7	25.5	26.2
Nonfuel	–9.5	1.5	–9.4	–7.9	–6.6	–2.3	–0.9	–0.7	2.9	3.8	2.9	1.5
of which, primary products	–5.5	–7.0	–12.2	–15.6	–16.9	–7.6	–7.7	–10.5	–7.9	–3.4	–2.2	–7.0
By external financing source												
Net debtor countries	–13.2	–2.7	–13.6	–13.7	–12.2	–7.0	–5.6	–5.0	–1.8	–0.5	–1.1	–2.7
of which, official financing	–15.4	–1.5	–12.6	–9.3	–9.1	–2.5	5.3	1.6	–0.8	0.6	0.9	–1.5
Net debtor countries by debt-servicing experience												
Countries with arrears and/or rescheduling during 1997–2001	–21.2	0.7	–18.6	–18.8	–22.1	–13.3	–5.2	–6.9	–2.4	1.5	3.0	0.7
Other groups												
Heavily indebted poor countries	–29.9	–18.2	–28.3	–30.7	–36.0	–39.0	–27.2	–23.6	–21.7	–17.8	–17.4	–18.2
Middle East and north Africa	–3.0	23.5	4.7	3.8	–15.2	3.9	23.0	14.4	10.1	16.8	23.2	23.5
Memorandum												
Median												
Other emerging market and developing countries	–11.9	–7.8	–11.3	–12.2	–16.7	–11.4	–10.3	–10.0	–9.7	–8.6	–7.8	–7.8

[1]Mongolia, which is not a member of the Commonwealth of Independent States, is included in this group for reasons of geography and similarities in economic structure.

Table 29. Other Emerging Market and Developing Countries—by Region: Current Account Transactions

(Billions of U.S. dollars)

	1996	1997	1998	1999	2000	2001	2002	2003	2004	2005
Other emerging market and developing countries										
Exports	1,197.2	1,283.9	1,195.0	1,287.5	1,616.9	1,581.3	1,721.3	2,098.6	2,565.5	2,837.8
Imports	1,194.2	1,273.3	1,214.3	1,194.7	1,411.2	1,428.6	1,535.9	1,853.0	2,251.9	2,542.5
Trade balance	3.0	10.6	–19.3	92.8	205.7	152.7	185.4	245.7	313.6	295.2
Services, net	–49.7	–56.2	–46.7	–50.6	–57.8	–59.2	–56.8	–62.2	–61.1	–64.7
Balance on goods and services	–46.6	–45.6	–66.1	42.2	147.9	93.5	128.6	183.4	252.6	230.5
Income, net	–83.7	–91.8	–99.5	–114.3	–118.3	–116.9	–124.5	–137.3	–156.9	–152.8
Current transfers, net	44.2	52.1	49.2	53.2	56.7	63.0	80.0	102.7	105.7	105.5
Current account balance	**–86.1**	**–85.3**	**–116.3**	**–18.9**	**86.3**	**39.5**	**84.2**	**148.9**	**201.3**	**183.2**
Memorandum										
Exports of goods and services	1,449.1	1,560.7	1,464.0	1,545.9	1,901.9	1,875.6	2,034.4	2,448.8	2,974.1	3,284.9
Interest payments	121.1	126.6	136.7	135.7	140.6	134.0	124.3	124.1	135.3	149.0
Oil trade balance	167.3	157.1	102.0	155.5	253.8	208.7	221.2	277.2	370.2	379.5
Regional groups										
Africa										
Exports	110.4	114.0	98.2	105.9	135.5	126.3	129.7	163.2	196.8	214.8
Imports	98.8	103.5	101.1	102.0	106.3	108.6	116.6	141.8	163.8	176.6
Trade balance	11.6	10.5	–2.9	3.9	29.2	17.7	13.1	21.4	33.0	38.2
Services, net	–9.9	–10.4	–11.7	–11.0	–11.1	–11.6	–11.9	–13.6	–16.3	–17.0
Balance on goods and services	1.7	0.1	–14.5	–7.1	18.1	6.1	1.2	7.8	16.8	21.2
Income, net	–17.9	–17.2	–16.1	–18.0	–23.5	–20.2	–21.9	–26.0	–33.4	–35.6
Current transfers, net	11.2	11.1	11.3	10.1	11.6	12.8	14.1	17.8	19.4	19.4
Current account balance	**–4.9**	**–6.0**	**–19.3**	**–15.0**	**6.3**	**–1.3**	**–6.7**	**–0.4**	**2.8**	**5.0**
Memorandum										
Exports of goods and services	131.5	135.2	119.6	128.2	157.6	149.5	153.9	192.3	228.7	248.2
Interest payments	16.2	15.4	15.6	15.3	14.9	13.3	12.3	13.3	13.6	13.8
Oil trade balance	29.5	29.1	18.8	26.1	46.0	38.0	40.2	55.7	76.0	86.5
Central and eastern Europe										
Exports	140.6	151.7	161.5	157.5	178.3	197.6	224.9	289.9	356.6	390.5
Imports	180.8	197.2	208.9	200.4	232.4	231.9	263.2	339.7	420.0	456.5
Trade balance	–40.2	–45.5	–47.4	–42.8	–54.1	–34.3	–38.3	–49.9	–63.4	–66.0
Services, net	14.5	19.1	21.6	11.2	14.9	14.0	12.0	15.4	19.2	20.9
Balance on goods and services	–25.6	–26.4	–25.8	–31.6	–39.2	–20.2	–26.3	–34.5	–44.3	–45.1
Income, net	–1.7	–5.2	–6.4	–6.6	–5.6	–8.1	–11.2	–14.9	–16.7	–18.7
Current transfers, net	9.6	10.5	12.9	11.6	12.2	12.0	13.5	14.2	16.7	18.6
Current account balance	**–17.8**	**–21.1**	**–19.3**	**–26.6**	**–32.6**	**–16.3**	**–24.0**	**–35.1**	**–44.2**	**–45.2**
Memorandum										
Exports of goods and services	193.6	211.6	227.6	213.5	240.6	259.3	287.9	366.8	448.2	490.2
Interest payments	11.1	11.7	11.5	11.8	12.9	14.1	14.3	16.8	19.9	23.1
Oil trade balance	–17.5	–17.5	–14.3	–14.1	–20.4	–19.5	–19.5	–23.8	–28.6	–29.1

Table 29 ***(concluded)***

	1996	1997	1998	1999	2000	2001	2002	2003	2004	2005
Commonwealth of Independent States[1]										
Exports	126.8	125.0	107.4	107.5	147.2	145.9	155.0	196.6	258.5	274.0
Imports	113.7	118.3	99.4	73.8	84.3	97.0	106.3	133.8	163.1	181.4
Trade balance	13.1	6.7	8.0	33.7	62.9	48.9	48.7	62.7	95.4	92.7
Services, net	−3.0	−4.7	−3.7	−3.8	−7.0	−10.2	−11.0	−12.9	−16.3	−19.8
Balance on goods and services	10.0	2.0	4.3	29.9	55.9	38.7	37.7	49.8	79.2	72.9
Income, net	−8.8	−12.0	−15.2	−11.6	−11.9	−8.0	−8.3	−16.0	−20.7	−21.4
Current transfers, net	1.3	1.2	1.3	2.3	2.3	2.0	2.8	2.8	3.0	2.1
Current account balance	**2.5**	**−8.8**	**−9.6**	**20.7**	**46.3**	**32.8**	**32.2**	**36.6**	**61.4**	**53.6**
Memorandum										
Exports of goods and services	147.5	147.1	127.2	123.5	164.8	165.2	177.9	223.7	290.2	306.8
Interest payments	10.3	13.9	17.0	12.7	12.9	10.5	9.3	9.6	13.8	15.1
Oil trade balance	21.3	20.4	13.5	20.0	39.0	36.8	42.3	56.0	82.2	90.7
Developing Asia										
Exports	415.7	466.5	455.3	493.8	604.0	593.3	676.2	831.7	996.8	1,172.9
Imports	445.1	449.2	387.9	422.9	541.4	537.0	607.1	761.8	950.3	1,127.8
Trade balance	−29.3	17.3	67.3	70.9	62.6	56.3	69.1	69.9	46.5	45.1
Services, net	−6.6	−11.0	−12.5	−10.6	−10.1	−10.0	−4.7	−10.0	−4.6	−1.0
Balance on goods and services	−36.0	6.3	54.9	60.3	52.4	46.3	64.3	59.9	41.9	44.0
Income, net	−23.9	−24.1	−28.0	−37.8	−35.4	−37.9	−33.7	−26.0	−24.3	−24.8
Current transfers, net	22.1	28.1	22.0	25.7	28.5	30.2	39.7	52.1	51.2	49.2
Current account balance	**−37.8**	**10.3**	**48.9**	**48.2**	**45.6**	**38.5**	**70.4**	**85.9**	**68.8**	**68.5**
Memorandum										
Exports of goods and services	504.6	564.9	538.0	576.5	698.2	693.6	789.1	950.1	1,140.3	1,338.7
Interest payments	30.4	27.9	31.8	33.7	33.4	31.2	28.9	27.5	30.0	32.4
Oil trade balance	−17.8	−20.5	−12.4	−19.6	−37.5	−34.9	−39.8	−51.3	−71.2	−87.6
Middle East										
Exports	176.1	177.0	132.4	172.9	252.3	231.5	245.1	296.6	369.4	383.7
Imports	127.4	134.1	132.9	130.9	143.1	155.6	168.6	189.9	212.4	230.1
Trade balance	48.7	42.9	−0.5	42.0	109.2	75.9	76.5	106.7	157.1	153.6
Services, net	−33.2	−34.1	−25.1	−24.6	−31.8	−27.7	−32.0	−33.4	−34.6	−37.4
Balance on goods and services	15.5	8.8	−25.6	17.4	77.3	48.3	44.5	73.3	122.5	116.2
Income, net	11.4	13.8	16.4	11.3	11.7	10.8	4.2	3.4	3.1	13.9
Current transfers, net	−15.6	−14.9	−16.2	−17.2	−19.9	−20.4	−19.6	−19.1	−22.0	−21.9
Current account balance	**11.4**	**7.8**	**−25.4**	**11.6**	**69.2**	**38.7**	**29.1**	**57.6**	**103.5**	**108.2**
Memorandum										
Exports of goods and services	198.6	202.8	159.4	202.2	282.6	263.7	279.3	335.0	413.6	430.1
Interest payments	6.8	7.3	7.4	6.6	7.2	6.7	7.0	5.0	5.2	6.0
Oil trade balance	126.1	120.8	80.8	119.0	186.9	158.3	164.8	204.4	261.1	266.4
Western Hemisphere										
Exports	227.6	249.8	240.2	249.8	299.6	286.6	290.4	320.7	387.3	401.9
Imports	228.3	271.1	284.2	264.7	303.8	298.6	274.1	285.9	342.3	370.2
Trade balance	−0.8	−21.3	−43.9	−14.8	−4.2	−12.0	16.3	34.8	45.0	31.7
Services, net	−11.5	−15.1	−15.4	−11.9	−12.5	−13.7	−9.1	−7.6	−8.5	−10.4
Balance on goods and services	−12.3	−36.4	−59.3	−26.7	−16.7	−25.7	7.2	27.2	36.5	21.4
Income, net	−42.7	−47.1	−50.2	−51.5	−53.7	−53.5	−53.6	−57.8	−64.9	−66.3
Current transfers, net	15.6	16.1	18.0	20.6	22.0	26.3	29.6	35.0	37.3	38.1
Current account balance	**−39.4**	**−67.4**	**−91.6**	**−57.7**	**−48.4**	**−52.9**	**−16.8**	**4.4**	**9.0**	**−6.8**
Memorandum										
Exports of goods and services	273.4	299.2	292.1	301.9	358.2	344.3	346.4	380.9	453.2	471.0
Interest payments	46.3	50.3	53.4	55.5	59.3	58.2	52.5	51.9	52.8	58.6
Oil trade balance	25.7	24.8	15.5	24.2	39.9	30.1	33.3	36.1	50.8	52.7

[1]Mongolia, which is not a member of the Commonwealth of Independent States, is included in this group for reasons of geography and similarities in economic structure.

Table 30. Other Emerging Market and Developing Countries—by Analytical Criteria: Current Account Transactions

(Billions of U.S. dollars)

	1996	1997	1998	1999	2000	2001	2002	2003	2004	2005
By source of export earnings										
Fuel										
Exports	229.2	230.4	168.1	220.5	336.9	298.6	311.3	380.0	484.5	510.4
Imports	132.0	144.5	143.2	143.0	157.3	173.4	188.3	213.8	243.5	264.2
Trade balance	97.2	85.9	24.9	77.5	179.5	125.2	123.0	166.2	241.0	246.1
Services, net	–50.9	–51.6	–42.4	–44.2	–51.2	–48.1	–52.3	–56.5	–62.6	–66.1
Balance on goods and services	46.2	34.3	–17.5	33.3	128.4	77.1	70.7	109.7	178.4	180.0
Income, net	1.6	4.0	6.3	0.7	–2.8	–1.1	–10.1	–14.0	–20.6	–12.2
Current transfers, net	–19.8	–19.4	–21.0	–22.8	–25.4	–25.8	–25.2	–24.2	–27.1	–26.5
Current account balance	**28.0**	**18.9**	**–32.2**	**11.3**	**100.2**	**50.2**	**35.5**	**71.5**	**130.6**	**141.4**
Memorandum										
Exports of goods and services	240.9	245.3	184.1	236.6	354.1	317.5	332.7	404.6	511.8	539.1
Interest payments	14.0	15.7	16.3	14.2	15.1	14.4	13.7	12.0	12.5	13.5
Oil trade balance	177.8	173.3	116.2	167.2	269.1	227.3	232.3	287.0	373.9	390.9
Nonfuel exports										
Exports	968.0	1,053.5	1,026.9	1,067.0	1,280.0	1,282.7	1,410.0	1,718.6	2,081.0	2,327.4
Imports	1,062.2	1,128.8	1,071.2	1,051.7	1,253.9	1,255.2	1,347.6	1,639.2	2,008.4	2,278.3
Trade balance	–94.1	–75.3	–44.2	15.2	26.1	27.5	62.4	79.5	72.6	49.1
Services, net	1.3	–4.6	–4.3	–6.4	–6.6	–11.1	–4.5	–5.7	1.6	1.4
Balance on goods and services	–92.9	–79.9	–48.5	8.9	19.5	16.4	57.9	73.7	74.2	50.5
Income, net	–85.3	–95.8	–105.8	–115.0	–115.5	–115.8	–114.4	–123.3	–136.3	–140.6
Current transfers, net	64.1	71.5	70.2	76.0	82.1	88.7	105.2	127.0	132.8	132.0
Current account balance	**–114.0**	**–104.2**	**–84.1**	**–30.2**	**–13.9**	**–10.7**	**48.7**	**77.4**	**70.7**	**41.9**
Memorandum										
Exports of goods and services	1,208.2	1,315.4	1,280.0	1,309.3	1,547.8	1,558.2	1,701.8	2,044.1	2,462.3	2,745.8
Interest payments	107.1	110.9	120.4	121.5	125.5	119.6	110.6	112.0	122.8	135.5
Oil trade balance	–10.5	–16.2	–14.2	–11.7	–15.3	–18.6	–11.0	–9.8	–3.7	–11.5
Nonfuel primary products										
Exports	45.3	46.9	42.5	43.1	45.2	42.8	44.1	51.7	63.8	64.8
Imports	46.5	49.0	46.2	41.3	43.5	43.2	43.5	49.0	57.8	62.1
Trade balance	–1.2	–2.1	–3.7	1.8	1.8	–0.4	0.6	2.7	6.0	2.7
Services, net	–4.1	–4.3	–4.5	–4.5	–4.2	–4.2	–4.4	–5.0	–5.5	–6.2
Balance on goods and services	–5.3	–6.4	–8.2	–2.7	–2.5	–4.6	–3.8	–2.3	0.5	–3.5
Income, net	–6.1	–6.3	–4.9	–5.6	–6.6	–6.2	–6.3	–6.9	–10.4	–9.6
Current transfers, net	4.8	4.0	4.4	4.3	4.9	5.3	5.9	7.1	8.2	7.7
Current account balance	**–6.6**	**–8.7**	**–8.7**	**–3.9**	**–4.2**	**–5.5**	**–4.2**	**–2.1**	**–1.7**	**–5.4**
Memorandum										
Exports of goods and services	53.7	55.6	51.3	51.9	53.9	51.9	53.6	62.7	75.8	77.2
Interest payments	5.1	5.0	5.1	5.1	5.5	5.0	4.7	4.7	4.5	5.2
Oil trade balance	–2.4	–2.7	–2.6	–3.0	–4.6	–4.5	–3.7	–4.1	–4.3	–3.9

Table 30 *(continued)*

	1996	1997	1998	1999	2000	2001	2002	2003	2004	2005
By external financing source										
Net debtor countries										
Exports	745.1	804.2	781.6	823.7	978.0	960.2	1,022.4	1,198.2	1,426.5	1,531.8
Imports	867.4	929.2	882.5	867.1	1,011.8	990.8	1,030.7	1,198.3	1,432.6	1,564.5
Trade balance	−122.3	−125.0	−100.9	−43.4	−33.9	−30.6	−8.2	−0.1	−6.1	−32.8
Services, net	0.5	−4.2	−6.7	−3.4	−3.6	−7.2	−0.5	0.4	8.0	7.1
Balance on goods and services	−121.8	−129.2	−107.6	−46.8	−37.4	−37.8	−8.7	0.4	1.9	−25.7
Income, net	−70.7	−79.4	−80.4	−93.8	−102.6	−99.4	−104.8	−116.4	−132.6	−138.1
Current transfers, net	62.9	68.2	66.3	68.2	72.7	78.2	90.8	108.3	112.1	113.3
Current account balance	**−129.6**	**−140.4**	**−121.7**	**−72.5**	**−67.3**	**−59.0**	**−22.7**	**−7.7**	**−18.6**	**−50.5**
Memorandum										
Exports of goods and services	949.3	1,025.2	996.5	1,031.5	1,204.3	1,190.0	1,259.7	1,458.1	1,725.9	1,852.1
Interest payments	93.0	97.6	102.1	105.2	109.5	104.4	95.5	96.3	102.4	112.6
Oil trade balance	−1.8	−1.2	−1.5	12.2	23.6	15.4	19.8	24.9	31.8	35.6
Official financing										
Exports	122.3	133.7	119.3	126.5	162.7	149.5	154.8	181.0	208.8	220.8
Imports	129.1	135.2	120.0	118.3	137.2	135.1	145.3	168.2	190.8	207.2
Trade balance	−6.9	−1.5	−0.7	8.2	25.5	14.4	9.5	12.8	18.0	13.6
Services, net	−17.2	−19.1	−21.1	−13.3	−15.9	−16.5	−16.6	−20.6	−22.1	−23.4
Balance on goods and services	−24.0	−20.6	−21.7	−5.1	9.6	−2.1	−7.1	−7.8	−4.1	−9.8
Income, net	−12.1	−13.3	−11.3	−20.2	−23.2	−19.9	−23.3	−24.6	−28.9	−29.1
Current transfers, net	17.8	19.1	20.1	21.5	23.5	24.9	29.1	33.7	35.1	35.1
Current account balance	**−18.4**	**−14.9**	**−12.9**	**−3.8**	**9.9**	**2.8**	**−1.4**	**1.4**	**2.1**	**−3.8**
Memorandum										
Exports of goods and services	146.0	159.7	142.7	149.2	186.8	174.6	181.7	209.0	239.2	253.1
Interest payments	16.1	16.5	18.3	18.7	18.8	15.7	14.6	14.3	14.6	14.4
Oil trade balance	19.3	18.5	11.5	15.4	25.8	19.7	16.4	25.1	31.3	30.8
Net debtor countries by debt-servicing experience										
Countries with arrears and/or rescheduling during 1997–2001										
Exports	206.7	226.6	209.3	219.4	275.5	267.6	280.8	329.5	392.6	418.3
Imports	221.7	238.0	220.4	210.2	242.9	245.9	252.7	288.9	336.3	366.6
Trade balance	−15.1	−11.4	−11.1	9.2	32.6	21.7	28.1	40.6	56.3	51.7
Services, net	−22.5	−27.5	−30.1	−18.4	−21.2	−23.1	−19.8	−22.0	−24.7	−26.4
Balance on goods and services	−37.5	−38.9	−41.1	−9.2	11.4	−1.4	8.3	18.5	31.6	25.3
Income, net	−28.8	−32.5	−34.8	−44.8	−49.1	−44.9	−46.5	−49.3	−56.7	−59.3
Current transfers, net	20.3	20.4	20.1	19.3	20.8	24.7	30.2	36.4	38.5	37.6
Current account balance	**−46.0**	**−51.0**	**−55.8**	**−34.7**	**−16.8**	**−21.6**	**−8.0**	**5.6**	**13.4**	**3.5**
Memorandum										
Exports of goods and services	247.5	271.4	252.3	260.7	321.3	315.5	332.0	385.1	453.6	483.0
Interest payments	34.1	35.2	39.7	41.5	42.3	39.1	34.8	35.0	35.6	36.2
Oil trade balance	12.1	14.3	12.0	22.2	36.7	32.3	31.9	39.6	49.3	57.1

Table 30 *(concluded)*

	1996	1997	1998	1999	2000	2001	2002	2003	2004	2005
Other groups										
Heavily indebted poor countries										
Exports	25.1	25.5	25.2	24.6	28.2	28.2	30.5	35.7	42.8	46.6
Imports	28.4	29.9	32.2	32.6	32.3	33.8	35.9	40.8	47.6	51.5
Trade balance	–3.4	–4.4	–7.0	–8.0	–4.0	–5.7	–5.4	–5.1	–4.8	–4.9
Services, net	–4.4	–4.3	–4.8	–4.4	–4.6	–4.6	–5.1	–5.7	–7.2	–7.6
Balance on goods and services	–7.8	–8.7	–11.8	–12.5	–8.6	–10.3	–10.5	–10.8	–12.0	–12.6
Income, net	–7.2	–6.8	–5.6	–5.8	–7.6	–5.5	–6.0	–6.8	–7.9	–8.5
Current transfers, net	6.1	5.6	5.8	5.8	6.5	7.2	8.0	9.5	10.7	10.6
Current account balance	**–9.0**	**–9.9**	**–11.7**	**–12.5**	**–9.8**	**–8.6**	**–8.5**	**–8.1**	**–9.3**	**–10.5**
Memorandum										
Exports of goods and services	31.7	32.2	32.4	32.1	35.9	36.3	39.0	45.4	53.3	57.6
Interest payments	5.5	5.3	5.7	5.3	5.8	5.2	4.6	5.2	5.4	5.5
Oil trade balance	–0.5	–0.3	–0.5	–0.3	1.1	0.5	0.9	1.3	4.1	5.5
Middle East and north Africa										
Exports	202.9	204.5	156.4	199.8	289.5	266.5	280.9	340.7	424.5	443.8
Imports	154.9	160.6	161.1	159.9	173.4	186.9	203.4	229.8	260.9	281.9
Trade balance	48.0	43.9	–4.7	39.9	116.0	79.6	77.5	110.9	163.6	161.9
Services, net	–32.2	–33.0	–24.2	–23.8	–31.1	–26.5	–30.7	–31.9	–33.4	–36.2
Balance on goods and services	15.9	10.9	–28.9	16.0	84.9	53.1	46.8	79.0	130.2	125.7
Income, net	5.6	8.4	11.3	5.8	5.4	5.7	–1.0	–2.5	–5.5	5.1
Current transfers, net	–10.7	–10.2	–11.2	–12.6	–15.2	–14.5	–13.1	–11.0	–13.3	–12.9
Current account balance	**10.8**	**9.1**	**–28.8**	**9.3**	**75.1**	**44.3**	**32.7**	**65.5**	**111.4**	**117.9**
Memorandum										
Exports of goods and services	231.7	236.6	189.9	236.1	326.7	306.7	323.6	389.0	479.7	501.9
Interest payments	–12.1	–12.3	–12.1	–11.2	–12.3	–11.1	–10.9	–9.0	–9.2	–10.1
Oil trade balance	137.1	132.3	89.4	129.6	207.2	176.1	182.3	227.7	291.7	300.6

Table 31. Other Emerging Market and Developing Countries—by Country: Balance of Payments on Current Account

(Percent of GDP)

	1996	1997	1998	1999	2000	2001	2002	2003	2004	2005
Africa	**–1.1**	**–1.4**	**–4.5**	**–3.5**	**1.4**	**–0.3**	**–1.5**	**–0.1**	**0.4**	**0.7**
Algeria	2.7	7.2	–1.9	—	16.8	12.9	7.8	13.4	13.1	15.2
Angola	–4.4	–11.5	–29.7	–27.8	8.7	–16.0	–1.4	–4.9	9.2	14.5
Benin	–4.2	–7.4	–5.7	–7.6	–8.0	–6.7	–9.0	–8.5	–8.4	–9.1
Botswana	10.3	13.9	4.1	12.3	10.4	11.5	11.6	11.0	6.4	5.7
Burkina Faso	–9.1	–9.6	–8.6	–10.8	–12.3	–10.2	–9.1	–6.8	–8.4	–7.0
Burundi	–6.1	–2.8	–7.5	–6.1	–10.0	–6.8	–6.5	–6.2	–15.1	–17.7
Cameroon	–4.1	–2.8	–2.5	–4.3	–1.7	–4.1	–7.0	–2.5	–2.1	–2.3
Cape Verde	–6.9	–6.0	–11.0	–12.4	–11.2	–10.8	–12.0	–8.9	–8.9	–8.5
Central African Republic	–3.3	–3.0	–6.1	–1.6	–3.0	–2.5	–2.9	–5.2	–2.8	–2.2
Chad	–8.3	–9.0	–9.8	–15.9	–18.0	–35.1	–51.5	–39.0	–18.3	–10.9
Comoros	–12.7	–19.9	–8.4	–6.4	–1.8	1.8	–2.3	–4.5	–2.2	–0.1
Congo, Dem. Rep. of	–0.5	–3.1	–9.0	–2.6	–4.6	–4.9	–2.8	0.6	–3.0	–5.9
Congo, Rep. of	–32.7	–12.9	–20.6	–17.1	7.9	–3.2	–0.3	–0.1	1.6	1.6
Côte d'Ivoire	–1.7	–0.8	–2.6	–1.3	–2.8	–1.1	6.1	3.6	–0.2	1.4
Djibouti	–3.3	–2.3	–0.6	–0.4	–7.2	–5.6	–6.3	–6.2	–10.7	–18.6
Equatorial Guinea	–107.7	–37.5	–78.5	–43.6	–29.0	–34.4	–7.2	–0.3	18.3	34.5
Eritrea	–7.1	2.1	–23.8	–28.2	–11.7	—	0.3	–15.3	–9.9	–3.5
Ethiopia	1.1	–3.0	–1.6	–7.9	–5.1	–3.6	–5.7	–4.7	–3.8	–8.5
Gabon	15.6	10.0	–13.8	8.4	19.7	11.0	5.2	9.6	11.6	10.9
Gambia, The	–13.1	–3.7	–2.4	–2.8	–3.1	–0.4	–5.5	–5.2	–6.1	–6.8
Ghana	–3.1	–14.4	–5.0	–11.6	–8.4	–5.3	0.5	1.7	0.3	–1.0
Guinea	–8.5	–7.0	–8.5	–7.6	–7.3	–2.7	–4.3	–3.3	–2.9	–2.8
Guinea-Bissau	–16.5	–8.8	–13.2	–12.0	–13.2	–22.2	–10.7	–3.5	–2.2	–4.8
Kenya	–2.1	–4.2	–4.9	–2.2	–2.7	–4.1	—	–2.5	–7.7	–8.3
Lesotho	–30.2	–30.9	–25.0	–22.8	–18.2	–13.2	–17.0	–11.1	–6.4	–6.5
Madagascar	–5.0	–5.5	–7.4	–5.4	–5.6	–1.3	–6.0	–6.0	–8.6	–7.2
Malawi	–7.1	–11.9	–0.4	–8.2	–5.4	–6.9	–7.0	–8.1	–10.0	–8.6
Mali	–9.1	–6.5	–6.8	–8.8	–10.0	–10.4	–3.1	–4.2	–5.0	–7.2
Mauritania	–1.6	1.7	–0.7	3.0	–2.7	–10.6	1.5	–10.0	–23.1	–30.3
Mauritius	–0.6	0.4	–2.8	–1.5	–1.6	3.4	5.4	2.6	2.6	0.5
Morocco	0.1	–0.3	–0.4	–0.5	–1.4	4.8	4.1	3.1	0.2	–1.3
Mozambique, Rep. of	–17.7	–12.5	–14.4	–22.4	–19.2	–22.4	–21.2	–14.7	–9.3	–13.3
Namibia	3.6	1.7	2.4	6.9	9.3	1.7	3.8	4.0	5.5	3.6
Niger	–5.5	–7.2	–6.9	–6.5	–6.2	–4.8	–6.5	–6.2	–7.9	–6.4
Nigeria	6.9	5.1	–8.9	–8.4	10.3	2.6	–11.1	–2.8	2.9	1.7
Rwanda	–6.7	–9.5	–9.6	–7.7	–5.0	–5.9	–6.7	–8.4	–6.8	–8.2
São Tomé and Príncipe	–53.3	–30.9	–30.8	–45.4	–48.9	–54.2	–44.8	–36.1	–59.9	–77.2
Senegal	–4.2	–4.2	–4.1	–5.6	–6.1	–4.9	–6.0	–6.4	–7.3	–6.6
Seychelles	–13.2	–10.7	–16.5	–19.8	–7.2	–23.5	–16.3	–2.8	1.0	2.1
Sierra Leone	–12.5	–0.4	–2.6	–11.1	–15.2	–16.2	–4.8	–7.6	–12.1	–9.4
South Africa	–1.3	–1.5	–1.7	–0.4	–0.2	—	0.6	–0.8	–2.0	–2.1
Sudan	–16.5	–13.7	–14.9	–15.8	–15.1	–15.5	–9.6	–8.2	–6.8	–4.8
Swaziland	–3.9	–0.2	–6.9	–2.6	–4.7	–4.3	–3.9	–4.1	–6.0	–6.2
Tanzania	–2.3	–5.3	–11.0	–9.9	–5.3	–5.3	–3.8	–2.4	–5.2	–6.2
Togo	–6.5	–11.1	–10.6	–9.5	–17.4	–17.3	–14.3	–11.7	–8.6	–6.7
Tunisia	–2.4	–3.1	–3.4	–2.2	–4.2	–4.3	–3.5	–2.9	–2.8	–3.0
Uganda	–6.4	–2.5	–5.3	–7.4	–4.7	–5.8	–6.0	–5.9	–1.2	–5.3
Zambia	–3.7	–6.1	–16.7	–13.7	–18.2	–20.0	–15.4	–13.3	–10.8	–10.9
Zimbabwe	–1.1	–8.0	–4.7	2.5	0.2	–4.5	–2.6	–4.4	–7.1	–10.9

Table 31 ***(continued)***

	1996	1997	1998	1999	2000	2001	2002	2003	2004	2005
Central and eastern Europe	**–3.1**	**–3.6**	**–3.0**	**–4.3**	**–5.3**	**–2.7**	**–3.5**	**–4.2**	**–4.4**	**–4.2**
Albania	–6.3	–8.7	–3.9	–3.9	–4.4	–3.2	–6.5	–5.1	–5.5	–5.2
Bosnia and Herzegovina	. . .	. . .	–8.6	–9.3	–13.3	–16.7	–22.1	–19.0	–19.0	–18.2
Bulgaria	7.3	10.1	–0.5	–5.0	–5.6	–7.2	–5.3	–8.4	–8.7	–8.3
Croatia	–4.8	–12.5	–6.7	–7.0	–2.5	–3.7	–8.4	–6.1	–5.8	–5.2
Czech Republic	–6.6	–6.2	–2.0	–2.5	–4.9	–5.4	–5.6	–6.2	–5.5	–4.9
Estonia	–8.6	–11.4	–8.6	–4.4	–5.5	–5.6	–10.2	–13.2	–11.2	–9.5
Hungary	–3.7	–4.5	–7.1	–7.9	–8.7	–6.2	–7.2	–8.9	–8.8	–8.2
Latvia	–3.8	–4.7	–9.0	–9.1	–6.4	–8.9	–6.5	–8.6	–9.3	–8.2
Lithuania	–5.0	–7.9	–11.7	–11.0	–5.9	–4.7	–5.2	–6.7	–7.1	–6.9
Macedonia, FYR	–8.8	–7.9	–7.5	–0.9	–2.1	–6.8	–8.5	–6.0	–7.7	–6.3
Malta	–12.2	–5.9	–6.2	–3.4	–13.4	–4.5	–1.1	–6.0	–4.0	–2.6
Poland	–2.1	–3.7	–4.1	–7.6	–6.0	–2.9	–2.6	–1.9	–1.7	–2.1
Romania	–6.7	–5.4	–7.1	–4.1	–3.9	–5.5	–3.4	–5.9	–5.2	–5.3
Serbia and Montenegro	. . .	. . .	–4.8	–7.5	–3.9	–4.6	–8.8	–10.2	–9.6	–8.5
Slovak Republic	–10.1	–9.2	–9.6	–4.8	–3.5	–8.4	–8.0	–0.9	–2.3	–2.6
Slovenia	0.2	0.3	–0.6	–3.3	–2.8	0.2	1.4	0.1	–0.6	–1.4
Turkey	–1.2	–1.1	1.0	–0.7	–4.8	2.2	–0.8	–2.9	–4.0	–3.5
Commonwealth of Independent States[1]	0.5	–1.7	–2.5	7.1	13.0	7.9	6.9	6.4	8.3	6.2
Armenia	–18.5	–16.6	–20.8	–16.6	–14.6	–10.0	–6.6	–7.1	–5.9	–5.2
Azerbaijan	–25.9	–23.1	–30.7	–13.1	–3.6	–0.9	–12.3	–28.3	–24.2	–8.1
Belarus	–3.6	–6.1	–6.7	–1.6	–2.7	–3.5	–2.6	–2.9	–3.6	–3.5
Georgia	–10.8	–10.5	–10.2	–7.8	–4.4	–6.5	–6.0	–7.5	–8.1	–8.4
Kazakhstan	–3.6	–3.5	–5.4	–0.1	4.2	–4.0	–3.5	–0.2	2.1	–0.7
Kyrgyz Republic	–23.2	–8.3	–22.9	–15.7	–5.3	–2.0	–2.2	–2.3	–3.7	–5.7
Moldova	–11.1	–14.2	–17.3	–6.0	–9.0	–4.9	–6.0	–9.3	–6.6	–6.3
Mongolia	–2.1	9.0	–5.8	–4.7	–5.7	–7.6	–7.1	–5.6	–3.3	–2.8
Russia	2.1	–0.6	–0.8	11.3	17.2	10.9	8.9	8.3	9.9	7.8
Tajikistan	–6.7	–5.0	–8.3	–3.4	–6.3	–7.1	–2.7	–1.3	–2.2	–2.5
Turkmenistan	0.1	–21.6	–32.7	–14.8	8.4	1.7	6.5	4.6	5.4	4.7
Ukraine	–2.7	–3.0	–3.1	2.6	4.7	3.7	7.5	5.8	10.2	4.1
Uzbekistan	–8.8	–4.0	–0.8	–0.8	1.6	–1.0	1.2	8.9	8.2	5.5

Table 31 ***(continued)***

	1996	1997	1998	1999	2000	2001	2002	2003	2004	2005
Developing Asia	**–1.9**	**0.5**	**2.6**	**2.4**	**2.1**	**1.7**	**2.9**	**3.1**	**2.2**	**2.0**
Afghanistan, I.S. of	. . .	. . .	. . .	. . .	. . .	. . .	. . .	. . .	. . .	. . .
Bangladesh	–2.4	–1.6	–1.1	–0.9	–1.5	–0.8	0.6	0.4	–0.5	–1.3
Bhutan	6.6	8.3	5.6	0.9	–1.6	–1.1	–2.0	–6.0	–5.0	–2.0
Brunei Darussalam	37.2	35.7	44.7	48.1	81.7	83.7	72.9	80.8	77.9	78.0
Cambodia	–5.6	–1.1	–5.9	–5.2	–2.9	–1.2	–0.9	–2.4	–3.3	–4.2
China	0.9	4.1	3.3	1.6	1.9	1.5	2.8	3.2	2.4	2.8
Fiji	3.5	1.6	–0.3	–4.5	–6.3	–3.6	–2.3	1.5	1.9	1.8
India	–1.6	–0.7	–1.7	–0.7	–1.1	–0.2	1.0	1.1	0.5	—
Indonesia	–3.2	–1.8	4.2	4.1	5.3	4.8	4.5	3.5	2.9	1.9
Kiribati	–12.1	22.0	35.2	12.4	13.3	3.2	7.7	–21.5	–12.5	–13.6
Lao PDR	–12.6	–10.5	–4.7	–4.0	–1.4	–3.3	–5.5	–4.5	–3.7	–7.1
Malaysia	–4.4	–5.9	13.2	15.9	9.4	8.3	8.4	12.9	12.4	10.1
Maldives	–1.7	–6.8	–4.0	–13.4	–8.2	–9.4	–5.6	–6.5	–9.2	–10.9
Myanmar	–10.3	–12.8	–14.8	–8.8	1.4	–4.3	3.5	1.0	–0.2	–0.8
Nepal	–5.4	–1.0	–1.0	4.3	3.8	4.8	4.5	1.8	3.0	0.9
Pakistan	–6.5	–4.2	–3.2	–2.8	–1.9	0.4	4.5	3.5	0.3	–0.3
Papua New Guinea	5.5	–5.4	0.6	2.8	8.7	7.0	–0.7	11.2	16.2	10.0
Philippines	–4.6	–5.2	2.3	9.5	8.4	1.9	5.8	4.9	2.8	1.8
Samoa	5.0	–3.6	–3.4	–8.6	–6.1	–11.7	–8.1	–1.9	–1.1	–0.3
Solomon Islands	6.9	–5.6	–1.6	3.1	–10.6	–12.8	–6.9	1.4	–0.6	–9.5
Sri Lanka	–4.9	–2.6	–1.4	–3.6	–6.4	–1.1	–1.4	–0.6	–3.2	–3.5
Thailand	–7.9	–2.1	12.8	10.2	7.6	5.4	5.5	5.6	3.8	2.0
Timor-Leste, Dem. Rep. of	. . .	. . .	. . .	2.1	14.9	14.0	11.6	12.7	12.3	8.9
Tonga	–5.9	–0.9	–10.5	–0.6	–5.9	–9.2	4.9	–2.9	0.8	–0.5
Vanuatu	–2.4	–1.0	2.5	–5.2	2.0	0.8	2.4	–0.7	–3.7	–3.4
Vietnam	–9.9	–6.2	–3.9	4.5	2.1	2.2	–1.2	–5.1	–4.5	–3.6
Middle East	**2.2**	**1.4**	**–5.0**	**2.1**	**10.9**	**6.0**	**4.5**	**8.1**	**12.7**	**12.5**
Bahrain	4.3	–0.5	–12.5	–1.4	10.4	2.8	–6.1	–5.5	3.1	3.8
Egypt	–0.3	0.2	–3.0	–1.9	–1.2	—	0.7	2.4	3.2	1.8
Iran, I.R. of	4.7	2.1	–2.2	6.3	12.9	5.2	3.1	1.5	3.4	1.6
Iraq	. . .	. . .	. . .	. . .	. . .	. . .	. . .	. . .	. . .	. . .
Jordan	–3.2	0.4	0.3	5.0	0.7	—	4.5	11.2	5.6	1.8
Kuwait	22.6	25.9	8.5	16.6	39.6	24.5	12.1	18.1	28.8	29.6
Lebanon	–37.1	–33.6	–28.1	–18.3	–17.9	–21.5	–13.8	–13.1	–12.2	–10.0
Libya	4.4	0.7	–1.2	5.4	20.8	10.2	–2.0	13.6	21.3	24.1
Oman	1.3	–1.2	–22.3	–3.1	16.1	9.9	8.7	6.6	10.0	6.9
Qatar	–24.0	–25.6	–21.5	6.8	18.0	19.9	16.5	27.6	36.2	35.4
Saudi Arabia	0.1	–0.1	–8.7	0.3	7.6	5.0	6.2	13.5	19.5	20.1
Syrian Arab Republic	–0.4	1.9	–0.3	0.6	4.4	4.8	6.7	3.5	3.3	3.3
United Arab Emirates	9.1	10.1	1.8	1.6	17.3	9.4	4.9	8.5	14.2	16.9
Yemen	1.7	1.6	–2.8	2.7	13.2	5.3	5.4	1.8	3.5	–1.1

Table 31 *(concluded)*

	1996	1997	1998	1999	2000	2001	2002	2003	2004	2005
Western Hemisphere	**−2.2**	**−3.4**	**−4.6**	**−3.3**	**−2.5**	**−2.8**	**−1.0**	**0.3**	**0.5**	**−0.3**
Antigua and Barbuda	−18.9	−14.7	−10.8	−9.2	−10.6	−7.0	−11.1	−13.2	−13.1	−13.1
Argentina	−2.5	−4.2	−4.9	−4.2	−3.2	−1.4	9.0	6.2	1.1	−1.4
Bahamas, The	−7.2	−16.9	−23.8	−5.3	−10.5	−11.9	−6.8	−8.1	−10.9	−13.6
Barbados	3.6	−2.2	−2.4	−6.0	−5.6	−3.7	−6.6	−7.8	−10.0	−7.7
Belize	−1.1	−3.5	−6.0	−10.4	−20.6	−22.6	−20.2	−19.5	−14.7	−11.1
Bolivia	−4.5	−7.0	−7.9	−5.9	−5.3	−3.4	−4.2	0.5	2.7	1.1
Brazil	−3.0	−3.8	−4.2	−4.8	−4.0	−4.6	−1.7	0.8	1.2	0.4
Chile	−4.1	−4.4	−4.9	0.1	−1.2	−1.6	−1.3	−0.8	0.5	−1.9
Colombia	−4.8	−5.4	−4.9	0.8	0.8	−1.4	−1.8	−1.9	−1.1	−2.2
Costa Rica	−3.8	−4.8	−5.3	−5.2	−4.4	−4.5	−5.7	−5.3	−5.3	−5.0
Dominica	−20.7	−16.4	−9.0	−12.9	−19.5	−18.2	−15.0	−18.1	−15.0	−12.1
Dominican Republic	−1.6	−1.1	−2.1	−2.4	−5.1	−3.4	−3.7	5.2	5.6	3.5
Ecuador	−0.7	−3.0	−9.3	5.7	6.3	−2.4	−5.0	−1.7	2.8	3.0
El Salvador	−2.0	−0.9	−0.9	−1.9	−3.3	−1.1	−2.9	−4.9	−4.6	−4.0
Grenada	−19.6	−24.9	−23.0	−8.0	−20.3	−17.6	−25.8	−27.0	−26.1	−25.2
Guatemala	−2.9	−3.5	−5.2	−5.5	−5.4	−5.9	−5.3	−4.3	−4.4	−3.9
Guyana	−7.6	−14.2	−13.7	−11.4	−15.3	−17.6	−14.8	−11.5	−15.9	−23.1
Haiti	1.1	−6.9	−5.5	−7.2	−6.6	−6.6	−4.2	−3.6	−1.5	−1.4
Honduras	−4.1	−3.1	−2.4	−4.4	−4.0	−4.7	−3.1	−3.7	−6.2	−3.6
Jamaica	−1.4	−5.2	−3.1	−4.9	−5.2	−9.5	−12.5	−11.5	−9.9	−7.8
Mexico	−0.8	−1.9	−3.8	−2.9	−3.1	−2.9	−2.2	−1.5	−1.2	−1.5
Netherlands Antilles	−10.3	−2.6	−3.6	−9.2	−2.7	−5.5	−2.2	0.2	−3.1	−2.2
Nicaragua	−35.3	−36.1	−39.5	−39.7	−37.1	22.9	−20.3	−19.6	−20.5	−19.4
Panama	−2.1	−5.0	−9.3	−10.1	−5.9	−1.5	−0.8	−3.2	−2.1	−1.9
Paraguay	−3.7	−6.8	−1.9	−2.1	−2.1	−3.9	2.3	2.5	1.3	0.2
Peru	−6.5	−5.8	−6.0	−3.0	−2.9	−2.2	−2.0	−1.7	−0.4	−0.7
St. Kitts and Nevis	−30.4	−21.1	−14.3	−21.7	−19.8	−28.9	−33.5	−21.8	−14.4	−15.0
St. Lucia	−10.1	−11.8	−11.8	−12.5	−12.5	−9.1	−12.7	−18.8	−10.2	−10.1
St. Vincent and the Grenadines	−14.0	−28.5	−29.7	−21.8	−8.4	−11.8	−11.8	−12.4	−13.1	−13.9
Suriname	−1.3	−6.4	−14.3	−19.0	−9.5	−19.8	−10.0	−15.5	−11.8	−5.7
Trinidad and Tobago	1.2	−9.9	−10.6	0.5	6.6	5.0	0.9	12.5	6.2	4.5
Uruguay	−1.1	−1.3	−2.1	−2.4	−2.8	−2.9	1.6	0.7	0.1	0.2
Venezuela	12.7	4.2	−4.6	1.8	10.0	1.6	7.9	11.3	13.5	12.1

[1]Mongolia, which is not a member of the Commonwealth of Independent States, is included in this group for reasons of geography and similarities in economic structure.

Table 32. Summary of Balance of Payments, Capital Flows, and External Financing
(Billions of U.S. dollars)

	1996	1997	1998	1999	2000	2001	2002	2003	2004	2005
Other emerging market and developing countries										
Balance of payments[1]										
Balance on current account	–86.1	–85.3	–116.3	–18.9	86.3	39.5	84.2	148.9	201.3	183.2
Balance on goods and services	–46.6	–45.6	–66.1	42.2	147.9	93.5	128.6	183.4	252.6	230.5
Income, net	–83.7	–91.8	–99.5	–114.3	–118.3	–116.9	–124.5	–137.3	–156.9	–152.8
Current transfers, net	44.2	52.1	49.2	53.2	56.7	63.0	80.0	102.7	105.7	105.5
Balance on capital and financial account	122.7	146.5	146.5	70.3	–35.7	5.3	–65.1	–178.7	–209.5	–191.6
Balance on capital account[2]	7.8	21.1	5.9	7.9	8.2	8.9	4.8	5.1	5.9	6.7
Balance on financial account	114.9	125.4	140.6	62.4	–43.9	–3.5	–69.9	–183.8	–215.4	–198.3
Direct investment, net	118.3	147.5	155.2	158.5	158.5	178.1	152.3	135.4	147.6	157.8
Portfolio investment, net	75.8	58.0	21.3	8.0	–29.9	–61.2	–54.5	–22.6	–41.7	–43.9
Other investment, net	–1.1	6.6	–35.8	–68.6	–99.2	–35.7	–15.6	1.0	–22.8	–57.2
Reserve assets	–78.1	–86.8	—	–35.6	–73.3	–84.7	–152.1	–297.7	–298.6	–254.9
Errors and omissions, net	–36.6	–61.2	–30.2	–51.4	–50.6	–44.9	–19.1	29.8	8.2	8.4
Capital flows										
Total capital flows, net[3]	192.9	212.2	140.6	98.0	29.4	81.2	82.2	113.8	83.2	56.6
Net official flows	–0.1	14.7	52.5	26.5	–20.5	24.5	8.9	–13.2	–20.1	–31.7
Net private flows[4]	183.9	209.1	93.8	57.8	33.3	62.6	73.0	130.1	96.5	79.0
Direct investment, net	118.3	147.5	155.2	158.5	158.5	178.1	152.3	135.4	147.6	157.8
Private portfolio investment, net	74.1	61.2	22.7	6.4	–12.9	–54.0	–49.6	6.7	–18.3	–15.8
Other private flows, net	–8.5	0.4	–84.1	–107.2	–112.3	–61.5	–29.7	–12.0	–32.8	–63.0
External financing[5]										
Net external financing[6]	277.7	354.1	265.5	237.8	220.9	164.8	175.9	241.1	235.0	245.7
Non-debt-creating flows	155.3	196.3	166.4	170.3	179.4	175.2	146.7	149.5	167.1	179.9
Capital transfers[7]	7.8	21.1	5.9	7.9	8.2	8.9	4.8	5.1	5.9	6.7
Foreign direct investment and equity security liabilities[8]	147.5	175.2	160.5	162.4	171.2	166.4	141.8	144.4	161.2	173.2
Net external borrowing[9]	122.4	157.8	99.1	67.5	41.5	–10.5	29.3	91.5	67.9	65.8
Borrowing from official creditors[10]	2.8	12.0	51.1	31.8	4.8	28.7	13.9	14.6	6.7	1.1
of which, credit and loans from IMF[11]	0.7	3.3	14.0	–2.4	–10.9	19.0	13.4	1.8	. . .	. . .
Borrowing from banks[10]	8.0	6.4	10.5	–15.3	–11.0	–3.7	–2.0	29.9	31.1	31.8
Borrowing from other private creditors[10]	111.6	139.3	37.5	51.0	47.7	–35.5	17.4	47.0	30.2	32.9
Memorandum										
Balance on goods and services in percent of GDP[12]	–0.8	–0.7	–1.1	0.7	2.4	1.5	2.0	2.6	3.1	2.6
Scheduled amortization of external debt	212.4	255.5	262.9	295.7	307.7	313.9	328.7	354.0	351.6	349.3
Gross external financing[13]	490.1	609.6	528.4	533.5	528.7	478.6	504.7	595.1	586.6	595.0
Gross external borrowing[14]	334.8	413.3	362.0	363.2	349.3	303.4	358.0	445.6	419.5	415.1
Exceptional external financing, net	33.4	–7.7	28.3	24.5	17.7	15.3	32.5	28.2	19.3	24.4
Of which,										
Arrears on debt service	–5.6	–29.8	11.9	8.5	–18.0	3.0	0.9	15.7	. . .	. . .
Debt forgiveness	11.0	16.2	1.8	2.0	2.2	2.7	4.6	1.6	. . .	. . .
Rescheduling of debt service	27.5	2.8	8.2	11.8	1.4	9.1	15.3	6.9	. . .	. . .

[1]Standard presentation in accordance with the 5th edition of the International Monetary Fund's *Balance of Payments Manual* (1993).

[2]Comprises capital transfers—including debt forgiveness—and acquisition/disposal of nonproduced, nonfinancial assets.

[3]Comprise net direct investment, net portfolio investment, and other long- and short-term net investment flows, including official and private borrowing. In the standard balance of payments presentation above, total net capital flows are equal to the balance on financial account minus the change in reserve assets.

[4]Because of limitations on the data coverage for net official flows, the residually derived data for net private flows may include some official flows.

[5]As defined in the *World Economic Outlook* (see footnote 6). It should be noted that there is no generally accepted standard definition of external financing.

[6]Defined as the sum of—with opposite sign—the goods and services balance, net income and current transfers, direct investment abroad, the change in reserve assets, the net acquisition of other assets (such as recorded private portfolio assets, export credit, and the collateral for debt-reduction operations), and the net errors and omissions. Thus, net external financing, according to the definition adopted in the *World Economic Outlook*, measures the total amount required to finance the current account, direct investment outflows, net reserve transactions (often at the discretion of the monetary authorities), the net acquisition of nonreserve external assets, and the net transactions underlying the errors and omissions (not infrequently reflecting capital flight).

[7]Including other transactions on capital account.

[8]Debt-creating foreign direct investment liabilities are not included.

[9]Net disbursement of long- and short-term credits, including exceptional financing, by both official and private creditors.

[10]Changes in liabilities.

[11]Comprise use of International Monetary Fund resources under the General Resources Account, Trust Fund, and Poverty Reduction and Growth Facility (PRGF). For further detail, see Table 36.

[12]This is often referred to as the "resource balance" and, with opposite sign, the "net resource transfer."

[13]Net external financing plus amortization due on external debt.

[14]Net external borrowing plus amortization due on external debt.

Table 33. Other Emerging Market and Developing Countries—by Region: Balance of Payments and External Financing[1]

(Billions of U.S. dollars)

	1996	1997	1998	1999	2000	2001	2002	2003	2004	2005
Africa										
Balance of payments										
Balance on current account	–4.9	–6.0	–19.3	–15.0	6.3	–1.3	–6.7	–0.4	2.8	5.0
Balance on capital account	7.0	9.4	3.2	3.2	1.9	2.8	2.4	2.7	3.0	2.9
Balance on financial account	–2.4	–3.0	15.6	12.8	–7.3	–2.4	5.3	–3.9	–6.6	–8.3
Change in reserves (– = increase)	–5.9	–10.5	3.3	–2.9	–12.8	–12.3	–7.6	–20.0	–22.9	–23.4
Other official flows, net	–2.6	–6.4	1.8	1.5	0.9	0.5	3.7	5.2	2.3	2.6
Private flows, net	4.5	12.3	8.3	12.2	5.6	13.5	11.9	14.8	16.6	13.7
External financing										
Net external financing	17.2	28.6	26.1	30.1	16.3	19.9	18.7	20.6	22.9	23.5
Non-debt-creating inflows	14.3	25.5	19.9	22.3	11.5	20.6	15.2	16.8	18.8	19.9
Net external borrowing	2.9	3.0	6.2	7.8	4.8	–0.7	3.5	3.8	4.1	3.7
From official creditors	–1.8	–5.6	2.9	2.5	0.4	–1.5	2.4	3.3	1.0	2.0
of which, credit and loans from IMF	0.6	–0.5	–0.4	–0.2	–0.2	–0.4	–0.1	–0.8	. . .	. . .
From banks	1.2	0.8	–1.3	2.3	0.5	–0.2	1.0	0.7	1.0	–2.5
From other private creditors	3.5	7.9	4.6	2.9	3.9	1.0	0.1	–0.3	2.1	4.1
Memorandum										
Exceptional financing	13.1	13.1	4.5	9.5	6.8	6.1	6.4	6.7	—	5.1
Sub-Sahara										
Balance of payments										
Balance on current account	–5.7	–8.8	–17.6	–14.4	–1.6	–9.1	–11.7	–10.0	–6.8	–6.4
Balance on capital account	6.8	9.3	3.1	2.8	1.9	2.6	2.2	2.7	2.9	2.8
Balance on financial account	1.1	1.7	14.5	11.2	0.5	5.7	10.4	5.8	2.9	3.0
Change in reserves (– = increase)	–3.2	–5.5	2.2	–3.3	–6.1	–2.2	–3.2	–10.5	–14.4	–11.7
Other official flows, net	–1.6	–4.6	3.2	3.0	3.2	2.7	6.3	7.4	4.6	4.1
Private flows, net	5.7	11.7	8.7	11.3	7.3	11.5	12.5	14.7	18.2	14.1
External financing										
Net external financing	16.8	26.8	24.6	27.4	15.2	16.0	16.9	19.2	22.1	21.5
Non-debt-creating inflows	13.0	23.6	18.2	20.3	9.9	16.0	12.8	13.9	16.2	17.5
Net external borrowing	3.8	3.2	6.4	7.0	5.3	—	4.1	5.3	5.9	4.0
From official creditors	–1.5	–4.6	3.4	3.1	1.3	–0.4	3.7	4.6	1.9	2.4
of which, credit and loans from IMF	0.1	–0.5	–0.3	–0.1	—	–0.2	0.2	–0.4	. . .	. . .
From banks	0.9	—	–1.3	0.9	0.2	–0.7	0.1	—	1.0	–2.7
From other private creditors	4.4	7.8	4.3	3.0	3.8	1.1	0.2	0.7	3.0	4.3
Memorandum										
Exceptional financing	8.5	9.4	3.5	8.8	6.8	6.0	6.3	6.7	—	5.1
Central and eastern Europe										
Balance of payments										
Balance on current account	–17.8	–21.1	–19.3	–26.6	–32.6	–16.3	–24.0	–35.1	–44.2	–45.2
Balance on capital account	1.2	10.2	0.4	0.3	0.5	0.7	0.7	0.4	1.6	2.8
Balance on financial account	15.1	6.3	18.5	23.1	37.8	24.0	33.0	32.2	36.1	37.5
Change in reserves (– = increase)	–7.4	–10.6	–9.5	–11.3	–3.3	5.8	–14.4	–13.6	–9.4	–5.7
Other official flows, net	0.1	–3.3	0.3	–2.6	1.6	5.5	–7.6	–5.5	–6.6	–5.5
Private flows, net	23.0	20.2	27.2	36.7	39.1	12.1	55.3	51.5	53.2	49.3
External financing										
Net external financing	24.8	40.2	33.9	47.1	52.7	27.7	46.1	54.3	56.0	54.7
Non-debt-creating inflows	13.4	23.8	21.1	21.5	24.8	25.1	24.7	17.7	23.3	27.1
Net external borrowing	11.4	16.3	12.8	25.6	27.9	2.6	21.4	36.7	32.7	27.5
From official creditors	–0.2	–3.3	0.5	–2.5	1.8	5.9	–7.6	–5.6	–7.1	–5.8
of which, credit and loans from IMF	–0.8	0.4	–0.5	0.5	3.3	9.9	6.1	—	. . .	. . .
From banks	5.3	1.2	2.6	2.0	4.0	–7.3	2.8	8.7	5.8	6.4
From other private creditors	6.4	18.4	9.7	26.1	22.1	4.0	26.3	33.5	34.1	26.9
Memorandum										
Exceptional financing	1.4	0.2	0.4	0.6	0.3	0.1	0.1	0.3	0.1	—

Table 33 *(continued)*

	1996	1997	1998	1999	2000	2001	2002	2003	2004	2005
Commonwealth of Independent States[2]										
Balance of payments										
Balance on current account	2.5	–8.8	–9.6	20.7	46.3	32.8	32.2	36.6	61.4	53.6
Balance on capital account	0.1	–1.1	–0.3	–0.5	–0.6	–0.7	–0.6	–1.0	–1.0	–1.0
Balance on financial account	5.3	21.0	21.3	–10.3	–36.0	–21.0	–23.4	–28.4	–49.2	–42.3
Change in reserves (– = increase)	2.2	–3.8	7.5	–2.2	–17.1	–11.2	–11.8	–33.6	–27.8	–34.7
Other official flows, net	10.6	8.4	9.9	–0.1	–4.0	–4.2	–1.5	–4.7	–2.6	–2.5
Private flows, net	–3.8	19.6	7.2	–6.1	–12.6	–1.7	–9.2	15.2	–19.2	–5.8
External financing										
Net external financing	33.3	54.3	31.3	10.3	3.0	–5.3	11.6	34.5	24.6	32.1
Non-debt-creating inflows	4.8	6.6	5.5	4.4	2.7	3.2	3.3	9.3	10.1	11.0
Net external borrowing	28.4	47.7	25.9	5.9	0.2	–8.4	8.3	25.2	14.5	21.1
From official creditors	8.8	6.8	8.3	–1.1	–5.2	–5.0	–1.9	–1.9	–1.5	–1.3
of which, credit and loans from IMF	4.5	2.1	5.8	–3.6	–4.1	–4.0	–1.8	–2.3	. . .	. . .
From banks	7.4	15.7	0.1	–1.3	0.8	3.4	11.0	23.1	13.9	23.9
From other private creditors	12.3	25.2	17.5	8.3	4.6	–6.8	–0.8	4.0	2.1	–1.4
Memorandum										
Exceptional financing	12.2	–21.1	7.4	7.3	5.7	1.8	1.8	–1.8	0.2	0.1
Developing Asia										
Balance of payments										
Balance on current account	–37.8	10.3	48.9	48.2	45.6	38.5	70.4	85.9	68.8	68.5
Balance on capital account	0.8	0.8	0.6	0.6	0.4	0.5	0.4	0.4	0.5	0.5
Balance on financial account	67.2	34.9	–27.6	–26.1	–21.0	–30.4	–73.0	–106.6	–82.0	–80.2
Change in reserves (– = increase)	–37.4	–28.8	–20.7	–31.3	–17.8	–62.2	–114.0	–163.5	–180.3	–121.7
Other official flows, net	–3.1	11.3	21.4	22.2	11.4	6.0	5.6	–2.6	6.5	4.2
Private flows, net	107.7	52.5	–28.3	–17.0	–14.6	25.7	35.5	59.5	91.8	37.3
External financing										
Net external financing	108.4	106.4	41.0	55.8	70.6	47.9	67.3	85.2	93.8	75.6
Non-debt-creating inflows	69.1	62.3	52.5	54.0	62.1	53.2	58.9	66.5	74.0	75.0
Net external borrowing	39.4	44.2	–11.5	1.8	8.4	–5.3	8.5	18.7	19.8	0.6
From official creditors	–3.1	11.3	21.4	22.2	11.4	6.0	5.6	–2.6	6.5	4.2
of which, credit and loans from IMF	–1.7	5.0	6.6	1.7	0.9	–2.2	–2.7	–0.6	. . .	. . .
From banks	27.9	13.5	–12.5	–11.8	–22.3	–6.4	–8.3	0.7	6.2	3.6
From other private creditors	14.6	19.4	–20.5	–8.7	19.3	–4.8	11.1	20.7	7.1	–7.3
Memorandum										
Exceptional financing	0.7	0.5	14.6	7.1	5.6	6.6	7.6	6.2	2.9	2.9
Excluding China and India										
Balance of payments										
Balance on current account	–38.9	–23.7	24.3	35.8	30.2	21.9	30.1	33.6	27.0	18.8
Balance on capital account	0.8	0.8	0.6	0.6	0.5	0.6	0.5	0.5	0.5	0.5
Balance on financial account	50.8	33.8	–19.5	–28.9	–17.8	–18.3	–25.6	–34.1	–24.0	–17.5
Change in reserves (– = increase)	–3.0	11.6	–11.7	–16.7	–1.2	–6.2	–19.7	–20.8	–14.0	–16.4
Other official flows, net	–5.4	9.7	15.9	15.2	11.9	5.0	3.6	2.0	3.1	2.7
Private flows, net	59.3	12.5	–23.7	–27.3	–28.5	–17.3	–9.6	–15.3	–13.1	–3.9
External financing										
Net external financing	53.4	27.4	–1.5	1.7	0.6	–4.1	1.5	–1.0	0.7	4.1
Non-debt-creating inflows	24.6	10.6	9.6	13.1	6.4	2.6	6.5	5.1	7.7	7.5
Net external borrowing	28.9	16.8	–11.1	–11.4	–5.8	–6.7	–4.9	–6.1	–7.0	–3.4
From official creditors	–5.4	9.7	15.9	15.2	11.9	5.1	3.6	2.0	3.1	2.7
of which, credit and loans from IMF	–0.4	5.7	7.0	2.1	1.0	–2.2	–2.7	–0.6	. . .	. . .
From banks	24.0	6.2	–15.4	–9.8	–15.7	–6.5	–10.4	–6.5	–1.2	–0.2
From other private creditors	10.3	0.9	–11.6	–16.7	–1.9	–5.2	1.9	–1.6	–8.9	–6.0
Memorandum										
Exceptional financing	0.7	0.5	14.6	7.1	5.6	6.6	7.6	6.2	2.9	2.9

Table 33 *(concluded)*

	1996	1997	1998	1999	2000	2001	2002	2003	2004	2005
Middle East										
Balance of payments										
Balance on current account	11.4	7.8	–25.4	11.6	69.2	38.7	29.1	57.6	103.5	108.2
Balance on capital account	0.2	0.5	0.3	1.1	2.9	2.9	1.3	1.2	–0.1	–0.1
Balance on financial account	–14.2	–0.3	24.0	3.7	–63.4	–25.7	–28.3	–60.7	–107.5	–110.1
Change in reserves (– = increase)	–14.6	–6.8	12.1	0.7	–27.0	–9.8	–2.7	–31.2	–45.4	–56.2
Other official flows, net	2.4	–2.4	0.2	–1.0	–24.3	–9.7	–13.3	–28.4	–27.5	–30.7
Private flows, net	–2.2	7.0	12.6	–5.2	–23.9	–9.2	–22.0	–10.9	–42.6	–29.7
External financing										
Net external financing	3.5	13.6	23.0	9.2	14.7	—	4.9	11.4	2.4	10.6
Non-debt-creating inflows	3.5	3.2	2.3	4.5	7.5	5.3	4.0	4.9	3.3	6.6
Net external borrowing	—	10.4	20.7	4.7	7.1	–5.3	0.9	6.6	–1.0	4.1
From official creditors	0.9	0.4	0.6	0.6	–0.5	–0.1	–1.1	–0.2	–0.6	0.4
of which, credit and loans from IMF	0.1	0.2	0.1	0.1	–0.1	0.1	—	–0.1	. . .	. . .
From banks	–8.2	–3.1	6.0	0.9	–0.9	–0.3	0.2	0.3	1.3	—
From other private creditors	7.4	13.1	14.0	3.1	8.5	–4.9	1.8	6.4	–1.6	3.6
Memorandum										
Exceptional financing	1.0	0.3	0.4	0.2	0.4	0.3	1.0	2.5	0.7	1.5
Western Hemisphere										
Balance of payments										
Balance on current account	–39.4	–67.4	–91.6	–57.7	–48.4	–52.9	–16.8	4.4	9.0	–6.8
Balance on capital account	–1.5	1.5	1.7	3.3	3.0	2.6	0.6	1.4	1.8	1.6
Balance on financial account	43.8	66.5	88.9	59.2	46.0	52.1	16.5	–16.4	–6.1	5.1
Change in reserves (– = increase)	–15.0	–26.3	7.3	11.3	4.7	4.9	–1.6	–35.7	–12.7	–13.2
Other official flows, net	–7.4	7.1	18.8	6.5	–6.1	26.5	22.0	22.7	7.8	0.2
Private flows, net	54.8	97.4	66.6	37.3	39.6	22.2	1.4	—	–3.3	14.2
External financing										
Net external financing	90.5	111.0	110.2	85.3	63.7	74.6	27.4	35.0	35.4	49.2
Non-debt-creating inflows	50.2	74.9	65.1	63.5	70.7	67.9	40.7	34.4	37.6	40.3
Net external borrowing	40.2	36.1	45.1	21.7	–7.0	6.7	–13.3	0.6	–2.2	8.9
From official creditors	–1.8	2.5	17.3	10.0	–3.1	23.4	16.6	21.5	8.5	1.6
of which, credit and loans from IMF	–2.0	–4.0	2.5	–0.9	–10.7	15.6	11.9	5.5	. . .	. . .
From banks	–25.4	–21.8	15.5	–7.5	6.8	7.1	–8.8	–3.6	2.9	0.3
From other private creditors	67.4	55.4	12.3	19.3	–10.6	–23.9	–21.1	–17.3	–13.6	7.1
Memorandum										
Exceptional financing	5.0	–0.6	0.9	–0.2	–1.1	0.4	15.6	14.4	15.4	14.8

[1]For definitions, see footnotes to Table 32.
[2]Mongolia, which is not a member of the Commonwealth of Independent States, is included in this group for reasons of geography and similarities in economic structure.

Table 34. Other Emerging Market and Developing Countries—by Analytical Criteria: Balance of Payments and External Financing[1]

(Billions of U.S. dollars)

	1996	1997	1998	1999	2000	2001	2002	2003	2004	2005
By source of export earnings										
Fuel										
Balance of payments										
Balance on current account	28.0	18.9	–32.2	11.3	100.2	50.2	35.5	71.5	130.6	141.4
Balance on capital account	3.2	—	—	0.5	1.1	1.4	0.4	—	–0.9	–1.5
Balance on financial account	–34.6	–8.9	29.7	4.6	–90.3	–32.2	–31.8	–68.8	–132.5	–141.4
Change in reserves (– = increase)	–15.8	–27.9	18.4	4.9	–42.8	–13.6	–1.5	–39.7	–65.1	–78.8
Other official flows, net	–2.9	1.1	3.0	–0.4	–26.6	–8.6	–5.7	–20.6	–27.2	–33.3
Private flows, net	–17.6	17.0	12.4	–11.2	–38.2	–9.0	–23.5	–5.9	–45.6	–37.6
External financing										
Net external financing	–5.8	33.0	29.4	13.7	18.4	4.3	6.6	11.0	2.2	11.4
Non-debt-creating inflows	9.4	7.8	9.1	9.8	12.2	12.8	11.5	15.5	14.6	17.2
Net external borrowing	–15.2	25.2	20.4	3.9	6.2	–8.5	–5.0	–4.5	–12.5	–5.8
From official creditors	–3.7	3.4	1.9	2.2	—	–1.1	1.1	1.4	–1.7	–1.3
of which, credit and loans from IMF	0.9	–0.1	–0.5	–0.4	–0.7	–0.3	–0.4	–0.5	. . .	. . .
From banks	–9.7	–3.9	2.1	—	–2.4	–1.6	–2.0	–1.1	–0.2	–3.5
From other private creditors	–1.8	25.7	16.4	1.8	8.6	–5.8	–4.0	–4.9	–10.6	–1.1
Memorandum										
Exceptional financing	8.9	7.9	6.1	4.5	2.2	1.2	2.5	2.0	–4.7	1.8
Nonfuel										
Balance of payments										
Balance on current account	–114.0	–104.2	–84.1	–30.2	–13.9	–10.7	48.7	77.4	70.7	41.9
Balance on capital account	4.6	21.1	5.9	7.4	7.1	7.5	4.4	5.2	6.8	8.2
Balance on financial account	149.5	134.3	110.9	57.8	46.4	28.6	–38.1	–115.0	–82.8	–56.9
Change in reserves (– = increase)	–62.3	–58.9	–18.4	–40.6	–30.5	–71.1	–150.7	–258.0	–233.5	–176.1
Other official flows, net	2.8	13.6	49.5	26.9	6.0	33.1	14.5	7.3	7.1	1.5
Private flows, net	201.5	192.1	81.4	69.1	71.5	71.6	96.5	136.0	142.1	116.6
External financing										
Net external financing	283.4	321.0	236.1	224.1	202.6	160.5	169.4	230.1	232.9	234.3
Non-debt-creating inflows	145.9	188.5	157.3	160.5	167.2	162.4	135.1	134.1	152.5	162.7
Net external borrowing	137.6	132.6	78.7	63.5	35.3	–2.0	34.2	96.0	80.4	71.6
From official creditors	6.5	8.6	49.2	29.6	4.8	29.8	12.8	13.2	8.3	2.3
of which, credit and loans from IMF	–0.1	3.4	14.5	–2.0	–10.2	19.3	13.8	2.3	. . .	. . .
From banks	17.7	10.4	8.3	–15.2	–8.7	–2.1	—	31.0	31.2	35.3
From other private creditors	113.4	113.6	21.2	49.2	39.2	–29.7	21.4	51.9	40.8	34.0
Memorandum										
Exceptional financing	24.5	–15.5	22.3	20.0	15.5	14.1	30.0	26.2	24.0	22.6
By external financing source										
Net debtor countries										
Balance of payments										
Balance on current account	–129.6	–140.4	–121.7	–72.5	–67.3	–59.0	–22.7	–7.7	–18.6	–50.5
Balance on capital account	8.5	22.1	6.3	7.5	6.1	6.4	3.9	4.9	6.2	7.5
Balance on financial account	137.1	130.5	119.6	78.3	85.8	67.7	34.1	–14.8	12.2	40.9
Change in reserves (– = increase)	–35.7	–19.4	–15.0	–28.2	–10.0	–14.6	–61.9	–111.7	–71.3	–54.3
Other official flows, net	–13.4	5.6	37.3	24.1	12.0	39.0	18.8	11.6	3.2	–1.4
Private flows, net	173.6	153.4	96.9	77.9	87.8	50.7	79.5	87.0	83.9	98.4
External financing										
Net external financing	217.2	217.4	198.7	179.9	148.4	129.4	117.0	145.7	145.3	148.7
Non-debt-creating inflows	113.0	143.3	118.3	127.5	119.6	123.0	93.0	90.4	100.3	107.5
Net external borrowing	104.2	74.1	80.4	52.5	28.8	6.4	24.0	55.3	45.0	41.1
From official creditors	–7.1	2.3	38.0	27.8	9.1	34.4	15.1	16.8	1.9	–2.0
of which, credit and loans from IMF	–3.0	1.7	9.1	1.6	–7.5	23.3	15.3	4.1	. . .	. . .
From banks	6.8	–11.8	6.2	–11.7	–2.8	–6.1	–12.9	1.5	11.3	3.7
From other private creditors	104.5	83.6	36.2	36.4	22.5	–22.0	21.8	37.0	31.8	39.5
Memorandum										
Exceptional financing	17.9	10.3	20.2	17.5	12.2	14.1	30.9	30.1	19.3	24.4

Table 34 ***(continued)***

	1996	1997	1998	1999	2000	2001	2002	2003	2004	2005
Official financing										
Balance of payments										
Balance on current account	–18.4	–14.9	–12.9	–3.8	9.9	2.8	–1.4	1.4	2.1	–3.8
Balance on capital account	3.1	10.8	3.9	3.6	3.6	3.8	3.1	3.4	3.4	3.5
Balance on financial account	20.7	2.7	8.7	–0.8	–11.9	–7.1	–2.2	–3.4	–6.4	–1.2
Change in reserves (– = increase)	2.1	–11.4	–2.3	–3.4	–12.1	–5.1	–11.0	–13.5	–10.6	–11.0
Other official flows, net	–1.6	–3.2	13.1	18.7	14.9	7.2	8.1	9.9	0.4	4.2
Private flows, net	19.4	15.9	–1.8	–17.7	–16.5	–8.5	–0.6	–2.1	3.9	5.9
External financing										
Net external financing	22.3	25.6	16.3	11.9	17.6	8.1	19.6	18.9	13.5	17.3
Non-debt-creating inflows	13.1	15.8	10.0	13.2	12.3	14.1	17.5	16.8	17.3	19.2
Net external borrowing	9.1	9.8	6.3	–1.3	5.4	–6.1	2.1	2.1	–3.8	–1.9
From official creditors	–1.2	–2.5	13.0	19.5	15.9	6.9	8.8	11.1	0.3	4.1
of which, credit and loans from IMF	0.2	3.2	6.0	1.8	1.1	–0.7	–0.7	0.2	. . .	. . .
From banks	16.2	14.6	0.7	0.7	–7.7	–2.4	–5.6	–2.2	1.4	1.7
From other private creditors	–5.9	–2.2	–7.4	–21.5	–2.8	–10.6	–1.1	–6.9	–5.5	–7.7
Memorandum										
Exceptional financing	8.8	8.2	21.9	14.5	10.1	11.4	12.9	11.0	3.8	7.2
Net debtor countries by debt-servicing experience										
Countries with arrears and/or rescheduling during 1997–2001										
Balance of payments										
Balance on current account	–46.0	–51.0	–55.8	–34.7	–16.8	–21.6	–8.0	5.6	13.4	3.5
Balance on capital account	5.5	10.2	4.4	5.7	4.4	4.0	1.9	2.9	2.6	2.7
Balance on financial account	48.3	46.9	56.3	32.8	16.1	21.2	8.5	–7.3	–13.1	–4.1
Change in reserves (– = increase)	–9.0	–4.3	7.7	3.0	–7.5	–13.9	–13.1	–27.2	–14.2	–16.2
Other official flows, net	–8.2	–5.4	22.9	25.3	8.4	16.0	21.0	10.9	–1.9	–2.3
Private flows, net	66.0	56.1	27.0	3.8	20.6	26.3	5.1	13.5	10.2	19.3
External financing										
Net external financing	73.4	63.9	69.4	48.1	49.9	52.2	39.1	40.8	23.3	32.0
Non-debt-creating inflows	36.4	48.6	47.9	55.6	55.7	48.8	40.0	37.0	38.0	43.3
Net external borrowing	37.1	15.3	21.5	–7.5	–5.8	3.3	–0.9	3.8	–14.6	–11.3
From official creditors	–8.4	–5.1	22.3	25.7	5.8	12.4	18.8	12.7	–5.5	–4.7
of which, credit and loans from IMF	0.9	3.3	10.8	5.9	–6.3	5.4	10.2	4.9	. . .	. . .
From banks	14.8	28.8	9.5	–7.7	–10.7	–1.8	–13.0	–5.3	1.6	–1.8
From other private creditors	30.7	–8.4	–10.3	–25.4	–0.9	–7.3	–6.7	–3.5	–10.7	–4.8
Memorandum										
Exceptional financing	14.9	10.3	19.5	16.8	11.6	13.3	16.6	13.0	3.4	8.1
Other groups										
Heavily indebted poor countries										
Balance of payments										
Balance on current account	–9.0	–9.9	–11.7	–12.5	–9.8	–8.6	–8.5	–8.1	–9.3	–10.5
Balance on capital account	1.2	10.3	4.0	4.6	3.6	4.7	1.8	4.2	4.5	4.5
Balance on financial account	7.8	–1.8	8.4	7.0	5.9	2.6	7.5	4.7	5.3	6.5
Change in reserves (– = increase)	–0.9	–0.1	1.2	—	–0.1	–1.7	–3.0	–2.5	–2.2	–2.0
Other official flows, net	2.2	–4.4	4.1	3.5	1.8	0.3	3.7	5.0	0.9	4.3
Private flows, net	6.2	2.1	2.9	3.4	4.1	4.4	7.7	2.7	6.3	4.5
External financing										
Net external financing	10.3	8.9	11.7	11.7	9.3	8.6	11.7	11.6	12.3	13.2
Non-debt-creating inflows	3.5	13.8	8.1	9.0	7.1	8.7	7.0	9.6	9.7	10.1
Net external borrowing	6.8	–5.0	3.6	2.7	2.2	—	4.7	2.0	2.6	3.1
From official creditors	2.4	–4.1	4.3	3.6	2.0	0.1	3.3	4.8	1.0	4.2
of which, credit and loans from IMF	—	–0.1	0.3	0.2	—	–0.2	0.1	–0.4	. . .	. . .
From banks	1.0	–0.1	–0.4	1.3	1.0	—	0.6	0.2	0.1	0.4
From other private creditors	3.4	–0.8	–0.3	–2.2	–0.8	–0.2	0.8	–3.0	1.4	–1.4
Memorandum										
Exceptional financing	8.5	6.1	–0.2	5.9	5.0	5.1	6.3	5.1	0.6	3.5

Table 34 ***(concluded)***

	1996	1997	1998	1999	2000	2001	2002	2003	2004	2005
Middle East and north Africa										
Balance of payments										
Balance on current account	10.8	9.1	–28.8	9.3	75.1	44.3	32.7	65.5	111.4	117.9
Balance on capital account	0.3	0.6	0.4	1.3	3.0	3.1	1.5	1.3	0.1	0.1
Balance on financial account	–16.7	–3.7	26.9	6.8	–69.9	–32.4	–32.5	–69.1	–115.4	–119.8
Change in reserves (– = increase)	–17.3	–11.8	13.2	1.0	–33.8	–19.9	–7.5	–41.3	–54.3	–68.4
Other official flows, net	2.4	–3.0	0.1	–1.1	–25.3	–11.0	–15.1	–29.8	–28.9	–31.4
Private flows, net	–3.2	7.8	13.1	–3.9	–25.3	–6.4	–21.7	–9.5	–42.9	–28.8
External financing										
Net external financing	4.9	16.7	26.2	13.2	17.1	5.2	7.9	14.5	5.3	14.8
Non-debt-creating inflows	4.9	5.4	4.7	6.6	9.4	10.5	7.1	9.0	7.5	10.6
Net external borrowing	0.1	11.3	21.6	6.6	7.7	–5.3	0.8	5.6	–2.1	4.1
From official creditors	1.5	0.5	1.2	1.2	–0.2	–0.5	–1.9	–0.8	–0.7	0.8
of which, credit and loans from IMF	0.6	0.3	–0.1	—	–0.3	–0.2	–0.3	–0.6	. . .	. . .
From banks	–7.9	–2.3	6.1	2.4	–0.6	0.2	1.0	1.1	1.3	0.2
From other private creditors	6.5	13.1	14.2	3.0	8.5	–5.1	1.7	5.2	–2.8	3.1
Memorandum										
Exceptional financing	6.8	5.3	2.9	2.3	1.9	1.3	1.8	3.3	1.4	1.9

[1]For definitions, see footnotes to Table 32.

Table 35. Other Emerging Market and Developing Countries: Reserves[1]

	1996	1997	1998	1999	2000	2001	2002	2003	2004	2005
					Billions of U.S. dollars					
Other emerging market and developing countries	**638.9**	**700.8**	**699.7**	**726.5**	**815.7**	**910.5**	**1,088.5**	**1,412.6**	**1,711.2**	**1,966.1**
Regional groups										
Africa	31.9	43.8	41.5	42.4	54.6	64.8	72.6	90.9	113.8	137.2
Sub-Sahara	21.6	29.5	28.0	29.6	35.7	36.0	36.6	40.6	55.1	66.8
Excluding Nigeria and South Africa	16.4	16.9	16.3	17.6	19.4	19.2	23.1	26.8	31.1	34.1
Central and eastern Europe	71.8	77.4	89.7	94.9	97.3	98.9	132.0	160.9	170.3	175.9
Commonwealth of Independent States[2]	19.9	22.3	15.1	16.5	33.2	44.2	58.2	92.7	120.5	155.2
Russia	12.0	13.7	8.5	9.1	24.8	33.1	44.6	73.8	93.9	124.8
Excluding Russia	7.9	8.6	6.6	7.4	8.4	11.0	13.5	18.8	26.6	30.4
Developing Asia	231.1	249.6	274.5	307.7	321.8	380.4	496.9	670.1	850.4	972.1
China	107.7	143.4	149.8	158.3	168.9	216.3	292.0	409.2	557.9	654.6
India	20.8	25.3	27.9	33.2	38.4	46.4	68.2	99.5	117.1	125.7
Excluding China and India	102.6	80.9	96.8	116.1	114.5	117.7	136.6	161.4	175.4	191.8
Middle East	127.2	137.1	125.5	121.6	152.6	163.0	167.6	201.9	247.3	303.5
Western Hemisphere	157.0	170.6	153.4	143.4	156.1	159.2	161.3	196.2	208.8	222.1
Brazil	58.5	51.0	34.4	23.9	31.5	35.8	37.7	49.1	46.5	48.0
Mexico	19.4	28.8	31.8	31.8	35.5	44.8	50.6	59.0	63.9	69.0
Analytical groups										
By source of export earnings										
Fuel	115.9	133.8	117.5	111.9	158.7	172.0	173.3	218.1	283.2	362.0
Nonfuel	522.9	567.0	582.1	614.6	657.0	738.6	915.2	1,194.5	1,428.0	1,604.1
of which, primary products	29.9	32.0	30.0	29.1	29.7	29.3	32.3	34.9	37.7	37.2
By external financing source										
Net debtor countries	412.5	419.6	430.8	453.8	476.8	502.6	585.9	716.6	788.0	842.3
of which, official financing	42.4	46.0	50.7	57.4	66.0	68.8	78.8	92.9	103.6	114.6
Net debtor countries by debt-servicing experience										
Countries with arrears and/or rescheduling during 1997–2001	115.2	112.8	98.8	96.2	111.9	124.4	138.7	168.7	182.9	199.1
Other groups										
Heavily indebted poor countries	9.4	10.3	10.2	11.0	11.9	13.0	16.9	19.7	22.0	24.0
Middle East and north Africa	137.8	151.8	139.3	134.8	172.2	192.3	204.5	253.5	307.9	376.3

Table 35 ***(concluded)***

	1996	1997	1998	1999	2000	2001	2002	2003	2004	2005
				Ratio of reserves to imports of goods and services[3]						
Other emerging market and developing countries	**42.7**	**43.6**	**45.7**	**48.3**	**46.5**	**51.1**	**57.1**	**62.4**	**62.9**	**64.4**
Regional groups										
Africa	24.6	32.4	30.9	31.3	39.1	45.2	47.5	49.3	53.7	60.5
Sub-Sahara	21.8	27.9	27.3	28.8	33.6	33.1	31.9	28.9	34.7	39.1
Excluding Nigeria and South Africa	30.3	29.7	28.5	30.5	33.6	31.3	36.3	35.9	36.3	37.1
Central and eastern Europe	32.8	32.5	35.4	38.7	34.8	35.4	42.0	40.1	34.6	32.9
Commonwealth of Independent States[2]	14.4	15.4	12.3	17.6	30.5	34.9	41.5	53.3	57.1	66.3
Russia	13.8	14.9	11.5	17.2	40.6	45.4	53.7	72.0	75.1	89.5
Excluding Russia	15.6	16.2	13.6	18.2	17.6	20.7	23.7	26.4	30.9	32.2
Developing Asia	42.8	44.7	56.8	59.6	49.8	58.8	68.6	75.3	77.4	75.1
China	69.9	87.2	91.6	83.4	67.4	79.7	89.0	91.1	96.4	90.7
India	37.5	43.4	47.0	52.9	51.1	61.7	85.7	111.4	103.4	95.7
Excluding China and India	31.0	24.1	37.2	44.1	35.8	39.1	43.1	45.9	43.2	43.4
Middle East	69.5	70.7	67.8	65.8	74.4	75.6	71.4	77.1	85.0	96.7
Western Hemisphere	55.0	50.8	43.6	43.7	41.7	43.0	47.6	55.5	50.1	49.4
Brazil	87.2	66.0	45.4	37.6	43.5	49.2	61.1	77.0	60.4	57.1
Mexico	28.1	33.8	33.4	30.3	27.6	35.2	40.1	45.8	42.6	43.2
Analytical groups										
By source of export earnings										
Fuel	59.6	63.4	58.3	55.0	70.3	71.5	66.1	74.0	84.9	100.8
Nonfuel	40.2	40.6	43.8	47.3	43.0	47.9	55.7	60.6	59.8	59.5
of which, primary products	50.7	51.7	50.3	53.4	52.6	51.8	56.2	53.7	50.1	46.1
By external financing source										
Net debtor countries	38.5	36.3	39.0	42.1	38.4	40.9	46.2	49.2	45.7	44.9
of which, official financing	24.9	25.5	30.8	37.2	37.2	39.0	41.7	42.9	42.6	43.6
Net debtor countries by debt-servicing experience										
Countries with arrears and/or rescheduling during 1997–2001	40.4	36.3	33.7	35.6	36.1	39.3	42.8	46.0	43.3	43.5
Other groups										
Heavily indebted poor countries	23.7	25.4	23.1	24.7	26.6	27.9	34.1	35.1	33.7	34.2
Middle East and north Africa	63.8	67.2	63.7	61.3	71.2	75.8	73.9	81.8	88.1	100.0

[1]In this table, official holdings of gold are valued at SDR 35 an ounce. This convention results in a marked underestimate of reserves for countries that have substantial gold holdings.
[2]Mongolia, which is not a member of the Commonwealth of Independent States, is included in this group for reasons of geography and similarities in economic structure.
[3]Reserves at year-end in percent of imports of goods and services for the year indicated.

Table 36. Net Credit and Loans from IMF[1]

(Billions of U.S. dollars)

	1995	1996	1997	1998	1999	2000	2001	2002	2003
Advanced economies	**–0.1**	**–0.1**	**11.3**	**5.2**	**–10.3**	**—**	**–5.7**	**—**	**—**
Newly industrialized Asian economies	—	—	11.3	5.2	–10.3	—	–5.7	—	—
Other emerging market and developing countries	**17.3**	**0.7**	**3.3**	**14.0**	**–2.4**	**–10.9**	**19.0**	**13.4**	**1.8**
Regional groups									
Africa	0.8	0.6	–0.5	–0.4	–0.2	–0.2	–0.4	–0.1	–0.8
Sub-Sahara	0.6	0.1	–0.5	–0.3	–0.1	—	–0.2	0.2	–0.4
Excluding Nigeria and South Africa	0.6	0.1	–0.1	0.1	–0.1	—	–0.2	0.2	–0.4
Central and eastern Europe	–2.4	–0.8	0.4	–0.5	0.5	3.3	9.9	6.1	—
Commonwealth of Independent States[2]	7.5	4.5	2.1	5.8	–3.6	–4.1	–4.0	–1.8	–2.3
Russia	5.5	3.2	1.5	5.3	–3.6	–2.9	–3.8	–1.5	–1.9
Excluding Russia	2.0	1.3	0.5	0.5	—	–1.2	–0.2	–0.3	–0.4
Developing Asia	–1.5	–1.7	5.0	6.6	1.7	0.9	–2.2	–2.7	–0.6
China	—	—	—	—	—	—	—	—	—
India	–1.2	–1.3	–0.7	–0.4	–0.3	–0.1	—	—	—
Excluding China and India	–0.3	–0.4	5.7	7.0	2.1	1.0	–2.2	–2.7	–0.6
Middle East	—	0.1	0.2	0.1	0.1	–0.1	0.1	—	–0.1
Western Hemisphere	12.9	–2.0	–4.0	2.5	–0.9	–10.7	15.6	11.9	5.5
Brazil	—	–0.1	—	4.6	4.1	–6.7	6.7	11.2	5.2
Mexico	12.1	–2.1	–3.4	–1.1	–3.7	–4.3	—	—	—
Analytical groups									
By source of export earnings									
Fuel	–0.1	0.9	–0.1	–0.5	–0.4	–0.7	–0.3	–0.4	–0.5
Nonfuel	17.4	–0.1	3.4	14.5	–2.0	–10.2	19.3	13.8	2.3
of which, primary products	0.6	0.2	–0.1	0.3	–0.1	–0.2	–0.2	0.1	–0.3
By external financing source									
Net debtor countries	12.3	–3.0	1.7	9.1	1.6	–7.5	23.3	15.3	4.1
of which, official financing	0.5	0.2	3.2	6.0	1.8	1.1	–0.7	–0.7	0.2
Net debtor countries by debt-servicing experience									
Countries with arrears and/or rescheduling during 1997–2001	2.2	0.9	3.3	10.8	5.9	–6.3	5.4	10.2	4.9
Other groups									
Heavily indebted poor countries	0.6	—	–0.1	0.3	0.2	—	–0.2	0.1	–0.4
Middle East and north Africa	0.2	0.6	0.3	–0.1	—	–0.3	–0.2	–0.3	–0.6
Memorandum									
Total									
Net credit provided under:									
General Resources Account	15.633	0.291	14.355	18.811	–12.856	–10.741	13.213	12.832	1.738
PRGF	1.619	0.325	0.179	0.374	0.194	–0.140	0.114	0.575	0.017
Disbursements at year-end under:[3]									
General Resources Account	52.832	51.396	62.301	84.541	69.504	55.368	66.448	85.357	95.143
PRGF	8.284	8.336	7.997	8.733	8.708	8.128	7.952	9.206	10.080

[1]Includes net disbursements from programs under the General Resources Account and Poverty Reduction and Growth Facility (formerly ESAF—Enhanced Structural Adjustment Facility). The data are on a transactions basis, with conversion to U.S. dollar values at annual average exchange rates.
[2]Mongolia, which is not a member of the Commonwealth of Independent States, is included in this group for reasons of geography and similarities in economic structure.
[3]Converted to U.S. dollar values at end-of-period exchange rates.

Table 37. Summary of External Debt and Debt Service

	1996	1997	1998	1999	2000	2001	2002	2003	2004	2005
					Billions of U.S. dollars					
External debt										
Other emerging market and developing countries	**2,196.7**	**2,314.0**	**2,522.9**	**2,562.5**	**2,503.3**	**2,471.4**	**2,533.3**	**2,724.3**	**2,763.0**	**2,830.1**
Regional groups										
Africa	299.8	286.6	284.9	282.8	269.4	255.6	259.7	278.0	275.0	278.5
Central and eastern Europe	224.0	236.3	269.4	286.6	309.7	315.0	372.6	460.3	488.5	514.7
Commonwealth of Independent States[1]	171.8	199.1	222.8	218.9	198.9	193.3	196.9	218.9	230.7	251.1
Developing Asia	607.8	659.6	695.7	692.9	663.5	668.5	664.6	695.7	717.3	728.2
Middle East	252.5	259.3	283.9	294.3	294.7	295.5	301.5	312.4	315.9	321.9
Western Hemisphere	640.8	673.0	766.3	787.0	767.1	743.4	737.8	759.0	735.7	735.7
Analytical groups										
By external financing source										
Net debtor countries	1,772.0	1,849.5	1,998.7	2,039.2	2,011.7	1,969.1	2,033.9	2,177.0	2,187.3	2,218.0
of which, official financing	358.5	371.3	393.4	392.2	377.7	366.7	361.8	373.9	367.3	366.0
Net debtor countries by debt-servicing experience										
Countries with arrears and/or rescheduling during 1997–2001	727.4	766.1	836.0	838.4	815.1	783.2	785.7	804.2	776.5	765.2
Debt-service payments[2]										
Other emerging market and developing countries	**311.5**	**361.0**	**376.5**	**400.0**	**415.6**	**421.0**	**400.9**	**437.8**	**443.8**	**454.2**
Regional groups										
Africa	26.7	31.8	26.6	25.9	26.2	25.8	26.9	25.2	26.8	24.7
Central and eastern Europe	38.0	40.8	45.9	49.5	55.2	64.7	65.1	76.9	86.8	93.5
Commonwealth of Independent States[1]	16.0	25.5	29.8	27.2	27.7	32.8	32.1	29.4	36.7	43.6
Developing Asia	70.1	84.6	98.0	94.4	97.2	100.6	109.5	105.5	101.2	108.2
Middle East	33.1	27.1	24.0	24.0	24.0	27.4	20.9	26.4	29.1	30.4
Western Hemisphere	127.6	151.2	152.2	179.0	185.3	169.7	146.4	174.3	163.2	153.8
Analytical groups										
By external financing source										
Net debtor countries	248.1	289.3	300.5	325.2	341.0	335.7	322.0	356.2	350.9	354.2
of which, official financing	37.5	52.3	53.2	43.5	48.4	48.7	52.3	45.6	45.9	41.8
Net debtor countries by debt-servicing experience										
Countries with arrears and/or rescheduling during 1997–2001	72.1	102.3	115.5	128.1	118.7	111.0	112.3	112.3	115.1	109.0

Table 37 *(concluded)*

	1996	1997	1998	1999	2000	2001	2002	2003	2004	2005
	Percent of exports of goods and services									
External debt[3]										
Other emerging market and developing countries	**151.6**	**148.3**	**172.3**	**165.8**	**131.6**	**131.8**	**124.5**	**111.3**	**92.9**	**86.2**
Regional groups										
Africa	228.0	212.1	238.1	220.6	170.9	171.0	168.8	144.6	120.2	112.2
Central and eastern Europe	115.7	111.7	118.3	134.2	128.7	121.5	129.4	125.5	109.0	105.0
Commonwealth of Independent States[1]	116.5	135.4	175.2	177.2	120.7	117.0	110.7	97.9	79.5	81.8
Developing Asia	120.5	116.8	129.3	120.2	95.0	96.4	84.2	73.2	62.9	54.4
Middle East	127.1	127.9	178.1	145.5	104.3	112.1	108.0	93.2	76.4	74.8
Western Hemisphere	234.4	224.9	262.3	260.7	214.2	215.9	213.0	199.3	162.3	156.2
Analytical groups										
By external financing source										
Net debtor countries	186.7	180.4	200.6	197.7	167.0	165.5	161.5	149.3	126.7	119.8
of which, official financing	245.6	232.5	275.6	262.9	202.2	210.0	199.1	178.9	153.5	144.6
Net debtor countries by debt-servicing experience										
Countries with arrears and/or rescheduling during 1997–2001	293.9	282.3	331.3	321.6	253.6	248.3	236.7	208.8	171.2	158.4
Debt-service payments										
Other emerging market and developing countries	**21.5**	**23.1**	**25.7**	**25.9**	**21.8**	**22.4**	**19.7**	**17.9**	**14.9**	**13.8**
Regional groups										
Africa	20.3	23.5	22.2	20.2	16.6	17.2	17.5	13.1	11.7	10.0
Central and eastern Europe	19.6	19.3	20.2	23.2	22.9	25.0	22.6	21.0	19.4	19.1
Commonwealth of Independent States[1]	10.8	17.3	23.5	22.0	16.8	19.9	18.0	13.1	12.6	14.2
Developing Asia	13.9	15.0	18.2	16.4	13.9	14.5	13.9	11.1	8.9	8.1
Middle East	16.7	13.3	15.0	11.9	8.5	10.4	7.5	7.9	7.0	7.1
Western Hemisphere	46.7	50.5	52.1	59.3	51.7	49.3	42.3	45.8	36.0	32.7
Analytical groups										
By external financing source										
Net debtor countries	26.1	28.2	30.2	31.5	28.3	28.2	25.6	24.4	20.3	19.1
of which, official financing	25.7	32.8	37.2	29.2	25.9	27.9	28.8	21.8	19.2	16.5
Net debtor countries by debt-servicing experience										
Countries with arrears and/or rescheduling during 1997–2001	29.1	37.7	45.8	49.1	36.9	35.2	33.8	29.2	25.4	22.6

[1]Mongolia, which is not a member of the Commonwealth of Independent States, is included in this group for reasons of geography and similarities in economic structure.

[2]Debt-service payments refer to actual payments of interest on total debt plus actual amortization payments on long-term debt. The projections incorporate the impact of exceptional financing items.

[3]Total debt at year-end in percent of exports of goods and services in year indicated.

Table 38. Other Emerging Market and Developing Countries—by Region: External Debt, by Maturity and Type of Creditor

(Billions of U.S. dollars)

	1996	1997	1998	1999	2000	2001	2002	2003	2004	2005
Other emerging market and developing countries										
Total debt	**2,196.7**	**2,314.0**	**2,522.9**	**2,562.5**	**2,503.3**	**2,471.4**	**2,533.3**	**2,724.3**	**2,763.0**	**2,830.1**
By maturity										
Short-term	321.2	339.9	343.1	320.8	298.8	314.0	322.3	377.9	404.6	426.2
Long-term	1,874.8	1,972.8	2,178.0	2,239.7	2,202.4	2,155.5	2,209.3	2,344.9	2,357.1	2,402.9
By type of creditor										
Official	960.0	947.5	1,008.3	1,012.0	969.6	976.1	1,002.4	1,021.9	1,011.1	1,000.8
Banks	620.2	692.8	732.4	734.5	706.8	679.0	678.2	722.1	757.4	795.1
Other private	613.8	669.2	775.0	808.3	818.1	807.2	839.9	960.0	972.9	1,010.9
Regional groups										
Africa										
Total debt	**299.8**	**286.6**	**284.9**	**282.8**	**269.4**	**255.6**	**259.7**	**278.0**	**275.0**	**278.5**
By maturity										
Short-term	30.7	33.9	36.3	38.1	16.7	14.9	17.9	19.4	21.5	23.9
Long-term	269.1	252.8	248.7	244.7	252.7	240.6	241.8	258.6	253.5	254.6
By type of creditor										
Official	218.7	204.1	206.8	204.2	198.5	194.8	199.5	213.1	209.1	209.1
Banks	47.9	50.8	47.9	47.9	44.4	40.7	39.8	42.5	41.5	42.0
Other private	33.1	31.8	30.2	30.6	26.5	20.2	20.5	22.4	24.5	27.4
Sub-Sahara										
Total debt	**232.9**	**224.9**	**222.3**	**222.9**	**214.7**	**205.3**	**207.6**	**222.4**	**222.4**	**227.2**
By maturity										
Short-term	28.4	31.9	33.8	35.2	14.0	12.3	15.1	16.3	18.2	20.6
Long-term	204.5	192.9	188.5	187.6	200.7	193.1	192.5	206.1	204.2	206.6
By type of creditor										
Official	170.4	158.8	160.3	160.3	157.9	157.2	159.4	169.4	167.9	169.0
Banks	37.9	40.5	36.9	35.8	33.1	29.7	28.5	30.6	30.1	30.8
Other private	24.6	25.6	25.1	26.8	23.7	18.4	19.7	22.4	24.5	27.4
Central and eastern Europe										
Total debt	**224.0**	**236.3**	**269.4**	**286.6**	**309.7**	**315.0**	**372.6**	**460.3**	**488.5**	**514.7**
By maturity										
Short-term	43.4	48.8	56.4	60.1	65.7	56.4	63.9	90.5	96.6	103.4
Long-term	180.6	187.5	213.0	226.5	244.0	258.6	308.7	369.8	391.9	411.3
By type of creditor										
Official	80.0	77.1	79.5	75.8	77.6	83.1	76.5	73.3	66.6	61.4
Banks	54.3	78.5	94.3	101.9	114.0	99.6	128.2	156.0	166.5	173.9
Other private	87.0	76.1	88.3	101.2	109.3	123.2	155.1	210.7	233.7	256.0
Commonwealth of Independent States[1]										
Total debt	**171.8**	**199.1**	**222.8**	**218.9**	**198.9**	**193.3**	**196.9**	**218.9**	**230.7**	**251.1**
By maturity										
Short-term	5.4	14.7	23.6	15.0	15.3	15.7	15.7	22.8	23.3	23.8
Long-term	165.8	183.0	197.3	201.8	181.5	175.7	179.6	194.6	206.1	226.2
By type of creditor										
Official	92.9	102.6	114.2	113.8	106.6	101.5	96.8	91.5	86.0	81.0
Banks	33.6	33.6	35.8	35.3	18.2	22.4	21.2	44.0	57.9	81.7
Other private	45.3	62.9	72.7	69.7	74.2	69.4	78.9	83.4	86.8	88.4

Table 38 *(concluded)*

	1996	1997	1998	1999	2000	2001	2002	2003	2004	2005
Developing Asia										
Total debt	**607.8**	**659.6**	**695.7**	**692.9**	**663.5**	**668.5**	**664.6**	**695.7**	**717.3**	**728.2**
By maturity										
Short-term	110.5	99.3	88.7	70.1	59.2	88.7	87.1	106.3	123.0	129.3
Long-term	497.3	560.3	607.0	622.8	604.2	579.8	577.6	589.4	594.3	599.0
By type of creditor										
Official	253.7	274.9	296.6	302.9	286.0	281.1	287.7	292.6	293.4	292.7
Banks	200.6	209.9	202.5	197.1	182.5	178.1	168.4	161.9	167.9	171.3
Other private	153.5	174.9	196.6	192.9	195.0	209.3	208.4	241.3	256.0	264.1
Middle East										
Total debt	**252.5**	**259.3**	**283.9**	**294.3**	**294.7**	**295.5**	**301.5**	**312.4**	**315.9**	**321.9**
By maturity										
Short-term	26.5	31.4	44.3	46.2	44.7	44.9	43.1	49.2	53.8	56.2
Long-term	226.0	228.0	239.6	248.1	250.0	250.6	258.4	263.2	262.1	265.7
By type of creditor										
Official	139.4	132.6	134.6	136.6	136.1	137.2	143.8	147.0	146.9	149.1
Banks	91.4	106.2	121.9	127.2	129.1	126.4	124.8	131.9	136.3	139.5
Other private	21.8	20.6	27.3	30.6	29.5	32.0	32.9	33.5	32.7	33.3
Western Hemisphere										
Total debt	**640.8**	**673.0**	**766.3**	**787.0**	**767.1**	**743.4**	**737.8**	**759.0**	**735.7**	**735.7**
By maturity										
Short-term	104.7	111.8	93.8	91.2	97.1	93.4	94.6	89.7	86.6	89.6
Long-term	536.0	561.2	672.5	695.8	670.0	650.1	643.2	669.3	649.2	646.1
By type of creditor										
Official	175.5	156.2	176.6	178.7	164.9	178.4	198.0	204.5	209.3	207.6
Banks	192.3	213.8	229.8	225.0	218.7	211.9	195.8	185.8	187.3	186.6
Other private	273.0	303.0	359.8	383.3	383.5	353.1	344.0	368.7	339.2	341.6

[1]Mongolia, which is not a member of the Commonwealth of Independent States, is included in this group for reasons of geography and similarities in economic structure.

Table 39. Other Emerging Market and Developing Countries—by Analytical Criteria: External Debt, by Maturity and Type of Creditor
(Billions of U.S. dollars)

	1996	1997	1998	1999	2000	2001	2002	2003	2004	2005
By source of export earnings										
Fuel										
Total debt	**320.5**	**321.8**	**354.1**	**362.4**	**359.9**	**359.7**	**361.6**	**370.0**	**359.2**	**361.2**
By maturity										
Short-term	35.5	44.1	56.0	58.1	36.7	37.0	36.0	42.0	45.6	48.4
Long-term	284.3	276.4	296.2	302.3	321.0	320.8	324.0	326.5	312.4	311.7
By type of creditor										
Official	165.3	161.0	164.5	168.4	168.8	170.2	180.6	186.4	179.6	179.8
Banks	92.3	104.5	118.1	121.0	120.3	116.4	110.4	114.4	113.6	115.0
Other private	62.8	56.4	71.5	73.1	70.7	73.1	70.6	69.2	66.0	66.4
Nonfuel										
Total debt	**1,876.2**	**1,992.2**	**2,168.8**	**2,200.0**	**2,143.5**	**2,111.7**	**2,171.7**	**2,354.3**	**2,403.8**	**2,468.9**
By maturity										
Short-term	285.7	295.8	287.0	262.6	262.1	277.0	286.3	335.9	359.0	377.8
Long-term	1,590.5	1,696.4	1,881.8	1,937.4	1,881.4	1,834.6	1,885.3	2,018.4	2,044.7	2,091.2
By type of creditor										
Official	794.7	786.5	843.8	843.6	800.8	805.9	821.8	835.6	831.5	821.0
Banks	527.8	588.3	614.3	613.5	586.5	562.6	567.8	607.7	643.8	680.1
Other private	550.9	612.8	703.5	735.2	747.4	734.1	769.2	890.8	906.8	944.5
Nonfuel primary products										
Total debt	**115.8**	**116.6**	**118.9**	**121.3**	**121.8**	**120.1**	**120.2**	**126.5**	**129.9**	**132.6**
By maturity										
Short-term	12.3	11.2	7.7	6.7	8.0	7.0	7.7	9.7	10.3	10.8
Long-term	103.5	105.4	111.1	114.5	113.8	113.1	112.4	116.8	119.6	121.8
By type of creditor										
Official	83.6	77.3	79.1	78.6	76.8	76.9	74.9	78.1	79.5	79.3
Banks	18.7	20.7	20.0	21.6	21.4	21.1	21.3	21.4	21.6	20.9
Other private	13.4	18.7	19.8	21.1	23.6	22.0	23.9	27.0	28.7	32.4
By external financing source										
Net debtor countries										
Total debt	**1,772.0**	**1,849.5**	**1,998.7**	**2,039.2**	**2,011.7**	**1,969.1**	**2,033.9**	**2,177.0**	**2,187.3**	**2,218.0**
By maturity										
Short-term	277.4	279.1	266.6	254.7	232.3	217.1	224.1	250.0	259.0	273.9
Long-term	1,494.6	1,570.4	1,732.1	1,784.5	1,779.4	1,752.0	1,809.8	1,927.1	1,928.3	1,944.1
By type of creditor										
Official	789.4	762.9	810.9	826.3	800.6	814.5	841.4	858.8	849.3	839.6
Banks	505.4	568.1	590.8	585.7	575.8	549.5	554.6	572.3	586.9	595.3
Other private	474.5	513.9	589.7	619.4	626.5	595.9	625.1	725.7	729.4	759.7
Official financing										
Total debt	**358.5**	**371.3**	**393.4**	**392.2**	**377.7**	**366.7**	**361.8**	**373.9**	**367.3**	**366.0**
By maturity										
Short-term	35.2	32.4	39.3	38.5	15.9	14.5	10.7	12.3	14.5	16.7
Long-term	323.3	338.9	354.1	353.7	361.8	352.2	351.1	361.6	352.8	349.4
By type of creditor										
Official	246.6	241.4	252.0	261.3	253.7	250.7	258.7	273.0	267.2	264.0
Banks	48.5	58.9	61.1	58.6	51.4	50.2	42.3	40.0	39.6	40.6
Other private	63.4	71.1	80.3	72.3	72.6	65.8	60.8	60.9	60.5	61.5
Net debtor countries by debt-servicing experience										
Countries with arrears and/or rescheduling during 1997–2001										
Total debt	**727.4**	**766.1**	**836.0**	**838.4**	**815.1**	**783.2**	**785.7**	**804.2**	**776.5**	**765.2**
By maturity										
Short-term	78.4	76.3	70.7	70.8	45.8	44.4	36.4	34.8	30.2	32.3
Long-term	649.0	689.8	765.3	767.7	769.2	738.8	749.3	769.4	746.3	732.9
By type of creditor										
Official	408.6	405.5	435.9	455.4	438.9	442.7	469.6	491.3	479.3	469.9
Banks	195.8	225.6	239.2	236.9	227.1	219.1	196.3	183.2	180.8	179.7
Other private	122.9	135.1	160.9	146.1	149.1	121.4	119.8	129.7	116.3	115.6

Table 39 *(concluded)*

	1996	1997	1998	1999	2000	2001	2002	2003	2004	2005
Other groups										
Heavily indebted poor countries										
Total debt	**162.6**	**151.6**	**152.1**	**151.9**	**145.9**	**143.5**	**139.9**	**145.8**	**145.3**	**148.9**
By maturity										
Short-term	5.1	5.2	3.9	3.8	3.3	3.4	3.5	3.3	3.5	3.6
Long-term	157.5	146.4	148.2	148.1	142.6	140.2	136.4	142.5	141.8	145.3
By type of creditor										
Official	139.9	131.1	135.3	133.5	129.2	128.5	126.2	132.0	132.3	134.7
Banks	15.5	15.2	11.0	12.4	11.6	11.4	10.4	10.8	9.5	9.8
Other private	7.2	5.3	5.8	6.0	5.2	3.7	3.3	3.0	3.5	4.4
Middle East and north Africa										
Total debt	**342.6**	**344.6**	**371.3**	**379.4**	**371.8**	**369.1**	**379.5**	**394.5**	**396.2**	**402.7**
By maturity										
Short-term	28.9	33.5	46.9	49.1	47.4	47.6	46.0	52.3	57.0	59.5
Long-term	313.7	311.0	324.4	330.3	324.4	321.5	333.6	342.2	339.1	343.3
By type of creditor										
Official	206.2	196.2	200.4	200.3	195.8	194.4	205.9	213.4	211.7	214.4
Banks	105.1	120.4	137.3	143.4	143.0	140.1	139.1	146.7	150.8	154.0
Other private	31.3	27.9	33.6	35.6	33.0	34.6	34.6	34.4	33.6	34.2

Table 40. Other Emerging Market and Developing Countries: Ratio of External Debt to GDP[1]

	1996	1997	1998	1999	2000	2001	2002	2003	2004	2005
Other emerging market and developing countries	**37.8**	**37.8**	**43.2**	**45.1**	**40.5**	**39.5**	**39.8**	**38.1**	**33.8**	**31.8**
Regional groups										
Africa	69.0	64.5	66.8	66.1	61.8	59.1	57.5	49.9	43.4	40.7
Sub-Sahara	70.3	65.4	68.9	69.1	65.3	63.5	61.2	52.7	46.7	44.0
Central and eastern Europe	39.0	40.5	42.4	46.5	50.2	52.2	54.1	54.7	48.7	47.9
Commonwealth of Independent States[2]	34.2	38.0	58.1	75.2	56.0	46.7	42.5	38.4	31.2	28.9
Developing Asia	31.2	32.6	37.2	34.3	30.7	29.8	27.4	25.4	23.4	21.5
Middle East	48.2	47.3	55.5	52.6	46.6	45.7	46.8	43.8	38.7	37.2
Western Hemisphere	35.0	33.6	38.1	44.4	38.9	38.8	43.6	43.9	38.4	36.4
Analytical groups										
By source of export earnings										
Fuel	54.1	51.2	60.3	56.6	48.7	47.0	48.6	44.1	36.0	34.0
Nonfuel	35.9	36.2	41.3	43.6	39.4	38.5	38.6	37.3	33.5	31.5
of which, primary products	62.1	59.5	63.2	67.1	69.6	70.7	65.6	67.2	60.0	58.7
By external financing source										
Net debtor countries	43.8	43.7	49.3	52.4	48.5	48.4	50.0	48.0	42.9	40.4
of which, official financing	64.2	67.3	92.3	82.4	75.6	73.1	63.8	58.4	52.2	48.1
Net debtor countries by debt-servicing experience										
Countries with arrears and/or rescheduling during 1997–2001	51.0	52.4	63.7	77.3	68.4	69.9	68.3	63.2	54.3	49.5
Other groups										
Heavily indebted poor countries	126.9	114.4	111.2	109.9	108.1	105.0	95.0	86.9	78.1	74.4
Middle East and north Africa	53.8	52.1	59.1	56.0	49.4	47.9	49.1	45.4	39.8	38.1

[1]Debt at year-end in percent of GDP in year indicated.
[2]Mongolia, which is not a member of the Commonwealth of Independent States, is included in this group for reasons of geography and similarities in economic structure.

Table 41. Other Emerging Market and Developing Countries: Debt-Service Ratios[1]

(Percent of exports of goods and services)

	1996	1997	1998	1999	2000	2001	2002	2003	2004	2005
Interest payments[2]										
Other emerging market and developing countries	**7.9**	**7.6**	**8.8**	**8.3**	**7.0**	**6.7**	**5.4**	**4.3**	**4.0**	**4.0**
Regional groups										
Africa	9.3	9.0	8.5	7.7	6.1	6.5	7.9	4.1	3.5	3.4
Sub-Sahara	7.9	8.1	7.3	6.7	5.4	6.3	8.5	3.8	3.4	3.4
Central and eastern Europe	5.9	5.6	6.2	6.1	6.0	6.2	5.2	4.6	3.9	4.4
Commonwealth of Independent States[3]	6.9	9.4	13.4	10.3	7.8	6.4	5.2	4.3	4.7	5.0
Developing Asia	6.0	5.0	5.9	5.5	4.6	4.1	3.2	2.6	2.6	2.4
Middle East	3.0	3.1	3.9	3.1	2.4	2.3	1.9	1.5	1.3	1.4
Western Hemisphere	16.1	15.5	17.2	17.9	15.9	16.2	12.5	10.8	9.7	10.4
Analytical groups										
By source of export earnings										
Fuel	4.9	4.6	5.8	4.8	3.3	3.6	2.4	2.2	1.7	1.8
Nonfuel	8.5	8.2	9.3	8.9	7.8	7.4	6.0	4.7	4.5	4.5
of which, primary products	5.9	5.7	6.3	6.4	7.7	6.6	14.5	3.8	3.7	4.4
By external financing source										
Net debtor countries	9.2	9.1	9.9	9.5	8.5	8.3	6.8	5.5	5.1	5.3
of which, official financing	9.5	9.8	10.6	8.9	7.7	6.9	6.9	4.0	4.9	4.6
Net debtor countries by debt-servicing experience										
Countries with arrears and/or rescheduling during 1997–2001	12.3	12.0	13.6	12.8	10.8	10.3	9.1	6.8	6.5	6.4
Other groups										
Heavily indebted poor countries	8.5	10.9	6.4	6.2	6.8	5.7	16.7	3.6	4.1	3.8
Middle East and north Africa	4.4	4.3	5.2	4.1	3.1	2.9	2.5	2.0	1.6	1.7
Amortization[2]										
Other emerging market and developing countries	**13.6**	**15.5**	**16.9**	**17.6**	**14.9**	**15.7**	**14.3**	**13.6**	**10.9**	**9.8**
Regional groups										
Africa	11.0	14.6	13.7	12.5	10.5	10.7	9.6	9.0	8.2	6.6
Sub-Sahara	9.6	13.8	11.5	10.3	9.2	9.3	7.4	7.7	6.9	5.6
Central and eastern Europe	13.7	13.7	14.0	17.1	16.9	18.7	17.4	16.4	15.5	14.7
Commonwealth of Independent States[3]	3.9	8.0	10.1	11.7	9.0	13.5	12.8	8.8	7.9	9.2
Developing Asia	7.9	10.0	12.3	10.8	9.4	10.4	10.7	8.5	6.2	5.7
Middle East	13.7	10.2	11.1	8.7	6.1	8.1	5.6	6.4	5.7	5.6
Western Hemisphere	30.6	35.0	34.9	41.4	35.9	33.1	29.8	34.9	26.3	22.3
Analytical groups										
By source of export earnings										
Fuel	13.9	12.6	14.0	10.8	7.3	9.3	6.9	8.0	6.6	5.7
Nonfuel	13.6	16.1	17.3	18.8	16.6	17.0	15.7	14.7	11.8	10.6
of which, primary products	15.4	18.7	11.4	13.0	15.1	15.7	15.8	13.2	13.1	10.9
By external financing source										
Net debtor countries	16.9	19.1	20.3	22.0	19.8	19.9	18.8	19.0	15.3	13.9
of which, official financing	16.2	23.0	26.6	20.3	18.2	21.0	21.9	17.8	14.2	11.9
Net debtor countries by debt-servicing experience										
Countries with arrears and/or rescheduling during 1997–2001	16.9	25.7	32.2	36.3	26.1	24.9	24.7	22.3	18.9	16.2
Other groups										
Heavily indebted poor countries	14.1	24.7	14.1	11.0	12.0	12.2	7.9	6.6	8.6	6.4
Middle East and north Africa	14.0	11.1	12.5	10.1	7.1	8.9	6.8	7.2	6.5	6.1

[1]Excludes service payments to the International Monetary Fund.

[2]Interest payments on total debt and amortization on long-term debt. Estimates through 2003 reflect debt-service payments actually made. The estimates for 2004 and 2005 take into account projected exceptional financing items, including accumulation of arrears and rescheduling agreements. In some cases, amortization on account of debt-reduction operations is included.

[3]Mongolia, which is not a member of the Commonwealth of Independent States, is included in this group for reasons of geography and similarities in economic structure.

Table 42. IMF Charges and Repurchases to the IMF[1]

(Percent of exports of goods and services)

	1996	1997	1998	1999	2000	2001	2002	2003
Other emerging market and developing countries	**0.7**	**0.6**	**0.6**	**1.2**	**1.2**	**0.7**	**1.1**	**1.2**
Regional groups								
Africa	0.4	0.9	1.1	0.5	0.2	0.3	0.4	0.3
Sub-Sahara	0.2	0.7	0.8	0.2	0.1	0.1	0.2	—
Excluding Nigeria and South Africa	0.4	0.4	0.5	0.4	0.3	0.3	0.5	0.1
Central and eastern Europe	0.6	0.3	0.4	0.4	0.3	0.8	2.7	0.8
Commonwealth of Independent States[2]	0.8	0.9	1.7	4.9	3.2	3.1	1.2	1.1
Russia	1.0	1.1	1.9	5.9	3.1	3.8	1.4	1.3
Excluding Russia	0.4	0.5	1.2	2.9	3.4	1.4	0.7	0.6
Developing Asia	0.4	0.2	0.2	0.2	0.2	0.6	0.6	0.3
Excluding China and India	0.2	0.2	0.2	0.3	0.4	1.2	1.4	0.8
Middle East	0.1	—	—	0.1	0.1	0.1	—	—
Western Hemisphere	1.6	1.9	1.1	3.2	4.2	0.6	2.0	5.3
Analytical groups								
By source of export earnings								
Fuel	0.3	0.4	0.6	0.5	0.3	0.2	0.1	0.1
Nonfuel	0.7	0.7	0.6	1.3	1.4	0.9	1.3	1.4
By external financing source								
Net debtor countries	0.8	0.8	0.6	1.2	1.5	0.7	1.6	1.8
of which, official financing	0.4	0.3	0.5	0.7	0.6	1.5	1.9	1.2
Net debtor countries by debt-servicing experience								
Countries with arrears and/or rescheduling during 1997–2001	0.4	0.3	0.4	1.6	2.9	1.1	2.6	4.2
Other groups								
Heavily indebted poor countries	0.8	0.6	0.6	0.3	0.2	0.3	0.7	0.2
Middle East and north Africa	0.2	0.3	0.4	0.3	0.1	0.1	0.1	0.2
Memorandum								
Total, billions of U.S. dollars								
General Resources Account	9.495	9.986	8.809	18.531	22.863	13.849	22.352	29.381
Charges	2.264	2.200	2.510	2.829	2.846	2.638	2.806	3.015
Repurchases	7.231	7.786	6.300	15.702	20.017	11.211	19.546	26.366
PRGF[3]	0.750	0.866	0.881	0.855	0.828	1.035	1.206	1.215
Interest	0.046	0.039	0.040	0.042	0.038	0.038	0.040	0.046
Repayments	0.703	0.827	0.842	0.813	0.790	0.997	1.166	1.169

[1]Excludes advanced economies. Charges on, and repurchases (or repayments of principal) for, use of International Monetary Fund credit.
[2]Mongolia, which is not a member of the Commonwealth of Independent States, is included in this group for reasons of geography and similarities in economic structure.
[3]Poverty Reduction and Growth Facility (formerly ESAF—Enhanced Structural Adjustment Facility).

Table 43. Summary of Sources and Uses of World Saving

(Percent of GDP)

	Averages										Average
	1982–89	1990–97	1998	1999	2000	2001	2002	2003	2004	2005	2006–09
World											
Saving	22.8	22.9	23.0	23.2	23.8	23.2	23.1	23.9	24.5	24.9	25.1
Investment	24.0	24.0	23.4	23.1	23.5	23.0	22.8	23.5	24.2	24.4	25.1
Advanced economies											
Saving	21.9	21.1	21.8	21.4	21.6	20.5	19.3	19.0	19.5	20.2	20.3
Investment	22.5	21.8	21.7	21.8	22.1	20.8	20.0	19.9	20.5	20.6	21.1
Net lending	–0.6	–0.7	0.1	–0.4	–0.5	–0.3	–0.6	–0.9	–1.0	–0.4	–0.9
Current transfers	–0.3	–0.4	–0.5	–0.5	–0.5	–0.5	–0.5	–0.6	–0.5	–0.5	–0.5
Factor income	–0.2	–0.5	—	0.1	0.6	0.5	0.1	0.1	—	0.6	0.1
Resource balance	—	0.3	0.6	—	–0.6	–0.3	–0.2	–0.4	–0.5	–0.5	–0.4
United States											
Saving	17.9	15.9	18.3	18.1	18.0	16.4	14.2	13.5	14.0	15.6	15.4
Investment	20.3	18.3	20.3	20.6	20.8	19.1	18.4	18.4	19.5	19.4	20.1
Net lending	–2.5	–2.4	–2.0	–2.6	–2.7	–2.8	–4.2	–4.9	–5.4	–3.8	–4.7
Current transfers	–0.5	–0.4	–0.6	–0.5	–0.6	–0.5	–0.6	–0.6	–0.5	–0.5	–0.5
Factor income	0.3	–0.9	0.5	0.8	1.7	1.3	0.4	0.2	0.1	1.5	0.1
Resource balance	–2.3	–1.1	–1.9	–2.8	–3.9	–3.6	–4.0	–4.5	–5.1	–4.9	–4.3
Euro area											
Saving	. . .	21.4	21.7	21.8	21.8	21.3	20.9	20.3	20.9	21.2	21.8
Investment	. . .	21.2	21.1	21.4	22.0	21.0	20.1	19.7	19.9	20.1	20.8
Net lending	. . .	0.2	0.7	0.4	–0.3	0.4	0.8	0.7	1.0	1.1	1.0
Current transfers[1]	–0.4	–0.6	–0.7	–0.6	–0.7	–0.7	–0.7	–0.8	–0.8	–0.8	–0.8
Factor income[1]	–0.6	–0.5	–0.8	–0.5	–0.3	–0.5	–0.9	–0.9	–0.8	–0.8	–0.8
Resource balance[1]	1.1	1.2	2.0	1.4	0.6	1.4	2.3	2.0	2.2	2.3	2.2
Germany											
Saving	23.4	22.3	21.2	20.5	20.3	19.4	19.5	19.7	21.1	21.9	22.8
Investment	20.6	22.7	21.8	21.7	21.6	19.4	17.3	17.5	16.9	17.5	19.4
Net lending	2.8	–0.4	–0.5	–1.1	–1.4	0.1	2.2	2.2	4.2	4.4	3.3
Current transfers	–1.5	–1.6	–1.4	–1.3	–1.4	–1.3	–1.3	–1.4	–1.5	–1.5	–1.5
Factor income	0.5	0.4	–0.5	–0.8	–0.5	–0.8	–1.1	–0.9	–0.5	–0.5	–0.5
Resource balance	3.9	0.7	1.4	1.0	0.5	2.2	4.6	4.5	6.2	6.4	5.4
France											
Saving	21.0	20.5	21.7	22.5	22.4	22.1	20.6	19.3	19.3	19.4	19.7
Investment	21.6	19.9	19.1	19.6	21.0	20.4	19.6	19.0	19.9	20.1	20.2
Net lending	–0.5	0.6	2.7	2.9	1.4	1.6	1.0	0.3	–0.6	–0.6	–0.5
Current transfers	–0.7	–0.7	–0.9	–0.9	–1.1	–1.1	–1.0	–1.1	–1.0	–1.0	–1.0
Factor income	–0.2	–0.4	0.6	1.3	1.2	1.1	0.3	0.4	0.5	0.5	0.5
Resource balance	0.3	1.6	2.9	2.5	1.3	1.6	1.7	0.9	–0.1	–0.2	—
Italy											
Saving	21.1	20.2	20.0	20.3	19.7	19.6	19.4	18.1	18.6	18.6	19.4
Investment	22.9	19.8	19.3	19.7	20.2	19.7	20.0	19.6	19.7	19.4	19.4
Net lending	–1.8	0.4	0.8	0.7	–0.5	–0.1	–0.6	–1.5	–1.1	–0.8	—
Current transfers	—	–0.5	–0.6	–0.5	–0.4	–0.5	–0.5	–0.6	–0.6	–0.6	–0.6
Factor income	–1.8	–1.6	–1.9	–0.9	–1.1	–0.9	–1.2	–1.5	–1.1	–1.0	–0.8
Resource balance	—	2.5	3.3	2.1	1.0	1.4	1.1	0.6	0.6	0.8	1.4
Japan[2]											
Saving	32.0	32.2	29.8	28.6	28.8	27.8	26.7	27.2	27.6	27.7	28.3
Investment	29.4	30.0	26.8	26.0	26.3	25.7	23.9	24.0	24.2	24.5	24.9
Net lending	2.6	2.2	3.0	2.5	2.5	2.1	2.8	3.1	3.4	3.2	3.4
Current transfers	–0.1	–0.2	–0.2	–0.3	–0.2	–0.2	–0.1	–0.2	–0.2	–0.2	–0.2
Factor income	0.5	0.9	1.3	1.3	1.2	1.7	1.6	1.6	1.7	1.7	1.7
Resource balance	2.3	1.5	1.9	1.6	1.5	0.6	1.3	1.7	1.9	1.7	1.9
United Kingdom											
Saving	17.6	15.4	17.7	15.1	15.0	15.0	14.9	14.6	14.8	14.8	15.1
Investment	19.0	17.1	18.1	17.8	17.5	17.3	16.7	16.5	16.9	16.8	16.8
Net lending	–1.4	–1.6	–0.5	–2.7	–2.5	–2.3	–1.7	–1.9	–2.0	–1.9	–1.7
Current transfers	–0.7	–0.8	–1.0	–0.8	–1.0	–0.7	–0.8	–0.9	–0.9	–0.9	–0.9
Factor income	—	—	1.5	–0.1	0.5	1.2	2.1	2.0	2.1	2.1	2.1
Resource balance	–0.8	–0.9	–1.0	–1.8	–2.1	–2.8	–3.0	–3.0	–3.3	–3.1	–2.9
Canada											
Saving	19.8	16.4	19.1	20.7	23.6	22.0	21.5	22.1	22.7	22.7	23.3
Investment	21.2	19.0	20.4	20.3	20.2	19.1	19.6	20.1	19.8	20.3	21.0
Net lending	–1.4	–2.5	–1.3	0.4	3.4	2.9	2.0	2.0	2.9	2.4	2.4
Current transfers	–0.1	–0.1	0.1	0.1	0.1	0.1	0.1	—	—	—	—
Factor income	–3.2	–3.6	–3.3	–3.3	–2.4	–2.9	–2.5	–1.9	–2.0	–1.9	–1.6
Resource balance	1.9	1.1	1.9	3.6	5.7	5.7	4.3	3.9	4.8	4.3	4.0

Table 43 *(continued)*

	Averages 1982–89	Averages 1990–97	1998	1999	2000	2001	2002	2003	2004	2005	Average 2006–09
Newly industrialized Asian economies											
Saving	33.8	34.0	33.3	32.2	31.5	29.5	29.6	30.6	30.9	30.5	29.8
Investment	27.8	32.4	25.9	26.9	28.0	24.9	24.0	23.4	24.6	24.5	25.1
Net lending	6.0	1.6	7.4	5.3	3.5	4.6	5.6	7.2	6.3	6.0	4.7
Current transfers	0.2	–0.1	—	–0.3	–0.4	–0.6	–0.6	–0.8	–0.7	–0.7	–0.6
Factor income	0.4	0.9	–0.2	—	0.4	0.8	0.9	1.3	0.7	0.6	0.6
Resource balance	5.3	0.9	7.5	5.6	3.5	4.4	5.3	6.7	6.4	6.1	4.8
Other emerging market and developing countries											
Saving	24.1	25.4	24.6	25.6	26.9	26.7	28.0	29.9	30.7	30.5	30.4
Investment	25.9	27.2	25.7	25.0	25.3	26.0	26.5	28.0	28.7	28.9	29.7
Net lending	–1.7	–1.8	–1.1	0.6	1.6	0.7	1.5	1.9	2.0	1.5	0.8
Current transfers	0.7	1.1	1.0	1.0	1.2	1.4	1.7	1.9	1.7	1.6	1.4
Factor income	–2.0	–1.9	–1.9	–1.9	–2.1	–2.0	–2.1	–1.9	–1.7	–1.5	–1.2
Resource balance	–0.5	–1.0	–0.1	1.5	2.5	1.4	1.9	2.0	1.9	1.5	0.6
Memorandum											
Acquisition of foreign assets	0.4	2.4	2.9	4.0	5.0	3.3	4.5	5.5	4.9	4.1	3.1
Change in reserves	–0.1	1.3	0.2	0.8	1.3	1.9	3.0	4.7	4.2	2.9	2.0
Regional groups											
Africa											
Saving	18.6	17.1	16.1	16.4	19.1	18.5	18.4	19.9	19.7	20.2	20.7
Investment	22.2	20.1	21.1	20.5	19.1	19.6	20.0	20.3	20.0	20.6	20.8
Net lending	–3.7	–3.0	–5.1	–4.1	0.1	–1.0	–1.6	–0.4	–0.2	–0.4	–0.2
Current transfers	1.8	3.0	2.9	2.6	3.1	3.4	3.5	3.9	3.9	3.6	3.3
Factor income	–4.9	–4.6	–3.9	–4.2	–5.2	–4.3	–4.4	–4.2	–4.8	–5.0	–3.8
Resource balance	–0.6	–1.4	–4.0	–2.5	2.1	–0.1	–0.7	—	0.6	1.0	0.4
Memorandum											
Acquisition of foreign assets	0.1	0.8	1.1	2.7	4.1	4.7	2.8	3.5	3.5	3.6	3.2
Change in reserves	—	0.9	–0.7	0.7	2.5	2.7	2.1	3.8	3.3	3.1	2.4
Central and eastern Europe											
Saving	26.3	20.8	20.7	18.6	18.8	18.6	18.7	18.5	19.0	19.8	21.2
Investment	27.5	23.1	24.6	23.5	24.7	21.8	22.8	23.1	23.6	24.1	25.1
Net lending	–1.2	–2.3	–3.9	–5.0	–5.8	–3.1	–4.1	–4.6	–4.5	–4.3	–3.9
Current transfers	1.7	1.8	2.0	1.9	2.0	2.1	2.1	1.8	1.8	1.9	2.2
Factor income	–3.1	–1.9	–1.7	–1.6	–1.5	–1.7	–2.1	–2.1	–1.8	–1.9	–2.5
Resource balance	0.1	–2.1	–4.3	–5.2	–6.4	–3.6	–4.1	–4.3	–4.6	–4.4	–3.6
Memorandum											
Acquisition of foreign assets	1.7	2.4	1.8	3.0	2.9	1.7	3.1	2.0	1.2	0.9	1.5
Change in reserves	0.2	1.1	1.4	1.8	0.8	–1.0	2.2	1.7	1.0	0.5	1.1
Commonwealth of Independent States[3]											
Saving	...	...	14.4	24.1	31.8	29.7	27.5	27.1	28.8	27.3	25.6
Investment	...	...	16.8	16.2	19.0	22.2	20.9	21.5	21.3	22.1	23.4
Net lending	...	...	–2.4	8.0	12.8	7.5	6.6	5.6	7.5	5.2	2.1
Current transfers	...	...	0.4	0.8	0.7	0.7	0.8	0.7	0.7	0.4	0.3
Factor income	...	...	–3.6	–3.8	–3.4	–2.1	–2.0	–3.3	–3.2	–2.9	–2.5
Resource balance	...	...	0.9	11.0	15.4	8.9	7.8	8.1	10.1	7.7	4.3
Memorandum											
Acquisition of foreign assets	...	...	5.0	10.1	12.7	5.9	8.3	10.2	10.2	8.2	4.9
Change in reserves	...	...	–2.0	0.8	4.7	2.8	2.5	5.7	4.0	3.8	2.2

Table 43 *(continued)*

	Averages 1982–89	Averages 1990–97	1998	1999	2000	2001	2002	2003	2004	2005	Average 2006–09
Developing Asia											
Saving	25.3	31.1	31.5	31.7	31.6	32.2	34.2	36.9	37.0	36.7	36.5
Investment	27.3	32.0	29.5	29.2	29.3	30.5	31.3	33.8	34.9	34.6	35.0
Net lending	–2.0	–0.9	2.0	2.5	2.2	1.7	2.8	3.1	2.2	2.0	1.5
Current transfers	1.0	1.2	1.3	1.4	1.5	1.5	1.8	2.1	1.8	1.6	1.2
Factor income	–0.4	–0.9	–1.4	–1.1	–1.0	–1.4	–1.1	–0.6	–0.5	–0.4	–0.2
Resource balance	–2.6	–1.2	2.2	2.2	1.7	1.5	2.1	1.6	0.8	0.8	0.5
Memorandum											
Acquisition of foreign assets	0.6	3.4	4.2	4.6	5.1	3.3	5.5	6.2	5.0	4.0	3.1
Change in reserves	0.1	1.8	1.1	1.4	0.9	2.8	4.7	6.0	5.9	3.6	2.3
Middle East											
Saving	17.0	22.4	21.0	25.1	28.8	26.3	24.9	26.9	30.8	31.1	29.2
Investment	22.5	25.5	25.5	23.3	22.6	24.0	25.8	25.8	24.4	25.1	25.2
Net lending	–5.4	–3.1	–4.4	1.8	6.1	2.3	–0.9	1.2	6.4	6.0	3.9
Current transfers	–1.4	–2.4	–5.1	–5.8	–3.9	–2.0	–1.4	–1.0	–0.8	–0.6	–0.7
Factor income	–0.3	–0.4	0.1	–0.6	–4.3	–2.1	–4.5	–4.3	–2.1	–1.1	0.3
Resource balance	–3.7	–0.2	0.6	8.2	14.3	6.4	5.0	6.4	9.3	7.7	4.4
Memorandum											
Acquisition of foreign assets	–1.7	–2.4	1.0	4.0	12.5	5.9	5.4	8.0	9.8	10.1	7.5
Change in reserves	–1.8	1.0	–1.9	0.1	4.1	1.8	1.3	3.6	4.7	5.1	3.2
Western Hemisphere											
Saving	19.3	18.5	17.6	16.9	18.0	16.7	18.7	19.7	20.8	20.5	20.3
Investment	20.8	20.8	22.1	20.2	20.6	19.9	18.9	19.1	20.0	20.5	21.5
Net lending	–1.5	–2.3	–4.5	–3.3	–2.7	–3.2	–0.2	0.7	0.8	—	–1.2
Current transfers	0.7	1.1	1.1	1.3	1.3	1.5	1.7	2.0	1.9	1.9	1.8
Factor income	–4.7	–2.9	–2.4	–2.9	–2.8	–3.1	–3.2	–3.5	–3.2	–3.0	–2.7
Resource balance	2.5	–0.5	–3.2	–1.7	–1.2	–1.5	1.3	2.1	2.0	1.1	–0.3
Memorandum											
Acquisition of foreign assets	0.1	1.8	0.4	1.0	0.5	1.3	0.8	2.6	2.2	1.7	1.2
Change in reserves	–0.2	1.3	–0.3	–0.7	–0.3	–0.2	–0.3	2.0	0.5	0.5	0.4
Analytical groups											
By source of export earnings											
Fuel											
Saving	19.2	23.3	21.7	25.5	32.7	28.5	26.8	29.7	33.2	33.4	31.6
Investment	23.0	25.1	27.4	24.6	23.0	24.9	27.3	27.5	25.4	25.4	24.9
Net lending	–3.8	–1.8	–5.7	0.8	9.6	3.6	–0.5	2.2	7.7	8.1	6.6
Current transfers	–2.2	–3.4	–5.0	–5.9	–4.1	–2.5	–2.1	–1.6	–1.5	–1.3	–1.2
Factor income	–1.0	–2.5	–1.5	–2.3	–6.2	–3.6	–6.4	–6.4	–4.9	–4.4	–2.5
Resource balance	–0.6	4.1	0.9	9.0	20.0	9.7	8.0	10.2	14.2	13.7	10.3
Memorandum											
Acquisition of foreign assets	–1.5	–0.4	–0.2	3.3	15.0	7.1	4.9	8.1	10.3	11.3	8.5
Change in reserves	–1.6	0.3	–2.6	–0.7	6.5	2.7	1.1	4.5	6.5	7.0	4.3
Nonfuel											
Saving	24.5	25.6	24.9	25.6	26.4	26.5	28.0	29.9	30.5	30.3	30.3
Investment	26.2	27.3	25.6	25.0	25.5	26.1	26.4	28.0	29.0	29.2	30.0
Net lending	–1.5	–1.8	–0.7	0.6	0.9	0.5	1.6	1.9	1.5	1.1	0.3
Current transfers	1.0	1.5	1.4	1.6	1.6	1.7	2.0	2.2	2.0	1.8	1.5
Factor income	–2.2	–1.8	–2.0	–1.9	–1.8	–1.9	–1.8	–1.6	–1.4	–1.3	–1.1
Resource balance	–0.5	–1.4	–0.2	0.9	1.1	0.7	1.5	1.3	0.9	0.5	–0.1
Memorandum											
Acquisition of foreign assets	0.6	2.6	3.1	4.1	4.2	3.0	4.5	5.3	4.4	3.5	2.7
Change in reserves	—	1.4	0.5	1.0	0.9	1.8	3.2	4.7	4.0	2.6	1.8

Table 43 ***(concluded)***

	Averages 1982–89	Averages 1990–97	1998	1999	2000	2001	2002	2003	2004	2005	Average 2006–09
Net debtor countries											
Saving	20.3	20.6	19.3	19.9	20.6	19.9	20.8	21.4	21.6	21.6	22.0
Investment	22.6	23.6	21.9	20.9	21.5	20.9	20.6	20.9	21.4	22.0	22.9
Net lending	−2.1	−3.1	−2.6	−1.0	−0.9	−1.0	0.2	0.5	0.3	−0.4	−1.0
Current transfers	1.3	1.9	1.6	1.6	1.9	2.2	2.5	2.7	2.5	2.3	2.1
Factor income	−2.9	−2.9	−2.1	−2.0	−2.3	−2.3	−2.3	−2.2	−2.1	−2.0	−1.9
Resource balance	−1.0	−2.6	−2.1	−0.5	−0.5	−0.9	0.1	—	−0.1	−0.7	−1.3
Memorandum											
Acquisition of foreign assets	0.2	1.4	1.6	2.7	2.3	2.2	2.9	3.4	2.6	1.8	1.5
Change in reserves	−0.2	1.1	0.6	0.9	0.5	0.7	1.8	2.7	1.5	1.0	1.0
Official financing											
Saving	15.6	19.6	16.4	19.3	21.3	20.9	20.1	20.4	20.2	20.0	20.8
Investment	21.5	23.5	19.6	17.1	18.4	19.3	18.8	19.3	19.6	20.2	21.3
Net lending	−5.9	−3.9	−3.2	2.2	2.9	1.6	1.3	1.1	0.6	−0.2	−0.5
Current transfers	2.5	3.4	4.0	4.1	4.4	4.7	5.2	5.4	5.2	4.9	4.3
Factor income	−3.7	−3.7	−3.3	−1.1	−2.4	−2.5	−2.6	−2.3	−2.4	−2.2	−1.7
Resource balance	−4.7	−4.6	−3.9	−0.8	0.8	−0.6	−1.3	−2.1	−2.2	−2.9	−3.1
Memorandum											
Acquisition of foreign assets	0.4	1.0	0.9	1.2	4.3	1.7	3.9	3.5	1.9	1.4	1.0
Change in reserves	−0.1	0.8	1.1	0.8	1.8	1.1	2.4	2.2	1.1	1.1	1.2
Net debtor countries by debt-servicing experience											
Countries with arrears and/or rescheduling during 1997–2001											
Saving	18.5	19.5	16.1	17.4	19.4	18.9	19.3	20.4	20.7	20.4	20.4
Investment	21.4	23.1	20.4	18.5	19.6	20.0	19.1	19.4	19.5	20.2	21.1
Net lending	−2.9	−3.6	−4.3	−1.1	−0.2	−1.1	0.2	1.0	1.2	0.2	−0.7
Current transfers	0.8	1.7	0.9	0.6	1.4	2.4	2.9	3.2	3.1	2.8	2.5
Factor income	−2.9	−2.9	−3.7	−3.0	−4.1	−3.7	−3.4	−3.1	−3.2	−3.2	−2.7
Resource balance	−0.8	−1.7	−1.5	1.3	2.5	0.2	0.8	0.9	1.3	0.6	−0.5
Memorandum											
Acquisition of foreign assets	−0.4	0.5	1.2	1.5	3.2	2.7	3.1	3.9	2.6	2.0	1.3
Change in reserves	−0.2	0.8	—	0.1	0.8	1.4	1.5	2.2	1.0	0.9	0.9

Note: The estimates in this table are based on individual countries' national accounts and balance of payments statistics. For many countries, the estimates of national saving are built up from national accounts data on gross domestic investment and from balance-of-payments-based data on net foreign investment. The latter, which is equivalent to the current account balance, comprises three components: current transfers, net factor income, and the resource balance. The mixing of data sources, which is dictated by availability, implies that the estimates for national saving that are derived incorporate the statistical discrepancies. Furthermore, errors, omissions, and asymmetries in balance of payments statistics affect the estimates for net lending; at the global level, net lending, which in theory would be zero, equals the world current account discrepancy. Notwithstanding these statistical shortcomings, flow of funds estimates, such as those presented in this table, provide a useful framework for analyzing development in saving and investment, both over time and across regions and countries. Country group composites are weighted by GDP valued at purchasing power parities (PPPs) as a share of total world GDP.

[1]Calculated from the data of individual euro area countries.

[2]Annual data are calculated from seasonally adjusted quarterly data.

[3]Mongolia, which is not a member of the Commonwealth of Independent States, is included in this group for reasons of geography and similarities in economic structure.

Table 44. Summary of World Medium-Term Baseline Scenario

	Eight-Year Averages		Four-Year Average					Four-Year Average
	1986–93	1994–2001	2002–05	2002	2003	2004	2005	2006–09
	Annual percent change unless otherwise noted							
World real GDP	**3.2**	**3.7**	**4.0**	**3.0**	**3.9**	**5.0**	**4.3**	**4.3**
Advanced economies	2.9	3.0	2.6	1.6	2.1	3.6	2.9	3.0
Other emerging market and developing countries	3.5	4.6	5.8	4.8	6.1	6.6	5.9	5.8
Memorandum								
Potential output								
Major advanced economies	2.9	2.6	2.6	2.7	2.6	2.6	2.6	2.6
World trade, volume[1]	**5.4**	**7.3**	**6.1**	**3.3**	**5.1**	**8.8**	**7.2**	**6.6**
Imports								
Advanced economies	5.8	7.4	4.9	2.6	3.7	7.6	5.6	5.8
Other emerging market and developing countries	3.7	7.2	10.4	6.0	11.1	12.8	11.9	9.1
Exports								
Advanced economies	5.6	6.8	4.8	2.2	2.6	8.1	6.3	5.8
Other emerging market and developing countries	5.4	8.8	9.7	6.6	10.9	10.8	10.6	8.8
Terms of trade								
Advanced economies	0.9	–0.2	0.2	0.9	1.0	–0.6	–0.5	0.2
Other emerging market and developing countries	–3.1	0.5	1.2	0.8	1.2	3.0	–0.2	–0.8
World prices in U.S. dollars								
Manufactures	5.8	–1.4	6.0	2.4	13.2	7.5	1.5	1.0
Oil	–5.9	4.7	11.2	2.5	15.8	28.9	—	–2.8
Nonfuel primary commodities	1.5	–1.0	4.9	0.6	7.1	16.8	–3.9	–1.5
Consumer prices								
Advanced economies	3.8	2.1	1.9	1.5	1.8	2.1	2.1	2.1
Other emerging market and developing countries	58.9	20.6	5.9	6.0	6.1	6.0	5.5	4.1
Interest rates (in percent)								
Real six-month LIBOR[2]	3.6	3.7	–0.1	0.2	–0.6	–0.7	0.7	3.2
World real long-term interest rate[3]	4.4	3.5	2.3	2.9	1.9	2.0	2.6	3.4
	Percent of GDP							
Balances on current account								
Advanced economies	–0.2	–0.2	–0.8	–0.8	–0.8	–0.8	–0.8	–0.7
Other emerging market and developing countries	–1.5	–0.9	2.0	1.3	2.1	2.5	2.1	1.0
Total external debt								
Other emerging market and developing countries	31.5	40.7	35.9	39.8	38.1	33.8	31.8	28.4
Debt service								
Other emerging market and developing countries	4.2	6.1	5.7	6.3	6.1	5.4	5.1	4.6

[1]Data refer to trade in goods and services.
[2]London interbank offered rate on U.S. dollar deposits less percent change in U.S. GDP deflator.
[3]GDP-weighted average of 10-year (or nearest maturity) government bond rates for the United States, Japan, Germany, France, Italy, the United Kingdom, and Canada.

Table 45. Other Emerging Market and Developing Countries—Medium-Term Baseline Scenario: Selected Economic Indicators

	Eight-Year Averages		Four-Year Average					Four-Year Average
	1986–93	1994–2001	2002–05	2002	2003	2004	2005	2006–09
			Annual percent change					
Other emerging market and developing countries								
Real GDP	3.5	4.6	5.8	4.8	6.1	6.6	5.9	5.8
Export volume[1]	5.4	8.8	9.7	6.6	10.9	10.8	10.6	8.8
Terms of trade[1]	–3.1	0.5	1.2	0.8	1.2	3.0	–0.2	–0.8
Import volume[1]	3.7	7.2	10.4	6.0	11.1	12.8	11.9	9.1
Regional groups								
Africa								
Real GDP	1.7	3.4	4.4	3.5	4.3	4.5	5.4	4.9
Export volume[1]	4.4	6.0	5.2	1.1	6.1	4.9	8.9	6.2
Terms of trade[1]	–4.2	0.9	3.1	0.3	4.4	6.2	1.6	–1.3
Import volume[1]	2.0	5.7	7.3	4.8	7.0	7.8	9.8	5.7
Central and eastern Europe								
Real GDP	0.1	3.0	4.8	4.4	4.5	5.5	4.8	4.7
Export volume[1]	2.5	9.9	9.2	5.5	11.3	11.8	8.5	8.0
Terms of trade[1]	0.4	0.3	–0.1	0.7	–0.7	–0.8	0.3	–0.1
Import volume[1]	5.3	9.7	9.8	7.8	11.9	11.7	8.1	7.3
Commonwealth of Independent States[2]								
Real GDP	. . .	–1.0	6.9	5.4	7.8	8.0	6.6	5.4
Export volume[1]	. . .	3.6	8.4	6.8	12.9	8.1	6.1	6.4
Terms of trade[1]	. . .	2.3	4.2	–0.8	8.1	11.4	–1.5	–2.2
Import volume[1]	. . .	3.2	13.0	9.4	20.5	12.5	9.7	8.0
Developing Asia								
Real GDP	7.3	6.9	7.2	6.6	7.7	7.6	6.9	6.8
Export volume[1]	11.0	12.1	14.7	12.1	15.4	15.2	16.1	11.8
Terms of trade[1]	–1.0	–0.8	—	1.2	–0.3	–1.3	0.5	—
Import volume[1]	8.5	8.7	15.7	11.7	17.4	16.8	17.1	12.4
Middle East								
Real GDP	2.8	3.8	5.0	4.3	6.0	5.1	4.8	4.9
Export volume[1]	8.1	5.2	6.1	4.7	8.9	4.8	5.9	5.8
Terms of trade[1]	–8.4	3.7	2.7	0.7	0.2	12.7	–2.0	–3.4
Import volume[1]	–0.3	4.5	6.0	8.7	1.6	6.1	7.5	5.8
Western Hemisphere								
Real GDP	2.7	2.8	2.5	–0.1	1.8	4.6	3.6	3.5
Export volume[1]	5.3	8.4	3.9	0.1	3.1	8.1	4.5	5.3
Terms of trade[1]	–1.5	–0.4	1.7	1.2	3.2	3.3	–1.0	–0.9
Import volume[1]	9.1	7.3	2.7	–7.6	1.2	10.9	7.1	5.9
Analytical groups								
Net debtor countries by debt-servicing experience								
Countries with arrears and/or rescheduling during 1997–2001								
Real GDP	2.1	3.0	4.3	3.5	3.3	5.4	5.1	5.0
Export volume[1]	4.3	7.3	6.8	5.0	8.6	7.2	6.6	6.0
Terms of trade[1]	–2.7	–0.7	0.7	–0.1	–0.4	3.6	–0.1	–0.9
Import volume[1]	2.3	6.2	6.1	1.4	5.7	8.9	8.7	6.7

Table 45 *(concluded)*

	1993	1997	2001	2002	2003	2004	2005	2009
			Percent of exports of goods and services					
Other emerging market and developing countries								
Current account balance	–13.2	–5.5	2.1	4.1	6.1	6.8	5.6	1.7
Total external debt	188.5	148.3	131.8	124.5	111.3	92.9	86.2	70.7
Debt-service payments[3]	20.5	23.1	22.4	19.7	17.9	14.9	13.8	11.4
Interest payments	8.5	7.6	6.7	5.4	4.3	4.0	4.0	3.7
Amortization	12.0	15.5	15.7	14.3	13.6	10.9	9.8	7.7
Regional groups								
Africa								
Current account balance	–10.1	–4.5	–0.9	–4.3	–0.2	1.2	2.0	0.7
Total external debt	270.4	212.1	171.0	168.8	144.6	120.2	112.2	96.3
Debt-service payments[3]	26.2	23.5	17.2	17.5	13.1	11.7	10.0	8.9
Interest payments	8.5	9.0	6.5	7.9	4.1	3.5	3.4	3.1
Amortization	17.7	14.6	10.7	9.6	9.0	8.2	6.6	5.8
Central and eastern Europe								
Current account balance	–9.5	–10.0	–6.3	–8.3	–9.6	–9.9	–9.2	–6.3
Total external debt	153.6	111.7	121.5	129.4	125.5	109.0	105.0	90.8
Debt-service payments[3]	17.8	19.3	25.0	22.6	21.0	19.4	19.1	16.5
Interest payments	6.2	5.6	6.2	5.2	4.6	3.9	4.4	4.3
Amortization	11.6	13.7	18.7	17.4	16.4	15.5	14.7	12.3
Commonwealth of Independent States								
Current account balance	0.2	–6.0	19.8	18.1	16.3	21.2	17.5	7.8
Total external debt	125.8	135.4	117.0	110.7	97.9	79.5	81.8	98.3
Debt-service payments[3]	6.9	17.3	19.9	18.0	13.1	12.6	14.2	16.5
Interest payments	5.3	9.4	6.4	5.2	4.3	4.7	5.0	6.9
Amortization	1.6	8.0	13.5	12.8	8.8	7.9	9.2	9.6
Developing Asia								
Current account balance	–11.1	1.8	5.6	8.9	9.0	6.0	5.1	2.7
Total external debt	155.9	116.8	96.4	84.2	73.2	62.9	54.4	37.9
Debt-service payments[3]	18.2	15.0	14.5	13.9	11.1	8.9	8.1	4.9
Interest payments	7.0	5.0	4.1	3.2	2.6	2.6	2.4	1.8
Amortization	11.1	10.0	10.4	10.7	8.5	6.2	5.7	3.0
Middle East								
Current account balance	–16.2	3.8	14.7	10.4	17.2	25.0	25.1	17.1
Total external debt	147.1	127.9	112.1	108.0	93.2	76.4	74.8	73.7
Debt-service payments[3]	9.0	13.3	10.4	7.5	7.9	7.0	7.1	8.2
Interest payments	3.5	3.1	2.3	1.9	1.5	1.3	1.4	1.7
Amortization	5.5	10.2	8.1	5.6	6.4	5.7	5.6	6.5
Western Hemisphere								
Current account balance	–25.3	–22.5	–15.4	–4.8	1.1	2.0	–1.4	–8.2
Total external debt	287.7	224.9	215.9	213.0	199.3	162.3	156.2	138.2
Debt-service payments[3]	39.4	50.5	49.3	42.3	45.8	36.0	32.7	31.2
Interest payments	18.2	15.5	16.2	12.5	10.8	9.7	10.4	10.5
Amortization	21.3	35.0	33.1	29.8	34.9	26.3	22.3	20.7
Analytical groups								
Net debtor countries by debt-servicing experience								
Countries with arrears and/or rescheduling during 1997–2001								
Current account balance	–11.8	–18.8	–6.9	–2.4	1.5	3.0	0.7	–4.2
Total external debt	344.8	282.3	248.3	236.7	208.8	171.2	158.4	122.9
Debt-service payments[3]	30.3	37.7	35.2	33.8	29.2	25.4	22.6	15.7
Interest payments	12.0	12.0	10.3	9.1	6.8	6.5	6.4	5.6
Amortization	18.3	25.7	24.9	24.7	22.3	18.9	16.2	10.1

[1]Data refer to trade in goods and services.
[2]Mongolia, which is not a member of the Commonwealth of Independent States, is included in this group for reasons of geography and similarities in economic structure.
[3]Interest payments on total debt plus amortization payments on long-term debt only. Projections incorporate the impact of exceptional financing items. Excludes service payments to the International Monetary Fund.

WORLD ECONOMIC OUTLOOK AND *STAFF STUDIES FOR THE WORLD ECONOMIC OUTLOOK*, SELECTED TOPICS, 1994–2004

I. Methodology—Aggregation, Modeling, and Forecasting

	World Economic Outlook
The New *Balance of Payments Manual*	May 1994, Box 13
The Difficult Art of Forecasting	October 1996, Annex I
World Current Account Discrepancy	October 1996, Annex III
Alternative Exchange Rate Assumptions for Japan	October 1997, Box 2
Revised Purchasing Power Parity Based Weights for the *World Economic Outlook*	May 2000, Box A1
The Global Current Account Discrepancy	October 2000, Chapter I, Appendix II
How Well Do Forecasters Predict Turning Points?	May 2001, Box 1.1
The Information Technology Revolution: Measurement Issues	October 2001, Box 3.1
Measuring Capital Account Liberalization	October 2001, Box 4.1
The Accuracy of *World Economic Outlook* Growth Forecasts: 1991–2000	December 2001, Box 3.1
On the Accuracy of Forecasts of Recovery	April 2002, Box 1.2
The Global Current Account Discrepancy and Other Statistical Problems	September 2002, Box 2.1
The Global Economy Model	April 2003, Box 4.3
How Should We Measure Global Growth?	September 2003, Box 1.2
Measuring Foreign Reserves	September 2003, Box 2.2
The Effects of Tax Cuts in a Global Fiscal Model	April 2004, Box 2.2

	Staff Studies for the World Economic Outlook
How Accurate Are the IMF's Short-Term Forecasts? Another Examination of the *World Economic Outlook* *Michael J. Artis*	December 1997
IMF's Estimates of Potential Output: Theory and Practice *Paula R. De Masi*	December 1997
Multilateral Unit-Labor-Cost-Based Competitiveness Indicators for Advanced, Developing, and Transition Countries *Anthony G. Turner and Stephen Golub*	December 1997

II. Historical Surveys

	World Economic Outlook
The Postwar Economic Achievement	October 1994, Chapter VI
Non-Oil Commodity Prices	October 1994, Box 10
The Rise and Fall of Inflation—Lessons from Postwar Experience	October 1996, Chapter VI
The World Economy in the Twentieth Century	May 2000, Chapter V
The Monetary System and Growth During the Commercial Revolution	May 2000, Box 5.2
The Great Depression	April 2002, Box 3.2
Historical Evidence on Financial Crises	April 2002, Box 3.3
A Historical Perspective on Booms, Busts, and Recessions	April 2003, Box 2.1
Institutional Development: The Influence of History and Geography	April 2003, Box 3.1

	Staff Studies for the World Economic Outlook
Globalization and Growth in the Twentieth Century *Nicholas Crafts*	May 2000
The International Monetary System in the (Very) Long Run *Barry Eichengreen and Nathan Sussman*	May 2000

III. Economic Growth—Sources and Patterns

	World Economic Outlook
Why Are Some Developing Countries Failing to Catch Up?	May 1994, Chapter IV
The Postwar Economic Achievement	October 1994, Chapter VI
Business Cycles and Potential Output	October 1994, Box 5
Economic Convergence	October 1994, Box 11
Saving in a Growing World Economy	May 1995, Chapter V
North-South R&D Spillovers	May 1995, Box 6
Long-Term Growth Potential in the Countries in Transition	October 1996, Chapter V
Globalization and the Opportunities for Developing Countries	May 1997, Chapter IV
Measuring Productivity Gains in East Asian Economies	May 1997, Box 9
The Business Cycle, International Linkages, and Exchange Rates	May 1998, Chapter III
The Asian Crisis and the Region's Long-Term Growth Performance	October 1998, Chapter III
Potential Macroeconomic Implications of the Year 2000 Computer Bug	May 1999, Box 1.2
Growth Divergences in the United States, Europe, and Japan: Long-Run Trend or Cyclical?	October 1999, Chapter III
How Can the Poorest Countries Catch Up?	May 2000, Chapter IV
Trends in the Human Development Index	May 2000, Box 5.1
Productivity Growth and IT in the Advanced Economies	October 2000, Chapter II
Transition: Experience and Policy Issues	October 2000, Chapter III
Business Linkages in Major Advanced Countries	October 2001, Chapter II
How Do Macroeconomic Fluctuations in the Advanced Countries Affect the Developing Countries?	October 2001, Chapter II
Confidence Spillovers	October 2001, Box 2.1
Channels of Business Cycle Transmission to Developing Countries	October 2001, Box 2.2
The Information Technology Revolution	October 2001, Chapter III
Has the IT Revolution Reduced Output Volatility?	October 2001, Box 3.4
The Impact of Capital Account Liberalization on Economic Performance	October 2001, Box 4.2
How Has September 11 Influenced the Global Economy?	December 2001, Chapter II
The Long-Term Impact of September 11	December 2001, Box 2.1
Is Wealth Increasingly Driving Consumption?	April 2002, Chapter II
Recessions and Recoveries	April 2002, Chapter III
Was It a Global Recession?	April 2002, Box 1.1
How Important Is the Wealth Effect on Consumption?	April 2002, Box 2.1
A Household Perspective on the Wealth Effect	April 2002, Box 2.2
Measuring Business Cycles	April 2002, Box 3.1
Economic Fluctuations in Developing Countries	April 2002, Box 3.4
How Will Recent Falls in Equity Markets Affect Activity?	September 2002, Box 1.1
Reversal of Fortune: Productivity Growth in Europe and the United States	September 2002, Box 1.3

Growth and Institutions	April 2003, Chapter III
Is the New Economy Dead?	April 2003, Box 1.2
Have External Anchors Accelerated Institutional Reform in Practice?	April 2003, Box 3.2
Institutional Development: The Role of the IMF	April 2003, Box 3.4
How Would War in Iraq Affect the Global Economy?	April 2003, Appendix 1.2
How Can Economic Growth in the Middle East and North Africa Region Be Accelerated?	September 2003, Chapter II
Recent Changes in Monetary and Financial Conditions in the Major Currency Areas	September 2003, Box 1.1
Accounting for Growth in the Middle East and North Africa	September 2003, Box 2.1
Managing Increasing Aid Flows to Developing Countries	September 2003, Box 1.3
Fostering Structural Reforms in Industrial Countries	April 2004, Chapter III
How Will Demographic Change Affect the Global Economy?	September 2004, Chapter III
HIV/AIDS: Demographic, Economic, and Fiscal Consequences	September 2004, Box 3.3
Implications of Demographic Change for Health Care Systems	September 2004, Box 3.4

	Staff Studies for the World Economic Outlook
How Large Was the Output Collapse in Russia? Alternative Estimates and Welfare Implications *Evgeny Gavrilenkov and Vincent Koen*	September 1995
Deindustrialization: Causes and Implications *Robert Rowthorn and Ramana Ramaswamy*	December 1997

IV. Inflation and Deflation; Commodity Markets

	World Economic Outlook
The Rise and Fall of Inflation—Lessons from Postwar Experience	October 1996, Chapter VI
World Oil Market: Recent Developments and Outlook	October 1996, Annex II
Inflation Targets	October 1996, Box 8
Indexed Bonds and Expected Inflation	October 1996, Box 9
Effects of High Inflation on Income Distribution	October 1996, Box 10
Central Bank Independence and Inflation	October 1996, Box 11
Recent Developments in Primary Commodity Markets	May 1998, Annex II
Japan's Liquidity Trap	October 1998, Box 4.1
Safeguarding Macroeconomic Stability at Low Inflation	October 1999, Chapter IV
Global Liquidity	October 1999, Box 4.4
Cycles in Nonfuel Commodity Prices	May 2000, Box 2.2
Booms and Slumps in the World Oil Market	May 2000, Box 2.3
Commodity Prices and Commodity Exporting Countries	October 2000, Chapter II
Developments in the Oil Markets	October 2000, Box 2.2
The Decline of Inflation in Emerging Markets: Can It Be Maintained?	May 2001, Chapter IV
The Global Slowdown and Commodity Prices	May 2001, Chapter I, Appendix 1
Why Emerging Market Countries Should Strive to Preserve Lower Inflation	May 2001, Box 4.1
Is There a Relationship Between Fiscal Deficits and Inflation?	May 2001, Box 4.2
Inflation Targeting in Emerging Market Economies: Implementation and Challenges	May 2001, Box 4.3

How Much of a Concern Is Higher Headline Inflation?	October 2001, Box 1.2
Primary Commodities and Semiconductor Markets	October 2001, Chapter I, Appendix 1
Can Inflation Be Too Low?	April 2002, Box 2.3
Could Deflation Become a Global Problem?	April 2003, Box 1.1
Housing Markets in Industrial Countries	April 2004, Box 1.2
Is Global Inflation Coming Back?	September 2004, Box 1.1
What Explains the Recent Run-Up in House Prices?	September 2004, Box 2.1
	Staff Studies for the World Economic Outlook
Prices in the Transition: Ten Stylized Facts *Vincent Koen and Paula R. De Masi*	December 1997

V. Fiscal Policy

	World Economic Outlook
Structural Fiscal Balances in Smaller Industrial Countries	May 1995, Annex III
Can Fiscal Contraction Be Expansionary in the Short Run?	May 1995, Box 2
Pension Reform in Developing Countries	May 1995, Box 11
Effects of Increased Government Debt: Illustrative Calculations	May 1995, Box 13
Subsidies and Tax Arrears	October 1995, Box 8
Focus on Fiscal Policy	May 1996
The Spillover Effects of Government Debt	May 1996, Annex I
Uses and Limitations of Generational Accounting	May 1996, Box 5
The European Union's Stability and Growth Pact	October 1997, Box 3
Progress with Fiscal Reform in Countries in Transition	May 1998, Chapter V
Pension Reform in Countries in Transition	May 1998, Box 10
Transparency in Government Operations	May 1998, Annex I
The Asian Crisis: Social Costs and Mitigating Policies	October 1998, Box 2.4
Fiscal Balances in the Asian Crisis Countries: Effects of Changes in the Economic Environment Versus Policy Measures	October 1998, Box 2.5
Aging in the East Asian Economies: Implications for Government Budgets and Saving Rates	October 1998, Box 3.1
Orienting Fiscal Policy in the Medium Term in Light of the Stability and Growth Pact and Longer-Term Fiscal Needs	October 1998, Box 5.2
Comparing G-7 Fiscal Positions—Who Has a Debt Problem?	October 1999, Box 1.3
Social Spending, Poverty Reduction, and Debt Relief in Heavily Indebted Poor Countries	May 2000, Box 4.3
Fiscal Improvement in Advanced Economies: How Long Will It Last?	May 2001, Chapter III
Impact of Fiscal Consolidation on Macroeconomic Performance	May 2001, Box 3.3
Fiscal Frameworks in Advanced and Emerging Market Economies	May 2001, Box 3.4
Data on Public Debt in Emerging Market Economies	September 2003, Box 3.1
Fiscal Risk: Contingent Liabilities and Demographics	September 2003, Box 3.2
Assessing Fiscal Sustainability Under Uncertainty	September 2003, Box 3.3
The Case for Growth-Indexed Bonds	September 2003, Box 3.4
Public Debt in Emerging Markets: Is It Too High?	September 2003, Chapter III

Has Fiscal Behavior Changed Under the European Economic and Monetary Union?	September 2004, Chapter II
Bringing Small Entrepreneurs into the Formal Economy	September 2004, Box 1.5
HIV/AIDS: Demographic, Economic, and Fiscal Consequences	September 2004, Box 3.3
Implications of Demographic Change for Health Care Systems	September 2004, Box 3.4
Impact of Aging on Public Pension Plans	September 2004, Box 3.5

	Staff Studies for the World Economic Outlook
An International Comparison of Tax Systems in Industrial Countries *Enrique G. Mendoza, Assaf Razin, and Linda L. Tesar*	December 1993

VI. Monetary Policy; Financial Markets; Flow of Funds

	World Economic Outlook
Information Content of the Yield Curve	May 1994, Annex II
Saving in a Growing World Economy	May 1995, Chapter V
Saving and Real Interest Rates in Developing Countries	May 1995, Box 10
Financial Market Turmoil and Economic Policies in Industrial Countries	October 1995, Chapter III
Financial Liberalization in Africa and Asia	October 1995, Box 4
Policy Challenges Facing Industrial Countries in the Late 1990s	October 1996, Chapter III
Using the Slope of the Yield Curve to Estimate Lags in Monetary Transmission Mechanism	October 1996, Box 2
Financial Repression	October 1996, Box 5
Bank-Restructuring Strategies in the Baltic States, Russia, and Other Countries of the Former Soviet Union: Main Issues and Challenges	October 1996, Box 7
Monetary and Financial Sector Policies in Transition Countries	October 1997, Chapter V
Dollarization	October 1997, Box 6
Interim Assessment (Focus on Crisis in Asia—Regional and Global Implications)	December 1997
Financial Crises: Characteristics and Indicators of Vulnerability	May 1998, Chapter IV
The Role of Hedge Funds in Financial Markets	May 1998, Box 1
International Monetary System: Measures to Reduce the Risk of Crises	May 1998, Box 3
Resolving Banking Sector Problems	May 1998, Box 6
Effective Banking Prudential Regulations and Requirements	May 1998, Box 7
Strengthening the Architecture of the International Monetary System Through International Standards and Principles of Good Practice	October 1998, Box 1.2
The Role of Monetary Policy in Responding to Currency Crises	October 1998, Box 2.3
Summary of Structural Reforms in Crisis Countries	October 1998, Box 3.2
Japan's Liquidity Trap	October 1998, Box 4.1
How Useful Are Taylor Rules as a Guide to ECB Monetary Policies?	October 1998, Box 5.1
The Crisis in Emerging Markets	December 1998, Chapter II
Turbulence in Mature Financial Markets	December 1998, Chapter III
What Is the Implied Future Earnings Growth Rate that Would Justify Current Equity Prices in the United States?	December 1998, Box 3.2
Leverage	December 1998, Box 3.3
The Near Collapse and Rescue of Long-Term Capital Management	December 1998, Box 3.4
Risk Management: Progress and Problems	December 1998, Box 3.5

Supervisory Reforms Relating to Risk Management	December 1998, Box 3.6
Emerging Market Banking Systems	December 1998, Annex
International Financial Contagion	May 1999, Chapter III
From Crisis to Recovery in the Emerging Market Economies	October 1999, Chapter II
Safeguarding Macroeconomic Stability at Low Inflation	October 1999, Chapter IV
The Effects of a Zero Floor for Nominal Interest Rates on Real Output: Selected Simulation Results	October 1999, Box 4.2
Asset Prices and Business Cycle	May 2000, Chapter III
Global Liquidity and Asset Prices	May 2000, Box 3.2
International Capital Flows to Emerging Markets	October 2000, Chapter II
Developments in Global Equity Markets	October 2000, Chapter II
U.S. Monetary Policy and Sovereign Spreads in Emerging Markets	October 2000, Box 2.1
Impact of the Global Technology Correction on the Real Economy	May 2001, Chapter II
Financial Market Dislocations and Policy Responses After the September 11 Attacks	December 2001, Box 2.2
Investor Risk Appetite	December 2001, Box 2.3
Monetary Policy in a Low Inflation Era	April 2002, Chapter II
The Introduction of Euro Notes and Coins	April 2002, Box 1.3
Cross-Country Determinants of Capital Structure	September 2002, Box 2.3
When Bubbles Burst	April 2003, Chapter II
How Do Balance Sheet Vulnerabilities Affect Investment?	April 2003, Box 2.3
Identifying Asset Price Booms and Busts	April 2003, Appendix 2.1
Are Foreign Exchange Reserves in Asia Too High?	September 2003, Chapter II
Reserves and Short-Term Debt	September 2003, Box 2.3
Are Credit Booms in Emerging Markets a Concern?	April 2004, Chapter IV
How Do U.S. Interest and Exchange Rates Affect Emerging Markets' Balance Sheets?	April 2004, Box 2.1
Does Financial Sector Development Help Economic Growth and Welfare?	April 2004, Box 4.1
Adjustable- or Fixed-Rate Mortgages: What Influences a Country's Choices?	September 2004, Box 2.2

	Staff Studies for the World Economic Outlook
The Global Real Interest Rate *Thomas Helbling and Robert Wescott*	September 1995
A Monetary Impulse Measure for Medium-Term Policy Analysis *Bennett T. McCallum and Monica Hargraves*	September 1995
Saving Behavior in Industrial and Developing Countries *Paul R. Masson, Tamim Bayoumi, and Hossein Samiei*	September 1995
Capital Structure and Corporate Performance Across Emerging Markets	September 2002, Chapter II

VII. Labor Market Issues

	World Economic Outlook
Fostering Job Creation, Growth, and Price Stability in Industrial Countries	May 1994, Chapter III
Capital Formation and Employment	May 1995, Box 4
Implications of Structural Reforms Under EMU	October 1997, Annex II

Euro-Area Structural Rigidities	October 1998, Box 5.3
Chronic Unemployment in the Euro Area: Causes and Cures	May 1999, Chapter IV
Labor Market Slack: Concepts and Measurement	May 1999, Box 4.1
EMU and European Labor Markets	May 1999, Box 4.2
Labor Markets—An Analytical Framework	May 1999, Box 4.3
The OECD Jobs Study	May 1999, Box 4.4
The Effects of Downward Rigidity of Nominal Wages on (Un)employment: Selected Simulation Results	October 1999, Box 4.1
Unemployment and Labor Market Institutions: Why Reforms Pay Off	April 2003, Chapter IV
Regional Disparities in Unemployment	April 2003, Box 4.1
Labor Market Reforms in the European Union	April 2003, Box 4.2

	Staff Studies for the World Economic Outlook
Evaluating Unemployment Policies: What Do the Underlying Theories Tell Us? *Dennis J. Snower*	September 1995
Institutional Structure and Labor Market Outcomes: Western Lessons for European Countries in Transition *Robert J. Flanagan*	September 1995
The Effect of Globalization on Wages in the Advanced Economies *Matthew J. Slaughter and Phillip Swagel*	December 1997
International Labor Standards and International Trade *Stephen Golub*	December 1997
EMU Challenges European Labor Markets *Rüdiger Soltwedel, Dirk Dohse, and Christiane Krieger-Boden*	May 2000

VIII. Exchange Rate Issues

	World Economic Outlook
Striving for Stability: Realignment of the CFA Franc	May 1994, Box 8
Currency Arrangements in the Former Soviet Union and Baltic Countries	May 1994, Box 10
Exchange-Rate-Based Stabilization	May 1994, Box 11
Exchange Market Reforms in Africa	October 1994, Box 3
Currency Convertibility	October 1994, Box 7
Currency Substitution in Transition Economies	October 1994, Box 8
Exchange Rate Effects of Fiscal Consolidation	October 1995, Annex
Exchange Rate Arrangements and Economic Performance in Developing Countries	October 1997, Chapter IV
Asymmetric Shocks: European Union and the United States	October 1997, Box 4
Currency Boards	October 1997, Box 5
The Business Cycle, International Linkages, and Exchange Rates	May 1998, Chapter III
Evaluating Exchange Rates	May 1998, Box 5
Determining Internal and External Conversion Rates for the Euro	October 1998, Box 5.4
The Euro Area and Effective Exchange Rates	October 1998, Box 5.5
Recent Dollar/Yen Exchange Rate Movements	December 1998, Box 3.1
International Financial Contagion	May 1999, Chapter III
Exchange Rate Crashes and Inflation: Lessons for Brazil	May 1999, Box 2.1
Recent Experience with Exchange-Rate-Based Stabilizations	May 1999, Box 3.1
The Pros and Cons of Dollarization	May 2000, Box 1.4

Why Is the Euro So Undervalued?	October 2000, Box 1.1
Convergence and Real Exchange Rate Appreciation in the EU Accession Countries	October 2000, Box 4.4
What Is Driving the Weakness of the Euro and the Strength of the Dollar?	May 2001, Chapter II
The Weakness of the Australian and New Zealand Currencies	May 2001, Box 2.1
How Did the September 11 Attacks Affect Exchange Rate Expectations?	December 2001, Box 2.4
Market Expectations of Exchange Rate Movements	September 2002, Box 1.2
Are Foreign Exchange Reserves in Asia Too High?	September 2003, Chapter II
How Concerned Should Developing Countries Be About G-3 Exchange Rate Volatility?	September 2003, Chapter II
Reserves and Short-Term Debt	September 2003, Box 2.3
The Effects of a Falling Dollar	April 2004, Box 1.1
Learning to Float: The Experience of Emerging Market Countries Since the Early 1990s	September 2004, Chapter II
How Did Chile, India, and Brazil Learn to Float?	September 2004, Box 2.3
Foreign Exchange Market Development and Intervention	September 2004, Box 2.4

	Staff Studies for the World Economic Outlook
Multilateral Unit-Labor-Cost-Based Competitiveness Indicators for Advanced, Developing, and Transition Countries *Anthony G. Turner and Stephen Golub*	December 1997
Currency Crises: In Search of Common Elements *Jahangir Aziz, Francesco Caramazza and Ranil Salgado*	May 2000
Business Cycle Influences on Exchange Rates: Survey and Evidence *Ronald MacDonald and Phillip Suragel*	May 2000

IX. External Payments, Trade, Capital Movements, and Foreign Debt

	World Economic Outlook
The Uruguay Round: Results and Implications	May 1994, Annex I
The Recent Surge in Capital Flows to Developing Countries	October 1994, Chapter IV
Currency Convertibility	October 1994, Box 7
Trade Among the Transition Countries	October 1995, Box 7
World Current Account Discrepancy	October 1996, Annex III
Capital Inflows to Developing and Transition Countries—Identifying Causes and Formulating Appropriate Policy Responses	October 1996, Annex IV
Globalization—Opportunities and Challenges	May 1997
Moral Hazard and IMF Lending	May 1998, Box 2
The Current Account and External Sustainability	May 1998, Box 8
Review of Debt-Reduction Efforts for Low-Income Countries and Status of the HIPC Initiative	October 1998, Box 1.1
Trade Adjustment in East Asian Crisis Countries	October 1998, Box 2.2
Are There Dangers of Increasing Protection?	May 1999, Box 1.3
Trends and Issues in the Global Trading System	October 1999, Chapter V
Capital Flows to Emerging Market Economies: Composition and Volatility	October 1999, Box 2.2
The Global Current Account Discrepancy	October 2000, Chapter I, Appendix II

Trade Integration and Sub-Saharan Africa	May 2001, Chapter II
Sustainability of the U.S. External Current Account	May 2001, Box 1.2
Reducing External Balances	May 2001, Chapter I, Appendix 2
The World Trading System: From Seattle to Doha	October 2001, Chapter II
International Financial Integration and Economic Performance: Impact on Developing Countries	Ocober 2001, Chapter IV
Potential Welfare Gains From a New Trade Round	October 2001, Box 2.3
Critics of a New Trade Round	October 2001, Box 2.4
Foreign Direct Investment and the Poorer Countries	October 2001, Box 4.3
Country Experiences with Sequencing Capital Account Liberalization	October 2001, Box 4.4
Contagion and Its Causes	December 2001, Chapter I, Appendix
Capital Account Crises in Emerging Market Countries	April 2002, Box 3.5
How Have External Deficits Adjusted in the Past?	September 2002, Box 2.2
Using Prices to Measure Goods Market Integration	September 2002, Box 3.1
Transport Costs	September 2002, Box 3.2
The Gravity Model of International Trade	September 2002, Box 3.3
Vertical Specialization in the Global Economy	September 2002, Box 3.4
Trade and Growth	September 2002, Box 3.5
How Worrisome Are External Imbalances?	September 2002, Chapter II
How Do Industrial Country Agricultural Policies Affect Developing Countries?	September 2002, Chapter II
Trade and Financial Integration	September 2002, Chapter III
Risks to the Multilateral Trading System	April 2004, Box 1.3
Is the Doha Round Back on Track?	September 2004, Box 1.3
Regional Trade Agreements and Integration: The Experience with NAFTA	September 2004, Box 1.4

	Staff Studies for the World Economic Outlook
Foreign Direct Investment in the World Economy *Edward M. Graham*	September 1995
Trade and Financial Integration in Europe: Five Years After the Euro's Introduction	September 2004, Box 2.5

X. Regional Issues

	World Economic Outlook
Adjustment and Recovery in Latin America and the Caribbean	May 1994, Annex III
European Economic Integration	October 1994, Annex I
Adjustment in Sub-Saharan Africa	May 1995, Annex II
Macroeconomic and Structural Adjustment in the Middle East and North Africa	May 1996, Annex II
Stabilization and Reform of Formerly Centrally Planned Developing Economies in East Asia	May 1997, Box 10
EMU and the World Economy	October 1997, Chapter III
Implications of Structural Reforms Under EMU	October 1997, Annex II
The European Union's Stability and Growth Pact	October 1997, Box 3
Asymmetric Shocks: European Union and the United States	October 1997, Box 4

Staff Studies for the World Economic Outlook

XI. Country-Specific Analyses

	World Economic Outlook
Adjustment and Recovery in Latin America and the Caribbean	May 1994, Annex III
Poland's Economic Rebound	May 1994, Box 9
Foreign Direct Investment in China	October 1994, Box 6
Factors Behind the Financial Crisis in Mexico	May 1995, Annex I
New Zealand's Structural Reforms and Economic Revival	May 1995, Box 3
Brazil and Korea	May 1995, Box 5
The Output Collapse in Russia	May 1995, Box 8
Foreign Direct Investment in Estonia	May 1995, Box 9
September 1995 Economic Stimulus Packages in Japan	October 1995, Box 1
Uganda: Successful Adjustment Under Difficult Circumstances	October 1995, Box 3
Changing Wage Structures in the Czech Republic	October 1995, Box 6
Resolving Financial System Problems in Japan	May 1996, Box 3
New Zealand's Fiscal Responsibility Act	May 1996, Box 4
Deindustrialization and the Labor Market in Sweden	May 1997, Box 7
Ireland Catches Up	May 1997, Box 8
Foreign Direct Investment Strategies in Hungary and Kazakhstan	May 1997, Box 12
China—Growth and Economic Reforms	October 1997, Annex I
Alternative Exchange Rate Assumptions for Japan	October 1997, Box 2
Hong Kong, China: Economic Linkages and Institutional Arrangements	October 1997, Box 9
Russia's Fiscal Challenges	May 1998, Box 9
Japan's Economic Crisis and Policy Options	October 1998, Chapter IV
Brazil's Financial Assistance Package and Adjustment Program	December 1998, Box 1.1
Recent Developments in the Japanese Financial System	December 1998, Box 1.2
Malaysia's Capital Controls	December 1998, Box 2.1
Hong Kong's Intervention in the Equity Spot and Futures Markets	December 1998, Box 2.2
Is China's Growth Overstated?	December 1998, Box 4.1
Measuring Household Saving in the United States	May 1999, Box 2.2
Australia and New Zealand: Divergences, Prospects, and Vulnerabilities	October 1999, Box 1.1
The Emerging Market Crises and South Africa	October 1999, Box 2.1
Structural Reforms in Latin America: The Case of Argentina	October 1999, Box 2.3
Malaysia's Response to the Financial Crisis: How Unorthodox Was It?	October 1999, Box 2.4
Financial Sector Restructuring in Indonesia, Korea, Malaysia, and Thailand	October 1999, Box 2.5
Turkey's IMF-Supported Disinflation Program	May 2000, Box 2.1
Productivity and Stock Prices in the United States	May 2000, Box 3.1
India: Reinvigorating the Reform Process	May 2000, Box 4.2
Risky Business: Output Volatility and the Perils of Forecasting in Japan	October 2000, Box 1.2
China's Prospective WTO Accession	October 2000, Box 1.3
Addressing Barter Trade and Arrears in Russia	October 2000, Box 3.3
Fiscal Decentralization in Transition Economies: China and Russia	October 2000, Box 3.5
Accession of Turkey to the European Union	October 2000, Box 4.3
Japan's Recent Monetary and Structural Policy Initiatives	May 2001, Box 1.3
Japan: A Fiscal Outlier?	May 2001, Box 3.1

Financial Implications of the Shrinking Supply of U.S. Treasury Securities	May 2001, Box 3.2
The Growth-Poverty Nexus in India	October 2001, Box 1.6
Has U.S. TFP Growth Accelerated Outside of the IT Sector?	October 2001, Box 3.2
Fiscal Stimulus and the Outlook for the United States	December 2001, Box 3.2
Argentina: An Uphill Struggle to Regain Confidence	December 2001, Box 3.4
China's Medium-Term Fiscal Challenges	April 2002, Box 1.4
Rebuilding Afghanistan	April 2002, Box 1.5
Russia's Rebounds	April 2002, Box 1.6
Brazil: The Quest to Restore Market Confidence	September 2002, Box 1.4
Where Is India in Terms of Trade Liberalization?	September 2002, Box 1.5
How Important Are Banking Weaknesses in Explaining Germany's Stagnation?	April 2003, Box 1.3
Are Corporate Financial Conditions Related to the Severity of Recessions in the United States?	April 2003, Box 2.2
Rebuilding Post-Conflict Iraq	September 2003, Box 1.4
How Will the U.S. Budget Deficit Affect the Rest of the World?	April 2004, Chapter II
China's Emergence and Its Impact on the Global Economy	April 2004, Chapter II
Can China Sustain Its Rapid Output Growth?	April 2004, Box 2.3
Quantifying the International Impact of China's WTO Accession	April 2004, Box 2.4
Structural Reforms and Economic Growth: New Zealand's Experience	April 2004, Box 3.1
Structural Reforms in the United Kingdom During the 1980s	April 2004, Box 3.2
The Netherlands: How the Interaction of Labor Market Reforms and Tax Cuts Led to Strong Employment Growth	April 2004, Box 3.3

	Staff Studies for the World Economic Outlook
How Large Was the Output Collapse in Russia? Alternative Estimates and Welfare Implications *Evgeny Gavrilenkov and Vincent Koen*	September 1995

World Economic and Financial Surveys

This series (ISSN 0258-7440) contains biannual, annual, and periodic studies covering monetary and financial issues of importance to the global economy. The core elements of the series are the *World Economic Outlook* report, usually published in April and September, and the semiannual *Global Financial Stability Report.* Other studies assess international trade policy, private market and official financing for developing countries, exchange and payments systems, export credit policies, and issues discussed in the *World Economic Outlook.* Please consult the IMF *Publications Catalog* for a complete listing of currently available World Economic and Financial Surveys.

World Economic Outlook: A Survey by the Staff of the International Monetary Fund

The *World Economic Outlook,* published twice a year in English, French, Spanish, and Arabic, presents IMF staff economists' analyses of global economic developments during the near and medium term. Chapters give an overview of the world economy; consider issues affecting industrial countries, developing countries, and economies in transition to the market; and address topics of pressing current interest.

ISSN 0256-6877.
$49.00 (academic rate: $46.00); paper.
2004. (April). ISBN 1-58906-337-6. **Stock #WEOEA200401.**
2003. (April). ISBN 1-58906-212-4. **Stock #WEOEA0012003.**
2002. (Sep.). ISBN 1-58906-179-9. **Stock #WEOEA0022002.**
2002. (April). ISBN 1-58906-107-1. **Stock #WEOEA0012002.**

Global Financial Stability Report: Market Developments and Issues

The *Global Financial Stability Report,* published twice a year, examines trends and issues that influence world financial markets. It replaces two IMF publications—the annual *International Capital Markets* report and the electronic quarterly *Emerging Market Financing* report. The report is designed to deepen understanding of international capital flows and explores developments that could pose a risk to international financial market stability.

$49.00 (academic rate: $46.00); paper.
September 2004 ISBN 1-58906-337-6. **Stock #GFSREA0022004.**
April 2004 ISBN 1-58906-328-7. **Stock #GFSREA0012004.**
September 2003 ISBN 1-58906-236-1. **Stock #GFSREA0022003.**
March 2003 ISBN 1-58906-210-8. **Stock #GFSREA0012003.**
December 2002 ISBN-1-58906-192-6. **Stock #GFSREA0042002.**
September 2002 ISBN 1-58906-157-8. **Stock #GFSREA0032002.**

Emerging Local Securities and Derivatives Markets

by Donald Mathieson, Jorge E. Roldos, Ramana Ramaswamy, and Anna Ilyna

The volatility of capital flows since the mid-1990s has sparked an interest in the development of local securities and derivatives markets. This report examines the growth of these markets in emerging market countries and the key policy issues that have arisen as a result.

$42.00 (academic rate: $35.00); paper.
2004. ISBN 1-58906-291-4. **Stock #WEOEA0202004.**

Official Financing: Recent Developments and Selected Issues

by a staff team in the Policy Development and Review Department led by Martin G. Gilman and Jian-Ye Wang

This study provides information on official financing for developing countries, with the focus on low-income countries. It updates the 2001 edition and reviews developments in direct financing by official and multilateral sources.

$42.00 (academic rate: $35.00); paper.
2003. ISBN 1-58906-228-0. **Stock #WEOEA0132003.**
2001. ISBN 1-58906-038-5. **Stock #WEOEA0132001.**

Exchange Arrangements and Foreign Exchange Markets: Developments and Issues

by a staff team led by Shogo Ishii

This study updates developments in exchange arrangements during 1998–2001. It also discusses the evolution of exchange rate regimes based on de facto policies since 1990, reviews foreign exchange market organization and regulations in a number of countries, and examines factors affecting exchange rate volatility.

ISSN 0258-7440
$42.00 (academic rate $35.00)
2003 (March) ISBN 1-58906-177-2. **Stock #WEOEA0192003.**

World Economic Outlook Supporting Studies

by the IMF's Research Department

These studies, supporting analyses and scenarios of the *World Economic Outlook,* provide a detailed examination of theory and evidence on major issues currently affecting the global economy.

$25.00 (academic rate: $20.00); paper.
2000. ISBN 1-55775-893-X. **Stock #WEOEA0032000.**

Exchange Rate Arrangements and Currency Convertibility: Developments and Issues

by a staff team led by R. Barry Johnston

A principal force driving the growth in international trade and investment has been the liberalization of financial transactions, including the liberalization of trade and exchange controls. This study reviews the developments and issues in the exchange arrangements and currency convertibility of IMF members.

$20.00 (academic rate: $12.00); paper.
1999. ISBN 1-55775-795-X. **Stock #WEOEA0191999.**

Available by series subscription or single title (including back issues); academic rate available only to full-time university faculty and students. For earlier editions please inquire about prices.

The IMF *Catalog of Publications* is available on-line at the Internet address listed below.

Please send orders and inquiries to:
International Monetary Fund, Publication Services, 700 19th Street, N.W.
Washington, D.C. 20431, U.S.A.
Tel.: (202) 623-7430 Telefax: (202) 623-7201
E-mail: publications@imf.org
Internet: http://www.imf.org